LIFEBOAT GALLANTRY

Commander Charles Howe Fremantle was awarded the first gold medal of
the Institution in 1824.
Reproduced from a miniature in a private collection

LIFEBOAT GALLANTRY

*The Complete Record of
Royal National Lifeboat Institution
Gallantry Medals and
how they were won
1824 – 1996*

Edited by
BARRY COX
*Honorary Librarian
Royal National Lifeboat Institution*

SPINK

London 1998

© Spink & Son Ltd and the RNLI 1998

Published by Spink & Son Ltd
5, 6, & 7 King Street, St James's
London SW1Y 6QS

ISBN 0 907605 89 3

British Library Cataloguing in Publication Data
A CIP catalogue record is available from the British Library

Set in 10.5 pt Times by Columns Design Ltd, Reading
Printed and bound in Great Britain by
Butler & Tanner Ltd, Frome and London

Contents

This work is based upon
original research
undertaken by
Major D.V. Henderson, GM

Foreword

The founding of the RNLI in 1824 saw the establishment of the first national voluntary organisation dedicated to the saving of lives from disaster at sea. The continuing saga of bravery and endurance shown by lifeboat crews and others in rescuing their fellows from certain death is one which excites admiration from people in all walks of life, whether they are connected with the sea or not.

This book lists those men and women whose endeavours have been recognised by the award of one of the Institution's medals. These represent but a few of the thousands of volunteers who, since 1824, have risked their lives to save others. This unselfish service is worthy of the highest praise. Men and women still today give of their time and energies at lifeboat stations around our coasts, and their courage and dedication is an example to all. Together with those who work at lifeboat stations ashore and backed up by our supporters throughout the country, they provide a service second to none. Long may it continue.

Lieutenant Commander Brian Miles, CBE RD FNI CIMgt RNR
Director and Secretary RNLI

DEDICATED to those men and women who go out in lifeboats in all weathers ignoring the risks involved: to those who provide the back-up so necessary to ensure an efficient service: to the countless thousands who provide the financial support to keep the RNLI afloat. Thank you all.

Introduction

'At great risk to life' and 'without consideration of the risk involved' are phrases which occur repeatedly in the Minute Books of the R.N.L.I. when awards were being considered. Time and again there are reports of men setting out in small boats to battle against the fury of the elements and in mountainous seas. One cannot but have the utmost admiration for the courage, endurance and tenacity of the men, and occasionally women, who risked all to save their fellows from shipwreck.

Since its foundation on 4 March 1824 and up to 31 December 1996, the Institution has awarded:

118 Gold Medals
1548 Silver Medals
760 Bronze Medals (from 1917 only)

Whilst the majority of these are for individual services, for many years it was the practice to award silver medals, mainly to Coxswains, on retirement or resignation from a station after many years service. The last such medal was awarded in 1907 only shortly after the first motor lifeboats came into service. When, however, one bears in mind the conditions in which services were so often carried out, then the medals were well merited. One gold medal only was awarded to a Coxswain on retirement – to Charles Fish of Ramsgate in 1891. Two silver medals were awarded to the Institution's District Inspectors on retirement. The one to Lieutenant Gartside-Tipping (voted 12 May 1892) is included in the gallantry medals. The other, however, voted on 13 September 1886 to Commander Clement La Primaudaye is included in the Honorary Medals. A gold medal was awarded to Vice-Admiral John Ross Ward on 7 June 1883 on his retirement as Chief Inspector. This is also included in the Honorary Medals.

Included in the medal statistics are some anomalies. In the early years, on three occasions silver medals were reported lost or stolen, and replacements were issued. At the time these re-issues were classed as new awards and so included in the total number of medals awarded for gallantry. In 1840, the retiring Honorary Secretary of the North Devon Humane Society Bideford Branch wrote in to request a silver medal to go with a silver snuff box the local Association had given him. He had been awarded a silver medal for gallantry for a service in December 1833 when he had gone out in a lifeboat, but this second medal was for many years listed in the Annual Reports as an Honorary Award, although in fact it is included in the gallantry numbers.

The youngest person to have been awarded a medal was Frederick Carter. He was only 11 when he and 16 year old Frank Perry were each awarded a silver medal in 1890 for a rescue at Weymouth. At least fifteen other boys between the ages of 12 and 19 have received medals. Other young men may have received medals but no indication has been given of age when terms such as midshipman or apprentice suggest youth. The last teenager to receive a medal was Simon Peter Hall of Robin Hood's Bay, awarded a bronze medal for a rescue on 10 June 1979.

The first woman to be awarded a medal was Grace Darling, of whom much has been written, awarded a silver medal in 1838. Nineteen other silver medals have been awarded to women, the last in 1888, over one hundred years ago.

Few medals have been awarded posthumously – in all 2 gold, 4 silver, and 27 bronze medals. The first was to Captain J.M. Boyd R.N. who lost his life in a service in 1861. The last were those awarded to the crew of the Penlee lifeboat so tragically lost in 1981.

A certain number of Honorary gold and silver medals have been awarded to individuals (including one posthumous silver medal) and to other lifeboat organisations:

29 Gold Medals
8 Silver Medals

These are listed on pages 405 to 407.

Awards for gallantry are listed in date order of the service involved. Normally the date of the vote of the medal (shown on the right hand side of the page under the class of medal) is shortly after the date of the service. In some instances a longer time elapsed, but it is interesting to note how soon after the service an award was voted in the early days. The postal services were really most efficient, and Committee Meetings were held more regularly with fewer members. In two cases, medals have been awarded only two days after the event. A service at Padstow on 2 April 1872 was reported to the Wreck and Reward Committee on 4 April, and a medal recommended which was confirmed by the Committee of Management the same day. Medals for services at Ramsey on 7 and 11 November 1890 were awarded on 13 November. The longest gap between a service and an award was the exceptional case of the service at Fraserburgh in January 1912 when the medal was awarded on 21 February 1929.

An alphabetical list of recipients of medals will be found at the end of the book in the 'Index of Medal Awards' starting on page 425.

God help our men at sea

The Medals of The RNLI

The 'National Institution for the Preservation of Life from Shipwreck' was founded on 4 March 1824. Various resolutions concerning the organisation and administration of the Institution were proposed and passed that day.

Resolution 2 was proposed by Mr William Wilberforce M.P. and seconded by Captain Deans Dundas R.N. 'that Medallions or Pecuniary rewards be given to those who rescue Lives in cases of shipwreck'.

On 20 March, the Chairman of the Institution, Mr Thomas Wilson M.P. reported that 'His Grace the Archbishop of Canterbury had communicated to him His Majesty's most Gracious command that the Institution be hereafter authorised to take the name of the 'Royal National Institution for the Preservation of Life from Shipwreck'. King George IV was the first Patron, and the Archbishop of Canterbury, Dr Manners Sutton, had presided at the inaugural meeting at the City of London Tavern.

The first medals were voted by the Committee on 10 July. The award to Captain Fremantle was referred to as a 'Gold Medallion' and that it 'be presented to that gentleman as soon as the same can be prepared'. Consideration was already being given to the design of the awards as on 5th June it was minuted that 'The Chairman would communicate with Mr Cock respecting the design for the Medallion proposed by Mr Howard; it was thought the Medallion should be about the size of the Waterloo Medal, – but need not be so thick'.

On 25 August, the Committee was read a letter from Mr Secretary Robert Peel signifying 'that His Majesty was graciously pleased to comply with the Committee's request to have His Majesty's Head borne on the Medals of the Institution as patron thereof'. At the same meeting Mr William Wyon (1795–1851), of the Royal Mint, was recommended 'as the Artist being the best Engraver of Human figures and also of the Head of His Majesty, which he had executed for the Coins'.

Wyon designed the reverse of the Medal, from a sketch by Henry Howard R.A. (1796–1847), Secretary and later Professor of Painting at the Royal Academy. This represents the lifeboat, in which are three sailors, rescuing a fourth from the sea. Two of the sailors are steadying the boat, whilst the other, stooping, draws in the shipwrecked sailor. The inscription on the reverse reads 'Let not the deep swallow me up' and was adapted from the Authorised Version of the Bible, Psalm 69, verse 15 – 'Let not the waterflood overflow me, neither the deep swallow me up'. The figure of the sailor helping the shipwrecked sailor is reputed to be a portrait of the artist himself.

The medals were not forthcoming immediately. On 1 December the Secretary reported on a visit to Mr Wyon, who had said that 'the work would necessarily take a considerable time to execute, and that his reputation as an artist (particularly in the situation in which he was, as Engraver to the Mint) was at stake in its being done in a satisfactory manner, and that he really could not undertake to promise its being completed in less than 6 months'.

Mr Wyon's account for engraving the medal dies and for the first medals is dated 24 June 1825. He charged £105 for 'engraving a pair of medal dies', whilst the gold medals cost £6. 18s. 0d. each, the silver 10 shillings. The medals had been sent to recipients shortly before as the Committee Minutes of 29 June 1825 record that letters of thanks had been received from 'several persons to whom Medallions and Medals had been sent'.

Mr Howard, on whose sketch the reverse of the medal was based, put in a bill for 7 guineas. The Secretary was instructed on 13 July 1825 to write to suggest that 'as this is a charitable institution, he will consider 5 guineas a sufficient charge'. A rather sharp reply was received from Mr Howard: 'he cannot conceive the fairness of appealing to him on the score of Charity; and that he should be unjust to himself and his profession if he consented to reduce his charge'. He was sent a draft for 7 guineas.

In 1854, to avoid confusion with the Shipwrecked Fishermen and Mariners' Benevolent Society, the Institution changed its name to the 'Royal National Life-Boat Institution – founded in 1824 for the Preservation of Life from Shipwreck'. No change was made to the medals.

The R.N.L.I. was granted a Charter of Incorporation by Queen Victoria on 24 April 1860. Consideration was then given to replacing the head of George IV on the obverse of the medal. Advice was sought from Leonard Charles Wyon (1826-1891), son of William Wyon, and now Engraver at the Mint. He wrote on 14 February 1862 that 'The Royal Academy of Arts had changed the obverse of its Medal with each different Reigning Monarch'. On 6 March, the Committee decided that 'the obverse of the Medal be changed for a portrait of Her Most Gracious Majesty The Queen, Patroness of the Institution'. The Committee approved the new design by Leonard Wyon on 2 October 1862.

With the advent of Edward VII to the throne, the medal was changed completely. The obverse showing the King as Patron was designed by G.W. de Saulles, appointed Engraver at the Mint in 1893. The Wyon design on the reverse was also changed, for a completely new one, showing 'the figure of Hope assisting a Coxswain – Superintendent of a Lifeboat to buckle on his life-belt, and wishing him and his crew 'God speed', with the lifeboat manned in the distance ready to launch, and awaiting the instructions of the Coxswain – Superintendent'.

The Edward VII medal was used for a short time only. In 1912, a head of George V by Bertram MacKennal A.R.A. was substituted on the obverse, and Wyon's design restored to the reverse where it is still in use today.

Shortly after his accession in 1936, George VI decreed that his effigy should appear only on medals for which he had given his sanction as sovereign. The obverse was therefore changed to bear the head of the Institution's founder, Sir William Hillary. This was designed by the Reverend A.G. Wyon (1882–1962), a distant relative of William Wyon. And so the design remains to-day.

When the first instance of a second award was considered, the Committee, on 28 March 1827, informed Lieutenant Jobson that it intended 'to adopt some further emblem, as an appendage to the Gold Medallion, for a second signal service in the cause of the Institution, and which was suggested by H.R.H. the Duke of Sussex at the Past Anniversary Dinner'. When the Committee voted a second gold award to Sir William Hillary on 16 January 1828, the additional emblem was referred to as 'a boat' which would be hung below the original medal.

The practice for additional awards to be recognised by the issue of a clasp started in 1852. The first reference to such an award was that voted on 11 November 1852 to James Kearney White.

On 29 June 1825, the Committee decided that 'a gold or silver loop or ring be attached to every Medal voted' and 'that a Navy Blue Ribbon be sent with each Medal'. Since 1852 the medal has been supported by two dolphins, their heads facing. The ribbon in use today is nearer the Garter blue.

Finally, at a Committee of Management meeting held on 9 March 1917, it was decided to institute a Bronze Medal, to be awarded to crews of lifeboats and others in recognition of conspicuous gallantry in life-saving.

The medals are now engraved on the edge with the name of the recipient and the date the medal was voted. It is not clear from the Institution's records when the practice was started, as certainly some of the earliest medals awarded were not so engraved. On additional service clasps, the reverse of the bar is engraved with the date of the vote.

A fuller description of the variations in the design of the medals will be found in Appendix One.

The Launch – awaiting a chance

The Launch

List of Medal Recipients

(in date order of service)

FREMANTLE Charles Howe, Commander, R.N.
   Commander H.M. Coastguard, Lymington   **GOLD**

10 July 1824

8 March 1824: The Swedish brig *Carl Jean*, Peter Wabrood, Master, bound from Alicante to Gefle, laden with salt and casks of wine, was seen to be in difficulties broadside on to the shore at Whitepit, near Christchurch, Hampshire.

   The mainmast was overside and the vessel striking so heavily that it looked as if she would break up. Commander Fremantle managed to reach her by swimming through the surf with a line fastened to his body. Although he had the ship's boats cut clear, heavy seas filled them, rendering them useless. When he proposed other rescue measures, the brig's crew refused to act on them. He returned to the shore only with the help of a shore line by which he was hauled in, exhausted and insensible. Eventually, after the ship broke up, her crew reached shore using the wreck of the mainmast.

   In 1829, when in command of the frigate H.M.S. Challenger, *he was specially selected to take possession of Western Australia, and the port of Fremantle is named after him. He commanded the Channel Fleet and became Commander-in-Chief at Devonport in 1861, and afterwards was knighted.*

ROWE William, Seaman   **SILVER**
FREEMAN James, Seaman   **SILVER**

10 July 1824

27 April 1824: The Tenby brig *Olive* , wrecked at Halzephron, near Gunwalloe, in Mount's Bay, Cornwall, on passage from Tenby to Littlehampton, had been driven ashore under a perpendicular cliff, some 200 feet high, after a hurricane had driven her into the bay. She anchored, but the cable soon parted. Seeing the brig's plight, Messrs. Rowe and Freeman went to her aid and, after a rope was got aboard, saved eight survivors including a woman.

WATTS Charles, Master Mariner   **SILVER**

10 July 1824

15 June 1824: After a disaster overtook a Brighton pleasure boat off the Sussex coast, Mr. Watts saved three survivors, including a woman, out of the six people that had been on board.

FOWLER James, Master Mariner   **SILVER**
TINDALL Smith , Master Mariner   **SILVER**

17 November 1824

11 October 1824: The brig *Hebe* of Sunderland came on shore in a gale about a mile to the south of Scarborough Harbour with men clinging to the rigging. Fowler and Tindall, both Masters of Ships,

volunteered their services as steersmen and managers of the lifeboat which proceeded a mile through broken water. The Master and all the crew – a total of seven persons – were rescued successfully.

GREY George, Farm Servant   **SILVER**

25 January 1826

11 October 1824: Mr Grey plunged into the sea and saved four seamen and the Master from the vessel *Economy* which had been driven ashore at Heselden, near Hartlepool, Co. Durham. He made five journeys to the wreck, boarding her and saving one man on each occasion.

PRESTON Benjamin, Chief Officer, H.M. Coastguard, Newton-by-the-Sea   **SILVER**

24 November 1824

11 October 1824: Mr. Preston led the Coastguard team which saved the 15 man crew from the New York vessel *Robert Burns* bound for home. She had been wrecked near Dunstanburgh Castle, near Newton-by-the-Sea, Northumberland. Making communication by Manby rocket apparatus, the coastguards reached the wreck by boat.

FOSTER Joseph, Boatman, H.M. Coastguard, Sizewell Gap   **SILVER**

24 November 1824

12 October 1824: En route from St. Petersburg to London, the ship *Diligence* was wrecked off Aldeburgh, Suffolk. Four coastguards put off in a small boat led by Mr. Foster and rescued the six man crew.

CLARKE Joseph, Lieutenant, R.N. Coast Blockade, Birling   **GOLD**

8 December 1824

18 November 1824: On passage from Jersey, Channel Islands to Glasgow, the brig *Juno* was forced to run before a storm and went ashore at Birling Gap, near Beachy Head, Sussex. Braving the tremendous seas, Lieutenant Clarke, with eight members of the Coast Blockade stationed at Birling, helped to save the brig's Master, Mate, three seamen and the Pilot. No rockets were available so he knotted a number of hammock strings together and, after several attempts, got the line on board to achieve the rescue.

MIDDLETON John, Master, Boat *Po*   **SILVER**
NORRIS Benjamin, Master, Boat *Canning*   **SILVER**
MINTER Ockady, Master, Boat *Ox*   **SILVER**
ERRIDGE Edward, Master, Boat *Sparrow*   **SILVER**

8 December 1824

23 November 1824: The vessel *Belina*, London to Grenada, was driven ashore on the south end of the Goodwin Sands, off Deal, Kent. In spite of the sea and heavy gales, the Masters of the four boats put off in them at 4 a.m. but had to haul off until daybreak. Then, with seas breaching over the wreck and people hanging on to the rigging, they bore up all four in a line and tried to get

alongside before conditions became impossible. Using their knowledge of the tides, they saved the Master, Second Mate, three seamen and a boy from the wreck. All boats sustained damage. The wreck parted and broke up soon afterwards. Thirteen men had perished when the vessel was driven on to the Sands.

*GRANDY Samuel, Lieutenant, R.N. H.M. Coastguard, Portsmouth Harbour   GOLD
PEAKE Thomas Ladd, Captain, R.N.
    Inspecting Commander, H.M. Coastguard, Portsmouth   GOLD
FESTING Benjamin Morton, Lieutenant, R.N. H.M.S. *Brazen*   SILVER
WALKER Leven Charles, Lieutenant, R.N. H.M.S. *Brazen*   SILVER

*9 February 1825
2 March 1825

23 November 1824: The transport ship *Admiral Berkeley*, on passage to Cape Coast Castle, South Africa, was wrecked at Portsmouth, Hampshire, with 195 persons on board – troops, officers, women and crew. Captain Peake directed and helped to land the troops and women, while Lieutenant Grandy and his Coastguard boat's crew put out from the shore. The Captain spent six hours on the beach wholly exposed to the violence of the storm, drenched by the sea and in a stream of water dashing over the causeway. By 8 a.m., the survivors were in uncommon peril, as the ship filled from the dashing of the sea against the wall. Escape from the jib boom was not possible as the ship was driven along the beach for three hours until her masts were cut away. Lieutenants Festing and Walker made a raft and, with a crew from their ship, helped Lieutenant Grandy to land survivors. The rescue was completed without casualties.

BARNES George   **SILVER**
CURTIS Stephen   **SILVER**

8 December 1824

23 November 1824: En route to Southampton from Swanage, the Southampton vessel *Hero* went ashore in bad weather off Christchurch Head, Hampshire. Six crew perished, but two seamen were saved by Messrs. Barnes and Curtis, who had witnessed the tragedy. They volunteered to be lowered down the Head from a height of 70–100 feet.

CURTEIS William, Chief Officer, H.M. Coastguard, Stokes Bay   **SILVER**

12 January 1825

23 November 1824: The ship *Madras*, on passage from London to Madras and Bengal, was driven on shore in Stokes Bay, Hampshire just to the west of the entrance to Portsmouth Harbour. Despite the atrocious conditions, the Chief Officer led his team in the successful rescue of the nine passengers.

BENETT Charles Cowper, Captain, R.N   **GOLD**
*PORTER William, Seaman   **SILVER**
*FREEMAN John, Seaman   **SILVER**

5 January 1825
*12 January 1825

23 November 1824: On voyage from Lyme, Dorset to London, the brig *Unity* was wrecked between Lyme Regis and Charmouth, Dorset. Captain Benett provided himself with ropes and lines from his yacht, then proceeded along the shore to a point opposite the casualty. There he got down on a projecting point of the cliff and, followed by his men, went on board and rescued the Master, two men and a boy. One man fell from the rigging into the sea; Captain Benett descended the cliff and rushed into the water to recover the body.

EDDY Richard, Pilot   **SILVER**

30 June 1825

23 November 1824: A violent storm caused at least 22 vessels to be wrecked off Plymouth, Devon. Mr. Eddy launched his skiff to try to save as many people as possible. The *Coromandel* had been upset off the Eddystone Reef and had drifted for some hours before striking the breakwater off Plymouth, two of her crew being washed overboard and drowned. With his crew, Mr. Eddy saved four survivors from the ship, which had been in passage from Faro to the Downs.

CRAGGS James, Boatman, H.M. Coastguard, Yealm   **SILVER**

12 January 1825

23 November 1824: During a storm, the ship *John*, Leghorn, Italy to London, was wrecked in Wembury Bay, south-east of Plymouth, Devon. At daybreak, it was discovered that the officers and crew had drowned, the sole survivor being the Master's wife, Mrs. Wills, who was seen clinging to

the vessel's side with the sea breaking over her with great violence. Mr. Craggs, waiting his opportunity, plunged into the heavy seas and succeeded in getting on board the wreck from which he brought her to safety.

MILLER John, Boatman, H.M. Coastguard, Cawsand   **SILVER**

12 January 1825

23 November 1824: Inward bound from Surinam, Dutch Guiana to Hamburg, the Dutch brig *Harmonie* was driven ashore in Porlorn (Palhawn) Cove, Whitsand Bay, near Devonport. Six of her crew were lost. When at 5 a.m. cries were heard, a Coastguard crew led by Mr. Miller repaired to the spot instantly with a light. Using great exertion they climbed down the very high cliff and succeeded in making the Dutchmen understand that they would be saved if they were patient and remained on board. Eventually they were brought ashore and accommodated at Coastguard houses for four days.

ELWIN Joseph, Lieutenant, R.N. H.M. Coastguard, Lymington   **SILVER**

19 January 1825

23 November 1824: The *Lark*, a small vessel from Christchurch, Hampshire, was driven ashore under a high sandy cliff at Flag Head, Branksea Island (now Brownsea Island). Her two man crew was rescued by Lieutenant Elwin and two of his men, possibly with the Manby rocket apparatus.

Whilst the Committee Minutes refer only to Flag Head, Branksea, the first Annual Report mentions Branksea Island. It is possible the rescue took place near what is now Flaghead Chine, Canford Cliffs.

De St. CROIX Francis, Gentleman   **GOLD**
De St. CROIX Jean, Gentleman   **GOLD**
De St. CROIX Philip, Gentleman   **GOLD**
*NICOLLE Philip, Gentleman   **SILVER**

27 July 1825

*31 August 1825

9 January 1825: One evening, seeing the French boat *Fanny* of St. Malo strike on the rocks off Jersey, Channel Islands, in thick, hazy weather, the four gentlemen put off in a boat, which was kept to help vessels in danger. In two trips, they saved 13 people before the wreck broke into pieces. The dangerous swell of the sea was so great that a pilot boat, which arrived, dared not venture into the surf breaking over the casualty.

RANDALL Henry, Lieutenant, R.N. H.M. Coastguard, Elie   **GOLD**

9 February 1825

17 January 1825: After the schooner *Devoran* had been wrecked at Bridge of Don, north of Aberdeen, her Mate was washed overboard and was drowned. The wreck was seen at 6 a.m.;

Lieutenant Randall set up the Manby rocket apparatus on the beach and succeeded in throwing a line on board the casualty at the fourth or fifth attempt. This enabled a boat, manned by coast-guards, to bring off the four survivors.

LEWIS Edmund, Seaman **SILVER**
16 March 1825

2 February 1825: In a violent gale the crew of the vessel *Neptune*, New Orleans to Liverpool, abandoned her in Cardigan Bay, North Wales leaving her drifting in a sinking condition under the high cliffs. Seven Barmouth men went to her assistance but, having boarded her, were unable to leave, and she was driven ashore by a flood tide three miles from Barmouth, Merioneth. The ship parted, her upper works drifting under the cliffs, and the men were given up for lost. Mr. Lewis, attaching himself to a rope, descended an awe-inspiring precipice to board the wreck. Using ropes that he brought down for the purpose, he helped to haul all the men up the cliffs to safety.

ALLAN James, Pilot **SILVER**
6 April 1825

18 March 1825: Crimston Rock is nine miles south-east of Holy Island off the Northumberland coast. Here at 4 a.m., on her way from Hull via Leith to the River Plate, the Argentina ship *Thomas Jackson* was wrecked in a gale. Mr. Allan was prominent among the 12 fishermen who went off in two cobles to rescue the survivors. They reached Staples Lighthouse in a heavy sea where the keeper said it would be impossible to reach the wreck with the flood tide running so violently against the wind. Nonetheless they carried on and rescued the Master and six men and landed them safely at Holy Island.

ROSS Richard, Chief Boatman, H.M. Coastguard, Curracloe **SILVER**
9 November 1825

20 October 1825: The *Mary and Eliza* was wrecked on passage from Bangor to Wexford at Curracloe Island at 5 a.m., and four seamen were drowned. Mr. Ross and his crew of six men carried their gig on their shoulders to a point opposite the wreck off Wexford Harbour, Co. Wexford, Ireland. The gig was swamped and her side completely stoved in, whilst the casualty's mast and upper works separated from her hull. Heavy seas broke over both craft, and the res-cuers were given up for lost by those on shore. The damaged gig reached the shore safely, and the coastguardmen immediately launched a strand cot and, after many attempts, rescued the Master and one seaman, the former apparently dead but he was revived.

JOY George, Master, Revenue Cutter *Mermaid* **GOLD**
WILSON Thomas, Pilot, Holy Island **SILVER**
13 September 1826

30 October 1825: At 10 a.m. the sloop *John and Jessie* ran for Holy Island in distress and, in trying to take the bar, was wrecked on shore within Parton Stell. The violent sea washed four young ladies, the Master and one seaman to their deaths. Three of the crew were seen at the masthead

with half the mast under water and, on arrival at the scene, Mr. Joy found 100 spectators standing idly by, refusing to attempt rescue. Eventually, with the help of his own crew and men from a fishing smack, he brought a fishing coble overland and launched it with the help of four of his men, a fisherman and a Pilot. Although driven back several times with the boat full of water, they succeeded in bringing off the survivors just before the mast was washed away. During all this time the violent gale was blowing with hard sleet over heavy breakers.

HUTCHINSON Henry, Chief Officer, H.M. Coastguard,
Orford Ness Lighthouse **SILVER**

28 December 1825

8 November 1825: The Coastguard put out to the Newcastle ship *Traveller* which had been driven ashore near Aldeburgh, Suffolk, in heavy weather on a very dark night. Mr. Hutchinson saved the Master and three seamen, but eight others were lost. The survivors were floating on parts of the wreck ; the first was saved by a grapnel thrown on to it, while others were pulled from the breakers into which they had thrown themselves.

FOY Thomas, Coxswain, Rossglass Lifeboat **SILVER**

15 November 1826
*11 April 1827

2 December 1825: At 2 a.m. the vessel *Usk* was wrecked in violent weather off Rossglass, Co. Dublin, Ireland. She struck a sharp rock and heavy seas washed over her. With five other men, Mr. Foy launched a fishing boat through tremendous surf and took the Master, the Mate, one seaman and three passengers from the wreck. The boat was taken half a mile along the beach and launched again, but before they could reach the wreck, two of three men left aboard were washed off and drowned; the other man was brought ashore safely.

   *The medal was originally voted to John Kerr on 15 November 1826 who, having heard the sounds of distress, summoned help, but it was transferred to Mr. Foy on 11 April 1827.

LLOYD Owen, Boatman, H.M. Coastguard, West Lulworth **SILVER**

28 December 1825

14 December 1825: The Master, four seamen and two boys were drowned when the ship *Vigilant* was wrecked at Lulworth Cove, east of Weymouth, Dorset. Coastguardmen, led by Mr. Lloyd, threw a rope and were able to drag the Mate up the high, crumbling cliff. The vessel went to pieces soon afterwards.

CRONEN Dennis **SILVER**

1 February 1826

21 December 1825: When the vessel *Britannia* was wrecked in Ballycotton Bay, Co. Cork, Ireland, her Master, who was the only survivor, lashed himself to a rock. Seven hours later, cold and exhausted, he was rescued by Mr. Cronen who, in spite of the sea conditions, helped the survivor ashore and up a high cliff, then accommodated him for four days.

BARRY Garrett, Lieutenant, R.N. H.M. Coastguard, Sandy Island **SILVER**

22 February 1826

15 January 1826: In a gale and heavy seas, the vessel *Eliza* was wrecked at 4 a.m. on Sandy Island, Kinsale, Co. Cork, Ireland. At daylight, by putting off in a boat through heavy surf, Lieutenant Barry with five coastguards was able to save all of her crew except for one boy. Lieutenant Barry had to make two trips and, at times, the boat was nearly swamped.

CULMER George, Chief Officer, H.M. Coastguard, Shoeburyness **SILVER**

1 March 1826

17 February 1826: With two men of his boat's crew, Mr. Culmer saved two men clinging to the Leith vessel *Friendship* which at daybreak had been observed upset and ashore in a heavy southerly gale off Shoeburyness, Essex. They launched the boat over the sands through heavy surf with the tide at half ebb. The victims were exhausted to the point of insensitivity, and one died before reaching shore.

MORRIS John Row, Captain, R.N. H.M. Coastguard, Newcastle, Co. Down **GOLD**
DOUGLAS Alexander, Boatman, H.M. Coastguard, Newcastle, Co. Down **SILVER**

5 April 1826

6 March 1826: The barque *Richard Pope*, Liverpool to Sierra Leone, was driven ashore in Dundrum Bay, near Newcastle, Co. Down, northern Ireland in a strong gale and amid tremendous surf. A galley with Captain Morris aboard was launched from the shore at 1 p.m. but, nearing the casualty, because of the gale and only being able to row with the lee-side oars, the galley filled with water and drifted ashore. Another boat then made an unsuccessful rescue attempt but was compelled to return. A boat launched from the barque was upset and four of the five occupants drowned. Alexander Douglas almost drowned when he swam through the surf and just failed to save a seaman. The surf continued to be very heavy until after dark and, during the night, another survivor drowned. By day break the sea had abated; the coastguardmen and shoreboatmen then combined to save the remaining ten men aboard the barque.

WOOD Thomas Lamb, Chief Officer, H.M. Coastguard, Dunany **SILVER**

7 June 1826
*11 March 1840

25 March 1826: Three fishermen of Augher Head set sail in their boat from Cooly to return home, but a violent easterly gale and tremendous seas made it impossible to weather Dunany Point, north of Clogher Head, Co. Louth, Ireland. The fishing boat bore up for the bay.

The boat was twice upset by the sea, and this was seen by the Coastguard who made two unsuccessful attempts to launch their own boat. Being the only man amongst his crew that could swim, Mr. Wood then stripped, swam off from the shore with a rope tied round his waist. He was able to rescue one man, but the two others had drowned.

*Some years later Mr. Wood reported the theft of his medal, and on 11 March 1840 a replacement medal was voted. At the time this was counted as a separate award and was included in the overall number of medals awarded.

ELSE John, Lieutenant, R.N. H.M. Coastguard, Polkerris **GOLD**
18 October 1826

26 August 1826: The sean boat *Providence* of Par was driven among the rocks outside Polkerris Harbour, near Fowey, Cornwall; the alarm was raised about 3 p .m. but already the crew of eight had been washed overboard. Giving orders for the Coastguard gig to be manned, Lieutenant Else and another man launched a 14 foot punt and managed to get three of the distressed boat's crew on board before the punt was driven into the rocks by heavy surf. Lieutenant Else was injured so badly that he could take no further active part. The punt was retrieved with its survivors still on board, and the gig brought the other five ashore under Lieutenant Else's supervision.

MILLER William, Boatman **SILVER**
13 September 1826

7 September 1826: The *Eliza and Jane* was wrecked on the Goodwin Sands in heavy weather. Mr. Miller, with a crew of 12, launched his boat from Ramsgate beach at 6 a.m., reached the Sands and then hoisted out a small boat. In three trips the Master, his wife and five crew were rescued – they had been lashed to the rigging for four hours, the vessel being completely under water. On the first trip, the Master's wife and the clothes belonging to the crew were transferred. All were landed safely at Ramsgate at 1.30 p.m.

SULLIVAN John, Seaman **SILVER**
13 December 1826
*28 February 1827

15 November 1826: A boat from H.M.S. *Hyperion* carrying four men struck the piles of the Newhaven, Sussex, bridge, capsized and threw the men into the water. One man was drowned, the others were left clinging to the bridge supports. Mr John Grinder, Master of the smack *Favourite* lying nearby, launched their small boat and, with John Sullivan, managed to save the three men who were struggling for their lives in the strong current.

*The medal, originally voted to John Grinder on 13 December 1826, was transferred to Mr Sullivan on 28 February 1827.

BURNEY Robert, Chief Officer, H.M. Coastguard, Banff **SILVER**
3 January 1827

25 November 1826: The ship *Rival* was wrecked on the coast at Pennan, Aberdeenshire near Banff, and the Master and eight seamen were saved by Mr. Burney and other coastguardmen using ropes.

BOWEN Charles Holcombe, Lieutenant, R.N.
   H.M. Coastguard, Fraserburgh **GOLD**
31 January 1827

2 January 1827: The weather was the most serious it had been for many years when the ship *Rose* was wrecked near Fraserburgh, Aberdeenshire. Lieutenant Bowen and a Coastguard team set up

the Manby rocket apparatus. The third shot pitched alongside the mainmast, and a hawser was sent from the wreck enabling the exhausted survivors – three men, two women and a child – to be rescued. The rescuers worked for seven hours up to their waists in freezing water.

LINDSAY James, Lieutenant, R.N. H.M. Coastguard, Fort George   **GOLD**
CORK William, Boatman, H.M. Coastguard, Fort George   **SILVER**
GRAY Alexander, Boatman, H.M. Coastguard, Fort George   **SILVER**
7 February 1827

2 January 1827: The Inverness sloop *Lively* went on shore during severe weather near Fort George, Nairn, with the Master, two seamen and one female passenger on board. Using *Lively*'s boat, which had been driven ashore, Lieutenant Lindsay and his two men went alongside. Soon the boat was swamped and went to pieces, and they were forced to board the sloop where they remained for two hours. With the sea running over the vessel, Lieutenant Lindsay had continually to hold on to the female passenger to prevent her being swept overside. The bottom of the sloop was out by this time and, half an hour after they were finally taken off by the Coastguard boat, she broke up.

JOBSON Christopher, Lieutenant, R.N. H.M. Coastguard, Arbroath   **GOLD**
7 March 1827

17 February 1827: When the *Clyde Packet*, on passage from Glasgow to Aberdeen, was wrecked in a strong snow filled gale on rocks at Arbroath Harbour entrance, Fife, the Manby rocket apparatus was used in a successful attempt to get a boat to the wreck. During its return the boat was swamped and capsized throwing three men passengers, two women and two children into the water. Lieutenant Jobson and a Coastguard team rushed into the water and got them all ashore. The remaining survivors stayed on board and, when the packet drifted ashore, they landed after the tide had receded.

STAP Randall, Chief Officer, H.M. Coastguard, Dunbar   **SILVER**
11 April 1827

4 March 1827: Two seamen were washed overboard and lost when the sloop *Brothers* was wrecked at Dunbar, East Lothian. Chief Officer Stap waded out about 50 yards through heavy surf and putting the Master on his own back brought him ashore in spite of a strong gale and thick snow .

DONKIN Alexander   **SILVER**
10 May 1827
*3 October 1833

7 March 1827: The sloop *James* was wrecked at 9 p.m. on shore near Cullercoats, Northumberland, in a heavy easterly gale. A boat, manned by nine fishermen, made two unsuccessful attempts to reach the wreck. Meanwhile Mr. Donkin plunged in amongst the breakers and swam until he reached a rock some 40 yards from the wreck. He was then able, after much difficulty, to save the

Master of the sloop, James Marr, who had jumped off the wreck. The two men were then taken off by the nine men in the local boat which had been pulled over the rocks to launch from a new site.

Mr. Donkin reported the medal as lost and, on 3 October 1833 , a replacement medal was voted. At the time this was counted as a separate award and was included in the overall number of medals awarded.

JOBSON Christopher, Lieutenant, R.N. H.M. Coastguard, Arbroath   **GOLD BOAT(2)**

28 March 1827

8 March 1827: The vessel *Alice* of Garthwaite was driven ashore near Abroath at 2 a.m. in a severe gale accompanied by snow. The Manby apparatus was got down, but as the vessel was 300 yards away 10 or 12 oz charges were used which caused the line to break several times. The second discharge laid a line over the main boom, but the crew of two men and one boy were so exhausted they could not help and the line slipped off into the water.

Lieutenant Jobson, together with 11 excellent seamen, then manned the lifeboat, and they were able to rescue the Master. The other man drowned and the boy died of cold.

SUTTER John, Master Mariner   **SILVER**

MACKINTOSH Alexander, Master Mariner   **SILVER**

WALLACE James, Master Mariner   **SILVER**

15 August 1827

August 1827: In severe weather Messrs. Sutter, Mackintosh and Wallace, together with six Coastguardmen, put off in a boat and saved two men from an open boat which had been driven out to sea near Peterhead, Aberdeenshire.

The Committee 'made this award rather with the view of exciting others to follow the example of the parties herein referred to in saving lives (in which it appears there was a most unworthy indifference in their case) than from any particular risk incurred by them'. In addition to the silver medals, the Chief Coastguard Boatman received two guineas and the five crew one guinea each.

DEANE Henry, Chief Officer, H.M. Coastguard, Cemaes   **SILVER**

10 October 1827

22 September 1827: In a boat manned by coastguardmen, Mr. Deane saved the crew, four men and a boy, of the sloop *Phoenix* which had been wrecked on a rock known as West Mouse at Cemaes, Anglesey. The vessel became a total wreck.

MATTHEWS Robert Bates, Lieutenant, R.N. H.M. Coastguard, Lowestoft   **GOLD**

24 October 1827

12 October 1827: The *Lord Duncan* was driven ashore at Lowestoft, Suffolk, at midnight between the 11th and 12th October. Using the Manby rocket apparatus, Lieutenant Matthews was instrumental in saving the Master and the six crew.

During his coastguard service, he was responsible for saving a total of 31 lives.

HILLARY Sir William, Bart	**GOLD BOAT(2)**
HILLARY Augustus William	**SILVER**
ROBINSON Robert, Lieutenant, R.N	**SILVER**
STRUGNELL William Baker, Lieutenant, R.N. H.M. Coastguard,	
Cruiser *Swallow*	**SILVER**
	16 January 1828

10 December 1827: The Swedish ship *Fortroendet*, Marseilles to Glasgow, having called at Derbyhaven, Isle of Man, was trying to make a sheltered anchorage in Douglas Bay, but the storm tore out her anchor soon after it dropped. After an unsuccessful attempt to make the harbour mouth, a spare anchor was dropped to prevent her running on to rocks. Meanwhile, efforts were being made on shore to get a line on board; they were too late, and she drove on to the rocks of St. Mary's Isle. The Douglas lifeboat *True Blue* was launched, followed by the coastguard cutter *Swallow*. In a very difficult operation the lifeboat, with Sir William at the helm, his son and Lieutenant Robinson among her crew, took off 17 men but, seriously overloaded, she transferred eight of them to the cutter commanded by Lieutenant Strugnell. Both boats made their way back to the harbour and landed all survivors.

Sir William was voted a first Gold Medal as Founder of the Institution on 10 March 1825. This is included in the list of Honorary Medals.

BROAD William, Lloyd's Agent, Falmouth	**GOLD**
	10 June 1829

7 January 1828: The 150-ton brig *Larch*, Newfoundland to Poole, with a cargo of fish, blubber and furs, encountered a heavy gale and, at noon, ran for Falmouth, Cornwall. She brought up too close to the shore and hoisted distress signals when, three hours later, she dragged her anchors. Mr. Broad and a Pilot went out in a six-oared gig and, boarding the vessel, tried to save her but, their efforts proving ineffectual, she was driven on to the rocks at New Quay pier, which put her crew in extreme danger. With the onset of darkness, the inhabitants of Flushing, a suburb of Falmouth, provided light by setting fire to furze and tar barrels on a nearby hill. Efforts to save the ship included cutting away her masts and running a cable ashore by means of which the crew and three passengers were brought to safety, all except the Master suffering from frostbite.

The brig was later discharged of her cargo and salvaged only to be again overtaken by disaster in 1831.

CLAYBOURN Thomas, Coxswain, Scarborough Lifeboat	**SILVER**
	30 January 1828

9 January 1828: With four other men, Mr. Claybourn went off in a boat in very difficult conditions and rescued the Master and seven crew members of the Sunderland ship *Centurion* which had gone aground at Osgodby, near Scarborough. One other crew member was rescued but he died soon after he was landed.

USHER John, Landlord, Tiger Inn. Coxswain, Bridlington Lifeboat   **SILVER**

23 April 1828

10 January 1828: In a tremendous gale, heavy seas and a blizzard with snow two feet deep on the uncovered low tide sand, the 120-ton Montrose schooner *Fox*, on passage from Pillau, East Prussia to Yarmouth with a cargo of linseed, was driven ashore south of Bridlington, Yorkshire. Three apprentices took to the sloop's boat but drowned. Although it was by then dark and conditions still bad, the Master, Mate and a seaman were brought ashore to safety in the lifeboat.

BAKE John Woolland, Lieutenant, R.N. H.M. Coastguard, Bovisand Bay   **SILVER**

13 February 1828

13 January 1828: When the ship *Mary Ann* was wrecked in Bovisand Bay near Plymouth, Devon, in heavy seas, Lieutenant Bake directed the rescue by rope of her Master, Mate, crew of 16 seamen and boys, and seven passengers. The ship was inward bound from St. Kitts, Leeward Isles, West Indies.

SMITH William, Fisherman   **SILVER**

13 February 1828

16 January 1828: The brig *Reaper*, en route from Pillau, East Prussia to London, went ashore through heavy seas at Thorp Gap, near Aldeburgh, Suffolk. All her crew except one seaman was swept overboard and drowned. As the mortar apparatus was ineffective, Mr. Smith waded out into the pounding surf and brought to safety the survivor, who had clung to a piece of the stern frame and drifted in.

Mr. Smith was awarded £2 for this service on 30 January 1828 which he returned to the Institution for its funds. He was then awarded the silver medal.

MORRISON Richard James, Lieutenant, R.N. H.M. Coastguard, Youghal   **SILVER**

27 February 1828

February 1828: Bound for Cork from Newport, Monmouthshire, the sloop *Mermaid* was wrecked in Whiting Bay, near Youghal, Co. Cork, Ireland. Lieutenant Morrison and five of his men saved the Master and four seamen by using ropes.

BAILLIE Henry, Lieutenant, R.N. H.M. Coastguard, Great Yarmouth   **SILVER**

27 February 1828

February 1828: As rescue by mortar apparatus was not possible, Lieutenant Baillie and crew put off in a boat and saved the Master and all the nine men from the Sunderland brig *Crofton* which had been wrecked off Caister, north of Great Yarmouth, Norfolk.

KIDD Daniel, Fisherman   **SILVER**

12 March 1828

9 February 1828: When the schooner *Fancy* was driven ashore at Broughty Ferry, near Dundee, Angus, Mr. Kidd with eight other fishermen put off and saved the Master and two seamen who had had to take refuge in the rigging. Two others had drowned.

LAKE Andrew, Chief Officer, H.M. Coastguard, Wick   **SILVER**

23 April 1828

22 February 1828 The brig *St. Nicholas*, on passage from St. Petersburg to Liverpool, was wrecked at Freswick Bay, near Wick, Caithness. The Coastguard boat was launched in an attempt to rescue the crew, but conditions were so severe that it could not reach the casualty. The rescuers then waded through heavy surf and brought off the exhausted Master, Mate and nine seamen who had drifted ashore on pieces of the wreckage after the brig had broken up.

BLOIS John Ralph, Captain, R.N. Inspecting Commander,
   H.M. Coastguard, Glynn   **GOLD**

20 August 1828

18 March 1828: At 9 p.m. a boat belonging to the steam packet *Venus* of Glasgow came ashore at Glynn, Co. Wexford, Ireland, with the Master, a lady and seven others aboard. The steam packet had been left in a sinking condition with 16 people on board. Captain Blois put off in a small Coastguard boat to try to effect a rescue. There was a gale blowing over a very heavy sea so this proved impossible. Captain Blois then sought the help of two fishing boats, but they each refused to put to sea even though a light could be seen which it was assumed belonged to the wreck. By this time the light had disappeared, so the coastguardmen returned to the shore and gave comfort to the people who had managed to reach safety in the steam packet's boat. Captain Blois ordered that a most strict lookout be maintained through the night and, at dawn, after the masts had been sighted, he launched and ten survivors were brought ashore.

CARTER John, Chief Officer, H.M. Coastguard, Skerries   **SILVER**

23 April 1828

26 March 1828: The ketch *British Oak* was wrecked on the South strand of the Skerries off Balbriggan, Co. Dublin, Ireland, while on passage from Liverpool to Dublin. With another coastguardman and five fishermen, Mr. Carter launched a yawl and saved the Master, Mate and two seamen who were clinging to the wreck's masthead with a tremendous sea breaking over them.

BRUNTON John, Lieutenant, R.N. H.M. Coastguard, Newton-by-the-Sea   **GOLD**

10 December 1828

1 December 1828: A little before daybreak, two miles north of Newton-by-the-Sea, Northumberland, during a severe easterly gale, the Arbroath schooner *Triton*, on passage from Libau, Russia, to Newcastle, with a cargo of rye, ran ashore. All attempts to get a rocket line aboard failed due to the distance involved. Lieutenant Brunton volunteered to make another attempt using a local coble. With four fishermen, he succeeded in launching it at the third attempt through violent surf. Alongside the wreck the sea was so turbulent that all, together with a survivor who had dropped

into the boat, were thrown out but they managed to regain hold on her. Using the rope that had been attached to it, the the coble was pulled ashore with the rescuers and rescued. By this time the schooner had broken up and the remainder of her crew perished.

WEEKES William Wall, Master, Smack *Fortitude*   **SILVER**

10 December 1828

1 December 1828: The Barking fishing smack *Fortitude* was on passage from the North Sea to the London market with a cargo of fish. Just after noon in a violent north-easterly storm with wind and rain in mountainous seas, the smack was forced to haul off the lee shore. At midnight she had reached the Swin or King's Channel and about an hour later saw a light on the sandbank known as Middle Ground, off Lowestoft, Suffolk. After tacking back and forth for two hours, she managed to come up with the Prussian brig *Graf von Essen* which had been wrecked there for some hours. A boat containing a number of people suffering from exposure was attached to the wreck so the *Fortitude* let go her anchor to try to get near the brig but could not manage to do so. After circling the casualty, Mr. Weekes managed to get a rope aboard and, although most of the survivors were unable to help themselves, he and his crew of four were able to rescue the Master, crew of ten and the Pilot. The brig had been on passage from Danzig to London with a cargo of wheat.

STRAHAN Henry, River Pilot   **SILVER**

7 January 1829

1 December 1828: A tide surveyor and four men, who had been upset in the River Tyne at Newcastle in a Custom House boat, would certainly have perished had not Mr Strahan and his son gone to their assistance in a boat not exceeding 14 feet long. All five were brought safely to shore.

HANNING Nicholas, Boatman, H.M. Coastguard, Minnard   **SILVER**

JEFFERS Richard, Boatman, H.M. Coastguard, Minnard   **SILVER**

MARK William, Boatman, H.M. Coastguard, Minnard   **SILVER**

RENOWDEN Joseph, Boatman, H.M. Coastguard, Minnard   **SILVER**

ROWE William, Boatman, H.M. Coastguard, Minnard   **SILVER**

24 December 1828

7–8 December 1828: In stormy weather the Belfast brig *Veronica* was driven ashore on the sands outside Inch Bar in Dingle Bay, Co. Kerry, Ireland, while on passage from Liverpool to Charleston, U.S.A. The vessel soon became a total wreck, and her crew and a passenger were forced to take to the rigging with the mountainous seas breaking over them. It was impossible for rescuers to get near her and, after a short time, the wreck was driven into deeper water where it sank with the mainmast gone, and her foretop out of the water with all the survivors clinging to it. The Coastguard four oared gig launched and got clear, but filled and had to be bailed out. Still she managed to take on board the brig's Master, Mate, Second Mate, Carpenter, 13 seamen and a passenger. The gig then paddled or drifted to the shore, a journey lasting two and a half hours, which ended with the gig being overturned and everybody having to be recovered from the surf.

In the original report, Rowe's name is given as Roe.

QUIRK George, Water Bailiff   **SILVER**
BRINE Thomas, Lloyd's Agent   **SILVER**
CARRINGTON William Henry, Comptroller of Customs   **SILVER**

24 December 1828

7–8 December 1828: The Liverpool 200 ton wooden steam packet *Earl of Roden* was driven on to rocks at Derbyhaven, Isle of Man, in a dark and stormy night with heavy seas running; some 60 passengers, mostly Irish labourers, were on board. The Castletown lifeboat was launched at 1 a.m. next morning with Messrs. Quirk, Brine and Carrington supplementing her crew. Unfortunately, the lifeboat was prevented by heavy surf from approaching nearer than 40 yards, and the packet's Master and crew experienced the greatest difficulty in stopping the unruly passengers, some of whom had been firing weapons in the air, from jumping overboard. However, the three men managed to persuade them that, with the tide falling, the vessel would hold together until low water and that the lifeboat would stand by for that period. All were landed safely at 6 a.m., and the steam packet was safely refloated on 22 December.

GIMAR Edward, Captain, French Brig *Le Norman*   **SILVER**

7 January 1829

18–21 December 1828: En route from Bourbon to Havre, off Cap d' Antifer, Département Seine Maritime, France, the brig *Le Norman* came across the brig *Auguste* which had been dismasted 12 days before some 350 miles out into the Atlantic, while on passage from Cherbourg to Sète in the Mediterranean. The vessel was driving fast on shore, and two men had already been washed overboard. Captain Gimar decided to get a line on board and tow her off. He succeeded but, in a heavy gale during the night of the 19th, lost two topsails and was injured himself. As his crew were worn out, he lay to all night and resolved to try to gain refuge in Dieppe. The morning of the 20th brought high seas and a gale at tide time, so that no Pilot would put out which forced them to lay off all night and make sail to prevent being driven ashore. The following morning found them off Dungeness, where a Pilot was taken aboard and the casualty towed to safety to Ramsgate harbour. Captain Gimar declined to claim salvage or any other reward. The French Consul (a Briton) applied to the 'Royal Institute for Preserving Lives from Shipwreck' for its medal to be awarded as an expression of international appreciation of the fact that he had saved six lives as well as the vessel.

LITHABY Philip, Chief Boatman, H.M. Coastguard, Ballywater   **SILVER**
ASKIN James   **SILVER**
*MORRISON William, Branch Pilot   **SILVER**

18 February 1829
*15 April 1829

30 December 1828: In a very strong wind and heavy sea, the steam packet *Sheffield*, Liverpool to Belfast, was seen to be on Scullmartin Rock, about one and half miles from the shore, at Ballywater, near Donaghadee, Co. Down, northern Ireland with a distress signal flying. The Coastguard manned their boat; among her crew was Mr. Askin who had volunteered to fill a vacant seat. Because of the wind, the sea and the boat's weight, it took an hour and a half to reach the rock. Meanwhile three other boats had been manned, the lead being taken by Mr. Morrison but, on arrival, it was seen that

the sea was breaking over the rock with great force and rushing through numerous gullies and chasms that intersected it. Mr. Lithaby succeeded in getting hold of a buoy with a rope attached, by which he was drawn on board the steamer. With the Master, he organised the passage of women and children passengers across a boom on to the rock where the surf was breaking with such force that great judgement was needed to bring the boats alongside. However, in six hours the Master, two Mates, two Engineers, 16 seamen and 24 passengers were landed safely.

LLOYD Samuel, Lieutenant, R.N. Chief Officer, H.M. Coastguard, Ballycotton   **GOLD**
HENNESSEY John, Extra Man, H.M. Coastguard, Ballycotton   **SILVER**
18 February 1829

25 January 1829: At about 2 p.m. the Spanish brig *Capricho*, bound for Bristol from Bilbao with a cargo of wheat, struck on a small island off Ballycotton, Cloyne, Co. Cork, Ireland. Lieutenant Lloyd and Mr. Hennessey put off in a four oared boat. In their anxiety to get alongside the wreck, they were driven by a violent sea on to a rock that stove them in amidships. They managed to return to shore, where a fisherman's whaleboat was commandeered, and put out again to find that the brig's Master and crew were now on the rock. All efforts to rescue them failed. Twenty minutes later, another boat was seen to put out from the shore with armed men intent on plunder but, under Lieutenant Lloyd's orders, this boat was used to save the brig's crew. The Master was twice washed off the rock and saved by Mr. Hennessey who dived into the water. The brig had first got into difficulty when she sprung a leak and her pumps had become choked. The Master had been trying to make Cork but, failing to recognise the correct route because of heavy snow, he had run his ship ashore. Although the Master and all nine crew were saved, the task of the Coastguard was not yet finished as, for six days, they had to protect the vessel's remains from thousands of locals intent on plunder.

LLEWELLYN David, Chief Officer, H.M. Coastguard, Roberts Cove   **SILVER**
1 April 1829

25 January 1829: Mr Llewellyn and his crew saved the entire complement of Master and ten seamen from the Portuguese schooner *Souza and Bastos*, wrecked at Rocky Bay, Cove District, Co. Cork, Ireland.

HENRY John Alphonso, Lieutenant, R.N. H.M. Coastguard, Groomsport   **SILVER**
18 March 1829

26 January 1829: The sloop *Friends* was wrecked in bad weather on Cockle Island, off Groomsport, Co. Down, northern Ireland and, hearing cries, Lieutenant Henry put off with his seven man crew. As the ridge of rocks completely encircling the vessel made it impossible to reach her, he landed on the island and burned two blue lights. The night was very dark with snow showers, but he went from rock to rock with seas breaking over them until he reached a point 15 to 20 yards from the survivors. He persuaded the crew – the Master, Mate and two seamen – to get into their own boat but as it reached the spot where Lieutenant Henry waited, it upset, and the men were then dragged on to the rocks and saved.

FLETCHER Thomas, Chief Boatman, H.M. Coastguard, Rosslare   **SILVER**
10 June 1829

24 April 1829: In severe weather the brig *Two Brothers* was wrecked near Rosslare, Co. Wexford, Ireland. Mr. Fletcher led eight coastguards to the rescue of the Master, seven crew and two passengers. Seven vain attempts were made to get a line on board by rocket, before four of his men launched a small punt in which, after three unsuccessful attempts in tremendous seas, all the survivors were brought ashore in three further trips.

LINGARD John, Lieutenant, R.N. H.M. Coastguard, Robin Hood's Bay   **GOLD**
19 August 1829

1 December 1828: In violent seas and a fierce north-easterly gale the brig *Henry* was driven ashore near Robin Hood's Bay, six miles south of Whitby, Yorkshire. Through high broken seas, Lieutenant Lingard led the rescue of her Master and the five crew members.

28 April 1829: Again, near Robin Hood's Bay, another brig, the *Esthers*, was wrecked and in a tremendously heavy easterly gale, Lieutenant Lingard, with four others, saved the Master, his wife and the five man crew.

HUGHES Thomas, Boatman, 1st Class   **SILVER**
8 July 1829

28 April 1829: Two brigs were wrecked on the same day off Holyhead, Anglesey, the *Fame* on passage from Barbados to Liverpool, and the *Harlequin*, to the same port from Palermo, Sicily. They had drifted on to rocks directly opposite the pier while trying to enter harbour in a heavy north-westerly gale. In both incidents, lines fastened to pieces of wood were thrown into the sea, which ended up among the rocks. Making use of the lines, both full crews were brought to safety – 24 men and boys in all. Hughes was the senior Boatman who led a party of 22 boatmen in the rescue.

MULLIGAN James   **SILVER**
8 July 1829

28 April 1829: With two other men James Mulligan saved two crew of the smack *Peggy* which was wrecked at Sligo, Co. Sligo, Ireland. He waded into the heavy surf and brought them ashore after their boat was upset while coming to land. One man died soon after the rescue.

MUDD William, Master, Smack *Samuel*   **SILVER**

WORDLEY Samuel, Master, Smack *Lively*   **SILVER**

13 May 1829

30 April 1829: At 7 a.m. the Aberdeen brig *Superb* was seen by William Mudd wrecked on Shipwash Sand, near Harwich, Essex. There were three men in the rigging, and the sea was breaking with great violence over the hull. Since the boats of the *Samuel* and *Lively* were too small, Mudd sought help from the London smack *Paul Pry* which proved to have a larger boat. Mudd and two of his crew together with two from the *Paul Pry* pulled to the wreck, with the *Lively* standing by. With great difficulty they managed to get two men on board, but the Master of the *Superb* was very weak and before he could be got on board, the *Paul Pry* boat was upset. Mudd and three men were thrown on to the wreck where they clung to the rigging. The remaining men in the boat managed to reach the *Lively* – bailing all the while and with a jacket stuffed in a hole.

Wordley from the *Lively,* with two of his own crew, then launched their boat and finally succeeded in getting everyone off. The nearly senseless Master of the *Superb* and the rescued men were finally landed at 10 p.m. the same day. The rescue had lasted 15 hours, but the three remaining crew of the *Superb* had been in the rigging since 10 p.m. on the 28 April. Two others had drowned.

William Mudd was drowned with his crew in January 1833 trying to save the crew of the brig Eslington *on Gunfleet Sand.*

BAILEY James, Boatman   **SILVER**

13 May 1829

30 April 1829: The brig *Perseverance* was driven on to the Goodwin Sands. Mr. Bailey, Acting Master of the *Sparrow* of Deal, with seven other men launched a boat at 4 a.m. and finally managed to get to windward of the wreck when they saw men in the rigging. Anchoring, they wore down keeping the boat's head to the wind, then hailed the men to come down the forestay to the bowsprit. Using the lead line, they had managed to get off the Master, three men and an apprentice when the brig then fell over on her beam ends. The remaining four men were lost.

During this service, some boats from Ramsgate had been hovering about the *Superb* but had made no attempt to render any assistance.

LOVELL Patrick   **SILVER**

5 August 1829

July 1829: After a boat was upset off Bellmullet, Co. Mayo, Ireland, spilling its occupants into the sea, Mr. Lovell launched a small leather curragh and saved three men and a woman. Three other men had drowned.

HUTCHISON William , Lieutenant, R.N. H.M. Coastguard, Kingstown   **GOLD**

11 November 1829

14 August 1829: The brig *Duke* was driven ashore in an easterly gale at 4 a.m. at Dalkey, in Sandy Cove, near Kingstown (now Dun Laoghaire), Co. Dublin, Ireland, with the crew and passengers, five men, three women and three children on board. In spite of the danger of being dashed to

pieces against rocks or the brig, Lieutenant Hutchison, with a crew of three coastguards and nine other men, put out through tremendous surf and saved all eleven from the wreck. Immediately afterwards the masthead was washed away and the brig broke up completely.

PYM Richard Elsworthy, Lieutenant, R.N.
   Chief Officer, H.M. Coastguard, Whitby   **GOLD**

16 September 1829

14 August 1829: Lieutenant Pym launched the Redcar lifeboat, manned by a double crew, on the night of the 14th to the rescue of the brig *Aurora*, laden with coal, which had been wrecked in a heavy gale and tremendous seas off the mouth of the River Tees. Despite seas sweeping over the lifeboat so strongly that there was an ever-present danger of the crew being washed overboard, they saved the Master, his wife, the Mate, Carpenter and six seamen. The seas were so violent that, to prevent them being washed out, the lifeboatmen had to lash everybody to their seats.

CROSSWELL Thomas, Chief Officer, H.M. Coastguard, Porthpean   **SILVER**

14 October 1829

19 August 1829: When the sean boat *Diligence* was observed sinking off Fowey, Cornwall, Mr. Crosswell went off in the Coastguard gig with five others and, carrying all possible sail, drove through the surf in a heavy gale. A lugger had saved the Master and four seamen two minutes before their arrival, but two of those saved were brought into the gig as the former was over-loaded.

SMITH Owen Nile Riordon, Master Mariner   **SILVER**
BRINKSMEAD William, Master Mariner   **SILVER**
GUY Philip, Master Mariner   **SILVER**

11 November 1829

11 September 1829: The Bristol packet *Daniel*, bound to Waterford, was thrown on to the South Tail in Bideford Bay, Devon in a severe north west gale. The Bideford Branch Association of North Devon lifeboat *Volunteer*, based at Appledore, was launched into the river and, manned by five volunteers including three Masters of vessels, fought her way over the bar through a maelstrom of violent sea. Reaching the *Daniel*, the lifeboat made two trips to shore saving ten passengers and crew.

The Master, who had the whole of his property in the Daniel *not insured, insisted on being brought ashore separately with a box containing some of his possessions. Whilst rewarding the lifeboat volunteers for the first two trips, the Committee of Management decided that the Master (one Thomas Williams) should remunerate himself those men that made the third trip to save him and his property.*

SIMS Andrew, Lieutenant, R.N. H.M. Coastguard, Peterhead   **SILVER**

14 October 1829

28 September 1829; An action involving the Manby rocket apparatus took place when the sloop *Frazer* went aground near Peterhead, Aberdeenshire; it was used to save her Master, Mate and two seamen. Lieutenant Sims was hurt in the process.

GRAHAM Philip, Commander, R.N.	**GOLD**
JOHNSON William Ward Percival, Lieutenant, R.N.	
H.M. Coastguard, Walmer	**GOLD**
WATTS William Stephen, Lieutenant, R.N. H.M. Coastguard, Walmer	**GOLD**
DURBAN John	**SILVER**

10 February 1830

24 November 1829: On passage from the Cape of Good Hope to London, the brig *Mountaineer* went on to Walmer Beach, near Deal, Kent. Lieutenants Johnson and Watts boarded the vessel and lowered down some of the crew over the side to Commander Graham who spent four hours in the surf carrying those rescued to the shore. He was repeatedly knocked down by the surf. The crew of 13 men and boys, a Pilot and three Deal boatmen were got on shore, but the Pilot, one boatman and two of the crew were dead. Local boatmen also rendered assistance. Amongst them was John Durban who was the first to get on board from the shore and helped in lowering the crew over the side.

CASEY Michael	**SILVER**
PHILLIPS John	**SILVER**

24 February 1830

4 December 1829: Messrs. Casey and Phillips were volunteers in the crew of the Coastguard boat which, with three other boats including the Rossglass lifeboat, saved the Master and 12 seamen from the *Sir James Kempt* which was wrecked in Dundrum Bay, Co. Down, northern Ireland, while on passage from New Brunswick, Canada to Liverpool. A woman and her infant child were also saved during the service.

ARMSTRONG William, Pilot	**SILVER**

27 January 1830

10 December 1829: On a dark night in a gale of wind and a heavy sea, the brig *Perseverence* was wrecked at Blyth, Northumberland. Armstrong and three other men went out in a boat and took off her Master, Mate, five seamen and two passengers. Soon afterwards the wreck fell over and broke up.

CLEAVE Robert, Master, Smack *New Union*	**SILVER**

27 January 1830

24 December 1829: The brig *Craig Elachie* was driven on to Gunfleet Sand, off Harwich, Essex at night in a heavy gale and snowstorm, with a crew of six men and a boy. Five died from cold and fatigue, but the other two were saved by Mr. Cleave in his boat; both were in a state of exhaustion.

MORGAN John, Chief Boatman, H.M. Coastguard, Staxigor	**SILVER**

10 February 1830

11 January 1830: Mr. Morgan saved the Master, Mate and three seamen, the full crew of the Stornoway, Lewis brig *Mary*, which had gone ashore at Thurso, Caithness in a storm. With two other coastguardmen Mr. Morgan rigged a rope and brought them ashore to safety. They had been in the rigging upwards of seven hours.

HILLARY Sir William, Bart   **GOLD BOAT (3)**
27 January 1830

14 January 1830: The Glasgow sloop *Eclipse* struck in Douglas Bay, Isle of Man, at daybreak. Four of the sloop's crew had taken to a small boat which, with the help of a line, drifted ashore safely. Conditions deteriorating, the sloop filled with water as heavy seas broke over her and the Master and two seamen were still on board. Sir William and a crew took the new lifeboat intended for Ramsey, lacking some of her buoyancy tanks, to the casualty. Reaching the sloop, with the lifeboat full of water, the last three survivors were taken off and landed.

JAMES Horatio, Lieutenant, R.N., H.M.S. *Hyperion*   **GOLD**
PRATTENT John, Lieutenant, R.N., H.M.S. *Hyperion*   **GOLD**
10 March 1830

19–20 January 1830: At Fairlight, near Hastings, Sussex, the French lugger *La Constance* was wrecked in a heavy gale and snow storm. On the morning of the 20th, Lieutenants James and Prattent led a number of Coast Blockade men into the very heavy surf and saved the Master and eight members of her crew when the ship broke up.

SANDERSON John Proctor, Lieutenant, R.N. H.M. Coastguard, Bridge of Don   **SILVER**
LANGTON Thomas William, Lieutenant, R.N. H.M. Coastguard, Belhelvil   **SILVER**
10 March 1830

21 January 1830: The smack *Fame* was driven ashore in Aberdeen Bay and wrecked. Fourteen people, the Master, Mate, seven seamen and five passengers (two of them women), were saved, five of them by boat and nine by rocket apparatus.

JONES Richard, Lieutenant, R.N. H.M. Coastguard, Whitby   **GOLD**
10 February 1830

18 January 1830: The local brig *Smalls* was driven on to the sands near the West Pier at Whitby, Yorkshire during an east-north-east gale, and the crew had taken to the rigging. The lifeboat could not make any way because of a strong flood tide, therefore Lieutenant Jones launched a small gig and, with four men, succeeded in reaching the wreck. The gig was almost immediately swamped. Lieutenant Jones then secured the crew of the brig who would otherwise have been washed overboard. At 2 p.m., when the tide changed, the lifeboat was able to come to their assistance and saved everyone – the Master, Mate, eight men and boys and Lieutenant Jones and his four men.

23 January 1830: Two Dundee smacks *William George* and *Catherine and Ann* were wrecked on Whitby Rocks in a gale. Lieutenant Jones with seven men, launched the coastguard gig through heavy seas but were forced to send for the lifeboat, which saved the Master, Mate and three seamen from each smack.

GRIFFITH David, Seaman, Beaumaris   **SILVER**

5 May 1830

16 April 1830: The emigrant ship *Newry* was wrecked at Bardsey Island, off the Lleyn Peninsula, Gwynedd, whilst on passage from Newry, Co. Down, northern Ireland to Quebec with 400 emigrants on board. At the time of the disaster, the passengers were in their berths, most of them seasick. Confusion and terror resulted. The Master ordered the mainmast cut down to form a bridge between the ship and shore but, as soon as this had been done, his entire crew, except for the Mate and one seaman, fled without thought for their passengers. As they vanished, David Griffith crossed the makeshift bridge and commenced rescuing the freezing men, women and children, taking them ashore using ropes. Three hundred and seventy-five survivors were saved, 40 to 50 of them by Griffith with the help of three labourers.

WILSON Ralph, Ruler of Pilots, Holy Island   **SILVER**

16 June 1830

9 May 1830: The Holy Island private lifeboat was launched by Mr. Wilson and a crew of 10 men and was towed by cobles through the surf when the brig *Jubilee*, Shields to London, was wrecked on Holy Island, Northumberland. The Master, eight seamen and one passenger were saved.

SHAW Charles, Lieutenant, R.N. H.M. Coastguard, Redheugh   **SILVER**

22 September 1830

28 August 1830: During bad weather, the Peterhead sloop *Peggy* went ashore on Tyne Sands near Dunbar, East Lothian. The Master, Mate, a seaman and a boy were rescued by Lieutenant Shaw and the Coastguard team using the Manby rocket apparatus.

TULLY William, Pilot   **SILVER**

9 May 1832

16 September 1830: The sloop *Friendship* ran on to rocks at Spanish Battery, near the entrance to Shields Harbour, Co. Durham, and drifted higher up on them so that it became unsafe for a lifeboat to attempt rescue. Mr. Tully, with three others, tried in a coble but it was impossible in the high seas; he landed from his boat and swam from rock to rock until he could throw the rope on to the vessel, which made it possible to save the Master and two seamen.

HILLARY Sir William, Bart   **GOLD BOAT (4)**
ROBINSON Robert, Lieutenant, R.N.   **GOLD**
CORLETT William, Steam Packet Agent   **SILVER**
VONDY Isaac, Coxswain, Douglas Lifeboat   **SILVER**

15 December 1830

20–21 November 1830: During the evening of the 20th, the Royal Mail Steamer *St. George*, entering Douglas Harbour, Isle of Man from Liverpool, was forced to anchor off the entrance by a south-west gale. During the night, the gale backed to south-east and increased dramatically so that, at 5.a.m., the chain cable parted and she was driven between the Pollock and St. Mary's Isle on to rocks. The vessel struck so violently that she began filling immediately, settling forward. Although the new lifeboat had not been commissioned, Sir William assembled a crew consisting of the Coxswain, 14 men, Lieutenant Robinson and Mr. Corlett who, after two hours' rowing, dropped anchor to veer down on the casualty's weather quarter. Disregarding advice from the casualty that the unsuccessful attempts should be suspended pending improvement in the weather, the lifeboat was brought, with great difficulty, into the narrow channel between the lee side of the wreck and the rocks. The lifeboat sustained serious damage, a number of oars were broken, and Sir William and three others were washed out of the boat. The three were recovered with all speed, but Sir William had been flung against the lifeboat's stern, sustaining six broken ribs among other serious injuries. Lieutenant Robinson, by now on the wreck, leaned overside and grasped him, then, with help, got him on board. The *St. George*'s foremast had been cut away to form a bridge ashore, but this created a formidable obstacle to freeing the lifeboat from her prison. Two hours of desperate work with an axe and knives cleared the tangle and, with the rising tide, she was able to reach open water with 22 aboard. On her way to the shore she was met by two boats, one of which took on the survivors, the other taking her in tow.

THOMPSON Robert Kirkpatrick, Chief Officer,
 H.M. Coastguard, Clogher Head **SILVER**

15 December 1830

20 November 1830: Across the Irish Sea, violent weather was causing trouble at Drogheda, Co. Louth, Ireland, where the brig *Raven* had grounded at night near the bar on the River Boyne. Mr. Thompson and a crew of fishermen double banked the oars of a country boat and put out. They succeeded in taking off the brig's crew, the Master and four men, who had been in the rigging for several hours.

HYNES Bartholomew, Boatman, H.M. Coastguard, Galway **SILVER**

15 December 1830

20 November 1830: On Ireland's Atlantic coast, the brig *Lillies* was wrecked on Black Rock, off Galway, Co. Galway. Two men were drowned, but the Master and four men remained aboard in the violent weather. Both a Coastguard boat and a boat from a man-o-war failed to save them and, during their several hours awaiting rescue, the survivors contrived, vainly, to build a raft. Finally, Mr Hynes and a crew of nine fishermen took them off in a sailing boat.

SERGEANT John, Lieutenant, R.N., H.M. Coastguard, Budleigh Salterton **SILVER**

5 January 1831

6 December 1830: The brig *Unity* was driven ashore near Exmouth, Devon, during a violent storm. The Manby rocket apparatus failed because the line broke. Lieutenant Sergeant went into the surf with a rope and with the assistance of two of his crew and several inhabitants succeeded in saving the whole crew of seven.

JAMES William, Lieutenant, R.N.   **GOLD**

5 January 1831

6 December 1830: The French Brig *Le Bon Père*, en route from Guadaloupe, Leeward Isles to Havre, was discovered during a heavy and destructive gale, manoeuvring near the coast and fast drifting on to shore. About 5 a.m. in darkness she struck violently on a reef of rocks off Towan, near Falmouth, Cornwall (two miles east of St. Anthony's Head) and, soon afterwards, beat over them to the beach. The tide was rising so rescue was urgent. Lieutenant James, a visitor to the neighbourhood, stripped naked and swam off through tremendous surf towards the vessel with a rope around his body, only to be overwhelmed by the raging sea when near the stricken vessel. He was dragged back to the shore, but swam off again, this time reaching the ship. He was able to bring a rope ashore by which the Master, Mate, a French Lieutenant and seven seamen safely reached the shore.

JONES Richard, Lieutenant, R.N. Chief Officer,
    H.M. Coastguard, Whitby   **GOLD BOAT(2)**

5 January 1831

12 December 1830: The sloop *Northfield* was stranded in severe weather off the beach at Whitby, Yorkshire. Watching the receding sea for an opportune time, Lieutenant Jones dashed into the surf and swam to the wreck. He brought ashore a rope by means of which the Master and three seamen, all the crew, were saved.

LEIGH Thomas, Lieutenant, R.N. Chief Officer,
    H.M. Coastguard, Winterton   **GOLD**

21 September 1831

26 November 1830: In tremendous gale conditions, the collier brig *Annabella* was driven on shore off Winterton, Norfolk with water breaking over her and the crew in danger of drowning. With much difficulty Lieutenant Leigh and his crew put out in a boat and rescued seven men.

24 December 1830: On passage from Hull to London, the brig *Henry* went ashore off Winterton in bad weather. In great difficulty and danger, Lieutenant Leigh and his men took off the Master and three seamen by boat.

DABINE Thomas Dymock Jones, Lieutenant, R.N.
    H.M. Coastguard, Wicklow   **SILVER**

2 March 1831

31 January 1831: During the night, with the sea making a complete breach over her, the schooner *Jane* was wrecked off the port of Wicklow, Co. Wicklow, Ireland. Entering the surf with ropes attached to their bodies, Lieutenant Dabine and his team of six coastguardmen tried to throw a boathook, with a lead line attached, to the schooner. After two hours unremitting effort, they succeeded in taking off the Master and three seamen. At daybreak, they boarded the schooner to find only one dead seaman lashed to the foremast. One other seaman had drowned.

STEANE John, Lieutenant, R.N. Coast Blockade, Camber   **GOLD**

EARLE Edward Charles, Lieutenant, R.N. Coast Blockade, Camber   **GOLD**

4 May 1831

1 February 1831: The brig *Fame*, on passage from Messina, Sicily to London, came ashore and was wrecked on Camber Sands, near Rye Harbour, Sussex. As soon as the brig was discovered the Lieutenants Steane and Earle, together with six coastguards and five local seamen, alternately went off in their boats four times, but failed to reach the wreck because of the wind, sleet and snow. The fourth attempt ended with the boat's bottom stove in, but the rescuers reached safety. After the tide had fallen and the sea had become less turbulent, they managed to reach the casualty. The only sign of the brig's crew was two dead bodies entangled in the rigging. They recovered gold worth £3,000 from the wreck.

TURNER Charles, Lieutenant, R.N   **GOLD**

1 June 1831

5 May 1831: When the sloop *Janet* was wrecked off Fraserburgh, Aberdeenshire, attempts were made to save the Master, Mate and a single seaman by rocket apparatus. A line reached the vessel at the second attempt but broke. Seeing another line astern of the wreck, Lieutenant Turner made several attempts to swim off but was pounded by heavy seas; he had to be taken home. Earlier, he had also helped to get the local private lifeboat afloat and tried to board the casualty, without success. After Lieutenant Turner had been taken home, the lifeboat did manage to save the three crew members.

The lifeboat belonged to the town of Fraserburgh and was kept up by a charge of sixpence per man, on all seamen entering the harbour.

LEWIS WALKER William, Collegian   **SILVER and SILVER BOAT(2)**

WILLIAMSON Ralph, Captain, Yacht *Campeadora*   **SILVER and SILVER BOAT(2)**

21 December 1831

18 August 1831: The steam packet *Rothsay Castle*, on passage from Liverpool to Beaumaris Bay, Anglesey, was wrecked at night on Dutchman's Bank, Anglesey, but news of the disaster did not reach shore until 4 a.m. next morning. In the horrendous conditions and with delay in help arriving, only 20 men and two women survived. Mr. Williamson, whose yacht was anchored off Beaumaris, gave help with his crew and boats and, in the morning, rescued two men found floating on pieces of wood, one of whom had gone blind. Mr. Lewis Walker, who happened to be on the Green at Beaumaris, saw nine people drifting in the Bay on part of the wreck. He raised the alarm and, when the lifeboat was launched, he took part in the rescue. Boatmen rescued four survivors and the Penmon Pilots seven more.

No particular reason is given for the double awards other than that they were 'for their very meritorious exertions in the cause of humanity'.

BAKER Gustavus Spicker, Lieutenant, R.N.
H.M. Coastguard, Folkestone

SILVER

30 November 1831

2 November 1831: The coal laden brig *Brothers and Sisters* went on shore at 1.45 a.m. close to No. 24 Martello Tower, near Folkestone, Kent. The Coastguard launched their galley immediately, but the boisterous conditions rendered their efforts ineffective; twice the boat was nearly swamped. Lieutenant Baker and his men took their boat along the shore until they were opposite the wreck, where they lit port fires to encourage the crew. When the weather slackened at 3.30 a.m., they launched and closed the brig in the dark, proposing to take the crew ashore two at a time. Unfortunately the Master and the five seamen jumped into the rescuers' boat at the same time and it sank on a sandbank – so they all had to wade ashore.

LYONS William, Lieutenant, R.N. H.M. Coastguard, Ardrossan

SILVER

30 November 1831

10 November 1831: The brig *Lady Montgomerie*, laden with coal, was seen to go down, one mile from shore, off Saltcoats Harbour, near Ardrossan, Ayrshire. The Master, Mate and one seaman were drowned. The local private lifeboat launched with Lieutenant Lyons and a crew of ten men; they reached the wreck through a severe gale and heavy seas and saved two apprentices.

PARRY Howard Lewis, Lieutenant, R.N.
Inspecting Commander, H.M. Coastguard, Rye

GOLD

25 January 1832

21 November 1831: At daybreak, a large French lugger fishing boat *L'Aimée* was found ashore in Rye Bay, east Sussex with her French colours flying and a light in her shrouds. Lieutenant Parry manned his galley, brought it half a mile overland to a point opposite and launched with four coastguardmen in the face of a violent storm. In four hazardous trips, 21 survivors were brought ashore. By this time, the galley was so damaged that it was no longer seaworthy then, using a rope that he had brought ashore from the lugger, he saved the ten remaining survivors.
Lieutenant Parry had been a Boy seaman at Trafalgar.

DESMOND John, Farmer

SILVER

21 December 1831

26 November 1831: The sloop *Shaw Stewart* was driven ashore under cliffs on the River Shannon in Oyster Haven, Co. Limerick, Ireland. It was dark, but Mr. Desmond was lowered over a tremendous precipice with a rope and lantern and, in very hazardous conditions, was able to save five men.

MARIOLE Jean Baptiste, Honfleur Pilot

SILVER

21 December 1831

9 December 1831: Mr Mariole, in his own fishing smack, came across the dismasted sloop *Pyramus* of Dartmouth off Fairleigh, Sussex, and took her in tow, delivering her safely at Ramsgate, Kent, with her Master and crew.

AUTRIDGE Charles, Lieutenant, R.N. H.M. Coastguard, Doonbeg　　　**SILVER**

25 January 1832

21 December 1831: In strong westerly winds and a heavy running sea the Whitehaven brig *Cyclops* was discovered at daybreak ashore at Doonbeg, Co. Clare , Ireland, with her foremast and bowsprit gone, apparently waterlogged and her crew in the rigging. Lieutenant Autridge launched his gig with a crew of five coastguardmen and pulled for three hours before he succeeded in reaching the brig which he found to be a complete wreck with the sea making a complete breach over her. At the third attempt, during a lull in the weather, he pulled alongside and took off seven men and two boys. The Master had been washed overboard, and the Carpenter had died in the rigging.

DUFFY Michael, Boatman　　　**SILVER**

14 March 1832

5 February 1832: In a dark, tempestuous night, the pleasure boat *Caroline* (9 tons) was upset and sank near Sligo, Co. Sligo, Ireland, with two men on board. One was saved in difficult and dangerous conditions by Mr. Duffy, a Mullaghmore boatman, who went off in a Norway yawl with five other boatmen.

HILDEBRAND Henry, Bailiff　　　**SILVER**

14 March 1832
*7 March 1850

12 February 1832: The timber laden ship *Huntley* foundered on 4 February 500 miles west of Ireland; her Master and crew of 14 men took to their boat. After nine nights and days without a compass, suffering great privations, they were cast up on the Island of Bopphin, near Westport, Co. Mayo, Ireland, so emaciated and frost-bitten that they could not render themselves the slightest assistance. The people of the coast, fearing cholera, would not go near them until Mr. Hildebrand (Bailiff to the Marquis of Sligo) went forward and, by example and influence, succeeded in getting them all safely landed. He then took them to his own house and offices where they were fed and looked after. Unfortunately two of them died next morning.

　*Mr. Hildebrand reported his medal as lost, and on 7 March 1850 a replacement was voted. At the time this was counted as a separate award and was included in the overall number of medals awarded.

CARRINGTON Lawrence George, Lieutenant, R.N.
　H.M. Coastguard, Sheephaven　　　**SILVER**

14 March 1832

26 January 1832: The Dublin brig *Bittern*, laden with coal, was wrecked at Dunfanaghy, Co. Donegal, Ireland, and her Mate and three seamen were drowned. After several attempts, Lieutenant Carrington and five local men put off in a boat and saved the Master and three other men.

TUVACHE ... , Captain, French Brig *Le Cotonnière*   **SILVER**

18 July 1832

29 February 1832: The 450 ton ship *St. Andrew* was on passage from Sierra Leone with a cargo of elephant's teeth (tusks) when the *Le Cotonnière* (also reported as *Le Collinièrre*) came up with her 900 miles west of Cape Finisterre at 2 p.m. on 29 February. Her Master reported that his ship was ungovernable and, after verifying this, Captain Tuvache took the Master and 19 men and boys aboard and conveyed them to his destination although he could hardly feed them.

Apparently, this was an instance of meritorious service rather than gallantry.

McCULLOCH Kenneth, Chief Boatman, H.M. Coastguard, Elie   **SILVER**

14 March 1832

6 March 1832: When the sloop *Vine* struck the bar at Elie Harbour, Fife and was wrecked, Lieutenant Randall and five men, Mr. McCulloch among them, put off in a gig and saved the Master and his two seamen.

JENNINGS William, Master, Smack *Spy*   **SILVER**

14 March 1832

6–7 March 1832: In a heavy gale thick with rain, Captain Jennings saw the brig *Faithful* of Sunderland on the Cork Sand, off Harwich, Essex and reached her position at 6 p.m. Manning his boat with himself and five men, he pulled towards the casualty but, with the heavy sea driving on to the sand, was compelled to return to his smack. He got her under way and, at 10 p.m., went around to the south of Cork Sand and manned his small boat for the second time but had to return once more. After midnight, he made a third attempt, but found the wreck bilged and full of water. Three men had drowned in the longboat and the jolly boat was gone. The survivors – the Master and four seamen – were taken aboard his smack at 1.30 a.m. and later were landed safely at Harwich.

EDWARDS David, Master Mariner	**SILVER**
MEARNS Robert (Junior), Master Mariner	**SILVER**
NICHOL John, Master Mariner	**SILVER**
COUL Alexander, Fisherman	**SILVER**
COUL Charles, Fisherman	**SILVER**
FINLAY William, Fisherman	**SILVER**
JAPP Robert, Fisherman	**SILVER**
PEART John, Fisherman	**SILVER**
WATT Alexander, Fisherman	**SILVER**

11 April 1832

8 March 1832: In violent weather a number of vessels were in difficulties off Montrose, Angus, and, after the private lifeboat had been to their aid, it was re-manned by a fresh crew of three Masters and 13 seamen. Helped by the six fishermen in a salmon coble, the new crew saved, with considerable difficulty, the Master and four others from the smack *Ann* which was being driven on shore at Annat, near Montrose.

HAMONO Abel, Master, French Brig *Le Francais de St. Brieux*   **SILVER**

18 July 1832

17 March 1832: The French brig *Le Francais de St. Brieux*, en route from Marseilles to Honfleur, Département Eure, fell in with the St. Ives galliot *Economy* on passage from Naples to London with a cargo of brandy and wine. The galliot was flying a distress signal and on fire in a high wind and sea, endangering the cargo. Manoeuvring carefully, Captain Hamono took three men from a boat and then the Master and two others from the galliot. Due to constantly contrary winds, he did not land the survivors at Honfleur until 20 April.

HUMPHREYS David, Second Mate, Steam Packet *St. Patrick*   **SILVER**

11 April 1832

25 March 1832: The *St. Patrick* was heavily bilged off Waterford, Co. Waterford, Ireland and filled rapidly. It was feared that she would soon become a complete wreck. Mr. Humphreys, nearly 60 years old, volunteered to swim ashore with a line.Despite the risk of being dashed on to the rocks, he was successful, and a hawser was brought ashore enabling all the passengers and crew to be rescued.

As a result of his action, Mr. Humphreys contracted a painful lingering illness, which prevented him from working again.

JONES Thomas, Second Mate, Packet *Escape*   **SILVER**

9 May 1832

8 April 1832: In bad weather and a heavy sea, the sloop *John and William* was wrecked on Baldogle Sand, near Howth, Co. Dublin, and soon filled. Mr. Jones and three men took a small harbour boat and pulled through the surf to rescue the sloop's Master and three seamen

ADAM John, Chief Officer, H.M. Coastguard, Blackwater   **SILVER**

SAWTELL Edwin, Chief Officer, H.M. Coastguard, Cahore   **SILVER**

9 May 1832

8 April 1832: In a strong gale and heavy sea, the brig *Hawk* was wrecked on Blackwater Bank, off the coast of Co. Wexford, Ireland. When she struck, five of her crew got a boat off and made for land. Seeing this, Mr Adam and others brought their galley down to the water's edge, but when the *Hawk*'s boat reached the outer bank, she swamped and her occupants were washed away. The galley put out to the wreck and took off the Master, two men and a boy. Meanwhile, Mr. Sawtell also rescued a seaman who had set out from the wreck with a rope.

SPARK Anthony, Captain, Ship *Chieftain*   **SILVER**

18 June 1834

July 1832: The Sunderland brig *Chieftain* came up with the ship *Isabella*, which, on passage from Galway to New York, was flying a distress signal, and took off 34 passengers and five crew, who were landed later at Quebec, Canada. The remainder of the crew and passengers were taken off by the *Nancy* of Shields next day one hour before the casualty sank.

HENSLOW Frederick John Francis, Lieutenant, R.N.,
   H.M. Coastguard, Dungeness   **SILVER**

20 September 1832

27 August 1832: A large American ship, the *Richmond*, was in distress in a gale and thumping on the ground near Fort Moncrieff Station, Littlestone-on-Sea, Kent. Nearby, the Ostend brig *Osiris* was seen to be drifting on her beam ends. Lieutenant Stuart, R.N., with his crew of nine men, then dragged a punt and a galley two miles to reach a point closer to the two ships. The punt capsized when launched. Lieutenant Stuart then saw the *Osiris* strike: the crew got away to the *Richmond*. Meanwhile, the Institution lifeboat stationed at No. 27 Tower, Dymchurch, had been launched by Lieutenant Henslow and six Coastguardmen. They reached the *Richmond*, but the Master refused assistance. The ten crew of the *Osiris* were taken in to the lifeboat and landed safely at Fort Montcrieff Station where they were looked after by Lieutenant Stuart.

ANNIS Mentor, Chief Officer, H.M. Coastguard, Redheugh   **SILVER**

24 October 1832

5 October 1832: When the smack *Forfarshire* was driven ashore in a storm at Fast Castle, St. Abb's Head, Berwickshire, the Chief Officer, Mr. Annis, and his crew took off six passengers – two men, two women and two children – in the Coastguard boat.

THOMAS James, Boatman, H.M. Coastguard, Atherfield   **SILVER**
STUBBS Henry, Boatman, H.M. Coastguard, Atherfield   **SILVER**

24 October 1832

8 October 1832: Just before daybreak, in a violent gale with severely surging seas, the 430 ton ship *Bainbridge* was driven on to rocks a quarter of a mile off Atherfield, Isle of Wight. With the ship striking at every heave and the sea making a complete breach over her, the fore and main masts were cut away to improve her stability and, at daylight, the crew was seen in her stern looking for help. With the immense waves breaking in quick succession any thought of a boat rescue was out, and four attempts by the Manby rocket apparatus failed. The Dennett's rocket apparatus was set up and succeeded, first time, in getting a line aboard; this was used to transfer a rope from the shore. Boatmen Thomas and Stubbs volunteered to man the Coastguard boat which was hauled to the wreck through the surf and used to bring the Master, passengers and crew – 19 in all – ashore.

DAVIES George, Lieutenant, R.N., H.M. Coastguard, Jury's Gap **SILVER**

5 December 1832

11 November 1832: The sloop *Dartmouth* was wrecked at Camber, near Rye, Sussex, and her Master and five others were drowned. Lieutenant Davies and six other men put off in a fishing vessel, but were driven back by the extraordinary violent weather. They carried the boat along the shore to a more convenient position and launched again to rescue the solitary survivor clinging to the rigging.

STABLES Robert, Coxswain, Holyhead Lifeboat **SILVER**
OWEN William, Master Mariner **SILVER**
ANTHONY Owen, Master Mariner **SILVER**

6 February 1833

3 December 1832: In severe weather the ship *Iphegenia*, en route from New Brunswick to Newry, Co. Down, northern Ireland, struck rocks to the leeward of Holyhead Harbour, Anglesey, but was not discovered until she was set fast on them. The Harbour Master's boat was nearby when the ship's hawsers parted, and he was able to rescue all the crew except one, who was taken off by the lifeboat after the ship had gone on the rocks. Captains Owen and Anthony helped man the lifeboat.
   Owen had been an African trader: Anthony in the West Indies trade.

CAREY Henry, Esq **SILVER**

27 March 1833

21 January 1833: The brig *Fame*, from Londonderry, was wrecked on Inishowen Head, Co. Donegal, Ireland, but the wreck was not discovered until the following morning. Mr. Carey, with four men, went off in his boat even though the sea was very high and the danger was very great and no Pilot boats would set out. He reached the brig and took off the crew of six who had been waiting ten hours with the sea completely breaching. They were landed safely. Had there been a half hour delay, the rescue would not have been possible.

RANDALL Henry, Lieutenant, R.N. H.M. Coastguard, Elie **GOLD BOAT(2)**
McCULLOCH Kenneth, Chief Boatman, H.M. Coastguard, Elie **SILVER BOAT(2)**

21 May 1834

2 February 1833: When the schooner *Wanderer* was wrecked at Elie, Fife, in a violent storm Lieutenant Randall and Mr. McCulloch put off in the Coastguard gig with two other men and, at the third attempt, rescued the Master and six men. They were landed under a salute of three cheers from several hundred spectators on the beach.

VONDY Isaac, Coxswain, Douglas Lifeboat **SILVER(2) and SILVER BOAT(3)**

13 March 1833

2–3 February 1833: On her maiden voyage from Douglas to Liverpool, the 500 ton ship *Parkfield* ('the largest and finest vessel ever built at the Isle of Man') suddenly encountered a storm when ten miles out. Her ballast of large paving stones shifted, at one time bringing the ship on her beam ends. The Captain decided to return to Douglas Bay, reaching there shortly after midnight. There the ship struck on St Mary's Rock – site of the recently completed Tower of Refuge. She let go her anchors but, in half an hour, was driven on to the Black Rocks. The plight of the ship was seen from the shore and Sir William Hillary was informed. As soon as a crew could be mustered, he sent off 'the lesser lifeboat', following himself shortly after in 'the larger lifeboat'. Waiting for high tide, the whole of the persons on board – some 60 crew and passengers including women – were taken on the boats and landed at the pier before sunrise without the loss of a single life. Sir William commended the services of the Coxswain, Isaac Vondy, who was exceptionally awarded a silver medal and a silver boat. This was Sir William's last active service in a lifeboat .

RAWSTONE James, Lieutenant, R.N. H.M. Coastguard, Newhaven   **SILVER**

GRANDY Samuel, Lieutenant, R.N. H.M. Coastguard, Newhaven   **SILVER**

*MORGAN Thomas. Commanding Revenue Cutter *Stork*   **SILVER**

8 May 1833

*12 June 1833

11 February 1833: The Jersey smack *John* was wrecked in Seaford Bay, Sussex, during a heavy gale and driven ashore where the beach was very steep. The sea was running tremendously high and began engulfing her. The Manby rocket apparatus was mounted at the scene and succeeded in getting a line aboard the vessel at the second attempt. The three officers played leading parts in the rescue, helped by 21 coastguardmen, and took off the smack's Master, Mate, one seaman and the two owners.

WAKE Baldwin Arden, Midshipman, R.N. H.M.S. *Forrester*   **SILVER**

27 March 1833

13 February 1833: A hurricane during the night drove H.M.S. *Forrester* on to the Crow Bar, north of St. Mary's, Isles of Scilly, from where she drifted on to Crowther Point. Gripping a line in his mouth, Midshipman Wake swam through high seas to the shore; this enabled an officer and 16 men to be brought to safety.

FIELD William, Farmer, former Master Mariner   **SILVER**

12 June 1833

20 February 1833: On passage from the Clyde to Leghorn, Italy, the Sicilian brig *Felicita* was wrecked in Sandy Haven Bay, west of Milford Haven, Pembrokeshire, during the night of the 19–20th; her Master and six seamen were washed off and drowned. About 7 a.m. Mr. Field saw the wreck on the sands near his house, the hull broken in two, all her masts gone, surf breaking over her and survivors in the lower rigging. Obtaining the services of two volunteers, he went over the reef and swam to the wreck and, helped by one of the men, brought two seamen safely ashore in separate journeys. With the other volunteer assisting them, they brought the remaining survivors (including two passengers) ashore, but one seaman and a boy died later. All the survivors were rendered helpless by exhaustion; the passengers were all badly cut by being thrown against the rocks.

MAY Augustus Charles, Mate, R.N. H.M.S. *Rover* — **SILVER**
STRONG Francis M., Second Master, R.N. H.M.S. *Spartiate* — **SILVER**
HUSS Thomas, Master's Assistant, R.N. H.M.S. *Rover* — **SILVER**

13 March 1833

20 February 1833: In a most violent gale the brig *Erin*, on passage from Liverpool to Savannah, Georgia, was wrecked on the breakwater at Plymouth, Devon. Boats from *Spartiate* and *Rover* put off to rescue any survivors, but, having lifted the Master, Mate and eight seamen, ran into grave difficulties. The gale was so violent that they could neither reach their ships nor any shore on which it would be possible to land. Particularly affected by the atrocious conditions were the officers and men in the *Rover*'s boat who had volunteered to leave their ship at a time of great risk to themselves and wearing scarcely any clothes. Drifting to the leeward with no chance of escape, the fatigued crews of both boats were saved solely by the efforts of the Master and crew of the fishing smack *Rebecca*.

CHAPPELL William, Master Mariner — **SILVER**

7 November 1833

6 March 1833: On 20 February, during a tremendous gale, the Truro schooner *Delabole*, homeward bound from Newport, Monmouth, with a cargo of coal and iron, stranded on Saunton Sands in Bideford Bay, Devon. Swept by heavy seas the crew were lucky to get ashore. Thinking the schooner to be a wreck, her owners sold her to two Braunton merchants who sent a crew and labourers on board to discharge the coal and patch the hull. During the night of 5–6 March, a heavy northerly gale sprang up and, at daylight, after signals from the wreck were seen, Bideford No. 2 lifeboat *Assistance* launched with Captain Chappell at the steering oar. With great skill he went alongside and took off the Master and eight men crew and labourers and landed them safely.

LEIGH Thomas, Lieutenant, R.N. H.M. Coastguard, Winterton — **GOLD BOAT(2)**

24 April 1833

20 March 1833: The ship *Crawford Davison* was totally wrecked in a heavy gale on Winterton Beach, Norfolk, north of Great Yarmouth. In conditions of great difficulty and danger, the Winterton lifeboat (Norfolk District Committee) launched with Lieutenant Leigh and a crew of 25 men. The ship's Master and his crew, 16 in all, were saved. The rescuers had been engaged on the beach from daybreak to 2 p.m. sometimes up to their chests in water; they then manned the lifeboat, landing the survivors at 4 p.m. just as the wreck rolled over and broke up.
   Lieutenant Leigh was also awarded the Royal Humane Society's Silver Medal.

MANN Adrian Thomas, Lieutenant, R.N. H.M. Coastguard, Devonport — **SILVER**

8 May 1833

26 April 1833: The barge *James* was wrecked in bad weather off Plymouth, Devon, and a boat put off with a crew of four men to give help, but capsized on the way. Lieutenant Mann with two of his men set off in the Coastguard punt to try to rescue the four erstwhile rescuers and the barge's two man crew. He picked up three men, two others swam ashore and one man drowned.

READ James, Lieutenant, R.N. H.M. Coastguard, Newhaven   **SILVER**

18 July 1833

16 June 1833: On passage from Arundel to London, the sloop *Industry* was wrecked near Newhaven, Sussex, in a south-west gale and heavy surf. The Master, his wife and a seaman took to the rigging. Lieutenant Read and two of his men then got a rope aboard and went through the surf to rescue the survivors despite twice being taken out of their depth.

HENIN Pierre, Mariner   **SILVER**

3 October 1833

31 August 1833: The chartered convict ship *Amphitrite*, en route from Woolwich for New South Wales with 108 female prisoners, 12 children, a Surgeon, his wife and a crew of 14, was over-crowded and undermanned when she ran into a violent gale off Dungeness, Kent. The ship was carried across the Channel to the French coast near Boulogne, Département Pas de Calais. In view of her helpless state, the Captain ran her ashore at 4.30 p.m. on a spit of sand three-quarters of a mile from the shore hoping to refloat her on the next tide. Onlookers and officials ashore were at best apathetic, but a local Pilot ran his boat close to the casualty and offered assistance. The Captain, fearful that some of his charges might seize the opportunity to escape, refused. Nothing further happened until 6.30 p.m. when Mr. Henin, who was a strong swimmer, stripped off on the beach and entered the water with a rope. However, the Captain obstinately refused to allow it to be used and the exhausted swimmer had to return to the shore. Finally, just after 7 p.m., the ship broke up with her crew in the rigging and, everybody, except three seamen, per-ished – a total loss of 133 souls.

Monsieur Henin was also awarded 250 francs (then equivalent to £10). The local Pilot also received 250 francs.

CHAPLIN ... , Captain, Steam Packet *Royal William*   **SILVER**

19 September 1833

2–4 September 1833: On 31 August, the brig *Shipwright* was in a tempestuous gale and, on the following day, lost her foremast, bowsprit, bulwarks up to the foremast and water cask. She con-tinued, deprived of water, and with the sea making a breach over her, until she was seen at 5 a.m on 2 September off Yarmouth, Norfolk by Captain Chaplin. After considerable difficulty the Master and seven crew of the brig were saved, and the *Shipwright* was towed into Yarmouth on the 4th.

BEVAN John, Captain, Schooner *Gower*   **SILVER**

7 November 1833

14 October 1833: With a tremendous gale blowing the brig *Ann and Margaret* was seen at 4.40 p.m. on shore a little to the east of the bar at Aberavon, Glamorgan. Captain Bevan ordered his jolly boat to be manned and went with four of his men to a point as near to the wreck as possi-ble. Seeing something rolling in the water, he swam to it with a lead line around his waist – it was a man, whom he brought safely to land. He returned immediately to the wreck, lying in the surf off the beach, and took off the exhausted Captain and the other three men.

CHAPPELL Thomas	**SILVER**
TUCKFIELD Thomas	**SILVER**
POPHAM Henry	**SILVER**

29 January 1834

24 November 1833: In a west-south-west gale, the topmasts of a sunken brig were seen on Northam Sands, off Bideford, Devon. The Bideford lifeboat *Assistance* was launched to the wreck which was found to be the deserted Exeter brig *Mary Ann*. Later, a movement in the rigging led to the lifeboat being launched again with a second crew, but, while lying-to alongside the wreck, the lifeboat was overturned by a big breaker and three of her crew were trapped, two being drowned. The second Bideford lifeboat, *Volunteer*, was launched and saved four men who had scrambled back on the upturned boat. Mr. Tuckfield and Mr. Chappell led the rescue attempts.

It is not clear from R.N.L.I. records what part Mr. Popham took in this service.

ROBERTS Robert, Harbour Surveyor   **SILVER**

12 December 1833

29 November 1833: On passage from Liverpool to Marseilles, the brig *Susan* ran aground on Abermenai Point in Menai Strait, off Caernarvon, North Wales, in a tremendous gale. Caernarvon lifeboat was launched with Mr. Roberts and nine men aboard. With great difficulty, they reached the brig just as night was falling and took off the brig's Master, his wife, two passengers and nine seamen. They were landed safely that night and, when dawn broke next day, not a vestige of the wreck remained.

SUMNER Richard, Surgeon   **GOLD**

12 December 1833

29 November 1833: Stormy weather caused an unusual sequence of events off the coast of Lancashire to which Pilot Boat No. 1 of Liverpool, *Good Intent*, was being driven with a number of Pilots aboard. The boat gave a lurch during the night and her punt was washed off its stowage on the deck into the belly of the sail, splitting it so that the wind blew it into ribbons. She became unmanageable and drove on to Formby Beach, 13 of her complement being drowned and nine remaining alive. Mr. Sumner obtained a bottle of rum, tied it round his neck and, finding that no boat could possibly get near the wreck, stripped and swam to it, then administered the bottle's contents to the survivors. Afterwards, he helped bring the eight men and a boy to safety, then exercised his medical skill in reviving them.

GILES William, Master Mariner   **SILVER**

12 December 1833

29 November 1833: The brig *Albion*, on passage from Youghal to London, ran on to Doombar Sands off Padstow, Cornwall, in a most violent gale with heavy ground sea. The harbour boat, going to help manned by volunteers, was upset. Mr. Giles and seven seamen volunteered to man the lifeboat and took off four men from the wreck. He tried also to persuade the Master to leave but, after half an hour, the line parted and the ship fell over and sank, drowning the man before he could change his mind.

EVANS Thomas, Lieutenant, R.N. Lloyd's Agent, Fishguard   **SILVER**

9 April 1834

29–30 November 1833: The sloop *Ranger*, at anchor near rocks, was wrecked in a very heavy sea off Fishguard, Pembrokeshire. Lieutenant Evans and his boat's crew put off in the Fishguard lifeboat and saved the Master and crew. Lieutenant Evans had constructed the lifeboat to his own plan in 1822 and paid for it himself apart from £50 granted by Lloyd's.

MURRAY Andrew, Boatman, H.M. Coastguard, Elie   **SILVER**

MASON John, Boatman, H.M. Coastguard, Elie   **SILVER**

5 March 1834

3 December 1833: The schooner *John* was in difficulties during bad weather off the coast of Fife, near Elie. Boatmen Murray and Mason put off in a boat and rescued her crew of five men.

GALE William, Captain, Smack *Active*   **SILVER**

8 January 1834

16 December 1833: The Sunderland brig *Sisters* finished on her beam ends after being wrecked in a storm near Near Warp Light, off Yarmouth, Norfolk, but her crew of 13 remained on board in great peril. Captain Gale, whose smack could not get near enough, launched his boat with three of his men and took off the survivors in two trips in which the boat's bows were stove in. The survivors were landed at Yarmouth.

BARLACH Henry, Captain, Ship *Everhard* (Bremen)   **SILVER**

21 May 1834

15 December 1833: Captain Barlach came across the collier brig *Advena*, dismasted and in a sinking condition, in the North Sea and saved her Master and seven man crew. He took them on board his own vessel, and fed and clothed them until 10 January 1834. He fell in with an English fishing smack but , only after considerable discussion, would her Master accept the survivors for passage.

BURNARD Thomas, Honorary Secretary, North Devon Humane Society   **SILVER**

8 January 1834

17 December 1833: In a violent storm the Liverpool ship *Elizabeth*, on passage from Calcutta, struck on Northam Sands, off Bideford, Devon. Mr. Burnard was first on board one of the two Bideford lifeboats, *Assistance* and *Volunteer*, which after launching had a strenuous pull through the surf. One boat took off ten survivors, the other rescued eight.

BAILLIE Henry, Lieutenant, R.N. H.M. Coastguard, Spittal   **SILVER(2)**

8 January 1834

26 December 1833: Five fishing cobles, manned by Lieutenant Baillie, three coastguardmen and 11 Pilots were launched to help the Swedish schooner *Cupido*, en route from Göttenburg to

Grangemouth. The vessel had stranded on Spittal Beach, near Berwick-on-Tweed with the sea running tremendously over the bar in a south-easterly gale. They brought off her whole crew of Master and five men.

EVISON John Crouchley, Lieutenant, R.N.
  H.M. Coastguard, Lowestoft   **SILVER**

29 January 1834

8 January 1834: At 10 a.m. the sloop *William and Ann* was observed near the breakers south of Lowestoft Harbour, Suffolk, in a south-south-easterly gale, but it was impracticable for any boat to approach her. Lieutenant Evison ordered horses for the Manby rocket apparatus which was moved to a point near the vessel where a first shot was fired. However, a Pakefield boat was dragged through the surf from the place where the rocket apparatus stood and boatmen succeeded in boarding the sloop and rescuing her Master, Mate and a seaman.

EDDY Richard, Pilot   **SILVER(2) and SILVER BOAT(3)**

19 March 1834

13–14 January 1834: The ship *Königsberg*, en route from Memel, Prussia to Lisbon, Portugal, was driven on to rocks near Plymouth, Devon during the night, and Mr. Eddy, with others, reached her with two large boats at 1 a.m. then tacked about until daylight when they anchored. Their two small boats were hoisted out and, in six trips each, the the whole crew of the Master, Mate and ten men were brought off, one of the boats being upset on the third trip. This service seems to have been a family affair as included among Mr. Eddy's crew were three sons and two sons-in-law.

MORGAN Richard, Lieutenant, R.N. H.M. Coastguard, Rye   **SILVER**
SOMERVILLE John, Lieutenant, R.N. H.M. Coastguard, Rye   **SILVER**

5 March 1834

23 January 1834: The Dutch brig *Conrad*, Batavia to Rotterdam, was wrecked near Rye, Sussex, and four men were drowned. After she had broken up, part of the wreck drifted into the surf and Lieutenants Morgan and Somerville, helped by 25 coastguardmen, waded into the surf, and, getting on board with ropes, saved the Master and seven men.

SNELL George, Lieutenant, R.N. H.M. Coastguard, No. 31 Tower, Rye   **GOLD**

29 January 1834

24 January 1834: During the stormy night of 23–24 January, the brig *Pioneer*, on passage from Yarmouth to Venice with a cargo of 70 barrels of herrings, drove on to the shore between Camber and Dungeness Lighthouse, Kent, with a tremendous sea running and broken water extending two miles out. The casualty was reported, shortly before daylight, to Lieutenant Snell who, with six of his men, launched the lifeboat stationed at No. 31 Tower. On the way to the wreck the lifeboat filled three times, two of her crew were washed out then recovered. Overwhelmed by a sea, the lifeboat struck the ground and filled, again two men were washed out and recovered, but the

wreck was found empty. Lieutenant Snell then, because of the deteriorating weather, beached the lifeboat in spite of the violent surf. The brig's Master and five men had reached safety during the night, losing a boy in the process.

SAUVAGE Charles, Master, French Fishing Boat *Isabelle*   **SILVER**

5 March 1834

19 February 1834: The ship *Amy*, Sunderland to New York, was seen ashore at 6 a.m. by the Kentish Knock, north of Margate, Kent, in a heavy sea and hard gales. Captain Sauvage abandoned his lines and tackle, then sailed as near to her as his draught would allow and waited in position while the ship's Master, ten men and one passenger reached him in a damaged boat. They were landed safely at Ramsgate next morning.

McDONALD William, Master Mariner   **SILVER**
ORR Robert, Master Mariner   **SILVER**
PEEBLES John, Master Mariner   **SILVER**

26 March 1834

27 February 1834: The brig *Ann*, manoeuvring near Troon Harbour, Ayrshire, missed stays and struck at low water, filling instantly. The ship's boat was lowered, but was swamped and the Mate, who had jumped on board, was drowned. The Master and four men took to the rigging where they remained until a boat was brought overland from the harbour to the beach opposite. Crewed by the three Masters and two others, the boat was launched and rescued the five men.

RAY John, Boatman   **SILVER**

14 January 1835

22 October 1834: The sloop *Mary*, at anchor at Tenby, Pembrokeshire, foundered when swamped by a rising sea, and the crews of three shore boats made desperate attempts to get alongside. Eventually, one was successful and took two men from the sloop's leeside but a third man, trying to keep his feet in seas sweeping over the vessel, fell overboard on the weather side. Seeing this, Mr. Ray, a former Ceylonese pearl-diver, jumped into the sloop's shrouds, climbed across the steeply canted deck and down the weather side. Rising and falling with the waves, he seized hold of the seaman's clothing but lost him in the maelstrom, an action which he repeated more than a dozen times, only to see the lifeless body sink out of sight.

GRAY George   **SILVER(2)**

5 November 1834

24 October 1834: The Peterhead sloop *Eagle* was stranded on the beach near Bridlington, Yorkshire, in a storm and her boat capsized. Mr. Gray, immediately, rode out on a horse into the surf to the sloop and was passed a rope by which a warp was hauled to the shore. He dismounted and went into the surf on foot and, holding the warp, helped ashore the survivors – the Master, crew of four and a passenger – in spite of being buried by waves several times.

TRESILIAN Robert, Master of Yawl   **SILVER**

3 December 1834

29 October 1834: The hooker *Kitty*, while trawling off Dumwordly, Co. Cork, Ireland, struck a hidden rock and her crew's cries were heard. 'By the exertions of Mr. Tresilian, assisted by ten men in his own yawl, the *Kitty* was towed to shore on the Strand, and her crew of four men thereby rescued from a watery grave'.

WILLIAMS Owen, Coxswain, Cemlyn Lifeboat No. 1   **SILVER**

14 January 1835

31 October 1834: In squalls and a strong tide, the steam packet *Leeds*, on passage from Liverpool to Dublin, struck Harry Furlong's Rock, off Cemlyn, Anglesey, and, with the tide continuing to flow, was forced off to seaward with the loss of her rudder. She was making water fast and signalled to the steamer *Commerce* which was nearby. With the assistance of boats from both steamers, some 40 of the 60 passengers were got on board the *Commerce*. Coming on to blow with squalls and a strong tide running, a boat from the *Leeds* with three men on board was unable to reach either vessel or to return to shore. The No. 1 lifeboat stationed at Cemlyn was launched and with close reefed sails reached the *Leeds* boat through a dangerous cross sea and rescued the three men and landed them at Cemlyn. The stricken *Leeds* was taken in tow by the *Commerce* and towed to Holyhead where they arrived after nine hours. The *Leeds* sank five minutes after the last passengers had been taken off.

STUART Thomas, Lieutenant, R.N. H.M. Coastguard, Cushenden   **SILVER**

3 December 1834

7 November 1834: The sloop *James* was stranded 400 yards outside a bed of rocks in Cushenden Bay, Co. Antrim, northern Ireland, and the Coastguard station was informed. Lieutenant Stuart, with a crew of coastguardmen and fishermen, dragged their boat along the beach to the sloop's lee. With the sloop's crew taking refuge in the shrouds, ropes were thrown over and several unsuccessful attempts were made to get through the surf. Eventually the boat was worked alongside the wreck and took off her Master and five men but, on returning to the shore, capsized. The occupants were dragged through the surf to safety.

SINCLAIR Benjamin, Merchant   **SILVER**

14 January 1835

8 December 1834: At Thurso, Caithness, the Leith schooner *Hunter* was driven on to the rocks with seas breaking over her; the crew was seen clinging to the rigging. Mr. Sinclair and eight others volunteered, went off in a boat, and rescued the Master and the crew of five persons .

ANNIS Mentor, Chief Officer
   H.M. Coastguard, Redheugh   **SILVER(2) and SILVER BOAT(3)**

18 March 1835

19 January 1835: During severe weather, the schooner *Bell* was wrecked near Redheugh, near St. Abbs, Berwickshire; her Master and two seamen drowned. Mr. Annis and three of his men got a

rope to board her and saved the two other men. On this, and several other occasions, Mr. Annis had behaved with great spirit and humanity.

PEDDER William, Lieutenant, R.N. H.M. Coastguard, Dungeness **SILVER**

11 February 1835

18 January 1835: In a strong gale and tremendous seas, the brig *Lord Exmouth*, on passage from Sierra Leone, struck on the flat near Dungeness, Kent, at 6 p.m. By 10 p.m., she had drifted to within half a mile of the beach with the state of the sea worsening and breaching completely over her. By midnight, mountainous seas had swept everything off her deck, and the crew took to the rigging with their future seemingly hopeless. Lieutenant Pedder and his team tried to launch the Coastguard galley several times, but it kept capsizing. However, after two hours, six of the brig's crew were taken off and, on another trip, the remaining four. Later, he went into the surf with another man and threw a rope on board the Penzance schooner *Cornubia*. Four men were saved, but the Master had drowned, .

FITZJAMES James, R.N. Euphrates Expedition **SILVER**

11 February 1835

1 February 1835: The Liverpool ship *George Canning* was part of an expedition to the Euphrates in what is now known as Iraq. While leaving the Mersey, a man fell overboard near Liverpool and was carried rapidly astern. Mr. Fitzjames, an officer with the expedition, jumped into the freezing water clad in his heavy greatcoat, swam to the man, and supported him until a boat came to pick them up.

DARRAGH Hugh, Chief Officer, H.M. Coastguard, Innisbofin, Co. Galway **SILVER**

20 May 1835

22 April 1835: The boat belonging to the Lighthouse on Tory island was upset when crossing Ballyness Bar and two men, a boy and two women were drowned. Mr. Darragh and four men put off in the Coastguard galley and rescued two men who still clung to the upturned boat.

WILLIAMS James, The Reverend, Llanfairynghornwy, Anglesey **GOLD**

7 October 1835

7 March 1835: The Belfast smack *Active*, anchored in Ramsey Bay, Isle of Man during a north-westerly gale, started to drag her anchors then drifted out to sea as soon as they had been hauled up. Many hours later, the smack drifted into Cemaes Bay, Anglesey, and tried to anchor but grounded a long way from the shore with every successive wave breaking over her. The Reverend Williams arrived after several unsuccessful attempts had been made to launch a boat and, ignoring the mountainous seas, rode a horse into the surf and drew near enough to throw a grappling hook over the smack's bowsprit. They were then able to launch a boat and pull out to the wreck whose crew of five were found in the cabin, too exhausted to move. All were landed safely.

18 September 1835: He was summoned hastily to Trescastell, near Aberffraw, south Anglesey, from where, four miles away, the Liverpool ship *Sarah* could be seen drifting to destruction. Reverend Williams directed the rescue operations which resulted in all the crew being saved.

The Committee of Management also took into consideration his invention of the self-inflating life-buoy.

LEIGH Thomas, Lieutenant, R.N. H.M. Coastguard, Winterton   **SILVER**
7 October 1835

30 April 1835: When the collier *Blackbird*, Sunderland to London, went ashore near Winterton, Norfolk, in severe weather, the Master, Mate and two men were drowned. Lieutenant Leigh and a crew put out in the local private lifeboat and took off three seamen.

SCOTT James, Captain, Schooner *Sarah*   **SILVER**
28 October 1835

4 August 1835: Near Fraserburgh, Aberdeenshire, a Coastguard boat got into difficulties. Captain Scott, who had witnessed the incident, went off in his own boat together with his Mate, rowed a mile and a half and rescued the men who by then had been an hour in the water.

OWEN William, Captain, Brig *Stanley*   **GOLD**
MORRIS Richard, Lifeboat Keeper   **SILVER**
7 October 1835

10 September 1835: In a heavy north-westerly gale the American ship *Plutarch*, New Orleans to Liverpool, without any sail set, anchored at dusk about three-quarters of a mile from Holyhead Pier, Anglesey apparently unable to hold her ground. Holyhead No. 2 lifeboat was taken to the pierhead, but with the tremendous sea running, it was thought that no boat could live in it. Captain Owen, whose ship was anchored in the harbour, offered to take command if others would volunteer. Selecting eight men he launched, but, in the dark with torrential rain and high seas, had to return without reaching the casualty. A second attempt was successful and, with the ship drifting fast on to the rocks, with only one mast standing, the First Mate, Second Mate and nine seamen were taken off; her Master and some of her crew had died on the voyage.

SOMERVILLE John, Lieutenant, R.N. H.M. Coastguard, Littlestone-on-Sea   **GOLD**
28 October 1835

2 October 1835: At midnight 1–2 October, Lieutenant Somerville saw a light drifting gradually eastward, about two miles to the west of Littlestone-on-Sea, New Romney, Kent, Coastguard station, until it became stationary opposite him. Assuming it to be a vessel dragging her anchors, he positioned lights and men along the beach to give help should the crew decide to take to the boats. At daybreak, he identified the brig *Industry* on her beam ends with her crew clinging to the foretopmast shrouds. Fearing that the Dungeness lifeboat would not arrive in time, he launched his galley with four of his men and, despite high seas, took off the Master, Mate and four seamen. Returning to the beach, the galley was upset but the occupants were all helped ashore.

COX Henry, Lieutenant, R.N., H.M. Coastguard, St. Andrews   **GOLD**

FULTON Robert, Master, R.N., H.M. Coastguard, St. Andrews   **SILVER**

28 October 1835

4 October 1835: The Dundee schooner *Tid*, bound for Glasgow, struck the rocks off St. Andrews, Fife, and sank shortly afterwards, the crew boarding their boat just in time. They were seen from the Coastguard station at dusk and Lieutenant Cox, Mr. Fulton and four men launched a fishing boat from south of the pier and, reaching the schooner's boat, took the survivors on board. Then, mindless of the dangers, the fishing boat was taken in stern first and everybody landed safely without being swamped.

SOUTHEY William, Lieutenant, R.N., H.M. Coastguard   **SILVER**

2 December 1835

9 October 1835: The French brig *Charles*, laden with coal and on passage from Sunderland to her home port of Cherbourg, went ashore near No. 31 Tower, Rye and set off distress signals. Lieutenant Southey and six men launched the lifeboat through heavy surf and reached the *Charles*. He managed to refloat the brig but her rudder was gone and she was taking in water. Lieutenant Southey therefore beached her near No. 28 Tower. With the Captain's permission, he hove out part of the coal and at high water got her safe into Rye Harbour with the Master and six crew (two other crew had drowned).

EVANS William, Master, Pilot Boat *William*   **SILVER**

23 December 1835

26 October 1835: On passage from Swansea to Gloucester, the sloop *John* was driven on shore near the river mouth at Neath, Glamorgan, in a very heavy gale. Her general cargo included copper, stone, coal and oysters. One man was drowned trying to swim ashore, and the Master and the other crewman took to the rigging in order to escape the full fury of the waves. The Masters of several larger decked boats refused to help. Mr. Evans with four of his men, rowed off in his smaller, open boat and, doggedly persevering, took off the two men.

BAKER William Henry, Lieutenant, R.N., H.M. Coastguard, Fort Moncrieff   **SILVER**

2 December 1835

9–10 November 1835: During a severe gale, a ship was discovered in the offing about five miles away, apparently without her rudder and sinking. Lieutenant Baker at the Coastguard station near Dymchurch, Kent prepared to launch his punt. In two unsuccessful attempts, the punt filled with water and was thrown back, but he finally got through the surf and reached the ship – the 450-ton *Bristol*, Quebec to London, which was beating the sand between West Hythe and Dymchurch. Her Master had left in a smack for Dover. Lieutenant Baker remained on board until 5 a.m. and landed the remaining 18 men through overwhelming surf.

ROSS Richard, Chief Boatsman, H.M. Coastguard, Dunmore   **SILVER(2)**

23 December 1835

24 November 1835 The brig *Collins*, Quebec to Liverpool, was wrecked near Dunmore Pier, Co. Waterford, Ireland. Mr. Ross and five of his men launched a boat but were obliged to turn back by the violence of the weather. Getting on to a rock abreast of the wreck, they succeeded in passing ropes on board by which the crew were hauled ashore one by one; the coastguardmen had other ropes fastened around their bodies. When the rope around the Master broke and he was swept away, one of the coastguardmen plunged in and saved him; nearly lifeless, both were hauled on to the rocks. A total of 11 men were saved.

COFFEY Patrick, Farmer   **SILVER**

23 December 1835

25 November 1835: The French schooner *Deux Soeurs*, on passage from Nice to Rouen, went ashore on Tramore Beach, near Waterford, Co. Waterford, Ireland; the weather was severe and the sea turbulent. Mr. Coffey rode through the surf on a horse and brought a rope to shore from the wreck, then he rode off again and helped the crew to launch her boat, by means of which all were saved.

EDINGTON Charles, Chief Officer, H.M. Coastguard, Knockadoon   **SILVER**

17 February 1836

25 November 1835: On passage from Newport to Youghal, the schooner *Ann and Elizabeth* was wrecked near Youghal, Co. Cork, Ireland in violent weather. Collecting seven local men, Mr. Edington launched a boat and saved the Master and four men.

AVISSE Jacques Nicholas, Captain, *Le Jeune Louis*   **SILVER**

17 February 1836

18 December 1835: The Portsmouth vessel *Hope* was wrecked on the coast of Spain with the Master and four men on board. Coming across the wreck, Captain Avisse, from Boulogne, took them off and landed them safely at Boulogne.

   The British Consul at Boulogne brought the 'very generous and humane conduct' of Captain Avisse to the attention of the Committee.

GRAHAM George, Lieutenant, R.N. H.M. Coastguard, Winterton **SILVER**
10 March 1836

19 December 1835: The vessel *Ann and Mary*, Selby to London, was wrecked during a gale at Winterton, Norfolk. Lieutenant Graham deployed his Manby rocket apparatus, set it up on the beach, and used it to bring off the Master and two men.

JELLARD William John, Captain, Brig *Angerona* **GOLD**
HILL William, Mate, Brig *Angerona* **SILVER**
FOWELL John, Seaman, Brig *Angerona* **SILVER**
HICKS Samuel, Seaman, Brig *Angerona* **SILVER**
10 March 1836

22 December 1835: Five days out from St. John's, Newfoundland the brig *Angerona* came across the *Francis Sparght*, dismasted and waterlogged, in position 47° North, 37° West, 800 miles east of Newfoundland. A strong gale was blowing and a tremendous sea running, breaking over the vessel frequently. Noticing a number of people on the poop, Captain Jellard, with three other men, lowered their only boat and made for the wreck. In two trips they took off 11 survivors who, miserable and helpless, had been without provisions and water for 19 days. Three men had been washed overboard when the vessel first became a wreck. On the 15th day lots were drawn for a victim to satisfy their hunger, and ultimately in four cases 'human blood had been shed for the sustenance of the survivors'. On 7 January 1836 the survivors were landed at Falmouth.

 The medals were awarded exceptionally since the service did not take place 'on the coasts of the United Kingdom'.

JONES Richard, Lieutenant, R.N. H.M. Coastguard, Kessingland **SILVER**
20 January 1836

19 December 1835: During a severe gale, the brig *Royalist* went ashore near Kessingland, Suffolk, and was wrecked. Lieutenant Jones and a party of his men waded through the heavy surf and saved her Master and five seamen, six men from the schooner *Stansfield*, and three men from wrecked colliers.

EVANS Thomas, Captain. R.N. Lloyd's Agent, Fishguard **SILVER(2)**
19 June 1844

17 February 1836: The Fishguard lifeboat with Captain Evans on board was launched after the schooner *Trieve* was wrecked near Fishguard, Pembrokeshire, and saved her Master and six men.

 In 1844 Captain Evans made inquiries about a medal for this service, when an award of £10 was made to the lifeboatmen, and possible reimbursement for having built the lifeboat in 1822, two years before the R.N.L.I. came into being, and keeping her in an efficient state of repair thereafter at a personal cost of £500. During the period 25 lives had been saved using the lifeboat. The medal was voted 'for long continuing exertions in the cause of humanity' and was to be double gilt with a gold swivel ring. (Mr. Evans' first medal was voted on 9 April 1834.)

JOACHIM Richard, Lieutenant, R.N. H.M. Coastguard, Lowestoft　　　　**SILVER**

17 August 1836

18 February 1836: A terrific storm on the east coast drove 23 vessels on to the shore between Lowestoft and Kessingland, Suffolk, stranding them. Lieutenant Joachim and his Coastguard crew set up their rocket apparatus, got a line on board the sloop *Janet*, on passage from Inverkeithing to London, and saved her three man crew. They then rescued the six man crew of the Weymouth sloop *Venus*, taking two trips in their boat to achieve success.

WATTS William, Captain, Smack *Brothers*　　　　**SILVER**

4 May 1836

28 March 1836: During a violent gale, the Newcastle brig *Thomason* went ashore near Woodbridge, Suffolk. The disaster was seen by Captain Watts, who jumped overboard from his own vessel with a line attached to his body. He then swam to the wreck which he boarded and, using the rope, saved the Master and nine men.

SUPERVILLE, Captain, French Ship *Clorinde*　　　　**SILVER**

8 October 1840

5 June 1836: The *Jane Scott*, bound for London from Portugal, was run down by the Swedish ship *Harmonie* of Stockholm 250 miles north-west of Cape Ortegal and left in a disabled state. Soon afterwards she was encountered by the French Indiaman *Clorinde*, which had seen her distress signals. On passage from India to Bordeaux, the Indiaman shortened sail, hove to and took on board the casualty's Master and her four man crew and landed them at Bordeaux.

The Committee presented the silver medal 'in consideration of his kind and humane conduct on the occasion'.

SIMS Andrew, Lieutenant, R.N., H.M. Coastguard, Peterhead　　　　**SILVER(2)**

4 November 1836

13 October 1836: The schooner *Helen* was totally wrecked near Peterhead, Aberdeenshire, in severe weather. Lieutenant Sims and his men set up the Manby rocket apparatus and brought ashore the Master and six men.

WADE Mitchell Brown, Captain, Brig *Dew Drop*　　　　**SILVER**

22 December 1836

23 November 1836: During a severe gale, the Jersey smack *Britannia* and the Swansea schooner *Jane* ran for Padstow, Cornwall on the ebb tide. The latter, obviously in a bad way, had lost her mainsail, mainboom, foretopsail and boat and was also partly full of water. The two vessels made the shelter of Stepper Point, but baffling cross winds caused them to collide, and, locked together, they drifted on to Dogger Bank. As the schooner struck bottom, they parted and the smack drove further ashore. After attempts were made to reach the casualties with rockets, the Harbour Association's lifeboat was launched with Captain Wade at the steering gear, and manned by a

mixed crew of coastguardmen and fishermen. The schooner broke up, drowning all of her crew including the smack's Master who had leapt on board. The lifeboat took off the smack's Mate and two seamen, who were clinging to the rigging, and brought them ashore.

DAY Thomas, Coxswain, Bideford Lifeboat   **SILVER**

22 December 1836

29 November 1836: The Plymouth schooner *Henrietta* was wrecked off Bideford, Devon, and the North Devon Humane Association's lifeboat *Volunteer* launched. Perhaps unwisely, she went alongside under the wreck's lee and, after the Master and five seamen were taken aboard, an incoming heavy sea rolled he wreck over on top of her, forcing her under water. The schooner righted immediately and the lifeboat rose on her air cases; everybody reached the shore safely.

THOMPSON Robert Kilpatrick, Chief Officer,
H.M. Coastguard, Clogher Head   **SILVER(2)**

11 January 1837

25–26 December 1836: At 7 p.m. on Christmas Day, during a heavy gale, the sloop *Isabella*, Liverpool to Dundalk, was stranded on the north side of Clogher Head, Co. Louth, Ireland and sank soon afterwards. Some local fishermen brought a boat from the harbour, a mile and a half away, using a cart. Manned by Mr. Thompson, three coastguardmen and five fishermen, the boat went off through heavy surf and, despite intense frost, reached the wreck at 3 a.m., where three men had been in the rigging since 8 p.m. One man had died from cold and fatigue, but the Master and another man were rescued.

STUART James, Lieutenant, R.N. H.M. Coastguard, Littlestone-on-Sea   **SILVER**

8 February 1837

26 December 1836: The Hull barque *Dixon*, on passage from St. John, New Brunswick, was seen at anchor off Littlestone-on-Sea, Kent, driving fast toward shore. At 10 a.m., she struck and came on shore, the sea tremendous on half flood. Lieutenant Stuart, with the whole of his crew and officers and men from other stations, went to the scene. The gale was so violent that they could hardly walk against it. He selected a few resolute men who took off their clothes and, with lifelines fastened around them and a man attending each, entered the water. The Second Mate threw himself into the sea and was brought safely on shore, but the Master, in trying to follow, drowned. The Mate and nine men, in a helpless state from extreme cold, were brought off to safety.

LOUCHET Louis Pierre Anton Bernard, Captain   **SILVER**

10 January 1838

9 January 1837: The Penzance schooner *Cornubia* was wrecked in a violent south-westerly gale in the Baie de l'Authie, 30 miles south of Boulogne, France. In the raging sea, the Master and six crew were saved by Captain Louchet and the crew of the Custom House Boat.

WHEELER John, Fisherman   **SILVER**

1 March 1837

11 February 1837: About noon, at the height of a gale, the 80 ton French lugger *Jean Marie* was wrecked in Chale Bay, on the south coast of the Isle of Wight. Each tremendous wave was fetching up at the cliff, and the lugger had been thrown high on the beach with two of her crew already drowned. Mr. Wheeler fastened a rope around himself which was held by three or four men at the bottom of the cliff. After a receding wave, he dashed to throw a line on board the lugger. Using this, the three men remaining on board were brought ashore just before the vessel broke up.

TRIPHOOK Richard, Captain, Revenue Cutter *Hamilton*   **SILVER**

19 April 1837

14 February 1837: The Kilrush brig *Leda*, on passage to London, was wrecked at Kilrush, Co. Clare. Captain Triphook and six of his crew went off and saved the Master and Mate; the rest of the crew had previously quitted the brig in its boat.

WALSH Martin W., Captain, Schooner *Alicia*   **GOLD**

16 August 1837

15 February 1837: On 8 February, the 423 ton American ship *Glasgow* left Liverpool with 17 crew and 80 passengers, bound for New York, but she was held up in the channel until the 14th by contrary winds and haze. She sighted the Tuskar Rock Lighthouse, about 11 miles off Carnsore Point, Co. Wexford, Ireland, late in the day. The night became hazier, and she struck a sunken rock at 5 a.m. next morning; the violence of the impact swung her around so that her stern struck the same rock, unshipping her rudder. With her sails set, the ship struck for the third time and was swept over the rocks into deep water. Captain Walsh bore up towards her, the schooner running under her lee quarter and started rescuing people from the seriously damaged vessel. Most of the women and children were rescued after oars had been provided for the schooner's boats, but, with the wind rising and the *Glasgow* certain to sink, Captain Walsh lay alongside. A collision soon occurred, which carried away the schooner's bulwarks and doing other damage. After the third strike, he sheered off, then stayed in the area to pick up 82 survivors, landing them at Wexford.

STARK Peter, Lieutenant, R.N. H.M. Coastguard, Broughty Ferry   **SILVER**

3 May 1837

11 April 1837: The Kirkcaldy vessel *Two Sisters* with a cargo of coal was wrecked at 4.30 a.m. on the banks of the River Tay between Angus and Fife and sank, leaving her crew of Master and two men clinging to her rigging in the high seas. Lieutenant Stark, a coastguardman, and 14 fishermen put off in the Broughty Ferry lifeboat and saved the three men.

ROBERTSON James Hector McKenzie, Lieutenant, R.N.
   H.M. Coastguard, Ballinacourty   **SILVER**

21 June 1837

30 April 1837: A small hooker set out from the isle of Lattermore, off the coast of Galway, Ireland, loaded with seaweed and potatoes, and at 1.30 a.m. was wrecked in Greatman's Bay, near Currack in a hard south-west gale. At 11.30 a.m., her two man crew was seen on a rock. Lieutenant Robertson and four men launched a local boat; it was two hours before high tide and they had to make four attempts before they were successful, even then they had to keep bailing during the rescue of the two men.

MILBURN William   **SILVER**

6 October 1837

19 May 1837: In a wildly tempestuous sea, the schooner *Vernon* was driven on to rocks in Laxey Bay, five miles north of Douglas, Isle of Man, in a position which could only be approached by boat. Mr. Milburn and a crew of six men launched their boat from Laxey but, getting off the beach, were upset. Righting their boat, they set off again and succeeded, in two trips, in rescuing the Master, two passengers and five seamen.

NOTT Edward Bunbury, Lieutenant, R.N.
   Commanding Revenue Cutter *Mermaid*   **SILVER**

6 October 1837

27 August 1837: At 6.30 a.m. the Newcastle sloop *Thomas*, in passage to Inverness with coal, was riding off the bar outside the harbour at Holy Island, Northumberland, trying to clear shoals. She struck and steered for the beach south-west of the harbour in a heavy gale. Lieutenant Nott, four Pilots, a coastguardman and nine men from the revenue cutter manned the Holy Island lifeboat and took off the Master and a seaman, but a heavy sea struck the sloop, dismasting her and filling the lifeboat which was forced to return to the shore, leaving a boy on board the wreck. Putting off again, they made six attempts to rescue him, but failed.

STRAINS John, Chief Officer. H.M. Coastguard, St. John's Point	**SILVER**
***BROWNE Philip R.M., Captain. R.N**	**SILVER**
ADAIR William, Boatman. H.M. Coastguard, St. John's Point	**SILVER**
ADAM John, Chief Officer. H.M. Coastguard, St. John's Point	**SILVER(2)**
HOGG William, Boatman. H.M. Coastguard, St. John's Point	**SILVER**

1 November 1837

**15 November 1837*

11 September 1837: The Liverpool ship *Coeur de Lion* on passage to Montreal, Canada, encountered stormy weather and was driven ashore at the lower end of Dundrum Bay, Co. Down, northern Ireland. With the regular crew of the Newcastle lifeboat absent in the herring fleet, a volunteer crew was assembled by Captain Browne. Mr. Strains volunteered to take command. They reached the wreck through heavy surf and, while they were bailing out, another boat from the shore took off six

of the ship's crew, but was upset immediately and a number of the occupants drowned. The lifeboat and shore boats, in which Messrs. Adam, Adair and Hogg helped, saved the Master, one passenger and 23 seamen.

WESTBROOK Edmund Barford, Lieutenant R.N
  H.M. Coastguard, Chichester Harbour   **SILVER**

7 February 1838

30 November 1837: A gale was blowing over the shoals off Chichester, Sussex, raising heavy surf, when the Portsmouth sloop *Ann* was driven on to them, the Master having drowned. Lieutenant Westbrook and three local Pilots put out in a small boat and rescued three men from the rigging of the sunken vessel.

STUART Thomas, Lieutenant, R.N. H.M. Coastguard, Dunmore   **SILVER(2)**

10 January 1838

19 December 1837: On the night of 19th December, in a westerly gale, the Cork sloop *Edward* was seen at anchor, but at dusk she was being driven towards the rocks at Ballyman, near Dunmore, Co. Waterford. The coastguards showed lights from the shore from a gap between the rocks. The Master of the sloop cut the anchor adrift and ran the vessel towards the lights. When the vessel struck, the three crew got on to the bowsprit and were saved by Lieutenant Stuart and his men. While saving the Master, Lieutenant Stuart was washed off the rocks, but he was caught by one of his men and was saved from drowning.

BRITTAIN George Sherras, Lieutenant, R.N. H.M. Coastguard, Whitby   **SILVER**

10 January 1838

21 December 1837: On the night of the 20th and the morning of the 21st, a heavy north-east gale was blowing, and the brig *Middlesbrough*, of Middlesbrough, was driven on shore about half a mile north of Whitby. On seeing this, Lieutenant Brittain immediately launched the Whitby (West Side) lifeboat with a crew of 14 coastguardmen and proceeded to the wreck. After great difficulty and danger, they succeeded in saving eight of the ten crew.

BULLEY John, Lieutenant, R.N. H.M. Coastguard, Atherfield   **SILVER**

10 January 1838

25 December 1837: On the morning of the 25th December, the man on watch at Atherfield Coastguard station heard a cracking as of a vessel breaking up and, on looking seawards, observed a vessel on shore. There was a thick fog and it was blowing a fresh gale. Lieutenant Bailey and four coastguardmen immediately proceeded to the wreck, the Norwegian brig *Enigheden*, which was in Chale Bay under a 100ft perpendicular cliff. They were unable to use the Dennett's rockets because of the cliff. Together with three fishermen, the coastguardmen persuaded the crew of the brig to throw a rope on shore, which was done by the Master, by which means all six crew were saved.

HOED Francis Philip W., Captain, Ship *Phenomene*   **GOLD**

6 June 1838

28 January 1838: The 500 ton Liverpool ship *Columbia* sailed from Bombay with 34 crew and passengers. The ship experienced very tempestuous weather, she lost her rudder and became so leaky the crew and all on board were exhausted by continual pumping. Another ship was sighted on 26 January but this did not respond to distress signals. On the next day, however, they were seen off the Azores by the Dutch ship *Phenomene*, on passage from Batavia to Rotterdam. Being nearly dark, blowing a gale and a very heavy sea, the *Phenomene* was forced to stand by all night. On the morning of the 28th, Captain Hoed, at the risk of his own life, managed to rescue all 34 persons from the *Columbia*. It took all day to effect the rescue, and they were safely landed at Plymouth on 13 February.

This gold medal was awarded despite the fact that the rescue took place way outside British waters.

FIELD William George, Lieutenant, R.N.   **SILVER**

9 May 1838

14 February 1838: A tremendous hurricane had been blowing for 24 hours when, with the wind at its height, two men were seen on board a coal hulk in Falmouth Harbour, Cornwall, trying desperately to pump her out. A coal bag was hoisted to a spar indicating distress. Realising that the vessel's hold was leaking, those on shore considered the two men to be in great peril. Lieutenant Field, acting commander of the South Australian Commission's brig *Rapid*, bribed a crew to take out a six-oared boat. Together they rescued the men from the hulk.

HOLMAN Thomas Holloway, Lieutenant, R.N. H.M. Coastguard, Bovisand   **SILVER**

21 March 1838

14 February 1838: The Liverpool vessel *Thetis* was wrecked on Plymouth breakwater, Devon, in the evening in a violent gale with a strong flood tide. Cries for help were heard, and Lieutenant Holman, with eight men, went off in the Coastguard galley and found the Master and four men together on the Rock. Another man was stuck lower down where he could not be reached without going round with the boat but, in spite of the risk of the galley being swamped, everybody was taken off safely, although the last man saved died shortly thereafter.

ESSELL William Folkes, Lieutenant, R.N. H.M. Coastguard, Carnsore   **GOLD**

28 February 1838

February 1838: When the sloop *Ann and Elizabeth* went aground off Carnsore Point, Co. Wexford, Ireland, in a gale, she became a complete wreck with her crew lashed to the rigging with no hope of rescue unless immediate steps were taken. Lieutenant Essell, without waiting for his own men, swam off with a rope but was nearly drowned. Nothing daunted, he swam off again and got the rope on board, enabling the crew (number unknown) to be rescued.

CAMPBELL James   **SILVER**

21 March 1838

15 February 1838: In a heavy gale and high seas, the Master and 14 man crew of the Liverpool vessel *John Stump* took to the rigging after she had been wrecked near Leestone, Co. Down, northern Ireland. In a partial lull, Mr. Campbell, with seven others, went out in a boat but, during the rescue operation, the rope broke just after two men had been hauled on board. The boat was forced to return to the shore, and the remainder of the crew was then brought ashore in two more trips.

BINGHAM William   **SILVER**

9 May 1838

20 February 1838: During a violent storm the schooner *Douglas*, Limerick to London, went on shore in a most perilous position among the breakers at Bellmullet, Co. Mayo, Ireland, on the west coast. Mr. Bingham, a resident nearby, helped a number of others to rescue her Master, Mate and nine seamen in two boats which were launched through tremendous surf. Practically all of the survivors were disabled by exposure to wet and cold.

WYLDE Sydenham, Lieutenant, R.N. H.M. Coastguard, Caister   **SILVER**

21 March 1838

25 February 1838: With two coastguardmen he saved the crew of the Shields schooner *Lapwing*, when she went aground in a storm at Caister, Norfolk. He got a rope on board the schooner, enabling a hawser to be hauled ashore, by which the Master and eight men were saved. Lieutenant Wylde himself narrowly escaped drowning.

STARK Peter, Lieutenant, R.N. H.M. Coastguard, Banks of Tay   **GOLD**

21 March 1838

4 March 1838: At daybreak, a wreck was reported on the Elbow Bank off the Firth of Tay. Lieutenant Stark manned his gig with eight hands and pulled down the river, accompanied by a fishing yawl, to the Broughty Ferry lifeboat. This they manned with a mixed crew of coastguard-men, Pilots and fishermen and succeeded in reaching the wreck, the Perth schooner *Ranger*. The sea was running very high, but they rescued the Master and crew of four men.

PARSONS William, Lieutenant. H.M. Coastguard, Swanage   **SILVER**

9 January 1839

7 April 1838: The French vessel *L'Aimable Mère*, in passage from Bordeaux to Dunkirk, was wrecked during stormy weather off St. Aldhelm's Head on the Dorset coast. Lieutenant Parsons, with a crew of seven of his men, launched his galley from Swanage and saved the Master and six men, bringing them safely ashore.

RYMER David, Lieutenant, R.N. H.M. Coastguard, Spittal **GOLD**

9 May 1838

8 April 1838: At 7.30 a.m., the Dundee schooner *Margaret*, seen in distress in a heavy sea at low water, finally went on to the beach near Spittal, south of Berwick-on-Tweed. Both Manby's life saving apparatus and Dennett's rocket apparatus were manned by men of the Coastguard. Lieutenant Rymer launched the Berwick lifeboat, crewed by seven fishermen, and went off through heavy surf to the wreck. The Master was injured and could not leave unaided; in trying to reach him one of the lifeboat crew was washed overboard then recovered. With six survivors on board, the lifeboat had to return to the shore. The Master drowned before the lifeboat could return to the ship, which became a total wreck.

ROBERTS Owen, Pilot **SILVER**

6 June 1838

15 April 1838: In heavy northerly squalls the Liverpool vessel *Scotia*, Liverpool to Demarara, British Guiana, was seen in the Menai Strait, Anglesey, with all yards gone and only her jib set. Completely unmanageable, she dropped anchors and swung round near New Menai Lighthouse. Mr. Roberts launched the Penmon lifeboat (Anglesey Lifesaving Association No. 4), crewed half by boatmen, half by fishermen and, with the help of the casualty's crew, launched her long boat just as the vessel sank. Some of the survivors jumped into the lifeboat and some into the long boat, but, in the absence of thole-pins, this had to be towed by the rescuer. The Master, the Mate, 14 seamen and a passenger were landed at Penmon.

ROTHERY John, Lieutenant, R.N. H.M. Coastguard, Sidmouth **SILVER**

6 June 1838

19 May 1838: Lieutenant Rothery, with five of his crew and a fisherman, launched the Coastguard boat to go to the assistance of the Guernsey schooner *Agnes* which was seen to be in distress. When they got near the stern of the schooner, their boat was swamped and the men washed out. All managed to reach the shore, very exhausted, and some were injured. The schooner soon after drove on shore and the Master and crew of six all saved.

KENNEDY Henry, Yacht Owner **SILVER**

30 January 1839

23 May 1838: A pilot boat was upset at night in a heavy squall in Belfast Lough, near Carrickfergus, Co. Antrim, northern Ireland; Mr. Kennedy launched his boat and saved one man.

24 May 1838: Another boat was upset in Belfast Lough, and Mr. Kennedy saved a man although four others drowned.

LANE William, Lieutenant, R.N. H.M. Coastguard, Dartmouth   **SILVER**

9 August 1838

29 June 1838: When, in stormy conditions and heavy seas, the French fishing boat *Victoire* was wrecked near Dartmouth, Devon, her crew of five men was rescued by a boat manned by Lieutenant Lane and nine men.

REEVE John, Master, Schooner *Wave*   **SILVER**

19 September 1838

24 July 1838: The St. Ives sloop *Feronia*, with a cargo of Cornish copper, was wrecked on the Mixen, off Swansea, Glamorgan. The three crew of the pilot boat *Victoria*, assisted by three crew of the pilot boat *Sarah Jane*, rescued the Master and two crew of the *Feronia*. Mr Reeve, Master of the schooner *Wave* (the name of the boat in the Minutes is not easy to read – it might be *Mane*) acted with great humanity in taking the rescued men on board his vessel and providing them with hammocks and other assistance and comforts.

NOTT Edward Bunbury, Lieutenant, R.N.
  Commanding Revenue Cutter *Mermaid*   **SILVER(2)**

19 September 1838

September 1838: When the schooner *Diana* was wrecked by driving on shore near Berwick-on-Tweed, launching the lifeboat was ruled out because the casualty was positioned among rocks. Lieutenant Nott went off with six men in a fishing coble and saved the Master, four men, one woman and three children.

DARLING William, Lighthouse Keeper   **SILVER**
DARLING Grace Horsley, Miss   **SILVER**

24 October 1838

7 September 1838: The weather in the North Sea was dark and stormy when, early on 6 September, the 270 ton paddle steamer *Forfarshire* developed boiler trouble off Flamborough Head, Yorkshire. She was on passage, with cargo and 63 people aboard, between Hull and Dundee and, under the tyranny of her timetable, her Master decided to press on rather than make for Shields. Later in the day the weather worsened to one of the most violent gales experi-enced up to then on the north-east coast, so a defective boiler was brought back into use. Operating conditions on board deteriorated until, at 1 a.m. on the 7th, the engines stopped and, off St. Abb's Head, the sails with which the ship was equipped were set but she was still blown ashore. The Master made for shelter but, in spite of dropping anchor, the ship went on to the Harcar Rocks on Inner Farne Island off Bamburgh, Northumberland, with her bows completely crumpled in. Eight of the crew and a passenger got away in a boat to be picked up 24 hours later, but the steamer broke in two very soon afterwards with only seven passengers and six of the crew left alive. During the night two children and two men died from exposure and, at dawn, the nine survivors crept on to the rocks. Their plight was seen by Miss Darling from the Longstone Lighthouse, a mile away on Farne (or Houss) Island. With her father, William, she put off in the coble and rowed through the howling gale, the boiling seas tossing them about like

a cork. Reaching the rocks where the seas were surging over the survivors, William jumped overside, leaving his daughter to manage the boat single handed. Five survivors were taken back to the lighthouse where Grace tended them, while her father and two of the men returned to bring off the other four. The ferocity of the weather was such that two days were to elapse before the survivors could be taken to the mainland.

DOOLEY Daniel, Lieutenant, R.N. H.M. Coastguard, Holy Island   SILVER
*WILSON William, Master Pilot   SILVER

24 October 1838
*9 January 1839

12 October 1838: In a north-north-west gale which grew to hurricane force, the Arbroath vessel *Isabella*, out of Sunderland, lost her sails and, at daybreak, was found to be on fire. This obliged her Master to make for Holy Island harbour off the Northumbrian coast about 3 p.m., but she grounded on the bar in tremendous surf. The Holy Island lifeboat launched, manned by Lieutenant Dooley, the Master Pilot, five Pilots and two coastguardmen. Although damaged in launching, the lifeboat fought her way to the wreck to take off the Master and four men, suffering two broken oars and filling with water up to the thwarts in the process. A coble also rendered invaluable help.

BROWNE Philip R.M., Captain, R.N   GOLD

15 November 1838

23 October 1838: The schooner *Bloom*, Bangor to Londonderry, drove ashore at St. John's Point, Dundrum Bay, Co. Down, northern Ireland, and became a total wreck in the severe weather and heavy sea. Captain Browne and others got ropes aboard and saved the Master, Mate and one seaman. Three others had drowned.

BRITTAIN George Sherras, Lieutenant, R.N.
H.M. Coastguard, Whitby   GOLD

15 November 1838

29 October 1838: Flying distress signals in a violent northerly gale, the coal laden Whitby brig *Jupiter* ran on shore during the morning between Whitby and Upgang, Yorkshire. Lieutenant Brittain, with a ten man crew, launched the Whitby (West Side) lifeboat and fought their way to the wreck, filling twice on the way; they took off the Master and nine men from the rigging.

KING Sidney, Lieutenant, R.N. H.M. Coastguard, Shoeburyness   SILVER

15 November 1838

29 October 1838: The London barge *John* parted both cables when anchored near the Hope Light in heavy weather and fetched up near the Knock buoys in the Thames Estuary, off Southend. Lieutenant King put off in a boat with eight men and took off her Master and one seaman – her whole crew.

FRANKLIN Edward, Lieutenant, R.N. H.M. Coastguard, Hove   **SILVER**
12 December 1838

29 October 1838: During stormy weather, the coal-laden brig *Friends* was wrecked near Hove, Sussex, her crew taking to the rigging. Lieutenant Franklin and two men waded into the sea, threw ropes on board and took off the Master and seven men.

DELPIERRE John Antoine, Captain, Fishing Boat No. 89   **SILVER**
19 June 1839

29 October 1838: The Guernsey vessel *Albion* went aground on Galloper Sand, off Harwich, Essex, during a gale. Both of her boats were lost and she soon found nine feet of water in her hold. The Master of the Boulogne fishing vessel No. 89, in spite of the gale increasing to hurricane force, took off the casualty's crew of seven men and landed them at Boulogne on 31 October.

GIN Nicolas Francois, Captain, Fishing Boat No. 95   **SILVER**
19 June 1839

29 October 1838: During a gale the Sunderland vessel *Isabella* stranded on Long Sand, north of Margate, Kent, and five of her crew were drowned. The remaining two men were saved by Captain Gin and landed at Boulogne.

LETT Stephen Joshua, Lieutenant, R.N. H.M. Coastguard, Rosslare   **GOLD**
9 January 1839

25 November 1838: The ship *Ariadne*, timber laden, having made the Tuskar Rock Light off Wexford, Co. Wexford, Ireland, under a heavy press of sail, was trying to wear it when she struck on nearby rocks and was thrown on her beam ends; three of her crew were lost. Some time later, the fore and main topmasts carried away and she righted, full of water, her bottom partly knocked out and her boats and deck cargo swept overboard. The ship then drifted in the direction between Raven Point and Currycloe, the surviving crew having lashed themselves to the rigging. By 11 a.m. next morning, three more men had been lost. The cargo washed out, she finished about 200 yards from the shore. When Lieutenant Lett arrived with his six-oared boat and Manby lifesaving apparatus, heavy surf and the tremendous gale prevented any help being offered although two attempts were made. The weather having moderated at 2.30 p.m., the rescuers put off, and a second attempt from a different place was successful but, as the Master, Mate and one seaman took their places, the boat partly filled so, cutting the rope, they returned to the shore. With darkness approaching and the gale increasing again, they fought their way back and brought off the other five exhausted seamen.

JONES Owen, Chief Officer, H.M. Coastguard, Wicklow   **SILVER**
21 February 1839

27 November 1838: During a violent storm the French brig *Le Nouveau Destin*, on passage from Louçon to the Isle of Man, went ashore near New Town, Co. Wicklow, Ireland. Mr. Jones led seven coastguardmen into the sea, swam to the wreck and brought off the Master and five men.

JENNINGS William, Commissioned Boatswain,
   H.M. Coastguard, Looe   **SILVER**

12 December 1838

27 November 1838: The large London brig *Belissima*, bound for Amsterdam from Odessa with a cargo of linseed, staves and other goods, was blown on to rocks behind Looe Island, Cornwall. Attempts to reach her by rocket line failed. The brig soon showed signs of breaking up, thus Mr. Jennings volunteered to swim to her and, after persevering for some time, got a rope on board, enabling the Master and 12 seamen to be saved.

GRANDY James Samual William, Mate, Revenue Cutter *Harpy*   **SILVER**

21 February 1839

28 November 1838: The French brig *Le Colosse*, on passage from Dunkirk to Bordeaux, was wrecked in a storm at the entrance to Mill Bay, near Plymouth, Devon. Mr. Grandy and four men from his crew put off in a four oared galley and saved the Master and four men. The Mate had drowned attempting to swim to the shore.

SYMMES Henry Alfred Sydney, Lieutenant, R.N.
   H.M. Coastguard, Freshwater   **GOLD**

9 January 1839

29 November 1838: A French vessel, the brig *Claire*, en route from Marseilles to Honfleur, was seen off Freshwater Bay, Isle of Wight, soon after daybreak, under close reefed main top-sail and fore-sail. With the gale at its height, the sea was making a clear breach over her, and the crew had taken to the rigging when the brig struck two or three cables from the shore off Brooke. Lieutenant Symmes made three unsuccessful attempts to reach the stricken vessel by rocket apparatus then, using a boat washed ashore from the wreck, he put out with four of his men and managed to reach the brig which was nearly sinking. He took off her Master and two seamen as no more could be accommodated. On their way to shore, a heavy sea swamped the boat but they were saved by two men dashing into the water. Using a rope brought ashore from the brig, six other men were saved before the wreck went to pieces.

ROSS Thomas, Captain, R.N. Inspecting Commander
   H.M. Coastguard, Swords District   **GOLD**
JONES George C., Chief Officer, H.M. Coastguard, Dublin   **SILVER**
BEGG ..., Master of a Collier   **SILVER**

9 January 1839

29–30 November 1838: In a violent gale, heavy rain and mountainous seas, the brig *Gainsborough*, Liverpool to London, was wrecked on shore near Carrickhill Tower, Malahide, ten miles north of Dublin. Captain Ross sent for a galley and a small fishing boat, which did not arrive until 2 p. m. By this time the gale had increased, blowing directly on shore with seas breaking as high as her mast tops; the galley was launched, manned by Captain Ross and seven volunteers, Mr. Jones and Captain Begg among them. Four attempts were necessary as the galley filled with water, was driven back and damaged, with her oars broken. The Master, two seamen and one boy were saved, three others drowned.

COPPIN Frederick, Lieutenant, R.N. H.M. Coastguard, Pelter Brig   **SILVER**

17 April 1839

22 December 1838: The Danish brig *Prince Christian*, on passage from Havana, Cuba to Amsterdam, Holland, was totally wrecked on a reef of rocks under very high cliffs between Folkestone and Dover, Kent, water rushing into her. Lieutenant Coppin and a team of coast-guards climbed down the cliff and, using a hawser and ropes, saved the Master and his ten man crew.

BERRIMAN James, Master Mariner   **SILVER**
PAYNTER, Richard, Master Mariner   **SILVER**
RICHARDS Edward, Master Mariner   **SILVER**
RICHARDS Thomas, Captain, Pilot   **SILVER**
WELSH, Michael, Master Mariner   **SILVER**

21 February 1839

24 December 1838: The Bristol schooner *Rivals*, Liverpool to London, with a cargo of salt, was seen two miles west of St. Ives, Cornwall, standing into danger in Porthmear Cove, but, after being signalled, she rounded the head and came to anchor at the back of St. Ives pier, striking the ground heavily. Attempts were made to rescue her crew with gigs, Manby rocket apparatus and seine boats, but all were unsuccessful. The seas continued to be extremely violent with very broken waters. Nothing daunted, a fishery tow-boat made a second attempt at 4.p.m., and a fresh crew succeeded in taking off the Master and four men, landing them on Porthminster Beach. Among more than 40 men who took part, the four Masters of vessels and the Pilot were out-standing.

RICHARDSON Andrew, Captain, Steam Packet, *Royal William*   **SILVER**

30 January 1839

24 December 1838: On 22 December, on passage from Hamburg to London, the vessel *Thetis* was stranded on a shoal off the coast of Holland, and her crew spent 56 hours in their own whale boat without water and with few provisions. Captain Richardson saved the vessel's Master and 12 man crew off Flamborough Head, Yorkshire, and landed them at Leith on 27 December. The medal was awarded 'in consideration of his humanity and kindness on the occasion'.

HOLLAND John, Lieutenant, R.N. H.M. Coastguard, Lough Swilly   **SILVER**

21 February 1839

7 January 1839: In hurricane force winds, the schooner *Venus* was wrecked, falling over on her beam ends on Inch Bank, Lough Swilly, Co. Donegal, Ireland. With her mastheads nearly under water, the Master and his eight man crew were left clinging to the rigging. Lieutenant Holland put off with six men in a boat and saved them.

WALKER Joseph, Farmer   **SILVER**

30 January 1839

7 January 1839: At dawn, the sloop *Mary Elizabeth* was seen to be stuck on sand in the River Humber, half a mile off West Halton, near Winterringham, Lincolnshire. With her hull nearly under water, her two man crew were in the rigging. A boat was taken on a cart to the most suitable place on shore and, with Mr Walker and three men aboard, launched through massive waves to save them.

*FOLEY Joseph, Captain, Schooner *Richard*   **SILVER**
HOWELL John, Master Mariner   **SILVER**
JENKINS Lewis, Pilot   **SILVER**
JONES Thomas, Captain, *Two Sisters*   **SILVER**
REES Arthur, Mate, *Galatea*   **SILVER**
SUTTON Charles, Master Mariner   **SILVER**

21 February 1839

7 January 1839: The brig *Thomas Piele,* laden with coal from Swansea to Dublin, was wrecked on a shallow shore near Port Talbot, Glamorgan and began to break up. After one of the crew swam ashore and raised the alarm, Captains Jones, Howell and Sutton, also Pilot Jenkins put off in a boat but, on nearing the wreck with its seven man crew, a heavy sea swept over the rescuers, breaking most of their oars and driving them back to the beach. Recovering their strength, Captain Jones and Pilot Jenkins put out again with Mr. Rees and a seaman, but they were washed out of their boat and back to the shore again. A third attempt led by Captain Foley with the Pilot and three seamen succeeded in taking off the Master and four men.
    *Recorded as Thomas *Foley by R.N.L.I.*

DUNN William, Captain, Vessel *Providence*   **SILVER**

13 September 1839

10 January 1839: The Hartlepool brig *Forster* was dismasted off Flamborough Head, Yorkshire, and soon requested a tow, but the weather made this impossible. Captain Dunn launched his boat with six of his crew and, in three trips, took off the brig's Master, ten crew, and one female passenger.

FRANKLYN George, Lieutenant, R.N. H.M. Coastguard, Newhaven   **SILVER**

7 August 1839

19 January 1839: Using a Coastguard boat, Lieutenant Franklyn took out a crew of six men in stormy weather to rescue the Master and five men from the brig *Zebra* on passage from Ipswich to Liverpool which had gone ashore near Rottingdean, Sussex. He also went out to the sloop *Ceres* driven ashore at the same place on the same day.

LOUGHOUR Rees   **SILVER**

7 August 1839

31 January 1839: The French lugger *Les Enfants Chéris* went ashore on Nash Sands, near Bridgend, Glamorgan, during severe weather. The Master and five man crew were saved by Mr. Loughour going in to the sea and bringing them off.

BATES Thomas, Chief Officer, H.M. Coastguard, Wexford   **SILVER**

17 April 1839

31 January 1839: During a storm the schooner *Thistle* drove on shore near Wexford, Co. Wexford, Ireland, and three men and two boys were marooned on board. Mr. Bates, two coast-guards and five fisherman put out in a boat and, with great difficulty, took off the crew.
   Mr. Bates was originally voted (21 February 1839) the sum of one pound, but appealed and was voted the silver medal.

DAVIES George, Lieutenant, R.N. Revenue Cutter *Tartar*   **SILVER(2)**
LEGGETT Edward, Gunner, R.N. Revenue Cutter *Tartar*   **SILVER**
STUBBS Charles, Seaman, R.N. Revenue Cutter *Tartar*   **SILVER**

17 April 1839

11 March 1839: The French brig *Le Jean Marie* from Bordeaux was in danger of being wrecked near Swanage, Dorset, with her Master and seven men on board. Lieutenant Davies and two men put off in a boat and brought the brig to port.

MACALISTER Robert   **SILVER**

7 August 1839

12 March 1839: The 270 ton brig *Thomas Dougall*, from Leith to Odessa, was driven on to rocks at Occmuster, ten miles south of Wick, Caithness, in a violent mid-morning gale. Mr. Macalister and eight men launched a small fishing boat. The brig's Captain and five men were drowned but four others had jumped on to a rock from where they were rescued by local people. The fishing boat had to launch through heavy surf but succeeded in reaching the casualty and took off three exhausted men clinging to the cross-trees on the broken mast.

THORP T., Rocket Storekeeper   **SILVER**

13 September 1839

12 March 1839: At 11 p.m. in a gale, the ship *Progress*, London to Newcastle, drove towards shore at Tynemouth, Northumberland and struck on sand a long way from shore. Mr. Thorp and five sailors set up the Dennett's rocket apparatus, but the ship's crew was unable to find the first two lines; the third shot being successful they bent on a warp by which four men were landed. The Master and six other men reached shore using the warp after the tide had fallen materially.

WILKIE Christopher, Captain, Ship *Indefatigable*   **SILVER**

13 September 1839

17 March 1839: When the schooner *Aurora*, on passage from London to St. John's, Newfoundland, foundered at 42° North, 36° West, 1400 miles west of Spain, her Captain and two men were drowned. The ship *Indefatigable*, en route from Liverpool to New York, came across her and took the Mate and seven seamen on board and landed them at its destination.

Captain Wilkie wrote to the Institution stating he had received the allowance from the Government for the support of the crew and 'now solicits a medal'. To this the Committee agreed, giving no reason for this exception to its rules.

GILLESPIE Andrew, Gunner, R.N. Revenue Cutter *Stork*   **SILVER**

17 April 1839

23 March 1839: The Plymouth sloop *Ann* was wrecked on Penlee Point, near Plymouth, Devon, with her crew of three men and a boy on board. Mr. Gillespie and six of his crew launched their six oared galley and brought them off.

THOMPSON Robert Kirkpatrick, Chief Officer,
**   H.M. Coastguard, Clogher Head**   **GOLD**

17 April 1839

31 March 1839: With the Master and three men on board, the Liverpool schooner *Minerva*, Bangor to Dundalk, was totally wrecked when she stranded on the north side of the bar near Drogheda, Co. Louth, Ireland. The men had been in the rigging for 12 hours when seen at 3 p.m. Mr. Thompson went to the spot and, deciding against using the rocket apparatus, ordered his boat and a shore boat to be made ready. With himself and eight coastguardmen in the first boat and a coastguardman and seven fishermen in the second, they set off in mutual support through the very heavy sea and brought the exhausted crew to the shore.

WEBLIN John, Boatman, H.M. Coastguard, Ballymacaw   **SILVER**

7 August 1839

22 June 1839: On passage from Newport to New York, the vessel *Prince Regent* was wrecked in very rough weather in Tramore Bay, Co. Waterford, Ireland. Dennett's rockets failed to throw a line the distance. Mr. Weblin then swam off to the wreck through tremendous surf with a rope by means of which the Master, crew and passengers – 40 men, women and children – were saved.

QUAYLE Edward, Captain, Steam Mail Packet *Mona's Isle*   **SILVER**

7 August 1839

19 July 1839: In stormy weather, the sloop *Nanny*, Liverpool to Dundalk, was driven ashore in Douglas Bay, Isle of Man, and was wrecked. Captain Quayle gathered a small crew of two lifeboatmen and two seamen, and manned the Douglas Palmer type lifeboat which took off the Master and two seamen. Very soon afterwards, the heavy sea caused the sloop to roll violently and she was dismasted before breaking up completely.

NORRIS James, Captain, Smack *Waterloo*   **SILVER**

12 December 1839

5 October 1839: Running into the River Humber Captain Norris found the Aberdeen brig *Manly* on its beam ends under water with survivors clinging to her side. Launching his small boat with three of his own crew, he rescued five men (two others had died from exhaustion), took them to his boat and landed them at Spurn Point, Yorkshire, that evening.

PARRY Henry, Quartermaster, H.M. Packet *Doberell*   **SILVER**

27 May 1840

14 November 1839: In very heavy weather, 20 miles west of Holyhead, Anglesey, the *Doberell* found the Bruges schooner *Rosalie*, Liverpool to Ostend, lying to, with eight feet of water in her hold and her long boat in pieces. Mr. Parry and two men made two trips in their boat through heavy surf and took off all nine people on board. When they left, the depth of water in the hold was 16 feet and the sea was making a fair breach over her.

COLLINS John, Captain, Ship *Roscius*   **GOLD**

8 January 1840

5 December 1839: The American packet ship *Roscius*, at position 46° North, 33° West, 1000 miles east of Newfoundland, fell in with the 600-ton timber ship *Scotia*, which had been en route from Quebec to Glasgow. The ship was lying waterlogged with 17 feet of water in her hold but, as Captain Collins tried to get near, the wreck pitched so heavily and staggered under the influence of the heavy sea that his command was seriously endangered. Drawing clear, he picked up all of the survivors from their own boats and succeeded in rescuing the Master and 23 men who were landed safely at Liverpool.

This medal was awarded in recognition of 'his admirable conduct on the occasion'.

COX Henry, Lieutenant, R.N. H.M. Coastguard, St. Andrews   **SILVER**

8 January 1840

20 December 1839: The St. Andrews, Fife, lifeboat with Lieutenant Cox and a crew of a coastguardman, a Pilot and ten fishermen put out through heavy surf to help the Aberdeen vessel *Isabella and Ann*, Shields to Dundee, in a very dangerous situation off that port. They rescued her Master and 12 men and took the vessel to port.

HICKS George, Boatman, H.M. Coastguard, Tyrella   **SILVER**

12 February 1840

13 January 1840: During a violent storm, the Liverpool schooner *Eagle* , laden with salt, was wrecked off Tyrella in Dundrum Bay, Co. Down, northern Ireland with breakers and surf reaching over her yards. A rope was sent ashore by buoy and, after it had been secured, Mr. Hicks succeeded in getting on board the wreck and sent the Master and crew of seven men to safety by the same rope which was held fast by six fishermen on shore, who stood up to their shoulders in the breakers.

FOLEY Joseph, Captain, Schooner *Richmond*   **SILVER(2)**

12 February 1840

20 January 1840: The vessel *Mary* was wrecked and completely lost near Port Talbot, Glamorgan, and one of her crew had drowned. Captain Foley stripped off his clothes, made his way through the surf with a line around his waist and succeeded in rescuing the Master and remaining man from the rigging. He fastened the line around each in turn, then passed them to other seamen who had approached as near as they could to the wreck.

ROBINS John Gunn, First Mate, R.N. Revenue Cutter *Active*   **SILVER**

27 May 1840

20–21 January 1840: At 9 p.m. on the 20th, the 800 ton ship *Brunswick*, London to Malta, was driven on to shingles near Hurst Castle, Hampshire at the west end of the Solent. The Coastguard galley, with Mr. Robins and five coastguardmen, was launched and reached the casualty at 1.30 a.m. next day. The ship had swung around and, under Mr. Robins' direction, the helm was put to starboard so she cleared the bank and got through the North Channel until just past Yarmouth Roads, off the Isle of Wight.

Mr. Robins reckoned that, had he been ten minutes later, the ship would have become a total wreck and the crew of 24 men and one woman would in all probability have been lost.

WRIGHT John, Captain, Smack *Samuel and Mary Ann*   **SILVER**

12 February 1840

27 January 1840: The smack *Samuel and Mary Ann* came across the Sunderland brig *Prospect*, on her beam ends, sinking in tremendous seas and hurricane force winds on the Dogger Bank in the North Sea. The smack shipped a heavy sea which split her trysail while she was taking off the brig's Master and 11 men. This was completed by 5 p.m. Captain Wright lay to all night, but by next morning the brig had disappeared.

QUADLING Barnabus Edward, Chief Officer,
   H.M. Coastguard, Courtmacsherry   **SILVER**

11 March 1840

21 February 1840: When the sloop *John and Ellen,* laden with coal, was nearing Courtmacsherry, Co. Cork, Ireland, from Newport, she was wrecked in very stormy conditions. Mr. Quadling and his men launched their gig, but the sea was too heavy and, with two oars broken and his boat nearly swamped, he was forced to give up. The sloop's crew of three men and a boy had been forced to take refuge in the cross trees and were rescued by a yawl.

METHERELL Richard Roe, Lieutenant, R.N. H.M. Coastguard, Youghal **GOLD**
15 April 1840

23 February 1840: Dennett's rockets used in the rescue attempt on the brig *Medora* proved not to have sufficient range when, on passage from Yarmouth to Swansea, the vessel was wrecked in Ardmore Bay near Youghal, Co. Cork, Ireland. The Youghal lifeboat was transported a distance of seven miles to a point where Lieutenant Metherell, with six coastguardmen and a seaman, launched through strong seas and took off the brig's Master and three men.

FISHER Simon, Captain, Smack *Alert* **SILVER**
15 April 1840

4 March 1840: The South Shields brig *Peace* got into difficulties off Aldeburgh, Suffolk. Their plight was seen by Captain Fisher in the smack *Alert* who came to their assistance. Captain Newbiggin of the *Peace* then hoisted out his long boat and transferred his crew (himself and eight men) to the *Alert*. Captain Fisher gave them a free passage to Gravesend, Kent, towing the longboat as well.

On arrival he gave the rescued crew £1 which was gratefully received. This sum was subsequently repaid by the Institution.

GRAY John, Captain, Ship *Eclipse* **SILVER**
9 November 1840

3 May 1840: The ship *Perseverence* was wrecked on the coast of Greenland and all on board – the Master and 45 men – took to the ice, from where Captain Gray took them off and distributed them among other ships to be brought home.

Although the service did not come within the qualifying conditions of the Institution's awards, the Management Committee voted the award in consideration of the extraordinary circumstances.

LYONS William, Lieutenant, R.N. H.M. Coastguard, Glenarm **SILVER(2)**
27 May 1840

10 May 1840: The sloop *Industry* of Belfast was wrecked in bad weather in Glenarm Bay, Co. Antrim, northern Ireland, and Lieutenant Lyons, with three coastguardmen and three other men, went off in a boat and saved her Master and the three man crew.

SMITH John, Thurso **SILVER**
27 May 1840

May 1840: Two fishing boats were wrecked in a heavy storm on rocks off Thurso, Caithness, and two men were drowned. Mr. Smith swam off from the shore in to the surf and, with two other men, saved seven survivors.

BLAIR Horatio, Lieutenant, R.N. H.M. Coastguard, Birling Gap   **SILVER**
15 July 1840

3 July 1840: Laden with salt, a French lugger was wrecked during a severe gale at Birling Gap, near Beachy Head, Sussex. Although it was extremely dark, Lieutenant Blair, with six other men, brought the Manby rocket apparatus into use and saved four men. A boy was drowned in the raging sea.

CAIN William, Boatman   **SILVER**
8 October 1840

16 September 1840: A sloop, the name of which has not been recorded, went ashore at Douglas, Isle of Man, during severe weather, and Mr. Cain put off in a boat with others and saved four men from her crew. One of his feet became entangled in a hawser attached to an anchor, which had been thrown overboard, and was torn off at the ankle. His leg was amputated later, just below the knee.

This case was brought to the attention of the Committee by Sir William Hillary, with whom he had gone off on several occasions to save lives. The Committee also voted £5 to help Cain support his wife and four children.

SEWELL Henry Frederick, Lieutenant, R.N.
    H.M. Coastguard, St. John's Point   **GOLD**
MACDONALD George, Boatman, H.M. Coastguard, St. John's Point   **SILVER**
9 November 1840

21 September 1840: In a strong gale, thick weather and a heavy sea, the smack *Sarah*, Swansea to the Clyde, was stranded and sank at St. John's Point, Dundrum Bay, Co. Down, northern Ireland, with the Master and four men on board. She was seen at daybreak. Lieutenant Sewell and Mr. Macdonald put off in the punt and rescued the crew from the smack's cross trees and yard, where they had been for three hours.

WARREN Charles Duncan, Lieutenant, R.N.
    H.M. Coastguard, Cromarty   **SILVER**
9 November 1840

18 October 1840: When the Fortrose sloop *Banff* was wrecked near Cromarty, Ross and Cromarty, Lieutenant Warren and his crew put off in the Coastguard boat and, in a difficult operation, saved the Master and one man – the vessel's full crew.

DEVEREUX Mark, Master Pilot   **SILVER**
17 December 1840

13 November 1840: In a very heavy gale the Wexford schooner *Mary* drove on shore at Windy Gap, near Rosslare, Co. Wexford, Ireland, where she was seen at daybreak with her crew in the rigging. One of the coastguardmen went for the rocket apparatus, but Mr. Devereux, who had ridden to the scene, rode into the surf to bring a rope from the schooner, and was thrown down once or twice by the violent sea before he achieved this. All the crew were brought off using the rope before the rocket apparatus arrived. One boy had to be saved a second time after he had lost his hold on the shore and was being carried out to sea.

MACNAMARA Timothy, Lieutenant, R.N.
  H.M. Coastguard, Littlehampton   **GOLD**
DAVIES George, Lieutenant, R.N. H.M. Coastguard, Littlehampton   **SILVER(3)**

17 December 1840

13 November 1840: In an extremely violent storm, the brig *Victoria* was driven ashore near Littlehampton, Sussex, with a crew of nine who drifted a line ashore. Lieutenants MacNamara and Davies, with their men, hauled a small boat out to the wreck three times and saved all the brig's crew. Shortly afterwards, the same thing happened to the Poole sloop *Lively*, Poole to Newhaven, and Lieutenant MacNamara and his men were quickly on the scene. In spite of huge waves crashing on to the beach, they waded into the sea with lines tied around them and saved all five members of the sloop's crew.

FRENCH Charles, Chief Officer, H.M. Coastguard, Ballymacaw   **SILVER**

21 January 1841

7 December 1840: When the vessel *Glencoe*, Glasgow to Calcutta, was wrecked near Waterford, Co. Waterford, Ireland, Mr. French, six coastguardmen and four local men placed themselves on nearby rocks with lifelines round their bodies. As the Master and his crew of 12 men dropped from the bowsprit and jib boom, they were dragged one at a time through the surf to safety.

MARSH Digby, Captain, R.N. H.M. Coastguard, Brighton   **GOLD**
PRIOR Thomas Henry, Lieutenant, R.N. H.M. Coastguard, Brighton   **SILVER**
NEWNHAM Nathaniel, Lieutenant, R.N. H.M. Coastguard, Brighton   **SILVER**
PRATT James, Lieutenant, R.N. H.M. Coastguard, Brighton   **SILVER**

17 December 1840

13 December 1840: The brigs *Mary* and *Offerton* and the schooner *Sir John Seale* were wrecked in a violent storm near Brighton, Sussex, leaving their crews in grave danger. The four Coastguard officers and their men established communication in the turbulent conditions and waded into the heavy surf to bring ashore all the Masters and crews – 22 men and boys – without loss.

BURNARD Thomas, Honorary Secretary, North Devon Humane Society   **SILVER(2)**

17 December 1840

Records show that this medal was 'presented to Mr. Burnard that it might accompany a silver snuff box given to him by the North Devon Humane Society on his retirement from the office of Honorary Secretary to that Society'.

Whilst included in awards for bravery, this is more properly an honorary award given in recognition of Mr. Burnard's work at Bideford with the lifeboats stationed at Appledore. Mr. Burnard was awarded a silver medal for the service to the Elizabeth *on 17 December 1833.*

STEEL Charles, Inspecting Commander, H.M. Coastguard, St. Mary's	**GOLD**
ROWE William, Boatman, H.M. Coastguard, St. Mary's	**SILVER**
O'NEIL Patrick, Boatman, H.M. Coastguard, St. Mary's	**SILVER**
HYDE James, Labourer	**SILVER**
HICKS Barnard, Seaman	**SILVER**

4 March 1841

4 January 1841: On passage from Dublin to London, the 500 ton Dublin steam packet *Thames* was seen just before 7 a.m. among the Western Rocks, Isles of Scilly, in very heavy seas and a severe westerly gale. Disabled, she soon ran aground on Jacky's Rock in the Brow of Pond's reef, and three gigs were launched from St. Agnes. Captain Steel, who had been instrumental in getting a lifeboat station at St. Mary's, had difficulty at first in manning the boat. The four men who were awarded silver medals were the first to volunteer. Eventually enough men were cajoled aboard and the lifeboat set out, as did the gigs, through massive seas and squalls of hail and sleet. The lifeboat reached St. Agnes but could proceed no further.

One of the gigs managed to rescue three women from the *Thames* who were transferred to a pilot cutter which landed them at St. Agnes at 3 p.m. The other rescue boats waited near the wreck for a lull in the weather, but none came. Improvised rafts had been made by the sailors on the *Thames*; these floated off when the wreck disintegrated, and some were dashed ashore on Rosevear island. One seaman survived, and he was rescued next morning. The lifeboat recovered eight bodies which were taken to St. Mary's. The figure for those lost was given variously as between 57 and 62.

QUAYLE Edward, Captain, Steam Mail Packet *Mona's Isle*	**SILVER(2)**
CANNELL Thomas, Coxswain, Douglas Lifeboat	**SILVER**

4 March 1841

6 February 1841: During severe weather, the smack *New Volunteer* from Whitehaven went to pieces off the Isle of Man. Captain Quayle mustered a boat's crew including Mr. Cannell and rescued the Master and three men.

BULLEY John, Lieutenant, R.N. H.M. Coastguard, Atherfield	**SILVER(2)**

4 March 1841

12 February 1841: The Russian brig *Castor*, Setubal, Portugal to Finland, was driven ashore near Chale Bay, Atherfield, Isle of Wight, very nearly at the same place at which the brig *Enigheden* was wrecked on Christmas Day 1837. Lieutenant Bulley managed to get lines aboard the brig using rocket apparatus and saved three of the crew of 22 men.

PROSSER Henry, Chief Officer, H.M. Coastguard, Nanny Water	**SILVER**

3 June 1841

31 March 1841: During a heavy westerly gale, at 5 a.m., the Skerries smack *Wellington* was reported sunk at Nanny Water, Co. Meath, Ireland, about two miles from the Coastguard station. Only part of the topmast with men clinging to it could be seen. Mr. Prosser launched his boat with five coastguardmen and rescued two men. The remainder of the smack's crew, including the Master- five in all – had been washed overboard and drowned.

MORTLEY Joseph, Chief Officer, H.M. Coastguard, Padstow **SILVER**

3 June 1841

31 March 1841: The brig *Britannia*, coal-laden on passage from Cardiff, was driven on to Doombar Sand, Padstow, Cornwall, in a dreadful sea. Only the tops of her rigging could be seen. Mr. Mortley and his men set up the Dennett's rocket apparatus and succeeded, first time, in throwing a line on board, and then brought a hawser ashore. The Master, Mate and four seamen were rescued one at a time and, to achieve this, the coastguardmen went out on to the rocks, the sea breaking over rescuers and rescued alike.

GRIFFITHS Griffith, Coxswain, Llanddwyn Lifeboat
(Station No. 5 of the Anglesey Lifesaving Association) **SILVER**

11 November 1841

18 October 1841: At half tide, during a strong north-north-west gale, the Liverpool ship *Mountaineer* was seen in distress on the North Bank, off Llanddwyn, south Anglesey, with a considerable sea breaking on the bank. In this first rescue by the second lifeboat at this station, Coxswain Griffiths mustered a crew and launched but, with conditions making it difficult to go alongside, he anchored close to the wreck and veered down. He took off the Master, his wife, three children and 12 of the crew, then landed them. A boy died in the rigging. The lifeboat lost her anchor and 12 fathoms of cable during the service.

GREGORY John, Boatman, H.M. Coastguard, St. Andrews **SILVER**
McNAUGHTON Neil, Boatman, H.M. Coastguard, St. Andrews **SILVER**
WILSON John, Pilot **SILVER**

11 November 1841

20 October 1841: The sloop *Thomas and George,* laden with coal from Newcastle for Eden, Fife, struck the east end of Barnstool Rocks, off St. Andrews, Fife, in a heavy north-easterly gale and hail storm. When seen she was nearly full of water, but a boat, manned by coastguards, a Pilot and fishermen, was launched which took off the Master and three men. Before high water the sloop became a complete wreck, bottom up and cargo all out.

KINCH Henry, Crew Member, Blyth Lifeboat **SILVER**

9 February 1842

28 October 1841: The Blyth Lifeboat Association Boat, on station since 1826, was attempting to take instructions to the brig *Sibsons* , anchored off-shore, when it was struck by heavy seas and capsized. Eight of the crew were drowned. Henry Kinch most particularly and heroically distinguished himself by his persevering and undaunted exertions in endeavouring to save his comrades. The two survivors had clung to the bottom of the lifeboat.

The Committee voted £20 to be distributed to Kinch and to the fund for the widows and orphans of those drowned.

HANSFORD John, Portland   **SILVER**

9 February 1842

30 November 1841: In a heavy south-west gale, the brig *Amyntas* was wrecked in West Bay, Portland, Dorset, on passage from Quebec to Exeter, laden with timber. She ground to a halt in heavy surf and her Master and three men were drowned in trying to reach the shore. Two others were saved by Mr. Hansford, a brave Portlander, who rushed into the breakers and brought them ashore.

CLAYTON James, Lieutenant, R.N. H.M. Coastguard, Paignton   **SILVER**

9 February 1842

7 January 1842: The Brixham sloop *Harmony* was stranded near Dartmouth, Devon, and the sea made a complete breach over her. Two of her crew took a boat to run out an anchor, but unable to return to the sloop they made for the harbour. Lieutenant Clayton put off in his boat with a Coastguard crew and saved the Master and a boy.

McQUEEN Alexander, Apprentice, Brig *Renown*   **SILVER**

13 April 1842

22 January 1842: The brig *Renown*, Newcastle to Greenock, was wrecked on the island of Lewin, Outer Hebrides, and all her boats were washed overboard. Master McQueen, aged 14, swam ashore with a deep sea lead line attached to a warp tied around his waist, which he succeeded in hauling to the rocks where it was made fast. Then, using this, all the crew were brought off.

WADDY John, Doctor, M.D   **SILVER**

9 February 1842

26 January 1842: In very heavy weather, the schooner *Sarah*, Llanelly to Barrow, was driven on shore at Bannow, near Wexford, Co. Wexford, Ireland, and started to break up, with her starboard side broadside on to the beach. Tremendous seas were breaking over the schooner and her rigging was over the larboard side. Although rocket apparatus was set up and four rockets were fired, four men were shaken out of the rigging and drowned. The only other survivor, who had nearly been killed in the breakers, was drawn on a rope through the surf and recovered by Doctor Waddy of Clough East Castle.

RICHARDSON William   **SILVER**

9 February 1842

January 1842: Four men were going out to lift fishing lines off Portrush, Co. Antrim, northern Ireland, when their boat was struck by a heavy sea and sank immediately. Three of the men were drowned. The other man was saved by the intrepid exertions of Mr. Richardson.

SEWELL John   **SILVER**

KENNEDY John   **SILVER**

16 March 1842

3 February 1842: At 3 p.m., a lighter working its way up to Belfast was seen to founder off Whitehouse between Mandon Point and White Abbey with scarcely time to place a ladder against the mast so that the crew could take refuge, water being already up to the shrouds. Master Sewell, aged 14, the son of Lieutenant H.F. Sewell, R.N., and Master Kennedy, aged 12, the son of Commissioned Boatman P. Kennedy, launched the Whitehouse Coastguard station punt and rowed three quarters of a mile to save two men from the sunken barge.

QUADLING Barnabas Edward, Chief Officer,

   H.M. Coastguard, Courtmacsherry   **GOLD**

13 April 1842

7 February 1842: Adverse winds forced the brig *Latona*, Alexandria to London, to the coast of Ireland and, in trying to enter harbour, she struck on the bar at Courtmacsherry Bay, broaching to in the breakers. Mr. Quadling and his crew launched and went alongside, but the brig's Captain urged him to shove off without delay as he expected the mast to go by the board as she was striking hard with seas going over her continually. The Coastguard boat, however, remained in the surf alongside the casualty from 1 p.m. to dusk and managed to prevail upon the Master and 13 crew to leave the wreck. They manned their longboat and gig, and the coastguards towed them ashore to safety.

McKINNON John, Captain, Steamer *Defiance*   **SILVER**

16 March 1842

February 1842: Captain McKinnon was informed that a boat with six men had gone off from the cutter *Chichester* on the river at Greenock, Renfrewshire. As most of his own crew were ashore, Captain McKinnon, with the assistance of a few gentlemen, got steam up and set out to find the boat. He was just in time as the men had been beating about for nearly three hours, the night was coming on and the gale increasing. The six men were landed safely back at the quay.

RANDLE John, Captain, Schooner *Heiress*   **SILVER**

13 April 1842

19 March 1842: The Dartmouth smack *Mariner* was wrecked near Lundy Island in the Bristol Channel off Bideford Bay in a strong north-west gale and heavy seas. Mr. Randle veered away his only boat by hawser to go alongside the sinking smack; helped by his two crew members, he brought off the Master and three seamen.

BEDWELL William, Captain, Smack *Sally*   **SILVER**

15 September 1842

4 August 1842: Herring boats were returning to Freswick, Caithness, from the fishing grounds and the *Success*, being well-laden, upset in the turbulence. Her crew gained the weather side of the boat, but one man was lost. Captain Bedwell went in his small boat, picked up the other five and landed them. The Master of the herring boat died soon after being landed.

GRIFFITHS Thomas, Boatman, H.M. Coastguard, Mulbay   **SILVER**

27 October 1842

3 September 1842: Three men, who had been fishing at Mulbay, Co. Clare, Ireland, remained on a rock until they were surrounded by the flood tide. Mr. Griffiths and three men went off in the Coastguard boat and saved them despite considerable difficulty and danger.

YOUNG Abraham, Chief Boatman, H.M. Coastguard, Fishersgate   **SILVER**

8 February 1843

13 January 1843: During severe weather, the smack *Prince Regent*, on passage from London to Portsmouth, was stranded at Copperas Gap, near Shoreham, Sussex. Mr. Young made himself fast to a rope flung from the smack and was then hauled on board through very heavy surf, helping the five crew to be landed safely.

'Sprang out into the Sea' from 'The Story of the Sea' edited by Sir Arthur Quiller-Couch 1895.

THOMPSON George   **SILVER**

8 February 1843

13 January 1843: In severe gales, a number of fishing boats from Annalong and Rossglass in Dundrum Bay, Co. Down, were blown out to sea and 74 men were lost. One boat managed to get within one mile of the shore, but the exhausted crew were forced to anchor. One boat with eight men went off from the shore in a rescue attempt but was compelled to turn back. To save the foundering boat's crew with a boat and oars was impossible as a hurricane was then raging. Mr. Thompson therefore lashed together the cobles of a number of fishing boats to haul a boat off with. Eight fishermen volunteered to go out in a boat with the cobles provided Mr. Thompson remained on shore to attend the ropes. In this manner the eight survivors of the fishing boat were warped on shore.

HUGHES John, Second Mate, Mail Packet *Princess*   **SILVER**

8 February 1843

13–14 January 1843: The schooner *Hale* was wrecked on Formby Bank, south of Formby, Lancashire, in a violent storm. All of her crew, except the Master, were washed away and drowned. Mr. Hughes put off from his ship with a boat's crew and saved the sole survivor.

BULLEY John, Lieutenant, R.N. H.M. Coastguard, Atherfield	**GOLD**
VICARY William, Lieutenant, R.N. H.M. Coastguard, Atherfield	**GOLD**
PITT Edward, Boatman, H.M. Coastguard, Atherfield	**SILVER**
DRAYSON Daniel, Boatman, H.M. Coastguard, Atherfield	**SILVER**
KENDALL William, Boatman, H.M. Coastguard, Atherfield	**SILVER**
HEAL John, Fisherman	**SILVER**
TRENT John, Fisherman	**SILVER**
WARN William (Senior), Fisherman	**SILVER**
WARN William (Junior), Fisherman	**SILVER**
WHEELER Charles, Fisherman	**SILVER**
WHEELER John, Fisherman	**SILVER(2)**
WHEELER Robert, Fisherman	**SILVER**

8 February 1843

14 January 1843: With a tremendous gale blowing on the night of 13–14th, the 320 ton brig *George*, outward bound from Shields to Grenada, West Indies, was seen to be driving ashore, her sails torn to ribbons and her anchor not holding. She fetched up on the Atherfield rocks some distance from shore. Lieutenants Bulley and Vicary were soon on the scene with their men and the rocket firing apparatus, but all the rockets were fired in vain and a fresh supply was obtained. At daylight a line was put aboard by which a man was hauled ashore and, when he regained consciousness, he reported that, although the Master and Mate had been washed overboard, ten men remained. Two small fishing boats were then hauled down the beach and launched. With Lieutenant Bulley in charge of one and Lieutenant Vicary the other, each had mixed crews of coastguardmen and fishermen. Lieutenant Vicary got to the wreck first, taking off six men then, on his way back, a cross sea struck his boat and it almost capsized. Lieutenant Bulley rescued the other four men, and they had barely escaped when the wreck broke up completely. The operations extended over 28 hours.

CUNNINGHAM John, Rocket Apparatus Superindendent   **SILVER**

8 March 1843

23 January 1843: In a severe south-east gale of almost hurricane force and much snow, the vessel *Constantia* was wrecked at Tynemouth, Northumberland. The rocket apparatus was set up on the beach within 25 minutes of the information being received by Mr. Cunningham. He put the first shot on board and saved an apprentice. The crew lost the hauling line and, before any more men could be landed, the North Shields lifeboat came alongside.

GILSON Thomas Andrew, Lieutenant, R.N. H.M. Coastguard, Holywell   **SILVER**

8 February 1843

28 January 1843: The schooner *L'Unione Fortunata*, Frierke to Dunkirk, was wrecked near Beachy Head, Sussex. Three coastguardmen and two fishermen launched a punt. They pulled between one and two miles in thick fog to a dangerous reef of rocks and found half the vessel sunk and the remaining mast and sails flat on the water with seas breaking over them. Three men in the cross trees and entangled rigging were taken off. A man's cries from the chains were heard, and they returned and took him off, the vessel breaking up soon afterwards. The Master, seven men and a military officer were lost. Lieutenant Gilson and five coastguardmen had gone out previously in the Coastguard boat, but it had been swamped when it smashed against the wreck.

LAZOIX ... , Lieutenant, French Marine, Dieppe   **SILVER**

8 March 1843

January 1843: The brig *Ver*, on passage from Tyne to Dieppe, Département Seine Maritime, France, was sunk in running for harbour at her destination. Lieutenant Lazoix waded up to his neck in the sea and succeeded in passing a rope to her by which means the Master and five men were saved.

GLOVER John, Captain, Smack *Atalanta*   **SILVER**
HURRY Stephen, Captain, Smack *New Gypsy*   **SILVER**
POWELL John, Master, Smack *Lord Howe*   **SILVER**

26 April 1843

18–19 February 1843: The brig *Traveller* was wrecked on Gunfleet Sand, off Harwich, Essex, on the 17th and was seen next morning by the two smacks *Atalanta* and *New Gypsy*, both of Colchester. She was breaking up fast and the crew had taken to the rigging. The gale continued all day with the sea running fearfully high; the smacks remained but were unable to do anything during that day or night. At daybreak on the 19th, the brig's crew were still to be seen in the rigging, so it was determined to attempt a rescue despite the fact that the sea had abated but little. A boat was launched from each smack, manned by Captains Glover and Hurry, John Powell, Master of the smack *Lord Howe,* and ten other men. After being buffeted for a considerable time they at length succeeded in reaching the wreck and took the whole crew from the rigging – six into the *New Gypsy* boat and four in the *Atalanta* boat. After clearing the Sand, they fell in with the steamer *Gazelle,* bound for London, and put the rescued men aboard her.

CORNISH John, Lieutenant, R.N. H.M. Coastguard, Bovisand   **SILVER**

16 November 1843

22 October 1843: When the schooner *Norman*, on passage from Alicante, Spain to London, was wrecked near Bovisand, Plymouth, Devon, the Master, three of his crew and eight passengers abandoned her as soon as she struck the rocks; two men were left behind. Lieutenant Cornish and four of his men launched the Coastguard boat at the height of the gale and took them off with seas breaking over her.

WILLIAMS J.M., Mate, Quarantine Cutter *Bee*   **SILVER**

16 November 1843

23 October 1843: The vessel *Andromache*, Quebec to the Humber, went on shore at the White Booth Middle and then drove on to Holme Sand, near Hull, Yorkshire, capsizing. Seven of her crew were trapped in the forecastle, clinging to their hammocks with the hatchways under water. The quarantine cutter was lying in harbour, three-quarters of a mile from the wreck; it was as dark as pitch, but she was manned by a crew taking hatchets, saws and a light. The search for the wreck took half an hour; Mr. Williams boarded and led the work of cutting a hole, through which six men escaped; a boy had drowned.

TREDWEN Richard, Shipbuilder   **SILVER**

13 December 1843

28 October 1843: In a very heavy gale, the Cork brig *Towan* ran for Padstow harbour, Cornwall, but tailed over on Doombar Sand. Her boat was stove in and, in the conditions, no Pilot would put out to her assistance. Mr. Tredwen and a crew of seven men manned a boat brought from the town and took ropes to the brig. He then boarded and saved the vessel as well as her crew.

CARBERRY Patrick, Master Mariner   **SILVER**

8 February 1844

25 December 1843: The Neapolitan brig *San Salvadore,* bound from Liverpool to Naples, was wrecked on the Blackwater Bank, off Wexford, Co. Wexford, Ireland. Captain Carberry launched a boat manned by ten fishermen in the raging sea, and they rowed seven miles to the north end of the Bank where they found the wreck, lying on her side with a heavy sea breaking over her and five of the crew in the rigging. The rescue boat shipped some water and it was difficult to avoid the rigging but the five men were taken into the boat; the Master and the other six crew members had to be abandoned because the rescuers could not get near them, which circumstances 'grieved them to the heart'.

ROBINSON James, Steam Tug Owner   **SILVER**

27 March 1844

24 February 1844: On passage from Shields to Aberdeen, the brig *Newcastle*, having been dismasted in the storm, sank at anchor in Aberdeen Bay. The local private lifeboat launched, manned by six Masters and Mates and six seamen of Mr. Robinson's steam tugs, and was then towed out to the wreck by the steam tug *Samson* with 14 Masters, owners and others on board. The crew – the Master and eight men – and two passengers were taken off and landed safely.

SMITH Thomas, Chief Boatman in Charge, H.M. Coastguard, Ballina SILVER
17 July 1844

16 June 1844: In tremendous seas, the schooner *Stormont*, Ballina to London, struck on the sands near Ballina, Co. Mayo, Ireland. Mr. Smith and four other coastguardmen launched their boat and rowed through part of her floating cargo of oats and pieces of wreckage to find the brig breaking up with sea washing over her and the crew – the Master and six men – in the rigging. They were taken off and then put on board a country boat to be landed safely.

BACON James, Captain, Smack *British Rover* SILVER
5 September 1844

14 July 1844: On passage from Quebec to London, the ship *Singapore* drove on shore near Rye, Sussex in a west-south-westerly gale and very heavy seas. She was seen at 5 a.m. by Captain Bacon. Her crew had taken to the ship's longboat, but it had no oars and they were obliged to hang on to the stern of the ship (then in 10 feet of water). Captain Bacon, at great risk to his vessel and crew, took his boat in among the breakers and heaved a buoy overboard with a line which was caught by the crew of the *Singapore*. Thus the Master and 12 men were saved.

BRITTON John, Captain, American Ship *Rochester* GOLD
30 July 1845

15 September 1844: The *Rochester* came across the British ship *Dorchester*, on passage from Liverpool to Boston, U.S.A., a total wreck and the sea breaking over her, in Latitude 50° Longitude 28° (about 1000 miles west of Land's End). Captain Britton took off the Master, 29 crew and some passengers (number unspecified) who were all landed at New York.

Whilst the Committee noted that this case did 'not come within the Rules of the Institution, which are limited to cases of shipwreck on the coasts of the United Kingdom', they voted the gold medal 'in consideration of the very laudable and humane conduct of Capt. Britton'.

BLACK Alexander, Chief Officer,
 H.M. Coastguard, Strangford, Co. Down SILVER
18 December 1844

6 October 1844: The schooner *William*, en route from Cardiff to Belfast, was driven ashore on Gun Island at the entrance to Strangford Lough in a violent gale. With great difficulty, Mr. Black and six of his men launched the Coastguard boat and went alongside the wreck from which they brought off the Master and seven men.

RIDGE John, Second Mate, Revenue Cutter *Kite* SILVER
18 December 1844

2 November 1844: A brig ran foul of a barque in Kingstown Harbour, Co. Dublin, Ireland, and both were driven on shore. A man fell overboard from the brig and another from the *Kite* jumped in after him. A heavy sea was running and both men were in peril. Mr. Ridge leaped overboard with a line and saved them.

BRUNTON John, Lieutenant, R.N.
   H.M. Coastguard, Alnmouth and Boulmer Detachment   **SILVER**

18 December 1844

3 November 1844: In very poor weather conditions, the brig *Iris* was wrecked on Boulmer Rocks, 25 miles south of Berwick-on-Tweed, on a journey from Danzig to London. The Master and seven men were on board. Lieutenant Brunton and the boat's crew launched the Boulmer lifeboat and took off the whole crew.

ACRAMAN John, Merchant   **SILVER**

8 January 1845

2 December 1844: Two vessels were driven on to the Goodwick Sands, near Fishguard, Pembrokeshire, with the sea running very high in severe weather; both showed distress signals. Mr. Acraman persuaded five men to help him drag a boat a great distance along the water's edge and then man it with him. They brought off the Master and five men from the schooner *Ann and Elizabeth*, then put out again and saved the Master and five men from the brig *Antelope*, aground further out.

TAYLOR James, Commissioned Boatman,
   H.M. Coastguard, Dundrum Bay   **SILVER**

12 February 1845

17 January 1845: The brig *Frolic*, Liverpool to Dordrecht, Holland, drove on shore in Dundrum Bay, Co. Down, northern Ireland, and was totally wrecked. The Master and his five crew had taken to the rigging. Mr Taylor, with three of his men and two fishermen, put out in the Coastguard boat but it was swamped coming alongside the wreck. Eight fishermen then put off in their boats to render assistance, and everyone was landed safely.

COVIN John   **SILVER**

12 March 1845

26 January 1845: A gale was blowing when the schooner *Hazelwood*, on passage from Sligo to Liverpool, was wrecked in Ramsey Bay, Isle of Man. The schooner *Mary* then collided with her and sank, her crew taking refuge on the *Hazelwood*. Both Masters drowned when a yawl, in which they were trying to reach shore, foundered. One man from the yawl was saved by Mr. Covin who, with others, then saved six men from a rock, using ropes, as it was impossible to launch a boat in the conditions.

BOLITHO Simon, Boatman, H.M. Coastguard, Bude   **SILVER**
PAUL Thomas, Boatman, H.M. Coastguard, Bude   **SILVER**
PERKINS James, Boatman, H.M. Coastguard, Bude   **SILVER**

12 February 1845

28 January 1845: Two days after her Master had been washed overboard and lost, the schooner *Margaret*, on passage from Cork to Porthcawl, was totally wrecked near Bude. Cornwall. She was

seen, dismasted, about seven miles from Bude and drifting towards the shore. The coastguardmen took their Dennett's rocket apparatus six miles along the coast and set it up. When the vessel came ashore, they fired a rocket over and saved three men and a boy, just before she broke up.

COMBE Matthew, Lieutenant, R.N. Chief Officer
    H.M. Coastguard, No. 2 Battery, Dungeness   **SILVER**

12 March 1845

31 January 1845: The vessel *William Harrington*, outward bound, grounded at Dungeness, Kent, at 9 a.m. in a severe snow storm at low water. When the weather cleared, she was seen by Lieutenant Combe who launched the Coastguard galley with four of his men. The sea was running very high and the north wind was strengthening, but the galley carried a short way over the sands at half water and got alongside. A rope was passed on board the vessel but the sea upset the galley, and the Coastguards were thrown into the water except for Lieutenant Combe who clung to the vessel's side. Two of the men were drowned, whilst the other two succeeded in getting hold of a rope and were saved. With the assistance of No. 1 Battery's boat and two Deal boats, the *William Harrington* was refloated later and taken to Portsmouth for repairs.

GOULD William, Lieutenant, R.N. H.M. Coastguard, Brooke   **SILVER**

30 July 1845

24–25 March 1845: On the 24th, the Coastguard boat manned by Lieutenant Gould and his men launched at 4 a.m. to the ship *Siam*, wrecked in Compton Bay, Isle of Wight, during a southwesterly gale. They could not lay alongside, so laid off a short distance away. At 11 a.m., the sea made a complete breach over the casualty and washed away her quarter boat in which were two men. One man was drowned, but the other was saved by the Coastguard boat.

On the following day, the weather was still adverse but, the Master and five of his crew still being aboard, Lieutenant Gould again launched and took them off, the ship breaking up soon afterwards.

MORRIS William E., Captain. Harbour Master, Portmadoc   **SILVER**

JONES Evan, Master Mariner   **SILVER**

GRIFFITHS Benjamin, Master Mariner   **SILVER**

PARRY Robert, Master Mariner   **SILVER**

30 July 1845

1 July 1845: During very severe weather, the 574 ton American ship *Glendower* went on to the bar at Port Madoc, Caernarvon, thumping violently with seas breaking over her. Her mast was cut away and the Master decided to abandon ship but, when a boat was lowered, this was swamped and driven against the ship's side. Local Pilots made two unsuccessful attempts at rescue then, after the gale had moderated, they took off all the crew of 15 men from the rigging. While this was going on, the Harbour Master and three Captains had set off to St. Tudwal's Road, 20 miles away near Abersoch on Lleyn Peninsula where, with others, they manned a lifeboat which they brought across Tremadoc Bay to find that the rescue had already been effected.

The Committee Minutes record that 'not only did they risk their lives but also sustained losses in having their coats and jackets washed away, which they pulled off to enable them the better to work the boat'.

PURDY Hugh, Chief Boatman, H.M. Coastguard, Tyrella   **SILVER**

10 December 1845

13 October 1845: The brig *Industry* drove on shore at Tyrella, Dundrum Bay, Co. Down, northern Ireland, while on passage from Belfast to Newport. Helped by 17 fishermen, Mr. Purdy used a hawser to save the Master and the crew of seven men in spite of the gale and heavy seas.

O'SULLIVAN Mortimer   **SILVER**

11 March 1846

19 November 1845: On the 18th, in very bad weather the schooner *Monkey* was driven into Bantry Bay, Co. Cork, Ireland where, approaching Bere Island with breakers ahead, she let go her anchors near the shore. Her masts were cut away and, on the next morning, the schooner showed distress signals. At 8 a.m., six men from Bere Island succeeded in taking off the Master, Mate, Second Mate, three seamen and a boy, but one man had been left behind. Mortimer O'Sullivan, aged 17, launched his father's whale boat and, with the same six men , tried to reach the casualty, but was driven back. The vessel was expected to break up, but the weather moderated and, at 3 a.m. on the 20th, coastguards boarded her and took off the survivor. The vessel was later salvaged.

GRIFFITH Robert, Seaman   **SILVER**
HIGHLAND Owen, Landsman   **SILVER**
OWEN Richard, Seaman   **SILVER**

11 March 1846

18 December 1845 ; On passage from Bahia, Brazil to Liverpool, the ship *Frankland* was wrecked at Cemaes, north Anglesey in a violent storm and very heavy seas. The Cemlyn lifeboat (Anglesey Lifesaving Association) launched and saved the Master and his 18 man crew, particular gallantry being shown by Messrs. Griffith, Highland and Owen.

WILLIAMS Joshua, Ship Owner. Retired Master Mariner   **SILVER**

30 April 1846

24 December 1845: The Bristol barque *Ness*, Demerara, British Guiana to Bristol with rum and sugar, was wrecked near Bideford, Devon, in heavy weather after 37 days at sea. The Bideford private lifeboat launched with Captain Williams as Coxswain and took off eight crewmen, the other eight being saved by the No. 2 lifeboat.

JONES Owen, Landsman   **SILVER**

11 March 1846

31 December 1845: During a violent storm the Dublin barque *Alhambra* was seen to be running before the gale on to some dangerous rocks off Holy Island, Anglesey. While the Rhoscolyn (Anglesey Lifesaving Association) lifeboat was being launched a landsman, Owen Jones, swam through the stormy sea to a small island, Ynys Traws, where he waved a flag and warned the barque of its peril. The crew reacted immediately and was able to bring up the barque only yards short of the rocks. When the lifeboat arrived, it was able to take off all 23 members of her crew.

WISHART James   **SILVER**

20 January 1847

16 March 1846: During a fierce storm, the sloop *Anna* was driven ashore near Thurso, Caithness and wrecked. Huge waves were pounding the beach, but Mr. Wishart waded out into the violent surf and brought the Mate to safety on the shore. The Mate was the only person saved.

LAVINGTON Thomas, Lieutenant, R.N. H.M. Coastguard, Bognor   **SILVER**

2 December 1846

13 October 1846: In a terrific gale, while en route from Aberystwyth to London, the sloop *Bellona* was wrecked on Bognor Rocks, near Bognor, Sussex. Lieutenant Lavington put off in the Coastguard galley with his crew to bring the Master and four men to safety.

EVANS John, Captain, Schooner *Royal George*   **SILVER**
*JENKINS William   **SILVER**

2 December 1846
*20 January 1847

22 October 1846: The sloop *Sir Peregrine*, Bangor to Cork, was driven on shore in foul weather near Fishguard, Pembrokeshire, and sank. With the sea breaking over her the whole time, the crew took to her top where they remained from 1 a.m. for eight hours. Captain Evans put off in his schooner's boat with Mr. Jenkins and some of his men. and rescued the sloop's Master and six men.

Mr. Acraman, Lloyd's Agent, who himself was voted a silver medal on 8 January, 1845, wrote of William Jenkins: 'A respectable young man of Fishguard (who went off) to rescue the crew of Sir Peregrine would be most gratified in having the Society's Medal, and it is not the first or second time that he has volunteered in saving the lives of distressed Mariners'.

McGLADERY John, Lieutenant, R.N. H.M. Coastguard, Dunfanaghy   **SILVER**

20 January 1847

22 October 1846: On passage from Liverpool to Westport, Co. Mayo, Ireland, the schooner *British Queen* was driven ashore in Sheep Harbour, near Dunfanaghy, Co. Donegal, Ireland. She was there for 12 hours before Lieutenant McGladery, with a crew of his men, put off at 5.30 a.m. in his galley and saved the Master and the crew of six men.

LLEWELLYN Margaret, Miss   **SILVER**
LLEWELLYN Martha, Miss   **SILVER**

29 April 1847

22 October 1846: When the smack *Margaret* of Barmouth was stranded on the beach at Fishguard, Pembrokeshire, in severe weather, three seamen were saved by the two ladies who waded into the surf with the help of two men.

CONEYS Anthony   **SILVER**

2 December 1846

November 1846: The 10 ton hooker *St. Michael* struck a sunken rock about a mile off Clifden, Co. Galway, Ireland. Mr. Coneys launched a boat with two other men, all others refusing to go out. The Master and two men were saved, and one minute later the hooker went to pieces.

KENNEDY Edward, Chief Boatman, H.M. Coastguard, Dunfanaghy   **SILVER**

20 January 1847

10–11 December 1846: In a severe northerly gale, the sloop *James Mackenzie*, Inverness to Liverpool, drove on shore at Mulroy Station, Co. Donegal, Ireland, and her five crew took to the rigging. Mr. Kennedy and his four men, helped by local inhabitants, carried the Coastguard galley one and a half miles across country to launch it. Nearing the wreck, the galley shipped a sea and was forced to return to the shore. They went out again next day and brought to safety the Master, who was near to death; the rest of his crew had drowned.

McKENZIE James, Chief Boatman, H.M. Coastguard, Galway   **SILVER**

11 March 1847

7 February 1847: The vessel *Sea Horse* was driven on shore near Galway, Co. Galway, Ireland, and Mr. McKenzie saved a man from the rigging.

TOWN John, Chief Boatman in Charge, H.M. Coastguard, Folkestone   **SILVER**

10 June 1847

12 March 1847: On passage from Swansea, the brig *Henry and Sarah* was wrecked under Lydden Spout, three miles west of Dover, Kent, and sank. Mr. Town launched the Coastguard galley with a crew of four men and took off the Master and seven men.

MILLS Charles, Chief Boatman, H.M. Coastguard, Clifden   **SILVER**

29 April 1847

20 March 1847: Mr. Mills was the only person who would put out to the brig *Halifax*, which had driven ashore from her anchorage in Ardbear Bay, near Clifden, Co. Galway, Ireland, on to rocks at the harbour entrance. With the help of four other men, the brig's Master and 16 seamen were taken off in three trips.

FISHER Georgia Vilhelmina C.A., Mrs., Clergyman's Wife   **SILVER**

29 April 1847

March 1847: The British ship *Marwood* was wrecked on the Faroe Islands (Danish territory, 250 miles north of Scotland). The crew, in attempting to land, were swamped in the surf and with great difficulty, scrambled up the rocks. One of the crew suffered so much he appeared lifeless. Of the rescuers, only Mrs. Fisher understood resuscitation and eventually, after a long period, she succeeded in reviving him.

WILLIAMSON Robert, Fisherman   **SILVER**

6 April 1848

23 August 1847: Mr Williamson was among the first on the scene when the vessel *Britannia* was wrecked at Thurso, Caithness, in a storm. In an operation lasting two and a half hours, he brought off five seamen by rope although he was knocked down repeatedly by the violence of the sea.

RAYE Henry Robert, Lieutenant, R.M. H.M. Coastguard, Donegal   **SILVER**

8 December 1847

18 September 1847: The sloop *Ninian Lindsay* was wrecked in a heavy gale on Tun Sandbank, near Londonderry, northern Ireland, and, after her masts were cut away became a total wreck. Lieutenant Raye, with a mixed crew of coastguardmen and fishermen, put off in a boat. In two trips, they saved seven men from the wreck on what was considered to be the worst sandbank in Ireland; the remainder of the sloop's crew saved themselves in their own boat.

ALLEN Luke James, Captain, Vessel *William and Mary*   **SILVER**
AGNES Samuel, Seaman, Vessel *William and Mary*   **SILVER**
COLE John, Seaman, Vessel *William and Mary*   **SILVER**
DYER Benjamin, Seaman, Vessel *William and Mary*   **SILVER**
DYER Benjamin (cousin), Seaman, Vessel *William and Mary*   **SILVER**

10 February 1848

27 October 1847: At midnight, on passage from Quebec in a heavy north-west gale, the Colchester vessel *William and Mary* with double-reefed sails, came across the wreck of the ship *Cambria*, also timber laden, 1000 miles west of Land's End. Though the wreck was exhibiting lights, the conditions made it impossible to board by boat during the hours of darkness, so the *William and Mary* sailed about until daylight. Four men then volunteered to go across by boat and got alongside where they found the casualty's First Mate, who had broken his leg, the Second Mate, cook and 11 seamen, all sheltering in the topgallant forecastle. They had been in this situation for four days and nights, during which the Captain, two apprentices and a seaman had drowned, and the exhausted crew had existed without fresh water on a quarter pint of vinegar per man per day. The survivors were taken off in two trips and landed at Colchester on 13 November.

The medals were awarded to the four seamen for their 'very laudable conduct', and to the Captain 'for his necessary sanction and encouragement to his men and for his attention to the shipwrecked crew during their voyage to Colchester'.

WOODHAM William Henry, Lieutenant, R.N. H.M. Coastguard, Banff   **SILVER**

8 December 1847

16 November 1847: With an extreme gale blowing right on shore at Banff, Banffshire, the schooner *Pearl*, Sunderland to Campbeltown, was wrecked with five men on board. After unsuccessful attempts had been made by rocket apparatus to get a line aboard her, a coble with seven men got alongside and took off two men but, returning through the furious surf, the coble capsized. Lieutenant Woodham brought the rocket apparatus into use again, and saved the Master and three men together with six from the coble.

WILLIAMSON William, Branch Pilot   **SILVER**

19 July 1848

21 November 1847: The Dundee sloop *Sisters*, laden with coal, got into difficulties at the entrance to Wick harbour, Caithness, and struck about 50 yards outside Quayhead. Mr. Williamson, with five others, put off in the pilot boat. The sloop had run ashore to the east of the harbour, but her Master and five men were taken off half an hour before she became a total loss.

DARK William, Captain, Smack *Rose*   **SILVER**
FOUND William, Captain, Schooner *Model*   **SILVER**
JOHNS William, Captain, Schooner *Liberty*   **SILVER**

10 February 1848

8 December 1847: The vessel *Marchioness of Abercorn*, on passage from Quebec to London, was wrecked near Padstow, Cornwall, and rescue attempts by rocket all failed. Captains Dark, Found and Johns launched a small boat, and pulled through tremendous rollers, reached the wreck and brought a line to the shore. Four survivors were brought to safety, but the boat capsized on the second trip and two men were drowned. Finally, using a hawser, the remainder of the crew – the Master and 20 men – were brought ashore.

BULLEY John, Lieutenant, R.N. H.M. Coastguard, Atherfield   **GOLD BOAT(2)**

10 February 1848

30 December 1847: Three miles from the Coastguard station at Atherfield, Isle of Wight, the ship *Llanrumney* ran ashore at 1 a.m. during a heavy gale. At 7 a.m., lines were fired without success. Lieutenant Bulley went back to his station and launched a lorette through the violent surf. A fisherman's boat which had preceded him lost two men when it overturned. The coastguardmen worked for one hour with surf breaking completely over them and, in two trips, took off the Master and 14 men plus one of the fishermen who had held on to the wreck.

DILLON James, Boatman, H.M. Coastguard, Arklow   **SILVER**

6 April 1848

27 February 1848: During a severe storm the ship *Calypso*, bound from Liverpool to Rio de Janiero, was driven ashore at Mizen Head, near Arklow, Co. Wicklow, Ireland, her crew taking refuge in the main and mizzen rigging. Mr. Dillon waded into the pounding surf but was twice thrown back on to the beach. He tried once again and succeeded in getting a line on board and with the sea breaking over the mizzen mast, the Master and all the crew were brought ashore safely.

GRAVES Joseph, Captain, Steamer *Victoria*   **SILVER**

18 January 1849

26 October 1848: The sloop *Banff*, on passage from Bangor, north Wales to Alnmouth, was wrecked on Robin Rigg Bank in the Solway Firth. With the hull under water, the Master and his three crew had taken to the cross trees. Captain Graves, who saw the wreck from two miles away,

proceeded towards her and then put 'part of the boldest of his crew into the steamer's boat'. With great difficulty, owing to breakers and a strong current, the boat's crew rescued the four men who had been in their perilous situation for 15 hours.

GRANBY Charles, Captain, Schooner *Nais*   **SILVER**

18 January 1849

13–14 November 1848: In a severe gale, en route from Bremen to New Orleans, the 700 ton American emigrant ship *Burgundy* was wrecked on the Long Sand, off the Thames Estuary. Captain Granby stood by for one night and one day and, with great exertion and danger, succeeded in saving 160 persons from the wreck and landed them at Ramsgate. He did not leave the wreck until he had seen all the rest of the passengers and crew safely on board the Revenue Cutter *Desmond* and some fishing smacks. The Master and crew of the smack *Trial* of Harwich are recorded as saving 70 passengers and received compensation for damage to their boat and lost equipment.

HEARD Richard, Chief Officer, H.M. Coastguard, Rutland   **SILVER**

2 May 1849

20 November 1848: The ship *Forest Monarch*, on passage from St. John, New Brunswick, to the Clyde, was wrecked on rocks off the island of Inneskeagh, Rutland, off the coast of Co. Mayo, Ireland, where she became a total wreck. Mr. Heard, with a mixed crew of coastguardmen and others, waded into the surf with ropes and brought off the Master and 35 men.

YOUNG Abraham Hart, Chief Boatman, H.M. Coastguard, Blatchington   **SILVER**

18 January 1849

29 November 1848: The Swedish ship *La Fayette*, from Setubal, Portugal, was wrecked off Newhaven, Sussex, on an excessively dark night with a very heavy sea. Mr. Young reached the wreck through the surf and, seeing a man washed from her, ran out on a receding wave and seized a piece of bulwark hanging by her side, but was trapped and seriously injured. The wreck's crew gave him the end of a rope and, in a lull, he ran for the shore; the rope was then used to bring five men ashore; two others were drowned.

FISH John, Acting Coxswain, Southwold Lifeboat   **SILVER**

14 March 1849

4 December 1848: The Sunderland schooner *Ury* grounded on the Barnard Sand in the early morning. By the time the Southwold private lifeboat *Solebay* reached the wreck, the schooner was on her beam ends, the decks torn out and a tremendous sea breaking over her. One man was rescued when the lifeboat veered down on the wreck. John Fish clambered on to a mast that was floating beside the wreck, to which it was still tethered by the standing rigging. By this means Fish reached a second survivor who was unconscious and got him safely on board the lifeboat. The two survivors, out of a crew of five, were landed at Lowestoft.

GLEESON Robin, Boatman, H.M. Coastguard, Fethard　　　　**SILVER**
31 January 1849

15 December 1848: En route from Constantinople to Liverpool, the Greek ship *Amaltea* was wrecked on Bannow Bar in Fethard Bay, Co. Wexford, Ireland, her mizzen and main topmasts going immediately. Her crew collected at the bow, clinging together. They were stranded on the first ebb of an extraordinarily high tide and, at low tide, Mr. Gleeson, whose station was half a mile from the wreck, launched his cot and went down the river. It was almost dark before he reached that part of the harbour when, hearing cries, his crew entered the water, held hands, and saved four survivors – all that remained of a 17 man crew.

MITTIN Philip, Captain, Boat *Zephyr*　　　　**SILVER**
ROSSITER Thomas, Captain, Boat *Steamer*　　　　**SILVER**
2 May 1849

18 December 1848: The American ship *Republic* , from Liverpool to Baltimore, was wrecked on Blackwater Bank, off Cahore Point, Co. Wexford, Ireland, and started going to pieces. Captain Mittin, with a crew of seven men, and Captain Rossiter, with a crew of 12 men, put off in their boats and saved the Master and 19 of his crew. Two crew had drowned.

SELLY William Henry, Chief Boatman, H.M. Coastguard, Penzance　　　　**SILVER**
18 January 1849

26 December 1848: The schooner *Kitty*, on passage from Newport to Plymouth, became a total wreck near Penzance, Cornwall, and her crew were seen hanging from the remains of her bulkheads, her foremast having gone by the board. A boat, belonging to fishermen on the spot, was launched with Mr. Selly and four fishermen on board; they brought the Master and six men ashore; a boy had drowned. The vessel broke up soon after.

REES William　　　　**SILVER**
14 March 1849

29 January 1849: In poor weather, the Gloucester brig *Lady Kenmure* was wrecked on Goodwick Sands, near Fishguard, Pembrokeshire, while on passage from the Clyde to Bristol, and she was totally destroyed. The Master and five men took to the rigging from where they were taken by Mr. Rees and eight men in a boat after six hours awaiting rescue.

LESLIE John, Master, *Wilhemina*　　　　**SILVER**
12 September 1849

4 April 1849: The schooner *Olive* of Hull was wrecked at the entrance to Stonehaven harbour, Kincardineshire, and the Master and her four-man crew were saved. The lifeboat sent off to the vessel had been upset, and two of the crew of ten had drowned. John Leslie, Master of the *Wilhemina* was acting as Master and Manager of the Lifeboat.

The Institution awarded £5 to each of the widows of the two men who had drowned – one a coastguard, the other a labourer.

PEPPER John, Chief Boatman, H.M. Coastguard, Hurst Castle   SILVER
30 May 1849

19 April 1849: At night, the brig *Love and Unity*, Shields to Poole, struck the Needles, off the Isle of Wight, and went to pieces, one boy being lost. At midnight, the Master and five men reached the top of a rock from her main top gallant yard and, at 10 a.m., were rescued by Mr. Pepper and four of his men in the Coastguard galley. The service was stated to have been carried out at considerable risk on the part of the coastguardmen.

TOOLE William, Captain, 40th Regiment of Foot   SILVER
12 September 1849

19 April 1849: The Dublin vessel *Prince Albert* was wrecked in a near hurricane on the Raven Strand near Curracloe House, Co. Wexford, Ireland, grounding at 5 a.m. and going down in the surf. Her crew took to the rigging, except for one who swam ashore. Captain Toole, the owner of Curracloe House, went, with men and horses, and launched a herring cot. After several failures, he reached the casualty between 6 and 7 p.m., and took off the other man and two boys, one other boy having died in the rigging.

COLLARD Stephen, Cinque Port Pilot, Deal   SILVER
2 May 1849

Awarded for long service, as on various occasions he had been foremost where life and property were to be saved from shipwreck. Lord Liverpool had made him a Gunner of Sandown Castle, Deal, Kent, for his meritorious conduct. Mr. Collard was between 70 and 80 years old, and still held that appointment.

GALLAGHER Patrick   SILVER
11 July 1849

10 June 1849: With a cargo of Indian corn, the smack *Emily Mary*, Liverpool to Donegal, was wrecked on a rock between Killibegs and St. John's Point , near Donegal, Co. Donegal, Ireland, sinking immediately in deep water. Mr. Gallagher and his boat's crew (tenants of Thos. Conolly, M.P. for Donegal) rowed to the wreck, took off the smack's Master and five men and brought them to Killibegs harbour.

DAND Middleton Henry, Land Owner   SILVER
14 October 1852

3 December 1849: The brig *Pedestrian,* of South Shields, sprang a leak during a heavy storm on the night of the 3rd December 1849 and most of her sails had blown away. Endeavouring to make for the Coquet roads, the boat drifted on to a reef of sunken rocks about half a mile from shore, called the Pan Bush, near Hauxley, Northumberland. Mr. Dand and the Harbour Master launched two cobles and were followed by eight other volunteers. They succeeded in getting within about 100 yards of the brig from which a buoy was streamed. The crew of nine men then left the vessel in their own boat and were taken into the cobles and brought on shore.

In reporting this incident to the Wreck & Reward Committee, it was stated that 'owing to the great press of business devolving upon Mr. Robert Plummer, Secretary to the Northumberland Branch Association, the case had lain in that gentleman's desk nearly three years unattended to, and that the consequence of that delay was, he had found at Hauxley great unwillingness in any of the fishermen to volunteer to form a crew for the new lifeboat for that place'. Apart from the silver medal to Mr. Dand, the Harbour Master was awarded one sovereign and the eight other men each received ten shillings.

TOWN John, Chief Boatman, H.M. Coastguard,
   No. 2 Battery, Dungeness   **SILVER(2)**
6 February 1850

21–22 December 1849: During stormy weather the Danish galliot *Margaretta Sabreana* was wrecked off Romney Hay, south-west of Folkestone, Kent. Mr. Town, with a crew of coastguardmen and others, launched the Coastguard galley and rowed to windward inshore of the heavy breakers abreast of the galliot, but was forced back on shore again. He remained abreast of the vessel all night and, at daybreak, launched again and took two men from the masthead just as his galley filled, forcing him to return to shore and bail out. Putting back to the wreck, he took off the other two men.

AGAR John, Chief Boatman, H.M. Coastguard, Morren Castle   **SILVER**
7 March 1850

12 January 1850: En route from Liverpool to New York, the ship *Hollinguer* (993 tons) drove on to the Blackwater Bank, off Arklow, Co. Wexford, Ireland, with the Master, four Mates, 28 seamen and 11 passengers on board. Some of them reached the shore in the ship's lifeboat, but the Master and 12 men drowned. Three boats were launched from the shore, among them the Coastguard boat with Mr. Agar and four men aboard which saved the Master's son and one woman passenger. Five seamen and nine passengers were saved by the other two boats.

ATKINS Thomas, Commissioned Boatman, H.M. Coastguard, Gibraltar Point   **SILVER**
9 May 1850

12 February 1850: In a severe storm, the schooner *Talisman* was wrecked on Knock Sand, near Wainfleet, 13 miles north-east of Boston, Lincolnshire. Mr. Atkins set off in a very small boat with two of his men and, rowing three miles through tremendous seas, took off the Master and his two man crew and landed them at Skegness.

MARSHALL John, Master Mariner   **SILVER**
WILLIAMS Joshua, Ship Owner, Retired Master Mariner   **SILVER(2)**
18 May 1850

23 March 1850: Captains Marshall and Williams put out from Bideford and saved four men from the brig *Dasher* just before she broke up; one other man had died in the rigging from exhaustion.

PEEBLES Thomas, Captain, *Earl of Errol*   **SILVER**

12 September 1850

25 August 1850: In a south-west gale, the Belfast schooner *Margaret Young*, Belfast to Irvine, ran ashore in Irvine Bay, Ayrshire, among the jettees or stones on the north side of the bar with the sea were making a breach over her. Captain Peebles launched his boat with four men and brought off the Master, Mate, one boy and a passenger.

TOWN John, Chief Officer, H.M. Coastguard, Castle Gregory   **SILVER(3)**

6 February 1851

19 November 1850: Mr. Town, with other men to help him, waded into the surf and took off ten of the 12 man crew from the Neapolitan brig *Enrichetta*, on passage from Barletta, south-west Italy to Limerick, which was wrecked at Kilshannig, Co. Kerry, Ireland.

LANDELLS Thomas, Tide Surveyor   **SILVER**

13 February 1851

19 November 1850: The Cork schooner *Maria*, weather bound in Milford Haven, Pembrokeshire, while on passage from Newport to Cork, parted from her anchor and was driven on to rocks at Pill Point. Mr. Landells, who was employed in the customs service, assembled a crew of three of his men and two volunteers and put out through the heavy surf to find the schooner sinking. At great risk, he managed to take off her Master, his wife and six men.

SUTHERLAND Daniel, Boatman, H.M. Coastguard, Katerline   **SILVER**

19 December 1850

19 November 1850: Running on to rocks at Cowie, near Stonehaven, Kincardineshire, the Thurso sloop *Nancy* was wrecked with the sea breaking over her and her crew in the rigging. Mr. Sutherland, coming more than five miles, took up position on a rock with the sea completely surrounding him, passed a rope to the wreck and with the help of others, brought the Master, Mate and a seaman ashore.

RUSSELL Richard, Esq. J.P.   **SILVER**
LIKELY Henry, Butler to Mr. Russell   **SILVER**
PREVEL Robert, Chief Officer in Charge, H.M. Coastguard, Kilkee   **SILVER**
McCARTHY James, Commissioned Boatman, H.M. Coastguard, Kilkee   **SILVER**
FLYNN Patrick, Boatman, H.M. Coastguard, Kilkee   **SILVER**
HARRINGTON Timothy, Boatman, H.M. Coastguard, Kilkee   **SILVER**
SHANNON Patrick, Assistant Boatman, H.M. Coastguard, Kilkee   **SILVER**
*WILSON John, Captain, Barque *Edmund*   **SILVER**

2 January 1851

*6 March 1851

20 November 1850: The 400 ton emigrant barque *Edmund*, on passage from Carrigaholt, Co. Clare, to New York, was struck by a violent gale on the 19th, which carried away two of her masts, making her unmanageable. Just before midnight on the night of the 20th, the barque struck in the Duggerna

Rocks off the Bay of Kilkee, Co. Clare, Ireland, but the force of the seas washed her off and drove her farther inshore where the remaining mast went by the board and the vessel broke in two. Fortunately the mast provided a bridge to the rocks and a total of 117 people clambered to safety helped by Mr. Russell, his butler, Mr. Prevel and four boatmen. The barque's Captain was awarded the silver medal for his humane and laudable exertions after the ship was wrecked.

GOSS Thomas, Lieutenant, R.N. H.M. Coastguard, Dunmanus	**GOLD**
BLISSENDON William M., Commissioned Boatman,	
H.M. Coastguard, Dunmanus	**SILVER**
CARR John, Chief Boatman, H.M. Coastguard, Dunmanus	**SILVER**
McNAMEE Patrick, Boatman, H.M. Coastguard, Dunmanus	**SILVER**
RODERICK Edward, Boatman, H.M. Coastguard, Dunmanus	**SILVER**
TUTT Edward, Boatman, H.M. Coastguard, Dunmanus	**SILVER**

16 January 1851

14 December 1850: On passage from Quebec, Canada, to Newport laden with timber, the ship *Mountaineer* got into trouble on the 13th and drifted toward some rocks in Dunmanus Bay, Co. Cork, Ireland. Next morning, Lieutenant Goss launched the Coastguard whaleboat through thick haze, tremendous thunder and lightning in a hard gale and proceeded to the ship's assistance. With the wind blowing up the bay, he was at a loss which side of the ship to go down with the life apparatus. A party sent to the north side of the bay reported the *Mountaineer* to be within 40 yards of the rock off Dunmanus Point. Lieutenant Goss went there himself (a distance of nine miles) with the apparatus and was abreast of the ship about 5 p.m.. He resolved, with his men, to attempt to rescue the crew and, in a local boat, succeeded in getting alongside the ship. They were hauled on board, and the boat was smashed, losing with it their clothing and Lieutenant Goss' sword. Finally, Lieutenant Goss managed to run the ship aground on soft mud and so saved the Master, Mate and 26 crew.

PINCOMB Thomas (Junior), Pilot, Exmouth	**SILVER**

13 February 1851

5 January 1851: Shortly after leaving Exmouth harbour, the brig *Maria* was struck by a sudden gale from the south west, losing her foretopmast and jib boom. A local pilot boat put off to help the brig return to port. On nearing the brig, three Pilots got into their rowing boat, when a heavy sea filled the boat. Two of the Pilots sprang back to the pilot vessel, but Thomas Pincomb was unlucky and was in the water for three-quarters of an hour before his comrades were able to rescue him. The Pilots then boarded the brig and were instrumental in saving the *Maria* from disaster.

DAVIES George, Captain, R.N. Inspecting Commander,	
H.M. Coastguard, Penzance	**GOLD**
BURNE James, Commissioned Boatman, H.M. Coastguard, Penzance	**SILVER**
SELLY William Henry, Commissioned Boatman,	
H.M. Coastguard, Penzance	**SILVER(2)**
EASTAWAY Robert, Boatman, H.M. Coastguard, Penzance	**SILVER**
KERLEY Thomas, Boatman, H.M. Coastguard, Penzance	**SILVER**
FORWARD Thomas Randall, Commander, Revenue Cutter *Sylvia*	**GOLD**
CARR Charles S., Gunner, Revenue Cutter *Sylvia*	**SILVER**
JONES Henry, Mariner, Revenue Cutter *Sylvia*	**SILVER**
RICHARDS Henry, Mariner, Revenue Cutter *Sylvia*	**SILVER**
RICHARDS James, Mariner, Revenue Cutter *Sylvia*	**SILVER**
SURRY William, Mariner, Revenue Cutter *Sylvia*	**SILVER**
WARD James, First Class Boy, Revenue Cutter *Sylvia*	**SILVER**

30 January 1851

12–13 January 1851: On the morning of the 11th, the 250 ton Whitby brig *New Commercial* struck the Brisons rocks off Cape Cornwall, four miles north of Lands End, and broke up immediately in thick fog and high seas. The nine men aboard and the Master's wife managed to scramble on to a rock shelf, but a massive wave swept seven of the men to their deaths. Captain Sanderson and his wife managed to get back on the rocks. The other man, a mulatto, grasped a piece of wreckage and was later saved by fishermen from Sennen Cove. Captain Davies, meanwhile, had ordered the *Sylvia* out from Penzance in atrocious conditions and, on arrival at the scene, an unsuccessful attempt was made to take off the two survivors by a small boat; she only just made it back to the cutter which then lay off all night to give the victims hope. Next morning, with the wind having veered a little and the seas slightly calmer, five other boats arrived, one manned by the coastguard, three by fishermen and the fifth was a preventative boat containing Captain Davies and a rocket apparatus. Using this, he managed to fire a line which the two on the rock secured and the Master's wife was hauled aboard but, sadly, she died very quickly from exposure and the buffeting. The other survivor, Captain Sanderson, was brought aboard safely and landed at Sennen Cove together with the bodies which had been recovered.

MITCHELL John, Pilot, Guernsey	**SILVER**

30 January 1851

16 January 1851: In the evening, the cutter *Adele*, St. Malo to Guernsey, was making for St. Peter Port, but, unable to reach the port, let go her anchor after she had passed Castle Cornet. The south-east gale broke the cutter from her moorings and drove her north on to the Soubreaux Rocks by which time the wind was almost a tempest. Mr. Mitchell launched his boat with four men and reached the cutter just when she bottomed on the rocks. Already one of the cutter's crew had drowned. The Pilot ran his boat under her bowsprit. As the vessel fell over and went down stern first, the Master, one seaman and the cabin boy jumped aboard. The Pilot pushed off just before the cutter sank.

KENNEDY Arthur, Lieutenant, R.N. H.M. Coastguard, Cushenden	**SILVER**

6 March 1851

16 January 1851: In a very heavy gale, the Coleraine schooner *Martin* parted her anchors at 3 p.m. and drove on to rocks off Rock Point, near Cushenden, Co. Antrim, northern Ireland. With the

schooner's boat broken to pieces by the seas passing over her, the crew of Master and four men took to a mast. Lieutenant Kennedy and his crew, unable to launch their boat, carried a country boat over the rocks to a position opposite the wreck and launched. They were forced to put back twice because of the very high seas breaking over them but rescued the schooner's crew at the third attempt.

WHEELER William, Thames River Pilot   **SILVER**

13 March 1851

8 February 1851: Whilst piloting the Danish brig *Margaretta* up the Thames, when off Erith Wheeler saw two of her crew thrown into the river from the ship's boat. He immediately leaped over the vessel's bows and saved one of the men, but the other man sank before Wheeler could reach him.

The Committee also took into consideration Wheeler's action in saving four of the crew of the brig *Percy* of Sunderland, wrecked on the rocks close under Tynemouth Castle about three years earlier.

ANDERSON John Gurnsdall, Chief Officer, H.M. Coastguard, Downderry   **SILVER**

3 April 1851

15 February 1851: On the previous day, in a heavy gale, the French brig *Fletan* was forced to cut down her larger mast but ran aground on the 15th in Whitsand Bay, Cornwall, and was wrecked. Mr. Anderson waded into the sea up to his arms, took a rope from one of the brig's crew who had jumped overside and then helped to bring off, by this means, the other eight crew members.

*CASTLE George, Broadstairs Lifeboat   **SILVER**
*HOLBORN Solomon, Coxswain, Broadstairs Lifeboat   **SILVER**
WALES George, Broadstairs Lifeboat   **SILVER**
CROUCH John, Broadstairs Lifeboat   **SILVER**
CHITTENDEN Edward, Broadstairs Lifeboat   **SILVER**
WALES John, Broadstairs Lifeboat   **SILVER**
HANSELL Paul Sackett, Broadstairs Lifeboat   **SILVER**
CROUCH Richard, Broadstairs Lifeboat   **SILVER**

*20 March 1851
3 April 1851

7 March 1851: At 8 a.m. on the 6th, the London brig *Mary White* was seen, by the lookout at Walmer Coast Guard Station, on the Goodwin Sands off the east Kent coast. A heavy northerly gale with the rising tide was making conditions so difficult that, although boats put off from Ramsgate and Broadstairs, nobody could approach the brig within half a mile. The Broadstairs private lifeboat was launched on the 7th and, in conditions of great difficulty, rescued seven of the brig's ten man crew.

This lifeboat had been presented to the town in 1850 by John and Robert White, shipbuilders of Cowes who were born in Broadstairs, and was then named Mary White *after this first successful rescue.*

WILLCOX John, Chief Officer, H.M. Coastguard, Lydd	**SILVER**
RIVERS Thomas, Boatman, H.M. Coastguard, Lydd	**SILVER**
	12 June 1851

21 March 1851: During severe weather, the Greek brig *Melpomene* was wrecked near Dungeness, Kent. Mr. Willcox, Mr. Rivers and two other coastguardmen set up rope communication and brought off four of her 14 man crew.

ARMSTRONG Robert, Fisherman	**SILVER**
ARMSTRONG William, Fisherman	**SILVER**
BROWN Henry, Fisherman	**SILVER**
DENT John, Fisherman	**SILVER**
JEFFERSON Philip, Fisherman	**SILVER**
	12 June 1851

22 March 1851: When 14 men drowned after four fishing cobles upset off Newbiggin, Northumberland, the five fishermen distinguished themselves by their lifesaving efforts in saving two men.

KELLY Edward, Lieutenant, R.N. Harbour Master,	
Port Louis, Mauritius	**SILVER**
	1 September 1853

26 June 1851: The 500 ton sailing vessel *Randolph*, an East India trader, left Port Louis, Mauritius, for Calcutta in June with 250 Indian coolies as steerage passengers, returning to their native country after a term of labour. Also aboard were a few other passengers including two Army officers. On the night of the 25th, sailing too close to the shore at the north-east end of the island, the vessel ran on to a reef in the darkness, going heavily aground and becoming a total wreck. Her masts were cut away, but this did not prevent the ship from rolling over on her beam ends and, at daylight, most of the survivors were transferred to the shore using the ship's boats. A shore boat manned by Lieutenant Kelly and others made four journeys and saved about 50 coolies and the Mate who were found huddled together on the fore part of the wreck.

The Wreck and Reward Sub-Committee recommended that an exception to the Rules of the Institution be made in this case.

HARRISON Jacob, Tyne Pilot	**SILVER**
BURN John (Senior), Tyne Pilot	**SILVER**
SMITH Joseph, Tyne Pilot	**SILVER**
MILBURN John, Tyne Pilot	**SILVER**
	26 June 1851

Minutes record that the Committee's attention had been 'called to the intrepid and successful exertions of the Pilots of the Tyne during the past nine years in saving lives from shipwreck'. The medals were voted to the four most deserving Pilots as recommended by the Treasurer of the Tyne Shipwreck Association. They had gone off in the lifeboat 48, 25, 22 and 16 times respectively.

HEIN John, Captain, Russian barque *John* SILVER
LARKIN Thomas, Mate, Russian barque *John* SILVER

30 October 1851

25 September 1851: The yacht *Owen Glendower* was wrecked off the Arran Isles at the entrance to Galway Bay, Ireland. The Russian barque *John*, on voyage to New York with emigrants, came across the wreck and for seven hours tried to render assistance. Because of the violence of the storm, they were unsuccessful. Then the Mate, Thomas Larkin, lowered the barque's long boat and, with five volunteers, made three trips to rescue the owner, three ladies and ten crew from the yacht. They were safely landed at Kilrush, where the Russian ship was delayed from continuing its voyage to New York by contrary winds. Captain Hein reckoned the delay cost him ú70 a week.

PEARCE Richard, Lloyd's Agent, Penzance SILVER

30 October 1851

For repeated services in saving life from shipwreck; Richard Pearce's exact period of serviced is not given although he took part in rescues from 46 vessels in 30 years, always as the leader. A specific service in which he participated was that on 24 May 1828 to the Plymouth brig *Albion*, laden with coal, which was driven on the beach to the east of Newlyn, Cornwall, during a heavy south-south-east gale. The brig was stern on to the beach, about a quarter of a mile out. When the sea made a breach over her and carried away her bulwarks, Mr. Pearce brought the rocket apparatus to the scene together with his gig. Using the gig, he saved the brig's Master and crew before the vessel broke up.

HOOD William, Coxswain, Seaton Carew Lifeboat SILVER

30 October 1851

Awarded for long service, during which he participated in 32 services to wrecks and had assisted in saving 120 persons.

MOODY Samuel , Coxswain, Skegness Lifeboat SILVER

27 November 1851

Recommended by the Lincoln County Association, for having 'personally assisted over a period of 21 years in saving 53 lives'.

EVANS Thomas, Coxswain, Magazines Lifeboat SILVER

27 November 1851

At the suggestion of the then President, the Duke of Northumberland, the Coxswains of five Liverpool Dock Trustees lifeboats were each awarded medals for having distinguished themselves in going off to save life – in Coxswain Evans' case 106 times. During this period services were given to the ships *Brighton* and *St. Andrews* (both 1839), schooner *Sally* and brig *Mary Bell* (both 1841), flat *Daniel* (1844) and brig *Harlequin* (1846).

CROPPER Peter, Coxswain, Liverpool Lifeboat   **SILVER**

27 November 1851

For long service in a Liverpool Dock Trustees lifeboat; he went out 96 times to shipwrecked vessels.

FORMBY Joseph, Coxswain, Formby Lifeboat   **SILVER**

27 November 1851

For long service in a Liverpool Dock Trustees lifeboat; he went out 70 times to save lives. During Joseph Formby's service lives were saved from the pilot boat *Good Intent* (1833), ship *Byrades* (1836) when the lifeboat capsized, brig *Harvest Home*, liner *The Pennsylvania*, and emigrant ship *Lockwood* (all 1839).

BECK Robert, Coxswain, Point of Ayr Lifeboat   **SILVER**

27 November 1851

For long service in a Liverpool Dock Trustees lifeboat; he helped to save lives in 60 launches. One rescue took place on 28 August 1831 from the ship *Burmese*, homeward bound from St. Petersburg, stranded at Talacre, Flintshire – this resulted in 19 lives being saved. Another service on 5 April 1844, to the steamer *Mermaid*, resulted in all passengers and crew being saved when she was wrecked on the West Hoyle Bank.

DAVIES George, Coxswain, Hoylake Lifeboat   **SILVER**

27 November 1851

For long service in a Liverpool Dock Trustees lifeboat; he went out to save lives 59 times in 11 years.

CHARD Joshua, Boatman   **SILVER**

8 January 1852

9 December 1851: The schooner *John* of Newcastle, laden with coal, was wrecked in severe weather on Thorpeness Reef on the coast of Suffolk. Joshua Chard launched his own boat with a crew of four men and 'at great peril' went off to the rescue of the schooner's crew of ten who had taken to their boats.

BROWN James, Commissioned Boatman, H.M. Coastguard, Dunbar   **SILVER**

5 February 1852

9 January 1852: In stormy weather, the schooner *Susan* of Fraserburgh was wrecked on the Yellow Carr Point, near Dunbar. The crew of four jumped on to a rock and, with assistance of a line and a grummet with corks on it belonging to the life apparatus, were dragged on shore. James Brown twice jumped into the sea to rescue the Master and one of his crew.

ROCKCLIFFE William, Coxswain, Southport Lifeboat　　　　**SILVER**

5 February 1852

For long service; he went out in the private lifeboat 20 times in 17 years and was present when 70 lives were saved.

KEARNEY WHITE James, Chief Officer, H.M. Coastguard, Blyth　　**SILVER**

4 March 1852

10 February 1852: The Sunderland sloop *William and Mary* was driven on shore in a north-easterly gale near Blyth, Northumberland and her crew took to the rigging. Mr. Kearney White, with a crew of six fishermen, put out in a fishing coble and, in the heavy sea, saved the four man crew. The men in the rigging were so helpless with cold that they had been unable to make use of a line fired to them by Dennett's rocket.

TURNBULL Robert , Fisherman　　　　　　　　　　　　　　　**SILVER**

1 April 1852

28 February 1852: During a gale, a fishing yawl was wrecked on rocks in Dunbar Harbour, East Lothian. Three of her crew were saved by rocket apparatus from a rock where they had gained refuge. Mr. Turnbull swam through the heavy surf with a rope tied round his body and landed on the rock. With the aid of the rope the skipper and his young nephew were hauled to safety.

COSTELLO Martin, Tide Surveyor　　　　　　　　　　　　　**SILVER**
DEVEREUX Mark, Master Pilot　　　　　　　　　　　　　　**SILVER(2)**

14 October 1852

18 September 1852: During thick and dirty weather, the emigrant ship *Bhurtpoor*, with 419 people aboard, bound for New Orleans , U.S.A., from Liverpool, went ashore on the Long Bank, off the coast of Co. Wexford, Ireland. Fishing smacks, the pilot cutter *Rapid* (Captain Mark Devereux) and the lifeboats from Rosslare and Kilmore put off to rescue the crew and passengers. Between them, 416 people were saved; one man and two infants had perished from the cold. The Kilmore lifeboat saved 30 lives.
　　The part played by Mr. Costello in the rescue is not detailed in the Minutes.

HOWE Robert, Chief Boatman, H.M. Coastguard, Ballygerig　　**SILVER**
PEIRSON Stephen Dodge, Commissioned Boatman,
　　H.M. Coastguard, Ballygerig　　　　　　　　　　　　　**SILVER**

14 October 1852

19 September 1852: About 6p.m., a disabled boat was seen drifting off Ballygerig Point, Co. Wexford, Ireland with two men on board. The two coastguardmen put off in a small punt from Greenore Point and managed to bring the two men ashore despite the very difficult conditions. The boat turned out to be a lifeboat belonging to the *Bhurtpoor* (see previous service). She had left Rosslare earlier that day with the Master and Mate of the ship and three men from a Jersey trawler

to go to the wreck. The Master and Mate had got aboard the *Bhurtpoor* when a sea struck the lifeboat, causing heavy damage and washing the Master of the trawler in to the sea where he drowned. The boat then drifted away.

BARNARD Addeley, Chief Officer, H.M. Coastguard, Clogher Head **SILVER**

11 November 1852

26 October 1852: In a gale from east-south-east, the Dublin brig *Fidelity* ran on to rocks near Clogher Head, Co. Louth, Ireland, and broke up. Mr. Barnard, with a mixed crew of coastguard-men and fishermen, put off in a Coastguard boat and rescued the eight man crew of the brig in two trips.

KEARNEY WHITE James, Chief Officer, H.M. Coastguard, Blyth **SILVER(2)**

11 November 1852

28 October 1852: In an easterly gale, the Russian barque *Victoria* was wrecked near Blyth, Northumberland, her main and mizzen masts going by the board. Her crew were nearly washed off the deck on several occasions, but Mr. Kearney White put off in the Blyth lifeboat and, in difficult conditions, saved the 14 men. The barque went to pieces shortly afterwards.

DAY Christopher, Captain, Steam Tug *Contractor* **SILVER**

6 January 1853

29 October 1852: The brig *Louisa* of Stettin, bound from Riga to Stockton, with a cargo of timber, had struck on the North Gar when attempting to enter the River Tees. It was blowing a strong gale from the east. About half an hour after she struck, the tug *Contractor* went to her assistance and by means of lines rescued five of the crew. Having lost all his lines, Captain Day went for the Seaton Carew lifeboat which he towed to within a quarter of a mile of the wreck. Unable to reach the wreck, the lifeboat returned to shore. The tug therefore returned again to the *Louisa* and saved two more men. The Redcar lifeboat then arrived and rescued the remaining three men. All were landed safely, the *Louisa* shortly after becoming a complete wreck.

WARD John Ross, Commander, R.N. Inspector of Lifeboats **SILVER**

11 November 1852

Awarded 'in consideration of the risk to life he had incurred while making some experimental trials with the new lifeboats, during rough weather, on the coast of Northumberland'.

In 1851 he was engaged by Algernon, the fourth Duke of Northumberland to try experiments with lifeboats.

On 5 February 1852 he was elected a member of the Committee of the Institution and appointed Inspector of Lifeboats in August. On his retirement in 1883 as Chief Inspector he was awarded an Honorary Gold Medal.

BARNARD Addeley, Chief Officer, H.M. Coastguard, Clogher Head　　　**SILVER(2)**

9 December 1852

11 November 1852: The Dublin schooner *William Pitt* was wrecked in a heavy east-south-east gale near Clogher Head harbour, Co. Louth, Ireland. Mr. Barnard launched a boat and, in two trips, saved her five crew.

McCARTHY James, Chief Boatman, H.M. Coastguard, Dundrum　　　**SILVER(2)**

9 December 1852

12 November 1852 During a heavy gale from the east, the Maryport schooner *Martha Grace* was driven on to Dundrum Bar in Dundrum Bay, Co. Down, northern Ireland, and wrecked. With four men, Mr. McCarthy put off first in the Coastguard punt, unsuccessfully, then in a whale boat. They rescued the three crew and brought them on shore.

BARRETT William, Chief Officer, H.M. Coastguard, Balbriggan　　　**SILVER**

BARRETT William, Junior, (his son)　　　**SILVER**

SYNGE Alexander, Reverend　　　**SILVER**

9 December 1852

14–15 November 1852: The Glasgow barque *Young England* was wrecked on Carabates Rocks near the Balbriggan coastguard station, Co. Dublin. William Barrett, with his son, the Reverend Synge, two coastguardmen and three fisherman, got to the coast opposite the wreck, and at 9 pm. saw articles from the ship coming ashore. After much difficulty, Mr. Barrett succeeded in launching his boat and about 1 am. reached the ship and took the Master and nine crew from the rigging. A second attempt failed. At daylight he made a third attempt from another spot with the Coastguard galley and, after three hours at the oars, rescued the six remaining survivors. Two of the crew had perished.

CHADDOCK John, Commissioned Boatman, H.M. Coastguard, Stonehaven　　　**SILVER**

*COLLISON Robert, Captain, *William and Mary*　　　**SILVER**

3 February 1853

*3 March 1853

26 November 1852: During a south-easterly gale, the Arbroath schooner *Christiana* was wrecked near Stonehaven, Kincardineshire. Mr. Chaddock and Captain Collison, with others, rescued her crew of six men using ropes. To carry this out they had had to swim to a rock from the main outcrop of rocks.

The award of a silver medal to Captain Collison took into account his previous services.

BRIDLE William, Master, Boat *Primrose*　　　**SILVER**

6 January 1853

26–27 December 1852: The emigrant barque *Heroine,* on passage from London to Australia, was wrecked off Beer Head, near Lyme, Dorset, during a hurricane. Two boats carrying 44 passengers and crew from the wreck were seen near Lyme Cobb. Seeing the perilous situation of these boats, a boat put off from the revenue cutter *Frances* manned by three of the cutter's men and two belonging to other vessels in the harbour. This boat capsized and all the men, except William Bridle, were drowned. The two boats from the *Heroine* came ashore safely.

PARSONS Thomas, Lieutenant, R.N. H.M. Coastguard, Bournemouth   **SILVER**

6 January 1853

27 December 1852: During a heavy south to south-east gale, the Poole barque *William Glenanderson*, inward bound from Quebec, Canada, came on shore at Boscombe. Lieutenant Parsons put out in the Coastguard galley with four men and saved the barque's crew of eight. A boat, from Sir Percy Shelley's yacht, which was also taking part, capsized, but the Coastguard galley saved four of the five persons on board..

BROOKS Arthur, Chief Boatman, H.M. Coastguard, Dungeness   **SILVER**

SIMS John, Boatman, H.M. Coastguard, Dungeness   **SILVER**

3 February 1853

27 December 1852: At 8 a.m., with 71 emigrants and ten crew aboard, the German brig *Louise Emilie* was wrecked during a hurricane at Dengemarsh, near Dungeness, Kent, and, in spite of the bitterly cold conditions, coastguardmen and local people made several attempts to secure a line aboard the vessel. Finally, this was achieved, after men had put their own lives at risk, wading into rough seas with the brig already breaking up. A gigantic wave swamped the vessel without warning and many were drowned. Only 41 persons survived, among them a little child whose parents perished. It took many days before all the bodies were recovered and buried.

PARKER William, Captain, Schooner *Pearl*   **SILVER**

PARKER John, Mate, Schooner *Pearl*   **SILVER**

3 March 1853

27 December 1852: During a heavy north-easterly gale (also described as a hurricane), the Exeter brigantine *Maria* was seen flying a flag of distress off Flamborough Head, Yorkshire. The two brothers launched their ship's boat and went to the casualty which foundered shortly after they had taken off the six crew.

SINNOTT Richard, Chief Boatman, H.M. Coastguard, Mullaghmore   **SILVER**

3 March 1853

10 February 1853: During a snow-laden gale varying from north-east to east-north-east, the Dutch galliot *Ida Gizena* was wrecked about 13 miles from Mullaghmore, Co. Sligo, Ireland. Under the command of Mr. Sinnott, the Coastguard boat was rowed a total distance of nearly 30 miles and brought to safety seven of the nine man crew.

REDFORD John, Coxswain, Cullercoats Lifeboat   **SILVER**

31 March 1853

26 February 1853: Cullercoats is located on an exposed part of the Northumberland coast between Whitley Bay and the mouth of the Tyne. A fishing boat, in trying to enter the Cullercoats Haven during a heavy gale, lost three of her crew overside, two of whom drowned. The third, a young boy , managed to hang on to a rock. Mr. Redford jumped into the surf with a rope tied around his body and swam to help the boy, who was hauled to safety by means of the rope.

TEGG Thomas, Captain, Sloop *Caroline* **SILVER**

31 March 1853

26 February 1853: The Cardiff schooner *Comet* was embayed in a north-north-westerly gale in Fistral Bay between Towan Head and Pentire Head, near Newquay, Cornwall. The coastguard managed to shoot a line over her and, by this means, a boat was hauled off to the wreck with a hawser. Mr. Tegg, with two of his own crew, went off in that boat and saved the brig's crew of four.

KNIGHT John T., Boatman, H.M. Coastguard, North Sunderland **SILVER**

5 May 1853

26 February 1853: The Goole schooner *Nisus* was wrecked during a north-easterly storm about 200 yards from the shore near North Sunderland, Northumberland, and attempts were made to rescue the crew. Mr. Knight particularly distinguished himself by going off four times, twice in the lifeboat and twice in a coble, but without success.

BRICE William, Commissioned Boatman, H.M. Coastguard, Greencastle Fort **SILVER**

2 June 1853

12 March 1853: The Londonderry schooner *Harmony* sank on a dark night during an east-south-easterly gale off Greencastle Harbour, Co. Donegal, Ireland, at the mouth of Lough Foyle. Three men and a woman were saved by a country yawl manned by ten men, one of whom was Mr. Brice who , on nearing the wreck, leapt out of the boat on to a rock hidden by the half-tide. From here he saved an exhausted seaman whom he pushed to safety in the boat and followed him in. It had been impossible to get the boat near the man because of rocks nearby and because the boat was swept away and back.

SANDS Robert, Master, Schooner *Oracle of Nassau* **SILVER**

7 July 1853

3 May 1853: The Commanding Officer of H.M. Troops in the Bahama Islands called the attention of the Institution 'to the laudable services of Mr Sands, a blackman, Master of the Wrecking Schooner *Oracle*, who was instrumental in saving 160 persons from the emigrant ship *William and Mary* of Bath, Maine, from Liverpool to New Orleans, which had struck on a coral reef near that place on the 3rd May and was rapidly sinking when Sands and his crew boarded her. The Master and his crew with the exception of two men, had taken to their boats and left the emigrants to their fate'.

The Wreck and Reward Sub-Committee made an exception to the Rules of the Institution in this case by recommending the silver medal. It also called the attention of the Board of Trade to 'the improper conduct of the Master and crew' of the William and Mary.

In one report Sands' first name is given as John.

STANNARD Francis, Captain, Sloop *Glenmoriston* **SILVER**

2 June 1853

12 May 1853: The Southwold steamer *William and Mary*, whilst running into Lowestoft Roads, off the Suffolk coast in an easterly gale, struck an anchored vessel and stoved in her own bows. She sank 20 minutes later; two of her crew drowned while two others reached a billyboy. The Master remained at the scene clinging to the sunken vessel's mast, from which position he was rescued by Mr. Stannard and two of his crew in their ship's boat.

STORR John, Fisherman, Whitby **SILVER**

7 July 1853

The Wreck and Reward Sub Committee on 30 May 1853 recommended a grant of two sovereigns be voted in aid of the fund being collected for the relief of John Storr who had been made a cripple by being thrown out of his boat while going off to a wreck in September 1851. On advising the authorities of this award, the reply came that 'Storr had on several occasions distinguished himself in saving life from wreck, and that £23 had been collected for him'. The Institution therefore decided to award the Silver Medal.

LUDLOW Isaac, Captain, Whaler *Monmouth* **GOLD**

5 January 1854

5 September 1853: The 579 ton sailing ship *Meridian*, an emigrant ship, sailed from London to Australia on 4 June 1853 with 84 passengers (including 41 children) and a crew of 23. On the night of 23 August in a heavy gale, she struck rocks at the south-west end of Amsterdam Island in the Indian Ocean, midway between South Africa and Western Australia. Her hatchways, not unnaturally in view of the season, were open and she flooded. The Captain, the cook and a passenger were washed overboard and, shortly afterwards, the vessel broke in two and sank. At day break, the survivors noticed that the mainmast formed a bridge to the rocks. They used this to get ashore from where, on the 28th, they espied a sail which proved to be that of the American whaler *Monmouth*. Conditions at the time prevented this vessel from approaching the wreck, a gale driving the whaler away from the island. The survivors trekked across the island taking three days to cover 12 miles, to find a more suitable landing place for the whaler. On Monday 5 September the *Monmouth* returned and was able to take off everyone, whom they landed at Mauritius 17 days later.

A full account of this wreck, covering six pages, appeared in the Lifeboat Journal of January 1854. It was written by one of the survivors.

TREGIDGO William Henry, Chief Boatman, H.M. Coastguard, Bude **SILVER**

3 November 1853

9 October 1853: Trying to make Bude Harbour, Cornwall, the Bideford smack *Margaret* ran on to the Chapel rocks at the entrance. The east-south-easterly wind was fresh and there was a heavy ground swell but, with the vessel sinking, the new Institution lifeboat was launched with a mixed crew of coastguardmen and volunteers. Although there was a tremendous sea running on the bar, the lifeboat soon reached the wreck in spite of very heavy waves and took off the two men on board the smack which sank immediately afterwards.

BONNER George, Boatman, H.M. Coastguard, Collieston	**SILVER**
RIOCH Robert, Boatman, H.M. Coastguard, Collieston	**SILVER**

3 November 1853

19 October 1853: Having sprung a leak, the Russian schooner *Elise* ran on to the shore by the River Ythan, near Collieston, Aberdeenshire; only four of her crew survived. These were rescued by the two boatmen, Bonner and Rioch, who, at great risk to themselves, put off in a small skiff.

AHERN John, Boatman, H.M. Coastguard, Kilmore	**SILVER**
COX William, Boatman, H.M. Coastguard, Kilmore	**SILVER**
DONOVAN Dennis, Boatman, H.M. Coastguard, Kilmore	**SILVER(2)**
GRAY Donald, Boatman, H.M. Coastguard, Kilmore	**SILVER**
REGAN Daniel, Boatman, H.M. Coastguard, Kilmore	**SILVER**
SMYTH Henry, Boatman, H.M. Coastguard, Kilmore	**SILVER**

7 February 1856

22 October 1853: The New Ross brigantine *Exile* was driven on to a reef of rocks in broken water and a strong tide near Kilmore, Co. Wexford, Ireland, with about 15 inches of water in her. Seven coastguardmen put off in their boat without their Chief Officer, who was ill, and took off the six man crew. The seventh coastguardman, J. Barrett, died before the medals were awarded; his widow received £2. This case was reported late because of the illness of the Chief Officer.

HERRINGTON Benjamin, Coxswain, Southwold Lifeboat	**SILVER**
WATERS William, Second Coxswain, Southwold Lifeboat	**SILVER**

5 January 1854

29 November 1853: The Southwold private Lifeboat saved the nine crew of the brig *Sheraton Grange* of Sunderland. The attention of the Institution was called to the frequent acts of gallantry of the two Coxswains of the boat. Herrington had been off ten times and had helped save 40 lives; Waters had been off nine times and had helped save 38 lives.

HAMILTON Henry Alexander, J.P.	**SILVER**

5 January 1854

19–21 December 1853: During a heavy gale, the Whitehaven brig *Agnes* was driven on shore at Benhead, Co. Meath, Ireland, between Drogheda and Balbriggan, and several attempts were made in shore boats, manned by Mr. Hamilton and others, to rescue the crew. Success escaped them, and a small lifeboat was then brought from Dublin by rail; this was manned by Mr. Hamilton and five other men. In two trips, they succeeded in bringing off three of the five survivors.

DAND Middleton Henry, Land Owner   **SILVER(2)**

2 February 1854

6–9 January 1854: In an easterly gale, the Shields brig *Earl of Newburgh* drove from her anchors in the Coquet Roads, off the coast of Northumberland, near Amble. She became a total wreck and the local Hauxley lifeboat, manned by Mr. Dand and 16 others, launched and saved six of the crew. In the following three days, during which the gale continued, the lifeboat took off 14 men from the vessels *Monarch* and *Heroine*, but the crew of the *Maria* perished before it could reach her.

JEFFERSON Philip, Coxswain, Newbiggin Lifeboat   **SILVER(2)**

2 February 1854

12 January 1854: The Kristiania (Oslo) brig *Embla* was disabled off Newbiggin-by-the-Sea, Northumberland, having been struck by a heavy sea which swept away all hands. No fisherman joined the Newbiggin local lifeboats, as they had been swayed by their wives' entreaties not to go. Eventually the lifeboat was launched with the Coxswain, four men and five boys, but weakly manned as it was, it failed in its attempt to reach the wreck.

FINLAY George, Chief Boatman, H.M. Coastguard, Lambay Island   **SILVER**

2 March 1854

21 January 1854: The 1,997 ton emigrant sailing ship *Tayleur* left Liverpool for Australia on 19 January with 71 crew and 501 passengers, many of them bound for the goldfields. As soon as she entered the Irish Sea, she encountered rough weather which worsened during the night, becoming so thick that, next morning, observations could not be taken. The combination of inaccurate navigation and an unsatisfactory crew meant that at 11.30 a.m. on the 21st she was to be found on a

dead lee shore with badly reduced visibility. The vessel dropped two anchors to try to ride out the south to south-westerly gale, but both cables snapped immediately and the ship drifted on to rocks at the east point of Lambay Island, off Howth Head, Co. Dublin, Ireland. Because of broken water, the boats could not be launched; a passenger then swam ashore with a line and, clinging to this, a number of people were saved, although many drowned in the attempt. A heavy sea washed the ship back and she sank in deep water taking with her 270 people, but one was seen to be still in the rigging from where he was rescued by the Coastguard galley which had been launched, manned by Mr. Finlay, three coastguardmen and a rescued passenger.

FITZPATRICK James, Chief Boatman, H.M. Coastguard, Malin Head   **SILVER**

2 March 1854

30 January 1854: When the Greenock brig *Lady Octavia* was wrecked near Malin Head, the northernmost point of Co. Donegal, Ireland, during a south-westerly gale, ten of her crew were saved in the ship's boat but, nearing the shore, this overturned and was dashed to pieces, one boy being drowned. The Master and three of his crew were saved from their refuge on the ship's bowsprit by Mr. Fitzpatrick and others who waded through the surf to them.

TERRETT Thomas, Sub-Constable   **SILVER**
HEAVY Patrick, Sub-Constable   **SILVER**
NICHOLSON Michael, Sub-Constable   **SILVER**

1 November 1855

19 September 1854: During a strong gale, in a heavy sea, a hooker's boat was seen to fill and sink near Knock, Co. Limerick, Ireland. After much difficulty in obtaining a boat, the three constables, Terrett, Heavy and Nicholson, with two reluctant volunteers from some 50 to 70 fishermen who were watching, put off in an attempt to save the crew. After much effort, they succeeded in reaching the boat from where they rescued two men, who were clinging to the masthead of the sunken vessel, and brought them to the shore.

JOACHIM Richard, Lieutenant, R.N. H.M. Coastguard, Lowestoft   **SILVER(2)**

4 January 1855

7–8 October 1854: On the evening of the 7th, the Norwegian brig *Dronningen* (180 tons) showed distress signals from Holm Sand, off Lowestoft, Suffolk, where she had grounded in an easterly gale. The Pakefield Institution lifeboat was launched with Lieutenant Joachim and a crew of 19 seamen an d was towed out over the sands by the Lowestoft steam tug. The lifeboat then made sail, but found that they could not close the brig to leeward, so they weathered the Sand and ran down to find the sea breaking heavily over her. They succeeded in boarding her, but found the eight man crew drunk and, in spite of the danger, they refused to leave. With the lifeboat in a perilous situation on the edge of the shoal and the sea breaking over her constantly, Lieutenant Joachim took the boat back to Lowestoft harbour. He returned next morning with a fresh crew to find the men on the brig now sober and glad to leave for the shore.

PRICE Thomas, Fisherman
                                                SILVER

2 November 1854

18 October 1854: The Aberystwyth sloop *Two Brothers* was stranded during a north-easterly gale in Red Wharf Bay, east Anglesey, with her crew of three men. Although no more than a mile offshore, it took four hours of unusual perseverance and gallantry for Mr. Price and eight others to effect their rescue in a shore boat.

MOODY Samuel, Coxswain, Skegness Lifeboat
    SILVER(2)

7 December 1854

18 October 1854: In a north-north-east gale, the Shields brig *Atalanta*, laden with timber, drove on shore three miles north of Skegness, Lincolnshire, with her Master, his wife, his child and eight men aboard. The Skegness private lifeboat was brought to the scene using six horses and, manned by her Coxswain and her usual crew, launched into the heavy sea and intense darkness. They succeeded in reaching the wreck and brought everybody ashore.

PEARCE Charles, Seaman
                                                     SILVER

1 March 1855

20 December 1854: During a northerly gale, the Exeter schooner *New Jane* was wrecked near Newquay, Cornwall, and started to break up with her bowsprit over the rocks. Mr. Pearce climbed out over the rocks and helped the crew to escape over the bowsprit but, tragically, was washed off the rocks when he was carrying the ship's boy. He recovered himself with great difficulty, but the boy was lost.

LEWIS William, Captain, Smack *Tyrall*
                                    SILVER
LEWIS John, Captain, Smack *Aurora's Increase*
                                   SILVER

1 February 1855

16–18 January 1855: On the 16th, the North Shields brig *Staunton* struck on Gunfleet Sand, off Clacton-on-Sea, Essex, and several smacks made unsuccessful attempts to tow her off. The smack *Aurora's Increase* took off her crew, except for an apprentice boy, and three men from another smack. The *Tyrall* and *Aurora's Increase* tried unsuccessfully to rescue them next day. Both smacks tried again on the 18th, helped by the steam tug *Amazon* and this time were successful but at the expense of one of their boats.

SALMON Charles, Fisherman
                                              SILVER
FLEMING George, Fisherman
                                           SILVER

1 March 1855

16 February 1855: The South Shields brig *Ann Moor* drove on to the Corton Sands, off the Norfolk coast, during the night of 15–16 February. The survivors were forced to take to the rigging, but the Master died during the night. The remaining eight men and two boys of the crew were seen at

daybreak, and a yawl put out from Gorleston, manned by 15 men. After six attempts, the yawl took off all the brig's crew who were exhausted and suffering from frozen limbs. One boy died after being landed. Charles Salmon and George Fleming particularly distinguished themselves in the rescue.

NEWSON William, Captain, Smack *Alfred*   **SILVER**

1 March 1855

20 February 1855: During cloudy weather and in a heavy sea, the Newcastle brig *Woodman* was driven ashore on the Shipwash Sand, near Harwich, Essex, and wrecked. In two trips in his ship's boat, Captain Newson and his crew rescued the brig's crew of 11 men.

CAHILL David Francis Sitwell, Esq., M.D.   **SILVER**

2 August 1855

17 June 1855: With a high sea rolling on shore, the result of gales on the previous day, a small boat with two people aboard was seen in peril passing the mouth of the River Tweed. In no doubt that they were heading for disaster, Dr. Cahill persuaded the Master of a small steam tug in Berwick-on-Tweed to go to their rescue. The Doctor and two other volunteers went with the Master and his two man crew. Making the best possible speed, they caught up with the boat just in time to save the seaman and his wife from destruction. Had they arrived ten or 15 minutes later, the boat would have reached a position where it would have been impossible for the tug to follow. The sea over the bar at the mouth of the river was so heavy that the tug was thrown on her broadside when crossing it on her return.

KISBEE Thomas, Commander, R.N. Chief Officer, H.M. Coastguard, Yarmouth   **SILVER**

5 July 1855

For long service 'in testimony of his services in saving 87 persons, who had been wrecked at different periods from ten wrecks on the coast of Norfolk'. Rescues had been effected by boat and the mortar and rocket apparatus.

GALBRAITH Eleanor, Mrs   **SILVER**
RAE William, Fisherman   **SILVER**

6 September 1855

6 August 1855: As four men, employed by a salmon fishery about one mile north of Whitburn, Co. Durham, were returning from floating their nets, a cross sea upset their boat and threw them in to the water. One of the men tried to cling to the boat but drowned. Mr. Rae, who was the only one of the men who could swim, helped the other two to a submerged rock. They were swept off but Mr. Rae bade them cling to his clothes and he swam for a short distance, but one of them fell off and drowned. By his strenuous exertions, Mr. Rae succeeded in bringing the other man into shallow water where he managed to gain a safe footing. Mrs. Galbraith, who had witnessed these events, scrambled, fully dressed, over precipitous and slippery rocks to their assistance and, entering the water, helped to bring the man, nearly dead from exhaustion, safely to the shore.

GRUER William, Boatman, H.M. Coastguard, Lossiemouth   **SILVER**

6 December 1855

2 October 1855: The Leith schooner *Thor* drifted from her anchors to a point among the breakers. Mr. Gruer first was able to bring on shore a lad in his boat. It then being quite dark, 'he swam to the vessel with a lifebuoy and a line. He found the Master was in a state of intoxication in the cabin, the door of which he had locked. Mr. Gruer broke it open, took the Master by force on deck, secured him to the lifebuoy and dropped him in to the sea and he was then pulled on shore. Mr. Gruer then assisted the other seaman on shore'.

HODGSON Joseph, Carver, Sunderland   **SILVER**

3 January 1856

For long service, 'in testimony of his extraordinary exertions, extending over a period of 12 years, in saving life. He had personally rescued ten persons from drowning and had assisted in lifeboats and other boats in saving about 17 others'.

DONOVAN Dennis, Chief Boatman, H.M. Coastguard, Kilmore   **SILVER**

3 January 1856

18 December 1855: In the night, a heavy gale drove the Cork brigantine *Isabella* on to rocks near the Coastguard station at Kilmore, Co. Wexford, Ireland. At 2 a.m., with three of his men, Mr. Donovan, showing great gallantry, put off in a boat and rescued five of the casualty's crew. Earlier, in the evening, another attempt had been made but, failing to cross the rocks, the rescuers gave up.

Mr. Donovan's second award clasp had been earned in October 1853, but was only voted on 7 February 1856.

JESSE Richard, Lieutenant, R.N. H.M. Coastguard, Tenby   **SILVER**

2 January 1856

20 December 1855: The Tenby lifeboat of the Institution, manned by 11 men, had saved three of the crew of the schooner *Agenoria* of Bideford which in a south-east gale had become a total wreck near St. Catherine's Rock. At 10 pm the same day, the lifeboat with the same crew put off to rescue the five man crew of the French schooner *Alexandre* of Havre, wrecked near Galler Point. Lieutenant Jesse had gone off both times in the lifeboat.

ROBERTS John, Clogwyn, Caernarvon   **SILVER**

3 January 1856

24 December 1855: The French brig *Charlotte*, was stranded near Harlech, Merionethshire. Bound from Havre to Cardiff in ballast, she had encountered bad weather and been driven up the Irish Sea into Cardigan Bay, going ashore at 3 p.m. The crew quit the vessel in the long boat, leaving the Master on board. The boat capsized and eight men were left struggling in the sea. Alone, Mr. Roberts managed to save four of the crew by plunging in to the surf. Meanwhile, the Criccieth lifeboat had been launched and taken off the Master, just before the brig began to break up.

HAMILTON George, Chief Boatman, H.M. Coastguard, Neds Point   **SILVER**

1 May 1856

7 February 1856: During a gale on the 6th, the barque *Augusta Jessie* was wrecked near the Coastguard station in Co. Donegal, Ireland. Mr. Hamilton and a crew of one coastguardman and five fishermen launched the Coastguard boat and, in the early hours of the next morning, saved the barque's 15 man crew.

TAW Charles, Captain, Schooner *Devonport*   **SILVER**

26 March 1856

8 February 1856: A French lugger, the *Bon Lion*, was seen waterlogged near Porthcawl, and a boat with four men on board had put out to investigate. The boat's crew found no-one on board the lugger, and on returning from the vessel their boat was upset near the shore. Two of the men perished. The other two were only saved through the intrepidity of Mr. Taw and five other men who waded into the sea to their rescue.

When acknowledging receipt of the medal, Mr. Taw asked if the Institution could use its influence with the Admiralty to get his son in to Greenwich School. This request was declined.

PARROTT Robert, Chief Boatman, H.M. Coastguard, Tenby   **SILVER**

6 March 1856

For long service covering 21 years in which the main services were to vessel *The Teignmouth* (1835), vessel *Joseph and Ann* (1840), brig *Ellen* (1850), vessel *Queen of the West* (1854) and schooners *Agenoria* and *Alexandre* (1855).

NORCOCK George Lowcay, Commander, R.N. Inspecting Commander
  H.M. Coastguard, Polkerris   **SILVER**
HENWOOD Thomas, Boatman, H.M. Coastguard, Fowey   **SILVER**
JOHNS Richard, Merchant Seaman   **SILVER**

5 June 1856

6 May 1856: When the small Ipswich schooner *Endeavour* was driven ashore by a gale in Polkerris Bay, near Fowey, Cornwall, members of the Coastguard station launched their boat and tried to reach her but were unable to weather Gribbon Point due to the severe conditions. Meanwhile, a small punt and some lines had been carted from Polkerris to the area where Commander Norcock was organising a rescue. The punt was securely slung and lowered 200 feet down the cliff to the rocks where the sole survivor was clinging. Three of the schooner's crew had made it to the rocks but two of them had drowned trying to swim to the shore. Commander Norcock jumped into the punt followed by two other men and, after a long struggle, they managed to rescue the exhausted survivor.

TAIT Grace, Miss   **SILVER**
PETRIE Ellen, Miss   **SILVER**

28 July 1856

23 May 1856: In bad weather, a small fishing boat capsized in Bluemull Sound between the north Shetland Islands of Unst and Yell. Miss Tait and Miss Petrie put out in a boat with Miss Tait's

father and saved two of the four man crew. They ran a considerable risk in so doing because of the speed of the tide in one of the most dangerous sounds in the islands. Mr. Tait received £2, as did each of the women.

CALLAWAY William, Seaman   **SILVER**

4 September 1856

22 August 1856: During squally weather near Lyme Regis, Dorset, the *Secret*, a small boat taking part in a regatta, capsized and filled, throwing three men in to the sea. The incident was seen by Mr. Callaway who was alone in another small boat. He turned back to the casualty and was able to rescue one of the men. He then took off his clothes, plunged in and tried vainly to save another man. Mr. Callaway had been thrown a rope by a trawler from the port but such was the speed of the boat that he was dragged under water and forced to let go of the man he was trying to save, who by this time was senseless and had drowned.

LEWIS William, Captain, Smack *Tyrall*   **SILVER(2)**

2 October 1856

14 September 1856: The Goole ship *Maria* was wrecked on Lang Sand, off Harwich, Essex, during a fresh breeze and thick weather. Captain Lewis and his crew of four men put off in their boat and, in considerable danger, rescued the sloop's three man crew before flood tide, when they would certainly have drowned.

THOMPSON Donald   **SILVER**

6 November 1856

26 September 1856: The Russian brigantine *Ahti* was wrecked during a gale near Dunnet Head, north-east of Thurso, Caithness. Mr. Thompson launched a boat with four other men and, at considerable risk, rescued the only two survivors. They had to put off twice because the Russians were frightened and would only consent to come off after the second attempt at persuasion.

WYRILL Henry, Boatman   **SILVER**

5 February 1857

14 November 1856: In stormy weather, the Sunderland brigantine *Elizabeth* was wrecked off Scarborough, Yorkshire. Mr. Wyrill took his boat out with five other men and brought off her crew of five.

HIPPLEWHITE Thomas, Captain. Harbour Master, Warkworth   **SILVER**

5 February 1857

4 January 1857: In the morning the Oporto brig *Sophie* was driven ashore in Druridge Bay, about three miles south of Hauxley Point, Northumberland, in a heavy easterly gale. The Hauxley Institution lifeboat was drawn by horses to a point abreast of the wreck and, manned by Hauxley fishermen with Captain Hipplewhite aboard, was launched through very heavy surf. The brig was

being swept by violent seas but the crew of 11 men were taken off and put on shore. In the afternoon, the Inverness schooner *Georgina* came ashore off Warkworth, and the lifeboat was launched for the second time that day and rescued her crew of five men.

YOUNG Thomas, Lieutenant, R.N. Chief Officer,
   H.M. Coastguard, Atherfield   **SILVER**

5 February 1857

4 January 1857: The London brig *Red Port* was wrecked during severe weather near Atherfield, Isle of Wight. Lieutenant Young put off with his crew in the Coastguard boat and, by skilful seamanship, saved both the brig and her crew of nine. On previous occasions also, he had rendered valuable services in saving life from shipwreck.

CLAYBOURN Thomas, Coxswain, Scarborough Lifeboat   **SILVER(2)**

5 February 1857

4 January 1857: An easterly gale was felt at Scarborough, Yorkshire, where the brigs *Thompsons* and *Northumberland*, both of Whitby, and *Wilsons* of Shields were wrecked. The Scarborough lifeboat launched on three different occasions and rescued a total of 23 men from these vessels. Thomas Claybourn had previously answered many calls in his 40 years as Coxswain in the old Scarborough lifeboat, and had saved many lives. He received a silver medal from the Royal Humane Society in 1828 in addition to his first silver medal from the Institution.

SHIELDON Robert, Coxswain, Redcar Lifeboat   **SILVER**

5 February 1857

5 January 1857: The Shields barque *Emma* was cast on to the Redcar Rocks, near the mouth of the River Tees, Yorkshire and wrecked. The Redcar lifeboat *Zetland* (the oldest in service in the British Isles) was launched and went out to the vessel. Although the lifeboat managed to get alongside twice and rescued the Master, the crew refused to leave, and the lifeboatmen returned to shore for rest and refreshment before putting out again to take off the eight man crew. The lifeboat was owned by the Tees Bay Life-boat Association.

JOACHIM Richard, Captain, R.N. H.M. Coastguard, Lowestoft   **SILVER(3)**

5 February 1857

5 January 1857: With vision obscured by a severe snow-storm, the Stockton brig *Tennant* ran on to the north-east Newcome Sands, off Lowestoft, Suffolk , where she soon was seen from the shore. The Lowestoft lifeboat, the Norfolk and Suffolk class *Victoria*, was launched with Captain Joachim and 19 men and, on reaching the casualty, veered down. The sea was breaking heavily, yet three men were soon got in to the boat then, in a tremendous squall, a cable parted. A strong rope was then secured and the other four men were taken off. During these operations, the brig's Master was washed overboard but was recovered nearly drowned. The brig, with her cargo of timber, was salvaged later by the beachmen and towed into Lowestoft harbour.

PILLAR William, Gunner, H.M. Revenue Cutter *Eagle*   **SILVER**

COCKROM William, Steward, H.M. Revenue Cutter *Eagle*   **SILVER**

BONGOURD Henry, Pilot. Pilot Cutter *Blonde*   **SILVER**

HUGHES George, Pilot. Pilot Cutter *Blonde*   **SILVER**

* CORBET Peter, Pilot. Pilot Cutter *Blonde*   **SILVER**

5 March 1857

*7 May 1857

5 January 1857: Soon after daybreak, the 415 ton North Shields barque *Boadicea*, on passage from Alexandria to Antwerp, was seen on the Tanteney Rock , off Guernsey, Channel Islands, but, because of the gale then raging, no boats ventured near her. Early in the morning, several men were seen on deck. The *Eagle* and the steam tug *Watt* set out from St. Peter Port and, after fighting a head wind, reached the wreck in heavy seas. The pilot cutter *Blonde* also arrived from St. Sampson and launched a boat which took off three survivors and transferred them to a tug. Two other men were seen still alive on the wreck, but another had already died. In spite of further efforts in the vicious seas amid rock-strewn waters the rescue vessels were forced to abandon their efforts and return to port; nine lives were lost.

HOUGHTON Henry, Joiner   **SILVER**

2 April 1857

14 January 1857: A north-easterly gale wrecked the Rochester brig *Eva* on the Black Halls Rocks at Castle Eden, four miles north of Hartlepool, Co. Durham. Mr. Houghton, a resident of West Hartlepool, waded into the surf and saved seven of the eight man crew. He also caught a line thrown from the brig. The Master of the *Eva*, heavy and benumbed with cold, fell into the sea, but was saved. Mr. Houghton was helped by H.A. Hamilton J.P. who had been voted a silver medal on 5 January 1854.

PICARD Pierre, Captain, Fishing Smack *Victoire Désirée*   **SILVER**

2 April 1857

8 March 1857: The Lyme Regis smack *Dart* foundered in stormy weather in the Portland Race, Dorset, and Captain Picard and his crew incurred considerable risk in rescuing five survivors – the three crew and two passengers.

AIKIN John, Commissioned Boatman, H.M. Coastguard, Cushendall   **SILVER**

4 June 1857

11 March 1857: At Cushendall, Co. Antrim, northern Ireland, a farmer tripped over a mooring chain and fell in to the sea. Mr. Aikin plunged in after him and, seizing a mooring chain, swam over to the place where the man had sunk. When the farmer came to the surface, the coastguardman grabbed him with one hand and supported him for at least five minutes by maintaining his grip on the chain with the other hand. He sustained a dislocated arm and severely damaged hand.

JONES John, Pilot	**SILVER**
PEARSE James, Pilot	**SILVER**
PEARSE Thomas, Pilot	**SILVER**
CLARK George, Seaman	**SILVER**

7 May 1857

29 March 1857: Shortly after midnight the St. Agnes schooner *Trevaunance* was wrecked in an easterly gale off Porthcawl, Glamorgan, and sank immediately. Her four man crew took to the masthead and remained there for several hours until daybreak. A boat launched with three Pilots and a seaman, but it could not reach the wreck as heavy seas were breaking over the sands at low tide. Later, in the dark, it became obvious that disaster was imminent, and the four men rushed into the surf and took off the three survivors – one other had already drowned.

POMEROY Henry, Chief Boatman, H.M. Coastguard, Mevagissey	**SILVER**
CLOKE William, Pilot	**SILVER**
LEY Joseph, Pilot	**SILVER**

6 August 1857

14 June 1857: The French schooner *Rochellaise*, Dunkirk to Cette (Sète), on the French Mediterranean coast, with a cargo of wine and salt, was trying to get into Mevagissey, Cornwall, in a gale when she stranded on Mevagissey Bar with the sea making a clear breach over her. Three small boats put off with the Chief Boatman, two Pilots and 14 other men and saved the schooner's crew of five and a boy.

INKSTER Peter, Captain, Schooner *William Tell*	**SILVER**
BLANCE John, Apprentice Boy, Schooner *William Tell*	**SILVER**

6 August 1857

17 June 1857: A small boat, which was returning from fishing at Grif Skerry, capsized in a squall off Whalsay Island, Shetland Isles with its six man crew. One man sank immediately, two got to the boat's side where one held a third by the collar, though not able to keep his head above water, and two others remained afloat on oars. They were seen after half an hour by Captain Inkster, who took his schooner to the scene where he and the apprentice rescued two of them in his small boat. The two men holding on to oars had floated away and drowned.

TURPIE James, Boatman, H.M. Coastguard, Salcombe	**SILVER**
WARDER David Thomas, Boatman, H.M. Coastguard, Salcombe	**SILVER**
WEDGE William, Boatman, H.M. Coastguard, Salcombe	**SILVER**

3 September 1857

27 August 1857: A boat capsized at night on Bantham Bar at the mouth of the River Avon, Devon, throwing its three occupants in to the water. The three boatmen launched their small boat and, in great danger, rescued two out of the three.

TUDOR John, Commander, R.N. Agent, British Fishery Society, Wick   **SILVER**

1 October 1857

9 September 1857: In very heavy seas and a near gale, the Hanoverian galliot *Vronia Santina* was running for Wick, Caithness, and, having narrowly missed Proudfoot Rocks, her Master decided to anchor in Wick Bay. The galliot tried to ride out the storm at anchor, but her situation remained so precarious that Captain Tudor, the Coxswain, decided to launch the B.F.S. lifeboat. He set out with a 14 man crew, but, when she was almost alongside the galliot, enormous waves swept them apart. Despite herculean efforts, the lifeboat was unable to close the galliot again, then a violent wave struck the lifeboat, wreaking havoc. The lifeboat filled with water, three of her crew were swept overside and most of her oars were broken or lost while the boat was swept ashore at the harbour entrance. Two men were eventually rescued but one was lost.

HOGBIN James, Coxswain, Ramsgate Lifeboat   **SILVER**

3 December 1857

26–27 November 1857: In a hard north-east gale, the Lisbon brig *Caminha* drove on to the Goodwin Sands, off the east Kent coast. The Ramsgate Harbour Trustee Beeching lifeboat *Northumberland* launched at 9 p.m. Under tow by the steam tug *Aid*, she went to the scene and, driving over the shoals through heavy surf, found the small Broadstairs lifeboat alongside with her crew on board the brig. As the brig's crew refused to leave, Coxswain Hogbin and his men remained alongside until the brig filled and began to break up, which damaged and disabled the small lifeboat. With their combined crews of 30 men and with the damaged lifeboat in tow, the *Northumberland* set sail across the shoals, striking heavily in the broken water. The two boats came into contact, which totally destroyed the damaged vessel, but the *Northumberland* reached Ramsgate harbour safely. The medal was awarded, also, in consideration of many previous rescues, mostly at night from the Goodwin Sands.

O'SULLIVAN Daniel, Chief Boatman, H.M. Coastguard, Ballycastle, Co. Antrim SILVER

7 January 1858

2 December 1857: The Russian barque *Sona Fratella* was wrecked in a south-westerly gale off White Ball Head, Co. Antrim. Two boats, manned by Mr. O'Sullivan and ten other men, put off and rescued the barque's crew of 11 men in circumstances of great danger.

TREGIDGO William Henry, Chief Boatman, H.M. Coastguard, Boscastle   **SILVER(2)**

STONE James, Chief Boatman, H.M. Coastguard, Boscastle   **SILVER**

SHARROCK John Pascoe, Commissioned Boatman, H.M. Coastguard, Boscastle SILVER

ELLIS Henry, Boatman, H.M. Coastguard, Boscastle   **SILVER**

MAY William Richard, Boatman, H.M. Coastguard, Boscastle   **SILVER**

6 May 1858

13 March 1858: The Liverpool ship *Defence* was wrecked in stormy weather on rocks below the cliffs at Beeney, St. Juliot, north of Boscastle, Cornwall. Using ropes, 16 crewmen and a Pilot were rescued by the Coastguard, in conditions of great danger.

WAUGH Edward, Boatman, H.M. Coastguard, Wexford **SILVER**

6 May 1858

6 April 1858: The brig *Arctic* was stranded during a south-south-east gale on Kilgormin Strand, on the coast of Co. Wexford, Ireland. At great risk to himself, Mr. Waugh swam out through the surf to catch a breaker (a small cask) and rope thrown overboard with which the seven man crew were ultimately saved. Nine other coastguardmen and nine fishermen also helped in the rescue

*JOHNSTON Bernard, Captain, Steamer *Enterprise*	**SILVER**
SHANKEY Robert, Chief Boatman	
H.M. Coastguard, Dundalk	**SILVER & SILVER CLASP (2)**
CONNICK John, Agent, Shipwrecked Fishermen and Mariners Society	**SILVER**
LEWIS Thomas, Mate, *Earle of Erne*	**SILVER**
GILMER William, First Mate, Steamer *Pride of Erin*	**SILVER**
CROSBY Nicholas	**SILVER**
ELPHINSTONE George	**SILVER**
*HYNDS John	**SILVER**
McARDLE Thomas	**SILVER**

6 May 1858
*3 June 1859

6–10 April 1858: The barque *Mary Stoddart*, standing from Carlingford, Co.. Louth, Ireland, into Dundalk Bay in a gale, was seen to be in distress by Captain Johnston who went to her assistance. Acting on his advice, the barque managed to anchor near the rocks and, after more than six hours, he returned to Dundalk with a high sea running. Next day, in another boat, Captain Johnston returned and managed to get aboard the casualty where the weather forced him to remain; his boat steamed off to seaward. By the end of the day the *Mary Stoddart* had dragged one and half miles and was aground in 12 feet of water, with five feet over her deck and the crew in her rigging. On the 8th, although the gale was still fierce and the sea very high, boats were manned with Mr. Connick in charge of one of them, but they were soon forced to return. The following morning found the gale blowing with great fury yet other boats made further rescue attempts, those led by Mr Lewis and Mr Gilmer among them. None was successful, except that at 1 p.m. a boat from Ballurgan got alongside the casualty but the survivors were too weak to do anything. Meanwhile, other attempts were being mounted and, at 5 p.m. a boat in the charge of Mr. Shankey put off from Gyles Quay and was able, three hours later, to land Captain Johnston and six men. Returning to the wreck with two fresh hands in his crew, Mr. Shankey brought ashore the remaining survivors at 6am on the 10th. Seven members of the barque's crew had perished. The other four medal winners had led rescue boats in the sustained efforts.

HAMILTON Henry Alexander J.P. Chief Boatman,
   H.M. Coastguard, Balbriggan. Honorary Secretary,
   Balbriggan R.N.L.I. **SILVER(2)**

5 August 1858

21 July 1858: The action of Mr. Hamilton was brought to the attention of the Institution in a letter from a Mrs Burden. She had been thrown out of a boat by accident near Kingstown (Dun Laoghaire), Co Dublin, Ireland, and he had dived into the water and saved her. The lady gave £300 to fund the stationing of an additional lifeboat on the Irish Coast.

MOAR May Stout Hectorson, Mrs.   **SILVER**

2 December 1858

9 September 1858: A boat with four men on board capsized off Burra Ness, Shetland Isles. Mrs Moar, with a rope attached to her, descended the cliff, and standing on a small shelf of rock succeeded in throwing a rope with a life-buoy to two of the men. They were drawn through the surf to the shore while two other women held the rope fast at the top of the cliff. The remaining two men were rescued by Mr. Moar – he was awarded ten shillings.

BEATSON Godfrey Bosville McDonald, Chief Officer
  H.M. Coastguard, Fraserburgh   **SILVER**

2 December 1858

8 October 1858: With a crew of ten men and the use of rocket apparatus, Mr. Beatson brought ashore the eight man crew of the Prussian schooner *Fortuna*, of Griefswald, wrecked during a heavy northerly gale off Fraserburgh, Aberdeenshire. During his efforts, he sustained serious injuries to a leg.

COLLOPY James, Boatman, H.M. Coastguard, Porthcawl   **SILVER**
SHEA Daniel, Chief Officer, H.M. Coastguard, Porthcawl   **SILVER**

2 December 1858

13 October 1858: The Plymouth schooner *Ajax* was wrecked on Kenfig Sands, west of Porthcawl in severe weather. Mr. Shea, Mr. Collopy and five other coastguards manhandled their gig along the foreshore then, without pausing for rest, put off. Battling through the surf, they went alongside the wreck and took off the six man crew.
  In one report, Shea's first name is given as James.

JOHNSON William   **SILVER**

4 November 1858

18 October 1858: The sloop *Queen,* with seven men on board, was wrecked off Yarmouth, Norfolk, during an easterly gale. Mr. Johnson went out from the shore in the breeches buoy using lines that the crew had rigged, to ensure that they were secure. Then, with four others, he took a boat to the vessel and rescued four of her seven man crew.

HAMILTON Henry Alexander J.P. Chief Boatman, H.M. Coastguard, Balbriggan
  Honorary Secretary, Balbriggan R.N.L.I.   **GOLD**

2 December 1858

17 November 1858: In an easterly gale on the 14th, the Austrian brig *Tregiste* stranded midway between Lambay Island and Portram, Co Dublin, Ireland. The Balbriggan lifeboat left at 11 a.m. on the 15th and tried to reach the brig but was compelled to put back to Rogerstown owing to the violence of the gale. Green seas continued to pour in to the lifeboat for two hours and threatened to wash out Mr. Hamilton and his crew. He remained at the Coastguard House watching for a favourable opportunity until 4 a.m. on the 17th, when he reached the hulk and took off 13 men.

DAVISON William, Coxswain, Sunderland Lifeboat   **SILVER**

2 December 1858

For long service, as Coxswain of the Sunderland lifeboat and otherwise during which time 94 people were saved from wrecks.

MOSS John, Boatman, Dungeness   **SILVER**

6 January 1859

19 December 1858: The lugger *Stornaway's* boat was run down off Dungeness, Kent, with two men in it; Mr. Moss, 'at the peril of his life', saved one of them.

RIDGE John, Chief Officer, H.M. Coastguard, Cadgwith   **SILVER**

3 March 1859

22 January 1859: On 21 January, the 937 ton iron, barque-rigged screw steamer *Czar*, en route from Woolwich Arsenal, London to the Malta Garrison and other destinations in the Eastern Mediterranean, got into difficulties west of Bishop Rock, Isles of Scilly, when she encountered a full west-south-west gale. Laden with 1600 tons of military stores, including guns and ammunition, she was rolling heavily in the deep troughs when she developed boiler trouble, and her Master decided to put about for Falmouth, Cornwall. The weather worsened and the afternoon of the 22nd saw the steamer lying close inshore trying to reach shelter under the cliffs east of the Lizard but, in rounding the headland, she struck Vroge Rock. Badly holed, broadside on to the sea, the vessel rolled so violently that her lower yards dipped into the water and, finally, she broke in two abaft the funnel. The two sinking halves drifted apart; two men were swept off the forecastle together with the occupants of a boat being lowered from the wreck. A second boat was launched successfully and reached Parnvoose Cove, south of Cadgwith, with three survivors and raised the alarm. Several shore boats put out together with the Coastguard cutter and succeeded in rescuing 31 survivors, 18 of them due to Mr Ridge's efforts.

RUDDOCK John, Boatman, Filey   **SILVER**

3 February 1859

For long service in testimony for his general valuable and gallant services in saving life from wrecks on different occasions, in the Filey lifeboat and in other boats.

SHEA Daniel, Coxswain, Padstow Lifeboat   **SILVER**

7 April 1859

8 March 1859: The French brig *Gonsalve*, of Nantes, driven towards the English coast, found herself unable to weather Trevose Head and was forced to run for Padstow harbour, Cornwall. As the brig reached the lee of Stepper Point eddy winds caught her and the tide and heavy seas drove her out on to Doombar Sand. The Institution lifeboat *Albert Edward* was launched and, although repeatedly filled by seas, took off the crew of seven before the brig went to pieces.

15 March 1859: The Ipswich schooner *Frederick William*, becoming embayed, ran for Padstow harbour in a very heavy north-west gale but, on approaching the narrow entrance, was taken aback by the baffling eddy winds and was carried by the heavy sea on to the Doombar Sand. The *Albert Edward* was launched through the terrific sea, and took off the four man crew and a Pilot.

BAIN Alexander, Seaman   **SILVER**

5 May 1859

28 April 1859: The French barque *Azaléa* of Nantes drove on to the rocks off Skerries, near Dublin, Ireland during a gale. In considerable danger, Mr. Bain waded in to the surf and conveyed a line aboard the wreck by which her crew of three men were saved. Several men of the Coastguard and other men helped in the rescue.

CRAGIE John, Acting Coxswain, Southwold Lifeboat   **SILVER**
*HERRINGTON Benjamin, Second Coxswain, Southwold Lifeboat   **SILVER(2)**

6 October 1859
* 3 November 1859

17 September 1859: During a strong gale and in a very heavy sea, the Prussian brig *Lucinde* was wrecked at night off Misner Haven, between Thorpeness and Dunwich, Suffolk. The Southwold *Harriet* lifeboat launched and rescued the crew of nine men and the Captain's wife.

SMITH Peter, Chief Boatman, H.M. Coastguard, Lydd   **SILVER**

1 December 1859

25 October 1859: The Norwegian brig *Caroline* was wrecked in a heavy gale off Lydd, Kent. Mr Smith and his crew of five men put out in their boat and took off the brig's Master and some of the crew.

MITCHELL Charles, Fisherman   **SILVER**

1 December 1859

25 October 1859: Mr. Mitchell was one of the crew of a boat that, at great risk, put off on three occasions, and he displayed great courage and perseverance in saving four men of the Newquay sloop *Busy*'s crew in a very heavy gale off Port Isaac, Cornwall.

RODGERS Joseph, Maltese Seaman   **GOLD**

3 November 1859

26 October 1859: The 2,719 ton auxiliary sailing ship *Royal Charter* had made a record journey from Melbourne, Australia, to Queenstown (Cobh) Co.Cork, Ireland, in 55 days carrying, as well as passengers, a valuable cargo which included gold. After transacting the normal maritime business at that port, the ship left with 386 passengers and 112 crew heading for Liverpool but, by popular request, was diverted to Holyhead, Anglesey. Heading up the Irish Sea, the wind freshened until, off Port Lynas, the seas were tempestuous and, running inshore as close as possible, she put

up rockets for a Pilot. Conditions were so bad that no pilot cutter could put to sea. At 10 p.m. on the 25th, both bower anchors were let go and the screw kept turning, but both cables parted at 2 a.m. and the ship began to drift towards the shore. In spite of the fore and main masts being cut away, the vessel continued to drift landwards until she swung broadside on to the sands of Moelfre Bay with her engines running in the hope that she would drive more firmly into them. The cordage from the fallen masts, however, became entangled with the screw, and she struck rocks where she became a total wreck. Mr. Rodgers volunteered to swim ashore with a line to facilitate the transfer of survivors and, although the seas were breaking violently amid broken spars and pieces of wreck were being tossed about in the near freezing sea, he succeeded, and a breeches buoy was rigged. A number of passengers had succeeded in getting ashore by this means when the ship was engulfed by a gigantic wave about 7 a.m. and she broke in two, taking with her a total of 479 persons, including the Captain and all of his officers.

DYER John   **SILVER**

2 February 1860

26 October 1859: After the Goole schooner *Beverley* had wrecked under Upton Cliff, south of Bude, Cornwall, during a gale, four men, by means of rocket apparatus, rescued six crew members. John Dyer particularly distinguished himself by wading in to the heavy surf, risking his life to save the Master.

TREGIDGO William Henry, Chief boatman, H.M. Coastguard, Newquay   **SILVER(3)**

5 January 1860

26 October 1859: Using two teams of his men in the Coastguard whaleboat, Mr Tregidgo rescued 11 men from the Vannes schooner *Union* and the St Vaast lugger *Anais,* both of which were forced ashore and wrecked off Newquay, Cornwall, in a gale.

THOMAS James, Chief Boatman, H.M. Coastguard, St Catherine's Point   **SILVER**

1 December 1859

1 November 1859: The London schooner *Lelia* was wrecked in a gale on Rocken End (St Catherine's Point) Isle of Wight. Mr. Thomas, with others, waded into heavy surf with ropes and rescued her crew of six men.

Testing self-righting lifeboat at Institution yards

HOOK Robert, Coxswain, Lowestoft Lifeboat	**SILVER**
BUTCHER James, Crew Member, Lowestoft Lifeboat	**SILVER**
BUTCHER Richard, Crew Member, Lowestoft Lifeboat	**SILVER**
COLBY Nathanial, Crew Member, Lowestoft Lifeboat	**SILVER**
LIFFEN Thomas, Crew Member, Lowestoft Lifeboat	**SILVER**
MEWSE Alfred, Crew Member, Lowestoft Lifeboat	**SILVER**
ROSE William, Crew Member, Lowestoft Lifeboat	**SILVER**
SMITH Francis, Crew Member, Lowestoft Lifeboat	**SILVER**

1 December 1859

1 November 1859: The Norfolk and Suffolk class lifeboat *Victoria* put off to the Dublin steamer *Shamrock*, which had been wrecked in a gale on the south end of the Holm Sands, off Lowestoft, Suffolk. Although seas were breaking over the mast head of the stricken vessel, the Coxswain was able to anchor and bear down upon her with seas swamping the lifeboat. A line was made fast to the wreck by which the crew of 14 was hauled, one at a time, through breakers. Account was also taken of the general gallant services rendered by the lifeboat's crew.

TALBOT Christopher Rice Mansel, Esq. M.P.	**SILVER**
WILLIAMS John, Farmer	**SILVER**

5 January 1860

2 November 1859: After the Jersey barque *Sunda* had been wrecked on Kenfig Sands, off Porthcawl, Glamorgan, Messrs. Talbot and Williams waded through pounding surf in the continuing gale and rescued the Master, his wife and four of the crew who had come ashore in a boat. The remainder of the crew was saved by other means.

BOYLE Robert Francis, The Hon. Lieutenant, R.N.	
Chief Officer, H.M. Coastguard, Tenby	**SILVER**
PARROTT Robert , Chief Boatman, H.M. Coastguard, Tenby	
Coxswain, Tenby Lifeboat	**SILVER(2)**

1 December 1859

7 November 1859: During a furious gale with hail squalls, the Sunderland brig *Policy* was wrecked in the evening, going on to Monkstone Rocks in Tenby Bay, Pembrokeshire. The Institution lifeboat was launched in the dark through tremendous seas with a mixed crew of coastguardmen and fishermen. In her position on a reef, the brig could only be approached from the windward. Before the lifeboat could veer down, a heavy roller struck her, carrying away her cable and breaking three oars, so she had to return to Tenby, three miles away. Lieutenant Boyle, with the lifeboat crew, made their way to a point near the wreck, set up their rocket apparatus and brought all the brig's crew ashore. The whole operation had taken several hours, three of which were spent on the rocket rescue.

BAKER Thomas, Extra Coastguardman, H.M. Coastguard, Brooke	**SILVER**

1 March 1860

4 December 1859: The Caernarvon schooner *Sentinel* was wrecked in a gale in Brighstone Bay, Isle of Wight. Mr. Baker readily took charge of one of the two boats responsible for saving four out of the six man crew of the schooner.

BOYD Henry, Coastguardman, H.M. Coastguard, St. John's Point **SILVER**

5 January 1860

9 December 1859: With five other men, Mr. Boyd put off in a fishing boat and, in three attempts, rescued the eight man crew of the Dublin brigantine *Water Lily* which had been wrecked in moderate weather but heavy surf in Dundrum Bay Co Down, northern Ireland.

RIDGE George Agar Ellis, Captain R.N. Inspecting Commander
   H.M. Coastguard, Newcastle, Co. Down **SILVER**

5 April 1860

14 December 1859: The Austrian brig *Tikey* was wrecked off St John's Point, Dundrum Bay, Co Down, northern Ireland, and her boat containing the crew capsized. A boat, manned by 12 men, put off to rescue them but also capsized. Captain Ridge then waded out through the surf and brought one of the men to safety.

WASEY Edward Frodesham Noel K., Captain R.N.
   Inspecting Commander, H.M. Coastguard, Fleetwood **SILVER**
FOX John, Chief Boatman, H.M. Coastguard, Fleetwood
   Coxswain, Fleetwood Lifeboat **SILVER**

2 February 1860

22 January 1860: With Captain Wasey aboard and Mr. Fox acting as Coxswain, the Fleetwood private lifeboat was towed four and a half miles by a steam tug to the Montrose schooner *Ann Mitchell* which had been totally wrecked at night during a gale off Fleetwood, Lancashire. She fought her way through mountainous seas to get alongside the schooner where, after seven attempts, one of the crew, the sole survivor, was rescued.

Lifeboat in tow

SHEA Daniel, Coxswain, Padstow Lifeboat   **SILVER(2)**

2 February 1860

22 January 1860: The Liverpool ship *James Alexander* was wrecked during a very heavy gale off Padstow, Cornwall. Mr. Shea and others assisted to save the crew. The lifeboat was not involved in the operation.

DAVIES Thomas, Captain, R.N. Inspecting Commander
    H.M. Coastguard, Great Yarmouth   **SILVER**
MILLIGAN George, Coxswain, Great Yarmouth Lifeboat   **SILVER**

1 March 1860

17 February 1860: During a heavy gale, Captain Davies and Mr Milligan put off with a crew of thirteen men in the surf lifeboat to rescue five men from the Yarmouth smack *John Bull*, which had parted her anchors and stranded on the north side of the harbour at night. The rescue needed two trips, and the Coxswain had to climb in to the smack's rigging on the second occasion and persuade the last survivor to leave.

WASEY Edward Frodesham Noel K., Captain R.N. Inspecting Commander
    H.M. Coastguard, Fleetwood   **SILVER(2)**

1 March 1860

19 February 1860: The Newry schooner *Catherine* was wrecked off Fleetwood, Lancashire, during a full gale, heavy snow squalls and in a violent sea. The lifeboat was launched and rescued her crew of four men.
    Captain Wasey had earned his second silver award less than a month after the first award..

LEESE Charles, Gunner, Coast Brigade, Royal Artillery   **SILVER**

5 July 1860

2 June 1860: A violent south-west gale struck the coast of Sussex and winds of hurricane force swept the area, forcing 12 vessels ashore between Blatchingdon and Newhaven. All but three crew members got ashore, but two men and a boy aged 12 remained aboard the Shoreham brig *Annie* and the Shields schooner *Woodside*. Gunner Leese and others of his unit waded through the surf and rescued them; he himself brought off the boy.

TROTT Thomas, Crew Member, Lugger *Diana*   **SILVER**

4 October 1860

25 September 1860: Early in the morning, a heavy gale stranded the Norwegian brig *Poseidon* of Arendal on the south end of the Goodwin Sands, and the Deal lugger *Diana* went to her assistance. While approaching the schooner, the lugger's rigging was fouled by that of the wreck. Mr. Trott jumped on to the brig, quickly cut away the gear and saved the rescue ship from disaster.

WASEY Edward Frodesham Noel K., Captain R.N.
Inspecting Commander, H.M. Coastguard, Fleetwood   **SILVER(3)**

1 November 1860

20 October 1860: During a violent west-north-west gale, the Nova Scotian barque *Vermont* of Halifax, was wrecked on Barnett's Bank, three miles off Fleetwood, Lancashire. The lifeboat, manned by Captain Wasey and 11 men, was launched in to tremendous seas and despite the difficulties, they managed to get alongside and took off the crew of 15 men and a Pilot. This was Captain Wasey's third award in eight months.

In November 1862, the new Peake design lifeboat placed on station at Fleetwood was named Edward Wasey.

TUDOR John, Captain R.N. Agent, British Fishery Society
Coxswain, Wick Lifeboat   **SILVER(2)**

6 December 1860

21 November 1860: On the 20th, a very heavy swell prevented the local sloop *Maria* from entering Wick harbour, and she was forced to seek shelter in Sinclair Bay, three miles to the north, where she dropped anchor. The weather was worsening and the conditions were appalling. Captain Tudor set out for Ackergill in a horse-drawn gig taking with him lines and lifebelts. Other arrangements were being made to obtain horses so that the lifeboat, on her carriage, could be hauled overland to a point near the sloop because Wick Harbour was closed. On reaching the shore at Sinclair Bay, Captain Tudor realised that immediate action was imperative; a Caithness Steam Shipping Co. boat was impressed and transported to a point on Shorelands Beach opposite the anchored sloop which was now being pounded by huge seas. The boat was launched with a crew of nine men and, despite massive waves sweeping over both vessels, the two man crew of the sloop was brought off and landed just as the Wick lifeboat arrived. Captain Tudor had, previously, saved by lifeboat six men from the Maryport vessel *Huntress*, wrecked in a heavy gale on 6 September 1859.

BROWN Thomas, Boatman   **SILVER**

3 January 1861

23 November 1860: The schooner *Julius* of Aalborg, Denmark, was wrecked on the Broad Carr Rocks (Broad Skear) off the Northumberland coast north of Newbiggin. The rocks were submerged by the incoming tide. She sank immediately and her crew could be seen in the rigging with her masts bending to near breaking point. Mr. Brown decided to attempt a rescue with his three sons, using his largest coble on which he had been forced to make temporary repairs to a hole which had been made by a fractious horse. Judging the right moment, he launched and came alongside the schooner in spite of difficult conditions. The crew of six were all saved although two broke their legs in jumping from the rigging. At the moment of rescue, a wave struck the wreck which broke up but, with great skill, Mr. Brown kept his own boat clear of the flying masts.

CORBERT William, Coxswain, Ardmore Lifeboat	**SILVER**
HALSE Richard, Boatman, H.M. Coastguard, Ardmore	**SILVER**
STEWART William, Boatman, H.M. Coastguard, Ardmore	**SILVER**
RODERICK John S.	**SILVER**

3 January 1861

26 December 1860: A south-east gale was blowing on Boxing Day, when the brigantine *Diana* of Frederickshavn, Denmark, en route from Bordeaux to Belfast with a cargo of wheat and brandy, struck a reef of rocks in Ardmore Bay, Co Waterford, Ireland. The Ardmore lifeboat launched through very heavy surf and Mr. Roderick took a vacant oar, but in spite of all their efforts they could not reach the wreck. The brigantine's crew veered a small boat to the shore on a line, although it swamped near the shore and had to be secured by men wading in to the surf. The Coxswain now took the lifeboat back, and a line from the vessel was made fast to the lifeboat's bow while another line was fired by rocket, this latter being secured to the stern. She was then hauled off to the brigantine and seven of the crew managed to get in to the lifeboat even though great seas were breaking over them. After the bow rope was cut, the lifeboat was drawn ashore and the survivors landed. An eighth man was left on the wreck by mistake but, as the brigantine was driven closer inshore, he threw himself into the sea with a small raft and retained his hold on it until he could be brought ashore by men wading into the sea.

WHITE Joseph	**SILVER**
FLANN William	**SILVER**

7 February 1861

30 December 1860: The Plymouth schooner *Norval* was wrecked on Chesil Beach, Portland, Dorset, in a gale. Messrs. White and Flann, in company with five others, put off in a boat and rescued her crew of five.

White had also assisted in saving 43 persons and Flann 57 from previous wrecks.

COOPER Hugh, Chief Boatman in Charge, H.M. Coastguard, Dingle Bay	**SILVER**

4 April 1861

24 January 1861: In a strong gale the Liverpool barque *Florence Graham* was wrecked on Inch Strand, Co Kerry, Ireland. Mr. Cooper, with three other men, launched a Coastguard boat and saved two survivors.

GOSS Thomas , Lieutenant, R.N.Inspecting Commander	
H.M. Coastguard, Queenstown	**SILVER**
STARKE John, Chief Boatman, H.M. Coastguard, Queenstown	**SILVER**

2 May 1861

27 January 1861: The Austrian brig *Uredon* drove on to outlying rocks on shore near Guilleen, Co Cork, Ireland, having missed Cork harbour during a heavy gale. Lieutenant Goss and Mr. Starke, with eight of their men, positioned the rocket apparatus and, by this means, saved 12 of the brig's 13 man crew.

*TOOMEY James	**SILVER**
HUTCHINSON William (Junior) Lieutenant, Royal Dublin City Militia	**SILVER**
PARSONS Richard, Lieutenant, 35th Regiment of Foot	**SILVER**

2 May 1861
*1 August 1861

9 February 1861: At great risk to himself, Mr. Toomey waded in to the surf and helped to save the Mate of the Whitehaven schooner *Industry*, which was wrecked off Kingstown, Co Dublin, Ireland, in a heavy gale. Lieutenants Hutchinson and Parsons also rushed in to the surf in attempting to save the Master.

BOYD John McNeil, Captain, R.N. H.M.S. *Ajax*	**Post SILVER**
* DYER Hugh McNeill, Lieutenant, R.N. H.M.S. *Ajax*	**SILVER**
*FARRIN George, Master Gunner, R.N. H.M.S. *Ajax*	**SILVER**

7 March 1861
*6 June 1861

9 February 1861: Captain Boyd, Lieutenant Dyer and Mr. Farrin, all serving in the screw steamer H.M.S. *Ajax* , assisted to save the crew of the brig *Neptune* wrecked during a heavy gale on the East Pier of Kingstown, Co Dublin, Ireland. Captain Boyd, with other members of his crew, was swept to his death off the pier. The silver medal, accompanied by a letter of condolence, was presented to his widow.

WALSH John, Lloyd's Agent, Dublin	**SILVER**

7 March 1861

9 February 1861: Mr. Walsh rendered general gallant services in helping to save lives from shipwreck over many years and his record was enhanced by the part he played in rescue attempts to the brig *Neptune* (see Captain Boyd, voted 7 March 1861) in which he sustained severe internal injuries.

*FREEMAN Henry, Crew Member, Whitby Lifeboat	**SILVER**
ROBINSON Thomas, Seaman	**SILVER**

7 March 1861
*4 April 1861

9 February 1861: At Whitby, Yorkshire, the fierce north-easterly gale which had been blowing for days continued to whip up violent seas but, in mid morning, the new West Pier lifeboat *Lucy*, with a crew of 12 men, was launched through very heavy surf, to the schooner *Gamma* which had been driven ashore 400 yards from the pier. She took off the schooner's four man crew and returned to shore to be called out shortly afterwards to the barque *Clara* which had been driven on to the beach just before noon. At 1 pm two more vessels were driven ashore – the brig *Utility* and the schooner *Roe*. The lifeboat was launched for the third time and battled her way out to save both crews. After the boat returned to station, more vessels were seen to be approaching the harbour, the first one, apart from a minor mishap, reaching it safely. The schooner *Merchant,* however, was driven ashore and the lifeboat was launched once more – this time to tragedy. Two waves met right

underneath her and she capsized in the violent mass of water. Mr. Freeman was the sole survivor on what had been his first day in the crew. Valiant efforts were made to save the others, and one of those prominent in the attempts was Mr. Robinson, who managed to get on the bottom of the lifeboat. Some men attempted to cut open the boat, but the hatchet unfortunately hit Mr. Robinson's hand and disabled him for life.

PARTRIDGE William Luke, Captain, R.N. Inspecting Commander
  H.M. Coastguard, Wexford   **SILVER**
BARRETT James, Chief Officer, HM Coastguard, Carnsore   **SILVER**

7 March 1861

10 February 1861: The Glasgow barque *Guyana*, bound for the West Indies, was driven ashore on the Carrig Rocks off Greenore Point, Co. Wexford, Ireland, in a north-easterly gale. The Carnsore lifeboat was called out at 3 a.m. The condition of the roads due to heavy rain and the circuitous route to be traversed by the horse-drawn wagon resulted in the lifeboat not reaching Greenore Point until 9 a.m. Then she had to be lowered down an 80 foot steep cliff, this being done under the direction of Captain Partridge. She was launched through high surf with Captain Partridge, Mr. Barrett and her crew aboard. The force of wind, tide and sea was so great that three attempts were needed before the wreck could be reached and the barque's crew of 19 men taken off. They were landed safely at 2.30 pm.

JOHNS Richard O., Coxswain, Tramore Lifeboat   **SILVER**
BUDD James, Esq, Honorary Secretary, Tramore Branch, R.N.L.I.   **SILVER**
READE William Morris, Esq, Tramore   **SILVER**
STEPHENS Alfred, Boatman, H.M. Coastguard, Tramore   **SILVER**

7 March 1861

17 February 1861: At daybreak the Greek brig *San Spiridione* from Galaxidhi on the Gulf of the Corinth, laden with coal, was seen ashore in Tramore Bay, Co Waterford, Ireland, where she had been driven during the night in a southerly gale. The Tramore lifeboat was launched through very high surf, but she had to return to shore with her crew exhausted. Replaced on her carriage, she was drawn to a better position and, manned by another volunteer crew, succeeded in almost closing with the wreck, but the brig's crew refused to leave her. The lifeboat was upset by a heavy wave, her crew was thrown in to the water – three of them regained the boat and the other five reached the shore. After a while, the brig started to break up and her crew was thrown in to the surf by the falling masts; the lifeboat was launched for a third time and saved two of them. Two others were saved by Mr. Budd and Mr. Stephens going into the surf, the former on his horse from which he was washed off twice. Mr. Reade was in the lifeboat when she upset and Mr. Johns went out in charge on all three occasions.

BEDDOE David, Fishguard   **SILVER**
FURLONG Albert, Fishguard   **SILVER**

7 March 1861

19 February 1861: The Cardigan sloop *Elizabeth and Mary* was wrecked during a heavy gale on the rocks off Carreg Onnen Island, west of Fishguard, Pembrokeshire. The two men climbed down nearby cliffs and, with a rope, swam out to the island despite considerable risk to their own lives.

They were able to rescue two of the crew, and all four men were then pulled back to the mainland. The youngest crew member, a 14 year old boy, had been swept away from the wreck and drowned.

LARGE John, Master Gunner, Royal Artillery　　　　　　　　**SILVER**

6 June 1861

19 February 1861: Mr. Large waded into the surf at great risk to himself and helped to rescue three of the crew of the Waterford brigantine *Harmony*, which had been wrecked in a gale at Freshwater West Bay, near Milford Haven, Pembrokeshire.

DOWER Augustin, Master Mariner　　　　　　　　　　　**SILVER**
BARRON Robert N., Esq　　　　　　　　　　　　　　**SILVER**

7 March 1861

19 February 1861: The Cork brigantine *Susan* was wrecked off Ballinacourty, ten miles from Dungarvan, Co Waterford, Ireland, during severe weather. Mr. Barron, Captain Dower and four other men put off and, at considerable risk to life, saved two out of the brigantine's crew of six men.

COX Joseph, Coxswain, Appledore Lifeboat　　　　　　　**SILVER**

4 April 1861

For long service: 'Coxswain Joseph Cox had been for many years past the Coxswain of the lifeboat of the Institution … in testimony of his long and gallant services'. It is probable that he was appointed in 1852 when the station was opened at Northam Burrows and, after that date, performed services to brig *Tonton Pierre* (1853), the snow *Felicity* (1858), the schooners *Caroline* and *Clifton* (1859) and the schooner *Druid* (1860) which resulted in a total of 27 lives being saved.

PUXLEY Henry, Esq　　　　　　　　　　　　　　　　**SILVER**

4 July 1861

7 June 1861: Six men were thrown into the sea from their boat which capsized in windy weather off Dunboy Castle, Berehaven, Co Cork, Ireland. Mr. Puxley swam off to a small boat, moored some distance from the shore, and used it to rescue four of the men.

BEAUCLERK Charles, Lord.　　　　　　　　　　　　**Post. SILVER**
HICK Michael, Ship Owner　　　　　　　　　　　　**SILVER**
ILES John.　　　　　　　　　　　　　　　　　　　**Post. SILVER**
RUTTER Joseph, Engineering Superintendent, Scarborough Railway Station　　**SILVER**
SARONY Oliver, Photographic Artist　　　　　　　　　**SILVER**
TINDALL William　　　　　　　　　　　　　　　　**Post. SILVER**

7 November 1861

2 November 1861: The South Shields schooner *Coupland*, laden with granite from Aberdeen, was totally wrecked in the late afternoon during a hurricane near Scarborough Pier, Yorkshire. Trying

to enter the harbour, she was taken aback, her sails disabled and, eventually, she struck on the rocks opposite the Spa, some 30 yards from the sea wall amid huge cataracts of water. The self-righting lifeboat *Amelia* (R.N.L.I.) had been manned and set out for the casualty. She was thrown against the wall a number of times, two of her crew were killed and others were thrown out. A rope was thrown from the promenade and then secured. The lifeboat was pulled through the surf to a landing place where members of the public rushed forward to help, but successive waves knocked them over and some were killed. Lord Beauclerk, prominent among them, died after being swept to the base of a nearby cliff in spite of Mr. Sarony and Mr. Rutter getting a line a round him and pulling him out of the water. The lifeboat, meanwhile, had suffered a heavy battering and was rendered useless; Mr. Tindall's body was found underneath it. Messrs. Iles and Hicks also played leading parts in the rescue attempts. The schooner's crew of six were all rescued by rocket apparatus.

ADAMS Thomas, Captain, Smack *Volunteer*	**SILVER**
BACON Henry, Seaman, Smack *Volunteer*	**SILVER**
LAMBETH Benjamin, Seaman, Smack *Volunteer*	**SILVER**
LAMBERT John, Seaman, Smack *Volunteer*	**SILVER**
SCARLETT Robert, Seaman, Smack *Volunteer*	**SILVER**
WYATT George, Seaman, Smack *Volunteer*	**SILVER**

2 January 1862

3 November 1861: At daybreak the South Shields barque *Darius* was seen to be aground on Long Sand, off Harwich, Essex, with the sea foaming around and breaking over her. The crew had taken to the rigging of the only mast left standing. At 7 a.m., the smack *Volunteer*'s boat was manned and approached the wreck but could not get near, so was brought up just clear of the Sand with the smack nearby. Other vessels without sails were seen, and two smacks left the area without offering help. Two men were seen to drop from the barque's rigging and disappear from view and, with the breakers getting worse, Captain Adams took his smack over the sands with her boat in tow, manned by the same men and bore up as near to the wreck as he could get it. The boat made an unsuccessful run and he picked it up again. It then made another desperate attempt and succeeded in reaching the wreck. Meanwhile the smack was hove to and had barely escaped a heavy sea and striking. The barque's Master, Chief Mate and four hands were taken off, almost senseless from cold, exposure and fatigue; three others had perished the day before in her long boat, The survivors were landed at Harwich at 7 p.m.

JOACHIM Richard, Captain, R.N. H.M. Coastguard, Lowestoft	**SILVER(3)**

5 December 1861

14 November 1861: Distress signals were seen to be flying from the pilot cutter *Whim* and the lugger *Saucy Lass* which were in a perilous position in a heavy gale near Holm Sand, off Lowestoft, Suffolk. Captain Joachim, with a crew of 19 men in the Lowestoft lifeboat *Victoria*, put off and helped save 18 men from the two vessels.

DONOVAN John, Chief Boatman, H.M. Coastguard, Old Head **SILVER**
GOUGH James, Fisherman **SILVER**

3 July 1862

22 January 1862: The Liverpool ship *Queen of Commerce* was wrecked in heavy weather on a rock 50 yards from cliffs in Tramore Bay, Co Waterford, Ireland. Mr. Gough swam off to the rocks through heavy surf closely followed by Mr. Donovan. They were able to take hold of a life-belt floated on a line from the wreck and, with seas savagely breaking over them, they took the line ashore followed by a hawser. By this means the 23 man crew and a Pilot were saved.

McMILLAN James, Mechanic **SILVER**

6 November 1862

13 October 1862: During a heavy gale, the London ship *Genoa* was wrecked in Glanmanuilt Bay, Mull of Kintyre, Argyll. Soon after, she began to break up and the crew took to pieces of wreckage, four of them being carried out to sea. The Mate, William Fordyce, climbed on to the poop and was driven inshore where he remained floating about among pieces of wreckage for nearly five hours. At last, being carried near the shore by a wave, he made a desperate effort to reach it but fell short inside a cleft of rock where he was seen by Mr. McMillan who, although 70 years old, rushed into the sea up to his shoulders and dragged the exhausted man ashore. The five men, with Mr Fordyce in charge, had served in a ship which had come across the crewless, waterlogged *Genoa* in Mid-Atlantic and volunteered to bring her in to port. Due to the severe weather and the loss of their sails and rigging they only just failed in their purpose..

GOLDRING William, Master, Smack *Ferret* **SILVER**
FARMER David, Seaman, Smack *Ferret* **SILVER**
SPRAGGS James, Seaman, Smack *Ferret* **SILVER**

6 November 1862

17 October 1862: When the Portsmouth sloop *Cygnet* sank near the Hampshire coast on the Woolsiner Sandbank, off Hayling Island, her crew of three men was seen clinging to her rigging with the sea washing over them. The sloop had become unmanageable after encountering a heavy gale, struck a shoal, was overwhelmed by heavy waves and began to break up. Captain Goldring made an unsuccessful effort to reach the casualty in his smack; he then launched her small 13 foot long skiff and with two of his crew rescued the three men who had been marooned for over five hours.

KING Thomas, Master, Smack *Paragon* **SILVER**

4 December 1862

19–20 October 1862: On the evening of the 18th during a gale and thick weather, the Goole schooner *Thrifty* ran on to the south-west end of Long Sand, off Clacton, Essex. About noon on the following day Captain King closed with the wreck and made two unsuccessful attempts to take off the crew; his vessel was nearly swamped. A third attempt from seaward of the Sand ended in the smack shipping a sea, and he was forced to return to Harwich. On the 20th, he reached the casualty at daylight and succeeded in rescuing the four crew still alive. In spite of damage to the smack, he spent part of the third day recovering the body of the Mate's wife from the wreck.

SWARBRICK William, Master, Steam Tug *Wyre*   **SILVER**

GERRARD Robert, Pilot   **SILVER**

1 January 1863

27 October 1862: The Glasson Dock, Lancashire barque *Pudyona* stranded during a heavy gale and high sea in Morecambe Bay, Lancashire, and the Fleetwood steam tug put out to assist. Great difficulty was experienced in getting close to the casualty but, with the help of Mr. Gerrard, Captain Swarbrick succeeded in taking off the barque's crew, 17 men in all.

JOHN William, Farmer, Limpert Farm   **SILVER**

5 February 1863

19 January 1863: The Russian barque *Henri Sorensin*, in ballast, bound from Bordeaux to Cardiff, was wrecked in a gale on Breaksea Point, west of Barry, Glamorgan. Driven ashore, the Captain and 12 man crew stayed on board all night but, in the morning, it was obvious that the barque was doomed. As their boat had been washed away, the men began to drop over the side at low tide, intending to swim and scramble ashore, but the breakers were driving ashore with a dangerous undertow. Mr. John dashed into the surf to help one man ashore and, with three others following his example, all the crew were brought ashore.

EVANS Thomas, Coxswain, New Brighton Lifeboat   **SILVER(2)**

EVANS Thomas , Junior   **SILVER**

EVANS William   **SILVER**

5 March 1863

20 January 1863: During a very heavy gale, the New York ship *John H. Elliott* stranded on the Great Burbo Bank in Liverpool Bay. Thomas Evans launched a shore boat with five other men and, along with the Liverpool steam tug *United States*, they saved 55 people, all the crew and passengers. Thomas Evans Jnr and William Evans incurred great risk of life, having waded over the sands to the ship, a distance of more than two miles.

MADDICK Henry, Master, Smack *Ruby*   **SILVER**

THOMPSON William, Apprentice, Smack *Ruby*   **SILVER**

5 March 1863

28 January 1863: Mr Maddick and his apprentice put off in their smack's boat to the Ipswich brigantine *Ganymede* which, during a violent gale, sank some miles off the coast. The other two men in the smack's crew had refused to go, but when Captain Maddick decided to go alone, his young apprentice volunteered. Together they succeeded despite great difficulty in bringing the six man crew safely back to the smack. It is not very clear where this rescue took place according to the report from the Collector of Customs, Ipswich; the *Ganymede* came from Ipswich and the *Ruby* was from Hull.

WILLIAMS David, H.M. Customs, Aberdovey **SILVER**

5 March 1863

8 February 1863: Mr. Williams put off with a crew of seven men in a heavy sea in the Institution's lifeboat to assist the Newport brig *Friends* stranded on the Aberdovey Bar in Cardigan Bay, at the mouth of the River Dovey. The brig's crew declined to leave and the lifeboat stood off for an hour but, with six oars broken, was in danger of being dashed against the stranded vessel's side. The gale broke afterwards and the brig drifted to the south, and her crew reached land in their own boat. David Williams had been involved in saving life from other shipwrecks; he was also Honorary Secretary Secretary of the Aberdovey branch of the Institution.

ROWLANDS Thomas, Master Mariner **SILVER**
LEWIS George, Commissioned Boatman, H.M. Coastguard, Goodick **SILVER**

7 May 1863

17 March 1863: The Cardigan sloop *Frances* sank on Newport Sands, near Fishguard, Pembrokeshire, in a heavy gale and high seas. Captain Rowlands and Mr. Lewis waded into the surf and, with six other men, brought the three man crew to shore.

BEATSON Godfrey Bosville McDonald,
   Inspecting Chief Officer, H.M. Coastguard, Fraserburgh **SILVER(2)**
FORBES Alexander, Shipbuilder, Peterhead **SILVER**

4 June 1863

12 April 1863: During a heavy gale and in high surf, the Liverpool ship *Genoa* was wrecked on Rattray Brigg Rocks, in Rattray Bay, north of Peterhead, Aberdeenshire. Together with five coastguardmen, Messrs. Beatson and Forbes saved 11 of the ship's crew of 14. The Fraserburgh lifeboat put off but, after 15 miles pulling against heavy seas and a headwind, arrived after the service had been completed.

HOOD Robert, Coxswain, Seaton Carew Lifeboat **SILVER**

7 May 1863

12 April 1863: The Whitby brig *Regalia* was wrecked off Seaton Carew, Co. Durham, in a gale and high seas when she was driven over the North Gare Sand on to the shore at the mouth of the River Tees. The Seaton Carew lifeboat *Charlotte* launched, took off her seven man crew and landed them. This medal was awarded also in testimony of Mr. Hood's long service in previous lifeboats during which he launched 43 times.

ALEXANDER William, Coxswain, Thorpeness Lifeboat **SILVER**

2 July 1863

12 June 1863: The coal laden London brig *Florence Nightingale* stranded on the Sizewell Bank, off Thorpeness, Suffolk, in a heavy south-south-westerly gale and became a total wreck. Her distress signal was seen just after midnight, and the Thorpeness lifeboat *Ipswich* was launched through a tremendous surf. The rescue was made very difficult by the brig's masts going by the board as the

lifeboat neared her. Coxswain Alexander veered down from windward and hauled off the six man crew using lines. During this service one of the lifeboat's crew was washed overboard but was recovered. The award of this medal was voted also in acknowledgement of Mr. Alexander's previous services in the former Thorpe lifeboats.

CANDLISH James, Coxswain, Lytham Lifeboat **SILVER**

7 January 1864

20–21 September 1863: The Liverpool barque *St. Lawrence*, in ballast to Cardiff, was stranded on Salthouse Sandbank at the mouth of the River Ribble, Lancashire, in a very strong west wind with a high sea running. The Southport lifeboat launched and took off the Master's wife, daughter and 12 of the crew, but the Master and three men refused to leave. The Lytham lifeboat later launched, but those on the casualty still refused to leave; Coxswain Candlish took his boat back to shore. Distress signals were seen next morning, so again the Coxswain took his boat out and found the barque abandoned with seven feet of water in her hold – the survivors had gone ashore in their own boat during the night. The Coxswain had the satisfaction of refloating the casualty and taking her to Lytham after several hours work. Reference was also made to Mr. Candlish's gallantry in almost 13 years of service.

KENNEDY Arthur, Lieutenant, R.N. H.M. Coastguard, Ballyheige **SILVER(2)**

7 January 1864

1 December 1863: With four of his men, Lieutenant Kennedy put off in an open boat and rescued the crew of five men from the Cardigan schooner *Gleaner* wrecked in a strong gale off Ballyheige, Co Kerry, Ireland.

CUBITT William, Honorary Secretary, Bacton Branch R.N.L.I. **SILVER**

7 January 1864

3 December 1863: During a heavy north-westerly gale, the North Shields barque *Ina*, laden with coal, went on shore about a mile south of Happisburgh Lower Lighthouse, Norfolk, at 1 p.m. after being seen without canvas and in an unmanageable condition. The Bacton lifeboat launched and bore away under sail for the wreck, five miles distant, and, on nearing her, found that coastguardmen were trying to reach her by rocket but without success. The lifeboat anchored within 100 yards of the casualty and dropped down under her stern then, after much difficulty in the storm, moved to her lee side where the Master, Pilot and 12 men were taken off. The Mate, under the influence of alcohol, could not be induced to leave, and he perished when the ship broke up.

Mr. Cubitt had gone off in the lifeboat to 'animate and encourage the crew'!

JARMAN Isaac, Coxswain, Ramsgate Lifeboat **SILVER**

7 January 1864

3–4 December 1863: On the evening of the 3rd during dreadful weather, rocket signals were seen coming from the Tongue Lightship, which indicated a ship in distress. The Ramsgate steam tug *Aid* set out at 8.45 p.m. with the Beeching class lifeboat *Northumberland* in tow. In mountainous seas and with a near hurricane raging, they reached the London to Melbourne emigrant ship *Fusilier* fast in the sand on the Girdler Bank some miles north of Herne Bay, Kent. Going alongside at 2 a.m., the lifeboat took off, one by one, 25 women and children and transferred them to the tug waiting nearly a mile away in Princes Channel. Returning to the casualty, the Coxswain repeated the operation three times during which, with huge seas sweeping over both vessels, 40 women and children and 36 men were transferred by 6 a.m. The Captain and crew remained on board in anticipation of refloating the ship at the next high tide. The tug left at daylight to land the survivors, but the lifeboat, which it must be remembered was an open one, continued to stand by, then, an hour and half later, saw the tug *Aid* returning. Sailing toward her, the Coxswain was informed that another casualty had been seen aground on the Shingles Bank, ten miles north of Margate. The Greenock ship *Demerara* was found on her beam ends with a shattered hull, and had her crew clinging to the rigging. Running across the broken waters on the sands, the lifeboat got alongside the wreck, took off the crew of 18 (including an 11-year-old boy) and the Pilot and put them aboard the tug. All reached Ramsgate safely. The lifeboat had been out for over 16 hours.

BUCK William Cumming, R.N. Chief Officer, H.M. Coastguard, Winchelsea   **SILVER**

3 March 1864

13 February 1864: The Jersey smack *Thetis* was wrecked during a heavy gale near Rye, Sussex. Mr. Buck, with a crew of five of his men, went off in a shore boat and was able to rescue one man. One coastguardman, George Terry, was washed overboard during the return trip and drowned.

Le GEYT Alice Bell, Miss   **SILVER**

1 September 1864

4 August 1864: After two boys had fallen into the sea from the outer pier at Lyme Regis, Dorset, Miss Le Geyt, a visitor who happened to be out in a pleasure boat with a lady friend, rowed through the surf and saved them.

CAMPBELL Angus, Carpenter, Edinburgh Board of Fisheries Cutter
   Princess Royal   **SILVER**

3 November 1864

22–23 October 1864: During a heavy gale, the Whitby brig *Eliza Hall* was wrecked on the rocks outside Granton Harbour breakwater, Midlothian in the night of the 22nd. A boat from the cutter tried to reach the vessel which was striking on the rocks, but could not get near enough to help. The sea made a complete breach over her and, after a time, her port quarter swung closer in. A line was secured around Mr. Campbell and he dashed down the outer slope of the breakwater, but the line proved too short. He was drawn back again, then re-entered the surf: communication being effected the eight men were brought to safety.

BYRNE Lawrence, Chief Officer, H.M. Coastguard, Tynemouth   **SILVER**

1 December 1864

24 November 1864: A fearful storm pounded the Northumberland coast on the night of the 24th, its force extending out to sea where the Colchester schooner *Friendship* and the Aberdeen screw-

steamer *Stanley* found themselves in difficulties, along with a number of other vessels. The schooner, deeply laden with coal and with a crew of five, sought shelter in the River Tyne but, at 4.25 p.m., was driven on to the Black Middens, rocks on the north shore near the Spanish Battery, Tynemouth. The steamer joined her nearby at 6 p.m., wave after wave breaking over both. The steamer with 30 passengers, 30 crew and a deck load of cattle had her bottom opened to the sea and her fires extinguished, so Mr. Byrne set up his rocket apparatus on the shore. His second shot was successful but only two men reached the shore, a lady and another seaman being drowned. By prompt action from Mr. Byrne and others, one other man was saved, the Chief Officer himself being almost swept away. Contact with the steamer was re-established after a fresh supply of rockets had been obtained; ten of the passengers (including two ladies) and 25 of the crew were then saved. In a simultaneous attempt by the self-righting Tynemouth R.N.L.I. lifeboat *Constance*, she was severely damaged and two of her men killed. Nobody was saved from the *Friendship*.

LUSK Andrew, Farmer   **SILVER**

5 January 1865

30 November 1864: During a heavy gale the Preston schooner *Havelock* was wrecked in the Solway Firth at Raeberry, near Kirkcudbright. Mr. Lusk and five of his servants working from the shore tried unsuccessfully to save the schooner's crew. One of Mr. Lusk's servants lost his life during the attempt.

BULKELEY John B., Coxswain, Teignmouth Lifeboat   **SILVER**

1 December 1864

For long service 'in testimony of his long and gallant services in assisting as Coxswain and by other means to save shipwrecked crews'. Among the 15 services concerned were those to a pilot boat (1857), a barge, the ship *Caroline*, the smack *Wonder*, fishing boats (1860), the sloop *Elizabeth*, the fishing yawl *John* (1862) the schooner *Victoria* and the fishing yawl *Hero* (1864). Three vessels and 18 persons were saved during these services.

FESTING Francis Worgan, Major, Royal Marine Artillery   **SILVER**

2 February 1865

14 January 1865: The Plymouth schooner *Ocean* was wrecked on Woolsiner Shoal, near Hayling Island, Hampshire, during a heavy gale, and was driven inshore and embayed by the force of the wind and heavy seas. In trying to tack close in upon the shoals, the schooner's heel touched the outer edge of the shoal and she missed stays. The crew let go both anchors immediately but she bumped heavily and filled rapidly, and the men took to the rigging. Once the tide had turned, a large ten oared cutter was launched from Fort Cumberland, with Major Festing at the helm and a crew of 12 local fishermen. The boat headed for the wreck and entered the breakers where, in spite of the spray hiding them, the Master, Mate and one man were saved. Another man and a boy had been washed overboard and drowned.

FELLOWES Thomas Hounsom Butler, Captain, R.N.
   Inspecting Commander, H.M. Coastguard, Penzance   **SILVER**

2 February 1865

29 January 1865: A strong southerly gale with heavy breaking seas caused the Plymouth brig *Willie Ridley* to drag her anchors and drive a considerable distance toward the shore off Penzance, Cornwall. She finished up 200 yards from a reef of rocks off the Western Beach. The Penzance Peake type lifeboat *Alexandra*, commanded by Captain Fellowes in the absence of her Coxswain, launched from the beach but, after breaking four or five oars, was driven back broadside on. After spare oars were obtained, a second attempt was made, but she was forced back again on the rocks. She was then loaded on to her carriage and taken to Newlyn where she launched once more. After some hard rowing, the lifeboat got alongside the brig where, in spite of the rising wind and sea, the Master and crew were taken off over the main boom. The wind moderated during the night and with the anchors holding, the crew were returned next day and the brig resumed her voyage.

DEVEREUX Mark, Master Pilot   **SILVER(3)**

6 April 1865

20 March 1865: Mr. Devereux put off in the Rosslare lifeboat and helped to save, under very difficult conditions, one man from the Goole schooner *Teazer*, which was totally wrecked during a heavy gale on the North Bar, Wexford, Co Wexford, Ireland.

FRANKISH Thomas H.   **SILVER**

2 November 1865

10 October 1865: In a heavy sea off the mouth of Bridlington Harbour, Yorkshire, Mr. Frankish, 'a youth', saved one of the men washed out of the coble *Fly* by allowing himself to be lowered in a lifebelt over the pier into the boiling surf, which threatened at all times to dash him against the wall.

MOORE James, Gunner, Coast Brigade, Royal Artillery   **SILVER**

7 December 1865

19 October 1865: In a gale, the French ship *Carioca* struck on rocks under the Hermitage Rock Battery, Point d'Else, Alderney, Channel Isles. Gunner Moore, with two of his colleagues, rescued all the crew of 17 men.

LEVETT Nicholas, Coxswain, St. Ives Lifeboat   **SILVER**

2 November 1865

28 October 1865: In a strong north-north-easterly wind with heavy ground sea, the 98 ton brig *Providence*, Cardiff to Dieppe, was seen aground three or four miles from St. Ives, Cornwall, on the western end of Hayle Bar. The self-righting Institution's lifeboat *Moses* launched immediately, but on her way to the schooner capsized twice. After great difficulty, in making the French crew understand and in fighting the prevailing conditions, four of the schooner's five man crew were brought ashore.

PASCOE Peter   **SILVER**

7 December 1865

24 November 1865: A southerly gale had been blowing for three days when the 300 ton
Sunderland barque *William*, from Odessa to Falmouth with a cargo of linseed, ran for the rock-
strewn harbour entrance at Porthleven, Mount's Bay, Cornwall. As the barque scraped past the
outer pier, one of her crew leaped on to the jetty but a wave swept him off. A local man rushed
into the water, but was swept into the sea before he could help, and Mr. Pascoe, his brother,
managed to drag him to safety before the brig was wrecked against the jetty.

HEATH Joshua, Chief Boatman, H.M. Coastguard, Fowey
  Coxswain, Polkerris Lifeboat   **SILVER**

7 December 1865

25 November 1865: During a heavy gale, the North Shields barque *Drydens* and the Sunderland
brig *Wearmouth* were seen in distress in St. Austell Bay, Cornwall, driving before the wind
toward Par Sands and both were soon grounded, broadside on to the fearful breakers. The self-
righting lifeboat *Catherine Rashleigh* had, meanwhile, launched but, having reached midway
with great difficulty, six of her oars were snapped short by a large sea. Mr. Heath allowed the
boat to drift to leeward for some distance and then hoisted sail. The lifeboat reached the pier at
Par from where she eventually saved the Master and 13 men from the barque and the Master and
eight men from the brig. This service took five hours.

KAVANAGH Peter, Coxswain, Arklow Lifeboat   **SILVER**

4 January 1866

26 December 1865: The Liverpool ship *Tenessarian* was wrecked on the Arklow Bank off the
coast of Co Wicklow, Ireland, during a northerly gale and began to break up. Both Arklow and
Wicklow lifeboats launched, but, when the Arklow Peake lifeboat *Arundel Venables* arrived, the
casualty's hull was totally submerged and her mainmast had been carried away. All survivors
were lashed to the fore-rigging; two had already perished. Coxswain Kavanagh took the lifeboat
in among the wreckage and brought off 34 survivors by lines. The award also took into account
'the repeated brave and zealous services at the saving of 82 lives on several occasions during a
period of nearly ten years'.

HILLS William, Coxswain, Padstow Lifeboat   **SILVER**
SHEA Daniel, Chief Officer, H.M. Coastguard, Padstow   **SILVER(3)**

4 January 1866

29 December 1865: When the Greenock barque *Juliet*, Demarara, British Guiana to London,
was seen anchored and flying a distress signal at the entrance to Padstow harbour, Cornwall near
Hell Bay, the self-righting lifeboat *Albert Edward* launched. She anchored within 100 yards of
the barque, which was rolling heavily in a very strong gale and, in spite of much difficulty and
danger, the 17 man crew were taken off and helped the lifeboat's crew to gain the harbour; the
barque later became a total wreck. Mr. Shea was awarded his clasp for his gallant conduct and
Coxswain Hill's medal was given for this rescue as well as his previous general gallant services.

TAYLOR William, Chief Officer, H.M. Coastguard, Robert's Cove SILVER

1 March 1866

29 December 1865 The Italian barque *Lidia* was wrecked at Robert's Cove, near Cork, Co Cork, Ireland, in a gale and terrific sea. Mr. Taylor and five of his men put off in the Coastguard galley and saved the 13 man crew.

HUGHES Evan (Senior), Master Mariner SILVER

1 February 1866

4 January 1866: A strong wind was blowing when the Liverpool ship *Palinurus* stranded in Cymyran Bay, Anglesey, south of Holy Island. Captain Hughes, with five other men, put off in a boat and at great risk saved the 24 man crew.

CARBIS Thomas, Coxswain, Penzance Lifeboat SILVER

1 February 1866

11 January 1866: The new screw-collier *Bessie* of Hayle went ashore on Hayle Bar in the estuary of the River Hayle, Cornwall, and became firmly embedded in the sand. Her nine man crew took to the foretop, and the St. Ives lifeboat *Moses* was taken to the spot together with rocket apparatus. In the mountainous seas, the range was too great for the rockets and the lifeboat had insufficient power to reach her, and a telegram was sent to Penzance seeking help from the self-righting class lifeboat *Richard Lewis*, which was despatched at once. After a journey of 50 miles around Land's End, Coxswain Carbis brought his boat into St. Ives and both lifeboats set off. The *Moses* was the first to reach the casualty and picked up one of her crew who had fallen overboard, then, after a long struggle, both boats returned to the shore with the Master and eight members of the crew.

LOVE Robert, Private, 63rd Regiment of Foot SILVER

1 March 1866

14 January 1866: When the North Shields brig *Medina* collided with s.s. *Arno* and foundered 16 miles east of the River Tees, Private Love, a young recruit , put off with two other men from s.s. *Arno* in a boat and helped save four men.

MORENO John, Captain, Austrian Barque *Eva* SILVER

1 March 1866

28 January 1866: A Pill yawl capsized and sank in squally weather and a rough sea near Walton Bay, Clevedon, Somerset. Captain Moreno went off in a small boat from his barque with four of his men and rescued three men from the casualty.

BUNT John, Chief Boatman in Charge, H.M. Coastguard, Sandown SILVER
*HAYDEN Francis SILVER

3 May 1866
*7 June 1866

24 March 1866: The Swedish brig *Fahli Bure* of Sundswell was totally wrecked during a heavy gale in Sandown Bay, Isle of Wight. Mr. Bunt put off, with eight men, in his Coastguard boat and, after several attempts, rescued five of the 12 man crew. Mr. Hayden went off in a small boat with three others and helped rescue some of the crew.

KERRNISH John, Commissioned Boatman, H.M. Coastguard, Bowness SILVER

3 May 1866

16 April 1866: Four men who had been working on a pile driving machine had been overtaken by the incoming tide on Drumburgh Marsh, Cumberland, at the mouth of the River Eden in the Solway Firth. Recognising their highly dangerous situation, Mr. Kerrnish swam 80 yards in the heavy sea to reach a shore boat in which he, with two other men, saved the trapped men.

MACKELL Patrick, Boatman, H.M. Coastguard, Batty's Cove SILVER

5 July 1866

8 June 1866: During stormy weather, the Kinsale brigantine *Anna* was wrecked at Hangman's Point, near Kinsale, Co Cork, Ireland. A woman and child were saved by the Coastguard galley. Mr. Mackell, one of the galley's crew, then waded through the sea and over some rocks and rescued five of the brigantine's crew by rope.

LEWIS Watkin SILVER

6 December 1866

10 September 1866: At Aberystwyth, Mr. Lewis swam out in a heavy sea and saved the life of his father who, with others, had been carried out to sea in a bathing machine by a heavy wave.

Mr Lewis had also on 25 March 1866 swum out at great risk to his life to the rescue of the six crew of the Bridgewater schooner *Rebecca*.

JONES Thomas, Captain, Steam Tug *Ely*   **SILVER**

1 November 1866

21 September 1866: When the Dartmouth sloop *Wool Packet* was wrecked on Bideford Bar, off Bideford, Devon, in a heavy gale from the west, Captain Jones went to the scene in his tug with his crew of eight men and rescued nine men from the casualty.

STEPHENSON Bartholemew, Coxswain, Boulmer Lifeboat   **SILVER**

1 November 1866

For 'his long and brave services as Coxswain … in assisting to save lives of a large number of shipwrecked persons' during 46 years. Bartholemew Stephenson's services included those to the brig *Robert Nicholl* (1853), the schooner *Montaguma* (1854), a fishing boat and the brig *Adelphi* (1859), the brig *Ann* and schooner *Active* (1860) and the schooner *Hortensia* (1861). The Boulmer lifeboat station had been taken over by the Institution in 1853.

NELSON William, R.N. Commanding H.M. Coastguard Cruiser *Eliza*   **SILVER**

7 March 1867

3 December 1866: In a strong gale, the Cork brigantine *Jane* got into difficulties off the coast of Co Waterford, Ireland, and became a total wreck on the beach at Tramore Bay. With a crew of four men, he put off from his cruiser in a small boat and saved the brigantine's five man crew.

ROWLANDS William, Coxswain, Holyhead Lifeboat   **SILVER**

6 December 1866

The Harbour Master at Holyhead wrote to the Institution stating that Rowlands had been the Coxswain of the lifeboat there for the past eight years and during that time had helped to save a large number of lives from shipwreck. The silver medal was awarded 'in acknowledgement of his long, valuable, and brave services as Coxswain'.

HARRINGTON James   **SILVER**

7 February 1867

1 January 1867: The Sunderland brig *Charlotte* was wrecked during a strong north-easterly gale on the East Scar, North Landing, Flamborough, Yorkshire. Mr. Harrington waded into the violent surf and, despite the cold and the risks, saved four men of the crew.

HIGGS Samuel (Junior), French Vice-Consul, Penzance   **SILVER**

17 January 1867

5 January 1867: In the morning, distress signals were seen from the direction of the village of Longrock between Penzance and Marazion on Mount's Bay , Cornwall. An east-south-easterly gale was blowing and there was a very heavy sea. The Penzance self-righting lifeboat *Richard Lewis* launched and found the Brixham schooner *Salome* drifting rapidly toward the shore near St. Michael's Mount. Five men and a boy were taken off the schooner just before she struck and broke up. More signals were seen in the pitch dark evening with a hurricane now blowing accompanied by very heavy rain over a fearful sea. The lifeboat launched again and returned within an hour carrying five crew from the Looe schooner *Selina Ann*. The lifeboat launched a third time to the Teignmouth schooner *Heiress* and rescued her six man crew. Mr. Higgs was on board the lifeboat for all three services.

REES Thomas Mortimer   **SILVER**

7 February 1867

5 January 1867: The Holyhead schooner *Two Brothers* was wrecked on a very dark and stormy night under some very high cliffs at Pointz Castle, a farm near Solva, St. Bride's Bay, Pembrokeshire. Mr. Rees, a local man, was lowered down the cliffs and was able to save four men from the schooner, who had originally put off in a boat which had then been smashed to pieces.

COBB Charles, M.A, Reverend, Rector of Dymchurch   **GOLD**
BATIST John, Boatman, H.M. Coastguard, Dymchurch   **SILVER**

17 January 1867

6 January 1867: The 59 ton Dieppe lugger *Courrier de Dieppe,* with four persons on board, was driven ashore in a strong gale at Dymchurch, Kent. She had got into difficulties off the English coast on the previous day and, failing to get help, her Master had run her on to the beach. Unfortunately the vessel's position was such that rocket apparatus failed to reach her. The Master, a seaman and a boy were washed overboard and drowned, leaving the Mate in the rigging. Wearing a cork life jacket attached to a rope, Mr. Batist tried to reach him , but had to be pulled back through the surf. The Rector then rushed into the water and, after one or two ineffectual attempts, reached the survivor. Mr. Batist followed him with a line and, between them, they brought the Mate safely ashore. Both men were awarded the Albert Medal, First and Second Class respectively.

ELTON William Hallam, Lieutenant, R.N. H.M. Coastguard, Lyme   **SILVER**

7 February 1867

8 January 1867: With his boat's crew of five men, Lieutenant Elton put off in a Coastguard galley during a heavy gale and saved two men from the schooner *Vulcan* and one from the schooner *Maria*. Both vessels were lying in dangerous positions off the beach near Lyme Regis, Dorset.

HUGHES William, Fisherman **SILVER**

6 June 1867

7 March 1867: After their fishing boat *John Milton* had been wrecked off Pittenweem, Fife, in a very heavy sea and a gale, two men took refuge on a rock. Mr. Hughes waded into the surf and, at the peril of his life, brought them safely to shore.

BARRETT James, Chief Officer, H.M. Coastguard, Carnsore
  Honorary Secretary, Carnsore R.N.L.I. **SILVER(2)**

6 June 1867

26 May 1867: In a strong wind and squally weather , the Liverpool vessel *Blanche Moore*, bound from Liverpool to Calcutta, India, was seen to be in distress on the Long Bank, off Wexford, Ireland. The Carnsore self-righting lifeboat *Gertrude* launched and saved the crew of 36 men in a service that extended to 16 hours. Mr. Barrett was in the lifeboat at the Coxswain's request.

HERBERT Auberon, The Honorable **SILVER**

5 September 1867

26 July 1867: When the Harwich sloop *Sutcliffe* was wrecked off Cromer, Norfolk, in a heavy sea and gale, the Cromer lifeboat launched with The Honorable Auberon Herbert as a member of the crew; some of the local boatmen had refused to help.

CUBITT William, Honorary Secretary, Bacton R.N.L.I. **SILVER(2)**

5 September 1867

14 August 1867: Mr. Cubitt of Bacton Abbey, Bacton, Norfolk entered the sea on horseback to save a young man who had been carried away from the beach while bathing.

KEARON Edward, Master Mariner **SILVER**

3 October 1867

11 September 1867: During a gale, it was reported that a boy was still on board the fishing smack *Kate and Mary*, riding at anchor in Arklow Bay, Co Wicklow, Ireland. The Arklow Peake type lifeboat *Arundel Venables* launched but, almost at once, was swept by a huge sea and swamped, twisting broadside on to the North Pier Head. Captain Kearon jumped on board from the pier and gave great encouragement, so that after two more strenuous attempts, the lifeboat broke through the surf and reached the smack, put her Master on board, who slipped the anchor and got the smack away safely.

JUNIPER William, Crew Member, Mundesley Lifeboat **SILVER**

6 February 1868

17 November 1867: The Sunderland brig *George* was seen in distress during a south-south-easterly gale off Mundesley, Norfolk, and the self-righting lifeboat *Grocers* launched. Meanwhile, in the

heavy seas the Master tried to beach his vessel but, full of water, she remained fast on the outer bank, out of reach of the rocket apparatus. The vessel broke up within an hour of striking, and six men drowned when the main mast fell. One man survived floating on a plank and was spotted when the lifeboat arrived after encountering great difficulties. Fully clothed, Mr. Juniper jumped overboard with a line and secured the seaman; both men were then hauled into the lifeboat.

McMAHON H.M.M., Lieutenant, East Clare Militia   **SILVER**
HARRIS Frederick, Inspecting Officer, H.M. Coastguard, Seafield   **SILVER**

6 February 1868

25 November 1867: During a heavy gale and in a very heavy sea, the French brigantine *Henriette* of Havre, stranded near Mutton Island, Mal Bay, Co Clare, Ireland. Lieutenant McMahon put off in a curragh but was driven back. Mr. Harris, with six others, put off in the Coastguard boat and, after two attempts, they saved two out of three men left on board.

ROWLANDS William, Coxswain, Holyhead Lifeboat   **SILVER(2)**

5 December 1867

1–2 December 1867: A terrific northerly gale was blowing on to Holyhead in the evening when, about 9 p.m., the Rouen barque *Bayadère* parted from her anchors and struck on the rocks near the Holyhead Lighthouse on Holy Island, Anglesey. The Holyhead self-righting lifeboat *Princess of Wales* soon launched in spite of the heavy sea and took off the barque's crew of 12 men; the vessel broke up soon after. The lifeboat then went out to the Liverpool ship *Lydia Williams* which had sunk near Salt Island and, in two trips, brought off 32 survivors, including a woman and her seven-month-old infant, all of whom had taken refuge in the rigging. They returned to the wreck a third time and rescued two more men who had been in the fore-rigging. At 5 a.m. next day, the lifeboat launched again to the Chester schooner *Seetland* but her crew were saved by ropes from the breakwater. She launched once more at 7 a.m. and brought ashore seven people from the Liverpool schooner *Elizabeth*. Coxswain Rowlands, *over* 70 years of age, rescued 53 people within a period of 24 hours.

JOHNS Richard O., Coxswain, Tramore Lifeboat   **SILVER(2)**
NORRIS Martin, Crew Member, Tramore Lifeboat   **SILVER**

6 February 1868

12–13 January 1868: Late in the evening of the 12th with a strong south-easterly gale blowing, the large iron ship *Oasis* of Liverpool was seen driving into Brown's Bay where she struck west of the Metal Man, Newtown Head, near Tramore, Co Waterford, Ireland. The Tramore self-righting lifeboat *Tom Egan* launched within half an hour but had great difficulty with the breakers. After prolonged exertions, she managed to reach the wreck at midnight. The Captain and two men had already been washed overboard from the casualty and drowned. Using an anchor, the lifeboat veered down and was able to take 20 survivors off the jib boom. The following day, they put out again after another man had been seen in the rigging. Mr. Norris boarded the wreck with difficulty and recovered the exhausted man; seven others had made the shore in the ship's longboat.

QUIGLEY William T., Chief Officer, H.M. Coastguard, Whitby   **SILVER**

7 May 1868

23 February 1868: During a dark and stormy night, the Whitby schooner *William Barker* was driven ashore and wrecked near the East Pier, Whitby. Mr. Quigley, with ten men, climbed down the precipitous cliff and, using hawsers, took off the three man crew.

ROE Robert, Esq., J.P., Lord of the Manor, Lynmouth   **SILVER**

3 September 1868

22–23 August 1868: The St. Andrew's, New Brunswick ship *Home*, engaged in the North American timber trade, was sailing from Bristol to Quebec in ballast, with a crew of 19. Early in the morning, near Lundy Island in the Bristol Channel, she encountered a progressively worsening north-west gale, and ran for shelter. She soon developed a list, lost most of her canvas, and anchored off-shore in Lynmouth Bay, North Devon. Her anchors failed to hold, her masts were cut away and four men made the shore in a small boat; her longboat reached the shore with ten more men. Four men remained on board the ship all night, until a light Coastguard galley was brought to the scene and saved three of them; the fourth had drowned. Mr. Roe took the lead in organising the people of Lynmouth in bringing the survivors ashore through the violent seas. Later in the day, a tug towed the disabled ship back to Bristol for repairs.

Following this event, the Institution established a lifeboat station at Lynmouth.

GRAY Edmund, Esq., Son of Sir John Gray, M.P., M.D.   **SILVER**
*FREENEY John, Coachman   **SILVER**

5 November 1868
*3 December 1868

25 September 1868: During a strong east-south-easterly gale and heavy sea, the Portmadoc schooner *Blue Vein* was stranded opposite Ballybrack Railway Station, Co Dublin, Ireland. The ship struck on some rocks about 200 yards out and, after various attempts, a line was floated ashore. After a number of difficulties the schooner's Captain and four men were brought ashore by Mr. Gray, who swam out several times; Mr. Freeney swam out and rescued one of the men.

BURY, The Right Honorable Viscount, M.P., P.C.   **SILVER**
PRIDE Charles , Boatman. H.M. Coastguard, Christchurch   **SILVER**

5 November 1868

6 October 1868: When the fishing boat *Alarm* capsized on Christchurch Bar, Hampshire in squally weather, Lord Bury and Mr. Pride went out in an open boat and saved one man.

MORRISON Sylvester, Chief Officer, H.M. Coastguard, Sennen Cove   **SILVER**
NICHOLAS Matthew, Coxswain, Sennen Cove Lifeboat   **SILVER**

5 November 1868

23–24 October 1868: The government lighter *Devon*, a strong seaworthy vessel, was trying to round Land's End in a hard gale on the 23rd, but she ran stern-on to the Brissons, a pair of rocks off Cape

Cornwall, near St. Just, Cornwall. Her Captain, 14 crew, a woman and two children were drowned. The Mate was washed half senseless, bleeding and bruised on to the Little Brisson, where he remained half frozen all night. He was seen early next morning and the self-righting lifeboat *Cousins William and Mary Ann of Bideford* was launched with rocket apparatus and anchored 180 yards to the leeward of the wreck. Mr. Morrison got a line over the rock with a buoy and brought the Mate into the lifeboat. Reaching the shore as fast as possible the Mate was revived before nightfall.

CAY Robert Barclay, Captain, R.N. Inspecting Commander **H.M. Coastguard, Penzance**	**SILVER**
BLACKMORE William, Chief Officer, H.M. Coastguard, Penzance	**SILVER**
HIGGS Samuel (Junior), French Vice-Consul, Penzance	**SILVER(2)**
CARBIS Thomas, Coxswain, Penzance Lifeboat	**SILVER(2)**
HIGGANS William, Second Coxswain, Penzance Lifeboat	**SILVER**

7 January 1869

6 December 1868: The Southampton barque *North Britain*, inward bound from Quebec with a 950 ton cargo of timber, mistook her position in the mist at daybreak, entered Mount's Bay and found herself embayed in the northern corner. She dropped anchor off St. Michael's Mount but the cable parted three times and, by noon, the barque was in the surf being driven ashore between the Mount and Longrock by a ferocious gale. The Penzance self-righting lifeboat *Richard Lewis* reached her in just over an hour, but seven lives had already been lost in an attempt by the barque's boat to reach safety; another four men had been saved by rocket apparatus when they neared the shore. A great sea struck the lifeboat as she was pulling under the barque's stern and capsized her nearly killing Coxswain Carbis who was trapped but was recovered in a disabled condition. Mr. Higgans, although barely able to stand, took control and, with Captain Cay's help, took the lifeboat back to the shore. A fresh crew was put on board with Mr. Blackmore as Coxswain and Mr. Higgs in the crew. They pulled through tremendous wind and sea to reach the wreck and took off the remaining eight men shortly before the masts went and the vessel broke up.

Some accounts give the name of the Second Coxswain as Higgins.

COX Joseph, Coxswain, Appledore Lifeboat	**SILVER(2) and SILVER(3)**
COX Joseph (Junior), Second Coxswain, Appledore Lifeboat	**SILVER**
KELLY John Moulton, Crew Member, Appledore Lifeboat	**SILVER**

7 January 1869

28 December 1868: Information was received that a vessel was embayed near Appledore, Devon. When it was confirmed that she had grounded, the self-righting lifeboat *Hope* was dragged to the nearest point and launched over Pebble Ridge into a terrific surf, reached the Austrian barque *Pace*, and made fast to her. The Master refused to let his crew leave, except that one boy ran to the side and dropped into the boat. After another five minutes, eight men rushed forward and dropped into the water from where all were saved just before a tremendous sea struck the lifeboat and drove her under the barque's counter. With the lifeboat's rudder carried away and the Coxswain bruised (his cork lifebelt saved him from serious injury or death), the boat returned to shore after another unsuccessful appeal to the barque's crew. Cox, the elder, raised another crew with his son, which again included Mr. Kelly. They set off once more, young Cox using an oar to steer. Just short of the wreck, they were swept by a huge sea which threw all the crew into the water. After some

difficulty everybody regained the boat which returned to the shore, where other crews volunteered. However, it was decided not to make a further rescue attempt in the lifeboat. The barque's Master and two men were taken off when the tide fell; three more had perished.

The Emperor of Austria awarded the three men the Silver Cross of Merit and made awards to others involved in the rescue.

CROWDEN James, Chief Officer, H.M. Coastguard, Muchalls   **SILVER**

4 February 1869

21 January 1869: During a gale, the Aberdeen schooner *Kinloss* was wrecked off Scateraw Fishery Creek, near Muchalls, north of Stonehaven, Kincardineshire. Mr. Crowden, with six others, put off in a coble and saved four men. He was also awarded the Albert Medal Second Class.

WRIGHT John, Seaman, Barque *Alceste*   **SILVER**

3 September 1874

15 June 1869: Mr Wright swam ashore from the Greenock barque *Alceste* with a line after she had gone ashore in a heavy sea at Portlaine Bay, Bingower, Co Donegal, Ireland. Fifteen crew members were rescued by this means.

No reason was given for the delay in bringing this service to the attention of the Institution.

DAWSON Thomas, Steam Tug Owner   **SILVER**

5 August 1869

16 June 1869: A sudden, heavy north-easterly gale put 51 Hartlepool fishing boats and their crews, 104 men in all, in danger off the mouth of the River Tees. Mr. Dawson ordered his three steam tugs to sea, and they helped all the boats back safely into Hartlepool harbour, Co. Durham. Most of the fishermen lost their nets.

BUMBY John, Chief Officer, H.M. Coastguard, Clovelly   **SILVER**

4 November 1869

12 September 1869: When the Italian barque *Odone* of Genoa was wrecked in a whole gale and heavy sea at Portledge Mouth, near Clovelly, Devon, her 12 man crew and a passenger put off in a longboat. Mr. Bumby put off with nine men in a shoreboat and brought the longboat to safety.

JOHNS Richard O., Chief Officer, H.M. Coastguard, Tramore   **SILVER(3)**

7 October 1869

'For long and gallant services in acting as Coxswain to save the lives of a number of shipwrecked men'. The medal was given when he left the station on promotion. Services in this period included those to the brig *San Spiridione* and schooner *Voador du Vouga* (1861), the brig *Marietta* (1863), the schooner *Sarah* (1864), the brig *Steffania* (1865), the schooner *Anemone* and the barque *Wild Horse* (1867) and the ship *Oasis* (1868).

THOMAS Richard J., Coxswain, New Brighton Lifeboat **SILVER**

6 January 1870

19 October 1869: At 7 a.m. the Ulverstone schooner *Elephant* ran aground on Taylor's Bank south-west of Formby, Lancashire. The New Brighton tubular lifeboat *Willie and Arthur* was towed out by the tug *Resolute* to approach the wreck from windward. Coxswain Thomas went alongside and rescued one man, then another was seen, lashed high up in the rigging, unable to move. Although the wreck was breaking up rapidly , the Coxswain jumped on board and had started to climb the rigging when the foremast gave way and crashed over the side , drowning the man. The Coxswain narrowly escaped.

ELYARD James, Captain. Honorary Secretary, Broadstairs R.N.L.I. **SILVER**

2 December 1869

20 October 1869: The North Shields barque *Frank Shaw* sought shelter in a very heavy gale in the Downs off the Kent coast, but was compelled to seek fresh anchorage off North Foreland. The vessel was forced to run before the wind but, about 2 p.m., struck on North Sand Head where she broke in two after 15 minutes; her masts, sails and rigging were washed away. All hands crowded aft and distress signals were made. The Broadstairs self-righting lifeboat *Samuel Morrison Collins* was soon on the scene, as well as the Ramsgate boat but they found it impossible to reach the wreck and as the tide fell they grounded on the Goodwins to leeward. Eight of the barque's crew were drowned but 21 reached the sands by various means where the Broadstairs lifeboat took on 19 of them. Both lifeboats were towed into harbour by the Ramsgate tug *Aid*, reaching there at 10 p.m. Captain Elyard had been one of the first to volunteer to go out in the Broadstairs boat.

DOBSON Thomas, Coxswain, Donna Nook Lifeboat **SILVER**

4 November 1869

27 October 1869: A severe northerly gale sprang up at Donna Nook, Lincolnshire, causing the Italian barque *Bartolemeo Cerruti* of Genoa, which had been riding at anchor in the Slate Run, to drift rapidly on shore with the sea making a complete breach over her. Although the self-righting lifeboat *North Briton* launched quickly, the sea, wind and tide driving to the southward forced her ashore again. The lifeboat was then transported to a more suitable location where another attempt produced the same result. Finally, using an anchor, she was able to drift under the wreck's bow where, securing herself to the bowsprit, the barque's 14 man crew was able to drop to safety just before the wreck broke up.

BANYARD John, Chief Officer, H.M. Coastguard, Hornsea **SILVER**

6 January 1870

28 October 1869: Mr. Banyard and two men tried unsuccessfully to reach the wreck of the Italian brig *Guiseppina* in a small boat to rescue the Master. Mr. Banyard then waded into the raging surf, swam out with a line and brought the Master safely ashore.

JARMAN Isaac, Coxswain, Ramsgate Lifeboat   **SILVER(2)**
FISH Charles Edward, Bowman, Ramsgate Lifeboat   **SILVER**

6 January 1870

For long service and in acknowledgement of Coxswain Jarman's and Bowman Fish's continued gallant services in the Ramsgate lifeboat. Outstanding services in this period included those to the brig *Zeeploeg* and the barque *Norma* (1865), the schooner *Zephyr* (1866), the schooner *Mizpah*, the barque *Aurora Borealis* and the brigantine *Amor* (1867), the brig *Britain's Pride* (1868) and the schooner *Chafton Winkel*, the brig *Carl*, the barque *Highland Chief* and the barque *Emilie* (1869).

WILLIAMS Owen Lloyd, The Reverend. Honorary Secretary,
  Abersoch R.N.L.I.   **SILVER**

3 February 1870

14–15 January 1870: The Liverpool ship *Kenilworth*, homeward bound from New Orleans with a cargo of cotton, was caught in a severe squall during a north-west gale and grounded on St. Patrick's Causeway, Cardigan Bay, north-west of Barmouth, Merioneth. Eight men were saved by the Barmouth lifeboat before it was forced to leave by rising seas and by the gale that had increased to hurricane force. The Abersoch self-righting lifeboat *Mabel Louisa* had launched from her station on the Lleyn Peninsula, Caernarvon, but was unable to find the casualty. Shortly after her return the Honorary Secretary arrived and with him on board, the lifeboat relaunched. After a three hour search in dreadful seas, they found the wreck and, going alongside, took off the 13 survivors in hazardous circumstances. The Reverend Lloyd Williams had been instrumental in saving 52 lives from various wrecks.

AMIS Edward, Coxswain, Palling Lifeboat   **SILVER**

3 February 1870

Given on Coxswain Amis' retirement, 'in testimony of his long and gallant services extending over eighteen years in assisting in the lifeboat to save the lives of a large number of shipwrecked men'. The following services, amongst others, were carried out in the period, those to the brig *Jane* (1862), the ship *Orso* (1865), the schooner *Laurel* (1866) and the brig *Zosteria* (1869).

ROBERTSON David, Captain, R.N. Assistant Inspector of Lifeboats   **SILVER**

3 March 1870

13 February 1870: The Venetian brig *Giovannina* was wrecked in a heavy easterly gale with snow squalls off Gorleston, Norfolk, and eight men were saved by the Gorleston self-righting lifeboat *Leicester* which included Captain Robertson in her crew.

14 February 1870: The heavy gale forced the Arbroath schooner *Favorite* ashore near the Wellington Pier, Great Yarmouth, Norfolk. Captain Robertson went out again, this time in the Norfolk and Suffolk Class Yarmouth lifeboat *Duff*, when four men were saved. He also helped with lines to rescue five of the crew of the North Shields barque *Victoria* wrecked on Gorleston beach.

McGENIS George, Seaman   **SILVER**

4 May 1871

29 May 1870: The London barque *Albany* was wrecked in a strong wind and stormy weather on McCarty's Island, near Cape Clear, Co Cork, Ireland. Mr. McGenis took a small line and, at an opportune moment, jumped overboard and succeeded in reaching the shore; this enabled all nine men on board to be rescued. (One report states 14 men were saved.)

STUGGINS William, Second Coxswain, Teignmouth Lifeboat   **SILVER**

2 June 1870

On Mr. Stuggins' retirement after 19 years service and 'for his long and gallant services in assisting in the Teignmouth lifeboat to save the lives of a large number of shipwrecked men'. Among the vessels concerned were the brig *Cheshire Witch* and the barque *Jessie* (1866), the brig *Anne* (1867) and the trawler *Start* (1869).

HILLS William, Chief Boatman, H.M. Coastguard, Padstow   **SILVER(2)**

7 July 1870

'In testimony of his long and gallant services in assisting as Coxswain of Padstow lifeboat to save a large number of lives from shipwreck'. Prominent among the services during this period were those to the brigantine *Nugget* (1861), the sloop *Loftus* (1862), the brigantine *Pandema* and the schooner *Betsy* (1863), the barque *Juliet* (1865), the smack *Jules Josephine* (1868), the brigantine *Thomas* and the schooner *Alexandrine* (1860) and the barque *Suez* (1870).

CUMMINS John, Coxswain, Arklow Lifeboat   **SILVER**

6 October 1870

2 September 1870: The Barrow schooner *Dove*, in violent seas and a severe south-south-west gale, ran aground on the Arklow Bank, off Arklow, Co Wicklow, Ireland, and sank. The Peake type lifeboat *Arundel Venables* launched through a very high sea and, after two hours strenuous effort, went alongside the wreck, the Coxswain constantly manoeuvring her, and took off five men by ropes, pulling them through the surf into the lifeboat.

SCOTT George R. , Boatswain, Ship *Beethoven*   **SILVER**

5 January 1871

16 October 1870: During a gale and in a very heavy sea, the St. John, New Brunswick ship *Beethoven* was under tow by a steam tug. As she approached Liverpool a perilous situation was developing. Mr. Scott, a volunteer, traversed the 70 fathom (420-ft.) tow rope to pass a message to the tug Master as a result of which his ship was saved from danger together with the 40 persons aboard.

MITCHELL Charles, Fisherman   **SILVER(2)**

1 December 1870

24 October 1870: During a heavy north-westerly gale, the Italian brig *Stephano Grosso* was driven against cliffs near Port Isaac, Cornwall, and started to break up. Rocket apparatus was set up on shore and saved all the crew except three before the lines broke. The self-righting lifeboat *Richard and Sarah* launched and brought off the three other men. Mr. Mitchell, who had been in charge of the rocket apparatus, was included in the lifeboat's crew.

GRANT William, Coxswain, Margate Lifeboat   **SILVER**

2 February 1871

26 January 1871: The Sunderland brig *Sarah*, during a heavy snow storm with a strong easterly wind, went on to Margate Sands, to the north-west of the town. When she was noticed at noon, her hull was under water; she had been there more than eight hours and her six man crew had taken refuge in the foretop. The Margate self-righting lifeboat *Quiver No. 1* went to the wreck, passing a lugger whose own rescue attempt had been unsuccessful, and took off her crew, two of whom had severely frost-bitten legs. As an indication of the weather encountered, it is recorded that snow some inches deep lay on the land.

TAYLOR William, Chief Officer, H.M. Coastguard, Dunny Cove   **SILVER(2)**

4 May 1871

7 February 1871: With four other men, Mr. Taylor put off in his small Coastguard boat through a heavy swell to save the eight man crew of the Liverpool brigantine *Cecil*, which was wrecked during a strong south-south-westerly wind in Rosscarbery Bay, Co Cork, Ireland.

CURNOW Paul, Coxswain, St. Ives Lifeboat   **SILVER**

2 March 1871

11 February 1871: During a heavy gale the Youghal brigantine *Queen* was trying to enter St. Ives harbour, Cornwall, and, in rounding the pier-head, she let go an anchor and the cable parted. She drifted about a mile to leeward and was brought up by a second anchor. The St. Ives self -righting lifeboat *Covent Garden* put out with some difficulty. After reaching and boarding the vessel, Coxswain Curnow helped to let go another anchor and took off the six man crew. The casualty continued to drift and went on to Carrack Gladden beach .

CAMPBELL Jane, Miss   **SILVER**

5 October 1871

27 September 1871: When the Whitehaven brig *Manly* was wrecked in a strong easterly gale on Drogheda Bar, off the River Boyne, Co Louth, Ireland, one of her crew used a lifebuoy to save himself. He floated some distance and was in a very exhausted state after his long ordeal. Miss Campbell saw him, rushed into the heavy surf, brought him out and resuscitated him.

SMALLRIDGE James Harvey, Coxswain, Braunton Lifeboat **SILVER**

7 December 1871

15 November 1871: Early in the morning in a strong gale, the New York brigantine *Nigretta* drove on to the Braunton Sands in Barnstaple Bay, North Devon. The self-righting lifeboat *George and Catherine* launched and, after a terrific struggle, went alongside and took off seven men; the Second Mate had been lost overboard.

READING Daniel, Master, Ramsgate Harbour Steam Tug *Vulcan* **SILVER**

4 April 1872

19 March 1872: The Ramsgate lifeboat *Bradford*, the steam tug *Vulcan* and the Broadstairs lifeboat *Samuel Morrison Collins* went out in a fresh north-north-east gale and a heavy sea and saved the crew of eight of the brig *Defender* of Sunderland which had gone on the Goodwin Sands. Reading was awarded the silver medal for this service and for 'his general gallant services in assisting to save lives from wrecks on the Goodwin Sands'.

CORKHILL William, Coxswain, Padstow Lifeboat **SILVER**
*BATE Samuel, Second Coxswain, Padstow Lifeboat **SILVER**

4 April 1872
*2 May 1872

2 April 1872: After a severe struggle, the self-righting lifeboat *Albert Edward* reached the wreck of the Sunderland barque *Viking*, which had gone ashore in a strong gale and tremendous sea in Harlyn Bay, west of Padstow, Cornwall. The lifeboat lay under the bowsprit with a single line to the barque. The Mate was the first man down the line with the Master's baby. The baby was snatched by the bowman, but the Mate missed his hold, was swept away and drowned. The lifeboat was forced to return to the shore after the line parted, and after landing the baby, they battled back to the *Viking* and rescued the Master, his wife and boy, and three others. The cook refused the lifeboat, lashed himself to a ladder and jumped overboard; he was washed ashore and survived. Three men had swum ashore and were saved by spectators on the beach.

BLAMPIED Charles, Farmer, St. Martin's, Jersey **SILVER**
BOUCHARD John, Labourer, St. Martin's, Jersey **SILVER**
WHITLEY Elias, Farmer, St. Martin's, Jersey **SILVER**

5 December 1872

2 November 1872: During a heavy westerly gale The Khristiania ship *Isabella Northcote* was driven on to the Ecrehos Rocks off the coast of Jersey, Channel Isles. Messrs. Blampied, Bouchard and Whitley put off twice in a small boat, a distance of seven miles and, under the most dangerous conditions, saved the 18 man crew and brought them ashore. They were looked after by a poor man Charles Pinet and his wife, who were most generous and hospitable to them.

HOOK Robert, Coxswain, Lowestoft Lifeboat   **SILVER(2)**

1 May 1873

13 November 1872: 'In testimony of his general brave services in saving life from shipwreck and particularly on the occasion of the large lifeboat saving the crew from … *Expedite*'. The Lowestoft Norfolk and Suffolk lifeboat *Loetitia* went off, towed by the steam tug *Rainbow*, to the Norwegian brig *Expedite* of Dröbak which had gone ashore on the Holme Sand, off Lowestoft, Suffolk. Heavy seas and a north-easterly gale made dangerous her approach among the wreck's fallen masts and yards, therefore the lifeboat anchored to windward and veered slowly down on the weather quarter deck. Waiting his chance, Coxswain Hook went in among the wreckage, took off all ten persons and landed them safely.

LEASK Robert (Junior), Farmer   **SILVER**

2 January 1873

28 November 1872: When a boat capsized in squally weather off Stromness, Orkney, Mr. Leask put off with his young son in their own boat and picked up two of the three men, although one of them died from exposure soon after reaching the shore.

JOHNS Richard, Mate, Schooner *John Pearce*   **SILVER**

6 February 1873

8 December 1872: The cutter *Mystery,* of Weston-super-Mare, stranded at the entrance to Cardiff harbour during a heavy west-south-west gale. Mr. Johns, in one of the boats from the *John Pearce* of Fowey, saved the lives of 13 of the cutter's men. These included a Royal Artillery Lieutenant and 11 artillerymen. The *Mystery* was being used to service various forts in the area.

MEARNS William, Coxswain, Montrose No. 1 Lifeboat   **SILVER**
MEARNS William (Junior), Coxswain, Montrose No. 2 Lifeboat   **SILVER**

2 January 1873

21 December 1872: The medals voted to Mr. Mearns and his son were in recognition of their long and gallant services in the lifeboats, but special attention was drawn to that to the East Prussian brig *Henriette*. On passage from Sligo, Ireland, to her home port of Memel she ran before the south-easterly wind and was driven on to the sands three-quarters of a mile north of Montrose, Angus. No. 1 lifeboat, the larger, *Mincing Lane*, a self-righting boat, was launched; going through the harbour mouth and across the dangerous Annat Bank, her Coxswain and three men were washed out. Another large sea took her close to the wreck, from which six men threw themselves into the lifeboat. She then went on to pick up the missing members of her own crew. No. 2 lifeboat, a North Country type, *Roman Governor of Caer Hun*, launched from the shore and took off from the wreck the three remaining survivors, including a little boy.

HOWORTH William, Captain, R.N. Inspecting Commander
   H.M. Coastguard, Penzance   **SILVER**
BLACKMORE William, Chief Officer, H.M. Coastguard, Penzance   **SILVER(2)**
DOWNING Nicholas B., Esq., Banker, Honorary Secretary,
   R.N.L.I. Penzance   **SILVER**

6 February 1873

26 January 1873: During a heavy southerly gale and high seas in Mount's Bay, the Norwegian brig *Otto* was driven ashore at Eastern Green, Penzance Bay, Cornwall. The lifeboat *Richard Lewis* launched through heavy seas, reached the wreck and took off the eight crewmen.

2 February 1873: When the seas were running very high, the French vessel *La Marie Emilie* of Lorient ran ashore with seas rolling over her, and the lifeboat, in trying to get to her, was driven back twice and had seven oars broken. Two more attempts resulted in the lifeboat being dashed against the wreck each time, but on the third attempt all four crewmen were saved.

MARTIN Charles, Chief Officer, H.M. Coastguard, St. Ives   **SILVER**
MURPHY James, Commissioned Boatswain, H.M. Coastguard, St. Ives   **SILVER**

6 February 1873

2 February 1873: The strong east-north-easterly gale and heavy sea brought three casualties to St. Ives Bay, Cornwall. On the night of 1–2nd, the Plymouth schooners *Rambler* and *Mary Ann* and the Porthcawl brig *Francis* were all driven ashore near the harbour. Considerable difficulty was experienced in launching the St. Ives self-righting lifeboat *Covent Garden* at low tide, and she was driven ashore, her crew exhausted. The lifeboat launched five times, each with a different crew and saved a total of 15 men; two others had drowned. Martin and Murphy acted as Coxswains, the latter having been in the boat on all five occasions.

BUCKETT James, Coxswain, Brighstone Grange Lifeboat   **SILVER**

6 March 1873

3 February 1873: The Norwegian iron screw steamer *Woodham*, on passage with a cargo of coal and soda from South Shields to New York, became disabled when the main shaft of her engine cracked. She was taken in tow by a passing steamer but, in the heavy seas that were running, the *Woodham* broke her tow no less than four times before being finally left to the mercy of the seas when she ran ashore on Chilton Ledge.

Signals of distress were fired and paraffin was lighted which led the spectators on shore to assume that she was on fire. The Brighstone Grange lifeboat *Rescue* was launched and made her way out to the wreck to find that some of the crew had already taken to the ship's boats. Persuaded by the lifeboat crew, they abandoned their boats, which were promptly smashed in the heavy seas, and in two journeys 18 men were brought to shore. The Master and the Mate, however, refused to leave but sometime later made signals of distress. By this time the lifeboat was rehoused and her crew on their way home when they were recalled for a third trip to take them off.

ROCKLIFFE William, Coxswain, Southport Lifeboat   **SILVER(2)**

6 February 1873

Voted on Coxswain Rockliffe's retirement 'in acknowledgement of his long and gallant services in saving life in the life-boat'. He was Coxswain for 25 years, and notable services included saving 22 from the ship *Diana* (1853), 21 from the ship *Melbourne* (1857), 17 from the barque *Tamworth* (1863) and 17 from the barque *Times* (1871). His previous silver medal was awarded in 1852 for long service – he had then already been in the lifeboat crew for 17 years.

WHITE James, Coxswain, Fishguard Lifeboat   **SILVER**

1 May 1873

'In acknowledgement of his gallant services in the boat on various occasions in assisting to save 50 lives from various wrecks'. Among the services in that period were those to the schooners *Albion* and *Emma* (1865), the schooners *Halwell, J.W.A., Ann Mitchell* and *Carnsew* (1871) and the smacks *Commerce* and *Lion* (1872).

JINKS Richard, Chief Officer, H.M. Coastguard, Cardigan   **SILVER**

2 October 1873

13 September 1873: 'In acknowledgement of his general gallant conduct in saving life from shipwreck in the lifeboats of the Institution', particularly for his services on the 13th when he put off twice in the Cardigan Coastguard boat and saved the crew of the smack *Ocean* of Milford, which had been driven on Cardigan Bar during a violent south-easterly wind and a heavy sea.

TAYLOR William, Chief Officer, H.M. Coastguard, Dunny Cove   **SILVER(3)**

2 April 1874

11 February 1874: In a south-easterly gale the Llanelli brigantine *Harriett Williams* ran ashore in Dunny Cove, Clonakilty Bay, Co Cork, Ireland, and was wrecked. Mr. Taylor put out in the Coastguard gig and helped save the crew of seven men, in the course of which he suffered a rupture.

URELL Joseph, Chief Officer, H.M. Coastguard, Hope Cove **SILVER**

2 July 1874

14 February 1874: The Hamburg brigantine *Theodor,* Venezuela to Falmouth with a cargo of cotton seed and dyewoods, was blown off course and wrecked at Thurlestone, South Devon; her Master and two men were lost. Mr. Urell and his crew put off in the Coastguard boat and saved the Mate and two men .

PARKER Edwin, Chief Boatman, H.M. Coastguard, Mothecombe **SILVER**

2 July 1874

14 February 1874: After the French steamer *Aivali* was wrecked near Mothecombe, South Devon, her nine man crew was saved by Mr. Parker and his crew in the Coastguard boat.

GRAY-JONES Charles, Captain, R.N. Second Assistant Inspector of Lifeboats **SILVER**

HILL James, Coxswain, Newcastle Co Down Lifeboat **SILVER**

5 March 1874

26 February 1874: At daybreak the Youghal schooner *Rose*, from Bridgewater to Dublin, was seen driving before the heavy south-easterly gale into Dundrum Bay, Co Down, northern Ireland and, while the Newcastle self-righting lifeboat *Reigate* was being launched, the schooner struck and filled immediately; one man was drowned. With Captain Gray-Jones on board, Coxswain Hill took the lifeboat through a heavy cross sea and tide, amid wreckage, and took off the other four crew members from the schooner's fore-rigging.

LANGAN Michael, First Officer, Steamer *Princess Alexandra* **SILVER**

McCOMBIE Thomas, Second Officer, Steamer *Princess Alexandra* **SILVER**

4 June 1874

13 April 1874: During a heavy west-south-westerly gale, the Dublin brig *Hampton* was wrecked on the Bull Sand, Dublin Bay, Co Dublin, Ireland. Three of her crew were saved by Mr. Langan and other men in the steamer's gig and by Mr. McCombie and others in her cutter. The steamer belonged to the Commissioners of Irish Lights.

SIMPSON James, Mate, Steam Tug *Aid* **SILVER**

WHARRIER William, Engineer, Steam Tug *Aid* **SILVER**

6 August 1874

'In acknowledgement of their gallant services extending over twenty years on occasions when the Ramsgate life-boats had been towed by that steamer to vessels in distress and have saved nearly five hundred lives from shipwreck on the Goodwin Sands'. Among the services which involved the tug *Aid* were those to the barque *Norma* (1865), the barque *Aurora Borealis* (1867), the ship *Highland Chief* and the barque *Emilie* (1869), the brig *Volunteer* (1870), the barque *India* (1871) and the barques *Ystroom* and *Amazon* (1873).

MARSHALL John (Junior), Second Coxswain, Seaham Lifeboat   **SILVER**

3 December 1874

29 November 1874: The Wells schooner *Lady Ann* was driven by heavy seas against Seaham North Pier, Co Durham, and wrecked. Three of her crew were saved by lines thrown on board from the Seaham lifeboat *Sisters Carter of Harrogate*, but her Master, entangled in the rigging, was too enfeebled to save himself. Mr. Marshall went on board, but, before he could reach him, the Master was washed overboard and lost.

MURPHY Adam, Coxswain, Tyrella Lifeboat   **SILVER**
GORDON John, Assistant Coxswain, Tyrella Lifeboat   **SILVER**

7 January 1875

29 November 1874: Bound for Belfast from Liverpool, the Belfast brigantine *Donna Maria* was wrecked during a strong south-east gale in Dundrum Bay, Co Down, northern Ireland. The lifeboat *Tyrella* launched in the middle of the night and succeeded in reaching the wreck and took off five survivors. Then a sixth man was found trapped by a log of timber which had fallen on one of his legs; therefore Mr. Gordon volunteered to remain on board with him. While the lifeboat landed the other survivors, he sawed through the log and freed the man. Both of them were then taken off and landed soon after daybreak when the gale had moderated.

GRAY-JONES Charles, Captain, R.N.
  Second Assistant Inspector of Lifeboats   **SILVER(2)**

7 January 1875

6 December 1874: A westerly gale and heavy sea drove the Padstow smack *Charlotte* into Widemouth Bay near Bude, Devon, where she was wrecked. Captain Gray-Jones rushed into the surf and helped save her Master.

16 December 1874: The Dublin brig *Annie Arby* was seen driving before a strong easterly gale with her topmast hanging in a tangle of rigging; the Ilfracombe self-righting lifeboat *Broadwater* launched under the command of Captain Gray-Jones and, with all possible sail, made the brig just as she was driving toward the shore under the cliffs north of Morte Point. The lifeboatmen helped to cut the wreckage and others worked the remaining sails until she wore clear. Under guidance from a man with local knowledge, she took a narrow passage through the rocks and came to anchor, where she waited for a tug while her seven man crew carried out emergency repairs. The lifeboat left but, during her return journey, picked up five men from the Workington brig *Utility* in a boat drifting helplessly off Rockham Bay. Their vessel had driven on to the rocky foreshore, filled and sunk so that all that they could do was scramble into their boat.

SHEADER William Tolladay G., Examining Officer, H.M. Customs   **SILVER**

7 January 1875

16 December 1874: While the Shoreham, Sussex lifeboat *Ramonet* was out on exercise in very rough weather and a very heavy sea, she capsized and one of her crew drowned. Mr. Sheader (also recorded as Streader), unaware the man was dead, swam out through the surf and brought his body ashore.

RITCHIE Alexander, Farmer   **SILVER**

4 March 1875

2 January 1875: In a gale and a heavy sea, the Glasgow barque *Perica* was wrecked on Sanday Island, Orkney Islands. Mr. Ritchie waded into the surf and rescued three of her crew. Afterwards, with three other men, he put off in a boat and saved another seven men from the same vessel.

PILCHER Stephen, Coxswain, Tramore Lifeboat
   Commissioned Boatman, H.M. Coastguard   **SILVER**

4 February 1875

3 January 1875: 'In acknowledgement of his long and gallant services in the Tramore boat saving sixty-three lives', particularly when the Salcombe schooner *Fanny,* bound for Barbados from Cardiff, was seen about noon on the 3rd, trying to beat out of Tramore Bay, Co Waterford, Ireland, in the face of a fresh breeze and heavy sea. Just before dark she anchored close in to the cliffs, having failed to weather Brownstone Head. Realising that she had no chance of holding her anchors, the lifeboat was launched. Before the schooner became a total wreck, the self-righting lifeboat *Tom Egan* had brought off her crew of seven men, returning to shore at 8 p.m.

LOSE John, Chief Officer, H.M. Coastguard, Swanage   **SILVER**

4 March 1875

23 January 1875: The Exeter brigantine *Wild Wave*, bound for Poole with a cargo of coal, was wrecked off Peveril Point, Dorset in a gale and heavy sea. The casualty was firmly jammed on the rocks, her main mast gone by the board. Twelve coastguards, with Mr. Lose, put off in two four-oared gigs to the rescue, but were unable to reach the wreck. At dawn five survivors were seen in the rigging; Mr. Lose again put out and, as the gale abated, was able to bring off four men and a boy. Shortly afterwards, the wreck slipped from the rocks and sank below the sea. The young boy, an orphan, was adopted by a Poole painter who apprenticed him to his own trade,
   As a direct result of this incident, the R.N.L.I. decided to place a lifeboat at Swanage.

CORKHILL William, Coxswain, Padstow Lifeboat   **SILVER(2)**

4 March 1875

Awarded 'on the occasion of his leaving that place, in acknowledgement of his long and valuable services in that boat'. Mr. Corkhill was Coxswain from 1870 to 1875 and during that time services included those to the *Viking* in 1872 for which he was awarded the silver medal, and to the schooners *Topaz* and *Huldah* and the brig *Thomas* (1874).

MONGER Thomas, H.M. Coastguard, Tenby. Coxswain, Tenby Lifeboat   **SILVER**

4 November 1875

'In acknowledgement of his long and intrepid services in that boat'. Mr. Monger was Coxswain from 1865 to 1875. Services included those to the smack *Mary* (1865), the smack *Queen Victoria* (1867), the brigantine *Nameless*, the schooners *Emily Ann* and *Carnsew* (1868) and the lugger *Marie* (1874).

WHITE James, Coxswain, Fishguard Lifeboat   **SILVER(2)**

2 December 1875

14 November 1875: About noon, in a terrific gale, distress signals were seen from vessels at anchor in Fishguard Roads, Pembrokeshire. The No. 1 lifeboat *Sir Edward Perrott* launched and saved three men from the Milford schooner *Elinor and Mary*, driven among breakers on Goodwick Sands, the crew of the Caernarvon smack *Laura*, the crew from the rigging of the schooner *Independence* and the crew in the rigging of the Caernarvon vessel *Princess Royal* – a total of 16 lives.

GEORGE Philip, Coxswain, Caister Lifeboats   **SILVER**
BISHOP S., Chief Boatman, H.M. Coastguard, Caister   **SILVER**

2 December 1875

19 November 1875: The Sunderland schooner *Wild Wave* was wrecked in a heavy sea on the beach near Caister, Norfolk. Mr. George and Mr. Bishop led a large number of coastguardmen and beachmen and saved the three man crew.

MOODY Samuel, Fisherman   **SILVER**
CHESNUTT George, Boatman, H.M. Coastguard, Skegness   **SILVER**

6 January 1876

5 December 1875: On passage from Hull to Poole, the Colchester barge *Star* was driven ashore at Winthorne Gap, near Skegness, Lincolnshire, in a fresh easterly gale with snow falling heavily. The lifeboat *Herbert Ingram* was pulled two miles along the beach by horses and, at 6 a.m., launched through heavy surf into an on-shore wind. Reaching the barge 20 minutes later, two crewmen were taken off, but the Master fell between the two vessels. Mr. Moody and Mr. Chesnutt jumped in after him and, hanging on to the lifeboat's life lines, held on to him while the boat was rowed to the shore.

BARTHOLEMEW R.J., Esq. of Rothesay   **SILVER**

1 June 1876

23 December 1875: While at anchor, the Russian barque *Tavernus* was run into and sank on Skelmorlie Bank in the River Clyde, off Skelmorlie, Lanarkshire. In spite of the gale and heavy sea, the Rothesay steamer *Argyll* launched a boat in which Mr. Bartholemew and three others rescued a seaman.

CARRINGTON John, Captain, Steam Tug *Liverpool*   **SILVER**

3 February 1876

7–8 January 1876: During an easterly gale on the 6th, the Norwegian barque *Hunter*, of Krageroe, was wrecked on Shipwash Sands, off Orford Ness, Suffolk. She was seen on the morning after and a call for help was relayed to Harwich. The steam tug *Liverpool* put out and arrived mid-afternoon. Captain Carrington and four men went off in a small boat and, during the night, took off the barque's crew of nine men while a gale was blowing and the weather so cold that the salt water spray froze. The Ramsgate lifeboat also responded to the call for help but took no part although at sea with her tug for 16 hours.

SHANAHAN Michael, Fisherman   **SILVER**

HARRINGTON Dennis, Fisherman   **SILVER**

4 May 1876

18 February 1876: The London brigantine *Joseph Howe* was wrecked during foggy and windy weather on Bere Island, Bantry Bay, Co Cork, Ireland. Messrs. Shanahan and Harrington descended a precipitous cliff, 200–300 feet high, and rescued four of the brigantine's crew.

ELYARD James, Major, 2nd Royal Surrey Militia

Committee Member, Broadstairs R.N.L.I.   **GOLD**

6 April 1876

12–13 March 1876: Bound from Hull to the Isle of Wight, the Goole schooner *Lion* was seen in distress at 5 p.m. driving before a heavy northerly gale off Broadstairs, Kent. The Broadstairs self-righting lifeboat *Samuel Morrison Collins* launched with Major Elyard, but an incomplete crew and, making all sail, caught up with and boarded the distressed vessel. Her condition aloft was deplorable but they took her, with her crew of four, into Dover Harbour on the following day. Major Elyard had been out on service 18 times and had helped to save 49 lives from different wrecks.

MURPHY Michael, Chief Boatman, H.M. Coastguard, Littlestone

Coxswain, New Romney Lifeboat   **SILVER**

4 May 1876

10 April 1876: Just after 7 p.m., the Dutch schooner *Tobina* of Pekala, from Sunderland, was seen to drag her anchors in a strong gale and heavy sea and strike on Roar Bank, off Littlestone-on-Sea, Kent. Her crew took to the rigging, part of the masts remaining above water at low tide. The lifeboat *Dr. Hatton* was launched over the widely extending soft sands and at 8.30 p.m. reached the wreck; two of her crew had already drowned. The five survivors were rescued just in time. The medal was also awarded 'in acknowledgement of Mr. Murphy's long and general gallant services' over a period of eight years.

BILLETT Richard, Chief Boatman, H.M. Coastguard, Dungeness
  Coxswain, Dungeness (Lydd) Lifeboat   **SILVER**

1 June 1876

18 May 1876: The Russian barque *Ilmatar* drove on shore during a freak east-north-easterly gale and heavy sea on the Brooks in West Bay, south of Lydd, Kent. Because insufficient coastguard-men were available to man the lifeboat, it was necessary to launch the small four oared Coastguard galley which took off the Master and his wife. At 2 p.m., the wind and sea worsened, the lifeboat *David Hulett* then launched and took off the barque's 15 man crew.

CAMERON Orford Summerville, Commander, R.N.
  H.M. Coastguard, Newcastle, Co Down   **SILVER**

1 February 1877

3 December 1876: During a strong south-easterly wind and very heavy sea, the Maryport brigantine *Fame* was wrecked off Newcastle, Co Down, northern Ireland. With two of his men, Commander Cameron put off in the Coastguard punt and saved the crew of four.

WELDRAKE Edward, Crew Member, Hull Trinity House Lifeboat,
  Spurn Point   **SILVER**

5 April 1877

24 December 1876: The Hull sloop *Grace Darling* was wrecked during a strong easterly gale on the Middle Banks, off Spurn Head, at the mouth of the River Humber. The Hull Trinity House lifeboat launched and, on nearing the wreck, Mr. Weldrake jumped into the sea and saved the sloop's Master.

PAYNE John, Chief Officer, H.M. Coastguard, Skerries, Co Dublin   **SILVER**

1 February 1877

2 January 1877: The Skerries fishing smack *Falcon* was wrecked in an east-south-easterly gale and very heavy sea. Mr. Payne twice swam out from the shore to the aid of the crew and was successful in rescuing one man who was unconscious.

CARR Henry, Examining Officer, H.M. Customs, Wexford   **SILVER**

1 March 1877

22 January 1877: During a strong south-south-westerly wind the Wexford fishing boat *Morning Star* stranded in a rough sea on Wexford Bar, off Wexford, Co Wexford, Ireland. Mr. Carr, with four other men, put off in a small boat and saved the six man crew.

WHITE James, Commissioned Boatman, H.M. Coastguard, Goodick
  Coxswain, Fishguard No. 1 Lifeboat   **SILVER(3)**

1 March 1877

23 February 1877: About an hour after midnight during a very heavy north-easterly gale and violent sea, three vessels showed distress signals from the roadstead off Fishguard, Pembrokeshire.

The No. 1 lifeboat *Sir Edward Perrott* launched and took off two men from the Newquay vessel *George Evans*, four from the Bridgewater dandy *Adventure* and three from the Newport vessel *Supply*, and landed them all at 4.30 a.m. They had to launch again immediately, with Mr. White still on board, to the New York brigantine *B.F. Nash*, which had been driven on to the beach, but when the tide ebbed the brigantine's crew elected to remain by her.

WHITE John, Coxswain, Howth Lifeboat **SILVER**

5 April 1877

26 March 1877: In a strong south-easterly gale, the Dublin barque *Eva*, on passage from Ardrossan, stranded on Baldoyle Strand, off Howth Head, Co Dublin, Ireland. The Howth lifeboat *Clara Baker* launched and found the sea making a clean breach over the casualty; five of her crew had put off in their own boat before she struck. The three others were lashed in the mizzen rigging and, despite filling several times, the lifeboat under Mr. White took them off and landed them at Baldoyle. Acknowledgement was also made for Mr. White's general gallant services in the boat including help given to the schooner *Liberty* (1862), the lugger *Castletown* (1864), the smack *Bessie* (1865), the smack *Favourite* (1866), the schooner *Adelaide* (1871), and the schooner *Tantivy* (1874).

MANIFOLD William, Assistant Coxswain, Arklow Lifeboat **SILVER**

3 May 1877

For service over the past eleven years … Assistant Coxswain Manifold had been out on service in that boat on twenty-two occasions and had assisted in saving forty-four lives. He served in two lifeboats, the *Arundel Venables* and the *Out Pensioner*, their services including those to the smack *Kate and Mary* (1867), the ship *Empire Queen* (1868), s.s. *Hellenis* (1869) and the schooner *Sensitive* and the barque *Roycroft* (1875).

LINAKER Hiram, Crew Member, New Brighton Lifeboat **SILVER**

5 June 1877

'In acknowledgement of his long and intrepid services as one of the original crew of the lifeboat'. In the 37 services in which Mr. Linaker had taken part, he had helped to save 96 lives. Prominent among these services were those to the brig *Levant* (1863), the brig *Corea* and the ship *Contest* (1864), the ship *Thornton* (1867), the barque *Empress* (1869), the barque *Ida Maria* (1870), the lugger *Vale of Nith* (1872), the ship *Dunmail* (1873) and the barque *Brothers Pride* (1876).

GRANT William, Coxswain, Margate Lifeboat **SILVER(2)**

6 December 1877

24–25 November 1877: The conditions on this date were described as being a 'strong gale increasing to a hurricane from the east-north-east, with heavy squalls of rain and sleet and a high sea'. Fifty to sixty vessels were in the roads off Margate, Kent, and, with some of them showing distress signals, the private lifeboat *Quiver No. 1* launched at 9.30 a.m. to come up to the North Shields barque *Hero*, that had parted from one anchor and was dragging the other while striking the ground. Mr. Grant took off the crew of 15 men before her second anchor parted and then went on to the Weymouth brigantine *Louisa*, where two of the lifeboat crew were put aboard. With her crew of seven the brigantine ran to Whitstable, 15 miles to the west, the lifeboat escorting her.

WILDS Robert, Coxswain, North Deal Lifeboat   **SILVER**

6 December 1877

1 December 1877: 'In acknowledgement of his gallant services in that lifeboat particularly to the Liverpool s.s. *Crusader* (991-tons)'. This ship had gone on shore on the Goodwin Sands at 7 a.m., while in passage from Quebec, Canada, to the Tyne with a cargo of timber. When the life boat *Van Kook* launched, some boatmen and some of the crew of a tug were already aboard the casualty, but she had eight feet of water in her hold and, as the tide ebbed, she settled by the stern, her mainmast fell over the side and her back broke. On arrival, under tow by the Cardiff s.s. *Royal Welsh*, the lifeboat took off the crew of 18 men and the four other men, bringing them ashore.

BOYLE Marcus, Coxswain, Wexford Lifeboat   **SILVER**

2 May 1878

25 April 1878: The Liverpool s.s. *Montagu* was seen to be ashore on the south side of East Bar Channel, off Wexford, Co Wexford, Ireland. The Wexford No. 2 lifeboat *Civil Service* launched at once and was towed out by the steam tug *Ruby* which had already made an unsuccessful attempt to help the casualty. Casting off, the lifeboat rowed through high seas to a point under the vessel's lee side from where she took off the passengers – four men, eight women and six children. The Master and crew remained on board.

This was the last service by this lifeboat which was the first of many which, over the years, have been paid for by the Civil Service, Post Office and British Telecom (CISPOTEL) Lifeboat Fund, which was founded in 1866.

WEBSTER John, Coxswain, Maryport Lifeboat   **SILVER**

7 November 1878

10 October 1878: The Liverpool barque *Carn Tual* sailed from Maryport, Cumberland, on the 6th and, at 9 a.m. on the 9th, was seen showing distress signals while riding in the Solway Firth between Robin Rigg and Dunrugh Banks, having lost one anchor. A strong west-south-westerly gale was blowing over a very rough sea. The Maryport lifeboat *Henry Nixson* launched and, unable to find the unlit barque after over five hours, returned to shore. She put out again next morning under tow by a steam tug. This time she was successful in locating the vessel and took off nine men, one of them insane through fear.

WILLIAMS Owen Lloyd, The Reverend,
   Honorary Secretary, Abersoch R.N.L.I.   **SILVER(2)**

2 January 1879

10 October 1878: The Reverend Williams came of a family devoted in every way to lifeboat service and took an active part in their activities. Not for him the Honorary Secretary staying ashore directing operations – he preferred to be in the thick of things and this award was made in recognition of his long co-operation and intrepid services.

A gale was blowing when the Liverpool barque *Dusty Miller*, St. John's, to Holyhead with a cargo of timber, was seen in distress riding at anchor near St. Patrick's Causeway in Cardigan Bay, off Barmouth, Merioneth. The Barmouth lifeboat could not launch in the gale, so the Abersoch lifeboat *Mable Louisa* put off and, arriving at the scene, was asked to stay alongside until the weather moderated. Despite the gale and heavy sea, the lifeboat, with the Reverend Williams on board, remained on station until a steam tug arrived at 6 a.m. and took the barque into St. Tudwall's Roads off Abersoch.

MACKAY James   **SILVER**

2 January 1879

16 November 1878: In a fresh gale and a heavy sea, two boys were trying to cross the Bar of Tongue, Kyle of Tongue, Sutherland, but their boat was swamped. Mr. Mackay swam out to the boat and saved both boys.

STEVENS Henry, Gunner, 10th Brigade, Royal Artillery   **SILVER**

6 February 1879

24 December 1878: When the brigantine *Princess Royal* was wrecked at Camden Fort, near Cork, Co Cork, Ireland, Gunner Stevens swam out twice trying to save some of her crew.

WEST William, Chief Boatman, H.M. Coastguard, Camber   **SILVER**

6 February 1879

8 January 1879: During a fresh east-south-east gale, the Gothenburg schooner *Marie Louise* was wrecked at Dymchurch, Kent, and five of her crew were saved by Mr. West and his crew.

KYLE Matthew, Coxswain, Holy Island Lifeboats   **SILVER**
KYLE George, Assistant Coxswain, Holy Island Lifeboats   **SILVER**

3 April 1879

20 March 1879: The s.s. *Darlington* was wrecked at False Emmanuel Head, Holy Island, during a fog and heavy sea. The Holy Island No. 1 lifeboat *Grace Darling* saved nine men from the wreck. Matthew Kyle was appointed Coxswain in 1879, but his medal and that to George Kyle were awarded 'in acknowledgement of their long and gallant services in saving lives from shipwreck'.

PRIDEAUX-BRUNE Ellen Frances, Miss   SILVER

PRIDEAUX-BRUNE Gertrude Rose, Miss   SILVER

PRIDEAUX-BRUNE Mary Katherine, Miss   SILVER

PRIDEAUX-BRUNE Beatrice May, Miss   SILVER

O'SHAUGHNESSY Nora, Miss   SILVER

2 October 1879

9 August 1879: A boat capsized in a wind squall off Bray Hill, Padstow Harbour, Cornwall and the occupants were thrown out. At the time, the five young ladies were in their rowing boat which was being towed behind a fishing boat. Asking to be cast off, they rowed through heavy surf to the scene where they saved a drowning sailor and only got him into their boat with the greatest difficulty.

DUNMORE The Earl of   SILVER

1 January 1880

22–23 September 1879: During a south-westerly hurricane on the 22nd, the Glasgow yacht *Astarte* sank in the Sound of Harris, between Harris and North Uist, Outer Hebrides and the seven passengers and crew took refuge on an island. On receipt of the news at 1 a.m. on the 23rd, the Earl of Dunmore and three fishermen put off in an open boat and rowed 11 miles through a very heavy sea and brought all seven to shore, where they were taken to his Lordship's residence at Rodel, Harris. The three fishermen were awarded £5.

MARKWELL George, Coxswain, Holy Island Lifeboat   SILVER

4 December 1879

Mr Markwell retired as Coxswain in 1879, and the medal was awarded 'in acknowledgement of his generally valuable and brave services in saving many lives from shipwreck'. During his period of office, there were services to the schooners *Mischief* and *Exchange* (1868), the sloop *Elizabeth* (1872), the schooner *Augustine Louise* and the steamer *Britannia* (1875) and the schooner *Dispatch* (1878).

CUBITT William Patridge (Junior), Crew Member, Bacton Lifeboat   GOLD

5 February 1880

20 January 1880: The Fleetwood schooner *Richard Warbrick* was in difficulties during severe weather off the coast of Norfolk and the Bacton lifeboat *Recompense* launched. While alongside, the lifeboat was capsized by an overwhelming sea and her Second Coxswain and a crew member were lost. To prevent further disaster, Mr. Cubitt, son of the Honorary Secretary, plunged into the sea and cut a rope which jammed the rudder of the lifeboat, so enabling her to reach the shore with survivors.

BICKERSTAFFE Robert, Coxswain, Blackpool Lifeboat   **SILVER**

4 March 1880

26 February 1880: In a gale and very heavy seas, the Fleetwood schooner *Bessie Jones*, Glasgow to Liverpool with a cargo of steel railway metals, was seen on Salthouse Bank, off Blackpool, Lancashire. Even with landsmen included, the Blackpool lifeboat *Robert William* had to launch short-handed but, under sail and shipping seas the whole time, the boat reached a point where the oars could be got out and, after two hours hard rowing, Coxswain Bickerstaffe took her alongside the casualty and removed four men. On her way back the lifeboat broached to on a sandbank, finishing on her beam ends, but was able to right herself and make St. Anne's safely.

SMITH Henry, Pilot, Gloucester   **SILVER**

6 January 1881

7 August 1880: In a gale and heavy seas, the yacht *Foam* got into a dangerous position in Cardiff Grounds, off the coast of Glamorgan. With the aid of another man, Mr. Smith saved the owner and two persons from her.

MURPHY James, Assistant Coxswain, St. Ives Lifeboat   **SILVER(2)**

7 October 1880

15 September 1880: In a strong northerly gale and heavy sea, the Plymouth schooner *Jane Smith*, Llanelly to Ipswich with a cargo of coal, ran for St. Ives Harbour, Cornwall, in distress. By the time that the St. Ives lifeboat *Exeter* reached her, she had struck on The Ridge, but the lifeboat managed to get alongside and six men were taken off and landed.
16 September 1880: During a service in which she was not needed, a vicious sea over the lifeboat's stern caused the drogue line to be trapped between the rudder and stern post. There being no other way, Mr. Murphy went over the stern and cleared the line.

HATCH Newbery George, Mate, Ship *Berkshire*   **SILVER**

4 November 1880

22 October 1880: The Whitby brig *Marys* was wrecked during a heavy east-north-easterly gale and high sea on Black Rock at the entrance to Falmouth Harbour, Cornwall. Mr. Hatch put off in a boat with four of his crew and saved two of the brig's crew.

FREEMAN Henry, Coxswain, Whitby Lifeboats   **SILVER(2)**

4 November 1880

28 October 1880: About noon with an east-north-east hurricane blowing and extremely high seas, the Douglas schooner *Reaper*, Ostend to Sunderland in ballast, was seen to be drifting rapidly on to Whitby Rocks, and the No. 1 lifeboat *Robert Whitworth* took off her four man crew. At 1.30 p.m. the Staithes fishing yawl *Good Intent* was running for Whitby Sands; the same lifeboat launched again and saved all her eight man crew. The Rye schooner *Elizabeth Austin*, Rye to Sunderland in ballast, also stranded on the beach at 3.15 p.m. No. 2 Lifeboat *Harriott Forteath* launched

immediately and took off all her crew of five men. The Great Yarmouth schooner *John Snell*, Great Yarmouth to Newcastle with a cargo of wheat, was seen at 4.30 p.m. making for the beach with tremendous seas continually sweeping over her. After she struck, No. 1 lifeboat launched for the third time, and saved her five man crew. Every one of these rescues was carried out under great difficulty and the Coxswain on each of them was Mr. Freeman.

TORRENS John Arthur Wellesley O'Neill, Lieutenant	
2nd Dragoons (Royal Scots Greys)	**GOLD**
COX Henry Lawrence, Surgeon, Army Medical Department	**SILVER**
SMITH William, Bombardier, Royal Artillery	**SILVER**
REILLY Patrick, Private, Army Service Corps	**SILVER**
HOWARD Francis, Private, 57th Regt. of Foot	**SILVER**

6 January 1881

28 October 1880: On the night of the 27th during an east-north-east gale and high seas, the Warrenpoint schooner *Robert Brown*, coal laden, was driven ashore near Pigeonhouse Fort, in Dublin Bay, Co Dublin, Ireland. Two of the schooner's four man crew were drowned; the other two secured themselves to her rigging where they were discerned at daylight. The normal Coastguard crew of the Poolbeg lifeboat being absent on training, a replacement crew was assembled composed of soldiers from the fort, a number of fishermen and seamen with Lieutenant Torrens as Coxswain. Under the guidance of Dr. Cox, the lifeboat was launched with great difficulty over a beach strewn with boulders and broken piles. After a half hour struggling through severe conditions, the two half-dazed survivors were brought to safety. Lieutenant Torrens was voted a silver medal on 2 December 1880 but this was replaced by a gold medal 'in consideration of his brave and conspicuous services'.

OWSTON John, Coxswain, Scarborough Lifeboat　　　　　　　　　**SILVER**

4 November 1880

28 October 1880: The severe storm on this day brought several casualties in the area of Scarborough, Yorkshire. The first of these, the South Shields brig *Mary*, was driven on shore while trying to make harbour. The Scarborough lifeboat *Lady Leigh* was launched at 9.30 a.m. and, after a severe struggle, saved the crew of six men and a boy. At 11 a.m., she went out and brought off five men from the Bideford schooner *Black-Eyed Susan* then, at 3 p.m., eight men from the Nantes brig *Jeune Adolphe*, ashore on South Sands. At 8.30 p.m., in the dark and with the gale worsening, the lifeboat took off four men and the Master's wife from the stranded Plymouth sloop *J. Prizeman*.
29 October 1880: On the following morning with the gale somewhat modified but still a very rough sea, the Dutch galliot *Herbruder* went ashore about noon, and three men were saved. All five rescues had been achieved with Mr. Owston as Coxswain.

BATE Thomas, Coxswain, Bude Lifeboat　　　　　　　　　　　　**SILVER**

7 April 1881

31 December 1880: The bude ketch *Stucley*, on passage from the Mumbles to Bude with coal, was wrecked in squally weather on Bude breakwater, Cornwall. Mr. Bate and his crew saved her crew of three men by means of lifelines and a hawser.

FISH Charles Edward, Coxswain, Ramsgate Lifeboat	GOLD
GOLDSMITH Richard, Second Coxswain, Ramsgate Lifeboat	SILVER
BELSEY Henry, Crew Member, Ramsgate Lifeboat	SILVER
BERRY David, Crew Member, Ramsgate Lifeboat	SILVER
COOPER Thomas (Senior), Crew Member, Ramsgate Lifeboat	SILVER
COOPER Thomas (Junior), Crew Member, Ramsgate Lifeboat	SILVER
FRIEND Thomas, Crew Member, Ramsgate Lifeboat	SILVER
GOLDSMITH John, Crew Member, Ramsgate Lifeboat	SILVER
GOLDSMITH Stephen, Crew Member, Ramsgate Lifeboat	SILVER
MEADER Henry, Crew Member, Ramsgate Lifeboat	SILVER
PENNEY Robert, Crew Member, Ramsgate Lifeboat	SILVER
VERION Charles, Crew Member, Ramsgate Lifeboat	SILVER
PAGE Alfred, Master, Steam Tug *Vulcan*	SILVER
WHARRIER William, Engineer, Steam Tug *Vulcan*	SILVER(2)
AUSTEN William, Crew Member, Steam Tug *Vulcan*	SILVER
KNIGHT Charles, Crew Member, Steam Tug *Vulcan*	SILVER
REVELL Edward, Crew Member, Steam Tug *Vulcan*	SILVER
WOODWARD George, Stoker, Steam Tug *Vulcan*	SILVER
YARE Richard, Stoker, Steam Tug *Vulcan*	SILVER

3 February 1881

6 January 1881: At 2 a.m. on the 5th in tense darkness, an easterly gale, frequent snow squalls and below freezing temperatures, the 1,238 ton barque *Indian Chief*, four days out from Middlesbrough, Yorkshire, and bound for Yokohama, Japan, grounded hard on Long Sand at the mouth of the Thames, off Clacton-on-Sea, Essex. During the day, apparently, she broke her back, lost her boats, and two men were drowned. She suffered further damage in a heavy sea at 5 p.m. The survivors took to the rigging but, by 3 a.m. on the 6th, only 12 remained after the mizzen mast fell. Following unsuccessful searches by the Harwich and Clacton lifeboats, the steam tug *Vulcan* arrived on the scene towing the Ramsgate lifeboat *Bradford*. Casting off, Charles Fish headed the lifeboat towards the wreck, then veered a piece of wood down on a number of ropes' ends, tied together. This enabled a hawser to be dragged aboard the wreck by which means the lifeboat's crew hauled their craft under the wreck's quarter. The lifeboat took off the 12 survivors, transferred them to the steam tug, which took the lifeboat in tow again and returned it to Ramsgate through heavy broken water, after 26 hours at sea.

Full graphic accounts of this service appeared in the *Daily Telegraph* on 11th and 18th January, and were reprinted in the *Lifeboat Journal* of 1st February. On February 11th, H.R.H. the Duke of Edinburgh, a member of the R.N.L.I.'s Committee of Management, presented all the medals at a ceremony at the Ramsgate Coastguard Station.

NEPEAN St. Vincent, Captain, R.N. District Inspector of Lifeboats.	SILVER
BRITTON William, Assistant Coxswain, Harwich Lifeboat	SILVER

3 February 1881

20–21 January 1881: The 438 ton Dutch screw steamship *Ingerid* of Rotterdam on passage from Norway to Naples, Italy, with a cargo of fish, struck the Sunk Sand, off Clacton, Essex, on 17 January. Seven men left the steamship next day in one of her boats, whilst two more men were lost overboard, which left the Master and six men lashed to the foremast in bitterly cold conditions. When the wreck was finally reported by the Cork lightship on the 20th, the Harwich lifeboat *Springwell* set out at 7 p.m., but the frost had been so severe that a way had to be cut through the ice right to the harbour mouth. After a difficult journey the lifeboat found the wreck between 4 and 5 a.m. and, at the second attempt, put a line aboard. The lifeboat crew, led by Mr. Britton and including Captain Nepean, boarded and helped the survivors into their boat which set off on the return journey. Arriving at the Cork lightship, they encountered the Lowestoft tug *Despatch* which took them in tow, and they reached Harwich, just before 10 a.m. on the 21st.

BLACKWOOD J. O'Reilly, The Reverend, Honorary Secretary, Ballywalter R.N.L.I.   SILVER

7 April 1881

4 March 1881: 'In acknowledgement of his general gallant services in the lifeboat', but particular attention was drawn to the following incident. Information was received at 1 a.m. that the Liverpool ship *Castlemaine*, bound from Rangoon, Burma, to the Clyde with a cargo of teak and bones, had stranded in Ballyherbert Bay, three miles south of the lifeboat station at Ballywalter, Co Down; a hurricane was blowing from the south-east with heavy sleet and rain. Horses were obtained and the Ballywalter lifeboat *Admiral Henry Meynell* was taken by road to the scene, great delay being occasioned by the weather and road conditions. With the Reverend Blackwood on board, the lifeboat was launched over a rough shore through very heavy surf, but was repeatedly driven back. A line drifted from the wreck and was seized, then by rowing and hauling they got under the ship's bow and took off 25 men who were delivered to the shore in two trips.

TURNER James, Chief Officer, H.M. Coastguard, Leysdown, Isle of Sheppey   SILVER

1 September 1881

31 July 1881: When the London steam launch *Edith* sank off Warden Point, Isle of Sheppey during squally weather and in a heavy sea the crew of six men took to their boat. Mr. Turner and four of his men put off in the Coastguard gig and brought them ashore at Bishopstone, fourteen miles east of Leysdown.

CUMISKY W.J., Honorary Secretary, Balbriggan R.N.L.I.   SILVER

6 October 1881

25 August 1881: During a strong south-south-westerly gale, the Whitehaven brig *Endeavour* went ashore in heavy seas outside Balbriggan Harbour, Co Dublin, and Mr. Cumisky put off with others in the Coastguard lifeboat and saved five persons from the wreck.

BROWN John, Coxswain, Newbiggin Lifeboat   SILVER

3 November 1881

14 October 1881: 'In recognition of his long and gallant services in the lifeboat' and particularly the service to the Newcastle s.s. *Northumberland*, which had run into the bay for shelter during a very severe storm and in very high seas. Distress signals were answered by the Newbiggin lifeboat *William Hopkinson of Brighouse*; she put off and transferred two men aboard to bring

the ship to an anchorage. With a kedge anchor run out, the *Northumberland's* four crewmen were taken ashore to reboard next day to take her to the Tyne. Other significant services were to the barque *King Oscar* and fishing boats (1864), the brigantine *Neptune* (1865), several fishing boats (1867 and 1870) and the steamer *Shotton* (1875). He had been appointed Coxswain in 1879, and in 1888 received a clasp to the silver medal for 35 years service.

*EVANS Daniel, Coxswain, Poolbeg Lifeboat	**SILVER**
*CARR Samuel, Chief Officer, H.M. Coastguard, Ring's End	
Honorary Secretary, Poolbeg R.N.L.I.	**SILVER**
WILLIAMS H., Coxswain, Kingstown Lifeboat	**SILVER**
LINDSAY Alexander John, Lieutenant, Royal Artillery	**SILVER**

1 December 1881

*5 January 1882

22 October 1881 and 31 October 1881: During a heavy south-easterly gale on 22 October, the St. John, New Brunswick, ship *George H. Oulton* stranded in heavy surf on the North Bull, off Clontarf, Co Dublin, Ireland. The Poolbeg lifeboat put out under the Coxswain and, with volunteers Mr. Carr and Lieutenant Lindsay aboard, proceeded to the wreck, but her services were not required – the Howth lifeboat had rescued the 16 man crew. On 31 October, the Poolbeg lifeboat rescued 11 riggers engaged in salvage from the same wreck – the Kingstown lifeboat also rendered assistance. Recognition was also given to Mr. Williams for long and gallant services.

LEGERTON Samuel James Robert, Coxswain, Clacton Lifeboat	**SILVER**

3 November 1881

23 October 1881: 'In recognition of his general gallant services' and particularly at the wreck of the Boulogne lugger *Madeleine* on Gunfleet Sands off Clacton, Essex, when the Clacton lifeboat *Albert Edward* rescued her crew of 16 men.

STEELE John, Esq., Provost   **SILVER**

5 January 1882

22 November 1881: 'For brave and valuable services in helping to man the Ayr lifeboat' on the occasion of the wreck of the brigantine *J.W. Harris* of Dublin during a severe gale. Three persons were saved.

NORSWORTHY William, Chief Officer, H.M. Coastguard, Caernarvon   **SILVER**
EVANS Henry, Police Constable   **SILVER**

2 February 1882

28 November 1881: In a whole gale, the German brigantine *Fritz von Gadow* of Barth stranded and capsized off Caernarvon. Mr. Norsworthy and Police Constable Evans put off in an open boat and, at great risk, they saved the brigantine's five man crew.

SCOTT Henry, Major. Chairman, Dover R.N.L.I.   **SILVER**

2 February 1882

9 December 1881: The Jersey barque *Chin Chin* went ashore at South Foreland near Dover, Kent, in a fierce gale and heavy seas. The Dover lifeboat *Henry William Pickersgill R.A.* was found to be one man short. Major Scott therefore took an oar and the boat was launched. A large amount of wreckage and spars were floating around the barque, but, in spite of this, the lifeboat went alongside and took off five men .

MURDOCH Peter, Fisherman   **SILVER**

2 February 1882

21 December 1881: During a gale, the Dundalk schooner *Circassian* became unmanageable and was wrecked at Glendrishaig, Ayrshire, where Mr. Murdoch, with three of his men, saved two crew using ropes.

WILDS Robert, Coxswain, North Deal Lifeboat   **SILVER(2)**

2 February 1882

'In recognition of his continued brave services in the boat' since 1877, when he was awarded the first silver medal, during which period he had helped to save 101 lives from various shipwrecks, including the ship *Crusader* and the barque *Hannah Rathkens* (1877), the brig *Royal Arch* (1878), the barques *Mia Madre E* and *Leda* (1879), the ship *Paul Boyton* (1880) and the ship *Ganges* (1881).

HEADON Richard, Coxswain, Clovelly Lifeboat   SILVER

6 April 1882

Coxswain Headon 'had been out in the lifeboat on all occasions when she had been afloat on service and had assisted to save 34 lives during the past 12 years'. The services concerned were those to the herring boat *Gem* and fishing boat *Sisters* (1870), the schooner *R.B.* (1871), the ketch *Minnie* and the brigantine *Elizabeth* (1874), the smack *Ebenezer* (1877), the ketch *Louisa* and the smack *Delabole* (1880) and the ketch *Bluebell* (1882).

ROBERTS Richard, Assistant Coxswain, North Deal Lifeboat   SILVER

3 August 1882

For going out on every occasion, except one, in 17 years, a total of 78 times in which Mr. Roberts helped to save 202 lives.

STOKES Richard, Coxswain, Poole Lifeboat   SILVER

7 September 1882

On his retirement, 'in acknowledgement of his long and gallant services' from 1865 when the station was established. He took part in services to the brigs *Antares* and *Contest* (1867), the lugger *Augustine* (1868) and the ketch *William Pitt* and the ship *Martaban* (1874). 63 lives were saved by the lifeboat *Manley Wood* during this period.

HALL George Edward, Captain, Fishing Boat *Trial*   SILVER

7 December 1882

28 October 1882: When the Caernarvon schooner *Prosper* was wrecked in the night off Lowestoft, Suffolk, in a heavy north-easterly gale, her Master and two of her crew escaped to the shore along a hawser. Another man, totally incapacitated by illness, was unable to follow. Captain Hall then went out along the hawser and brought him ashore.

NORSWORTHY William, Chief Officer, H.M. Coastguard, Caernarvon   SILVER(2)

1 March 1883

25 January 1883: During a west-north-westerly gale at night, the Caernarvon barge *Neptune* dragged her anchor and stranded on a sandbank at Caernarvon , North Wales. Mr. Norsworthy put off in a boat with four others and, in spite of being driven back four times, reached the wreck and took off her crew of one man and a boy.

JENKINS Jenkin, Coxswain, Mumbles Lifeboat   SILVER

1 February 1883

27 January 1883: The barque *Admiral Prinz Adalbert* of Danzig went ashore in a storm on Mumbles Head after a tug failed to tow her off into Swansea Bay. The lifeboat *Wolverhampton* was launched at 10 a.m. with Coxswain Jenkins at the helm. In the 12 man crew were four of his

sons, his son-in-law and a nephew. On reaching the wreck, two crew had just been rescued when a large sea struck the lifeboat, capsizing her. John and William, sons of the Coxswain, William MacNamara, his son-in-law, and crew member William Rogers were drowned. The four deceased men left widows and nineteen orphans, and the Institution gave £800 to the local fund in their aid. Jenkin Jenkins, who received £50 and the silver medal, had sustained a very serious scalp wound. Ultimately with the exception of the Carpenter, the barque's crew were saved.

BLACKWOOD J. O'Reilly, Reverend, Honorary Secretary,
   Ballywalter R.N.L.I.   **SILVER(2)**
PRIOR George, Chief Officer, H.M. Coastguard, Ballywalter   **SILVER**
                                                                      1 March 1883

6–7 February 1883: The Londonderry brig *Euphemia Fullerton*, Londonderry to Maryport with coal, was driven ashore in a fierce east-south-easterly gale on the north end of the Long Rock, off Ballywalter, Co Down, northern Ireland. After great difficulty the Ballywalter lifeboat *Admiral Henry Meynell*, with the Reverend Blackwood in charge, launched, but was driven ashore with three oars broken. At 3 a.m., a second launch was successful and the brig's six man crew were taken off from her rigging where they had been all night. During the launch Mr. Prior waded into the surf and rendered great help in launching and recovering the boat.

ARNOLD William H., Chief Boatman in Charge,
   H.M. Coastguard, Sandown   **SILVER**
                                                                      7 June 1883

10 February 1883: In the evening during a strong south-west gale, the French brigantine *Jeune Gustave*, of Brest, Département Finistère, was totally wrecked off Red Cliff, Sandown Bay, Isle of White. Mr. Arnold with five of his men launched the Coastguard boat and succeeded in taking off the crew, five men in all.

FELL Robert, Coxswain, Ramsey Lifeboat   **SILVER**
                                                                      1 March 1883

'In acknowledgement of his good services, being compelled by ill-health and advanced age to resign his office'. Outstanding services during that period were those to the brigantine *Jane* and the schooner *Prudence* (1868), the schooner *John Bell* (1870), the schooners *William* and *Rapid* (1871), the smack *Venus* (1874) and the schooner *John Wesley*, the brigantine *Victoire* and the brig *William Hill* (1880).

   He was Second Coxswain 1868 to 1873 and Coxswain 1873 to 1883.

WEBB William, Coxswain, Padstow Lifeboat   **SILVER**
                                                                      1 March 1883

On his retirement 'in recognition of his gallant services in the lifeboat during the past thirteen years'. These included services to the brig *Viking* and the schooner *Caroline Phillips* (1872), the schooner *Huldah* and the brig *Thomas* (1874), the brigantine *Immacolata* and the brig *Marie Josephine* (1875) and the schooners *Favorite* and *Mary Josephine* (1881).

HOOD Henry, Coxswain, Seaton Carew Lifeboat   **SILVER**
FRANKLIN John Henry, Crew Member, Seaton Carew Lifeboat   **SILVER**
FRANKLIN Matthew, Crew Member, Seaton Carew Lifeboat   **SILVER**

5 April 1883

11 March 1883: The Drammen schooner *Atlas* was driven on to the Long Scar Rocks off Seaton Carew, Co Durham, in a violent north-easterly gale accompanied by snow showers and a very heavy sea. The Seaton Carew lifeboat *Job Hindley* launched at once, but could find no signs of a wreck. Therefore Coxswain Hood and John Franklin landed on the reef, but darkness made a search extremely difficult. In spite of seas washing over them and, at one point, Mr. Hood being washed off, they found the wreck, then, joined by Matthew Franklin, managed to get a line on board her at the stern. The Coxswain rushed into the surf and rescued the schooner's Mate, and four others were brought off the wreck by line. All eight men regained the lifeboat and it was pulled back to shore. Mr. Hood also received the Albert Medal, Second Class.

ROBERTS Thomas, Coxswain, Holyhead Lifeboat   **SILVER**

5 April 1883

30 March 1883: When the Greenock brig *Norman Court* went on shore on Cymyran Bank, Anglesey, in a heavy south-south-westerly gale, her mainmast was carried away, she sank and her crew took to the fore-rigging. The Rhosneigr lifeboat *Thomas Lingham* went to help but became disabled and had to leave. Following this, the Holyhead lifeboat *Thomas Fielden* launched, and was taken in tow by s.s. *George Elliott* and then the steam tug *Challenger*. A mile from the wreck, the lifeboat cast off and tried three times under oars to reach the wreck, but had to return to Holyhead. Further attempts by the Rhosneigr lifeboat and rocket apparatus failed; the crew became so exhausted that the Holyhead crew were brought by special train to man the Rhosneigr lifeboat. In the dark Mr. Roberts led his crew in this boat through unknown waters and took off the 20 crewmen.

ADAIR Robert, Coxswain, Ballywater Lifeboat   **SILVER**

2 August 1883

Awarded 'on his retirement from the post of Coxswain in acknowledgement of his long and valuable services in assisting in the boat to save one hundred and twenty-six lives from different shipwrecks'. Prominent services during the period included those to the schooner *Brenton* (1870), the ship *Loch Sunart* and the schooner *Lady Land* (1879), the brigantine *John and Mary* (1880), the ship *Castlemaine* (1881), and the brig *St. George* (1882).

STROWGER George, Coxswain, Kessingland Lifeboats   **SILVER**

6 September 1883

'In recognition of his gallant services in these boats since the establishment of the station' (1855). His services included to the schooner *Centaur* (1865), the schooner *Admiral Jervis* (1868), the brigantine *Flora* (1870), the schooner *Jessie* and the brig *Sir William Pulteney* (1874), the schooner *Eliza* and the sloop *Firm* (1876), the brig *Lady Havelock* (1877), the barque *Cleopatra* (1879), the brig *Maria* (1881) and the brig *Marnhull* (1883).

   He became Coxswain in 1867 and served until 1897.

LEGERTON Samuel James Robert, Coxswain, Clacton Lifeboat **SILVER(2)**

7 February 1884

23–24 January 1884: In heavy seas and a cold wind, the Rochester barge *Jesse* lay at anchor near the Heaps Buoy, off Clacton, Essex, with her sails in tatters and showing distress lights. The Clacton lifeboat *Albert Edward* put out at 10 p.m. under close reefed canvas but, crossing the Gunfleet Sand, was struck by heavy seas and capsized, finishing on her starboard side. Freeing himself from the gear in which he was entangled, Mr. Legerton cut another man free. The anchor had fallen overboard bringing the boat up short, and two men were lost. The boat lay at her anchor in heavy seas until daylight with her surviving crew chilled through. Severely limited visibility forced the lifeboat to return to Clacton at 11.30 a.m., and the casualty was dealt with by the Harwich lifeboat.

The Institution gave £250 for the widow and six children under 14 years of age of the 2nd Coxswain James Cross, and £200 to the widow and three children under four years of age of crew member Thomas Cattermole.

Coxswain Legerton received his medal from the Princess of Wales at Marlborough House on 3 March. The Prince of Wales, President of the R.N.L.I., was also present.

HUGHES Rowland, Coxswain, Moelfre Lifeboat **SILVER**

7 February 1884

Awarded to Coxswain Hughes 'who, at the advanced aged of eighty-two years, was retiring from the post after 34 years' service, having assisted to save forty-nine lives'. In that period he served in three successive lifeboats and services to 17 wrecks, among them being incidents involving the brig *Carrs* and the schooner *Emma* (1852), the schooner *Douglas Pennant* (1868), the schooner *John* (1876) and the smack *Frens* (1883).

Coxswain Hughes also received his medal at Marlborough House on 3 March.

TEEL William, Coxswain, Plymouth Lifeboat **SILVER**

3 July 1884

Awarded 'on his retirement from that post after twenty-two years service' during which he had gone out to 13 boats and helped to save 82 lives. Services included those to the galliot *Aremana* (1862), the brigs *Espoir* and *Commerzieweathin Haupt* (1865), the schooner *Teaser* (1867), the brig *Flying Cloud* (1868), the brigantines *Laurel* and *Eliza* and the brig *Fearful* (1872), the ship *John Barbour* (1874), the steam ship *Hankow* and the schooner *Fortuna* (1880), the barque *Baron von Pallant* (1881) and the brig *Elise* (1883).

BOYLE Marcus, Coxswain, Wexford No. 2 Lifeboat **SILVER(2)**

3 July 1884

'In recognition of his good services in saving life from shipwreck during the twenty-six years he was Coxswain'. During this period the following services were prominent among approximately 30 in which more than 160 lives were saved; the smack *Shamrock* and men stranded on the Dogger Bank off Wexford (1866), the barque *Loretto* (1867), the barque *Paquita* (1871), the schooner *Gem* (1873), the brigantine *Emily Raymond* (1875), the smack *Mountain Hare* (1877), s.s. *Montagu* (1878) and yawl *Favourite* (1883).

SCANLAN Maurice, Chief Boatman, H.M. Coastguard, Belderig   **SILVER**

4 December 1884

9 October 1884: The Campbeltown brig *Mary Wilson* was wrecked in Belderig Bay, Co Mayo, Ireland, in a north-north-easterly gale and a very heavy sea. Mr. Scanlan, with three of his men, put off in the Coastguard whale boat and saved three of her crew – they capsized on their return to shore.

WHYTE, Mrs., Farm Labourer's Wife, Aberdour   **SILVER**

4 December 1884

28 October 1884: When the Dundee steamer *William Hope* was wrecked in Aberdour Bay, Fife, in a heavy gale, Mrs. Whyte went to the spot and took hold of a rope thrown to her by one of the crew. She then wound it around herself and, with waves washing around, planted her feet firmly on the beach, and enabled all six men to reach safety.

ARMSTRONG James, Coxswain, Hauxley Lifeboat   **SILVER**

7 May 1885

'In acknowledgement of his gallant services during the past twenty-five years in which period he has assisted to save one hundred and forty-one lives'. The services involved were those to the schooner *Prospect* (1861), the schooner *Little Aggie* (1862), the brig *Theophilus* (1863), the schooner *Tom Cringle* (1865), the schooner *Mary Jane* and the brig *Sundew* (1870), the brig *Osborne* (1871), the steamer *Anglio* (1874), the brig *Warkworth Castle* (1880), the smack *Belle*, s.s. *Amulet*, the brig *Catharine Regina* and the barque *Ross* (1882) and the steamer *Regian* (1884).

DUNCAN David, Coxswain, Montrose Lifeboats   **SILVER**

2 July 1885

Awarded 'on his resigning the post of Coxswain of the Montrose Lifeboat after many years good service'. Coxswain Duncan was Coxswain of the No. 2 lifeboat from 1876 to 1880, then Coxswain of the No. 1 Lifeboat 1880 to 1885.

ROBERTS Richard, Second Coxswain, Llanddulas Lifeboat   **SILVER**

4 February 1886

8 January 1886: The Runcorn flat *Dido* stranded at Penmaen-rhos, near Llanddulas, Denbighshire, in a strong gale and heavy sea. Helped by others, Mr. Roberts waded into the heavy surf and passed ropes by which the two man crew was brought off.

HAYTER John, Coxswain, Brooke Lifeboat   **SILVER**

4 February 1886

'For good service over a period of twenty-six years', since the station had opened in 1860. Prominent in this period were services to the barque *Cassandra* (1871), the brig *Hermoso-Habanero* (1874), the barque *Blanche Marguerite* (1875), the barque *Mignonette* (1876) and the steamer *Castle Craig* (1883).

LAWRENCE James, Coxswain, Selsey Lifeboat SILVER
6 May 1886

On his retirement, 'in acknowledgement of his long and valuable services in saving life from shipwreck'. In the 25 years since the station opened, lives had been saved from the brig *Governor Maclean* (1864), the brig *Sarah Ann* (1867), the schooner *Excel* (1872), the schooner *Henrietta* (1875), the barque *Sueine Meinde* (1878), the schooner *Kyanite* (1881) and the barque *Tranmere* (1883).

CANNON John, Coxswain, Happisburgh Lifeboat SILVER
6 May 1886

On his retirement, 'in acknowledgement of his long and valuable service in saving life from shipwreck'. In this period lives were saved from the schooner *Atalanta* (1868), the brigs *Launceston* and *Arctic Hero* (1871), the sloop *Richard and Elizabeth* (1875), the ketch *Rival* (1880) and the collier *Ludworth* (1881).

ROBERTS Thomas, Coxswain, Holyhead Lifeboat SILVER(2)
6 May 1886

On his retirement, 'in acknowledgement of his long and valuable services at saving life from shipwreck'. After his first award (voted 5 April 1883), the lifeboat *Thomas Fielden* went out on service to the brigantine *Wonder* and the schooner *Dorothy and Mary* (1883), s.s. *Caerleon* and the brig *Ebos* (1884), the brig *James Kenway* and the schooner *Lorn* (1886). In the first and last services the vessels were saved.

BRIMS John, Coxswain, Thurso Lifeboat SILVER
3 June 1886

'In recognition of his long and valuable services in the lifeboat'. His many services included those to the barque *Graces* (1863), the schooners *William Thompson*, *Blossom*, *Elizabeth Miller*, *Matilda Calder* and the brig *Supply* (1869), the brigantine *Mary Holland* and the brig *Eliza* (1872), the barque *Walker Hall* (1876), the vessel *Bella* (1883) and the schooner *Magnet* (1886).

CALLOW William, Coxswain, Castletown, Isle of Man Lifeboat SILVER
3 June 1886

'In recognition of his long and valuable services in the lifeboat', which included those to the lugger *Nimrod* and the schooner *Eliza Ann* (1861), the schooner *Water Lily* (1864), the schooners *Maria* and *Vision* (1868), the barque *Junak* (1877), the brigantine *Eugenie Auguste* (1882) and the schooner *John Perry* (1885).

GILBERT James, Coxswain, Tynemouth Lifeboats. **SILVER**
3 June 1886

'In recognition of his long and valuable services in the lifeboat'. Prominent among these services were those to the brig *Border Chieftain* and the brigantine *Burton* (1865), the brig *Emmanuel Boucher* (1867), the schooner *Viscount Macduff* (18 70), the brigs *British Queen* and *Valient* (1871), the barque *Iron Crown* (1881), and s.s. *Robert Boyd Watson* (1882).

HAMILTON Bernard, Coxswain, Dundalk Lifeboat **SILVER**
3 June 1886

'In recognition of his long and valuable services in the lifeboat'. Prominent services during his period of office were those to the barque *Frederick* (1861), the ship *Rock* (1862), the brigantine *Arion* and the schooner *Delila* (1863), the barque *Julia* (1866), the barque *Princess of Wales* (1873), the brigantine *Ida* (1875), the brigantine *Andover* (1880) and the brigantine *Jean Anderson* (1882).

KAVANAGH Patrick, Coxswain, Carnsore Lifeboat **SILVER**
3 June 1886

'In recognition of his long and valuable services in the lifeboat'. During this period, the significant services included those to the barque *Guyana* (1861), the ship *Blanche Moore* (1867), the brigs *Shields* and *Paquite de Terranova* (1875), the dandy *Fairy* (1878), the barque *Chevereul* (1879) the barque *John A. Harvie* (1880), and the ship *White Star* (1883).

TREVASKIS Edwin, Coxswain, Hayle Lifeboat **SILVER**
3 June 1886

'In recognition of his long and valuable services in the lifeboat'. In the period since the station opened in 1866 the lifeboat had been on services to the brigantine *Nicholas Harvey* (1866), the brig *Lizzie* and the schooner *Vigilant* (1869), the schooner *Bonne Adèle* (1880), the schooner *Constance* (1881), s.s. *Drumhendry* (1882) and the brigantine *Glynn* (1885).

PRINGLE Thomas, Coxswain, North Sunderland Lifeboat **SILVER**
3 June 1886

'In recognition of his long and valuable services in the lifeboat', including those to fishing cobles in 1870, the schooner *Don* (1872), the barque *John George* (1874), the schooner *Cairnduna* (1875), the fishing boat *Gem* (1876), the brig *Alice* (1880) and the schooner *Fergus* (1885).

WARFORD George, Coxswain, Pakefield Lifeboat **SILVER**
3 June 1886

'In recognition of his long and valuable services in the lifeboat'. Prominent among the rescues were those involving the brig *Amicizia* (1867), the brigantine *Douglas* (1868), the schooner *James Cuckow* (1869), the schooner *Levant* (1873), the steamer *Ludworth* (1877), the schooner *Effigo* (1880), the barque *Nimrod* and seven fishing boats (1882).

JONES Edward, Coxswain, Holyhead Lifeboat   **SILVER**

6 January 1887

9 December 1886: In a very heavy sea and a northerly gale among breakers in the south-eastern part of Holyhead Bay, Anglesey, the Liverpool ship *Pegasus*, laden with timber, fired distress signals at 6.30 a.m. She had dragged her anchors and drifted ashore on Treath-y-Gribin. The Holyhead lifeboat *Thomas Fielden* put out under tow by the tug *Challenger*, but soon had to be cast off. With the seas making a clean breach over the wreck, Coxswain Jones managed to position the lifeboat under her quarter deck and took off the 20 crewmen and the Pilot. After landing them, the lifeboat piloted a schooner, *Jane Anwyl*, to safety.

CLARKSON Thomas, Coxswain, Lytham Lifeboat   **SILVER**

20 December 1886

9–10 December 1886: The Hamburg barque *Mexico* was seen in distress in a violent gale and very heavy sea in the Ribble Estuary off Southport, Lancashire. At 10 p.m., the lifeboat *Charles Biggs* launched and, under sail and oars, reached a point to windward then rowed across the banks until, close to the wreck, she dropped anchor and veered alongside. The barque was on her beam ends, her fore and mains masts gone, and her 12 man crew lashed in the mizzen rigging. In spite of being filled and four of her oars broken, the lifeboat managed to land the survivors at 3 a.m. Two other lifeboats, those of Southport and St. Anne's, had launched to the *Mexico*. Both had capsized, 14 out of 16 perished in the Southport boat, and the total crew (13 men) of the St. Anne's boat were lost.

STARR Leonard George, Captain, s.s. *Juno*   **SILVER**
EASTAWAY Thomas, Second Mate, s.s. *Juno*   **SILVER**

9 June 1887

20 May 1887: During a strong north-west gale, the s.s. *George Moore* of Port Glasgow was wrecked on The Smalls, St. George's Channel in the western approaches to Milford Haven, Pembrokeshire. Captain Starr took his vessel as near as possible, then Mr. Eastaway put off in a boat with four of their crew, rescued the Master and his 15 man crew in two trips, and placed them on board the *Juno*, which was on passage from Cork to Bristol.

GEORGE Philip, Coxswain, Caister Lifeboats   **SILVER(2)**

9 June 1887

Awarded 'on the occasion of his having to relinquish his appointment on account of ill-health, for serving twenty-five years and assisting in saving a large number of lives'. Caister lifeboats dealt with nearly 150 casualties during this period and saved nearly 1000 lives, outstanding services were those to s.s. *Ontario* (1864), the ship *Hannah Petersen* (1869), the ship *China* (1875), the barque *Angostura* (1881), the barque *Canmore* (1882), and s.s. *Bedale* (1885).

McPHILLIPS Patrick, Sergeant, Royal Irish Constabulary　　　**SILVER**

1 September 1887

19 July 1887: A man suffering from delirium tremens was seen to be alone in a punt without sail or thole pins and was drifting on to a ledge of rocks off Aranmore Island, on the coast of Co Donegal, Ireland. With two other men, Sergeant McPhillips put out in a boat and rescued him.

BICKERSTAFFE Robert, Coxswain, Blackpool Lifeboat　　　**SILVER(2)**

4 August 1887

Awarded to Coxswain Bickerstaffe 'who had been compelled by ill-health to resign the office of Coxswain', which he had held since the establishment of the station in 1864. Prominent services were rendered to the brig *St. Michael* (1864), the barque *Susan L. Campbell* (1867), the schooner *Theodorus* (1868), the paddle steamship *Columbus* (1880) and the barque *Arethusa* (1881). He received his first medal for the service to the schooner *Bessie Jones* in 1880.

HORSFORD Maria, Miss　　　**SILVER**
HORSFORD Josephine, Miss　　　**SILVER**
SULLIVAN William C.L., Gentleman　　　**SILVER**

3 November 1887

12 August 1887: A sailing boat containing two ladies and two gentlemen capsized in Courtmacsherry Bay, Co Cork, Ireland. The Misses Horsford and Mr. Sullivan went out and rescued all four victims in spite of the smallness of their own boat.

BRADLEY William, Lightkeeper, Southend Pierhead　　　**SILVER**

1 December 1887

2 November 1887: During a strong breeze and rain in a moderate sea, the boat of the steam tug *Jubilee* capsized at Southend, Essex, at 11 p.m., and Mr. Bradley was called from his bed. Without waiting to dress, he lowered his boat, rowed to the victim who was clinging to the upturned boat and rescued him – all before midnight.

RIMMER Thomas, Coxswain, St. Anne's Lifeboat　　　**SILVER**

1 March 1888

26 January 1888: The Liverpool barque *Albert William*, bound from Talcahuano, Chile, to Fleetwood with a cargo of grain, was seen on the Horse Bank, off St. Anne's, Lancashire, in a gale. The St. Anne's lifeboat *Nora Royds* was launched. Despite repeatedly being filled by the heavy seas, the ten man crew of the barque was rescued. The medal was also awarded in recognition of 'his long and gallant services'.

BROWN John, Coxswain, Newbiggin Lifeboat   SILVER(2)

1 March 1888

Awarded to Coxswain Brown 'who has completed thirty-five years' service and has rendered many gallant services in the boats'. Since his last award in 1881, he assisted in the service to s.s. *Acaster* in 1886 and saved 19. Over the years, many fishing vessels were helped when the weather deteriorated after they had left port.

HAYTER John, Coxswain, Brooke Lifeboat   SILVER(2)

COTTON David, Crew Member, Brighstone Grange Lifeboat   SILVER

COTTON William, Crew Member, Brighstone Grange Lifeboat   SILVER

SALTER Frank, Crew Member, Brighstone Grange Lifeboat   SILVER

19 March 1888

9–10 March 1888: With a cargo of wheat and the Master, his wife, three children, a female servant and a crew of 26 men on board, the Glasgow ship *Sirenia*, bound from San Francisco for Dunkirk, stranded on the Atherfield Ledge off the Isle of Wight during a thick fog. The Brighstone lifeboat *Worcester Cadet* launched, took off and landed the Master's wife, three children, the female servant and an apprentice at Atherfield. She launched again in a very heavy sea , reached the wreck at low water, and took off 13 men, but was capsized by a huge breaker. The lifeboat righted, but lost two of her crew and two of the ship's crew. After landing the survivors at 2.30 a.m., she launched again at 12 noon to take off the remaining 13 men. Both Cottons and 16 year old Salter went off in all the launches. The Brooke lifeboat *William Stanley Lewis* had also launched but was struck by a heavy breaker which washed three of her crew overboard, one drowned; still she made persistent efforts to go alongside but, with several oars broken and her crew exhausted, the lifeboat was forced to return to the shore.

WALLACE William, Assistant Lightkeeper, Point of Ayre Lighthouse   SILVER

WALLACE, Mrs   SILVER

BLYTH Ellen, Miss   SILVER

CHRISTIAN T.A., Temporary Assistant Lightkeeper   SILVER

12 April 1888

11 March 1888: During a strong easterly gale and heavy seas, the Barrow schooner *Burns and Bessie* stranded under the Point of Ayre lighthouse, Isle of Man, Mr. Wallace, his wife, Miss Blythe (the Head Keeper's daughter) and Mr. Christian, using lines, saved the crew of four men.

MATTHEWS Edwin, Coxswain, Lizard Lifeboats   SILVER

12 April 1888

'In recognition of his long and gallant services as Coxswain'. During the 29 years that the station had operated 100 lives had been saved and the prominent services were to the schooner *Hurrell* (1861), the schooner *Selina* (1868), the barque *Formalhaut* (1873), the brig *Scotscraig* (1879), s.s. *Mosel* (1882), s.s. *Suffolk* (1886), the schooner *Gypsy Queen* (1887) and the barque *Lady Dufferin* (1888).

KELLY George Edward, Mariner   **SILVER**

14 June 1888

23 April 1888: Voted 'in recognition of his gallant and skilful services in rescuing four men from the sailing boat *Alice* of Castletown, Isle of Man, which capsized off that port during a strong easterly breeze and moderate sea'. The Thanks of the Institution on Vellum were awarded to the two men who assisted Mr. Kelly in the rescue.

NILES William, Coxswain, Cardigan Lifeboat   **SILVER**

12 July 1888

'In recognition of his long and faithful services as Coxswain' during which Mr. Niles helped save 53 lives from various wrecks. The vessels included the smacks *Oliver Lloyd*, *Turtle Dove* and *Coronation* (1867), the schooner *Dollart* (1873), the schooner *Johanna Antoinette* (1875), the brig *Wellington* (1882), the brigantine *Unda* (1884) and the fishing boat *President* (1886).

DINNEEN John, Chief Officer, s.s. *Albatross*   **SILVER**

14 March 1889

5 November 1888: After the Barrow schooner *Isabella Hall* stranded on Tongue Sand off Barrow-in-Furness, in a heavy sea, Mr. Dinneen put off from his ship in a boat, with four others, and saved four of the schooner's crew from the rigging. He was also awarded the Albert Medal 2nd Class for this service. The four men each received £1.10s.

WILLIAMS John O., Chief Officer, H.M. Coastguard, Holyhead. Honorary Secretary, Holyhead R.N.L.I.   **SILVER**

8 November 1888

'In acknowledgement of his valuable services for many years in the New Brighton, Milford and Fishguard lifeboats, in addition to assisting in other ways to save life from shipwreck'.
  He was Honorary Secretary at Holyhead from 1887 to 1890.

SUTCLIFFE Thomas, Sergeant, Royal Irish Constabulary   **SILVER**

14 February 1889

21 December 1888: The Belfast barque *Etta* stranded in Credan Bay, Co Waterford, Ireland. Sergeant Sutcliffe descended a cliff at great risk and rescued 12 of her crew and the Master's wife.

JONES Edward, Coxswain, Holyhead Lifeboat	**SILVER(2)**
JONES Robert, Assistant Coxswain, Holyhead Lifeboat	**SILVER**

14 March 1889

9 February 1889: After the Halifax, Nova Scotia barque *Glen Grant*, from Pensacola, Florida, parted from her cable in a gale while anchored in the New Harbour, Holyhead, Anglesey, she was seen among the rocks off Penrhos. Her 13 man crew was taken off by a line put aboard by rocket apparatus. The Holyhead lifeboat helped at the scene.

The medals were also awarded 'in recognition of their gallant services in the lifeboat, extending over many years'.

CURNOW Paul, Coxswain, St. Ives Lifeboat   **SILVER(2)**

11 April 1889

Awarded to Coxswain Curnow 'who had resigned the post of Coxswain which he had held for twenty years, having previously been Second Coxswain for six and a half years'. In that time, the boat had saved 52 lives from different wrecks. Services in the period were given to the brigantine *Queen* (1871), the schooners *Rambler* and *Mary Ann*, the brig *Francis* (1873), the schooner *Jane Smith* (1880) and the schooner *Rosa Josephs* (1881).

TREVASKIS Edwin, Coxswain, Hayle Lifeboat   **SILVER(2)**

9 May 1889

Awarded to Coxswain Trevaskis 'who had resigned the post of Coxswain of the lifeboat which he had held for twenty-four years. During that period lifeboats at the station had saved fifty-one lives from different wrecks'. The services involved were to the brigantine *Nicholas Harvey* (1866), the brig *Lizzie* and the schooner *Vigilant* (1869), the schooner *Bonne Adele* (1880), the schooner *Constance* (1881), s.s. *Drumhendry* and the schooner *Star of St Agnes* (1882), the brigantine *Glynn* (1885) and the brig *Albert Wilhelm* (1886).

WILLIAMS John O., Chief Officer, H.M. Coastguard Holyhead	
Honorary Secretary, Holyhead R.N.L.I.	**SILVER(2)**
OWEN William, Pilot	**SILVER**
JONES George, Boatman	**SILVER**
ROBERTS John, Farmer and Fisherman	**SILVER**
MORRIS John, Farmer	**SILVER**

9 January 1890

17 December 1889: The Liverpool barque *Tenby Castle* was wrecked in Caernarvon Bay on rocks off Penrhos Point, south of South Stack, Holyhead, beneath cliffs 150 feet high. There was a strong south-westerly breeze and a heavy sea that night. William Owen and George Jones put off three times in a boat and, at great risk, rescued, on the second occasion, three of the barque's crew. John Roberts and John Morris went out in the boat twice and helped save lives. Mr. Williams went in the boat on her final launch to attempt to save others, without success. The Holyhead lifeboat launched, but, by the time she reached the scene, the wreck was completely submerged. Eleven men of the *Tenby Castle* crew were lost.

BROWN Thomas, Coxswain, Cresswell Lifeboat   **SILVER(2)**

13 February 1890

Awarded to Coxswain Brown on his resignation as Coxswain, a post he had held for 15 years since the station was established. In that period the lifeboat had saved 33 lives from various wrecks. Services included those to the s.s. *Gustaf* (1876), the brig *Swift* (1882) and the schooner *Swift* (1886). Prior to the establishment of the station, Thomas Brown (Big Tom) had been prominent in saving life and had been awarded the silver medal on 3 January 1861 for a shore boat rescue from the schooner *Julius* on 23 November 1860.

WHARRIER William, Engineer, Ramsgate Steam Tugs   **SILVER(3)**

13 February 1890

Awarded to William Wharrier on his retirement 'who had held the position 44 years and during that period had been in charge of the engines on all occasions when the tugs had been out with the lifeboat'.

HUTCHINSON Henry, Fisherman   **SILVER**

8 May 1890

7 April 1890: A sudden northerly gale blew up as Mr. Hutchinson was returning to harbour at Bridlington Quay, Yorkshire in his coble. On his way, he picked up a rowing boat, took the six occupants aboard and towed their boat behind. Two other rowing boats capsized in the sudden squall and, noticing this, he lowered his sail, jumped into the boat that he was towing, and rescued them. With the eight rescued men on board, his coble returned to harbour in difficult conditions.

PERRY Frank   **SILVER**
CARTER Frederick   **SILVER**

12 June 1890

26 May 1890: In a strong easterly breeze and heavy surf, a boat capsized in Weymouth Bay, Dorset, and two men were thrown out. This was seen by two lads, Frank Perry, aged 16, and Frederick Carter, aged 11, who were in another boat in smooth water. They rowed into the broken water and saved one of the men.

POUNDER Thomas, Pilot   **SILVER**
METCALFE James, Pilot's Assistant   **SILVER**

7 August 1890

26 May 1890: A boat capsized in a strong north-north-easterly breeze and a rough sea near Longscarr Rocks off Hartlepool, Co Durham, throwing its two occupants into the water. Mr. Pounder and Mr. Metcalfe saved both lives.

DOUGLAS James (Junior)   **SILVER**

10 July 1890

25 June 1890: A boat capsized at Harrington, Cumberland, in a strong westerly gale, thick weather and a rough sea. Mr. Douglas swam out to assist and saved one of the occupants; the other was drowned while trying to reach the shore.

FERNIE Peter, Fisherman   **SILVER**
RIACH William, Fisherman   **SILVER**

11 December 1890

26 October 1890: The German smack *Industrie* was stranded near Cluny Harbour, Buckie, Banff, in a strong north-north-easterly gale. During the night Messrs. Fernie and Riach and five other men waded into the very rough sea and brought the smack's three man crew ashore.

ABBOTT Sidney, Fisherman   **SILVER**
HODGE Robert, Fisherman   **SILVER**

13 November 1890

5 November 1890: In a north-north-easterly gale and heavy seas, a boat capsized off Clovelly, Devon. Messrs. Gilbert and Hodge put off in a small boat and, after a tremendous struggle, rowing and bailing, they picked up the two exhausted men from the boat.

PRESTON William M., Treasurer and Honorary Secretary, Anglesey R.N.L.I.   **SILVER**
*ROBERTS Robert, Coxswain, Penmon Lifeboat   **SILVER**

13 November 1890
*11 December 1890

7 November 1890: Awarded to Mr. Preston 'in acknowledgement of his general gallant services in saving life from shipwreck' and to Mr. Roberts 'in recognition of his long and good services in the lifeboat extending over a period of thirty-four years'.

Both awards were made particularly for the help given to the wreck of the Plymouth schooner *Undaunted* on the Dutchman's Bank, near Penmaenmawr. The Penmon self-righting lifeboat *Christopher Brown,* already at sea, having launched on an earlier service, made for the schooner through mountainous, confused seas in shoal water. She took off five men from the schooner in spite of the mass of broken water around her. On her way back, the lifeboat was struck by an exceptionally heavy wave and capsized. Her mast struck the sand and broke off. When she righted, her crew and the rescued men got back in, but were helpless without their gear and oars. The lifeboat was swept on to the Lavan Sands in Conway Bay, half keeled over in the surf. With the anchor laid out, they made their way across the sands to Aber and thence by road to Penmon. Next day they were able to recover their boat. Mr. Preston was present in the lifeboat during this service.

JONES John, Quarryman	**SILVER**
*ROBERTS David, Mason	**SILVER**
ROBERTS John, Quarryman	**SILVER**
WILLIAMS Hugh, Labourer	**SILVER**
WILLIAMS William, Quarryman	**SILVER**
WILLIAMS William, Grocer	**SILVER**

13 November 1890

*11 December 1890

7 November 1890: In a north-westerly gale and mountainous seas, the Padstow schooner *Ocean Queen* was wrecked on rocks below the quarries at Penmaen Head, Llandulas, Denbighshire. She was first seen labouring heavily with her top-sails flying in shreds, completely out of control. After she went ashore with seas breaking clean over her, her crew of four men took to her rigging. It was not possible to launch the Llandulas lifeboat, probably because most of the local populace were at the scene of the wreck. As the Llandudno lifeboat was out on another service, some quarrymen managed to obtain a small boat, which they carried to a point opposite the wreck. Seven attempts to launch her through the vicious surf were unsuccessful, but the eighth brought success and all the crew were taken off. In the course of the successive attempts, the boat's crew was changed frequently.

FOGG James, Captain, Fishing Smack *Osprey*	**SILVER**
WILKINSON George, Seaman, Fishing Smack *Osprey*	**SILVER**

11 December 1890

7 November 1890: In a strong north-north-westerly gale and a heavy sea, the Wigton schooner *Jean Campbell* was seen to be in distress in Morecambe Bay, Lancashire. The *Osprey* was returning home having lost her jib and mainsail, but Captain Fogg took her as close to the schooner as possible. Mr. Wilkinson then put off with two others in a small punt and succeeded in taking off the schooner's three man crew. During her return, the punt was swamped. and Mr. Wilkinson was saved by Captain Fogg and his boy cook, the only ones still on board the smack. The other five men in the punt were lost.

KERR Edward Christian, Esq., Honorary Secretary, Ramsey R.N.L.I.	**SILVER**
GARRETT Robert, Coxswain, Ramsey Lifeboat	**SILVER**

13 November 1890

7 November 1890: A violent northerly gale together with a rough cross sea and heavy rain squalls put the steam dredger *Walter Bibby*, riding at anchor a mile and half south of Ramsey Harbour, Isle of Man, in serious danger. The Ramsey self-righting lifeboat *Two Sisters* launched and, despite violent gusts of wind and the rolling of the dredger, took off the 15 men on board and, as the boat was unable to regain her station, landed them south of Ramsey.

11 November 1890: The *Two Sisters* launched again in a gale with thick, very cold weather and rain, but, while being hauled off by warp, an immense wave caused damage. One of her crew was washed out, but he was saved by two of his comrades. Stern to the wind, the lifeboat rode on the warp until daylight. The Belfast vessel *Margaret*, Runcorn to Belfast with bricks and tiles, was seen a mile to the north and, by 8 a.m., her three man crew had been taken off and landed safely.

These awards were voted 'in acknowledgement of Messrs. Kerr and Garrett's gallant services in the boat' especially on the two occasions described here.

HUGHES John, Coxswain, Bull Bay Lifeboat   **SILVER**

11 December 1890

Awarded to John Hughes 'on resigning the post of Coxswain which he had filled for twenty-three years. During that period he had assisted in the lifeboat to save forty-two lives'. He was the first Coxswain at this station, appointed in 1868, and services included those to the schooner *Albion* (1871), boat of schooner *George IV* (1873), the schooner *Baltic* (1874), s.s. *Dakota* (1877), s.s. *Arabian* (18 79), the schooners *Pacific* and *Ocean Belle* (1886), and the barque *President Harbitz* (1889).

WRIGHT Robert, Coxswain, Fleetwood Lifeboats   **SILVER**

11 December 1890

Awarded to Coxswain Wright 'who had held that office twelve years and had been connected with the service, having been formerly one of the crew, more than thirty years'. During his period as Coxswain, services were given to the barque *Charles Challoner* (1878), the schooner *Elizabeth Ellen Fisher* (1879), the barque *Venus* (1882), s.s. *Eden* and the barque *Jenny* (1883), the barque *Blackwall* (1884), the sloop *Pennington* and the barquentine *Ruth Topping* (1886) and the barques *Labora* and *New Brunswick* (1890).

SMALLRIDGE James Harvey, Coxswain, Braunton Lifeboat   **SILVER(2)**

8 January 1891

Awarded to Coxswain Smallridge on his retirement after 32 years in charge, a period which included services to the brig *North Eske* (1859), the ship *Louisa* (1863), the brig *Ruth* (1867), the brigantine *Nigretta* (1871), the schooner *Caroline* (1874), the vessel *Chalciope* (1884) and the ship *Penthesilea* (1890).

CALLOW William, Coxswain, Castletown Lifeboat   **SILVER(2)**

12 February 1891

For 'good services during the long period in which he had served as Coxswain'. Since Coxswain Callow's previous service award in 1886, he had participated in rescues involving the trawler *Swift* and the schooner *Julia* (1886) and the schooner *Madryn* (1889).

WATT Frederick, Master Mariner   **SILVER**
HOPKINS John, Coxswain, Portrush Lifeboat   **SILVER**

12 March 1891

2–4 March 1891: On 28 February the Beaumaris schooner *Ellen Myvanwy*, bound from Runcorn for Ramelton, Co Donegal, with a cargo of salt, anchored in Skerries Roads, off Portrush, Co Antrim, northern Ireland, but, two days later, showed signs of distress as a north-west gale set in with a very heavy sea. The Portrush self-righting lifeboat *Robert and Agnes Blair* put out but, unable to reach her, returned to the shore. Next day, all attempts to relaunch the lifeboat failed, but, after sustained efforts, they succeeded on 4 March about 4 p.m. Then, under sail, they took off the schooner's three man crew and delivered them safely to the shore. Account was also taken of other services over a long period.

McALLISTER William, Carpenter   **SILVER**

9 April 1891

2 March 1891: Launching on service to the schooner *Ellen Myvanwy*, two lifeboatmen were washed overboard from the Portrush, Co Antrim lifeboat *Robert and Agnes Blair*. Mr. McAllister swam out through the heavy surf and rescued one of the men. The other man was also saved, whilst the lifeboat rescued three crew of the schooner.

STOUT Benjamin, Coxswain, Longhope Lifeboat   **SILVER**

9 July 1891

3 March 1891: The Sunderland s.s. *Victoria* (1960 tons), Hamburg to New York, was seen in distress in the Pentland Firth, five miles north of Dunnet Head. A heavy north-west gale was blowing with a tremendous sea and snow showers, but the Longhope self-righting lifeboat *Dickinson Edleston* launched at 4.30 p.m. She found the steam ship sinking, her fires extinguished, and took off the crew of 22 men, 11 of them German. They were landed at Widewell, South Ronaldsay, but the tremendous sea and adverse tide prevented the lifeboat from regaining Longhope on Hoy, therefore she was compelled to remain in Widewell Bay and only reached her station at 1.30 p.m. on the 5th.

THOMPSON Ralph, Coxswain, Sunderland No. 1 Lifeboat   **SILVER**

12 March 1891

'In acknowledgement of his services as Coxswain for twenty-six years, in which period the boat saved twenty-three lives'. Prominent services in that period included those to the steamer *Altona* (1875), and the schooner *Langdale* (1886).

GOURLAY James Grieve, Fisherman   **SILVER**

9 April 1891

5 April 1891: The Drammen schooner *Francis* became a total wreck in a very rough sea and heavy easterly gale in St. Andrews Bay, Fife. There were six men aboard. The Boarhills private lifeboat *John and James Mills* launched with a crew of 12 men, Mr. Gourlay in command, and took all of the schooner's crew to safety.

BOYD John, Seaman   **SILVER**
PATTON David, Fisherman   **SILVER**

14 May 1891

8 May 1891: While proceeding to a smack lying in Portrush Harbour, Co Antrim, northern Ireland, a boy was thrown out of his boat after running into another vessel's warp. This was seen by Mr. Boyd, who was on board a vessel about 100 yards away. Still wearing his clothes and heavy sea boots, he jumped in and swam to the boy, while Mr. Patton, who was twice as far away on shore, ran to the quay, threw off his coat and jumped in. Both men supported the boy until a boat from the shore reached them.

LEGERTON Samuel James Robert, Coxswain, Clacton Lifeboat   **SILVER(3)**

14 May 1891

Awarded to Coxswain Legerton who 'had resigned the post of Coxswain … He had held the office since the establishment of the station, about thirteen years ago, and assisted in saving many lives from shipwreck'. He had helped to save 169 lives and 13 vessels. These services included those to the ship *Hebe* (1879), the lugger *Madelaine* (1881) for which he received his first medal, the barque *Rome* (1883), the barge *Jesse* (1884) for which he received his second medal, the barque *Garland* (1885) and the steamer *Blonde* (1888).

COLLINS James, Coxswain, Rye Lifeboat   **SILVER**

14 May 1891

'In acknowledgement of his gallant services in the boat, in assistance to save forty-five lives during the past twelve years'. Included among the services were those to the French chassemarée *St. Anne* (1881), s.s. *Matin* (1882) and the fishing smack *Maid of Kent* (1885).

COX Joseph (Junior), Coxswain, Appledore Lifeboats   **SILVER(2)**

6 August 1891

Awarded to Coxswain Cox 'who had been Coxswain … for twenty-three years. He had previously served as Second Coxswain for thirteen years and as a member of the crew for six years. During the period he had served as Coxswain, the lifeboat had been launched twenty-one times on service and saved fifty lives'. The services included those to the schooners *Express*, *Annie Brooks* and *Mary Ann* and the brigantine *Spec* (1873), the brigantine *Waterloo* and the schooner *Heroine* (1878) and the smack *Mary Stevens* (1882).

FISH Charles Edward, Coxswain, Ramsgate Lifeboat   **GOLD(2)**

8 October 1891

A service award 'on his retirement through ill-health, from the post of Coxswain … He had been out in the lifeboats belonging to that station three hundred and fifty-three times during the past twenty-six years and had thus helped to save eight hundred and seventy-seven lives from different shipwrecks'. This was the first gold clasp to be awarded. Appointed Second Coxswain in 1866 and Coxswain in 1870 his previous gold medal was awarded for the *Indian Chief* service in 1881 and, in the subsequent period, major services included those to the ships *Attila* and *Ganges* (1881), the barque *Egmont* (1882), the barque *Georgia*, the ship *Wilhelmina* and s.s. *Boadicea* (1883), s.s. *Skandinavian* (1884), the barque *Rhuddlan Castle* (1885) and the barque *Frederike Carolina* (1886).

WOODS Edgar West, Coxswain, Gorleston No. 1 Lifeboat   **SILVER**

12 November 1891

13 October 1891: During a severe southerly gale with a very heavy sea the Portsmouth ketch *Ada*, coal-laden from Portsmouth to Seaham, was seen to be lying at anchor on Scroby Sand, off Gorleston, Suffolk. She had struck twice and was leaking badly; her Master burned everything possible as a signal. Mr. Woods, with two Pilots on board for advice, put out in the self-righting lifeboat *Mark Lane* and, under double-reefed storm sails, with difficulty, found the wreck, took off four men and landed them at 3.45 p.m. When the weather moderated later the lifeboat was used to take the ketch into Yarmouth harbour.

LUCAS James, Coxswain, Dungeness (Lydd) Lifeboat   **SILVER**

25 November 1891

11 November 1891: Hurricane force winds were lashing the coast when the Swedish brigantine *Aeolus* was driven on to a sandbank off Littlestone, Kent. In spite of many attempts, it was not immediately possible to launch the Dungeness self-righting lifeboat *R.A.O.B.* in the difficult conditions. After sustained efforts with the rocket apparatus, a line was fired on board but this broke. At the third attempt, the lifeboat was launched and was rowed to the wreck in terrifying conditions with Mr. Lucas in command. The force of the wind prevented the lifeboat coming alongside and she was blown a mile past when a heavy sea capsized her. Of the five crew thrown out, two were lost. After she made the shore, the lifeboat was pulled on to the beach by helpers. Survivors were later taken from the wreck by the Littlestone lifeboat which also had very great difficulty in launching.

HENNESSY Lawrence, Boatman, H.M. Coastguard, Hythe
    Coxswain, Hythe Lifeboat   **SILVER**
SADLER Albert, Commissioned Boatman, H.M. Coastguard, Sandgate
    Assistant Coxswain, Hythe Lifeboat   **SILVER**

25 November 1891

11 November 1891: The 2,033 ton Glasgow vessel *Benvenue*, outward bound for Sydney, Australia, was moving down the English Channel under tow, when the wind increased to hurricane force as she was off Folkestone, Kent. The tow parted at 5.30 a.m. and she was swept toward the

shore. She dropped her anchors just off Sandgate but, with seas breaching over her, she began to sink and her crew took to the rigging. The self-righting Hythe lifeboat *Mayer de Rothschild* was launched at Sandgate, but was driven back by the wind and a blinding blizzard. Attempts to put a line on board the casualty were made using rocket apparatus, but these failed. Hythe lifeboat was then launched from a point near the Coastguard houses at Hythe and set sail for Sandgate, but a huge wave turned her completely over and, when she righted, one man was missing. An unsuccessful attempt to leave harbour was made by the Dover lifeboat, but then, in the early evening, another attempt was made by the Hythe boat with a fresh crew of local fishermen as well as Messrs. Hennessey and Sadler, who had been in the original launch. With considerable difficulty the lifeboat went alongside the wreck and 27 survivors were taken off and landed at Folkestone soon after 10 p.m. Mr. Hennessy also received the Albert Medal, Second Class.

HENNESSY Lawrence, Boatman, H.M. Coastguard, Hythe
    Coxswain, Hythe Lifeboat   **SILVER(2)**
10 December 1891

11 November 1891: The schooner *Eider* stranded at 4.15 a.m. at Sandgate, Kent, in a whole gale from the south-south-east and a very heavy sea. By means of lines, Mr Hennessy, unaided, rescued four of the crew. Although this service took place before the *Benvenue* (see above) the second medal was awarded at the later date.
   It is also exceptional that separate awards were made for two services on the same day.

CABLE James, Coxswain, Aldeburgh Lifeboat   **SILVER**
MANN William, Assistant Coxswain, Aldeburgh Lifeboat   **SILVER**
10 December 1891

11 November 1891: 'In recognition of their several gallant services in the lifeboat' particularly on the occasion that the Norwegian barque *Winnifred* of Laurvig was seen running north in a south-south-westerly gale and a very heavy sea, with her main and mizzen masts gone and flying a distress signal. The self-righting lifeboat *Aldeburgh* was launched at 1.50 p.m., but the barque ran on to one of the sandbanks in Aldeburgh Bay, Suffolk, before she could be reached. With heavy seas sweeping over her, she was filling rapidly, when Mr. Cable went close enough to rescue the crew of 16 and a Pilot. Some of the crew were hauled through the water into the lifeboat, and the remainder were snatched off the jib boom. Assisted by Mr. Mann, the survivors were landed at 4.30 p.m.

TAYLOR William Henry, Labourer   **SILVER**
STANDING Edward, Labourer   **SILVER**
10 December 1891

11 November 1891: In a very heavy sea and a southerly gale, a Deal lugger was driven ashore between Littlestone and St. Mary's, Kent, Coastguard stations. Messrs. Taylor and Standing entered the water and saved two of the lugger's crew. On emerging from the water, both were greatly exhausted and had to be treated like those they had rescued.

LEE Charles, Coxswain, Worthing Lifeboat   **SILVER**

10 December 1891

11 November 1891: While a whole gale was blowing from the south-south-west, two vessels were seen, and, as it was evident that they would be driven ashore, the lifeboat *Henry Harris* launched at 9,45 a.m. Seven men were saved from the schooner *Kong Karl* of Khristiania en route from Liverpool with a cargo of coke, which had stranded half a mile west from Lancing. After landing these men, the lifeboat again launched and, in worsening weather, brought ashore seven of the crew of the barque *Capella* of Hamburg. Five other men from this vessel had landed in their own boat.

KAVANAGH Patrick, Coxswain, Carnsore Lifeboat   **SILVER(2)**

12 November 1891

Awarded to Coxswain Kavanagh 'who had been Coxswain of the lifeboat for thirty years. During that period he had assisted in the lifeboats on that station to save one hundred and thirty lives, having been out twenty-nine times on service'. After his 1886 award, the lifeboat went out on service to the barque *Samanco* (1886) and the smack *Rose* (1890).

ABBOTT John, Boatman, H.M. Coastguard, West Wemyss   **SILVER**
WEBB Edwin, Boatman, H.M. Coastguard, West Wemyss   **SILVER**

14 January 1892

13 November 1891: A moderate east-south-easterly gale was blowing, when the Stavanger schooner *Faavaret* stranded near West Wemyss, Fife. The two coastguardmen swam out in the heavy sea and rescued her crew of six men.

WOODGATE James, Coxswain, Dover Lifeboat   **SILVER**

10 December 1891

'In consideration of his valuable services during the twenty-one years he had occupied that position (Coxswain). During that period Coxswain Woodgate had been out in the boat sixteen times on service and assisted to save twenty-four lives'. Prominent among the services were those to the sloop *Edith* (1876), the barque *Chin Chin* (1881), the ship *Macduff* (1886) and the *Government Dredger No. 18* (1891).

WATSON Thomas James, Captain, Smack *Britain's Pride*   **SILVER**
BURTON William, Crew Member, Smack *Britain's Pride*   **SILVER**
HURLE Edwin, Crew Member, Smack *Britain's Pride*   **SILVER**
FISHER Arthur Edward, Crew Member, Smack *Britain's Pride*   **SILVER**

14 January 1892

12 December 1891: In a very heavy sea during a strong northerly gale, the Glasgow ship *Enterkin* was wrecked on Galloper Sands, off Harwich, Essex. Captain Watson and his crew were able to save an apprentice from the wreck.

FOREMAN William, Coxswain, Broadstairs Lifeboat   **SILVER**

14 January 1892

'In acknowledgement of his good services in saving life from shipwreck'. Prominent among the services were those to the ship *Frank Shaw* (1869), the barques *Anna* and *Fleetwing* (1875), the sloop *Pallas* and the schooner *Gleaner* (1877), the schooner *Star of the West* (1878), the schooner *Ocean Queen* (1879), the ship *Wilhelmina* (1883), the barque *Jane Kilgour* (1889) and the brigantine *Glance* (1891).

PAGE Alfred, Master, Ramsgate Harbour Steam Tugs   **SILVER(2)**

14 January 1892

Awarded to Captain Page, 'who has been Master ... since the 1st of April 1874 and has towed the Ramsgate lifeboat on every occasion of service since then'. Among his many services, were those to the barque *Bucephalus* (1875), the barque *Atlantic* (1876), the ships *Indian Chief* and *Ganges* (1881), the barque *Egmont* (1882), the barque *Georgia* and s.s. *Boadicea* (1883), the barque *Rhuddlan Castle* (1885), the barque *Frederike Caroline* (1886) and the fishing lugger *Verbena* (1889).

COTTON James, Coxswain, Brighstone Lifeboat   **SILVER**
COTTON William, Coxswain, Atherfield Lifeboat   **SILVER(2)**
HAYTER John, Coxswain, Brooke Lifeboat   **SILVER(3)**

11 February 1892

31 January–2 February 1892: On the night of Sunday 31st January, the four-masted s.s. *Eider*, of Bremen, 4,719 tons register, bound from New York for Southampton, en route for Bremen, stranded on the reef of rocks known as Atherfield Ledge in a thick fog, stormy weather, and a very rough sea. She fired signal rockets, and at about 11 o'clock the self-righting Atherfield lifeboat *Catherine Swift* was launched, proceeded to her, and at the request of the Master brought ashore telegrams for steam tugs. At daylight, the vessel again signalled, the lifeboat went to her, and found that the Master desired to land some of the mails which were therefore brought ashore. Meanwhile, intelligence of the stranding of the steamer had been sent to the neighbouring lifeboat stations at Brighstone and Brooke, and the lifeboats *Worcester Cadet* and *William Slaney Lewis* arrived as quickly as possible on the scene. The Master of the *Eider* ultimately decided that it would be best to land the passengers, and during the day the lifeboats made altogether eighteen trips to the ship, and safely landed two hundred and thirty three persons, specie and mails at Atherfield, where all the boats were afterwards drawn up for the night.

The next day, eleven journeys were performed by the lifeboats, and one hundrd and forty-six people were brought safely ashore, together with mails and specie, while on the two succeeding days, bars of silver, specie, the ship's plate, and passengers luggage were saved. Forty-one journeys in all were made by the gallant lifeboat crews, and three hundred and seventy nine persons were rescued by them. The Master and some of the crew remained on board the vessel, and on the 29 March, she was successfully towed off the rocks. On the following day the s.s. *Eider* was safely berthed in Southampton docks.

HICKS David, Coxswain, St. David's Lifeboat **SILVER**

11 February 1892

'In recognition of his gallant services during the time he occupied the office of Coxswain'. David Hicks was the first Coxswain and was in post for twenty-three years during which services were given to the flat *Chester* and the smacks *Prima* and *Anne Davies* (1870), the schooner *Amity* (1875), the brigantine *Mystic Tie* (1877), and the barque *Storjohann* (1882).

GARTSIDE-TIPPING Henry Thomas, Lieutenant, R.N.
    District Inspector of Lifeboats **SILVER**

12 May 1892

Awarded in 'high appreciation of his zealous and efficient services … in acknowledgement of the risk of life he frequently incurred in the Life-boat service'. Lieutenant Gartside-Tipping had filled the post of Inspector of the Irish District for 13 years and had resigned in consequence of private affairs.

He invented the Tipping's plates, named after him. These plates enabled a heavy lifeboat to be transported on her carriage over deep and soft sand. The plates were subsequently adapted to the needs of the artillery. At the outbreak of the 1914–1918 war, and at the age of 66, he volunteered for service in the navy. He was killed in action on 25 September 1915 whilst in command of the armoured yacht Sanda.

McKINSTRY John **SILVER**

8 September 1892

19 July 1892: In a rough sea during a period of squally weather from the north, a ferry boat plying between Larne Harbour and Island Magee, Co Antrim, northern Ireland, capsized about 200 yards from the Island Magee landing area. John McKinstry, aged 14, put off in a boat and saved three of the four people.

KENNEDY Malcolm, Captain, Fishing Skiff *Jessie* **SILVER**

8 December 1892

10 October 1892: The Port Ellen, Islay, fishing boat *Oag Van* was wrecked on the rocks at Rhugarton-taig, Islay, Inner Hebrides, in a moderate north-north-west gale and a heavy sea. Her three man crew was saved by Captain Kennedy and his men.

HAYTER John, Coxswain, Brooke Lifeboat **SILVER(4)**

10 November 1892

Awarded 'on his resignation of the post of Coxswain which he held for thirty-two years. During that period Coxswain Hayter had been out in the lifeboats on that station twenty-eight times on service and assisted to save two hundred and twenty-two lives'.

POTTER William, Coxswain, Cahore Lifeboat   **SILVER**

10 November 1892

'In recognition of the good services performed by him during the twenty-five years he had held that office. He had been out on the lifeboats on that station thirty-one times on service and saved forty-seven lives'. During that period services were given to the ship *R.H. Tucker* and the schooner *Vivid* (1868), the schooner *Handy* (1871), the barque *Edwin Basset* (1873), the barque *Nanta* (1877), the brigantine *Zephyr* (1888) and the schooner *Jewess* (1891).

SPINDLER Henry, Coxswain, Thorpeness Lifeboat   **SILVER**

8 December 1892

'In recognition of his gallant services during the ten years he held the office of Coxswain'. During that period Coxswain Spindler had been out in the boat 34 times on service and assisted in saving 93 lives.

PRESTON William M., Esq., Honorary Secretary, Penmon R.N.L.I.   **SILVER(2)**
ROBERTS Robert, Coxswain, Penmon Lifeboat   **SILVER(2)**

12 January 1893

9 December 1892: In a moderate north-east gale and a rough sea, the Dublin schooner *James and Mary*, laden with coal from Preston to Wicklow, struck on the Beacon Rock, near Penmon, Anglesey. The lifeboat *Christopher Brown* put out at 6.30 a.m. Reaching a position nearby, the lifeboat let go her anchor and veered down to the wreck, braving rocks in a very heavy sea which was breaking over the wreck. With Mr. Preston aboard, Mr. Roberts manoeuvred alongside the schooner and took off the Master, his wife, three children and the three man crew.

PESTELL Walter, Coxswain, Palling Lifeboat   **SILVER**

12 January 1893

'In acknowledgement of his long and good services in saving life from shipwreck. Coxswain Pestell had held the post for twenty-two years during which the boats had been out ninety-three times on service and saved three hundred and ninety-eight lives'.

KELLAND William Robert, Trinity Pilot   **SILVER**

9 February 1893

14 January 1893: During the night, a boat with five men aboard was seriously damaged in collision with the Pilot cutter at Dartmouth, Devon. With Mr. Kelland and another man aboard, the cutter's boarding boat put off to attempt rescue and, by means of a rope, saved an injured Pilot from the boat. The other four men were lost.

BISHOP George, Seaman	**SILVER**
PERRING Frederick, Seaman	**SILVER**
ROBINS Edwin, Seaman	**SILVER**
ROBINS William, Seaman	**SILVER**

9 March 1893

14 February 1893: The owner and the Master of the French smack *Dieu Protège* of Lannion were trying to enter Par Harbour, near Fowey, Cornwall, at the height of a heavy west-south-westerly gale in a very heavy sea when the boat capsized. The two men managed to swim to a buoy and clung to it. Their plight was seen, and the four seamen put off in a small open boat and brought them ashore.

KEANE Richard, Station Officer, H.M. Coastguard, Helen's Bay   **SILVER**

13 April 1893

26 February 1893: In a very heavy sea and a strong east-south-easterly gale, the Chester schooner *Clans* was stranded in Helen's Bay, Co Down, northern Ireland. Mr. Keane put off with five others in a shore boat and, in spite of being capsized several times, saved the three men on board the schooner.

HODDS William, Coxswain, Winterton Lifeboat   **SILVER**

9 March 1893

'In recognition of (his) gallant services for many years past in helping to save a large number of lives from different shipwrecks'.

HAYLETT James Henry (Junior), Coxswain, Caister Lifeboats   **SILVER**

9 March 1893

'In recognition of (his) gallant services for many years past in helping to save a large number of lives from different shipwrecks'. Rescues during this period included those from the dandy *Vanguard* (1887), the ship *Tay* and the barque *Vauban* (1888), the ketch *William and Sarah*, s.s. *Idlewild* and the brig *Eugenie* (1892) and the dandy *Energy* (1893).

BALL David Graham, Captain, s.s. *Gustav Bitter*   **SILVER**

9 March 1893

4 March 1893: The Newcastle-on-Tyne vessel *Gustav Bitter*, on passage from London to the Manchester Ship Canal, stranded in dense fog on the Callidges Rocks off Lizard Point, Cornwall. Both Polpear and Cadgwith lifeboats launched; the former saved three men from the ship's rigging, leaving one behind, while the latter came upon the ship's longboat with the Master and seven of his crew. They were taken on board the lifeboat and Captain Ball, hearing of the plight of the man left in the rigging and knowing him to suffer from rheumatism, seized a grapnel line, which had been thrown inboard, and swung himself on board the wreck. He helped the man into the lifeboat, but had to take refuge himself in the rigging as the heavy seas were breaking over the wreck. After two attempts to leave by the line, he plunged into the sea and swam to the lifeboat without benefit of lifebelt or line.

SUTCLIFFE Frederick, Private, 2848, 21st Hussars   **SILVER**

HOLMES John George, Lance Corporal, 9895, Rifle Brigade   **SILVER**

BYRNE Michael, Private, 2691, Royal Irish Regiment   **SILVER**

CARROLL James, Private, 3371, Royal Irish Regiment   **SILVER**

8 June 1893

1 May 1893: When a boat capsized in a heavy sea in Southampton Water, three men were thrown into the water. Four soldiers, patients in the Royal Victoria Hospital, Netley, Hampshire, invalided home from India, noticed the men's plight and set out in a skiff. They picked up the men, returned to land in an overloaded condition and risked further injury to their health from wet clothing and exposure to the cold wind.

VARLEY Thomas, Miner, Marsden Colliery   **SILVER**

14 September 1893

21 August 1893: The South Shields pilot coble *Polly* capsized in a squall during a west-south-west gale and a rough choppy sea near Marsden Bay, South Shields, Co Durham. Mr. Varley put off in a small boat, only eight feet long and, at great risk, saved two men.

CRAWFORD William, Honorary Secretary, Margate R.N.L.I.   **SILVER**

9 November 1893

Awarded 'on his retirement from the post of Honorary Secretary having held that office for many years and, previously, a member of the local committee. He had been out in the lifeboat on many occasions to the assistance of the crews of vessels in distress'.

TYRELL William, Coxswain, Harwich Lifeboat   **SILVER**

9 November 1893

'In recognition of his long and gallant services in saving life from shipwreck'. During this period, major services were given to the barque *Pasithea* (1879), the schooner *Rosita* and s.s. *Ingerid* (1881), the barque *Lorely* (1883), s.s. *Achilles* (1890), the schooner *Mercury* (1891) and s.s. *Helsingör* (1893).

KENT Frank, Chief Officer, H.M. Coastguard, Sandwich   **SILVER**

14 December 1893

18 November 1893: With four other men, Chief Officer Kent put off in the Coastguard gig in an attempt to help the Ramsgate ketch *Eclipse*, which had stranded at night in Minnis Bay, off Broadstairs, Kent, in a whole northerly gale and a heavy sea. Unable to reach the ketch because of the conditions, they lost sight of her, and returned to shore. They put off again at daylight, made contact with the casualty and rescued the only man aboard.

BUNT John, Boatman, Missions to Seamen   **SILVER**

FLORY John, Scripture Reader, Missions to Seamen   **SILVER**

8 February 1894

18 November 1893: In a strong north-easterly gale and a very heavy sea in the Severn Estuary, off Portishead, Somerset, the Jersey brig *Harriett* was stranded and soon filled. Messrs. Blunt and Flory put off three times and took off the four man crew – one of them deranged – from their refuge in the rigging.

TOSE George, Coxswain, Runswick Lifeboat   **SILVER**

14 December 1893

18 November 1893: In a furious north-easterly gale and tremendous seas, the Wyborg brig *Carula*, from Wyborg to Middlesbrough with pit props, tried to enter Runswick Bay, five miles north-east of Whitby, Yorkshire, but was driven ashore and broached to. The lifeboat *Cape of Good Hope* was launched and, after a very difficult operation, managed to get alongside and take off the six man crew. Running in to the beach, the lifeboat was hauled into a safe position up a small creek. This was essentially a service award, but it also took account of his long and gallant services in the boat.

BROWN Christopher, Fisherman   **SILVER**

BROWN Fred   **SILVER**

CLARK Thomas, Fisherman   **SILVER**

PURVIS Richard, Fisherman   **SILVER**

USHER John, Fisherman   **SILVER**

14 December 1893

20 November 1893: The strong northerly gale sweeping over the North Sea increased in strength in the evening and veered to the north-east. Just before 1 a.m., the Aberdeen vessel *Victoria* was seen to be driving on to the shelving beach in Bridlington Bay. Mr. Brown, his son and three other fishermen put off in a 24 foot coble and took off the Master and four men. Being told that another survivor remained aboard, they then managed to rescue him. The return journey was a nightmare experience, with snow and hail added to the fury of the wind and the sea, but everybody finally landed safely.

CABLE James, Coxswain, Aldeburgh Lifeboat   **SILVER(2)**

14 December 1893

20 November 1893: At 6.30 a.m. a waterlogged, dismasted hull was seen off Aldeburgh, Suffolk, with terrific seas breaking over her and in danger of drifting on to the outer shoals. The Norfolk and Suffolk class lifeboat *Aldeburgh* launched and found the wreck of the Russian barque *Venscapen* already breaking up but, within a few minutes, took off all the crew of 14 men. Running for Harwich, Essex, the lifeboat fell in with the damaged Hull Pilot cutter *Fox* and took her to that port. Later in the day, the lifeboat searched the Rough Sands for a casualty but found only wreckage. She returned to Harwich at midnight, and regained Aldeburgh at 1 p.m. on 21 November.

WOODGATE James, Coxswain, Dover Lifeboat **SILVER(2)**
14 December 1893

20–21 November 1893: The Norwegian barque *Johanne Marie* went aground on a sandbank in the early morning of the 20th, half a mile offshore at Lade, north of Dungeness, Kent. The morning was spent in efforts by the Littlestone and Dungeness lifeboats to try to reach her but, at 2 p.m., a telegram asking for help was received at Dover. The self-righting lifeboat *Lewis Morice* was launched and taken to the scene under tow by the steam tug *Lady Vita*. She arrived at 5.30 p.m. No attempt was possible that night, due to the intense darkness, torrential rain and a violent easterly gale. The lifeboat remained in the area all that wet and bitterly cold night until it sighted the wreck at 7 a.m. Mr. Woodgate went alongside and snatched seven survivors from the rigging (four others had drowned), and passed them to the tug which towed the lifeboat back to Dover. This service lasted 28 hours.

SCHOFIELD William, Coxswain, Clacton Lifeboat **SILVER**
14 December 1893

20–22 November 1893: With a gale blowing from the east-north-east, the self-righting lifeboat *Albert Edward* was launched at 8 a.m. in a very heavy sea to the three-masted schooner *Nora* of Mandal, from Nantes, France en route to Leith, which was drifting towards Gunfleet Sands. After the lifeboat's foremast had been broken by a sudden squall, a jury mast was rigged. The schooner, disabled with her sails blown away and only a foot of water under her, was eventually got into deep water and was accompanied by the lifeboat to Sheerness, Kent, where she was left in Queenborough Swale at 3 p.m. After two abortive attempts to rescue a vessel seen on the Barrow Sands, the life boat returned to Clacton at 3.30 a.m. Called out again at 5 a.m., she found the barque *Harald Haarfager* stranded near the Whittaker Beacon, full of water and breaking up fast, and took off 11 men; the s.s. *Aberdour* was then towed from the Swin Channel to the Gunfleet Spit buoy. After a most eventful period the *Albert Edward* returned to Clacton at 1.30 p.m. On the 22nd, she launched at 1.45 p.m. to the Copenhagen barque *Anna* stranded on West Gunfleet Sands, which by 8 p.m. had 12 feet of water in her hold. Her crew of ten men were taken off and landed at Clacton an hour later.

BRADFORD John **SILVER**
BRADFORD Uriah **SILVER**
PROWSE George **SILVER**
11 January 1894

4 January 1894: During a strong south-easterly gale, the Svendborg schooner *John Gronsünd* ran aground on the Pole Sands, off Exmouth, Devon, where heavy seas started to break over her. Although the lifeboat was called, the Bradfords and Mr. Prowse decided, because of the urgency of the situation , to go off in a small boat; they saved the schooner's six man crew.

BISHOP Thomas, Second Coxswain, Palling Lifeboat   **SILVER**

8 February 1894

5 January 1894: The Danish brigantine *Sophia* of Fredericia, on passage from Sundswall to Aberdovey with a cargo of timber, went ashore about a quarter of a mile from Hasborough (Happisburgh), Norfolk, in an east-south-east gale and a very heavy sea. The Palling No. 1 self-righting lifeboat *Good Hope* went out to the brigantine and, in spite of the heavy sea and floating wreckage, succeeded, after several attempts, in taking off the six crewmen and landing them safely. Mr. Bishop was in charge of the lifeboat on this service, and the award was also 'in recognition of his gallant services during the past 18 years in assisting to save 272 lives from shipwrecks'.

ROBERTS Richard, Coxswain, North Deal Lifeboat   **SILVER(2)**

11 January 1894

'In acknowledgement of his long continued services in the lifeboat with which he was connected for upwards of 30 years in which period he seems (sic) to have assisted in saving 409 lives'. Outstanding services were those to the barque *Louisa* (1873), the barque *Monte Carmelo* (1875), the barque *Hadvig Sophia* and the ship *Crusader* (1877), the barque *Mia Madre E* and the ships *Leda* and *Paul Boyton* (1879), the ship *Ganges* (1881) and the barque *Mandalay* and the steam trawler *Euphrates* (1891).

WARD Charles Edward, Bowman, Aldeburgh Lifeboat   **SILVER**

11 January 1894

'In consideration of his gallant services for many years past in the lifeboat and in shore boats in saving more than 100 lives. Mr. Ward served as Assistant Coxswain (to 1881) and Coxswain (1881–1888) of the lifeboat until compelled to resign because his fishing took him away so often from the station'. Up to the time of his resignation outstanding services were given to the schooner *Equity* (1881), the schooner *Rambler* (1882), fishing boats *Maggie* and *Australia* (1883), s.s. *Svend* (1887) and the barque *Hoppet* (1888). After his resignation he manned the lifeboat when his work allowed.

NICHOLLS Maurice, Crew Member, Clacton Lifeboat   **SILVER**
OSBORNE Robert, Crew Member, Clacton Lifeboat   **SILVER**
GRIER John, Crew Member, Clacton Lifeboat   **SILVER**

11 January 1894

Awarded to Messrs. Nicholls, Osborne and Grier who have been out on service in the lifeboat respectively 77, 74 and 67 times. They were out on 4 January 1894 when, in a very heavy sea and a whole gale, the Copenhagen brig *St. Alexia*, Valberg to Stranraer with wood, stranded on the Buxey Sand, south of St. Osyth, Essex. After many difficulties, due to wreckage around the vessel and ice over everything, the brig's crew of seven men were landed; the service had lasted for five and a half hours.

MIREHOUSE Richard William, Major, 4th Prince of Wale's North Staffordshire Regt.
  Honorary Secretary, Angle R.N.L.I.   **SILVER**
BALL Edward, Crew Member, Angle Lifeboat   **SILVER**
REES Thomas, Crew Member, Angle Lifeboat   **SILVER**

8 February 1894

30–31 January 1894: The Glasgow ship *Loch Shiel*, bound for Australia with a 1,600 ton general cargo, stranded in a heavy sea on Thorn Island, at the entrance to Milford Haven, Pembrokeshire, while making for shelter from a severe gale. The self-righting lifeboat *Henry Martin Harvey* was launched but, before she arrived, 27 people had taken refuge on the rocks and were at the mercy of the weather. On arrival, the lifeboat took off six men, including an invalid, from the mizzen top. Major Mirehouse, Mr. Ball and Mr. Rees then landed on the island with ropes and a lantern and, crawling along a narrow cliff, reached a point above the survivors, all of whom were hauled up. Twenty-six crew and seven passengers were landed in two trips.

FOLEY Winspeare   **SILVER**
MOORE Alexander, Divisional Carpenter, H.M. Coastguard, Ballycastle   **SILVER**

12 April 1894

20 February 1894: The Doonfeeney fishing boat *Mary* capsized in a south-east by south gale and a heavy sea at Ballycastle, Co Mayo, Ireland, and four men were thrown into the water. Messrs. Foley and Moore put off in a boat and saved them.

MARTIN William, Coxswain, New Brighton Lifeboat   **SILVER**

12 April 1894

For general gallant services, which included those to the ship *Ellen Southard* (1875), the barque *Brothers Pride* and the schooner *Wonder* (1876), s.s. *Anatolian* (1880), the ship *Nuncio* (1883) and the ship *Maxwell* (1892). William Martin was appointed Coxswain in January 1892, a post he held until 1900.

LONG James Harry, Honorary Secretary, Youghal R.N.L.I.   **SILVER**

11 October 1894

5 September 1894: The yacht *Seagull* foundered off Youghal, Co Cork, Ireland, leaving a young man, who was unable to swim, in danger of drowning. Mr. Long, the yacht's owner, went to his assistance. The young man clutched him by the neck, but was persuaded to get on his back. Losing his head, however, he got on to Mr. Long's shoulders, and shouted for help. Eventually, another yacht reached them and picked up the man, but over ran Mr. Long who caught hold of her bobstay. He was forced to release it, but five minutes later was picked up in an exhausted condition.

BRIMS John, Coxswain, Thurso Lifeboat   **SILVER(2)**

11 October 1894

'In recognition of his good services during the long period of thirty-five years in which he occupied the post of Coxswain'. Coxswain Brims had been out in the lifeboats at that station 32 times on service and assisted in saving 304 lives. In the period since the award of his first medal in June 1886, he had given service to the smack *Henry Florence* and the schooners *Margaret Garton* and *Lyra* (1886), the schooners *Janet Worthington* and *Lady Louison Pennant* and the ketch *Crest* (1887), the schooner *Debonair* (1888) and the schooners *Bonnie Lass*, *William Jones*, and *Sylph.*

SINCLAIR David, Coxswain, Irvine Lifeboat   **SILVER**

10 January 1895

29 December 1894: The self-righting lifeboat *Busbie* was called out to the Tönsberg ship *Frey* in distress near the Lady Isle, off Troon harbour, Ayrshire. It had been impossible to get the Troon lifeboat out of the harbour because of the terrific hurricane blowing from the north-west. Under sail, the Irvine lifeboat covered five miles in half an hour. At the wreck, 16 crewmen jumped into the water one by one and were dragged into the lifeboat by ropes. Coxswain Sinclair decided to land at the south beach, Troon, but nearing the beach, the lifeboat was overwhelmed by 12–15 feet waves and thrown on her beam ends. The Coxswain and three or four others were thrown out. When the boat was righted, all regained her except one of the rescued Norwegians who had been washed away; the shore was then finally reached safely. Coxswain Sinclair was 70 years old at the time of this service.

SIMMONS Arthur, Chief Engineer, Steam Lifeboat *Duke of Northumberland*   **SILVER**

10 January 1895

Awarded to Chief Engineer Simmons 'who had been in charge of the engines on each of the twenty-eight occasions when the boat had been on service and had thus contributed to the saving of fifty-one lives'. He was the original First Engineer appointed to this first steam lifeboat at Harwich in 1890; he stayed with her when she transferred to Holyhead in 1891 and to New Brighton in May 1893.

GOLDSMITH Edward William, Bricklayer   **SILVER**
PALMER Thomas Henry, Fisherman   **SILVER**
TOOK Alfred, Fisherman   **SILVER**

14 February 1895

13 January 1895: The North Shields vessel *James and Eleanor* was totally wrecked off Southwold, Suffolk, in a whole south-east by south gale. In spite of the very heavy sea and broken water, the three men swam out to the wreck and saved four of the crew, one of whom was found to be dead and another only lived a few seconds after being landed.

CRAGIE John, Coxswain, Southwold Lifeboats   **SILVER(2)**

11 July 1895

'In recognition of his long and gallant services during the period, about forty-eight years, in which he has been connected with the boats, firstly as one of the crew, afterwards as Second Coxswain and ultimately as Coxswain', a post John Cragie assumed in 1879. During this period, there were services to the barque *Nordenhavet* (1887), the brigantine *Vecta* (1890), the fishing boat *Mary Ann* (1892), the barque *Alpha* (1893), the barque *Nina* (1894) and the brig *James and Eleanor* (1895).

   Coxswain Craigie received his first silver medal for a service in 1859.

STROWGER George, Coxswain, Kessingland Lifeboats   **SILVER(2)**

14 November 1895

A second award for his long service – as Coxswain since 1867. Since the award of Coxswain Strowger's first medal in 1883, services included those involving the brig *Phillis* (1886), the steamer *Empress* (1890), the schooner *Kate and Elizabeth* (1891) and the brigantine *Alberta* (1894). He retired as Coxswain in 1897.

WRIGHT Robert, Coxswain, Fleetwood Lifeboats   **SILVER(2)**

14 November 1895

Awarded on his retirement for good services during his period in the boat and for the services, since the award of Coxswain Wright's first medal in 1890, involving s.s. *Odd* and the schooner *Theda* (1893) and the schooner *Annie Park* (1894).

POCKLEY Robert, Coxswain, Flamborough No. 1 Lifeboat   **SILVER**

12 December 1895

15 November 1895: Several miles off Flamborough Head, Yorkshire, in a strong south-easterly gale, the Flamborough fishing boat *Elizabeth* was struck by a heavy sea which washed her three man crew overboard. Mr. Pockley realised that launching a 19 foot coble would be quicker than launching the lifeboat, did this and, with two other men, battled out and saved the three men.

HAYNES James, Coxswain, Port Isaac Lifeboat   **SILVER**

12 December 1895

Awarded on Mr. Haynes' resignation from the post of Coxswain which he had held since the station opened in 1869. Services included those to the brig *Stephano Grosso* (1870), the fishing luggers *Castle* and *J.T.K.* (1872), the barque *Ada Melmore* (1877), the schooner *British Queen* (1882), four fishing boats (1883), s.s. *Indus* (1886), the schooner *Golden Light* (1890) and the barque *Antoinette* (1895).

JAMIESON James, Captain, Fishing Vessel *Wild Wave*   **SILVER**

13 February 1896

14 December 1895: While returning from fishing in a strong southerly gale, the Lerwick fishing boat *Jessie* was overwhelmed by a heavy sea and sank about half a mile from Oxna Island, south-west of Lerwick, Shetland. Captain Jamieson, with three other men, saved two of the fishing boat's crew. A third man had perished before help arrived.

McCOMBIE Thomas, Captain, s.s. *Tearaght*
  Commissioners of Irish Lights Vessel   **GOLD**

9 January 1896

24–26 December 1895: During a south-east gale on the 24th, the Finnish ship *Palme* dragged her anchors and went aground one and half miles north-north-west of Kingstown Harbour (Dun Laoghaire), Co Dublin. Three lifeboats responded to render assistance. The Kingstown No. 2 lifeboat *Civil Service No. 7* capsized about 600 yards from the *Palme*; the whole crew of 15 men lost their lives. The Kingstown No. 1 lifeboat *Hannah Pickard* also capsized, but righted – three men were thrown out but were recovered, and because of the damage sustained this boat had to return to shore. The Poolbeg lifeboat *Aaron Stark Symes* also went out but could not reach the wreck.

On Christmas Day, an attempt with the Poolbeg lifeboat and a tug failed, as did the efforts of the s.s. *Tearaght*. On the 26th, the *Tearaght* again went out, anchored ahead of the wreck, and lowered her port lifeboat with the Captain, his 15 year old son and eight of his crew on board. In two trips they saved the *Palme*'s Master, his wife and child and the 17 crew. Master McCombie of the *Tearaght* received a binocular glass, bearing a suitable inscription, for his part in the rescue.

WICKHAM Thomas, Coxswain, Wexford No. 1 Lifeboat   **SILVER**

12 March 1896

'For long and gallant services as Coxswain'. He was Second Coxswain 1881–1884, and became Coxswain in 1884. Services included those to the smack *Queen* (1886), the barque *Saltee* (1888), the schooner *Star of Hope* (1889), the schooner *Ruby* (1891), the yawl *Liberator* (1894) and the yawl *Annie* (3 March 1896).

McBAY James, Seaman, Fishing Lugger *Friendship*   **SILVER**

12 November 1896

26 September 1896: The fishing boat *Speedwell* was swamped in a southerly gale and rough sea at the mouth of Loch Nevis, near Mallaig, Inverness-shire, on the west coast of Scotland, and was seen by the *Friendship*'s Master, who went to help. While one man was being dragged on board, the two other men were drifting away. James McBay of the *Friendship* tied a rope around his waist and swam 50 yards to one of the helpless men, took him to the lugger and returned to do the same for the other man.

MORGAN John, Captain, Cardiff Pilot Boat *Cardiffian*   **SILVER**

12 November 1896

6 October 1896: Two barges were being towed to Spain, when, during a gale, they became separated from the towing steamer. The Cardiff Pilot cutter tried to tow them into port but could not do so. Captain Morgan then launched his cutter's punt and, with two assistants and an apprentice, rescued the crews of the barges, six men in all.

HOOKE William, Coxswain, Blakeney Lifeboat   **SILVER**

10 December 1896

Awarded on Mr. Hooke's retirement from the post of Coxswain during which period services were given to the barque *Amana* (1865), a Pilot coble (1866), the sloop *Emma* (1867), the schooner *Gypsy* (1869), the brigs *John and Mary* and *Ravensworth* (1870) and H.M.S. *Beaver* (1885).

FLETT James, Seaman, Fishing Boat *Betsy Hughes* of Pittenweem   **SILVER**

8 April 1897

6 February 1897: With a strong north-east breeze blowing over a heavy sea and in a hard frost, the St. Monans fishing boat *John and Agnes* was off the Fife coast, between Anstruther and Pittenweem, when a boy was struck by the sail and knocked overboard. The accident was seen by Mr. Flett, who took off some of his clothing, plunged overboard, swam to the unconscious boy and brought him back to the *Betsy Hughes*.

TREWHELLA H., Coxswain, Penzance Lifeboat **SILVER**

11 March 1897

On his retirement 'in acknowledgement of his long and gallant services in saving life from ship-wreck'. For the last six years, Mr. Trewhella served in the post of Coxswain, during which period services were given to the schooner *Joseph Nicholson* (1891), the schooner *Express* (1892), a man who fell from the quay (1892) and the barque *Lady Gladys* (4 March 1897).

CAULFIELD George, Seaman, Hooker *Storm King* **SILVER**
RICKARD Thomas, Seaman, Hooker *Storm King* **SILVER**
KELLY Christy, Seaman, Hooker *Maymaid* **SILVER**
McLAUGLAN James, Seaman, Hooker *Maymaid* **SILVER**
ROURKE Edward, Seaman, Hooker *Maymaid* **SILVER**

9 July 1897

11 May 1897: Off the Nose of Howth, Co Dublin, the Ringsend trawler *Dodger* sprang a leak and was taken in tow by the Howth hooker *Storm King*. The trawler began to sink immediately, so the hooker launched a boat with Mr. Rickard and Mr. Caulfield in it which took off the two man crew. Fouled by the trawler's boom, the boat was dragged partly down leaving the four men struggling in the water. They regained the boat and righted her, but she was capsized three times by the rough seas. The Howth hooker *Maymaid* launched a boat manned by Messrs. McLauglan, Kelly and Rourke and saved all four men.

HODDS William, Coxswain, Winterton Lifeboat **SILVER(2)**

13 January 1898

Awarded on Mr. Hodds' retirement from office of Coxswain. In the period since he was awarded his first medal, services included those to the steamer *Quantock* (1895), the shrimping boat *Adeline* (1896), the ketch *Isabella* and the brigantine *Hannah* (1897).

LEE Charles, Coxswain, Worthing Lifeboat **SILVER(2)**

13 January 1898

Awarded on Mr. Lee's retirement from office of Coxswain. Appointed in 1879, services included those to the brig *Albert H. Locke* (1888), the schooner *Yong Karl* and the brig *Capella* (1891), the brigantine *Halcyon* (1895) and the brig *Ophir* and the schooner *Flora Emily* (1896).

KYLE Matthew, Coxswain, Holy Island Lifeboat **SILVER(2)**

13 January 1898

Awarded on Mr. Kyle's retirement from office of Coxswain. Appointed in 1879, there were services to the barque *Jupiter* (1881), s.s. *Preston* (1882), the ketch *Mary Tweedie* and the fishing boat *Nancy* (1883) and the schooner *Flower of Ross* (1890). There were also many occasions of assistance to other vessels.

CRAGIE John, Coxswain, Southwold Lifeboat   **SILVER(3)**

10 March 1898

Awarded on Mr. Craigie's retirement from the post of Coxswain after many years in the boat. Only one service was rendered after his previous medal, that of assisting the ketch *Eliza and Alice* (1896).

TODD William, Coxswain, Gorleston No. 2 Lifeboat   **SILVER**

14 July 1898

Awarded on Mr. Todd's resignation from the post of Coxswain. Services were rendered to the smack *Sir John Astley* (1885), the dandy *Morning Star* (1888), the trawler *Favourite* and the dandy *Belinda* (1890), the yawl *Kate* (1891), the dandy *Hiram* (1893), the dandy *Fraternité* (1894), the dandy *Coquette* (1895) and the smack *Follow* (1897).

HOOD Henry, Coxswain, Seaton Carew Lifeboat   **SILVER(2)**

11 August 1898

Awarded on Mr. Hood's resignation of the post of Coxswain. He was awarded the silver medal as Coxswain in 1883 for the service to the *Atlas*. Since then there were services to the steam trawler *Express* (1886) and the galliot *Dina* (1896).

PAGE Alfred, Master, Ramsgate Harbour Steam Tugs   **SILVER(3)**

8 September 1898

Awarded 'on his retirement in consideration of his long and gallant services in towing the Ramsgate lifeboats'. During the period since the award of his last medal in 1892, services were given to the barque *Telegraph* (1892), the schooner *Sarah Elizabeth* (1893), the smacks *Blue Bell* and *Daisy*, the steamer *Almendral* and the brig *Hondeklip* (1894), s.s. *Beacon Light* and s.s. *Lady Wolseley* (1895) and the ship *Kommander Svend Foyn* and the smack *Ismene* (1898).

WARFORD George, Coxswain, Pakefield Lifeboat   **SILVER(2)**

13 October 1898

Awarded on Mr. Warford's resignation of the office of Coxswain. In the period from the award of his first medal in 1886, rescues were made from seven fishing vessels (1892), the dandy *Jolly Tar* and the brigantine *Kelpie* (1896) and the ketches *Magnet* and *Louise,* and the schooner *Natalie* (1897).

HILL James, Coxswain, Porthoustock Lifeboat   **SILVER**

10 November 1898

14 October 1898: On the evening of the 14th, having sailed from London for New York with 97 crew, 60 passengers (53 first class and seven cattlemen) and one stowaway, the 6,889 ton *Mohegan* was badly off course when she passed inshore of the Manacles Bell Buoy, off Manacle Rock, south of Falmouth, Cornwall. She struck Maen Voces Rock in the Varsis Ledge head on at speed in a

moderate east-south-east gale and a heavy sea. She immediately took on a port list and sank by the bow after 15 minutes, although some boats got away. Four other lifeboats went to the area, but were unable to find the wreck in the darkness and in the absence of any lights. Mr. Hill, who had seen the ship at the time of the disaster, launched the Porthoustock self-righting lifeboat *Charlotte* and saved 44 of the 51 survivors.

TINNING John William, Coxswain, Blyth No. 2 Lifeboat   **SILVER**

10 November 1898

16 October 1898: The self-righting lifeboat *Oswald, Sarah and Jane* was engaged on service when she was struck by two heavy seas; the second one knocked all the port oars out of the crutches. Before the men could recover, another sea struck her, capsized her and threw out all the crew. She righted immediately, some of her crew regained their positions while others swam to the shore, but the Assistant Coxswain was carried 40–50 yards to the seaward clinging to an oar. Contrary to regulations, he was not wearing a lifebelt. Mr. Tinning swam to him and got him to the shore where, sadly, he did not respond to efforts to revive him.

GILBERT James, Coxswain, Tynemouth Lifeboat   **SILVER(2)**

10 November 1898

Awarded on Mr. Gilbert's resignation of the post of Coxswain. Assistance since the award of his first medal had been given to s.s. *Napier* (1891) and some fishing boats (1895).

TAYLOR Andrew, Coxswain, Cullercoats Lifeboat   **SILVER**

10 November 1898

Awarded on Mr. Taylor's resignation from the post of Coxswain in the course of which the lifeboat assisted many fishing boats overtaken by bad weather after they had put out from harbour. Services were also rendered to s.s. *Libelle* (1883), s.s. *Niord* (1895) and the schooner *Luna* (1897).

PESTELL Walter, Coxswain, Palling Lifeboats   **SILVER(2)**

12 January 1899

Awarded on Mr. Pestell's resignation of the office of Coxswain. He joined the lifeboat at the age of 18 and, six years later in 1870, was appointed Coxswain in which post he served for 29 years, and assisted in saving 445 lives from shipwreck. Since he was awarded his first medal in 1893, services were given to the brigantine *Sophia* (1894), the ketch *Rival* (1896) and the barque *Hilda* and the brigantine *Craig Alvah* (1898).
   Mr Pestell died in 1931.

THOMAS James, Coxswain, Fishguard Lifeboats   **SILVER**

9 February 1899

Awarded in recognition of Mr. Thomas' general gallant services in saving life from shipwreck. In his period of office more than 200 lives were saved from over 50 vessels, particularly meritorious services being those to the brigantine *Osnabruck* (1880), the steamer *Udea* (1881), the brigantine *Xanthus* (1882), the ship *Troop* (1886) and the schooner *Mary Lloyd* (1898).

NICHOLLS Maurice, Crew Member, Clacton Lifeboat   SILVER(2)

OSBORNE Robert, Crew Member, Clacton Lifeboat   SILVER(2)

GRIGSON George (Senior), Crew Member, Clacton Lifeboat   SILVER

9 March 1899

Awards were made to three members of the lifeboat crew on their resignations, on account of old age, after one hundred and one, ninety-nine and sixty eight services respectively. Since the awards to Nicholls and Osborne on 11 January 1894 , there were services to the schooner *Betty Russel* (1895), the barquetine *Golgotha* (1896), the barquetine *Thyra* (1897), the schooner *Ornan* (1898) and the schooner *Robert Anderson* and the ship *Hawkesdale* (January 1899).

OLIVER Andrew, Coxswain, Hauxley Lifeboat   SILVER

12 October 1899

Awarded on Mr. Oliver's retirement as Coxswain during which period services included those to s.s. *Hayle* (1890), the coble *Lyra* (1893) and the fishing coble *Guiding Star* (1898). Mr Oliver was Coxswain from 1889 to 1899.

STRACEY Eustace William Clitherow, ex Lieutenant, R.N.   SILVER

14 December 1899

3 November 1899: In a strong south-south-west gale, while engaged in arranging a haul-off warp prior to exercising the Newburgh, Aberdeenshire lifeboat, the boat was swamped and the three men on board were cast into the water. Two men managed to reach the shore, but the third, who was the Assistant Coxswain of the boat, was obviously in difficulty. Mr. Stracey swam out and reached him just as he was sinking for the last time and then brought him ashore.

WATT James, Coxswain, Montrose Lifeboats   SILVER

9 November 1899

Awarded on Mr. Watt's retirement from the post of Coxswain during which period assistance was rendered to a great number of fishing boats trying to return to port in bad weather. Rescues included those from the schooner *Familiens Haab* (1885), the brig *Bazar* (1889), the brig *Frida* (1894), the schooner *Regina* (1896) and the ketch *Acacia* (1897).

WARD Charles Edward, Bowman, Aldeburgh Lifeboat   SILVER(2)

11 January 1900

7 December 1899: During a full east-south-easterly gale and in extremely violent seas, a vessel was reported aground on Shipwash Sands. The Norfolk and Suffolk Class lifeboat *Aldeburgh* launched. As the Coxswain and Second Coxswain were prevented by illness from going out in the boat, Mr.

Ward (a previous Coxswain) acted as Coxswain. Forcing her way through the extremely heavy surf, the lifeboat set sail to the south. Trying to cross the Inner Shoal, the lifeboat was capsized when two huge waves struck her broadside on, trapping six of her crew underneath. As soon as the lifeboat came ashore, efforts were made to get out the trapped men, and a hole was chopped in the upturned hull, but to no avail. Charles Ward was one of the first men washed ashore and, although badly shaken, he repeatedly went back into the heavy surf to help his comrades ashore. A seventh man died three months later from his injuries.

DEMPSEY Daniel, Lighthouse Boatman	**SILVER**
DEMPSEY Alexander, Fisherman	**SILVER**
DEMPSEY Daniel (Junior)	**SILVER**

8 February 1900

25 December 1899: The Campbeltown schooner *Sovereign*, in a strong north-west to north breeze, squally weather and a heavy cross sea, was totally wrecked on Sanda Island, south of Kintyre in the Firth of Clyde. Daniel Dempsey and his sons soon put off in a boat (at one stage he was washed out and only with great difficulty recovered) and rescued five men from the wreck.

STOUT Benjamin, Coxswain, Longhope Lifeboat	**SILVER(2)**

11 January 1900

Awarded on Mr. Stout's retirement from the office of Coxswain during which period services were given to s.s. *Ben Avon* (1884), s.s. *Victoria* (1891) for which he received his first medal, and the s.s. *Manchester City* (1898).

DANIELS Thomas, Sergeant, 4th Battalion, South Staffordshire Regiment	**SILVER**

8 March 1900

24 January 1900: With the wind blowing from west-north-west and in a moderate sea, Sergeant Daniels and two privates went by boat from Rocky Island to Spike Island, Co Cork, Ireland, but on returning at 7 p.m. the boat capsized. One of the soldiers was unable to swim. Sergeant Daniels swam to him and took him to the upturned boat, where the man was able to support himself until another boat from Spike Island picked him up. The Sergeant, meanwhile, searched without success for the other soldier, and was picked up himself in an exhausted condition.

CLEMENTS Francis George, Fisherman	**SILVER**
HUBBARD Samuel, Labourer	**SILVER**

8 March 1900

14 February 1900: When the West Hartlepool schooner *Lizzie and Edith* was totally wrecked in a strong north-easterly gale and very heavy sea at Eccles, Norfolk, Messrs. Clements and Hubbard rushed into the surf and saved her crew of four men.

HAYLETT James Henry (Junior), Coxswain, Caister No. 1 Lifeboat SILVER(2)

10 May 1900

Awarded on Mr. Haylett's retirement. Services since the grant of his first medal in 1893 included those to the s.s. *Resolven* and the barque *Glenhervie* (1896).

RYLE John, Constable, Royal Irish Constabulary SILVER

8 November 1900

9 July 1900: A fishing boat was wrecked at Boffin Island, Co Galway, Ireland, in a moderate gale and heavy surf. The accident was seen by Constable Ryle and another officer who, stripping off some clothing, went to the rescue. Two of the crew had managed to grasp hold of a rock, but two others were still struggling in the water. Constable Ryle swam out and supported one of them until a boat arrived; the other man was swept away. The men on the rock were rescued by the other policeman and another man.

CABLE James, Coxswain, Aldeburgh Lifeboat SILVER(3)

13 December 1900

15–16 February 1900: The lifeboat *Reserve* No. 1 was launched at 10.30 p.m., after a vessel had been reported on Sizewell Bank, off the coast of Suffolk, and headed through tremendous seas, heavy rain and sleet but could not find any trace of a casualty. An enormous sea sent her backwards and Coxswain Cable was knocked overboard, but he managed to get back inboard; the lifeboat dropped anchor. About 4 a.m. distress signals were seen, and the lifeboat found the London s.s. *Hylton*, which had lost her rudder and propeller. Coxswain Cable put two of his men aboard, and then went to Lowestoft to make arrangements for tugs to tow the vessel to Gravesend.

4 October 1900: This incident again took place on the Sizewell Bank. A southerly gale and very heavy seas meant that the hauling-off warp had to be used to launch the Aldeburgh lifeboat which was towed by the Hamburg s.s. *Minerva* to the Karlskrona (Sweden) barque *Antares*. Coxswain Cable dropped anchor and veered down to the stranded vessel, taking off 11 crewmen in three attempts.

James Cable had been Coxswain since January 1888. He had charge of the lifeboat on more than 20 occasions and had assisted in the rescue of 269 lives.

OWEN Richard, Assistant Coxswain, Moelfre Lifeboat SILVER

13 June 1901

'In recognition of his excellent services and conspicuous courage displayed on many occasions, especially in November last (6 November 1900) when he jumped overboard, although unable to swim, to disentangle a net which had fouled the boat's rudder'. He was appointed in 1887 and was involved in lifeboat services on 21 occasions during which 57 lives were saved.

REES David, Coxswain, Cardigan Lifeboat   **SILVER**

12 September 1901

7 November 1900: Awarded 'on his retirement from the office of Coxswain, in recognition of his long and gallant services in saving life from shipwreck, and especially of the rescue of the schooner *Mouse* of Cardigan on the 7th November'. The self-righting lifeboat *Lizzie and Charles Leigh Clare* was launched about 5 a.m., after the *Mouse*, bound from Chester River for Fishguard, had stranded on the Popit Sands, off Cardigan. Her crew had taken refuge in the rigging but rescue attempts were rendered futile by the tremendous waves washing over her. After a hard struggle, all three crew members were finally brought into the lifeboat using a block and lifebuoy.

PETTIT Jethro, Coxswain, Broadstairs Lifeboat   **SILVER**

1 August 1901

'In recognition of his good services in the boat during the period in which he held office' (1891–1901). Rescues were carried out from the schooner *Suomi* (1894), the ketch *Martin Luther* (1895), the brig *Flamingo* (1896), the ketch *Firefly* (1897), the schooner *Julia* (1899), the brig *Mary Kate*, the yawl *Dorothy* and the s.s. *Sir Robert Peel* (1900).

WOOD James, Boatswain, Steam Trawler *Marrs*   **SILVER**

12 September 1901

26 August 1901: A man was washed overboard from the Millom yacht *Dorcas*, which was in a water-logged condition in Morecambe Bay, Lancashire, with a moderate north-north-west gale blowing and a very rough sea. Mr. Wood plunged from his own vessel into the water and supported the man until both were picked up by the Piel (Barrow) lifeboat *Thomas Fielden*, which also rescued three men from the yacht.

HAYLETT James (Senior), Launcher, formerly Assistant Coxswain, Caister Lifeboat
  GOLD

12 December 1901

13–14 November 1901: When the Caister No. 2 Norfolk and Suffolk class lifeboat *Beauchamp* was launched to a casualty on the Barber Sands, Mr. Haylett was one of the helpers even though he was 78 years old. The launch took several hours due to the horrendous conditions, but eventually the boat succeeded in getting through the breakers. Three-quarters of an hour later, when cries were heard coming from the shoreline, Mr. Haylett went to the area and found the lifeboat upside down. With his grandson, he dashed into the water and brought three men to safety. One of the survivors was also a grandson and another a son-in-law, but he lost two sons in the incident. Altogether, he was on the beach for 12 hours in bitter cold weather, wet through and without food. He had served the lifeboats for 50 years and helped save hundreds of lives.

On 6 January 1902, King Edward VII, Patron of the RNLI, with the Prince of Wales, President, presented the gold medal to James Haylett at Sandringham. During the Board of Trade enquiry into the disaster, when asked if the lifeboat had abandoned the search for the casualty, Haylett replied: 'Caister lifeboatmen never turn back'.

HUGHES Hugh, Coxswain, Rhoscolyn Lifeboat **SILVER**

9 January 1902

8 December 1901: 'In recognition of his gallant services in that lifeboat and particularly on the occasion of the rescue of the schooner *J.W. Waring* in a whole north-west by north gale and very heavy sea'. The self-righting lifeboat *Ramon Cabrera* left her moorings at 4 p.m. for the schooner, which was in distress about six miles south-west of Rhoscolyn Point, Anglesey. She made three attempts to get a line on board, but a heavy sea put her on her beam ends. The lifeboat filled but righted and cleared herself, then, after getting lines on board, took two crewmen off; the other three jumped aboard the lifeboat just before the schooner drove on to Porth Saint Rocks and broke up.

OWEN Thomas, Coxswain, Moelfre Lifeboat **SILVER**

12 June 1902

Awarded on Mr. Owen's resignation, for his gallant conduct and skilful management on three special occasions:

2 March 1901: About 10 a.m., in a strong south-east breeze and rough sea, the Amlwch schooner *County of Cork*, on passage from Liverpool to Abersoch with coal and manure, showed distress signals. She was dragging her anchors and in danger of stranding on Moelfre Island. Her two man crew was taken into the self-righting lifeboat *Star of Hope* and landed and, when the weather had moderated, they were taken back by fishing boat.

25 August 1901: With a north-north-west gale blowing and a very heavy sea running, the Newry schooner *Edith*, Liverpool to Drogheda with coal, was lying, in thick weather, in the outer roads off Moelfre. Riding heavily at her anchors and in danger of being driven on to the rocks at Llanddona, she shewed distress signals at 12.35 p.m., and her four man crew was taken off by the reserve lifeboat temporarily replacing the *Star of Hope*.

25–26 January 1902: Conditions were very bad with a strong north-north-east gale, a heavy sea, very cold weather and snowstorms, when the Wicklow barquetine *Ethiopia* dragged her anchors for about two miles, and found herself in shoal waters on a lee shore. Her crew of six men was rescued by the lifeboat. Shortly after, at 1.45 a.m. three men were taken off the schooner *Lily Green* of Liverpool.

BRITTON Henry, Coxswain, Walton-on-Naze Lifeboat **SILVER**

10 July 1902

'In recognition of his gallant services. He had been Coxswain … since 1884 and assisted to save one hundred and thirty-two lives, going out in the lifeboat eighty-nine times; four of the services* were very gallant ones'. Prominent among the services during this period were those to the ship *Deike Rickmers** (1884), the ship *Constance* (1886), s.s. *Capri** (1887), the galliot *Edvard* (1889), the brigantine *Agnes Cairns*, the barque *Elphinstone** and the schooner *Branch* (1893), the brigantine *Lord Strangford* (1896), the brigantine *Green Olive** (1897), the ketch *Autumn* (1898), the schooner *Little Dorrit* (1899), the barque *Argo* (1900) and the barque *Halden* (1901).

DODD Thomas, Coxswain, Hoylake Lifeboat   **SILVER**

13 November 1902

15–17 October 1902: One of the worst storms for many years raged along the west coast of England, Scotland and Wales on the 15th and 16th and blew with exceptional severity in Liverpool Bay, where several ships were involved in disasters, and local lifeboats were heavily engaged. After being at sea for 11 hours on the night of the 15th, standing by s.s. *Heraclides* on Taylor's Bank, the Hoylake Liverpool class lifeboat *Coard William Squarey* returned to station at 10 a.m. on the 16th but was called out again after eight hours to the Riga barquetine *Matador*, ashore off Blundell Sands. The New Brighton lifeboat had arrived on the scene and had made several unsuccessful attempts to rescue the crew. Finally, despite violent seas, Coxswain Dodd got alongside and saved the barquetine's nine crewmen who were landed at New Brighton.

NARBETT William, Acting Coxswain, St. David's Lifeboat   **SILVER**

12 February 1903

27 January 1903: The Grimsby s.s. *Graffoe,* bound from Glasgow to Montevideo with a cargo of coal, experienced bad weather and at 11 p.m. on the 25th stranded on the southern end of Ramsey Island, off the coast near St. David's. Fourteen crew men got into one of the ship's lifeboats. Washed out to sea they were picked up 30 miles away by a steamer in the afternoon of the 26th and landed at Penarth. The remaining nine crew took refuge on the bridge and in the rigging, as it was impossible to launch the other lifeboat. The Master and Chief Engineer were washed away and drowned and only at 10 a.m. on the 27th was the wreck seen from the mainland. The St. David's lifeboat *Gem* launched with Acting Coxswain Narbett to the rescue. With great difficulty, a line was got aboard, and one by one the men were pulled through the water to the lifeboat. One of the seven died, but the remainder were safely landed at 2,15 p.m.

William Narbett was appointed full-time Coxswain later that year.

STEWART John, Sailor, Yacht *Tigris*   **SILVER**

ROBERTSON Hector, Sailor, Yacht *Tigris*   **SILVER**

13 August 1903

3 July 1903: In a south-westerly gale and very steep seas, the yacht *Valtos* foundered in Wemyss Bay, Renfrewshire, and three men were thrown into the water. The yacht *Tigris* went to their assistance, but the heavy seas made it impracticable to take them aboard. Messrs. Stewart and Robertson manned a 12 foot punt and picked up all three men. One was found to be dead and another exhausted and practically unconscious, but he recovered later.

ROWNTREE Thomas William, Coxswain, Hartlepool Lifeboat   **SILVER**

13 August 1903

6 July 1903: The Montrose ketch *Young John*, Middlesbrough to Fisher Row, Edinburgh, lost her mainsail in a northerly gale off Berwick-on-Tweed and ran back for Hartlepool, under her stay foresail. About 8.30 p.m., she was seen in Hartlepool Bay, unmanageable and drifting to leeward on to the Long Scar Rocks. The self-righting lifeboat *Charles Ingelby* was launched. She rowed across the bay and, after a great deal of difficulty, got alongside. A child, the Master's son, was at

once thrown from the ketch and was caught by one of the lifeboatmen; immediately after the three crew jumped into the boat. On her return journey, the lifeboat was frequently lost to sight in the waning daylight and heavy waves until, under the lee of the breakwater, she was taken in tow by a tug and eventually landed in the dark. The rescue was witnessed by thousands of people from the Hartlepool cliffs.

STONHAM Alfred, Fisherman   **SILVER**
9 June 1904

28 May 1904: Off Hastings, Sussex, the fishing boat *William and Maria* struck a submerged pile and sank immediately in the strong west-south-west breeze and a moderate sea. Her Master, clinging to a floating spar, was drifting rapidly to the east. Mr. Stonham ran down the beach, threw off his boots and clothes and swam out to save him. The other three men were saved by boat.

COOK Stephen, Coxswain Superintendent, Folkestone Lifeboat   **SILVER**
10 November 1904

5 October 1904: When the Folkestone fishing boat *Good Intent* was seen at 10.30 p.m. in trouble, being driven before a strong south-west gale, the self-righting Folkestone lifeboat *Leslie* was launched under considerable difficulty. On her way to the casualty, off Copt Point, to the east of the harbour, the lifeboat encountered a heavy wave which washed out two of her crew but they were soon picked up. Anchoring, Coxswain Cook veered her down to the casualty and took off the three crewmen just before the fishing boat was dashed on to the rocks.

HARRIS Sydney James, Coxswain Superintendent, Gorleston Lifeboats   **SILVER**
*SCLANDERS James, Chief Engineer, Gorleston Lifeboat   **SILVER**
9 February 1905
*9 March 1905

15–16 January 1905: After blowing for some days, the strong south-east wind increased to a furious gale on the night of 15–16th and, with a terrific sea and a below-freezing temperature, the conditions on the Gorleston bar were abysmal. Shortly after 6 p.m., the Lowestoft brig *Celerity* was reported in distress four miles to the south. The steam lifeboat *James Stevens No. 3* got up steam, slipped moorings, reached the brig and successfully took off the six man crew. As it was impossible to return over the bar at low tide, the lifeboat anchored outside in the biting cold and fury of the storm until she was able to make harbour at 2 a.m.

CLAYSON Stephen, Assistant Coxswain, Margate No. 1 Lifeboat   **SILVER**
9 February 1905

15 January 1905: At 3.15 a.m. on the 15th, the self-righting lifeboat *Eliza Harriett* put out, in a whole south-east gale and bitter cold, over a very heavy sea and sailed 23 miles to the Kentish Knock sands where the London ketch *Malvoisin* was aground. Bound from Gravelines, France to Goole with phosphates, the ketch was now stranded, her rudder and sails gone, her bulwarks

smashed and the sea breaking clean over her. Arriving at 8 a.m. the lifeboat, with Assistant Coxswain Clayson in charge, went alongside and took off the four exhausted crew, then battled back to Margate arriving at 1.30 p.m. After an unsuccessful attempt on the 16th, the lifeboat was able, with the help of a tug, to bring the ketch into port on the 17th.

JONES David, Coxswain Superintendent, Ferryside Lifeboat **SILVER**

9 November 1905

15 March 1905: In a moderate gale with very high seas, the Norwegian barque *Signe* of Kristiania went aground on Cefn Sidan Sands in Carmarthen Bay, off Towyn Burrows; the self-righting lifeboat *City of Manchester* launched under Coxswain Jones. When she arrived it was impossible to go alongside in the prevailing conditions. As it was clear that the crew would be able to walk ashore at low tide, the lifeboat set out to return, but had to shape its course for Burry Port, tackling seas so tremendous that, at one point, the lifeboat was under water on her beam ends and, at other moments, crewmen were washed out. All were recovered and she made Burry Port safely.

FAIRBAIRN Walter, Coxswain Superintendent, Dunbar Lifeboat **SILVER**

9 November 1905

13 October 1905: At 6 a.m. the Swansea s.s. *King Ja Ja*, on passage from Newcastle to Methil with a cargo of steam rails, was seen in a strong northerly gale close to rocks a few miles west of Cockburnspath, East Lothian. The Liverpool class lifeboat *William Arthur Millward* was launched and, as it was low water and with wind and sea against her, she had to be hauled by ropes to the new harbour's mouth where a very strong swell was encountered. On reaching the casualty, her machinery was found to be broken down so the lifeboat remained alongside for four hours while it was repaired. The ship got under weigh and the lifeboat returned to Dunbar at 1 p.m. but, in less than an hour, the steamer was in trouble again. With the northerly gale now creating much larger waves, the launch was much more difficult and dangerous but, aided by her sails, the lifeboat under Coxswain Fairbairn succeeded in reaching the casualty, now halfway between the Isle of May and St. Abb's Head, ten miles distance from Dunbar. Taking off the six man crew by lines took an hour and, in the face of sea and wind, the return journey took another three. The abandoned steamer ended up a wreck near Thorntonloch – almost back at the original spot where she had first been seen in distress.

HARRIS Sydney James, Coxswain Superintendent, Gorleston Lifeboats **SILVER(2)**

14 December 1905

11 November 1905: The Wick lugger *Fruitful* had been wrecked off Gorleston, Norfolk, on a cold stormy day with a crew of eight hands aboard. After two unsuccessful attempts to get a line aboard the *Fruitful*, Coxswain Harris entered the water in a heavy sea and secured a buoy which had been floated on a line from the vessel. Coxswain Harris had maintained his position in the water for an hour before being able to effect the communication by which means all hands were saved.

HANNAGAN Michael, Coxswain Superintendent, Youghal Lifeboat **SILVER**

11 January 1906

17 December 1905: In strong south-south-east gales and a very heavy sea, the Dungarvan schooner *Annetta*, coal laden, struck the bar off Youghal, Co Cork, Ireland, and drifted ashore, water-logged, opposite the railway station. The Youghal self-righting lifeboat *Mary Luckombe* was launched and the rocket apparatus was turned out, but this failed to reach the wreck. By the time that the lifeboat arrived the Master and one hand had been lost while the other three crewmen were in the rigging, exhausted. Coxswain Hannagan took the lifeboat *over* the wreck atop of the seas breaking over her and plucked the three men, in turn, to safety. One was so exhausted that three attempts alone were necessary to rescue him.

PENROSE William, Farmer **SILVER**

11 January 1906

31 December 1905: The Milford brigantine *Mary* was wrecked in a south-easterly gale at the mouth of Fowey harbour, Cornwall, and Mr. Penrose and his two brothers, all farmers, saw the incident. With a coil of rope they hastened to St. Katharine's Point, and arrived just as the vessel sank. Her Master reached the rocks, while the rescuers climbed down to save the other three crew members but were unsuccessful. William Penrose himself was washed off the rocks and had to be rescued by his brothers.

NICOL Francis (Rattie), Fisherman **SILVER**
NICOL Francis (Frankie), Fisherman **SILVER**
NICOL James, Fisherman **SILVER**
WATT Alexander, Fisherman **SILVER**

8 March 1906

11 February 1906: During a strong north-easterly gale, the Newcastle s.s. *Vigilant* was totally wrecked at Crovie, Banff, eight miles east of Banff town. A shore boat failed to reach the wreck because she was surrounded by jagged rocks, therefore the four fishermen manned an old disused flat-bottomed salmon coble. As it was Sunday, they were all in their best clothes. Before the coble put out, the steamer's Mate tried to land in the ship's boat but, as soon as it touched the water, it was swamped and he was saved by another man. The coble saved five men.

CHEYNE William, Fisherman	**SILVER**
FIDDLER Daniel, Fisherman	**SILVER**
GROAT William, Fisherman	**SILVER**
JAMIESON Edward, Fisherman	**SILVER**
TAYLOR Bremner, Fisherman	**SILVER**
TAYLOR William, Fisherman	**SILVER**

8 March 1906

16–17 February 1906: At 10 p.m. in a heavy west by south gale and snowstorm, the Sunderland s.s. *Dinnington* was wrecked on the Island of Switha, west of South Ronaldshay, Orkney, and broke in two. Two crewmen were washed overboard and drowned; the remaining nine took to the ship's boat which capsized and they were washed on to the rocks where they took shelter, wet through and semi-naked. Lights were seen and a shore boat was launched by six fishermen only to find the wreck deserted. Rocks were searched without success, as was the island of Flotta. They then returned to Switha and found the survivors who were taken to Harkness.

WICKHAM Edward, Coxswain, Wexford Lifeboat   **SILVER**

12 April 1906

18 March 1906: The Wexford yawl *Puffin* grounded on the west side of the bar at Wexford, Co Wexford, Ireland, as she was returning from the fishing grounds. The self-righting lifeboat *James Stevens No. 15* launched with a south-south-west gale blowing, a heavy confused sea, and the weather was getting worse. Anchoring to the west of the yawl, the lifeboat was unable to veer down because of the conditions. Finally, after three hours, a line was thrown to the wreck which was followed by a heavier rope and the lifeboat was able to work near. By this time the six hands were in the fore part of the vessel, wet and perished by the cold, and the yawl's decks were under water amidships. Waiting his chance, Coxswain Wickham got the six aboard and took them to Wexford. The yawl went to pieces shortly afterwards.

LANGLANDS Thomas, Coxswain Superintendent, Whitby Lifeboats   **SILVER**

14 June 1906

14 May 1906: Six fishing cobles were returning to Whitby harbour, Yorkshire, in a strong north-north-east breeze. Just before mid-day, four of them got in safely, but the fifth, *William and Tom*, encountered some nasty seas while passing the bar, and sank. Coxswain Langlands, who was in his own coble *Thankful*, the fourth in line, at once went to help and picked up one man. The other two men had seized a line thrown from the pier and were driven by the seas close to it but, even though his coble had lost two of her oars, Coxswain Langlands went in and picked them up and then transferred all three to the lifeboat *Robert and Mary Ellis*.

HAWKINS John, Harbour Boatman, Ramsgate   **SILVER**

11 October 1906

14 September 1906: An open boat capsized off the entrance to Ramsgate Harbour in a strong west-south-west breeze and rough sea. Of the five persons on board, only the boatman could swim. Seeing this, John Hawkins lowered himself by a rope from the East Pier and swam out. One lady

and a gentleman were clinging to the boat but the other two and the boatman were more or less under water. Hawkins got hold of the lady, swam with her into shallow water and dragged her unconscious on to a sand bank where 'he used the usual method of restoring the apparently drowned', with success. The other members of the party were picked up by two watchmen who had put out in a boat.

HAYLETT John, Coxswain Superintendent, Caister No. 2 Lifeboat	**SILVER**
PLUMMER John, Assistant Coxswain, Caister No. 2 Lifeboat	**SILVER**
BROWN Solomon, Crew Member, Caister No. 2 Lifeboat	**SILVER**
HAYLETT Walter , Crew Member, Caister No. 2 Lifeboat	**SILVER**

11 October 1906

18 September 1906: The Russian barque *Anna Precht*, of Mariehamm, on passage from Borga, Finland to Yarmouth with a cargo of wood, drove on to Cockle Sands and went to pieces immediately. The barque had been running for an anchorage in an east-north-east gale and very heavy sea, when she became unmanageable in a strong tide, and disaster struck so swiftly that there was not time to give orders. The first that anybody on land knew was when the Coastguard at Caister saw a small boat with three men aboard in the vicinity of the Sands. These men were rescued. It then became known that nine men remained on the wreck. The self-righting lifeboat *Nancy Lucy* was launched. At daybreak they found the Captain alone on what remained of the barque and after sailing through and searching the wreckage the lifeboat saved five more of the crew. One other man was saved by a steamer whilst two others had drowned. Plummer, Brown and Walter Haylett had jumped from the lifeboat on to the wreckage, broken the grasp of the helpless men and assisted them into the boat.

THOMAS James, Coxswain Superintendent, Fishguard Lifeboats	**SILVER(2)**

13 December 1906

Awarded 'on his resigning the post of Coxswain'. In the years since Captain Thomas's first medal was voted in 1899, his services included those to the ketch *Volunteer* and the schooners *Sarah Davies*, *Albion* and *Esther* (1900), the steamer *Prince Llewellyn* and the schooner *Mary Roberts* (1903) and the smack *Margaret and Ann* (1906).

SOTHERAN Shepherd, Coxswain Superintendent, Hartlepool No. 1 Lifeboat	**SILVER**
FRANKLIN John, Coxswain Superintendent, Seaton Carew Lifeboat	**SILVER(2)**

14 February 1907

31 January-1 February 1907: As the London s.s. *Clavering* (3,300 tons) was leaving Middlesbrough for Japan at 6 a.m., she encountered a fierce northerly gale and stranded near the North Gare breakwater at the approach to the sea, where she was swept from stem to stern by heavy seas. The Seaton Carew lifeboat *Charles Ingleby* was launched and landed 15 of the steamer's crew but, with the tide beginning to flow, further attempts to reach the wreck were unavailing even when, at 3.30 p.m., a fresh crew of West Hartlepool Pilots was shipped and a tug towed them as near as possible. The Hartlepool No. 1 self-righting lifeboat *Ilminster* was brought by road to Seaton Carew at 5.30 p.m. and, after waiting for the tide to ebb, both lifeboats left between 9–10 p.m. but had to

abandon their attempts at 2 a.m. Returning to their joint efforts at daylight with the weather moderating slightly, in a bitter wind and a keen frost they took off 24 survivors. The service was completed by 1 p.m.

PESTLE James (Junior), Crew Member, Palling No. 1 Lifeboat SILVER

13 June 1907

9 March 1907: Bound for the Tyne from London with a cargo of burnt ore, the Fowey schooner *Vixen* was wrecked on the beach, two and a half miles north of Palling, Norfolk, in a strong north-north-west gale and heavy sea. The self-righting Palling No. 1 lifeboat *54th West Norfolk Regiment* was transported along the beach and launched between 4–5 a.m., but the wreck's mizzen mast went by the board before she could be reached. In spite of the fallen mast and rigging five men were taken off, but one other remained. Mr. Pestle and the schooner's Master boarded the wreck and the lifeboatman climbed the tottering mainmast and took off the sixth man – a numbed and incapacitated Russian seaman. The lifeboat was washed away before Mr. Pestle could regain it, and he was forced to remain on the wreck for a considerable time until taken off.

VYVYAN Henry, The Reverend, Honorary Secretary, Cadgwith R.N.L.I. SILVER
RUTTER Edward, Coxswain Superintendent, Cadgwith Lifeboat SILVER
MITCHELL William Edward, Coxswain Superintendent, Lizard Lifeboat SILVER
*MITCHELL Edwin, Second Coxswain, Lizard Lifeboat SILVER
ANDERSON George Martin, Seaman, s.s. *Suevic* SILVER
WILLIAMS William, Seaman, s.s. *Suevic* SILVER

11 April 1907
*9 May 1907

17–18 March 1907: In a dense fog at 10.30 p.m. on the 17th, the s.s. *Suevic*, of Liverpool, ran on to the Maenheere Reef off the Lizard. A White Star liner of 12,000 tons, she was on her way home from Australia with 524 persons board (141 crew, 382 passengers, including 160 women and children, and one stowaway).

Two lifeboats immediately responded – the *Admiral Sir George Back*, Lizard and the *Minnie Moon*, Cadgwith. Two of the liner's boats were lowered and filled with women and children. One was taken in close to shore by the Lizard lifeboat, which then returned to the wreck. The other was picked up by the Cadgwith boat, and the Honorary Secretary, who was on board, jumped into the ship's boat to guide it ashore, so allowing the lifeboat to return to the wreck.

Meanwhile the Coverack lifeboat *Constance Melanie* and the Porthleven lifeboat *John Francis White* had also arrived on the scene. By noon all on board the *Suevic* had been rescued. The numbers rescued by the lifeboats were – Cadgwith 227, Lizard 167, Coverack 44, Porthleven 18. The remaining 68 were conveyed in the ship's boats to tugs which were in attendance. The two seamen, George Anderson and William Williams, specially distinguished themselves. They carried the children down rope ladders and, when the lifeboats, which were surging up and down, rose on the waves, dropped the children into the arms of the lifeboatmen who tended them until joined by their mothers. There were 60 children under three years of age on board.

SIMPSON John, Salmon Fisherman, Johnshaven   **SILVER**

11 July 1907

7 June 1907: When a boat was swamped and sank near Johnshaven, Kincardineshire, Mr. Simpson put off in a flat-bottomed surf boat and saved two men. His boat struck on rocks twice, but he jumped overboard and pushed it clear each time.

ROBERTS Richard, Coxswain Superintendent, North Deal Lifeboat   **SILVER(3)**

13 June 1907

Awarded 'on his resignation of the post of Coxswain Superintendent. Roberts had been Assistant Coxswain and Coxswain since the formation of the station, upwards of forty-two years'. Since the award of his second clasp on 11 January 1894, he had given service to the following: the brig *Franz von Mathies* and the schooner *Clacton* (1894), a boat from H.M.S. *Research*, a boat from the brigantine *G.L. Walters* and the schooner *Michael Kelly* (1895), the barque *Unione* (1897), the barque *Maria* (1901) and the dredger *Beaufort* (1907).

REES Daniel, Solicitor   **GOLD**

REES Ivor, Engineer   **SILVER**

11 July 1907

16 June 1907: When the small Mosquito class yacht *Firefly* capsized in winds varying from a strong breeze to a moderate gale and in a confused sea, three men were thrown into the water off Lavernock Point, south of Penarth, Glamorgan. Mr. Daniel Rees went off in a six feet dinghy and made for the victims who were now three miles offshore between the Point and Scully Island. Although his boat was shipping water, he took in two men and, with his dinghy very low in the water, remained by the third man for 20 minutes. His brother, Ivor, swam 200 yards to another Mosquito class yacht, brought it to the shore and, with his son, reached the casualty, now four miles away, and then took the three victims aboard before transferring them to a tug which arrived on the scene.

The award presentations were made by the Lord Mayor of Cardiff at a largely attended meeting at the Town Hall on the 14th October, when the heroes received a great ovation.

BURDEN William Joseph Newkey, Honorary Secretary, Teignmouth R.N.L.I.   **SILVER**

RICE George, Coxswain Superintendent, Teignmouth Lifeboat   **SILVER**

12 December 1907

10 October 1907: Shortly after mid-day, the Riga schooner *Tehwija* was seen to be driving dangerously near the outer end of the bar at Teignmouth, Devon, although the overnight south-south-west gale was moderating. The seas were still very heavy, but the Exmouth lifeboat was launched and, after several unsuccessful attempts to make for the schooner, was driven on to the Pole Sands. Although it was near low tide and the sea around the wreck was very turbulent and strewn with timber and wreckage, the Teignmouth self-righting lifeboat *Alfred Staniforth* was launched, with the Coxswain and the Honorary Secretary aboard. On nearing the wreck, the crew could be seen in the fore-rigging and the sea around was covered with timber and wreckage. The lifeboat anchored and veered down as near to the vessel as possible. Achieving communication by rope, the eight man crew was transferred from the schooner shortly before all three masts went by the board.

LAMING James, Coxswain Superintendent, Kingsdowne Lifeboat **SILVER**

14 November 1907

'In recognition of his long and gallant services in the lifeboat extending over a period of forty-one years (i.e. since the station was opened in 1866)'. Prominent services included those to the ship *Glendora* and the barque *Hony Sverne* (1870), the barque *Richard and Harriett* (1871), the s.s. *Sorrento* (1872), the brig *Dillwyn* (1877), the brig *Breeze* (1884), the steamer *Dolphin* (1885), the schooner *Excel* (1897), the brig *Unione* (1898), the s.s. *Carlotta* (1900), and the brig *Mersey* (1901).

This was the last occasion on which a medal was awarded on retirement.

GREIG Robert, Coxswain Superintendent, Stromness Lifeboat **SILVER**

9 January 1908

11 December 1907: About 6 a.m., the Hull steam trawler *Shakespeare*, homeward bound from the fishing grounds, went aground at Point of Spoil, near Breckness, Mainland, Orkney, in a fresh south-west breeze, and two of her crew were washed away. The self-righting lifeboat *Good Shepherd* launched but, by the time that she arrived, only the masts and funnel of the trawler could be seen above water and two more men had been lost from the rigging. Grapnel lines were got aboard, two men were taken from the foremast and another from the funnel. Three others were taken from the foremast by rocket apparatus.

HICKS Frederick Charles, Seaman, Gig *Slipper* **SILVER**

9 January 1908

13–14 December 1907: On the 13th, trying to ride out a vicious storm, the seven masted steel-hulled schooner *Thomas W. Lawson*, of Boston, anchored near Annet, one of the southern Isles of Scilly. Late in the afternoon, both St. Mary's and St. Agnes lifeboats were launched, but the schooner's Master refused to leave. For various reasons, both lifeboats returned to their stations. When they arrived back on the scene next morning, the schooner had struck Shag Rock and was reduced to a mass of floating wreckage. Her Master and Engineer had been washed on to Hellweather Rocks. When they were found there by the gig *Slipper*, Mr. Hicks jumped overboard and, taking a rope with him, swam into a deep gulley and took off the Master. Mr. Hicks' father had been killed on the schooner while acting as Pilot.

AITCHESON Alexander, Fisherman **SILVER**

12 March 1908

11 February 1908: When a fishing boat with two men on board capsized four miles north of Berwick, ten fishermen put out in a boat to rescue them. Mr. Aitcheson, aged 24, helped support his 64 year old companion until they were both rescued.

ROBSON James, Coxswain Superintendent, North Sunderland Lifeboat **SILVER**

12 March 1908

18 February 1908: The Norwegian steamer *Geir* of Bergen, in ballast for Blyth in a northerly gale and a heavy sea, stranded on Knavestone Rock, Farne Islands, off Bamburgh, Northumberland. The North Sunderland self-righting lifeboat *Forster Fawsett* launched at 7 p.m. In view of the

dangerous local conditions, Coxswain Robson, unable to go alongside the casualty, landed on an adjoining rock taking a lifebuoy with him. With the lifeboat standing off, he brought the steamer's 14 man crew to the rock using lines and, with the lifebuoy, they were hauled in the dark to the lifeboat and landed at North Sunderland at 11 p.m. The Coxswain was only 28 years old. The King of Norway conferred a silver medal for noble deeds, and a certificate on Robson.

OWEN William, Coxswain Superintendent, Holyhead Steam Lifeboat	**GOLD**
BROOKE Thomas W., Crew Member, Holyhead Steam Lifeboat	**SILVER**
JONES George, Crew Member, Holyhead Steam Lifeboat	**SILVER**
JONES Lewis, Crew Member, Holyhead Steam Lifeboat	**SILVER**
JONES Richard, Crew Member, Holyhead Steam Lifeboat	**SILVER**
JONES Samuel, Crew Member, Holyhead Steam Lifeboat	**SILVER**
LEE James, Crew Member, Holyhead Steam Lifeboat	**SILVER**
McLAUGHLIN William, Crew Member, Holyhead Steam Lifeboat	**SILVER**
MARSHALL Charles H., Crew Member, Holyhead Steam Lifeboat	**SILVER**
OWEN William (Junior), Crew Member, Holyhead Steam Lifeboat	**SILVER**
ROBERTS Lewis, Crew Member, Holyhead Steam Lifeboat	**SILVER**

12 March 1908

22 February 1908: The 75 ton s.s. *Harold*, bound from Teignmouth to Runcorn with china clay and a crew of nine, was drifting with the tide, in winds of hurricane force and violent seas, towards the rockbound shore of Anglesey between North Stack and South Stack. Having just returned from another service, the Holyhead steam lifeboat *Duke of Northumberland* put out but, on reaching the neighbourhood of the distressed steamer, it was found that she was anchored not very far from the shore. With tremendous seas around her it was quite impossible for the lifeboat to even get near her. Huge waves tossed the lifeboat about like a cork, but eventually, after two hours very skilful manoeuvring by Coxswain Owen and the slackening tide for which he had waited, the lifeboat was able to approach sufficiently near for communication to be effected by means of a rope. Seven of the crew of the ill-fated steamer were by the use of lines drawn through the water to the lifeboat, when a heavy sea suddenly carried her almost alongside the steamer and the two remaining men jumped on board. The rope was slipped and the lifeboat steamed clear, and it was a great relief to all when Holyhead was reached in safety.

On 4 May, the Prince of Wales (later George V), President of the R.N.L.I, presented Owen with the gold medal at Marlborough House.

MONAN Patrick **SILVER**

12 November 1908

26 September 1908: At night, in a south-easterly gale and very heavy sea, the Gothenburg barque *Trientalis* was wrecked at Ballyquinton Point, Co. Down, Ireland, and Mr. Monan, with four others, saved, at great risk to themselves, all the 11 man crew.

NICHOLAS Henry, Coxswain Superintendent, Sennen Cove Lifeboat   **SILVER**

14 January 1909

29 December 1908: The Liverpool ship *Fairport*, which had been under tow by the tug *Blazer*, was anchored in Porthcurno Bay, Cornwall, south-east of Land's End, in a southerly gale. The Sennen Cove self-righting lifeboat *Ann Newbon* launched but was forced to turn back. At 3 a.m., she set out again and was able to proceed only under close reefed foresail. With the rain falling in sheets in the pitch darkness, the lifeboat was filled by the following seas and did not reach the casualty until dawn; she then stood by until the weather moderated. The tug returned and with the help of the lifeboat a fresh hawser was passed, the ship slipped her cables and was towed away. The lifeboat then made for Penzance as she could not make her station in the prevailing conditions.

MARTIN Duncan, Master Mariner   **SILVER**

14 January 1909

29–30 December 1908: In the evening, during a whole gale with squalls of hurricane force, snow showers and a very heavy sea, the Campbeltown, Argyll, lifeboat *James Stevens No. 2* launched to the Larne schooner *Janes*, in distress off Campbeltown but in the conditions, she was unable to reach the schooner. Captain Martin, seeing the lifeboat's difficulties, raised a crew to man a line skiff which was then veered down to the wreck but, just as it reached her, two heavy seas carried the skiff away to the lifeboat. Scrambling aboard the lifeboat and abandoning the skiff, they were returned to the shore at 1.30 a.m. and changed into dry clothing. Between 6 and 7 a.m. during a lull, a fresh boat was manned by Captain Martin and his men, and they succeeded in rescuing two exhausted men and recovered one body.

NOBLE Andrew, Coxswain Superintendent, Fraserburgh Lifeboat   **SILVER**

12 August 1909

30 June 1909: About 10.30 a.m., as she was rounding the Fraserburgh breakwater in a strong north-east gale, the Nairn fishing boat *Henry and Elizabeth* was struck by a huge sea and almost submerged. Her mainsail burst and, after righting, the boat was washed on to the rocks and one man was drowned. The self-righting lifeboat *Anna Maria Lee* was launched and saved the remaining six men, although the rudder was broken and the yoke carried away during the service.

NOBLE Andrew, Coxswain Superintendent, Fraserburgh Lifeboat   **SILVER(2)**

14 October 1909

7 September 1909: A north gale of extraordinary ferocity swept the Buckie fishing boat *Zodiac* past Fraserburgh harbour entrance, and she was thrown on to rocks at the back of the south breakwater. Communication by rocket apparatus was achieved, but seeing the lifeboat approaching, the vessel's crew waited until she came alongside and all the seven man crew transferred to her. The lifeboat could make no headway on her return journey and was being carried to leeward, and an attempt by the harbour tug to put out was unsuccessful. Coxswain Noble hoisted sail and, with his crew at the point of exhaustion, finally managed to make headway. The Buckie steam drifter *Lively* then put out and was able to take her in tow.

PRITCHARD William, Coxswain Superintendent, Penmon Lifeboat   **SILVER**
BURTON James H., Esq., Honorary Secretary, Penmon R.N.L.I.   **SILVER**

11 November 1909

26–27 October 1909: The self-righting lifeboat *Christopher Brown* launched just after 6 pm. to the Liverpool ketch *William* which was in difficulties and had lost all her sails in a strong easterly gale and heavy sea in Red Wharf Bay, south of Moelfre, Anglesey. Coxswain Pritchard made numerous attempts before the lifeboat could get close enough for a line to be thrown on board the ketch, but her crew refused to leave, and the line parted. It proved to be impossible for the lifeboat to get close enough again so she stood by. Suddenly, the ketch's remaining anchor cable parted and she was driven on to the sands. The ketch was pounded by the seas to a total wreck and no further signs of the three crew could be found. The lifeboat itself was driven ashore and remained fast there for some hours before being refloated by the tide later in the morning. The crew, which included Mr. Burton, had been out for 15 hours.

HARRIS Sydney James, Coxswain Superintendent, Gorleston Lifeboats   **SILVER(3)**
HARRIS Ellery, Assistant Coxswain, Gorleston No. 1 Lifeboat   **SILVER**

11 November 1909

28 October 1909: The Aberdeen s.s. *Clunie* was seen on Cockle Shoal, off Gorleston, Norfolk, with her crew in the rigging. When the self-righting life boat *Mark Lane* reached her she was found to be drifting in the gale. Coxswain Harris anchored and veered down to the vessel, but only four men had been rescued when his cable was out at full length. Weighing anchor, he followed the vessel which was leaking badly, her fires extinguished and the remainder of her crew still on board. The situation was made more dangerous by wreckage and empty barrels which had broken adrift. A tug, which was in attendance, managed to establish a tow and, accompanied by the lifeboat, with some lifeboatmen on the *Clunie*, towed the ketch and the nine men aboard to safety.

PRITCHARD William, Coxswain Superintendent, Penmon Lifeboat   **SILVER(2)**

13 January 1910

21 December 1909: In a full gale, the Liverpool ketch *Willie* was wrecked at night on the lifeboat slipway at Penmon, Anglesey. In a rough sea and a blizzard, Coxswain Pritchard entered the pounding surf and threw a line on board by which means four men were saved.

ARMSTRONG John Dawson, Colliery Bank Keeper   **SILVER**

12 May 1910

18 April 1910: The Newbiggin coble *Sunbeam* was seen to capsize in a southerly gale in Druridge Bay, near Hauxley, Northumberland. Sending one of their number to alert the Hauxley lifeboat, Mr. Armstrong and four others put off in a small coble and succeeded in picking up the three men clinging to the casualty. With eight men on board, the rescue craft was seriously overloaded and, on the timely arrival of the lifeboat *Mary Andrew*, they transferred to her and were landed at Hauxley with despatch.

MORTIMER Sidney, Fisherman   **SILVER**

10 November 1910

3 October 1910: On the night of the 12th, while the Barnstaple ketch *Democrat* was riding in the lee of Ramsey Island, near St. David's, Pembrokeshire, the moderate north-north-easterly gale increased and her Master signalled for help. The St. David's self-righting lifeboat *Gem* arrived through heavy seas in a full gale and took off the three men from the ketch which was now dangerously close to the hazardous reef of rocks known as 'The Bitches'. This done, the Coxswain found it impossible to straighten up and the lifeboat was swept toward the reef where she was wrecked. The Coxswain and two crew members were drowned. Fifteen men, including the *Democrat*'s crew, got on to the rock but their fate was not known until 9 a.m. whereupon Mr. Mortimer, with two coastguardmen, put off through a heavy sea in his 20 ft open-boat *Wave Queen*. When they reached the scene, they had to lay off waiting for the tide to fall. By 3.30 p.m. however, in two trips he had taken off ten men and landed them on Ramsey Island, the other five being recovered by a second boat. In spite of his youth, he was 18 years old, Sidney Mortimer was elected to be Coxswain Superintendent of the next St. David's lifeboat, the youngest Coxswain in the British Isles.

Mortimer and the two coastguardmen were entertained to lunch at Buckingham Palace by King George V.

COWIE James, Fisherman   **SILVER**

10 November 1910

15 October 1910: The Banff steam drifter *Mistletoe* foundered 15 yards from the North Pier, Gorleston, Norfolk, in a strong east-north-easterly gale and very heavy sea. One man was drowned when entangled in nets on board. While one of the others was being hauled to the pier by lifebuoy and rope, the rope broke, and he fell into the water and was seen being washed out to sea by the ebb tide. Fully clothed, Mr. Cowie jumped in without line or belt and saved him.

O'SHEA John, The Reverend, Parish Priest, Ardmore   **GOLD**
BARRY Richard, Petty Officer, H.M. Coastguard, Ardmore   **SILVER**
NEAL Alexander, Leading Boatman, H.M. Coastguard, Ardmore   **SILVER**

13 April 1911

18 March 1911: During a terrific south-easterly gale, the Montrose schooner *Teaser* was driven ashore near Ardmore Bay, Co. Waterford, Ireland, in a very heavy sea. The rocket apparatus was brought to the scene and lines were thrown over the vessel, but her crew, exhausted and cold, could not make use of them. Aware of this, Messrs. Barry and Neal tried to swim out, but were beaten back to the shore. Father O'Shea then obtained a boat in which he put out with others, including the two coastguardmen. They boarded the wreck, but two of her crew were already dead and the other succumbed shortly afterwards.

CAMPBELL Duncan, Fisherman   **SILVER**

11 January 1912

21 October 1911: The Norwegian s.s. *Ena* of Kragero grounded during a thick fog on the 20th about 25 yards from the shore on the Mull of Oa, Islay, the southern-most of the Inner Hebrides, with an 18 man crew and one passenger on board. On the morning of the 21st, a strong gale developed into a whole gale with a very heavy sea, and 15 men escaped to the shore in a ship's boat. Mr. Campbell managed to reach a rock standing halfway between the wreck and the shore at high water, and the men on board floated a line to him and followed this with a wire rope to which a cradle was improvised. The four men were then brought ashore by this means.

STEVENSON Andrew, Rabbit Catcher   **SILVER**

14 December 1911

4 November 1911: In a severe north-westerly gale, the Finnish barque *Ocean* of Mariehaven was dismasted, driven ashore and broke in two at Kilchieran, Islay, Argyll. Four of her crew, including the Master, were lost. Five of the others were saved by Mr. Stevenson, who waded into the water and pulled them out, one by one. In doing this, he was nearly drowned when he slipped.

BAKER William Henry, Coxswain, Padstow Lifeboat   **SILVER**

14 December 1911

12 November 1911: Having already saved the five man crew of the schooner *Island Maid* of Belfast on Doom Bar at the mouth of Padstow harbour, Cornwall, the self-righting lifeboat *Arab* relaunched at 6 p.m. when the Brest brigantine *Angèle* struck on the same hazard in a strong west-north-westerly gale and heavy sea. In the gathering darkness and terrible sea, she failed in her attempt and returned ashore. After some difficulty, Coxswain Baker raised a fresh crew and put out again. By a desperate effort, the wreck, by now submerged with only the rigging visible, was reached and the schooner's Master saved. The other four men in her crew had already drowned.

HARDING Richard, Coxswain, Ballycotton Lifeboat   **SILVER**

14 December 1911

15 November 1911: On passage from Rotterdam to Cork during a strong south-easterly gale and very heavy sea, the Cork s.s. *Tadorna* (1,643 tons) was wrecked in Ballycotton Bay, Co. Cork, Ireland. The self-righting lifeboat *T.P. Hearne* launched immediately and, when some little distance from land, was taken in tow by a steam trawler. On reaching the wreck, it was impossible to board owing to the darkness and very heavy breakers on the ledge of rocks to seaward. At dawn, Coxswain Harding took the lifeboat through the reef and, boarding the wreck, took nine men off. The other 12 crew were saved by rocket apparatus.

SIM James Stuart, Second Coxswain, Fraserburgh Lifeboat **SILVER**

21 February 1929

14–15 January 1912: In the middle of the night, attempting to make Fraserburgh harbour, Aberdeenshire, in a very rough sea, the Dundee trawler *Clio* struck Beacon Rock, off Cairnbulg Briggs. The rocket apparatus was called out and the lifeboat *Lady Rothes* launched; the former proved ineffectual. The Coxswain took his boat to the scene but, in two attempts, could not get alongside for the seas sweeping over the wreck. The lifeboat anchored near the Beacon and, at 11 p.m., veered down closer to the wreck. The Second Coxswain jumped overboard with a line and swam to the rock, followed by three other men. With their help seven crew were taken off by the lifeboat and landed at Fraserburgh.

Due to the Honorary Secretary's serious illness at the time of the service, it was not fully reported but the circumstances were made known to the R.N.L.I. Secretary during a visit in 1928 and the award was voted after an interval of 17 years!

HUTCHISON John, Miner **SILVER**

LAWRIE David, Miner **SILVER**

LOWTH Thomas, Crane Driver **SILVER**

WALKER Alan A., Crane Driver **SILVER**

11 April 1912

16 January 1912: The Glasgow s.s. *Ashgrove* was totally wrecked on Methil Bank Dock Sea Wall, Fife, in a south-easterly gale and very heavy sea. A tremendous sea was breaking over the wall. In spite of the enormous risk, the four miners and crane drivers fought their way to the top of the parapet of the wall and led the rescue of 17 men from the ship.

CORIN John, Coxswain, Coverack Lifeboat **SILVER**

7 March 1912

10–11 February 1912: Over five hours after leaving Falmouth, during which time the weather had deteriorated to a whole gale from the south-east, the 2,354 ton steel, four masted Hamburg barque *Pindos* was driven ashore at Mear's Point, south-west of Coverack, Cornwall. The Liverpool class lifeboat *Constance Melanie* was launched about 10 p.m. and, on reaching the wreck, found seas breaking over her. Although four men were taken off, operations were suspended until daylight. In the meantime, however, a powerful acetylene lamp was brought to the scene, and rescue efforts were resumed. The remaining 24 men were taken off and all 28 landed.

HARRIS Sydney James, Coxswain Superintendent, Gorleston Lifeboats **SILVER(4)**

12 September 1912

27 August 1912: On passage from Antwerp to the Tyne with a cargo of concrete and iron, the 2,923 ton Glasgow s.s. *Egyptian* stranded on Cross Ridge, Scroby Sand, off Yarmouth, Norfolk, in a east-south-east gale. The Norfolk and Suffolk class lifeboat *Mark Lane* put out under tow, to find very heavy seas breaking around the casualty but, getting alongside, took off 13 people including the Master's wife and child. The remaining 20 men refused to leave, therefore Coxswain Harris left and landed those that he had on board at 10 a.m. Two further attempts to find the ship in the afternoon

were foiled by torrential rain. During the night, the lifeboat was called out again and, in very difficult circumstances, communication was effected by means of a bladder floated to the ship on the end of a rope; this was made secure and the men climbed down and were hauled through the water to the lifeboat. All 20 men were brought safely ashore.

CHISHOLM James, Coxswain, St. Andrews Lifeboat   **SILVER**

10 October 1912

29 September 1912: The Leith fishing boat *Resolute* was seen to be dragging her anchors close to St. Andrews Bar. The Rubie self-righting lifeboat *John and Sarah Hatfield* launched and reached the vessel in a very short time. Three minutes after the three crew had been rescued the *Resolute* was dashed to pieces on the rocks.

1 October 1912: During tempestuous weather, the Swedish barque *Princess Wilhelmina* of Halmstad, laden with firewood from Kemi to Dundee, attempted to round Fife Ness to enter the Firth of Forth. Because of heavy seas she failed and became embayed off St Andrews. About 11 p.m. on the 30th September, she let go both anchors about five miles north of St. Andrews. At 5 a.m. next day one anchor parted. Seen from the shore, the lifeboat crew were put on standby. At 8 a.m. the other cable parted and the vessel drove towards the rocks near St. Andrews Castle. Whilst rocket apparatus was tried, the lifeboat was taken to West Sands and launched. Thousands of onlookers saw the lifeboat reach the wreck through the treacherous rocks and rescue the nine man crew, bringing them safely to West Sands.

EGERTON Philip, Lieutenant, R.N.   **SILVER**
MAIN Alexander, Fisherman   **SILVER**

12 December 1912

26 November 1912: In a moderate east gale with a very heavy sea, the fishing boat *Gem* was trying to make the harbour at Helmsdale, Sutherland, but was swamped and sank with her crew of three hands. The Helmsdale Lifeboat Society lifeboat saved one of them, while Mr. Main dived from it and tried to save a lad but failed to secure him. Aware of the lad's danger, Lieutenant Egerton dived 20 feet from the breakwater but also failed in his attempt. Both would-be rescuers were picked up by the lifeboat; the third man had disappeared with the fishing boat.

BURTON Herbert Edgar, Captain, Royal Engineers,
    Mechanic, Tynemouth Lifeboat   **SILVER**
SMITH Robert, Coxswain, Tynemouth Lifeboat   **SILVER**
*NIXON Anthony, Coxswain, Cambois Lifeboat   **SILVER**

13 February 1913
*12 June 1913

11 January 1913: The Sunderland s.s. *Dunelm* stranded to the east of Blyth East Pier, Northumberland, at low water in a whole gale when a very heavy sea was running, and one of the crew swam ashore with a line. Using a rocket apparatus, the whole crew was rescued over the rocks except for two men who, with four rescuers, could proceed no farther because of the increasing depth of water. Using a small boat, Coxswain Nixon brought off two of them, three others were saved by other means, but one was swept away and drowned. A report of the casualty had been

made to Tynemouth, where Captain Burton assembled a reduced crew for the motor lifeboat *Henry Vernon* which set off through tremendous seas with Coxswain Smith aboard, and reached the wreck one and a quarter hours later, as the last man was rescued. The lifeboat returned to her station next day with Captain Burton at the tiller, as the Coxswain had been disabled en route. The Chief Inspector considered that this case demonstrated the immense value of a motor boat.

IRVINE Alexander, Captain, Fishing Boat *Spero Meliora*　　　　　**SILVER**
13 March 1913

7 February 1913: While returning from fishing, Captain Irvine saw the fishing boat *Chalcedony*, which had been totally wrecked near the entrance to St. Monans Harbour, Fife, in a moderate southerly gale and heavy sea. He dropped anchor, veered his vessel down to the quayhead, embarked four extra hands, hauled off, went into the breakers and took off seven men from the wreck.

STEPHENSON William, Coxswain, Boulmer Lifeboat　　　　　**SILVER**
10 April 1913

29 March 1913: In fog, the Boulogne steam trawler *Tadorne*, bound for the Icelandic fishing grounds with a crew of 30 on board, was wrecked in a very heavy sea near Howick Haven, Northumberland. The self-righting lifeboat *Arthur R. Dawes* found the wreck to be in a very awkward position with her decks just awash and the crew in the rigging. Three men had already put off in a boat, but two drowned and one reached the shore. Another man, who had been washed off the wreck, was rescued by the lifeboat on her way in but he died later shortly after being landed. Getting alongside, the lifeboat took off 20 men but, whilst doing so, the boat was repeatedly filled with water, and some of the crew were knocked about and dazed. With 21 rescued men on board it was decided to return to Boulmer, which was reached about 10.a.m. Putting out again, Coxswain Stephenson, with ten fresh men in his crew, took off four more men and landed them at Hawick Haven. The bodies of the two remaining crew of the *Tadorne* were brought ashore later.

BURGON Robert, Coxswain, Berwick-on-Tweed Lifeboat　　　　　**SILVER**
10 April 1913

29–30 March 1913: The Gothenburg barque *Jacob Rauers*, on passage to Grangemouth with a cargo of spars and pit-props, stranded on rocks near the 'Needle Eye' in Marshall Meadows Bay, Northumberland. At 9 p.m. in the pitch darkness, the self-righting lifeboat *Matthew Simpson* was despatched through the rough sea and reached the wreck just as attempts by the rocket apparatus were abandoned. Heavy seas were washing over the barque and the dangerous rocks, therefore the lifeboat was veered down to within 20 yards, a rope was then passed and the 11 men were dragged through the heavy seas and debris by lifebuoy. The lifeboat returned to station at 2 a.m.

MEARNS David, Captain, Steam Trawler *Southesk*　　　　　**SILVER**
12 June 1913

9 May 1913: With her engines broken down and sails blown away, the Portknockie steam drifter *Yarmouth* with a crew of nine was drifting through high seas with a strong south-east gale on

shore, near Montrose, Angus. When she was about a mile off Usan, the steam trawler *Southesk* steamed to her assistance and, achieving contact, towed her seawards, and maintained the tow for 26 hours before crossing the bar to safety.

PEDDLE William W., Captain, Trawler *Onyx*   **SILVER**

SEAWARD Andrew, Third Hand, Trawler *Onyx*   **.SILVER**

12 June 1913

30 May 1913: A strong south-west gale was blowing when the Milford trawler *Providence* was seen to be in distress near Carmarthen Bay, with a very heavy sea breaking over her. The *Onyx*, which was in the vicinity, went to her, and her 16 foot punt was lowered and, manned by Captain Peddle and his third hand, taken through the heavy sea. Shortly before the casualty foundered, her four man crew was taken off, this included her Master with a broken arm and one seaman with a wooden leg.

SMITH James (Junior), Coxswain, Portpatrick Lifeboat   **SILVER**

8 January 1914

15 December 1913: The Glasgow s.s. *Dunira*, which had broken from her tow, was drifting through a heavy sleet squall off Portpatrick, Wigtownshire, when she let go both anchors. Coxswain Smith took the self-righting lifeboat *Civil Service No. 3* alongside, and the steamer's Engineer and Mate jumped aboard just before the anchor chains parted and the drift toward the shore resumed. The Coxswain manoeuvred his boat alongside to rescue the remaining three crew when the steamer was only 100 yards from the rocks. The lifeboat was damaged by collision with the wreck and shortly after the foremast went by the board. Portpatrick was, however, reached safely.

DAVIES Daniel P., Pilot's Apprentice   **SILVER**

2 April 1914

22 February 1914: The Barnstaple ketch *Elizabeth Couch*, her sails blown away and burning flares for assistance, was driving before a south-west gale in very heavy seas near Nash Sands off Porthcawl, Glamorgan. Two men in the pilot cutter *Dawn* saw the ketch but, because of the severe weather, could not help immediately. They stood by for some hours during which time the ketch drifted into a dangerous position and was in danger of sinking. Daniel Davies, therefore, lowered the cutter's punt, rowed to the ketch and saved her two crew. Considerable risk was involved, not only because of the weather, but because the pilot cutter was in considerable danger of colliding with the ketch.

HOLMES Thomas, Commander, R.N. Chief Inspector of Lifeboats	**SILVER**
WICKHAM Edward, Coxswain, Wexford Lifeboat	**SILVER(2)**
DUGGAN William, Crew Member, Wexford Lifeboat	**SILVER**
WICKHAM James, Crew Member, Wexford Lifeboat	**SILVER**
POWER Walter, Coxswain, Dunmore East Lifeboat	**SILVER**

12 March 1914

20–23 February 1914: During a south-south-west gale and strong tide, the Norwegian schooner *Mexico*, bound from South America to Liverpool with a cargo of mahogany logs, lost her bearings and drove into Bannow Bay, Co. Wexford. There she struck on South Keenagh Island. About 3 p.m. on the 20th, the Fethard self-righting lifeboat *Helen Blake* put off to her assistance. When within 50 yards of the schooner, the lifeboat was struck by a heavy breaker and filled to the thwarts. The anchor was let go, but before it could bring her up three or four following seas struck her and hurled her against the rocks, where she was smashed to pieces. Of the 14 man crew, nine were washed away and drowned. The five survivors managed to scramble on to the island and, by means of rope, helped eight of the *Mexico*'s crew on to the island. Two other men from the *Mexico* had got away in a ship's boat and were washed ashore. As soon as news of the disaster reached London, Commander Holmes, the Chief Inspector of Lifeboats, was order to Fethard, and arrived there at 3 p.m. on Sunday, 22nd. In the meantime the lifeboats from Wexford, Kilmore and Dunmore East had made unsuccessful attempts to rescue the survivors. Shortly after his arrival, Commander Holmes led another unsuccessful attempt in the Dunmore East boat. At 6 a.m. on Monday 23rd, they set out again, came close to the island and got a line ashore by rocket. Two men were then dragged through the water to the lifeboat. The Wexford lifeboat arrived on the scene about 8.15 a.m., and two of her crew, James Wickham and William Duggan, volunteered to go off in a strong punt which they veered down on to the rocks. In five trips, bringing two men each time, they brought off the remaining survivors. During the second trip the punt was holed on the rocks which the men stopped with a loaf of bread and some packaging. The two lifeboats were then taken in tow by a tug which had brought out the Wexford lifeboat and returned the men and boats to their various stations.

During the whole of the time the survivors were on the island all they had to eat were two small tins of preserved meat and a few limpets: their only drink was a small quantity of brandy and half a pint of wine which the Captain of the *Mexico* had. With no shelter, they were exposed to a biting wind and were drenched by rain and spray. One of the *Mexico* crew, a Portuguese, died from exposure.

LANGLANDS Thomas, Coxswain, Whitby Lifeboats	**GOLD**
BURTON Herbert Edgar, Captain, Royal Engineers	
Superintendent, Tynemouth Motor Lifeboat	**GOLD**
SMITH Robert, Coxswain, Tynemouth Motor Lifeboat	**GOLD**
HALL Basil, Commander, R.N. District Inspector of Lifeboats	**SILVER**
EGLON Richard, Second Coxswain, Whitby Lifeboats	**SILVER**
BROWNLEE James S., Second Coxswain, Tynemouth Motor Lifeboat	**SILVER**
PEART George, Bricklayer	**SILVER**

12 November 1914

30 October-1 November 1914: The British India Steam Navigation Company's 7,400 ton steamer *Rohilla*, taken over early in the Great War as a hospital ship, was plying from Queensferry to Dunkirk to evacuate wounded. With 224 men (including medical staff) and five nurses on board,

in a terrific east-south-easterly gale at 4 a.m., she ran on to a dangerous reef off rocks at Saltwick Nab, near Whitby, Yorkshire, and lay at the mercy of a furious sea. When rescue operations finished on 1 November, 83 men had been lost. Lifeboats from Scarborough, Teesmouth, Tynemouth, Upgang and Whitby (Nos. 1 and 2) were involved. The self-righting Whitby No. 2 lifeboat *John Fielden* with her Coxswain and Second Coxswain saved 35. The Tynemouth motor lifeboat *Henry Vernon* with her Coxswain and Second Coxswain on board, as well as Captain Burton and Commander Hall, battled 45 miles down an unlit coast against the gale to save 50 lives. Fifty-six other survivors made their own way ashore and a number of onlookers, prominent among whom was Mr. Peart, rushed into the surf to drag them out.

SWAN John Thompson, Coxswain, Lowestoft Lifeboat SILVER

10 December 1914

22 November 1914: Early in the morning, the minesweeper H.M.S. *Spider* went on to the beach near Lowestoft, Suffolk, in a strong easterly breeze, and the Norfolk and Suffolk class lifeboat *Kentwell* launched. She found heavy seas breaking over the vessel, but veered down in broken water and took off the crew of 13 men. Later in the day, she was called out to another minesweeper H.M.S. *Condor* on Newçombe Sands, the crew of which was in the rigging. Again, with heavy seas breaking over the casualty, Coxswain Swan veered down and saved the nine man crew, striking the minesweeper five times in the process.

GRIGSON George James, Coxswain, Clacton Lifeboat SILVER

10 December 1914

2–5 December 1914: During a south-south-west gale and in very heavy seas, the 1,000 ton P. & O. steamer *Harlington*, bound from the Tees to London with iron and general cargo, went ashore on Gunfleet Sands, off Clacton, Essex. The Watson class motor lifeboat *Albert Edward* put out and helped the crew to lighten the stranded vessel by throwing 100 tons of cargo overboard, and stayed until the morning of the 4th, when they returned to Clacton for food and a rest. They set out again at 7.45 p.m. and stood by until 9 a.m. on the 5th, when it was found that the vessel had five feet of water in her holds and was not salvageable. The crew of 15 men was then taken off and landed at Clacton at 11.30 a.m.

CUNNINGHAM Andrew, Coxswain, Crail Lifeboat SILVER

14 January 1915

27 December 1914: During a severe south-east gale, the torpedo-boat destroyer HMS *Success* ran ashore in darkness on the rocky coast at Kingsbarns, Fife, about six miles south-east of St Andrews. The Crail lifeboat *Edwin Kay* was launched at 6 a.m., and it needed skilful seamanship to prevent the boat from being dashed to pieces on the rocks around the wreck. Unfortunately, the boat was badly holed, in spite of the care taken, and owing to the heavy seas, Coxswain Cunningham and another crew member were washed overboard, but recovered safely. The lifeboat pressed on, reached the *Success* and took off 20 men and landed them ashore. Despite the damage to the lifeboat, two more trips were made and 34 were more men brought to safety. The St Andrews lifeboat then arrived on the scene and took off the remaining 13 crew members.

BROWN Robert   **SILVER**

14 January 1915

1 January 1915: The strong south-east by east gale forced a naval seaplane down into the sea off Kingsbarns, near St Andrews, Fife. Mr. Brown put off in a small boat, with two other men, in a very heavy sea and saved the two airmen.

GRIGSON George James, Coxswain, Clacton Lifeboat   **SILVER(2)**
*SALMON Jesse Lord, Second Coxswain, Clacton Lifeboat   **SILVER**

14 October 1915
*10 March 1916

28–29 September 1915: At 3.40 p.m. the Guernsey barquentine *Leading Chief*, from London to Shields, was reported aground on the Sunk Sands, off Clacton. The Watson class motor lifeboat *Albert Edward* launched in a south-west breeze, but in a heavy sea, to render assistance. The lifeboat crew had helped to throw 40 tons of iron ore overboard when the wind increased in strength with seas beginning to break over the vessel. The hatches were replaced and all the lifeboatmen, except the Coxswain and three others, returned to the lifeboat. As high water approached, the barquentine began bumping heavily on the sands and started to take in water. Coxswain Grigson signalled for the lifeboat to return alongside. Second Coxswain Salmon, at the helm, had to make nine attempts, in very heavy seas and inky blackness, before everyone was rescued and the lifeboat had to be driven on to the deck of the sinking vessel. Coxswain Grigson was almost swept overboard but managed to hold on to a rope and two lifeboatmen were washed off the barquentine but were picked up safely by the lifeboat. Everyone landed safely at Clacton at 10 a.m. on the 29th.

JAMIESON James, Second Coxswain, Berwick-on-Tweed Lifeboat   **SILVER**

10 December 1915

10 November 1915: The Berwick-on-Tweed Lifeboat *Matthew Simpson* put to sea about 4 a.m. to assist the motor boat *Redhead* which was dragging her anchors. She had anchored in Berwick Bay the previous day to effect engine repairs, and overnight a strong southerly gale blew up. It was not until daylight that the lifeboat was able to make contact, and, at a second attempt, she managed to get alongside the *Redhead*. The six crew then jumped into the lifeboat. Great difficulty was experienced in returning to the pier at Berwick, and it was only finally with the help of six fishermen who put off in a boat from Spittal and brought a line from the pier that the lifeboat was hauled in.

MAINLAND James Prophet   **SILVER**

10 March 1916

6 December 1915: The Hull steam trawler *Jackdaw* was wrecked during a whole south-east gale at Basta Voe, Island of Yell, Shetland Isles, in a very heavy sea. Mr. Mainland and four other men put off in a shore-boat and saved eight of the trawler's crew.

CROSS Robert, Coxswain, Spurn Lifeboat   **SILVER**

14 January 1916

9 December 1915: The night was very dark, a strong gale was blowing and a terrible sea was running over the Middle Binks at the mouth of the River Humber, when s.s. *Florence* of Stockton, bound from London to Newcastle with a cargo of oil, stranded. The Liverpool class lifeboat *Charles Deere James* was launched but, due to the shallowness of the water over the sand bank, could not go alongside and grounded herself. Seas were sweeping over the steamer, and Coxswain Cross jumped into the sea with a rope, but had to be hauled back. He then went overside with another man and achieved contact with the casualty. Standing on the sands, completely smothered in the seas, he remained until the whole crew of the steamer, eight men in all, had been passed into the lifeboat, which took them to safety.

BUSHELL John, Coxswain, Blyth Lifeboat   **SILVER**

14 January 1916

10 December 1915: The North Shields steam trawler *Naval Prince* ran ashore in a whole south-easterly gale and very heavy sea off Cambois, two miles north of Blyth, Northumberland. The Cambois self-righting lifeboat *Dash* was launched, but was beaten back to the beach. Realising that the Blyth lifeboat would likewise be impossible to launch successfully, Coxswain Bushell obtained a shore-boat, put out with three other men and reached the trawler to bring off her crew of three.

STEVENS Thomas, Coxswain, St. Ives Lifeboat   **SILVER**

14 January 1916

27 December 1915: In a west-north-westerly gale and very heavy sea, the Liverpool s.s. *Taunton*, Newport to Rouen with a cargo of stores for the French Government, was riding to her anchors in St. Ives Bay, Cornwall. Her anchors were reported to be dragging about one mile from Gwithian Beach at the north end of the bay, and the self-righting lifeboat *James Stevens No. 10* was launched. The seas were too violent for her to go alongside in the very heavy ground swell on the lee shore, therefore Coxswain Stevens anchored and veered down near her. The ship's nine man crew was then taken off using an endless whip and lifebuoy, but the return journey of four miles took three and a half hours and they were not landed until 7.30 p.m. Returning next morning with the Padstow tug *Helen Peele*, the lifeboatmen helped save the vessel.

HOLBROOK John, Coxswain, Bembridge Lifeboat   **SILVER**

11 February 1916

3 February 1916: During fog on Ring Rocks, Bembridge Ledge, off the Foreland, the easternmost point of the Isle of Wight, s.s. *Empress Queen* stranded while on passage from Le Havre to Southampton with ammunition. The Bembridge self-righting lifeboat *Queen Victoria* launched and, as soon as the tide was favourable, made for the wreck but was unable to anchor and, after a long struggle, succeeded in retrieving a rope thrown from the wreck. During this operation Coxswain Holbrook sustained severe injury to a hand but, in four trips, 110 people, a cat and a dog were taken off and landed. During one of these trips, the lifeboat was severely damaged on the rocks and, on the last trip, was in a water-logged condition. The other nine men were taken off in a large fishing boat.

ADAMS William, Coxswain, North Deal Lifeboat   **SILVER**

11 February 1916

4 February 1916: After some difficulty, the self-righting lifeboat *Charles Dibdin* was launched at 5 a.m. in response to a distress signal from the steam trawler *De La Pole*, aground on the Goodwin Sands in tremendous seas. With seas breaking right over her, eight men were in her forerigging, three on her forecastle, and the Captain, up to his waist in water, was standing on his bridge. As the lifeboat was trying to get near, one of the trawlermen was washed overboard and drowned, but the other ten were taken off. Seeing no other way of being rescued, the Captain jumped into the sea and, at the second attempt, grabbed a line thrown from the lifeboat and was pulled aboard. All survivors were landed in the extremity of exhaustion at Broadstairs.

JACOBS Benjamin, Coxswain, Brooke Lifeboat   **SILVER**

14 April 1916

4 February 1916: In a south-westerly gale raging on the night of the 3rd, the Norwegian barque *Souvenir* of Trevisand was wrecked to the south-east of Brooke, Isle of Wight. She had already become derelict and unmanageable in the violent gale off St. Catherine's and drifted through the darkness, stranding hard and fast on the Great Stag Ledge in an area of comparatively shallow water studded with rocks. The self-righting lifeboat *Susan Ashley* launched just before 8.30 a.m., but was unable to get alongside the wreck. The barque's crew therefore donned lifebelts and jumped into the sea. Although they were carried in different directions, the lifeboat succeeded in picking up the nine crew, although the steward died shortly afterwards from exhaustion. The Master refused to leave his ship and stayed in his cabin. The vessel broke up before the lifeboat could return to try to save him, and his body was recovered next day.

This award was recommended in February but confirmed only in April after an investigation into certain details of the service.

HARRIS Sydney James, Coxswain Superintendent, Gorleston Lifeboats   **SILVER(5)**
BENSLEY Edward, Crew Member, Gorleston No. 1 Lifeboat   **SILVER**

14 April 1916

29 March 1916: When the Jersey schooner *Dart* sank off Corton, Suffolk, north of Lowestoft in blinding snow and a gale 'of almost unparalleled violence', her four man crew took to the rigging. The Gorleston No. 1 Norfolk and Suffolk class lifeboat *Mark Lane* put off and, nearing the wreck, anchored and veered down but was driven over her and had to haul back. Coxswain Harris held her in position and Mr. Bensley jumped into the schooner's rigging to transfer into the lifeboat the four men helpless from exposure, bitter cold and driving sleet.

Coxswain Harris is the only man to have received the silver medal five times.

LEMON Robert, Professional Diver   **SILVER**

7 July 1916

9 April 1916: While engaged in salvage work at Barnmouth, Co. Londonderry, northern Ireland, Mr Lemon saw the Glasgow s.s. *Corsewell* in distress and put off in his motor boat with two local men. After a short time, these men insisted on returning to the shore. He then went out alone and

came alongside the wreck, but a heavy sea filled his boat and stopped his engine. Fortunately he was able to reach another wreck and remained on it until rescued by the Portrush lifeboat. As a result of his brave action, Lemon lost his boat and gear, and a fund was opened locally to recoup him for his loss to which the Institution contributed £10.

CAMERON James, Coxswain, Peterhead Lifeboat   **SILVER**

10 November 1916

28–29 October 1916: At 7.15 p.m., the 6,000 ton s.s. *Kiev* of Odessa was reported ashore at Rattray Head, seven miles north of Peterhead, Aberdeenshire, and the Watson class motor lifeboat *John Ryburn* set off in intense darkness, through an extremely heavy sea and a strong southerly gale. After a prolonged search, the vessel was found about a mile from the shore, north of the Head, and 60 people were taken into the lifeboat. On the way back to Peterhead, a small boat holding 14 more was taken in tow. Ten more were saved by other means, but eight drowned. The lifeboat reached Peterhead at 4.30 a.m.

BADGER E., 2nd Lieutenant, Royal Engineers   **SILVER**
STEPHENS Frank Collyford, Lieutenant, R.N.R.   **SILVER**

8 December 1916

3 November 1916: After the 5,077 ton Fleet Auxiliary tanker *Ponus* stranded during a full southerly gale in very heavy seas on Gyllyngvase Beach, Falmouth Bay, Cornwall, some of her crew reached the shore in ship's boats with others being taken off by the Falmouth lifeboat. The Second Mate remained aboard, but the tanker later caught fire and he improvised a raft which, after he had boarded it, remained pinned against the burning vessel. Second Lieutenant Badger and Lieutenant Stephens put out in a dinghy, caught hold of the Second Mate, and brought him ashore tied to the dinghy's stern as it was too small to have him aboard.

ADAMS William, Coxswain, North Deal Lifeboat   **SILVER(2)**

12 January 1917

19–20 November 1916: At 8 p.m. with an east-south-east gale at hurricane force and mountainous seas on the Goodwin Sands, distress signals were seen coming from the Italian steamer *Val Salice* on passage from Sunderland to Savona. After an unsuccessful attempt to launch the Kingsdown lifeboat, the North Deal self-righting lifeboat *Charles Dibdin* was launched at 10 p.m. and, under storm sails, reached the wreck at midnight. At times, the seas were so violent that the lifeboat was lifted almost to the level of the steamer's mast heads. Assisted by the guardship's searchlight, 30 men (the whole crew) climbed down rope ladders and were pulled aboard the lifeboat and landed at Deal at 3 a.m.

CROMARTY George, Coxswain, Holy Island No. 2 Lifeboat   **SILVER**

8 December 1916

19–20 November 1916: The Gothenburg barque *Jolani* was seen to be drifting dangerously near to Emmanuel Head on Holy Island but succeeded in weathering it, and it became apparent that she would drive ashore in the neighbourhood of Goswick, Northumberland. The self-righting lifeboat *Edward and Eliza* was called at 2.40 p.m. Men and horses went to the boathouse two and a half miles away and transported the lifeboat on her carriage six miles over sands churned up by the waves. For four and a half miles of the journey, they were forced to wade through water two and a half feet deep. When they drew nearer the wreck, they saw her crew of 14 men gathered on her stern – the only part not submerged. Although repeatedly thrown back by the violence of the waves, the lifeboat was finally launched successfully. The wreck was drifting northwards in a raging east-south-east hurricane with seas breaking over her. After unsuccessful attempts, Coxswain Cromarty eventually managed to get a line aboard and all the 14 men were brought off, the lifeboat being beached at Cheswick, three miles further north. After being given rest and refreshment at the Goswick Golf Club House, the lifeboat crew went home by cart and returned in the afternoon to collect the boat.

SMITH Robert, Coxswain, Tynemouth Lifeboat   **SILVER(2)**

BROWNLEE James, Second Coxswain, Tynemouth Lifeboat   **SILVER(2)**

8 December 1916

19–21 November 1916: In a strong easterly gale and a very heavy sea, the Swansea 2,886 ton steel steamer s.s. *Muristan*, Tyne to Rouen, ran ashore on the 19th at Blyth Bay, Northumberland, when her steering gear was rendered useless. Her Master and another man were washed away and drowned. Big seas constantly swept over the wreck, which rendered the stem, funnel and after mast only occasionally visible. Three men managed to get ashore at daybreak on the 19th. The self-righting motor lifeboat *Henry Vernon* arrived on the scene in the late morning of the 20th but could do nothing. Trying to return to Tynemouth, the engine failed when she was struck by a tremendous sea. Putting into Blyth under sail, it was established that there were still survivors aboard the wreck. She therefore put out at daybreak on the 21st and, in a difficult and dangerous operation, took off 16 men.

STANTON William, Coxswain, North Deal Reserve Lifeboat   **SILVER**

COOPER William, Coxswain, Ramsgate Lifeboat   **SILVER**

PAY James, Coxswain, Kingsdowne Lifeboat   **SILVER**

HOLBOURN Robert, Second Coxswain, North Deal Reserve Lifeboat   **SILVER**

* READ Thomas William, Second Coxswain, Ramsgate Lifeboat   **SILVER**

8 December 1916

*12 January 1917

20–21 November 1916: Signals were seen at 7 a.m. from the New York s.s. *Sibiria* which had driven aground on the Goodwins in exceptionally bad weather. The North Deal Reserve lifeboat was launched and towed out to the wreck but, although she made four attempts, nearly capsizing on the first three and finishing on her beam ends on the fourth, she was unsuccessful. Her mizzen mast and sail were torn out of her and a thwart carried away, so she was forced to return to Deal. Meanwhile, the Ramsgate self-righting lifeboat *Charles and Susanna Stephens* was being towed out by the tug *Aid* and reached the scene at 11.3 0 a.m. She veered down across the Sands several times, constantly filling with water until one of her bollards was wrenched out, injuring two of her crew. With her cable parted, the lifeboat was compelled to return to Ramsgate which she reached at 4.30 p.m. Later, she received an urgent message to say that, with the crew still aboard, the *Sibiria*'s decks were almost under water. She set out again at 7.15 p.m. but found that the Kingsdowne lifeboat had fought her way through and had just taken off the last of the 52 man crew. They were landed at Kingsdowne at 12.45 a.m. on the 21st.

The North Deal Reserve Lifeboat Francis Forbes Barton *was a war emergency station boat based at Deal from 1915 to 1921.*

BECHER John Richard Hedge, M.A., The Venerable Archdeacon.
   Honorary Secretary, Baltimore R.N.L.I.   **SILVER**

SANDERSON Arthur Lakeland, Lieutenant, R.N.R.,
   H.M. Trawler *Indian Empire*   **SILVER**

12 January 1917

29–30 December 1916: The 2,244 ton s.s. *Alondra*, en route from Las Palmas to Liverpool, was wrecked on the Kedge Rock, off Baltimore, Co. Cork, Ireland. 16 of her crew left in one of the ship's boats, but drowned before they could reach the shore. Archdeacon Becher and some other volunteers launched a boat, but failed to land on Kedge Rock. They returned to Baltimore, but they put off again as some of the wreck's crew had made the Rock. Failing to reach the wreck with night closing in, they put back to the shore again. At daylight, they set out with the rocket apparatus. About the same time, two R.N. trawlers came upon the scene, and the combined efforts of all those present saved 23 survivors, some of whom had to be lowered down the sheer face of a 150 foot cliff.

CADOGAN Michael, Fisherman   **SILVER**

CADOGAN Tim, Fisherman   **SILVER**

DALY John, Fisherman   **SILVER**

DALY Tim, Fisherman   **SILVER**

12 January 1917

2 January 1917: On passage from Galveston, U.S.A. to Liverpool with a general cargo, the 6,395 ton s.s. *Nestorian* was wrecked on Cape Clear Island, the southernmost point of Co. Cork, Ireland.

Michael and Tim Cadogan and John and Tim Daly , with others, put out in a small boat and saved part of the crew. The lifesaving apparatus, in charge of Archdeacon Becher, was carried two miles over a mountain to the wreck.

*BLOGG Henry George, Coxswain, Cromer Lifeboat	**GOLD**
*DAVIES William, Acting Second Coxswain, Cromer Lifeboat	**SILVER**
*HOLMES Stewart, Private, 2/4th Battalion, Seaforth Highlanders	**SILVER**
ALLEN George, Crew Member, Cromer Lifeboat	**BRONZE**
ALLEN James, Crew Member, Cromer Lifeboat	**BRONZE**
ALLEN Edward Walter, Crew Member, Cromer Lifeboat	**BRONZE**
ALLEN William, Crew Member, Cromer Lifeboat	**BRONZE**
BALLS Henry, Crew Member, Cromer Lifeboat	**BRONZE**
COX Charles, Crew Member, Cromer Lifeboat	**BRONZE**
COX George, Crew Member, Cromer Lifeboat	**BRONZE**
HARRISON Leslie James, Crew Member, Cromer Lifeboat	**BRONZE**
KIRBY Tom, Crew Member, Cromer Lifeboat	**BRONZE**
MAYES Gilbert, Crew Member, Cromer Lifeboat	**BRONZE**
RIX Walter, Crew Member, Cromer Lifeboat	**BRONZE**
RIX William, Crew Member, Cromer Lifeboat	**BRONZE**

9 February 1917
30 March 1917

9 January 1917: The Liverpool class lifeboat *Louisa Heartwell* had already saved 16 men from the small Greek steamer *Pyrin*, in distress off Cromer, Norfolk, when a boiler exploded on the 1,326 ton Swedish s.s. *Fernebo* and the ship broke into two parts. The service to the first casualty had involved four trips, the last being completed at 3 p.m., and the lifeboat's crew were exhausted but, nevertheless, the decision was taken to relaunch. A strong north-easterly gale was blowing and there were very heavy seas – this lifeboat was normally launched over the open beach. Hundreds of servicemen helped the launch, many of them up to their necks in water, but it was impossible to get the lifeboat past the breakers and she was driven back on to the beach. A small boat had put out from the steamer with six survivors on board, but she capsized in the surf; all of the occupants were saved by the servicemen, prominent among whom was Private Holmes. By now (5 p.m.) both parts of the wreck had grounded, one mile apart, the aft end with the crew on board. The lifeboat put off again as bids by rocket apparatus had failed. After several attempts, the boat had to return with five oars broken and three lost. Spare oars were obtained and the lifeboat launched for another attempt just before midnight; 11 survivors were rescued. With wartime demands, lifeboat crews were nearly all over military age, and more than one in the Cromer lifeboat was approaching 70 years of age.

This was the first service for which bronze medals were voted.

MILLER William, Coxswain, Eyemouth Lifeboat   **BRONZE**

30 March 1917

6–7 March 1917: Shortly before noon, the Norwegian steamer *Livlig*, with a cargo of pit-props, was reported in difficulties off St. Abb's Head, Berwickshire, during a whole south-south-easterly gale. The self-righting lifeboat *Anne Frances* launched and got alongside after an hour in a very heavy sea to find the wreck, which had been on her beam ends, now righted with seven men in the rigging. One man had already drowned. After the lifeboat took the men on board, the weather prevented her from returning to Eyemouth so Coxswain Miller took her to Granton, near Leith, Midlothian, a journey occupying several hours with seas sweeping over the rescuers and rescued alike.

DEARMAN James, Coxswain, Hythe Lifeboat **BRONZE**
*GRIGGS Wright, Acting Second Coxswain, Hythe Lifeboat **BRONZE**
11 May 1917
*8 June 1917

2 April 1917: The 72 ton ketch *Mazeppa* of Harwich, at anchor in Hythe Bay, near Folkestone, Kent, dragged her anchor at 2.30 a.m. in a strong gale and drifted toward the shore. The self-righting lifeboat *Mayer de Rothschild* put out, kept the ketch under observation, then came up with her and managed to take off her two man crew. Mr. Griggs had retired earlier from the post of Second Coxswain, but volunteered to take the empty place on this launch.

CAMERON James, Coxswain, Peterhead Lifeboat **BRONZE**
11 May 1917

2–3 April 1917: With a strong east by south gale blowing over a very heavy sea, distress signals were seen in South Bay, Peterhead, Aberdeenshire. The Watson class lifeboat *John Ryburn* put out to deal with two steamers ashore in the bay: the s.s. *Tregarth* of Liverpool and the s.s. *Boscastle* of West Hartlepool. Anchoring in a suitable position, the lifeboat veered down and was about to make contact with them when her engine was stopped by a tremendous sea which she shipped. The water made it impossible to open the hatches, and the lifeboat was continually bumping on the rocks. She therefore hoisted her masts and sails and returned to harbour where her engine was put in working order. This done, she returned to the *Tregarth* and took off the 21 man crew and landed them. Coxswain Cameron then took the boat to the *Boscastle* and rescued the five men, the remainder electing to stay on board. Next day, they were found to be in danger; the lifeboat therefore returned and took off the 15 men left aboard.

RUDDOCK Arthur, Skipper, R.N.R. Steam Drifter *Heather Bell* **SILVER**
8 March 1918

16 December 1917: Off Whiting Bay, south-east Isle of Arran, Bute, the s.s. *Dragon* stranded in a full easterly gale and very heavy sea. She was sighted by Skipper Ruddock who launched a 14 foot dinghy and, with two other men, reached the wreck where the four man crew was in the rigging. After the men had been brought off, they were landed on shore as the sea was too heavy for the dinghy to return to the drifter.

GILL James, Acting Coxswain, Newquay Lifeboat **SILVER**
TREBILCOCK Richard James, Second Coxswain, Newquay Lifeboat **BRONZE**
11 January 1918

17 December 1917: When the large Danish steamer *Osten* was seen drifting in a helpless condition off Towan Head, Newquay, Cornwall, in a furious north-east gale, help was requested. The newly

appointed Coxswain of the self-righting lifeboat *James Stevens No. 5* stated that the conditions were too bad to launch, and the former Coxswain, Mr. Gill, then offered to take her out with Mr. Trebilcock. She launched, but a succession of heavy seas overpowered her after she had been thrown on her beam ends. She was swept on to rocks under cliffs and smashed to pieces. Onlookers rushed forward and, using lines, managed to save all the men in the boat. The steamer was brought to safety later. Trebilcock was promoted to Coxswain in recognition of his action.

GRIGSON George James, Coxswain, Clacton Lifeboat	**SILVER(3)**
SALMON Jesse Lord, Second Coxswain, Clacton Lifeboat	**BRONZE**
	11 January 1918

27–28 December 1917: Shortly before midnight, the Swedish 1,254 ton s.s. *Iris*, on passage from Gothenburg to Rouen, France, went ashore on the Longsand in a very rough sea and a strong easterly gale. When the Watson class lifeboat *Albert Edward* reached the wreck, she was found to have 11 feet of water in her engine room, but the Captain refused to abandon his ship. The lifeboat stood by all day in worsening weather. Eventually, the Captain, her 21 man crew and a Pilot were taken off through mighty waves and landed at Clacton at 11.30 p.m. By that time the whole of the crew were numbed from their 24 hours exposure in the icy cold weather.

HAMMOND William, Coxswain, Walton-on-Naze Lifeboat	**SILVER**
BYFORD John Charles, Second Coxswain, Walton-on-Naze Lifeboat	**BRONZE**
	11 January 1918

29–30 December 1917: In thick weather, sleet and rain and an east by north gale blowing, the 780 ton s.s. *Peregrine* en route from Rotterdam to London was stranded at 10.30 p.m. on the north-east part of the Longsand, off Clacton-on-Sea, Essex. The Norfolk and Suffolk class lifeboat *James Stevens No. 14* put out in tempestuous seas and, after a long and difficult search in the dark, got alongside at the sixth attempt. All 59 passengers and the Chief Steward were taken off and transferred to a patrol vessel. Then the lifeboat returned to the wreck, now in two parts. The other 32 crew members were taken off in an operation lasting all night and at 9 a.m. they left the wreck for Walton-on-Naze. The lifeboat was severely damaged during the service.

ESCOTT Henry, Company Quarter Master Sergeant,	
Royal Garrison Artillery	**SILVER**
	10 January 1919

29 September 1918: Owing to a sudden change in the north-north-east gale, one of H.M. motor launches was seen to be in difficulties near St. Ives, Cornwall. Before the lifeboat could get there, the launch struck the rocks, blew up, and ten men were killed. One man was saved from the water, and C.Q.M.S. Escott, after searching the rocks, saw another from the top of a cliff. With rope fastened around him, he was lowered into Clodgy Cove and managed to swim through the heavy sea. The ropes that he fastened to the survivor broke every time, and the man drowned; the C.Q.M.S. had himself to be rescued by a man lowered into the cove.

SWAN John Thompson, Coxswain, Lowestoft Lifeboat   **SILVER(2)**
AYERS George William, Second Coxswain, Lowestoft Lifeboat   **BRONZE**

11 October 1918

30 September 1918: The sloop H.M.S. *Pomona* was totally wrecked in a north-easterly gale and very heavy sea at Dunwich, Suffolk, five miles south of Southwold. The Norfolk and Suffolk class lifeboat *Kentwell* was called out, but when the crew was assembled two were over 70 years old, 12 over 60 and four over 50. Nevertheless, a few minutes after 5 a.m., they set out on a 17 mile journey and, when they reached the wreck at 7 a.m., it was completely under water with four men on top of the wheelhouse and five others on the foremast. Everybody was rescued after a number of attempts, but the Captain had drowned already; two others had been washed overboard but were rescued from the shore.

At the Annual General Meeting, reporting this service by veterans, it was stated that it was 'a most impressive sight to see these old men, grey haired and bent, and the majority afflicted with the attendant ills of old age, struggling in the darkness against the wind and rain'.

HART John, Master, Fishing Yawl *Mary Annie*   **SILVER**
McCARTHY Jeremiah   **BRONZE**
MURPHY Timothy   **BRONZE**

13 December 1918

10–11 November 1918: In a strong north-westerly wind and a very heavy sea, the Dublin motor fishing boat *Thomas Joseph* was wrecked on Shirkin Island, near Baltimore, Co. Cork, Ireland, at 10 p.m. She was on a trial trip with 11 people, including three young girls, on board. When he heard of the accident, Captain Hart put off in his punt with Messrs. Murphy and McCarthy and succeeded in saving three men clinging to the sunken vessel's mast. Seeing two other survivors clinging to rocks whom they could not save at that time, the three rescuers rowed to Heir Island, a mile away. There they obtained a large boat and with two extra men, saved a man and a girl from the rocks. Captain Hart and Mr. Murphy were nearly swept away in doing so.

JACKSON Alfred, Fisherman   **SILVER**
HICKS Thomas, Master, Motor Drifter *Ben-ma-Chree*   **BRONZE**
SLEEMAN David (Junior), Fisherman   **BRONZE**
SLEEMAN Edward, Fisherman   **BRONZE**

4 July 1919

17 March 1919: After striking the Lee Ore reef of the Runnelstone, an underwater granite pinnacle off Tol Pedn, Cornwall (two miles from Land's End), the Falmouth coaster s.s. *Falmouth Castle* beached at Porthcurno. On her way to the fishing grounds, the motor fishing vessel *Ben-ma-Chree* encountered a boat from the coaster, and the seven men in it were saved by Mr. Hicks and the Messrs. Sleeman in their small boat. Two others of the coaster's crew were saved by rocket apparatus. Before the Sennen Cove lifeboat arrived, Mr. Jackson put off from Porthgwarra in a 14 foot punt. Pulling through heavy seas he reached the wreck, over which the seas were making a clean breach, and took off the Captain's 68 year old wife, who was in a state of collapse, and landed her safely.

OWEN John, Coxswain, Llandudno Lifeboat   **BRONZE**

11 April 1919

27 March 1919: In a very heavy sea and north-westerly gale, the self-righting lifeboat *Theodore Price* launched to the Liverpool schooner *Ada Mary* which had lost her sails off Little Ormes Head, between Llandudno and Rhos-on-Sea, Caernarvonshire. With one cable parted, she was in danger of being driven on shore. Two attempts were necessary before the lifeboat could get alongside the casualty to take off the two men on board. Having been buried by the seas three times on her way to the wreck, she tried for two hours to beat back to Llandudno but was obliged to put into Colwyn Bay where the men were landed and the lifeboat drawn up.

BOWEN Thomas, Coxswain, Cardigan Lifeboat   **BRONZE**

11 April 1919

27 March 1919: In Cardigan Bay the London s.s. *Conservator* got into difficulties in a whole north-westerly gale, accompanied by cold weather, snow showers and a very heavy sea. Her distress signals were seen, and the self-righting lifeboat *Elizabeth Austin* was launched. When the lifeboat reached the ship, she was being driven toward the bar with both anchors dragging. Despite seas washing over both vessels, her ten man crew was taken off. Unable to regain her station, Coxswain Bowen took the lifeboat across the bar and up river to Cardigan , where the survivors were landed.

SLATER Charles, Petty Officer, H.M. Coastguard, Howth   **BRONZE**
RICKARD Patrick, Shop Assistant   **BRONZE**

4 July 1919

18 May 1919: A soldier fell over a cliff at Howth, Co. Dublin, Ireland, and Petty Officer Slater, Mr. Rickard and two others launched a motor boat in a strong south-south-east gale and rough sea. When they reached the area, Petty Officer Slater jumped overboard and swam to the rocks but found that the soldier had been killed. Mr. Rickard also entered the water and, together, they recovered the body.

ROBINSON William, Second Coxswain, Filey Lifeboat   **BRONZE**
BOYNTON George, Fisherman   **BRONZE**

4 July 1919

12 June 1919: In a whole south-south-west gale and a very heavy sea the fishing coble *Leslie* capsized off Filey, Yorkshire, throwing its two occupants into the water. Robinson and Boynton saw the accident from another coble and went to their aid and saved the two exhausted men in conditions of great risk.

HOLBROOK John, Coxswain, Bembridge Lifeboat   **SILVER(2)**

12 September 1919

28 August 1919: In the morning, during very heavy seas, thick rain and a strong south gale, the Los Angeles s.s. *Wakulla* was driven ashore on West Wittering shoal, near Chichester, Sussex, and the Bembridge self-righting lifeboat *Queen Victoria* put out. On nearing the wreck, she was taken

in tow by a government tug until she was to windward of the steamer, when she dropped down to her through a mile of heaving breaking seas. Going alongside with great difficulty, Coxswain Holbrook took off 13 men and, after landing them, returned to stand by the steamer all night but left at 4 a.m.; the wind had shifted and the weather had moderated. The lifeboat had been afloat in heavy seas for 19 hours.

BROWN John, Captain, Drifter *Bessie*   **BRONZE**

12 December 1919

18 September 1919: During severe weather, the lighter *Tom Telford* was totally wrecked at Digg, Staffin, Skye. Captain Brown, with his seven crew, saved the three hands on board. Great risk was incurred by the rescuers.

ADAMS William, Coxswain, North Deal Lifeboat   **SILVER(3)**
STANTON William, Coxswain, North Deal Reserve Lifeboat   **BRONZE**

14 November 1919

1–2 November 1919: The self-righting lifeboat *Charles Dibdin* launched after distress signals were seen from the Goodwin Sands. Even with two extra hands on board, she took three hours to reach the three masted Estonian schooner *Toogo* due to the east-north-easterly gale and strong head wind. Before the vessel could be reached she struck and sank, but nothing could be done in the darkness. The lifeboat therefore cruised among the wreckage until daybreak when two survivors, clinging to an upturned boat, were rescued. On reaching the shore, the lifeboat was taken over by Coxswain Stanton and the Reserve lifeboat's crew, who set out for the wreck of the London ketch *Corinthian*, which had struck while homeward bound from Antwerp. Reaching the ketch took nearly six hours, and the lifeboat was full of water nearly all the journey. The ketch's crew was found clinging to the rigging, where they had been for 16 hours. Three men were brought into the lifeboat by line, but one was found to be dead; one other had been washed away. The lifeboat returned to the shore, eight hours after she had put out.

*NICHOLAS Thomas Henry, Coxswain, Sennen Cove Lifeboat	**SILVER**
PENDER Thomas, Second Coxswain, Sennen Cove Lifeboat	**SILVER**
GEORGE Edmund, Crew Member, Sennen Cove Lifeboat	**BRONZE**
GEORGE Edward, Crew Member, Sennen Cove Lifeboat	**BRONZE**
GEORGE Ernest, Crew Member, Sennen Cove Lifeboat	**BRONZE**
GEORGE Thomas, Crew Member, Sennen Cove Lifeboat	**BRONZE**
NICHOLAS Edward, Crew Member, Sennen Cove Lifeboat	**BRONZE**
NICHOLAS Henry, Crew Member, Sennen Cove Lifeboat	**BRONZE**
NICHOLAS Henry (Junior), Crew Member, Sennen Cove Lifeboat	**BRONZE**
NICHOLAS Herbert, Crew Member, Sennen Cove Lifeboat	**BRONZE**
NICHOLAS James Howard, Crew Member, Sennen Cove Lifeboat	**BRONZE**
NICHOLAS John, Crew Member, Sennen Cove Lifeboat	**BRONZE**
PENROSE John, Crew Member, Sennen Cove Lifeboat	**BRONZE**
ROBERTS Robert, Crew Member, Sennen Cove Lifeboat	**BRONZE**

12 December 1919
9 January 1920

30 November 1919: En route from Queenstown (Cobh), Co. Cork, Ireland to Southampton in company with two other motor launches and a destroyer, H.M.M.L. *No. 378* was shipping water in a south-south-westerly gale off Land's End, when in the afternoon her engines stopped. One of the launches twice got a line to her, but each one parted and *No. 378* drifted, helplessly, toward the Longships reef. The lifeboat *Ann Newbon* launched and reached the casualty when she was almost on the reef. In desperation the motor launch's nine man crew put off in her dinghy, but it capsized, throwing them into the furious water. Four of them regained the motor launch to be flung with her on the rocks; the lifeboat was just in time to snatch four of the other five from the turbulent sea. The four men on the rocks, half-buried in water and frozen, were dragged on board the lifeboat as she manoeuvred close into the reef on her anchor; the slightest miscalculation would have meant disaster.

KNIGHTS George Henry, Coxswain, Kessingland Lifeboat	**SILVER**
SMITH Edward John, Second Coxswain, Kessingland Lifeboat	**SILVER**
SMITH Christopher Crispin, Bowman, Kessingland Lifeboat	**BRONZE**
BAGOT Ernest William, Crew Member, Kessingland Lifeboat	**BRONZE**
BLOWERS George, Crew Member, Kessingland Lifeboat	**BRONZE**
BROWN Sidney James, Crew Member, Kessingland Lifeboat	**BRONZE**
CATCHPOLE Richard, Crew Member, Kessingland Lifeboat	**BRONZE**
HART William, Crew Member, Kessingland Lifeboat	**BRONZE**
JEFFERY John B., Crew Member, Kessingland Lifeboat	**BRONZE**
KEMP Louis Henry, Crew Member, Kessingland Lifeboat	**BRONZE**
MUDDITT J.C., Crew Member, Kessingland Lifeboat	**BRONZE**
THACKER Herbert, Crew Member, Kessingland Lifeboat	**BRONZE**
UTTING Alfred, Crew Member, Kessingland Lifeboat	**BRONZE**
UTTING Arthur, Crew Member, Kessingland Lifeboat	**BRONZE**
WIGG Alfred, Crew Member, Kessingland Lifeboat	**BRONZE**
WIGG Wilfred, Crew Member, Kessingland Lifeboat	**BRONZE**

9 January 1920

11 December 1919: With a gale blowing and in a very rough sea, the Rye sailing smack *A.J.W.* stranded on Newcombe Sands, off Lowestoft, Suffolk. The Norfolk and Suffolk class lifeboat *St. Paul* launched only to be driven back after she had shipped three heavy seas and parted her haul-off warp. In a cold very dark night, the sunken smack was finally found with only two masts showing and four men clinging to the rigging. One man was taken off through seas breaking heavily over the wreck; the other three were snatched from their perches only after Coxswain Knights had driven the lifeboat over the sunken vessel between the two masts.

GALL Charles, Coxswain, Broughty Ferry Lifeboat **BRONZE**

21 May 1920

11 April 1920: During a strong easterly gale and a very heavy sea, the Dundee pilot cutter *Day Dream* ran on to the Gaa Bank at the mouth of the River Tay. It was just before 1 a.m. on a dark, cold night that the Watson class lifeboat *Maria* went down river to find the casualty lying in shallow, broken water, rolling in waves which were breaking over her. After an unsuccessful attempt, Coxswain Gall veered down and, in five more attempts, took off five men. He then searched for and found a sixth man, who had left in a dinghy.

O'MAHONEY John F. (age 12) **BRONZE**

17 September 1920

12 June 1920: Two boys, John F. O'Mahoney, son of the Chief of Customs at Fenit, and his friend Bernard Kelly, were bathing at Lighthouse Point, Tralee Bay, Co Kerry. Both were 12 years old, and neither could swim more than a few strokes. It was a cold day, with a moderate gale blowing off shore. Kelly got into difficulties, and O'Mahoney could not reach him but, with the help of some little girls, he launched a canvas canoe. The tide was ebbing and a strong off-shore wind swept him right past the drowning boy. O'Mahoney was finally rescued himself by a small war craft, HMS *Heather*

which had been alerted by the Coastguard. The canoe was eight miles out and the boy was lying naked and wet in the bottom.

Although it was not strictly an attempt at rescue from shipwreck, the Committee of Management felt it to be a case of so exceptional a character as to justify them in giving a generous interpretation to the rule governing the bestowal of the Institution's medals. O'Mahoney also received two War Savings Certificates.

BRUCE Hugh, Fisherman	**BRONZE**
BRUCE John, Fisherman	**BRONZE**
BRUCE Laurence, Fisherman	**BRONZE**
HUTCHISON Laurence, Fisherman	**BRONZE**
IRVINE William, Fisherman	**BRONZE**

18 November 1921

1 December 1920: The American three-masted sailing ship *Marion Chilcott*, Denmark to St. Thomas, Virgin Islands, in very thick weather and a strong south-easterly gale, was in danger of being wrecked on the Island of Yell, Shetland Isles with her Master, his wife and 26 men aboard. Her plight was seen by the five Scaw fishermen who launched their 15 foot sailing boat and, under sail, threaded their way through rocks. Mr. L. Bruce and Mr. Irvine boarded the distressed ship, took charge and piloted her safely into Blue Mull Sound, between Yell and Unst.

HOWELLS John, Coxswain, Fishguard Lifeboat	**GOLD**
DAVIES Thomas Oakley, Second Coxswain, Fishguard Lifeboat	**SILVER**
SIMPSON Robert Edwin, Motor Mechanic, Fishguard Lifeboat	**SILVER**
HOLMES Thomas, Crew Member, Fishguard Lifeboat	**SILVER**
DEVEREUX W., Crew Member, Fishguard Lifeboat	**BRONZE**
DUFFIN T., Crew Member, Fishguard Lifeboat	**BRONZE**
GARDINER J., Crew Member, Fishguard Lifeboat	**BRONZE**
MASON H.M., Crew Member, Fishguard Lifeboat	**BRONZE**
PERKINS Thomas, Crew Member, Fishguard Lifeboat	**BRONZE**
ROURKE John, Crew Member, Fishguard Lifeboat	**BRONZE**
THOMAS William John, Crew Member, Fishguard Lifeboat	**BRONZE**
VEAL R., Crew Member, Fishguard Lifeboat	**BRONZE**
WHELAN P., Crew Member, Fishguard Lifeboat	**BRONZE**

17 December 1920

3 December 1920: The three masted Dutch motor schooner *Hermina*, anchored outside Fishguard breakwater, Pembrokeshire, was dragging her anchors in a north-westerly gale. The self-righting motor lifeboat *Charterhouse* launched but, when she arrived, the schooner was grinding heavily on the rocks with tremendous seas making a clean breach over her. Veering down, in spite of great difficulties, seven men were taken off but the Master and the two Mates refused to leave. Coxswain Howells prepared to return to Fishguard, but the lifeboat had sprung a leak and it was found impossible to restart her engine. Her sail was hoisted, but she lost her mizzen sail, which left her with only the mainsail set. Second Coxswain Davies and crew member Holmes succeeded in setting the jib sail and, although waterlogged, the lifeboat managed to reach her station at midnight, three hours

later. Although flares were shortly after seen from the *Hermina*, the lifeboat was unable to return, and the schooner's Master and First Mate were rescued by life saving apparatus; the Second Mate had drowned.

In April 1921, Coxswain Howells, his crew and the lifeboat went on the train to London to receive their awards. Howells was 66 years old at the time of the service.

JOHNSTON William, Coxswain, Stromness Lifeboat   **BRONZE**

27 January 1922

1–2 January 1922: The Grimsby trawler *Freesia*, homeward bound with a large catch, sank in the morning off Costa Head, on Mainland, Orkney; her crew took to a small raft in the very heavy sea. Shore boats made unsuccessful attempts to give help and, when the self righting motor lifeboat *John A. Hay* arrived, she found some planks from the raft supporting two exhausted men whom she picked up and transferred to a shore boat. Nine other men had perished and two of their bodies were recovered on the return journey. In a service of nine hours, the lifeboat had travelled 50 miles, all the time on a lee shore with strong winds and heavy sea, her crew wet to the skin and perished with cold.

CROMARTY George, Coxswain, Holy Island Lifeboat   **SILVER(2)**
WILSON William, Second Coxswain, Holy Island Lifeboat   **BRONZE**
STEVENSON Thomas A., Bowman, Holy Island Lifeboat   **BRONZE**

17 February 1922

15–16 January 1922: At 8 p.m. in a strong south-easterly gale, heavy sea and a snow storm, the trawler *James B. Graham* went ashore on the rocks off False Emmanuel Head on the north side of Holy Island, off the Northumberland coast. The whole village turned out in the dark and snow to launch the lifeboat – it needed 60 helpers, and women waded out waist deep into the sea to help. When the self righting lifeboat *Lizzie Porter* arrived at the site of the wreck, the trawler was found lying in a perilous position by rocks and iron remnants of an old wreck. An unsuccessful attempt having been made, Coxswain Cromarty lay off for two hours for the tide to rise, but the next attempt also failed. After another hour, he veered his boat carefully down, took off the nine men and returned to station at 2 a.m.

CROSS Robert, Coxswain, Spurn Lifeboat   **BRONZE**

17 November 1922

18–19 October 1922: At 10 p.m., two vessels were seen to be aground on the Binks at the mouth of the River Humber. The Watson class motor lifeboat *Samuel Oakes* launched in a strong wind with squalls, a cold night and heavy sea. The first casualty was a fishing smack, which had sunk with only her mast above water; her crew was in the rigging with a terrific sea breaking over her. This carried the lifeboat over the submerged hull, but none of the survivors made any move and, when Coxswain Cross turned his boat, the mast and all four men had disappeared. After an abortive search he made for the second wreck, the Hull steam trawler *Mafeking*, which had also sunk with the sea breaking over her funnel, but her crew had taken to their boats and had been picked up by a Pilot Cutter.

SWAN John Thompson, Coxswain, Lowestoft Lifeboat	GOLD
FLEMING William George, Coxswain, Gorleston No. 1 Lifeboat	GOLD
CARVER Edward Sterling, Commander, R.D., R.N.R., District Inspector of Lifeboats	SILVER
SCOTT Ralph A.W., Mechanic, Lowestoft Lifeboat	SILVER
AYERS George William, Second Coxswain, Lowestoft Lifeboat	BRONZE(2)
ROSE John, Bowman, Lowestoft Lifeboat	BRONZE
ALLERTON H., Crew Member, Lowestoft Lifeboat	BRONZE
AYERS J., Crew Member, Lowestoft Lifeboat	BRONZE
BUTCHER W., Crew Member, Lowestoft Lifeboat	BRONZE
MEWSE C., Crew Member, Lowestoft Lifeboat	BRONZE
SPURGEON Albert, Crew Member, Lowestoft Lifeboat	BRONZE
SWAN F., Crew Member, Lowestoft Lifeboat	BRONZE
PARKER Samuel B. (Junior), Second Coxswain, Gorleston No. 1 Lifeboat	BRONZE
CHILVERS Charles W., Bowman, Gorleston No. 1 Lifeboat	BRONZE
FLEMING James, Crew Member, Gorleston No. 1 Lifeboat	BRONZE
GOSLING William, Crew Member, Gorleston No. 1 Lifeboat	BRONZE
HALFNIGHT Walter, Crew Member Gorleston No. 1 Lifeboat	BRONZE
HARRIS Arthur, Crew Member, Gorleston No. 1 Lifeboat	BRONZE
HARRIS Ellery, Crew Member, Gorleston No. 1 Lifeboat	BRONZE
HARRIS George Arthur, Crew Member, Gorleston No.1 Lifeboat	BRONZE
JOHNSON Charles Ambrose, Crew Member, Gorleston No. 1 Lifeboat	BRONZE
LEGGETT Harry, Crew Member, Gorleston No. 1 Lifeboat	BRONZE
MORLEY Thomas, Crew Member, Gorleston No. 1 Lifeboat	BRONZE
NEWSON Albert, Crew Member, Gorleston No. 1 Lifeboat	BRONZE
NEWSON William, Crew Member Gorleston No. 1 Lifeboat	BRONZE
STUBBS Ernest, Crew Member, Gorleston No. 1 Lifeboat	BRONZE
STUBBS James, Crew Member, Gorleston No. 1 Lifeboat	BRONZE

17 November 1922

19–21 October 1922: The Newcastle-upon-Tyne 2,348 ton s.s. *Hopelyn*, on passage from the Tyne to London with a cargo of coal, was wrecked on the north end of North Scroby Sands, off Yarmouth, Norfolk, on the night of the 19th during a strong north easterly gale and in a terrific sea. At 11 p.m. the Gorleston Norfolk and Suffolk class lifeboat *Kentwell* launched and was taken in tow by the tug *George Jewson*, but was unable to do anything until daylight. She then approached the wreck, only the amidship portion of which was above water, with very heavy seas sweeping right over. After two hours, Coxswain Fleming, coming to the conclusion that there were no survivors, returned to station at 9 a.m. An hour later, it was reported that a flag was being shown on the wreck; the Gorleston lifeboat returned to the scene but was unable to go alongside. At 3.45 p.m. the Lowestoft Norfolk and Suffolk class motor lifeboat *Agnes Cross* was called. She proceeded via Gorleston on Sea, where she picked up Commander Carver, and arrived at the wreck after dark. On the way, she met the tug and a damaged *Kentwell* returning to the station. After consultation, Coxswain Fleming transferred to the Lowestoft boat, but on reaching the wreck it was decided that the lifeboat should also return to Gorleston. The *Agnes Cross* put out again at 4.30 a.m. on the 21st in the face of a north-east gale with squalls and a rough sea. At the sands, the lifeboat veered down from windward and in spite of very great difficulties and dangers, took off 24 men and a black kitten, landing them at 7 a.m.

INNES John, Coxswain, Newburgh Lifeboat   SILVER
INNES James, Bowman, Newburgh Lifeboat   BRONZE
ESSAM Charles Albert William, Petty Officer, R.N., H.M.S. *Vampire*   SILVER

15 November 1923

19 October 1923: At 5.30 a.m., the Aberdeen trawler *Imperial Prince* drove ashore by Belhevie, north of Aberdeen, in a full southerly gale. At daybreak only her bow and stern could be seen. The Aberdeen private lifeboat, the self righting Rubie class Newburgh lifeboat *James Stevens No. 19*, and rocket apparatus were called out. The Aberdeen boat broached to and had to beach, her crew exhausted. Five rockets were fired by the apparatus, the fifth being secured to the trawler. Her crew were so exhausted they could not haul in the breeches buoy. During this time the Newburgh lifeboat was being dragged along seven miles of soft, sandy beach. When launched, she reached the wreck at 2 p.m. and took off two men. A third drowned as he was being dragged across to the lifeboat. After two further attempts, the lifeboat crew was so exhausted that help was sought from H.M.S. *Vampire* and H.M.S. *Vendetta*, destroyers lying in Aberdeen; a request was also sent to the Peterhead lifeboat. The Newburgh lifeboat put out again, manned by Coxswain Innes, Bowman Innes (his son), Petty Officer Essam and 11 other Royal Navy sailors and, in very difficult circumstances, took off the remaining five men. The Peterhead motor lifeboat journeyed 22 miles against the gale, but arrived just after the rescue was completed.

YOUNG Andrew, Acting Coxswain, Cloughey Lifeboat   BRONZE

21 February 1924

11–12 January 1924: In a strong south-south-easterly gale and heavy sea accompanied by showers of sleet and hail, the Plymouth brigantine *Helgoland* drove ashore off Tara Point, near Cloughey, Co. Down, northern Ireland. The Liverpool class lifeboat *John* was launched at 11.30 p.m. and found, on arrival at the scene, that the casualty had sunk, and her crew had taken to the rigging. Having stood by all night, the lifeboat veered down at daylight and took off the five men, landing them at 9 a.m. Acting Coxswain Young took the boat out because his brothers, the Coxswain and Second Coxswain, could not go due to illness; the latter died two hours after the launch.

STORRY John William, Fisherman   SILVER

27 June 1924

30 May 1924: A small pleasure boat, with five boys aged 8 to 17 aboard, tried to enter Whitby harbour, Yorkshire, just before 7 p.m. but capsized in a heavy swell on the Bar. The boys were all thrown into the water, 10–15 yards from the end of the Old West Pier. The incident was seen by Mr. Storry, who climbed down, jumped in to the sea, and brought three of the boys, all unable to swim, to the pier where he supported them, in spite of a sprained arm until a coble came to pick them up. The other two boys were able to swim to the pier.

CRAIG George (Senior), Fisherman   SILVER

22 January 1925

26 November 1924: On her way from the fishing grounds off Yarmouth, Norfolk, the Portgordon Trawler *Press Home* ran on to rocks inshore near Portlethen, Kincardineshire, six miles south of

Aberdeen, in a moderate gale, thick mist and a heavy swell. She broke up and three of her eight man crew managed to reach a rock ledge. Mr. Craig, in his 70th year, was one of those who responded to the disaster and, when there was difficulty in getting a rope to the survivors, he took it over submerged rocks in the rising tide, sometimes up to his waist in water, and brought the three men to safety.

GILLINGS James H., Decorator   **BRONZE**

22 January 1925

26 November 1924: In a south easterly gale, a Cromer fishing boat, trying to beach three quarters of a mile north of Southwold, Suffolk, was struck by a wave and broached to on the outer of two shoals. Two of her three man crew were washed overboard, but one managed to regain the boat, whilst the other was flung into deep water between the shoals. Mr. Gillings rushed into the sea fully clothed and, after a hard struggle up to his neck in water, brought the man, encumbered by his oilskins, safely ashore.

PAYNE Richard, Coxswain, Newhaven Lifeboat   **BRONZE**

18 December 1924

27 November 1924: While the cross channel steamer *Dieppe* was trying to enter Newhaven, Sussex harbour, in a full south westerly gale, she ran aground and two tugs went to her aid. The self righting motor lifeboat *Sir Fitzroy Clayton* was also launched, at 5.20 a.m., but found that the steamer did not require help. The tug *Richmere*, however, had been driven ashore, and the lifeboat went alongside her to take off her four man crew. While engaged in this, the tug rolled and ripped a large hole in the lifeboat as well as causing other damage. After landing the men, Coxswain Payne took the lifeboat out to stand by the steamer until she was refloated some three hours after she had grounded.

TOSE Andrew, Coxswain, Runswick Lifeboat   **BRONZE**
PATTON Thomas, Second Coxswain, Runswick Lifeboat   **BRONZE**

18 December 1924

27 November 1924: The Belgian s.s. *Princesse Clementine* went ashore on the 19th on Penny Steel, near Staithes, Yorkshire, and her 19 man crew was taken off by the self righting Rubie class lifeboat *Hester Rothschild*, but the Master remained aboard. On the 27th with a south-easterly gale blowing and a heavy sea sweeping right over the ship, he signalled for help when the ship started to break up at 6.30 a.m. The lifeboat launched and managed to go alongside; despite huge waves crashing over the wreck, she was able to take off the Master before returning to station.

CROSS Robert, Coxswain, Humber Lifeboat   **SILVER(2)**
DOBSON John Thomas, Coxswain, Donna Nook Lifeboat   **BRONZE**

17 December 1925

25 November 1925: With a northerly gale blowing, a heavy sea running and in heavy snow squalls, the Preston s.s. *Whinstone*, Hull to Berwick, was seen to be in distress off Saltfleet, Lincolnshire.

The self righting Donna Nook lifeboat *Richard* was launched, but found that the ship, although needing a tug, did not require her services. She returned to station, but the Humber (previously Spurn) Watson class motor lifeboat *City of Bradford* was advised to stand by. The latter was launched at 9.30 a.m. to find the ship at anchor, aground on the sands with seas breaking over her. In spite of being buried in the breaking seas nearly the whole time, six men (the whole crew) were brought into the lifeboat by breeches buoy.

FLEMING William George E.G.M., Coxswain, Gorleston Lifeboat   **BRONZE**

21 January 1926

22 December 1925: In a full north easterly gale and a very heavy sea, which had risen about 11 a.m., the Norfolk and Suffolk class motor lifeboat *John and Mary Meiklam of Gladswood* was launched to the Goole ketch *Henrietta* in the Yarmouth Roads, off the coast of Norfolk. Her anchors had parted and she was being driven towards the shore. When the lifeboat reached her, the ketch was on the edge of the breakers swept by heavy seas but, at the second attempt, the four man crew was able to jump to safety.

As part of the Centenary celebrations, on 30 June 1924 Coxswain Fleming, with other surviving gold medallists was received at Buckingham Palace by King George V and decorated with the Empire Gallantry Medal (E.G.M.). This was replaced by the George Cross in 1942. Coxswain Fleming's medals are now in the R.N.L.I. archives.

CLOUDSDALE T.L., Fireman, Steam Trawler, *Tenby Castle*   **SILVER**
VAUX Philip Edward, Lieutenant Commander, D.S.C., R.N.
  District Inspector of Lifeboats   **BRONZE**

22 April 1926

14–23 February 1926: With a heavy sea running, the Swansea Steam trawler *Tenby Castle* went ashore in the early morning of the 14th on the rocks in Clifden Bay, Connemara, Co. Galway, Ireland, a coast where there are many rocky islands. Her Master sent out a wireless message to say that he was abandoning ship and this was picked up by four other steam trawlers who started to search for survivors. The casualty was sinking rapidly: her boat was launched only to be swept away, but Mr. Cloudsdale dived into the sea, swam after it and clung to it until a line was thrown to him. The line wound round his neck and, enduring intense pain, he was hauled back to the wreck, where the whole crew boarded the boat and succeeded in reaching Inishark, an inhabited island. Meanwhile, the other trawlers continued their search together with a fishing protection cruiser and later, aeroplanes, but one of the trawlers, *Cardigan Castle*, struck on a rock just after midnight on the 14–15th. Her boat was also carried away and only one man managed to get into it, and he was rescued. No signs of the trawler or the remainder of her crew were found until on the 17th, a piece of wood bearing what appeared to be a message was discovered. Arriving late on the 19th Lieutenant Commander Vaux led and participated in a search of many islands by curragh and aeroplane demonstrating 'courage, initiative and tenacity' but no trace could be found save for two bodies. The search was abandoned on the 23rd.

ROBINSON William, Coxswain, Newbiggin Lifeboat   **BRONZE**
                                                                17 June 1926

28 April 1926: Although a moderate east-south-easterly breeze was blowing, there was a dense fog and a heavy sea, when the North Shields steam trawler *George R. Purdy* went on to rocks, north of Church Point, near Newbiggin, Northumberland, at 4.30 p.m. The lifeboat *Ada Lewis* launched and found the trawler, half a mile from shore, with very heavy surf breaking over her. When Coxswain Robinson veered down towards her, his boat filled with water. Shifting position, he managed to get through a very narrow channel and took off the nine man crew in spite of a falling tide.

SKINNER C.J., Decorator   **BRONZE**
                                                           16 September 1926

21 July 1926: A small yacht *Fidelity*, on passage to Newhaven from Cowes, was caught in a strong south-westerly gale and dismasted, then driven towards the Newhaven East Pier, where there was always a heavy sea. The self righting motor lifeboat *Sir Fitzroy Clayton* launched and went straight alongside, but the three people on the yacht refused to jump. Several heavy seas drove the yacht closer to the beach, where the lifeboat was unable to reach her. At that moment a passing motor cyclist, Mr. Skinner, saw the situation, obtained a rope, plunged into the water and took off the owner's wife and the deck hand. The owner drowned when he jumped into the water to try to get ashore.

JAGGER Geoffrey W.   **BRONZE**
MILLER Arnold, Bank Clerk   **BRONZE**
                                                           16 September 1926

25 July 1926: Mr Croft and Mr Scott went out fishing during the morning in a small foy boat which became unmanageable when it was struck by a squall. They tried to make South Shields harbour, but the wind and heavy seas swept them towards the Trow Rock. They succeeded in anchoring, but the cable parted, and their boat drove towards the shore, continually swept by the breakers. Two onlookers, Geoffrey Jagger and Arnold Miller, decided to launch a surf boat. As they neared the foy boat it was swamped; Croft was thrown into the sea, while Scott clung to the boat and was washed ashore. Then the rescuing boat was capsized throwing Jagger and Milner into the sea. Jagger swam towards Croft: Miller was able to get ashore, then turned to help save Croft, who was now unconscious. Once ashore first aid was rendered to Croft by a miner, Mr B. McReady.

CAMPBELL Michael, Ordinary Seaman, R.N.V.R. (Tyne Division)   **BRONZE**
                                                             21 October 1926

8 August 1926: At dusk a small boat went out to take passengers off a small pleasure steamer at Coble Landing, South Shields and, although she could only hold two or three people, seven tried to get into her. She capsized, but, fortunately, everybody except one man was able to reach safety. The man sank and was carried away. Ordinary Seaman Campbell threw off his coat and dived into the river. He reached the struggling man and kept him afloat until help arrived.

LETHBRIDGE Matthew, Coxswain, St Mary's Lifeboat	**SILVER**
JENKINS Charles, Coxswain, Motor Boat *Sunbeam*	**SILVER**
LETHBRIDGE James Thomas, Second Coxswain, St Mary's Lifeboat	**BRONZE**
ROKAHR John Henry, Mechanic, St Mary's Lifeboat	**BRONZE**
IVERS William E., Doctor	**BRONZE**
JENKINS Edward Reginald, Motor Boat *Sunbeam*	**BRONZE**
JENKINS William Edwin, Boat *Czar*	**BRONZE**
JENKINS Ernest, Motor Boat *Ivy*	**BRONZE**

17 November 1927

27 October 1927: In the afternoon in a dense fog the Italian 6872 ton s.s. *Isabo*, bound from Montreal to Hamburg with grain, stranded on the Scilly Rock, west of Bryher, Isles of Scilly. The first boats to respond to her siren were from Bryher – the 30ft open boat *Czar*, and two motor boats, *Ivy* and *Sunbeam*. With a gale developing over a very heavy sea, the *Czar* first rescued 11 men, and later another three. The *Ivy* picked up one man from the sea and took on board the eleven from the *Czar*. The *Sunbeam* arrived, and saved one man from the water. Launching a small dinghy, Charles Jenkins, with Edward Reginald Jenkins, saved another three men from the wreckage, then recovered another eight men before returning to shore.

The St Mary's motor lifeboat *Elsie* had been called out at 5 p.m., and finally reached the wreck about 9 p.m. after threading her way through treacherous waters. The sea was now breaking right over the *Isabo*, and men were clinging to her rigging. Coxswain Lethbridge made the difficult decision to wait until dawn to try to effect a rescue, and returned to New Grimsby for the night. Taking Dr. Ivers on board, the lifeboat reached the wreck at dawn and, with great difficulty, saved four men by means of line-throwing guns.

ROBERTS William, Second Coxswain, Moelfre Lifeboat	**GOLD**
JONES Owen, Captain, Crew Member, Moelfre Lifeboat	**GOLD**
WILLIAMS William, Bowman, Moelfre Lifeboat	**BRONZE**
FRANCIS Robert Richard, Crew Member, Moelfre Lifeboat	**BRONZE**
JONES Owen, Crew Member, Moelfre Lifeboat	**BRONZE**
JONES Thomas, Crew Member, Moelfre Lifeboat	**BRONZE**
MATTHEWS Hugh Lloyd, Crew Member, Moelfre Lifeboat	**BRONZE**
OWEN Hugh, Crew Member, Moelfre Lifeboat	**BRONZE**
OWEN John Lewis, Crew Member, Moelfre Lifeboat	**BRONZE**
OWEN Robert, Crew Member, Moelfre Lifeboat	**BRONZE**
OWENS Owen, Crew Member, Moelfre Lifeboat	**BRONZE**
ROBERTS William, Crew Member, Moelfre Lifeboat	**Post BRONZE**
THOMAS Hugh, Crew Member, Moelfre Lifeboat	**BRONZE**
THOMAS Richard, Crew Member, Moelfre Lifeboat	**BRONZE**
WILLIAMS Thomas, Crew Member Moelfre Lifeboat	**BRONZE**

17 November 1927

28 October 1927: During a whole gale in very cold weather, the Poole auxiliary ketch *Excel* was on passage from Birkenhead to Ireland with a cargo of coal, when she got into difficulties off Point Lynas, east of Amlwch, Anglesey. She started shipping water and her engines flooded. When the Watson class lifeboat *Charles and Eliza Laura* arrived at 5.30 p.m. she found the ketch made fast to a German steamer which, apparently, could do nothing to help and, as the lifeboat approached,

cut the tow rope. The ketch fell off to leewards, and the lifeboat tried to go alongside, but the attempt failed and, with desperate measures now necessary, Second Coxswain Roberts drove his vessel under full sail right over the water-logged wreck. The three men on board the ketch were grabbed and hauled aboard. In being hauled aboard, one of the three men received injuries from which he died. The lifeboat, badly damaged and also water logged, was swept away, her jib blown to ribbons. Shortly afterwards, the ketch sank and the German vessel left. With her sailing qualities badly impaired, the lifeboat struggled a distance of some 15 to 20 miles to Menai Straits and anchored by Puffin Island at 2 a.m. During this passage, William Roberts, one of the crew, collapsed and died of exposure.

She remained in this position until daylight, when the Beaumaris lifeboat came out, arriving at 8.30 a.m., and towed her into the harbour. The Second Coxswain remained at the tiller the whole 17 hours of the service (the Coxswain was away at the time of the call out). Captain Jones, an experienced Master Mariner, supported and sustained him during the whole time.

SPURGEON Albert, Coxswain, Lowestoft Lifeboat   **SILVER**

15 December 1927

21 November 1927: Shortly after 4p.m., the Lowestoft sailing smack *Lily of Devon* tried to enter Lowestoft harbour, Suffolk, in a whole easterly gale and very heavy sea. Caught by the tide, she missed the entrance and was carried into broken, shallow water where she began to bump heavily on the sand. On arrival, the Norfolk and Suffolk class motor lifeboat *Agnes Cross* found the smack being carried toward a concrete breakwater, with seas breaking clean over her and her crew of three men in the rigging. Coxswain Spurgeon veered down; in the very heavy seas the lifeboat struck the bottom and was thrown against the wreck. Although the lifeboat was damaged he took off the three men who were on the smack.

BLOGG Henry George E.G.M., Coxswain, Cromer Lifeboat	**GOLD(2)**
BALLS George, Second Coxswain, Cromer Lifeboat	**BRONZE**
DAVIES John James (Senior) Bowman, Cromer Lifeboat	**BRONZE**
DAVIES Robert, Mechanic, Cromer Lifeboat	**BRONZE**
DAVIES William Thomas, Assistant Motor Mechanic, Cromer Lifeboat	**BRONZE**
ALLEN Edward Walter, Crew Member, Cromer Lifeboat	**BRONZE(2)**
BAKER Richard J., Crew Member, Cromer Lifeboat	**BRONZE**
COX George, Crew Member, Cromer Lifeboat	**BRONZE**
DAVIES Harry William, Crew Member, Cromer Lifeboat	**BRONZE**
DAVIES James William, Crew Member, Cromer Lifeboat	**BRONZE**
DAVIES John James (Junior), Crew Member, Cromer Lifeboat	**BRONZE**
HARRISON Leslie James, Crew Member, Cromer Lifeboat	**BRONZE(2)**
HARRISON Sidney Charles, Crew Member, Cromer Lifeboat	**BRONZE**
FLEMING William George E.G.M. Coxswain	
Great Yarmouth and Gorleston Lifeboat	**SILVER**
UPCRAFT Frank, Coxswain, Southwold Lifeboat	**BRONZE**

15 December 1927

21–22 November 1927: At 8.30 p.m. information was received that the Dutch tanker *Georgia*, carrying oil from Abadan, Iran to Grangetown, was stranded on South Haisborough Sands, off the Norfolk coast, and had broken in two. The after part had drifted northwards with 16 men aboard and these had been taken off by s.s. *Trent*. The Norfolk and Suffolk class Great Yarmouth & Gorleston motor lifeboat *John and Mary Meiklam of Gladswood* reached the other section, but the weather was so wild that Coxswain Fleming could not attempt rescue that evening. He resumed the operation at daybreak on the 22nd but had to return to harbour at the end of the day exhausted after 21 hours at sea. Meanwhile, the Cromer Watson class motor lifeboat *H.F Bailey* had launched under Coxswain Blogg but, finding nobody on board the aft part, had returned, only to put out and stand by all night, returning to her station again at daybreak after 16 hours at sea. Another trip to investigate the empty boat was followed by orders to go to the Sands to reinforce Coxswain Fleming and, in fading light at 4.15 p.m. Coxswain Blogg located the wreck. To avoid having to stand by all night, he went alongside and took off the remaining 15 men. This done, the sea lifted the lifeboat on board the wreck but, with the next sea, she pulled herself off due to the sterling efforts of her Mechanic. Heavily damaged, she returned to station after being on duty for 28 hours. With the Lowestoft boat damaged in the *Lily of Devon* service, the Southwold Norfolk and Suffolk class lifeboat *Mary Scott* was called out but, going alongside in pitch darkness, found nobody on board. Coxswain Upcraft took her back to Yarmouth after 13 hours afloat.

Coxswain Blogg was another of eight surviving gold medallists awarded the Empire Gallantry Medal (EGM) during the Centenary celebrations in 1924.

BOYLE Thomas   **BRONZE**
                                                       15 March 1928

11 February 1928: Three men were marooned by a gale and heavy seas on Mutton Island off the coast of Co. Clare, Ireland. Mr Boyle and two other men put out from Quilty in a 24 foot canvas boat and rescued them through seas running very high. The three men had been on the island since the evening of the 8th, their only food a loaf of bread, no fire, their only shelter a ruin.

BAKER William John, Coxswain, Padstow Lifeboat   **BRONZE**
                                                       15 March 1928

11 February 1928: When the Oslo s.s. *Taormina* tried to enter Padstow harbour, Cornwall, at low tide in a gale with very heavy seas running, she struck on Doom Bar and lay there with seas breaking over her. The steam tug *Helen Peele* and the self righting lifeboat *Edmund Harvey* were called out, but found insufficient water in the channel. The smaller lifeboat *Arab* then put out. Under oars, she negotiated the dangerous Ketch Bank, took off the 18 man crew and landed them safely after a difficult return trip over the Bank. Of the *Arab*'s crew seven had not been out before.

MACKAY Hugh (Senior), Owner, Motor Yawl *Thrive*   **BRONZE**
                                                       24 May 1928

20 March 1928: In the afternoon, the motor fishing boat *Pearl* was trying to enter Balintore harbour, Ross-shire, on the Moray Firth, in a whole gale with a heavy sea running, when her engine failed. She was driven down on to salmon stakenets, where she was secured. With four others, Mr. Mackay put out in the gathering darkness in his motor yawl from Hilton of Cadboll. He succeeded in towing the casualty to the harbour entrance, but the tow rope parted, the fishing boat capsized and one man drowned. The other managed to reach the shore 15 yards away and owed his life to Mr. Mackay's efforts.

COTTON William H.B.   **BRONZE**

21 February 1929

27 August 1928: In the afternoon, the Cardiff s.s. *Kendy*, a small steamer, got into difficulties off Porthcawl, Glamorgan, and foundered. Her crew took to her boat but this capsized and drifted toward the shore with the men clinging to it. As there was a heavy surf breaking on the rocks, the coastguard rocket apparatus was brought into use but could not achieve communication. Preparations were then made to seize the survivors when they were washed up. One man was rescued by a boat, and Mr. Cotton, of Sandiacre, near Nottingham, a visitor to the town, plunged off the rocks in to the surf with a line, which he tried to pass to the steamer's Master who could not keep hold. Mr. Cotton's second attempt was prevented by the coastguards, who saved four survivors when the boat was carried in.

ROBINSON George, Coxswain, New Brighton No. 2 Lifeboat   **SILVER**
NICHOLSON John Rowland, Second Coxswain,
** New Brighton No. 2 Lifeboat**   **BRONZE**
CARMODY George James, Bowman, New Brighton No. 2 Lifeboat   **BRONZE**
SCOTT Ralph B., Mechanic, New Brighton No. 2 Lifeboat   **BRONZE**
GARBUTT Wilfred, Second Mechanic, New Brighton No. 2 Lifeboat   **BRONZE**
JONES Samuel J., Crew Member, New Brighton No. 2 Lifeboat   **BRONZE**
LIVERSAGE William, Crew Member, New Brighton No. 2 Lifeboat   **BRONZE**
MOORE John H., Crew Member, New Brighton No. 2 Lifeboat   **BRONZE**

20 December 1928

24 November 1928: The Mersey was suffering in a very heavy west-north-westerly gale, gusting to nearly 100 miles an hour, with very heavy seas and continuous blinding rain squalls. Owing to these conditions and shortage of fuel, the French s.s. *Emile Delmas* anchored four miles west-north-west of the Bar Light vessel where the Barnett class lifeboat *William and Kate Johnston* found her yawing wildly. Nevertheless, 23 men were taken off, followed by the Captain. Conditions on the return journey were appalling, the steamer's Chief Engineer washed out and drowned, and two of the lifeboat's crew had to be recovered after going overside. The damaged lifeboat crept back to station after six hours at sea.

The Mechanic, Scott, was at the time waiting to go in to hospital to undergo a serious operation. He nevertheless insisted on going out. On landing he was taken straight to hospital.

ATKINSON Joseph, Captain, Padstow Steam Tug *Helen Peele*   **BRONZE**

21 February 1929

27 November 1928: When, at 4.30 a.m. it was found that the Port Isaac fishing boat *Our Girlie* could not be accounted for in a west-north-westerly gale, the steam tug put out and, using her searchlight, found her anchored close to the shore near Portquin. In the very heavy seas she was in danger, if her cable broke, of being cast on to the rocks. Captain Atkinson caused oil to be released, which smoothed the waves, then stood in and anchored in two to three fathoms. He then manoeuvred the tug alongside and took off the five men, just before the boat was thrown on to the rocks.

JOHNSTON William, Coxswain, Stromness Lifeboat **BRONZE(2)**

21 March 1929

14 February 1929: The Barnett class lifeboat *J.J.K.S.W.* left Stromness harbour, Orkney, at 4.35 a.m. in a strong south-westerly breeze over a heavy sea and in bitterly cold weather. The Grimsby trawler *Carmania II* had gone ashore on Kirk Rocks in Hoy Sound, out of range of rocket apparatus. There was no hope of reaching her from seaward with seas breaking up to 150 yards before they reached her, and the water too shallow until the tide rose. After waiting for three hours, the lifeboat managed to get two lines on board the wreck, and five men were brought off. Then in spite of the lifeboat being swept by heavy seas, the remaining seven men were saved. Coxswain Johnston withdrew with great skill, landing everybody after a five hour service.

WICKHAM James, Coxswain, Rosslare Harbour Lifeboat **SILVER(2)**
MONCAS W.J.B., Honorary Secretary, Rosslare Harbour R.N.L.I. **BRONZE**

14 November 1929

20 October 1929: In a whole north by east gale, the Plymouth schooner *Mountblairy* was driven ashore at night in a very heavy sea at Carne, Co. Wexford about five miles from Rosslare Harbour. The Watson class motor lifeboat *K.E.C.F.* found her by searchlight and made a way between rocks and through broken water, got alongside and took off the five men on board, all of whom were injured. After Coxswain Wickham had turned the lifeboat around in very restricted space, he worked her clear of the rocks and brought her home through violent seas, arriving just before midnight. Mr Moncas went out in the lifeboat and, in looking after the rescued men, risked being washed overboard.

GRIGGS Henry Albert (Junior), Coxswain, Hythe Lifeboat **SILVER**
OILLER Douglas, Coxswain, Dungeness Lifeboat **BRONZE**

19 December 1929

11–12 November 1929: At 10.30 p.m. on 11 November the Dungeness self righting lifeboat *David Barclay* launched in a south-westerly gale, a very heavy sea and blinding rain and had great difficulty in getting away. She was trying to go to the help of the Rochester barge *Marie May*, but a search revealed nothing; therefore at 1 a.m. the lifeboat anchored. After 6 a.m. the wind veered and the weather moderated a little which enabled the search to be resumed at daybreak. After half an hour, the barge was sighted, crewless, two miles west of Hythe, Kent; Coxswain Oiller turned for home which after an exceptionally rough journey, was reached at 9.30 a.m. Meanwhile at Hythe, where flares had been seen still burning on the wreck, and in the absence of any information from the other lifeboat, the self righting lifeboat *Mayer de Rothschild* had launched about 3 a.m. under great difficulties and made for the wreck. Reaching the *Marie May* two hours later, Coxswain Griggs took off three men an hour before the Dungeness boat arrived.

WATKINS James, Coxswain, Angle Lifeboat **BRONZE**

19 December 1929

25–26 November 1929: The 3,809 ton s.s. *Molesey* left Manchester for Cardiff on the 24th with a crew of 33 plus three women. She ran into a south-west gale soon after leaving port. Off St David's

Head, Pembrokeshire, her propeller was damaged and she became helpless. She anchored in Jack Sound but dragged her anchors and went ashore in the afternoon of the 25th on Midland Island, between Skomar Island and the mainland. The Angle Watson class motor lifeboat *Elizabeth Elson* was launched but, searching a falsely reported area, found nothing and returned to station two hours later. The location was corrected and the lifeboat launched again at 7.45 p.m. but in the poor visibility failed to find the casualty. Launching a third time at 6.15 a.m. on the 26th, she discovered the wreck and in difficult and dangerous conditions took off 28 survivors, including two of the women, and landed them at Milford Haven at 11 a.m.

PAYNE Richard, Coxswain, Newhaven Lifeboat   **SILVER**

16 January 1930

7 December 1929: In a wild south-westerly gale and mountainous seas accompanied by torrential rain, the Danish schooner *Mogens Koch* of Rönne was wrecked at 7.30 a.m. east of Cuckmere Haven, Sussex, five miles from Newhaven. The self righting motor lifeboat *Sir Fitzroy Clayton* launched, and Coxswain Payne took her out through the heavy seas breaking across the harbour entrance and, after considerable difficulty, found the wreck. She was lying stern on to the seas, but after several attempts the lifeboat went alongside and took off the ten men, one at a time. Fighting her way back to Newhaven through horrific seas, the Second Motor Mechanic was washed overboard, but recovered. One crewman sustained a fractured jaw, one survivor dislocated his thigh and the Coxswain's back was so badly injured that he had to retire from the lifeboat service (he was appointed Bowman in 1911).

SWANSON John, Coxswain, Longhope Lifeboat   **SILVER**

20 March 1930

5 January 1930: When the Aberdeen steam trawler *Braconmoor*, bound for the fishing grounds, went ashore on Torness Point, Hoy, Orkney Islands, the Watson class motor lifeboat *K.T.J.S.* launched at 2 a.m. and reached the wreck after an hour. A south-east wind was blowing, and the night was very dark, with heavy rain. Coxswain Swanson found the wreck lying close to dangerous rocks in very heavy surf. At the third attempt in a very fierce tide, all nine men were hauled through the icy waters by breeches buoy; the Master died during this operation. The service took nearly five hours.

HOOD Robert, Coxswain, Hartlepool Lifeboat   **BRONZE**

20 November 1930

26 September 1930: With a very heavy gale blowing and a very heavy sea and rain, the three masted Danish schooner *Doris* tried to enter harbour at Hartlepool, Co. Durham. In ballast with only a small powered engine, she failed and was driven to leeward across Hartlepool Bay in heavy breaking seas, narrowly missing the Longscar Rocks. When she anchored, her anchors started to drag. The Watson class lifeboat *Elizabeth Newton* launched at 12.35 p.m. After five very difficult runs, the schooner's nine man crew jumped to safety in the lifeboat shortly before the *Doris* became a total wreck.

BARNES Frederick, Coxswain, Selsey Lifeboat   **BRONZE**

18 December 1930

2 November 1930: After launching at 10.30 a.m., the Watson class motor lifeboat *Canadian Pacific* found the motor yacht *Lucy B* of Rye in broken water, little more than a quarter of a mile from the shore. The yacht was in a small bay formed by 'The Streets' and 'The Hounds', two shoals west of Selsey Bill, Sussex. In the gale, hard squalls of wind and rain and a heavy sea, Coxswain Barnes took his boat into the breakers in six feet of water and went alongside. One of the two men on board was able to jump into the lifeboat before the yacht sheered away. It took two more attempts before the Coxswain got a line over and dragged the other man to safety. After reversing out of the shallows, the lifeboat returned to station where the seas were too heavy for her to be hauled up the slipway so she had to be placed on a mooring, and the two men were landed by shore boat.

CAHILL John, Fisherman   **BRONZE**
CAHILL Joseph, Fisherman   **BRONZE**
NOLAN John, Fisherman   **BRONZE**

18 December 1930

7 November 1930: In conditions rising at times to whole west-south-westerly gale force, the Tralee s.s. *Co-operator*, with a cargo of maize, began to founder a quarter of a mile from shore in Tralee Bay, Co. Kerry, Ireland, in a heavy cross sea. Seeing her plight the Messrs. Cahill and Nolan put off in a 13 foot pulling boat and, getting under the steamer's lee, took off the three men after several runs. The boat was now heavily loaded and so had little free board; it was swamped within a few feet of the land, but all six men scrambled ashore. The rescue had taken an hour and a half.

DAVIES John James (Senior) Bowman, Cromer Lifeboat   **BRONZE(2)**

19 March 1931

17 February 1931: The Sheringham fishing boat *Welcome Home*, overwhelmed by a heavy sea 200 yards from the shore, capsized and sank; one man was picked up by the Sheringham lifeboat. The Cromer Watson class motor lifeboat *H.F. Bailey* which had also launched, saved the other two; Bowman Davies jumped overboard to help one of them who was unconscious.

FENTON David, Coxswain, St Andrews Lifeboat   **BRONZE**

23 April 1931

9 March 1931: In the middle of the night, the Aberdeen steam trawler *Loch Long* went ashore in a heavy snow squall on a reef of rocks, known as Balcomie Briggs, near Fife Ness. The self righting Rubie class lifeboat *John and Sarah Hatfield* had to be launched over the beach due to the low tide and reached the trawler at 5.30 a.m., daybreak. Coxswain Fenton veered down and rigged a breeches buoy which took off one man. The other nine men were saved when the lifeboat got near enough for them to jump, and all were landed at 8 a.m. A party of 200 people, including women, had helped in the launch of the lifeboat.

McPHAIL Angus, Coxswain, Thurso Lifeboat   **BRONZE**

23 April 1931

18 March 1931: On a dark, foggy night in a strong breeze, the Chester schooner *Pet* was totally wrecked in a heavy ground swell on Brims Ness, five miles west of Thurso, Caithness. The Watson class motor lifeboat *H.C.J.* launched and veered down but could not get near. A breeches buoy was rigged and one man was taken off. Hearing that the other three men were too elderly to come off by this means, Coxswain McPhail managed to take the lifeboat alongside the wreck, lifted the men off and then drew clear. This service was the first occasion on which a night tracer was used, fitted on the projectile carrying the line, to show by its sparks the flight of the line. It was very successful.

SWANSON John, Coxswain, Longhope Lifeboat   **SILVER(2)**

10 March 1932

9–10 January 1932: After distress signals were seen off Tor Ness, Hoy, Orkney Islands, the Watson class lifeboat *K.T.J.S.* launched at 7.30 p.m. in a gale and a night which was exceptionally dark and bitterly cold with rain and sleet squalls. After an unsuccessful search along the shore by Tor Ness, Coxswain Swanson took the lifeboat out to search Pentland Firth. Meanwhile, three survivors had been discovered and saved by the searchers. It now became known that the stricken vessel was the Hull trawler *Dorbie*. Anxiety was being felt about the lifeboat but, when she eventually reached Dunett Head Shore Signal Station, she was apprised of the situation and returned to Tor Ness. By the time she arrived, the weather and sea had started to moderate, and they found the trawler about 150 feet from the cliff, lying on her port side. At the second attempt, the lifeboat got alongside and took off the remaining eight men, returning to Longhope at 1 a.m.

CAMPBELL John, Coxswain, Portpatrick Lifeboat   **BRONZE**

11 February 1932

13–14 January 1932: The 520 ton s.s. *Camlough* had left Belfast on the morning of the 12th bound for Birkenhead. Developing engine trouble off the Isle of Man, the Captain decided to return to Belfast. On the morning of the 13th a gale blew up, and the *Camlough* was driven towards the Wigtownshire coast. For six hours she was helpless in the gale until sighted by the s.s. *Moyalla*. A tow was established at 11.30 a.m. Six times the tow parted and made fast again. Answering a distress wireless message received by the Portpatrick Coastguard at 8.25 p.m, the Watson class lifeboat *J and W* put out through the notoriously difficult entrance to the harbour, reaching the casualty about 11.30 pm. The Coxswain decided to stand by until the steamers were in safe waters. For five hours the seventh tow held, whilst the *Moyalla* made for the comparative safety of Luce Bay. There the tow failed again. The *Camlough* dropped both anchors but they would not hold and the ship was quickly carried towards the rocks. The lifeboat anchored and then dropped down, stern first, to the weather side. A line was fired and a heavy rope then used to haul the lifeboat alongside, enabling the eight crew of the *Camlough* to jump into the lifeboat. This operation took 50 minutes, but so skilfully was she handled that she had not even scratched her paint.

BLOGG Henry George E.G.M., Coxswain, Cromer Lifeboat   **SILVER**

10 November 1932

14–16 October 1932: On October 14th the Watson class lifeboat *H.F. Bailey* was launched about 9.30 a.m. to the *Monte Nevoso,* of Genoa, aground on the Haisborough Sands. The Coxswain boarded the vessel, where the Captain told him that they had been aground since 4 a.m. The tug *Nordzee* was standing by. It was arranged that the lifeboat should render all assistance possible. The *Nordzee* started towing about 4.30 p.m.; five more tugs came up and all were engaged. The north-west wind reached gale force about 5 a.m., and about daylight two tugs broke their tow ropes and another had to be cut. About 8 a.m. all tugs were cast off as the vessel showed signs of breaking up, and the lifeboat was signalled to take off the crew. After about an hour the lifeboat succeeded in taking off 29 of the crew and also the man from the tug *Nordzee.* One of the crew misjudged the distance in jumping and fell into the sea but was quickly hauled into the lifeboat. The Captain, Chief Mate, Chief Engineer and Wireless Operator refused to leave the vessel, and Blogg proceeded to Yarmouth.

After obtaining dry clothes and petrol, the lifeboat went to sea again to try and persuade the four men to leave the ship. The lifeboat reached the vessel about 4.45 p.m, but the Captain still refused to leave. The Coxswain therefore returned to Gorleston, arriving about 7.30 p.m.

The Coxswain informed the Coastguard, and arranged to stay at the Mariners Refuge in readiness if the ship sent out an SOS. Nothing was heard, and the lifeboat put to sea at 5 a.m. on Sunday, and reached the vessel about 8 a.m., when it was found that the vessel had broken her back and the four men had left in their motor boat. Two dogs had been left on the ship, a big St. Bernard and a smaller one. The St. Bernard was taken off, but the smaller dog could not be caught. The lifeboat returned home, arriving about 1 p.m., some 52 hours after the original launch.

STANTON Bartholomew Stephenson, Coxswain, Boulmer Lifeboat   **BRONZE**

12 January 1933

21–24 December 1932: Shortly after 9 p.m. on the 21st, the self righting motor lifeboat *L.P. and St. Helen* launched to the Grimsby steam trawler *Fezenta,* aground on a reef of rocks off Seaton Point, near Boulmer, Northumberland, known as Boulmer South Ranges. The lifeboat stood by until the casualty settled down with the ebb tide then, with the crew in no immediate danger, returned to Boulmer at 1 a.m. Just before 2.30 a.m. another distress signal was seen, this time from the Grimsby steam trawler *Guillemot,* on the rocks near Cullernose Point, further north. She found the trawler lying among rocks and reefs, 100 yards from the cliffs; six of her crew had already been rescued by rocket apparatus. In a highly dangerous operation in the darkness, in less than five feet of water, Coxswain Stanton brought out the three men remaining aboard. After returning to the *Fezenta* to check that everything was still all right, the lifeboat returned to Boulmer at 8 a.m. Putting out again at 10.30 a.m. she stood by the *Fezenta* until 1.30 p.m. then went out to her again on the 23rd and to the *Guillemot* on the 24th, standing by during efforts to refloat them. The *Guillemot* was finally refloated on the 25th, and the *Fezenta* on the 26th.

STRACHAN John Reid, Coxswain, Peterhead Lifeboat   **SILVER**
WISEMAN David Falconer, Mechanic, Peterhead Lifeboat   **BRONZE**

9 February 1933

18–19 January 1933: Just before 10 p.m., the Aberdeen trawler *Struan* went ashore on Scotstown Head, three miles north of Peterhead. Aberdeenshire, in a moderate westerly wind and thick haze on a dark and extremely cold night. The Watson class motor lifeboat *Duke of Connaught* was launched and, with only a small hand signalling lamp working (the light connections had been damaged shortly after leaving Peterhead), reached the wreck at 10.40 p.m. The lifeboat anchored and veered down, but failed at the first attempt. In a second attempt, the Coxswain was swept out of the boat, by a very heavy sea which flung Mr. Wiseman, almost senseless, on to the fore end of the lifeboat's canopy. Regaining the boat, the Coxswain made a third attempt, and getting alongside, rescued all nine men in a protracted series of operations.

BARRETT Harry, Acting Coxswain, St Mary's Lifeboat   **BRONZE**

11 January 1934

28 November 1933: The Watson class motor lifeboat *Cunard* launched at 2 p.m. to the London schooner *Mynonie R. Kirby* drifting towards the shore in a strong south-easterly wind, accompanied by squalls, five miles to the south east of the Isles of Scilly. She had broken away from a tug towing her towards Falmouth. Bowman Barrett, acting Coxswain in the absence of the Coxswain and Second Coxswain, took his boat through a whole gale and heavy seas to find the schooner dismasted and water logged with one mast and its rigging hanging over each side, and the capstan hanging over the bow with the anchor and cable. He fired a line across her and rigged a breeches buoy. In fading light, he had to manoeuvre his boat constantly and succeeded in bringing off six men and a dog, landing them at 6.30 p.m.

BLOGG Henry George E.G.M., Coxswain, Cromer Lifeboat   **SILVER(2)**

11 January 1934

13 December 1933: The Cromer No.2 lifeboat *Alexandra* was launched at 8.30 a.m. to the barge *Sepoy* flying distress signals and dragging her anchors about one and a half miles east of Cromer Pier. Directly she was launched she was blown broadside on to the beach. After an hour's hard work she was got on to the carriage again and relaunched, but the crew could make no headway and she was again driven on to the beach. The crew, with the help of many voluntary helpers, got the lifeboat once more on to the carriage and dragged her about half a mile along the beach to get her to windward of the vessel, which was now near the shore, and launched her again about 1.30 p.m.

The heavy seas prevented the lifeboat from getting alongside the vessel, and they were again driven ashore. By this time Coxswain Blogg and the *H F Bailey* were seen coming back from Yarmouth, which they had made for after being launched about 4.30 a.m. to go to Haisborough to the assistance of a vessel; they had found the water too shoal to approach her and after the lifeboat had grounded and hauled off, Blogg stood by until he could see there was no further danger. About 8 a.m. the Coxswain made for Yarmouth, and when in Yarmouth Roads, met the Gorleston Lifeboat and was informed at 11.15 a.m. that a barge was in distress in Cromer. Coxswain Blogg then put about and with all speed made for Cromer, and found the barge at 3 p.m. lying stranded about 200 yards from the shore with heavy waves breaking over her. Blogg rounded her stern and came between barge and shore and made several attempts to lay alongside the vessel's rigging, her decks beneath under water. As it was impossible to hold the lifeboat in position, owing to the wind and tide, Blogg then ran the lifeboat's bows on top of the bulwarks abreast of the starboard rigging. One of the men was seized by some of the crew and hauled on board; then the lifeboat was washed astern, and the Coxswain repeated the manoeuvre and rescued the other man. The two men were quite exhausted and perished with cold, and the lifeboat crew had also suffered greatly from cold and exposure.

Coxswain Blogg decided to beach the lifeboat rather than face returning to Gorleston in the teeth of the gale.

REAY Thomas Quayle, Coxswain, Maryport Lifeboat   **BRONZE**

8 February 1934

17 January 1934: During the morning, the 2,500 ton Newcastle on Tyne s.s. *Plawsworth,* at anchor off Workington, Cumberland dragged her anchors in a south-west gale and went ashore. The self righting motor lifeboat *Priscilla Macbean*, which was five miles away, was launched at noon. She found the steamer head on to the wind and sea with her stern aground and her back broken. After examining the situation, Coxswain Reay anchored, veered down and got alongside the forepart of the ship. During this operation the helm was damaged, and, for the rest of the service, the Coxswain could use the helm only one way. In a slow and difficult operation with the lifeboat rising and falling through many feet, 13 men were taken off, but the Master and four others elected to stay aboard the wreck. At 3.30 p.m., on leaving Workington harbour to which the survivors had been taken, the lifeboat was recalled to the wreck but, with this now broadside on, there was insufficient water for her to go alongside. The Coxswain took the lifeboat back to Maryport at 5.15 p.m. and the five survivors waded ashore at low tide.

PATTON Robert, Coxswain, Runswick Lifeboat   **Post GOLD**

8 March 1934

8 February 1934: In a gale, heavy sea and rain the West Hartlepool salvage steamer *Disperser* was sinking five miles north-north-east of Staithes Nab, Yorkshire, after being under tow by a tug. Seven of her crew had been taken off by the tug, but one man, who was lame, was still on board. The Liverpool class lifeboat *The Always Ready* launched at 4.25 a.m. and reached the casualty an hour later. With very great difficulty Coxswain Patton took his boat alongside but, instead of jumping, the man lowered himself over the side and hung there. Seizing him, the Coxswain told him to let go, but the man clung all the tighter and, as the lifeboat veered away, Coxswain Patton was dragged out of the boat. Still holding the man, knowing him to be disabled, the Coxswain fell into

the sea and when the lifeboat was swept back, was crushed between it and the steamer. He was crushed twice more after the seaman had ben dragged inboard. Returning to Runswick at 6.15 a.m. the Coxswain was admitted to hospital, gravely injured. He died nine days later at the age of 46. In his own words – 'I could not lct the poor lad go, as he might have drowned'. The lifeboat was re-named *The Robert Patton – The Always Ready*.

BROWN Robert Charles, Assistant Mechanic, Swanage Lifeboat   BRONZE
19 April 1934

19 March 1934: When the yacht *Hally Lise* appeared to be in difficulties off Southbourne, eight miles east of Swanage, the self righting motor lifeboat *Thomas Markby* launched in a strong southerly gale and heavy seas. When she came up with the yacht at 1.30 p.m. it was near Boscombe Pier and close to the shore. The waves were eight feet high and, as the lifeboat approached, the yacht struck and was thrown on its beam ends. One of the two men on board was thrown into the sea, and Mr. Brown went overboard in oilskins, lifebelt and sea boots, seized him and held him until both were picked up. The other man was rescued from the shore by life saving apparatus.

POW George Henry Eastman, Second Coxswain, Appledore Lifeboat   BRONZE
14 March 1935

11 January 1935: In the afternoon, the Clovelly motor fishing boat *Lee Bay* was seen to be in serious difficulties in a west-north-westerly gale a mile inside Baggy Point, Devon, at the northern end of Bideford Bay. The self righting lifeboat *V.C.S.* launched at 4.37 p.m. In the absence of the Coxswain, Second Coxswain Pow took charge, putting out at low tide in the teeth of the gale, and safely negotiated the heavy seas over the bar. Coming up with the fishing boat, the Second Coxswain veered down twice in the darkness and a disabled man was lifted on board, the other two men jumping to safety. In view of the weather conditions, they were landed at Ilfracombe at 7.45 p.m.

JONES Archibald Claude, Honorary Secretary, Barry Dock R.N.L.I.   SILVER
ALEXANDER Stanley, Crew Member, Barry Dock Lifeboat   BRONZE
ALEXANDER Thomas, Crew Member,, Barry Dock Lifeboat   BRONZE
COOK William Richard, Crew Member, Barry Dock Lifeboat   BRONZE
HOBBS Henry James, Second Coxswain, Barry Dock Lifeboat   BRONZE
HOUSDEN Henry H., Crew Member, Barry Dock Lifeboat   BRONZE
SEARLE Frederick, Crew Member, Barry Dock Lifeboat   BRONZE
SWARTS Hewitt George, Motor Mechanic, Barry Dock Lifeboat   BRONZE
10 October 1935

17 September 1935: The French schooner *Goeland* of Paimpol, in passage from Brest to Swansea with a cargo of onions, was forced to make for Cardiff with her sails blown away in a strong west-north-westerly gale. Her ballast of sand shifted, and attempts were made to beach her in Porthkerry Bay. These failed and she was seen to be in difficulties off Rhoose Point. The Watson class motor lifeboat *Prince David* launched at 10.23 a.m. under Mr. Jones' command in the absence of her Coxswain. In a dangerous service, made worse by the schooner's condition, the lifeboat took off the six crew just before she struck and returned to station at 11.25 a.m. Mr. Jones was a retired dock pilot.

SINCLAIR Thomas Marshall, Coxswain, Aberdeen Lifeboat BRONZE
9 January 1936

25 December 1935: Returning from bunkering at Methil, Fife, the 141 ton Aberdeen trawler *George Stroud*, with a five man crew, was steaming up the channel into Aberdeen harbour at 8.05 p.m. when she grounded, swung around and remained fast about 50 feet from the wall of the North Pier. Within minutes, the line throwing gun had got a line aboard but, although they caught it, the trawler's crew refused to make use of it, demanding the lifeboat's attendance. The Barnett class motor lifeboat *Emma Constance* had already left her moorings and, in heavy seas under a strong south-easterly wind, Coxswain Sinclair took her between the pier wall and the trawler, but the crew still refused to leave their wheel house refuge. After a pause, however, one man did so and, while he was fastening a line, he was seized and dragged on board the lifeboat. Then a heavy sea broke and flung the lifeboat against the pier foundations and washed away the upper part of the trawler's wheel house. One man was then saved by the life saving apparatus. After five more attempts on one engine, the other having been damaged, and after an hour's search, the lifeboat could find no trace of the other three men.

MOGRIDGE William Harry Hayward, Coxswain, Torbay Lifeboat BRONZE
13 February 1936

30–31 December 1935: With a journey of 25 miles in a whole gale, heavy confused seas and a very strong tide ahead of her, the Barnett class motor lifeboat *George Shee* launched at 6.50 p.m. in answer to a call concerning the Cherbourg trawler *Satanicle*. Three other vessels had been standing by the casualty 15 miles east of Start Point, Devon, and one of them had taken off three men, leaving the Master still on board. In huge steep seas, Coxswain Mogridge got a line aboard, then hauled his boat in close enough for the man to jump. The lifeboat reached Torbay at 4.45 a.m. only slightly damaged, despite being twice flung against the *Satanicle*.

SIM James Stuart, Coxswain, Fraserburgh Lifeboat BRONZE
13 February 1936

18 January 1936: Shortly before 2 a.m. the Aberdeen trawler *Evergreen*, outward bound with a crew of nine went ashore in a snowstorm between Sandhaven and Rosehearty, four miles west of Fraserburgh, Aberdeenshire. She lay very dangerously deep among rocks into which she had run before stiking, and was 50 yards from the shore at an angle of 45 degrees, seas washing over her from end to end. With the tide rising, Coxswain Sim veered the self righting motor lifeboat *Lady Rothes* down and was hauled alongside. In five minutes, he took off the trawler's crew,then, hauling back on his anchor, returned to Fraserburgh at 4 a.m. During this period, the lifeboat crew had to endure a heavy ground swell in a very dark, cold night with frequent heavy snow showers.

BLEWETT Frank, Coxswain, Penlee Lifeboat BRONZE
13 February 1936

27 January 1936: In a strong gale and heavy sea, the 400 ton s.s. *Taycraig* drove on to Gear Rock in Mount's Bay, Cornwall, end on to the gale. When the Watson class motor lifeboat *W. and S.* arrived, she found the steamer with seas breaking over her, the after half submerged and the nine

man crew together on the forecastle. Coxswain Blewett veered his boat down and, with it rising and falling violently, took off all the crew, one at a time. He returned to station at 3.25 a.m. just 50 minutes after launching.

SLINEY Patrick, Coxswain, Ballycotton Lifeboat	**GOLD**
WALSH John Lane, Second Coxswain, Ballycotton Lifeboat	**SILVER**
SLINEY Thomas, Motor Mechanic, Ballycotton Lifeboat	**SILVER**
SLINEY John Shea, Crew Member, Ballycotton Lifeboat	**BRONZE**
SLINEY William, Crew Member, Ballycotton Lifeboat	**BRONZE**
WALSH Michael Coffey, Crew Member, Ballycotton Lifeboat	**BRONZE**
WALSH Thomas Flavin, Crew Member, Ballycotton Lifeboat	**BRONZE**

12 March 1936

11–13 February 1936: In a south easterly gale, verging on hurricane force, the Daunt Rock lightship, with eight men aboard, broke her moorings and, early on the 11th was reported drifting towards Ballycotton, Co. Cork. In intolerable conditions, Coxswain Sliney took out the Barnett class motor lifeboat *Mary Stanford*. The morning was spent searching, and the lightship was found at noon with two ships standing by her. One of the vessels left, but the lifeboat stood by for three hours before returning to Cobh. The other ship, the destroyer H.M.S. *Tenedos*, remained all night but, when the lifeboat returned early on the 12th, she left the scene. The lifeboat then stood by for 25 hours. After refuelling at Cobh early on the 13th, the lifeboat returned to find the Irish Lights vessel *Isolda* present. At 8 p.m. a huge wave carried away one of the lightship's warning lights. The vessel was drifting towards Daunt Rock and, at 9.30 p.m., with the Rock only 60 yards away, Coxswain Sliney commenced the rescue. With seas sweeping over the casualty, which was plunging wildly, he took his boat alongside more than a dozen times. Six of the crew jumped into the boat, but two had to be dragged off as they were transfixed with fear. The lifeboat returned to Cobh after being away for 76 hours, on service for 63 hours and at sea for 49 hours. The crew had been without food for 25 hours, and had sustained salt water burns and other injuries.

DASS William, Coxswain, Longhope Lifeboat	**BRONZE**

12 March 1936

21 February 1936: The French trawler *Neptunia* ran ashore on rocks known as The Tails of Brims at Brims Ness on the island of Hoy, Orkney Islands. It was an exceptionally dark evening with misty rain, sleet squalls and a strong south-easterly wind over the tide. Arriving at the scene, the Watson class motor lifeboat *Thomas McCunn* found the trawler lying nearly parallel to the shore, only a few yards away on her starboard side, and with a heavy list to port. Efforts to effect a rescue by rocket apparatus were unsuccessful. Coxswain Dass then took his boat in close to the wreck and, using a boat from the trawler, 41 men were taken off in five trips. They were landed at Longhope at 11.15 p.m.

MOGRIDGE William Harry Hayward, Coxswain, Torbay Lifeboat   **BRONZE(2)**

11 February 1937

23–24 January 1937: Early on 23 January, the 4000 ton s.s. *English Trader*, of London, owing to the temporary failure of her steering gear, ran ashore on Checkstone Ledge, at the entrance to Dartmouth Harbour. The ship, with a crew of 32, was bound from the Argentine to the Continent with a cargo of grain. The Barnett class lifeboat *George Shee* was launched and reached the steamer about 6.15 a.m. The Captain requested the lifeboat to stand by until efforts were made to refloat the steamer at high water in the afternoon. These efforts failed, and the Captain then asked the lifeboat to stand by all night. This she did, after refuelling at Kingswear. By 6 a.m., on the 24th, the wind had increased to a gale from the south-south-east, and the Captain decided to abandon ship. In darkness with the tide ebbing strongly and in danger from rocks and from seas breaking clean over the steamer, Coxswain Mogridge took the lifeboat alongside. One by one, the men on board were helped or lifted into the lifeboat. In addition to the 32 crew, also on board to help the salvage operation were 15 stevedores, three salvage officers, a Pilot and a naval signalman. All were safely rescued and landed at Dartmouth; the lifeboat then returned to Torbay at 12.15 p.m. She had been out for over 31 hours.

SINCLAIR Thomas Marshall, Coxswain, Aberdeen Lifeboat   **SILVER**

WEIR Alexander, Mechanic, Aberdeen Lifeboat   **BRONZE**

MASSON John, Crew Member, Aberdeen Lifeboat   **BRONZE**

11 March 1937

26–27 January 1937: With a whole south-east gale blowing over a very heavy sea, the 249 ton King's Lynn collier *Fairy,* with seven men on board, was seen at 4.30 p.m. in distress three and a half miles east of the Bridge of Don. The Barnett class motor lifeboat *Emma Constance* launched and found the steamer broken down with a German trawler trying to tow her. Another steamer, the s.s. *Montrose*, was then seen bearing down upon them, her steering gear carried away. The lifeboat first stood by the *Montrose* whilst repairs were effected. Returning to the other two vessels, Coxswain Sinclair found that the tow line had failed and the *Fairy* was drifting towards the heavy surf about two miles south of Belhevie. Although the steamer was rolling heavily and sheering about, the lifeboat veered down twice and took off the seven crew. One of them fell into the water and was rescued by Mr Masson at the risk of being dragged overboard between the steamer and the lifeboat.

RALPH George Alick, Captain, Fishing Boat *Barbara*   **BRONZE**

8 December 1938

27 January 1937: In an easterly gale, the Russian s.s. *Kingissepp* was anchored off Nairn harbour in the Moray Firth, when a small boat with three men on board was seen to put off and head for the harbour. It was obvious that it was being swept towards Fearn Rocks about a mile to the west. With the nearest available lifeboat too far away to help, Captain Ralph put out in his 48 ft motor fishing boat with his son and grandson. During a very risky operation in heavy broken water, he saved the three men and their boat just short of the rocks. Returning them to their ship, he piloted her to Invergordon, but as it was impossible to re-enter Nairn harbour in the prevailing conditions he stayed until the following afternoon.

It was only at the end of April 1938 that the rescue was brought to the notice of the Institution, and there was then delay in getting in full particulars as Mr Ralph had just left Nairn on a voyage to the West Indies.

LENG George, Coxswain, Flamborough Lifeboat   **SILVER**

13 March 1937

2–3 March 1937: In a heavy ground swell and a light south-west wind, the Grimsby steam trawler *Lord Ernle,* on passage from the White Sea to Grimsby, went ashore under Bempton cliffs, north of Flamborough Head, Yorkshire. 50 helpers launched the Liverpool class motor lifeboat *Elizabeth and Albina Whitley* over flat sand and rocks at 11.30 p.m. Swept continuously by the heavy breaking swell, Coxswain Leng veered down but found it impossible to get alongside. A line was fired on board the wreck with difficulty, and 15 men were taken off in three hours. The line parted twice and communication had to be re-established each time.

MATTHEWS John, Coxswain, Moelfre Lifeboat   **BRONZE**

11 November 1937

24 October 1937: With a gale blowing and a very heavy sea running, a vessel was reported in distress off Port Lynas, Anglesey. The Watson class motor lifeboat *G.W.* lanched at 1.20 a.m. Travelling in the teeth of the gale and repeatedly filled by the heavy seas, she searched for nearly three hours before finding the 80 ton Cardiff s.s. *Lady Windsor* nine miles from Port Lynas hoping to make Moelfre Roads. Standing by her for a further two hours, Coxswain Matthews eventually closed with her, came alongside and removed the five men, landing them at Moelfre at 8.40 a.m.

SINCLAIR Thomas Marshall, Coxswain, Aberdeen Lifeboat   **SILVER(2)**
FLETT George Allan, Second Coxswain, Aberdeen Lifeboat   **BRONZE**
ESSON Robert James Brown, Acting Mechanic, Aberdeen Lifeboat   **BRONZE**

9 December 1937

4–5 November 1937: With the regular Aberdeen lifeboat absent under overhaul, the Watson class reserve lifeboat *J. & W.* slipped her moorings at 10 p.m. and headed for a point two miles north of the River Ythan at Newburgh, Aberdeenshire. On a bitterly cold night in driving spray, Coxswain Sinclair searched the area, 13 miles north of his station, and found the 81 ton Aberdeen steam trawler *Roslin* aground in the boiling surf just south of the river mouth, and almost submerged with every passing sea sweeping over her. Unable to anchor and veer down, he took the lifeboat alongside, and six times ran her aboard the wreck before two survivors could be taken from the rigging; six others had drowned. The damaged lifeboat returned to her moorings at 5 a.m., her crew wearied by their efforts throughout the dreadful night.

REES John, Second Coxswain, Tenby Lifeboat   **SILVER**
COTTAM Alfred, Mechanic, Tenby Lifeboat   **BRONZE**

10 February 1938

15 January 1938: In a south-west gale, with frequent hurricane force gusts, a very rough sea and with rain and driving spray making visibility very poor, the Belfast s.s. *Fermanagh*, making for Llanelli, was driven aground on the Woolhouse Rocks, near Tenby, Pembrokeshire. Some time after the arrival of the Watson class motor lifeboat *John R. Webb*, the casualty floated off the rocks and drifted before the gale with her stern sinking and her bows in the air. Acting Coxswain Rees took his boat alongside and, in a few seconds, eight of the steamer's crew jumped on board and were landed

at 8.30 a.m. The lifeboat returned to the scene again to search for the Mate but found no trace of him and put back to Tenby at 10.45 a.m. The lifeboat's problems had not ended as, due to the severity of the weather, her crew had to remain on board until she could be rehoused at 4.15 p.m.

COCKING Thomas (Senior) Coxswain, St Ives Lifeboat	**SILVER**
PETERS William, Second Coxswain, St Ives Lifeboat	**BRONZE**
COCKING John Bassett, Assistant Mechanic, St Ives Lifeboat	**BRONZE**
BARBER Matthew Stevens, Bowman, St Ives Lifeboat	**BRONZE**
THOMAS John, Signalman, St Ives Lifeboat	**BRONZE**
BARBER William Bryant, Crew Member, St Ives Lifeboat	**BRONZE**
COCKING Thomas (Junior), Crew Member, St Ives Lifeboat	**BRONZE**
PAYNTER Phillip, Crew Member, St Ives Lifeboat	**BRONZE**
PETERS Henry, Crew Member, St Ives Lifeboat	**BRONZE**

10 February 1938

31 January 1938: On passage from South Wales to Italy with a cargo of coal, the 4,000 ton s.s. *Alba* drove ashore in bad weather near St Ives, Cornwall, after the engine began to give trouble. The self righting motor lifeboat *Caroline Parsons* launched at 7.30 p.m. and Coxswain Cocking found the casualty lying head on to the wind with heavy seas pounding her starboard side and went alongside in the comparative shelter of her port side. After some delay due to language and other difficulties, he took off her 23 man crew but, in reversing clear, the lifeboat was capsized by a huge wave and everybody, except three lifeboatmen, was thrown in the sea. The lifeboat righted herself, and the Coxswain and the rest of his crew regained the boat and set about recovering the men from the *Alba*. Her engine could not be restarted; she was swept on to the rocks and damaged beyond repair. Five men from the *Alba* had been lost but, with the help of many shore helpers, everybody else was brought to safety. Tragically, five of this lifeboat's crew lost their lives in a service on 23 January 1939.

PAGE Sidney Harry Bartlett, Coxswain, Southend-on-Sea Lifeboat　　**BRONZE**

10 November 1938

2 June 1938: In a very bad storm much of the shipping in the area of Southend-on-Sea, Essex, was in trouble, with no fewer than seven sailing barges and two larger motor barges going ashore near the Gas Works Jetty. Shortly after midnight, the Ramsgate class motor lifeboat *Greater London (Civil Service No. 3)* was called to the Ipswich yacht *Wimpie* as she was dragging her anchor; two men were taken off and landed on the pier steps. Receiving another call, Coxswain Page took the lifeboat to Shoebury Sands, where three men were taken from the rigging of the barge *Glen Rosa*. The barge *Maid of Munster* refused help, therefore the lifeboat went on to take off two men and a dog from the barge *Audrey*, adrift off the Nore Lightship with her rudder gone and her sails in ribbons.

GILL John, Coxswain, Galway Bay Lifeboat	BRONZE
DOYLE Joseph, Mechanic, Galway Bay Lifeboat	BRONZE
FLAHERTY Patrick, Bowman, Galway Bay Lifeboat	BRONZE
FLAHERTY Joseph, Crew Member, Galway Bay Lifeboat	BRONZE
FLAHERTY Thomas, Crew Member, Galway Bay Lifeboat	BRONZE
GILL Peter, Crew Member, Galway Bay Lifeboat	BRONZE
GORHAM William, Crew Member, Galway Bay Lifeboat	BRONZE

15 September 1938

16 August 1938: In the evening, a strong west-south-westerly wind was blowing through Gregory Sound over which a very heavy sea was running. The London steam trawler *Nogi* went ashore in a very exposed position, near the lighthouse on Straw Island, off Inishmore, Isles of Aran, in the mouth of Galway Bay. A small boat with two men on board was launched at once, but was carried away with one man; the other regained his ship. The steam trawler *Hatano*, anchored nearby, sent out an SOS and launched a boat with four men on board, but this was carried towards the rocks. The Watson class motor lifeboat *William Evans* was launched, took the four men from the boat, then went on to the *Nogi*. Coxswain Gill veered down using the *Hatano*'s boat which had been recovered, and 11 men were brought from the trawler in two journeys. A search was carried out for the man swept away in the small boat; he was found, dazed and exhausted, on Straw Island. The service lasted 14 hours.

JONES William Henry, Coxswain, New Brighton Lifeboat	SILVER
NICHOLSON John Rowland, Second Coxswain, New Brighton Lifeboat	BRONZE(2)
GARBUTT Wilfred, Mechanic, New Brighton Lifeboat	BRONZE(2)
MASON John E., Second Mechanic, New Brighton Lifeboat	BRONZE

8 December 1938

23 November 1938: The Barnett class motor lifeboat *William and Kate Johnston* launched at 9.55 a.m. and faced a whole west gale gusting up to 108 miles per hour with frequent, heavy rain and hail squalls. Putting out towards the Crosby Light Vessel, Coxswain Jones saw the Hoylake fishing boat *Progress* labouring heavily with a crew of three men and, also, the Annalong schooner *Loch Ranza Castle,* with a cargo of stone, drifting towards the shore, her sails blown away. The Coxswain decided to help the fishing boat first. Going alongside, after two or three attempts, the three men were rescued, shortly before the boat sank. He then set course for the schooner and caught up with her as she entered the surf. Dropping his anchor, he veered down to her, but she had already sunk. In three trips, during which the lifeboat was damaged in going over the wreck, four men were rescued from the rigging, one semi-conscious; they were landed at New Brighton just before 1 p.m.

CHATTEN George Edward, Coxswain, Aldeburgh Lifeboat	BRONZE

8 December 1938

23 November 1938: Just after 8 a.m. in a northerly gale and very heavy seas, the Watson (Beach) class lifeboat *Abdy Beauclerk* was launched to three barges seen to be in distress two and a half miles north east of the station. The Rochester barge *Grecian* refused help, but two men were taken off the Rochester barge *Astrild*, riding at anchor near Sizewell Bank, her topsail gone and with damage to her spars and rigging. The London barge *Decima* also refused help, therefore Coxswain Chatton returned to the *Grecian* and took off two men. By this time, it was impossible to make Aldeburgh and the lifeboat headed for Lowestoft arriving at 1.15 p.m.

JOHNSON Charles Ambrose, Coxswain
   Great Yarmouth and Gorleston Lifeboat   **BRONZE(2)**

8 December 1938

23 November 1938: When seven barges were in trouble, the Norfolk and Suffolk class motor lifeboat *John and Mary Meiklam of Gladswood* was out for over 11 hours. After helping the London barge *Ailsa* establish a tow to a tug, the lifeboat then took two men from the London barge *Britisher*, north east of Gorleston Harbour (they were returned after the arrival of a tug). Coxswain Johnson then took her out again to stand by the London barge *Royalty*, while she was taken in tow. He performed the same service near Scroby Sands for the London barge *Raybell*, which had earlier refused help. Then he set off in pursuit of the London barge *Cetus*, caught up with her opposite Winterton lighthouse and took off two men. Nearing Britannia Pier at Gorleston, he diverted to the London barge *Decima* and removed her two man crew just before she went on to Scroby Sands. Putting out once more from Gorleston, in the dark the lifeboat took off two men and a dog from the Ipswich barge *Una*, ashore on Yarmouth beach.

PAGE Sidney Henry Bartlett, Coxswain, Southend-on-Sea Lifeboat   **BRONZE(2)**

8 December 1938

26 November 1938: In very bad weather, during a very heavy gale and severe rain squalls, Coxswain Page took the Ramsgate class motor lifeboat *Greater London (Civil Service No.3)* out to three barges, two miles east of Southend pier head. The first one, the London *Lord Roberts*, refused help. He then went to the Rochester *T.F.C.* and, in two passes, took off her Master and Mate. He returned to the *Lord Roberts*, but help was again refused. Two passes were then needed to take off two men from the Rochester barge *Glenmore*. By this time the *Lord Roberts* had sunk, and her two man crew had to be rescued from the rigging. The lifeboat was back on station at 4.30 am, one and a half hours after launching.

MOGRIDGE William Harry, Coxswain, Torbay Lifeboat   **SILVER**

12 January 1939

9 December 1938: Early in the afternoon, a sudden gale overtook the Dartmouth crabber *Channel Pride*, off Coombe Point, Dartmouth, Devon; her engine had stopped because her propeller was fouled by a crab pot. She drifted toward the foot of the cliff, where huge, breaking seas were bursting 50 feet high. Fortunately, at the last moment, her anchor took hold, the wind veered and the back wash helped to keep her off. The conditions were terrible with visibility at its lowest and, in three hours of searching, the crew of the Barnett class lifeboat *George Shee* were unable to find the casualty. She was only sighted with the help of lights shining and burning on shore. Coxswain Mogridge took the lifeboat directly into the area and brought her up all standing alongside the crabber so that the crew was able to jump to safety. He then took the boat full ahead through violent seas and rocks to gain sea room and returned to Torbay at 7.45 p.m.

WHEATLEY Josiah, Coxswain, Blyth Lifeboat   **BRONZE**

20 April 1939

23 December 1938: Launched at 5.15 p.m., the Watson class motor lifeboat *Joseph Adlam* found the Sunderland Steamer *Skarv*, her boilers out of action, drifting towards Cambois Bay in a strong north-east wind. The Newbiggin motor lifeboat *Augustus and Laura* had also been called out, as well as a tug from Blyth. The tug could not get close enough for either of the lifeboats to pass a tow from her to the *Skarv*. The Blyth lifeboat then closed with the steamer and managed to take off three men before the lifeboat sustained severe damage to her rudder. Despite this, the Coxswain tried several more times to rescue the remaining crew but had to give up the attempt. The lifeboat then returned to shore; the Newbiggin boat returned but could not get near. Finally, the *Skarv* was driven ashore and the three survivors were taken off by rocket apparatus.

COCKING Thomas (Senior), Coxswain, St Ives Lifeboat	**Post BRONZE**
BARBER Matthew Stevens	
Acting Second Coxswain, St Ives Lifeboat	**Post BRONZE(2)**
BARBER William Bryant, Acting Bowman, St Ives Lifeboat	**Post BRONZE(2)**
STEVENS Richard Quick, Mechanic, St Ives Lifeboat	**Post BRONZE**
COCKING John Bassett, Assistant Mechanic, St Ives Lifeboat	**Post BRONZE(2)**
THOMAS John, Signalman, St Ives Lifeboat	**Post BRONZE(2)**
BASSETT Edgar, Crew Member, St Ives Lifeboat	**Post BRONZE**
FREEMAN William, Crew Member, St Ives Lifeboat	**BRONZE**

9 March 1939

23 January 1939: In an exceptionally violent west-north-westerly gale and heavy sea, a vessel (never identified) was seen to be in a dangerous position off Cape Cornwall. Although Sennen Cove is only six miles to the south, their lifeboat could not be got away, therefore the St Ives self righting motor lifeboat *John and Sarah Eliza Stych* launched at 2.50 p.m. with 11 miles to travel in the teeth of the gale. As she left the shelter of St Ives Bay, she met a heavy sea. Coxswain Cocking decided to keep her well clear of the headland then, avoiding the strong flood tide, turned west-wards but, one and a half miles north-north-east of Clodgy Point, she was capsized by a violent wave. When she righted herself, the Coxswain, the acting Bowman, the Signalman and Edgar Bassett were nowhere to be seen. Several times the engine restarted only to stall when it was put in gear and, with only four men in the boat, the mizzen mast and sail could not be raised. The lifeboat drifted across the bay, all attempts to recover power failed and, when she capsized again, the Mechanic was washed away. Continuing her drift towards Godrevy, she capsized a third time at 7.45 p.m. near the rocks. William Freeman was the only survivor, and he was able to crawl ashore and reach Godrevy Farm.

YOUNG Robert, Coxswain, Cloughey Lifeboat   **SILVER**

YOUNG George, Mechanic, Cloughey Lifeboat   **BRONZE**

13 July 1939

17–18 June 1939: The Bilbao s.s. *Arantzazu-Mendi* went aground on Butter Pladdy shoals outside Kearney Point, Co Down, northern Ireland. On the 17th with a salvage party on board, and with a strong south-south-westerly wind blowing, a distress signal was seen at 9.30 p.m. The self righting motor lifeboat *William Maynard* launched at 10 p.m. and, when she reached the wreck, 15 foot seas were sweeping clear over her from the bridge aft, with the 11 salvage men on the foredeck, knee deep in water. Coxswain Young had to veer the lifeboat down stern first on two occasions before he could use a line thrown from the wreck to pull alongside. All 11 men then dropped in to the boat, one or two at a time and it took three quarters of an hour for them to get aboard.

BLOGG Henry George E.G.M., Coxswain, Cromer Lifeboat	**SILVER(3)**
DAVIES John James (Senior), Second Coxswain, Cromer Lifeboat	**BRONZE(3)**
DAVIES Henry William, Mechanic, Cromer Lifeboat	**BRONZE(2)**
DAVIES James William, Assistant Mechanic, Cromer Lifeboat	**BRONZE(2)**

9 November 1939

9–10 October 1939: With a heavy sea running, the tide at half ebb in a south-east by east gale, mist and rain, the 4,275 ton Greek steamer *Mount Ida,* Vancouver to Hull with a cargo of grain and timber, was wrecked on Ower Bank, 32 miles east of Cromer, Norfolk. The Watson class motor lifeboat *H.F. Bailey* launched at 6.45 a.m. on a report that the wreck was on Haisborough Sands, but a revised signal added 19 miles to the journey. Arriving at 12.30 p.m. Coxswain Blogg made two unsuccessful approaches. After waiting for the tide to slacken, he made a third attempt at 2.15 p.m., maintaining position alongside by engine power. At 3.30 p.m. the last of 29 men was taken off; one had his leg crushed when the lifeboat smashed against the wreck. Reaching Cromer at 8 p.m. and, unable to land the men on the slipway, the Liverpool class No. 2 motor lifeboat *Harriett Dixon* was called to take the survivors ashore.

Coxswain Blogg had only just reached home, when he was called to a casualty off Bacton, ten miles south east of Cromer. Finding that the crew's rescue had already been effected by rocket apparatus, he took his boat to Lowestoft for repairs after almost 30 hours on service: 21 hours had been spent at sea and they had travelled over 100 miles.

CROSS Robert, Coxswain, Humber Lifeboat	**SILVER(3)**
MAJOR John Sanderson, Mechanic, Humber Lifeboat	**BRONZE**

14 December 1939

10 October 1939: At 4.55 a.m. the Watson class motor lifeboat *City of Bradford II* launched to the Grimsby steam trawler *Saltaire,* aground in a fresh south south west wind and very rough sea on the Inner Binks, off the Humber Estuary. The nine man crew was taken off and landed at 6.30 a.m. After the wind dropped, her crew and the owner's agent walked out to the trawler at low tide and preparations were made to tow her off at high water. As the tide rose, the wind swung to the east and freshened, the sea got up rapidly, and the trawler swung around and fell over to seaward. Coxswain Cross launched again at 2 p.m. and, using the breeches buoy, seven men were taken off and landed at 3.50 p.m. The other three were rescued by soldiers from the beach.

BLOOM Thomas Henry, Coxswain, Walton & Frinton Lifeboat   **SILVER**
OXLEY Walter Jonas, Second Coxswain, Walton & Frinton Lifeboat   **BRONZE**
BACON Fraser Thomas, Assistant Mechanic, Walton & Frinton Lifeboat   **BRONZE**
WILLIAMS Frederick John, Signalman, Walton & Frinton Lifeboat   **BRONZE**

9 November 1939

14 October 1939: The London barges *Esterel* and *Yampa*, en route from London to Norwich with cargoes of maize, encountered a gale off Orford Ness, turned back and both grounded on Cork Sands, off Harwich, Essex. The *Esterel* managed to get off, but, damaged and out of control, was soon driven ashore east of Walton Pier. The Ramsgate class motor lifeboat *E.M.E.D.* launched at 9.50 a.m. and found the barge lying about 100 yards from the shore in about six feet of water. Coxswain Bloom managed to get alongside and took off the Master, his wife, the Mate and a dog. Then by superb seamanship, he got the lifeboat clear. Pausing to land the survivors at Walton at 11.30 a.m., he made for the other casualty but, in a protracted search in very heavy seas, no survivors could be found. The lifeboat returned to station at 3 p.m.

MURFIELD James, Coxswain, Whitby No. 1 Lifeboat   **SILVER**
DRYDEN John Robert, Second Coxswain, Whitby No. 1 Lifeboat   **BRONZE**
PHILPOT James, Mechanic, Whitby No. 1 Lifeboat   **BRONZE**

14 December 1939

12 November 1939: In a dark, foggy night and a very heavy swell, the minesweeper H.M.M.S. *Cape Comorin* went ashore on the south side of East Pier, Whitby, Yorkshire, less than 100 yards from the cliffs, bow on to them and surrounded by foaming white water. The Watson class lifeboat *Mary Ann Hepworth* launched at 3.50 a.m. and found the wreck close under the Coastguard station; the District Officer was able to keep his searchlight trained on her all the time. Coxswain Murfield, unable to anchor, maintained a position alongside with the engines and took off 11 of the crew before a huge wave threw the lifeboat back. Two more attempts were necessary to take off the remaining seven men, the whole rescue having taken 40 minutes.

COTTON Walter Oliver, Coxswain, Yarmouth, Isle of Wight, Lifeboat   **BRONZE**

14 December 1939

14–15 November 1939: H.M. Trawler *British* went ashore off Brighstone, Isle of Wight, in the evening with a fresh breeze blowing over a moderate sea. It was raining heavily and very dark when the Watson class motor lifeboat *S.G.E.* launched at 9.15 p.m. Rounding the Needles in a full gale and very heavy sea, she found the trawler at midnight, but Coxswain Cotton decided to put back when he discovered that one of his crew was seriously ill. He put the sick man aboard the examination ship in Yarmouth Roads, resumed the service, and reached the trawler at 7.30 a.m. Anchoring, he veered the lifeboat down, took off the 12 crewmen in six attempts, and landed them at Yarmouth at 10.30 a.m.

ELLIS Charles Raymond, Coxswain, Clacton-on-Sea Lifeboat   **SILVER**

18 January 1940

19 November 1939: At 4 a.m. the Watson class motor lifeboat *Edward Z. Dresden* launched in rain squalls, a very rough sea and a gale. At daybreak, she found the Tollesbury smack *Charlotte Ellen* anchored and helpless in a very dangerous position at Swire Hole, four miles south of the Clacton, Essex, Coastguard station. As the smack's gear prevented any other approach, Coxswain Ellis brought the lifeboat between the smack and the sands, then took off her three man crew. Arriving back at Clacton at 8.50 a.m. he put out again and found the London barge *Lorna*, deeply laden with cotton seed, at anchor between south Whitaker and Middle Sands with seas breaking right over her. After an unsuccessful attempt to go alongside, the Coxswain ran the lifeboat on to the deck, his crew snatched the two crewmen aboard, and then the heavy sea washed the lifeboat off. They landed just before noon.

PARR William Reuben, Coxswain, Blackpool Lifeboat   **SILVER**

RIMMER Thomas Edward, Mechanic, Blackpool Lifeboat   **BRONZE**

PARKINSON John James, Coxswain, Lytham St Anne's Lifeboat   **SILVER**

HARRISON George, Mechanic, Lytham St Anne's Lifeboat   **BRONZE**

18 January 1940

26 November 1939: At midday on the 24th, the 434 ton pilot boat *Charles Livingstone* left Liverpool to cruise at a pilotage station with 32 men on board. At midnight 25–26th she was about one mile from the Liverpool Bar light vessel in bad weather with a strong breeze and rough sea. In a confused weather pattern she drove ashore at 3.42 a.m.; it was at first thought that this was on the north Coast of Wales. She was, however, finally located at 8.20 a.m. on Ainsdale beach, between Southport and Formby on the Lancashire coast. Five of the men on board were lost when the ship's boats were capsized in the surf, leaving the rest of the men stranded on board. Several men were washed out of the rigging, only four reaching shore alive. Arriving at Ainsdale Point in the Lytham Watson class motor lifeboat *Dunleary*, Coxswain Parkinson could see the casualty's mast and funnel, the vessel lying broadside on to the beach, embedded in the sand, her decks awash. He ran his boat in and made her fast under the wreck's lee but the nine survivors left on board refused to leave, hoping to walk ashore at low tide. *Dunleary* returned to station, her crew having been on duty for 24 hours. Shortly after she left the Blackpool Liverpool class motor lifeboat *Sarah Ann Austin* arrived at 2 p.m. and, going alongside in an ebbing tide, Coxswain Parr took off the six men now remaining on board and ran his boat straight on to the beach and landed them with the help of crowds of spectators. In this incident, 11 top Liverpool Pilots and 15 apprentice Pilots lost their lives.

BRYANT Colin H., Coxswain, Dover Lifeboat   **SILVER**

WALKER Richard, Lieutenant, R.N.R. Assistant King's Harbour Master   **BRONZE**

HILLS Sidney T., Second Coxswain, Dover Lifeboat   **BRONZE**

COOK Wilfred L., Mechanic, Dover Lifeboat   **BRONZE**

STOCK Christian R.T., Second Mechanic, Dover Lifeboat   **BRONZE**

18 January 1940

26 November 1939: While H.M. Trawler *Blackburn Rovers*, with 16 men on board, was on anti-submarine patrol near Dover, in rough seas and a south westerly gale, a wire fouled her propeller.

The crew let go the anchor, but this failed to hold and the boat began drifting towards a mine field. The Dover lifeboat men were summoned and the 64 ft. 'Special' lifeboat *Sir William Hillary* left harbour at 10 a.m., taking with her Lieutenant Richard Walker, R.N.R., the Assistant King's Harbour Master, who had a chart showing the minefields in the area. In the heavy seas, it took nearly one and a quarter hours for the lifeboat to reach the disabled trawler, by which time she was right on the edge of a deep minefield. Although the boat herself could drift through this area without touching a mine, there was a grave danger that her anchor cable would come into contact with a mine. There was then the added problem that even if she passed through this particular minefield safely, the trawler would then enter a shallow minefield.

Coxswain Bryant took the lifeboat alongside, and Lieutenant Walker instructed the trawler's crew to collect all the ship's papers together and as much of her secret gear as they could and to pass them all over to the lifeboat and, before they abandoned ship, they were to scuttle the vessel. The trawler was rolling violently in the heavy seas, which by that time were breaking clean over her, and she offered no lee at all for the lifeboat. Coxswain Bryant had to use all his skill to hold the lifeboat in position while the papers and gear were transferred, and his two Mechanics had great difficulty in remaining at the engine controls, so violent was the motion of the lifeboat.

By that time, they were all well aware that they were right in the middle of the minefield, but still the work went on of transferring the gear. At any moment, the trawler's anchor cable could have fouled a mine blowing them up. It took over an hour to get all the gear on board the lifeboat before the crew of 16 were rescued. Coxswain Bryant turned the lifeboat round and set course for home. They then had to face the full fury of the storm and speed had to be reduced to 6 knots. Coxswain Bryant had only recently recovered from a very serious illness, consequently he handed over the wheel to the Second Coxswain during the journey back. Huge seas repeatedly crashed over the lifeboat and it took them 3 hours to reach Dover Harbour, arriving there at 3.30 p.m.

JOHNSON Charles Ambrose, Coxswain,
   Great Yarmouth & Gorleston Lifeboat   **BRONZE(3)**

8 February 1940

2 December 1939: In a fresh and increasing southerly wind, H.M. Trawler *Resolvo* went aground on the eastside of Scroby Sands, off Great Yarmouth. When the Watson class motor lifeboat *Louise Stephens* reached the area it proved impossible to approach the casualty through the shallow water over the sands. Coxswain Johnson turned north-wards, found deeper water and went in from the east. He anchored, veered through heavy breaking seas, took off the ten man crew and returned to station after five and a half hours at sea.

COULL James, Coxswain, Broughty Ferry Lifeboat   **SILVER**
SMITH George Bell, Acting Second Coxswain, Broughty Ferry Lifeboat   **BRONZE**
GRIEVE John, Mechanic, Broughty Ferry Lifeboat   **BRONZE**

18 January 1940

5–6 December 1939: The Aberdeen steam trawler *Quixotic* went on to Bell Rock, near Lunan Bay, Angus, during the evening in a fresh north-east wind accompanied by sleet squalls. Two lifeboats were called, the Arbroath self-righting motor lifeboat *John and William Mudie* and the self-righting Broughty Ferry Watson class motor lifeboat *Mona*, launching at 9 p.m. and 8.15 p.m. respectively. The Arbroath boat, which had to travel nine and a half miles, arrived at 10 p.m. and made an unsuccessful attempt at rescue. When the Broughty Ferry boat arrived, Coxswain Coull took her in, threw a grapnel on board the wreck and, in half an hour of manoeuvring with seas washing over them, brought all nine men off and landed them at Broughty Ferry at 1.30 a.m.

DISTIN Edwin William, Coxswain, Salcombe Lifeboat   **SILVER**
CHANT Edwin, Second Coxswain, Salcombe Lifeboat   **BRONZE**
SHEPHERD Gerald, Bowman, Salcombe Lifeboat   **BRONZE**
ALLEN John, Mechanic, Salcombe Lifeboat   **BRONZE**
CHANT Phillip Edwin, Assistant Mechanic, Salcombe Lifeboat   **BRONZE**
CHEESEMAN Thomas, Crew Member, Salcombe Lifeboat   **BRONZE**
FIELD John, Crew Member, Salcombe Lifeboat   **BRONZE**
LAKE George John, Crew Member, Salcombe Lifeboat   **BRONZE**

8 February 1940

7–8 December 1939: When the 8,159 ton Dutch motor ship *Tajandoen* was torpedoed 40 miles north of Ile d'Ouissant (Ushant), France, 62 survivors were picked up by the Belgian ss *Louis Sheid* (6,000 tons) which in turn went ashore, early in the evening, at Bigbury Bay, Devon, in dark, squally weather. The Watson class motor lifeboat *Samuel and Marie Parkhouse* put out at 7.45 p.m. safely negotiating the heavy seas breaking over Salcombe Bar, only to find an increasing southerly wind and a rough sea when she left the shelter of the headlands. Reaching the wreck at 9.30 p.m. Coxswain Distin found her half a mile from the shore with no anchors down, head on to the wind and sea and with her engines going full ahead. Seas were breaking heavily around her in a full gale with heavy rain. His first attempt was aborted but, in the second attempt, 40 of the Dutch survivors were rescued and landed in Hope Cove inside Bolt Tail; a small pulling boat took them from the lifeboat eight at a time. The other 22 survivors were saved in the same manner. The 45 man Belgian crew were then landed by rocket apparatus. After waiting for conditions on Salcombe Bar to improve, the Coxswain brought his boat back to its station at 11 a.m.

MOGRIDGE William Harry Hayward, Coxswain, Torbay Lifeboat	**SILVER(2)**
PILLAR William, Second Coxswain, Torbay Lifeboat	**BRONZE**
SANDERS Frederick Collier, Bowman, Torbay Lifeboat	**BRONZE**
HARRIS Richard Trewaves, Mechanic, Torbay Lifeboat	**BRONZE**

8 February 1940

16 December 1939: When the Barnett class motor lifeboat *George Shee* arrived near the Truro schooner *Henrietta* at 3.15 p.m., she found her with one anchor down at the edge of the Skerries, a dangerous reef south of Dartmouth, Devon. A Dartmouth tug and a Brixham steam trawler stood by, helpless in the east-north-easterly gale and strong spring tide. With the light failing, Coxswain Mogridge carried out an exploratory run as a result of which he decided not to pursue rescue by breeches buoy. He ran in, secured to the starboard side of the violently rolling vessel, took off the seven men in three minutes, chopped away his ropes and drew clear. The survivors were landed at Torbay at 5.40 p.m.

SNELL John Charles, Coxswain, Falmouth Lifeboat	**SILVER**
WILLIAMS Charles H., Mechanic, Falmouth Lifeboat	**BRONZE**

8 February 1940

19 January 1940: In a south-easterly gale, very heavy sea and hazy weather, the West Hartlepool s.s. *Kirkpool* dragged her anchors off Castle Reach, Falmouth Bay, Cornwall, struck the beach and lay broadside on to the breaking seas. Coxswain Snell launched the Watson class motor lifeboat *Crawford and Constance Conybeare*, took her round the bows of the steamer and got between her and the shore. Once alongside, he took off an injured man on a stretcher and 13 firemen. These were landed at Falmouth. He then returned to rescue the remaining 21 men.

MATTHEWS John, Coxswain, Moelfre Lifeboat	**SILVER**
WILLIAMS Robert, Mechanic, Moelfre Lifeboat	**BRONZE**

14 March 1940

29–30 January 1940: In passage from Saigon to Liverpool with a cargo of maize, the 6,700 ton Glasgow m.v. *Gleneden* struck a mine off Bardsey Island, south of Lleyn Peninsula, Caernarvon. Her Captain decided to press on for Liverpool, but she went ashore on Dutchman's Bank, by Puffin Island at the mouth of the Menai Strait in Conway Bay. There she lay for three days. On the 28th the Llandudno lifeboat had gone out to her, but help was not needed. Next day, the Salvage Officer asked the Moelfre lifeboat to stand by as it was feared the ship would break in two. At 9 p.m., the Watson class motor lifeboat *G.W.* put out in extremely rough seas and arrived at the wreck. Coxswain Matthews went alongside without waiting for high water, took off 49 lascars and landed them at Beaumaris. Returning to the scene, he took off the ship's 11 officers.

GAWN Harry James, Coxswain, Bembridge Lifeboat	**BRONZE**

14 March 1940

29–30 January 1940: In a high wind, an easterly blizzard and a heavy sea with the tide at three-quarter ebb, the Watson class motor lifeboat *Jesse Lumb* put out at 5.20 p.m., and headed for No Man's Fort, off Selsey, Sussex. Failing to find anything, Coxswain Gawn was re-directed to a point between Ryde and Seaview on the Isle of Wight; he found a vessel, but it was in no danger. Returning to the Coastguard examination vessel once more, he was given yet more directions, this time to Chichester Bar where H.M.T. *Kingston Cairngorm* was found flooding fast. In an operation involving several approaches, her crew of 21 (including Lieutenant Commander P.E. Vaux R.D., R.N., Chief Inspector of Lifeboats recalled to service) was taken off and landed at Portsmouth. The lifeboat had been at sea for 14 hours with the Coxswain at the wheel all the time, and the weather was so bad that at the end of the service her deck was covered in ice.

PHILPOT James, Mechanic, Whitby Lifeboat	**SILVER**
MURFIELD James, Coxswain, Whitby Lifeboat	**BRONZE**
DRYDEN John Robert, Acting Second Coxswain, Whitby Lifeboat	**Post. BRONZE(2)**
WALE Christopher, Acting Bowman, Whitby Lifeboat	**Post. BRONZE**
WINSPEAR Matthew Leadley, Crew Member, Whitby Lifeboat	**BRONZE**
WALKER John William Cuthbeth, Crew Member, Whitby Lifeboat	**BRONZE**
DRYDEN William, Assistant Mechanic, Whitby Lifeboat	**BRONZE**

14 March 1940

3–4 February 1940: When the Belgian s.s. *Charles* was wrecked on Saltwick Nab, east of Whitby, Yorkshire, a south-easterly gale was blowing over a rough sea with the tide at half-flood. The Watson class motor lifeboat *Mary Ann Hepworth* launched at 9.20 p.m. in intense darkness and proceeded to the same spot on which the *Rohilla* was wrecked in 1914. Only the lights of the Coastguard life saving apparatus team enabled Coxswain Murfield to find the wreck, but his good fortune ran out when the lifeboat was thrown on to her beam ends and was damaged on her way in by a huge wave. He was badly injured, and two men were thrown out, and both drowned. The lifeboat returned to her station, where a second crew was assembled under a local fisherman John Storr; this included Mechanic Philpot who had been out on the first occasion. The new crew went out but returned because of the total lack of visibility. With the same scratch crew, they launched once more at 7.30 a.m. in an unsuccessful search for a liferaft reported to be in the area. Four survivors of the Belgian crew were hauled to safety by the life-saving apparatus.

The six bronze medals were awarded to the lifeboatmen who went out on the first launch. Mechanic Philpot went out on all three launches. John Storr was awarded the Thanks of the Institution on Vellum.

TAYLOR George Ralph, Second Coxswain, Newbiggin Lifeboat	**SILVER**

14 March 1940

4 February 1940: The Belgian m.v. *Eminent*, on her way to Newcastle-on-Tyne, found the bad weather had closed the port to shipping. She was forced to remain at sea and was later driven ashore half a mile north of Newbiggin Point, Northumberland. Just before 5 a.m., with Mr. Taylor acting as Coxswain, the Surf class lifeboat *Augustus and Laura* launched, through a south-easterly gale, high breaking seas, hard squalls of rain and sleet in a dark and intensely cold night. The hazardous conditions forced her to put back until, an hour later at daylight, an operation commenced to tow the lifeboat overland around the bay. This difficult task, dragging the boat up a cliff, over the town moor and across sand dunes involved 45 launchers, including many women. Arriving opposite the wreck at 8.10 a.m., the lifeboat launched for a second time. Lines were thrown aboard the wreck and the 11 crew were rescued and landed ashore.

HAY David, Coxswain, Fraserburgh Lifeboat	**BRONZE**
STEPHEN Andrew, Captain. Harbour Master	
Joint Honorary Secretary, Fraserburgh R.N.L.I. Station	**BRONZE**

11 April 1940

8 February 1940: In heavy rain and very heavy seas, the Danish m.v. *Bara Drangur* went ashore on the sands to the south of Fraserburgh, Aberdeenshire. Acting as Second Coxswain, Captain Stephen called out the Watson class motor lifeboat *John and Charles Kennedy*. Coxswain Hay took the lifeboat close to the wreck which was inside the broken water, her decks awash with heavy seas breaking over her. The five man crew were in the rigging, but, in a skilful and hazardous rescue, they were taken off the wreck just before midnight.

SWANKIE William, Coxswain, Arbroath Lifeboat	**BRONZE**

11 April 1940

9 February 1940: The self-righting motor lifeboat *John and William Mudie* was launched in a moderate sea and very hazy conditions to assist the 800 ton hopper barge *Foremost* on passage from Aberdeen to Methil, where she was scheduled to join a convoy. This vessel had already been attacked by a German aircraft when six miles south-east of Arbroath, Angus, and two of her crew were killed. As the lifeboat approached, the attack was continued by two aircraft but, despite machine-gun fire and bombs, the lifeboat went alongside the barge, took off the seven survivors and landed them at Arbroath.

CROSS Robert, Coxswain, Humber Lifeboat	**GOLD**
MAJOR John Sanderson, Mechanic, Humber Lifeboat	**SILVER**
JENKINSON William Robinson, Second Coxswain, Humber Lifeboat	**SILVER**
HOOD William James Jenkin, Bowman, Humber Lifeboat	**SILVER**
CROSS Samuel, Second Mechanic, Humber Lifeboat	**SILVER**
HOOPELL Samuel Frederick, Crew Member, Humber Lifeboat	**SILVER**

14 March 1940

12 February 1940: On a very cold, pitch dark night, in a strong westerly wind, with heavy and continuous snow, the Grimsby steam trawler *Gurth* struck on a sand bank as she returned from fishing grounds. The Watson class motor lifeboat *City of Bradford II* was launched, but with two crew short because of illness. With seas breaking continuously over her, in a co-ordinated use of engines, helm, cable and line, Coxswain Cross and his crew took off six survivors in 20 approaches in the dark. Even though one of her engines was stopped by a loose line around its propeller, the three remaining survivors were recovered in further approaches. The lifeboat, badly damaged and with only one engine working, was manoeuvred into comparatively calm water then, with the line cut free, the second engine was started and she was able to reach Grimsby.

Coxswain Cross was also awarded the George Medal.

HUGGETT Alec Francis, Crew Member, Eastbourne Lifeboat   BRONZE
ALLCHORN Thomas, Crew Member, Eastbourne Lifeboat   BRONZE

16 May 1940

20–21 March 1940: En route from Nova Scotia to London with a general cargo topped by a deck cargo of timber, the London s.s. *Barnhill* was bombed and set on fire by German aircraft in the English Channel, six miles off Beachy Head. The self-righting motor lifeboat *Jane Holland* was launched at 11.15 p.m., but found that 18 of the ship's crew had been rescued by a Dutch vessel. They were taken on to the lifeboat. Ignoring frequent explosions on the furiously blazing vessel, the lifeboat then took off ten men who had remained on board the vessel and landed everyone at Eastbourne. Almost two hours later, it was reported that an injured man was still on the vessel's forecastle. The lifeboat set out again with a doctor on board. Huggett and Allchorn boarded the wildly rolling, furiously blazing vessel and, ignoring the heavy and violent explosions, brought off the injured man. The lifeboat went out a third time to help a tug fight the fire.

STEPHEN Andrew, Captain. Harbour Master
  Joint Honorary Secretary, Fraserburgh R.N.L.I.   SILVER
DUTHIE George Flett, Mechanic, Fraserburgh Lifeboat   BRONZE
MAY John Downie, Crew member, Fraserburgh Lifeboat   BRONZE

14 November 1940

24 September 1940: The Grimsby trawler *Northward* was wrecked on the Cairnbulg Briggs, a reef of rocks two miles east of Fraserburgh, Aberdeenshire, in a fresh gale and violent sea. In the darkness with driving rain, the Watson class motor lifeboat *John and Charles Kennedy* was launched and found the trawler lying on a reef, far inside the broken water with seas breaking over and sweeping her full length. Captain Stephen, the acting Coxswain, dropped anchor but, after three attempts, failed to get alongside. At daylight, he anchored again and, veering down to within 50 feet of the wreck, brought off the whole crew of ten men by breeches buoy.

REAY Thomas Quayle, Coxswain, Maryport Lifeboat   BRONZE(2)

13 February 1941

9 October 1940: The wind had veered and strengthened to a full west-south-west gale with fierce squalls and blinding rain when herring drifters in the Solway Firth were making for Maryport – all that is except one, the Workington *Mourne Lass* whose nets had fouled her propeller. The Liverpool class motor lifeboat *Joseph Braithwaite* launched and found the drifter anchored with her sail split and the propeller still fouled. Coxswain Reay took off and brought to safety the four crewmen, who had abandoned all hope of rescue.

NELSON Samuel, Coxswain, Donaghadee Lifeboat   BRONZE

10 July 1941

21 November 1940: When the Watson class motor lifeboat *Civil Service No. 5* put out at 6.30 a.m. to the Liverpool s.s. *Coastville*, a mooring rope fouled one of her propellers and a half hour was spent clearing it. The wreck was marooned on the rocks at Ballymacormick Point in Belfast Lough,

in a north-westerly gale with heavy seas breaking over her. Coxswain Nelson took the lifeboat alongside through heavy broken water and took off seven men.

6 December 1940: During a gale, the Newcastle-on-Tyne s.s. *Hope Star* went ashore in shallow water surrounded by rocks at Ballyholme Bay. With rocket apparatus standing by on shore, Coxswain Nelson took the lifeboat in and rescued nine of the 43 men on board. The others refused to leave. After landing the nine men, he returned again and stood by until conditions moderated.

McAUSLANE William, Coxswain, Troon Lifeboat	**SILVER**
FERGUSON Albert John, Mechanic, Troon Lifeboat	**BRONZE**
	9 January 1941

6 December 1940: The 320-ton Belfast s.s. *Moyallon* was in difficulty off Dunure, Ayrshire, while sailing light from Larne to Ayr. The Watson class motor lifeboat *Sir David Richmond of Glasgow* launched at 2 p.m. On arrival, the lifeboat was asked to stand by while the steamer's anchor was lifted to enable her to make for shelter, but the anchor chains fouled and the engine broke down. The ship was now helpless in a whole north-westerly gale, heavy seas, fierce squalls of hail and heavy broken water. After trying other methods to take off the crew from the violently rolling and sheering ship, Coxswain McAuslane drove the lifeboat's bows hard against her and all seven crewmen jumped on board. During the rescue operation, Mechanic Ferguson worked in a cockpit full of water.

LEWIS David, Coxswain, Barry Dock Lifeboat	**BRONZE**
	9 January 1941

6 December 1940: The Watson class motor lifeboat *Rachel and Mary Evans* launched in a whole north-west gale to the 260 ton London s.s. *South Coaster*, in ballast from Penzance to Cardiff. The vessel was found dragging her anchors in very heavy seas near Breaksea lightship, off Breaksea Point, Glamorgan. Putting back to Barry, Coxswain Lewis arranged for a tug, but, because of heavy seas, it could not reach the steamer.

The lifeboat returned to the distressed vessel independently and got a line aboard in anticipation of the tug's arrival. However, when the tug's non arrival was realised, the lifeboat made two hazardous approaches and the ten man crew was able to jump to safety.

BOYLE John, Coxswain, Arranmore Lifeboat	**GOLD**
WARD Teague, Mechanic, Arranmore Lifeboat	**SILVER**
BOYLE Philip, Acting Second Coxswain, Arranmore Lifeboat	**BRONZE**
BYRNE Philip, Acting Bowman, Arranmore Lifeboat	**BRONZE**
BYRNE Neil, Assistant Mechanic, Arranmore Lifeboat	**BRONZE**
GALLAGHER Bryan, Crew Member, Arranmore Lifeboat	**BRONZE**
O'DONNELL Patrick, Crew Member, Arranmore Lifeboat	**BRONZE**
RODGERS Joseph, Crew Member, Arranmore Lifeboat	**BRONZE**
	17 April 1941

7 December 1940: After three days blowing hard, the north-north-west wind strengthened to hurricane force with fierce squalls accompanied by snow and sleet. The 2,500 ton Dutch s.s. *Stolwijk* was forced on to a reef of rocks at Inishbeg, east of Tory Island, 24 miles north of Arranmore Island. At

first light, the Watson class motor lifeboat *K.T.J.S.* put out with visibility reduced to 50 yards in the snow and, five and a half hours later, reached the wreck which was totally exposed to the fury of the Atlantic gales and seas which were breaking right over her. Ten of the steamer's crew had already drowned in an attempt to escape and the rest were huddled near the stern. Five of them were saved by breeches buoy before the rope chafed through, and ten more were brought into the lifeboat before it happened again; the last three were saved after communication had been established once more. The violence of the weather prevented the lifeboat returning to Arranmore, therefore all eighteen men were landed at Burtonport, Co. Donegal.

DAVIDSON Edwin Selby, Honorary Secretary,
    Tynemouth R.N.L.I.   **BRONZE**
LISLE George, Coxswain, Tynemouth Lifeboat   **BRONZE**

13 February 1941

8 December 1940: On 1 December, two merchant vessels were mined off Tynemouth and help was rendered by the Cullercoats and Tynemouth lifeboats; a number of survivors were landed. One of the vessels, the 20,000 ton Norwegian m.v. *Oslo Fjord*, grounded a mile south of Tyne South breakwater and salvage work soon commenced. At five past midnight on the 8th, distress signals were noticed, and Mr. Davidson assembled the crew of the Watson class motor lifeboat *John Pyemont*. She was launched at 12.30 a.m. in a very dark, stormy night and with a strong wind blowing. The seas breaking over the wreck were so heavy that she was starting to break up; two damaged lifeboats were hanging from their davits. Around her, the violently working seas were littered with wreckage. In an extremely hazardous and difficult operation, Coxswain Lisle was wholly occupied in handling his boat and Mr. Davidson was in charge of rescue activity; 21 men were taken off in an hour. After the lifeboat had returned to station, it was disclosed that the Chief Officer of the vessel had remained behind. Another trip was made later in the morning to bring him off.

PAGE Sidney Harry Barlett, Coxswain, Southend-on-Sea Lifeboat   **SILVER**
JURGENSON Frank Arthur, Mechanic, Southend-on-Sea Lifeboat   **BRONZE**
DEER William Arthur, Second Coxswain, Southend-on-Sea Lifeboat   **BRONZE**
MYALL Herbert George, Bowman, Southend-on-Sea Lifeboat   **BRONZE**
THOMAS Samuel Horace Gilson, Signalman, Southend-on-Sea Lifeboat   **BRONZE**
SANDERS Reginald Herbert, Assistant Mechanic,
    Southend-on-Sea Lifeboat   **BRONZE**

9 January 1941

6–11 December 1940: During a gale on the 5th, a number of barges were reported to be in difficulties and, on the following day, the Ramsgate class motor lifeboat *Greater London (Civil Service No. 3)* became engaged. The barge *Glencoe*, half a mile west of West Shoebury Buoy, refused service; two men were rescued from the rigging of the sunken Ipswich barge *Mistley*, followed by two men from each of the London barges *Cambria* and *Decima*, west of Southend Pier. Two ropes fouled both of the lifeboat's propellers and a sail was jury rigged to bring her back to her slipway, where the ropes were cleared away. The *Glencoe* once more refused service, and Coxswain Page took two men from the barge *Nelson* before the crew of the *Glencoe* finally agreed to be removed. On the 7th, after trying to give help to the *Cambria* which had now been carried against the pier, the lifeboat found that the crew of s.s. *Houston City* had already been saved. Two men were then rescued from the London barge

Verona west of Jenkin Buoy. On the 8th, the *Glencoe* was pumped out and brought in, and the *Cambria* was recovered on the 9th, followed by the *Decima* on the 11th.

BLOOM Thomas Henry, Coxswain, Walton and Frinton Lifeboat **BRONZE**
BROOKE Thomas Claude, Mechanic, Walton and Frinton Lifeboat **BRONZE**
13 March 1941

19 January 1941: With a south-easterly gale blowing, amid squalls of rain and snow, the Rochester barge *Martha* went ashore half a mile north of Walton pier, close to the shore. In the very dark night with heavy sea, she lay in six feet of water. The Ramsgate class motor lifeboat *E.M.E.D.* launched; Coxswain Bloom took her in among the breakers alongside the barge, took off the three man crew and brought them ashore.

GAMMON William John, Coxswain, Mumbles Lifeboat **BRONZE**
WILLIAMS Robert Trevor, Mechanic, Mumbles Lifeboat **BRONZE**
13 March 1941

20 January 1941: The 780 ton Liverpool s.s. *Cornish Rose* dragged her anchors in Swansea Bay, Glamorgan, in pitch darkness, mist and squalls of rain. The Watson class motor lifeboat *Edward Prince of Wales* launched through a whole gale and heavy breaking seas. Guided by a feeble lamp from the casualty, Coxswain Gammon took the lifeboat alongside straight away. The steamer had drifted very close to the shore which was thickly set with wartime iron rail defences but, ignoring the dangers, the Coxswain took off the ten man crew and landed them safely.

MURPHY Patrick, Coxswain, Newcastle Co. Down Lifeboat **BRONZE**
13 February 1941

19 and 21 January 1941: At 6.45 a.m., in a blinding snow-storm and gale through a very rough sea, the lifeboat *L.P. and St. Helen* launched to the Newcastle-on-Tyne m.v. *Hoperidge*, ashore between two reefs of rock at Minerstown, Dundrum Bay, Co. Down, northern Ireland. After arriving at the wreck, Coxswain Murphy responded to the request for medical assistance, returned to the shore, picked up an army doctor and medical orderly and put them on board the vessel. He stood by until they had completed their work, took them off and landed them at Newcastle. Hastily eating a hot meal, the Coxswain put out again taking the Honorary Secretary of the lifeboat station and another doctor to the casualty. He returned with them after once more standing by. Two days later, the lifeboat took part in an extended, unsuccessful attempt to refloat the motor vessel.

SLINEY Patrick, Coxswain, Ballycotton Lifeboat **BRONZE**
13 March 1941

30 January 1941: On the 27th, a large number of mines came ashore in Ballycotton Bay, Co. Cork, Ireland; four of them exploded and did considerable damage; the remainder drifted in along the coast. Three days later, mines were reported again in the bay and, just after 3 p.m., a report was received that a ship's boat had been seen off the land south of Flat Head, 17 miles away. The Barnett class motor lifeboat *Mary Stanford* launched at 3.15 p.m. After a long journey in thick fog

through a heavy, confused sea with a strong east-south-easterly wind blowing, she reached the boat, which was found to be from the Liverpool s.s. *Primrose*, which had turned turtle south-east of Daunt Rock. Eight men were in the water-logged boat and, as the lifeboat approached, a huge sea swept them into the water, but they were dragged aboard and revived. Braving the mines yet again, the lifeboat returned to station with the survivors.

MURPHY Patrick, Coxswain, Newcastle Co. Down Lifeboat   **BRONZE(2)**

AGNEW Robert, Mechanic, Newcastle Co. Down Lifeboat   **BRONZE**

13 March 1941

28–31 January 1941: On the 27th, the Newcastle-on-Tyne m.v. *Sandhill* was badly damaged off the English coast by a mine which exploded near her stern and put everything out of action. A south-easterly gale carried her across the Irish Sea. At 12.30 p.m. on the 28th, with seas breaking right into the harbour, the self-righting motor lifeboat *L.P. and St. Helen* launched to find the motor vessel anchored four miles south, about one and a half miles from a lee shore. After standing by, Coxswain Murphy returned to station at 3.30 p.m. With the gale increasing, he put out for the *Sandhill* again at 9.30 a.m. on the 30th to find her dragging toward the rocks. He took off her Captain and three men and landed them. After searching for nine soldiers reported adrift in a collapsible boat in Dundrum Bay, the lifeboat returned to the motor vessel, where Coxswain Murphy succeeded in rescuing the remaining ten men and landed them at 6 p.m. On the 31st, with the gale moderating, the lifeboat returned the crew to their vessel which was then taken under tow by a tug.

CROSS Robert G.M., Coxswain, Humber Lifeboat   **BRONZE(2)**

15 May 1941

27 February 1941: In a full south-south-easterly gale and heavy seas, the Watson class motor lifeboat *City of Bradford II* launched at 3.30 a.m. after a mine explosion in the Humber convoy anchorage was reported to have sunk a vessel. The lifeboat's search proved to be abortive and she was redirected to the air-raid balloon ship *Thora,* which had gone aground on the edge of the Trinity Sands with a cable around her propeller. Coxswain Cross took the lifeboat past the surf into shallow water and, in the dark and snowy night, brought off the eight man crew.

POWER Patrick, Second Coxswain, Dunmore East Lifeboat   **BRONZE**

10 July 1941

28 February-1 March 1941: In a gale and a very heavy sea, the Belgian motor trawler *Ibis* was caught on a lee shore close to Green Island, near Dunmore, Co. Waterford, Ireland, and dropped anchor. The Watson class motor lifeboat *C. and S.* launched at 11.15 a.m. and found the trawler 200 yards from a rocky shore with the seas breaking right over her. The vessel was sheering about violently, her gear in the way, and was surrounded by small submerged rocks. The Second Coxswain, who was at the wheel, took the lifeboat in five times by an indirect route, and the trawler's crew of seven men was able to jump aboard. The lifeboat assisted in the trawler's salvage on the next day.

CAMPBELL James, Coxswain, Boulmer Lifeboat   **BRONZE**

17 April 1941

27 March 1941: On the night of the 26th, the Glasgow s.s. *Somali* was seen to be on fire seven miles south-east of North Sunderland Point, but when the North Sunderland, Holy Island, and Boulmer lifeboats arrived, her crew had been taken off. After they had helped a tug to take the steamer under tow, the Holy island boat returned to her station at 9.30 a.m. with the other two boats remaining to stand by. After the steamer had been taken into the shelter of the Farne Islands, a salvage vessel arrived and the Boulmer Liverpool class motor lifeboat *Clarissa Langdon* put one of her officers and two seamen on to the still burning vessel. The tug continued to tow the damaged vessel and, at mid-day, the lifeboat took off the salvage vessel's officer and returned him to his own ship to which it was proposed to transfer the tow. To achieve this, the lifeboat approached the *Somali*, now one and a half miles off Beadnell, south of the Farne Islands. When only 70 yards away, a terrific explosion occurred in the casualty. The explosion lifted the lifeboat clear out of the water, blew the men flat, whirled away their caps, which were not seen again, and it emptied the jacket pockets of several of them. The stern of the *Somali* was still afloat with the two salvage men on board. Coxswain Campbell went in through the smoke and fumes and rescued the men who slid down a rope into the sea. Shortly afterwards, a piece of wreckage fouled the Boulmer lifeboat's propeller, and the North Sunderland lifeboat towed her from the danger area. After the obstruction was cleared, the two men were landed at Seahouses.

WRIGHT Jeffery, Coxswain, Fleetwood Lifeboat   **SILVER**

HILL Sydney Norman, Mechanic, Fleetwood Lifeboat   **SILVER**

9 October 1941

5 August 1941: After standing by for two hours, the Watson class motor lifeboat *Anne Letitia Russell* launched at 12.45 p.m., with a crew of six instead of the usual eight, to the 300 ton three masted schooner *Stella Marie*, carrying a valuable cargo of fresh fish and manned by Faroe Islanders. She had been in difficulties since the previous day and was now driving in a strong gale and very confused sea on to a sandbank off Fleetwood harbour. When the lifeboat arrived, the schooner was actually on the bank. Speed of action was vital. Coxswain Wright went alongside and, by various means, took off the eight man crew. The lifeboat's return was made more difficult by damage sustained by her rudder in the rescue.

BLOGG Henry George G.C., Coxswain, Cromer No. 1 Lifeboat	**GOLD(3)**
*DAVIES John James (Senior), Second Coxswain, Cromer No. 1 Lifeboat	**SILVER**
*DAVIES Henry William, Mechanic, Cromer No. 1 Lifeboat	**BRONZE(3)**
HARRISON Leslie James, Second Coxswain, Cromer No. 2 Lifeboat	**BRONZE(3)**
LINDER Harold V. , Mechanic, Cromer No. 2 Lifeboat	**BRONZE**
*JOHNSON Charles Ambrose, Coxswain,	
Great Yarmouth and Gorleston Lifeboat	**SILVER**
MOBBS George Frederick, Mechanic,	
Great Yarmouth and Gorleston Lifeboat	**BRONZE**

11 September 1941

*9 October 1941

6–7 August 1941: On the night of the 5th, in a north-north-westerly gale, poor visibility and a heavy, rough sea, six vessels in a south bound convoy went ashore on the southern end of the Middle

Haisborough Sands. At 8 a.m. next day, the Cromer No. 1 Watson class motor lifeboat *H. F. Bailey* launched and found the wrecked vessels close together and breaking up rapidly. Coxswain Blogg made for the London s.s. *Oxshott*, drove his boat on to her deck and took off 16 survivors. While he was transferring them, together with 31 survivors from the Rouen s.s. *Gallois*, to a destroyer, the Cromer No. 2 lifeboat *Harriot Dixon* (a Liverpool class motor boat) arrived. Coxswain Blogg transferred his Second Coxswain, J.J. Davies, to her, putting him in command. No. 1 boat then took off 19 survivors from the London s.s. *Deerwood* and 22 from the s.s. *Paddy Hendly* and, on her way to Yarmouth, passed the 41 survivors to a destroyer before returning to station so badly damaged as to be non-operational. The Watson class Great Yarmouth motor lifeboat *Louise Stephens* dealt with the Methil s.s. *Aberhill*, and took off 23 persons before returning to Gorleston. Cromer No. 2 lifeboat took off eight men from the Estonian s.s. *Taara*, then stood by while Coxswain Blogg dealt with *Paddy Hendly* and, after transferring her survivors to a destroyer, left the scene.

Coxswain Blogg was also awarded the British Empire Medal. Shortly before that, he received the George Cross substituted for the Empire Gallantry Medal awarded in 1924.

BAYNHAM Derek Hubert, Schoolboy	**SILVER**
WOOD John Leslie Stewart, Schoolboy	**SILVER**
WHYSALL Peter T., Second Lieutenant, Royal Artillery	**Post. BRONZE**
MOGER Alfred W., Battery Sergeant Major, Royal Artillery	**Post. BRONZE**
JACKSON C., Sergeant, Royal Artillery	**BRONZE**
TAYLOR T., Lance Bombardier, Royal Artillery	**BRONZE**
EATON Reginald, Gunner, Royal Artillery	**Post. BRONZE**
PARKINSON J.W., Gunner, Royal Artillery	**BRONZE**
THORNTON Clarence H., Gunner, Royal Artillery	**Post. BRONZE**
ATKINSON Albert E., Aircraftman 1, Royal Air Force	**BRONZE**
OWEN Arthur J., Second Officer, Merchant Navy	**Post. BRONZE**
JONES Evan, Boatman, H.M. Coastguard, Rhosneigr	**Post. BRONZE**
ARTHUR George C., Police Constable	**Post. BRONZE**

15 January 1942

28 August 1941: At 11 a.m., a Bristol Botha torpedo bomber from West Freugh (Stranraer), Kircudbright, crashed into the sea in shallow water off Rhosneigr, Anglesey, during a south-west gale. Its crew consisted of a Polish pilot and two airmen under training, all of whom got out on to the wings but, in the heavy seas, the two airmen were washed away and drowned. The Holyhead lifeboat was under overhaul, and the Porthdinllaen lifeboat attended, but was unable to reach the aircraft because the water was too shallow. The Polish airman was seen by two 17 year old schoolboys on holiday, who launched a small dinghy, reached the wreck after 45 minutes but were then capsized. Swimming to the airman, the boys managed to get him to their boat which was drifting to the shore some 500 yards away, but the badly weakened pilot drowned. Rescue efforts by boats and a whaler had all failed, and some of the rescuers had drowned. All members of the Royal Artillery who helped were serving with 226 L.A.A. Training Regt. and the R.A.F. men were stationed at R.A.F. Station Valley.

Both schoolboys were also awarded the George Medal.

BLOGG Henry George G.C., Coxswain, Cromer No. 1 Lifeboat	**SILVER(4)**
DAVIES John James (Senior), Second Coxswain, Cromer No. 1 Lifeboat	**BRONZE(4)**
DAVIES Henry William, Mechanic, Cromer No. 1 Lifeboat	**BRONZE(4)**
DAVIES James William, Assistant Mechanic, Cromer No. 1 Lifeboat	**BRONZE(3)**
DAVIES William Thomas, Bowman, Cromer No. 1 Lifeboat	**BRONZE(2)**
ALLEN Edward Walter, Signalman, Cromer No. 1 Lifeboat	**Post. BRONZE(3)**
DAVIES Henry Thomas, Crew Member, Cromer No. 1 Lifeboat	**BRONZE**
DAVIES James Richard, Crew Member, Cromer No. 1 Lifeboat	**BRONZE**
DAVIES John James (Junior), Crew Member, Cromer No. 1 Lifeboat	**BRONZE(2)**
DAVIES Robert C. , Crew Member, Cromer No. 1 Lifeboat	**BRONZE**
DAVIES William H., Crew Member, Cromer No. 1 Lifeboat	**BRONZE**
HARRISON Sidney Charles, Crew Member, Cromer No. 1 Lifeboat	**BRONZE(2)**
JOHNSON Charles Ambrose, Coxswain,	
Great Yarmouth and Gorleston Lifeboat	**BRONZE(4)**

13 November 1941

26–27 October 1941: In a full north-north-westerly gale with heavy squalls of rain, hail and sleet, s.s. *English Trader* went ashore on Hammond Knoll, 25 miles east of Cromer, Norfolk, and five of her crew were drowned. The Watson class motor lifeboat *H.F. Bailey* launched at 8.15 a.m. to find the casualty lying on the sands with her hull nearly under water in a welter of cross seas. The possibility of approaching the wreck was further diminished by swinging derricks and cargo washing out of open hatches; Coxswain Blogg stood off awaiting a suitable opportunity but, at the second attempt, a massive sea threw him and four others out of the boat. They were recovered, but Signalman Allen collapsed and died shortly afterwards. With her operational capability impaired by ropes around her propellers, the lifeboat limped to Yarmouth, and arrived at 6 p.m. with the crew exhausted. Her place near the wreck was taken by the Great Yarmouth and Gorleston Watson class lifeboat *Louise Stephens*, but she faced the same difficulties as the Cromer boat and, after five attempts to get alongside, returned to her station for the night. Coxswain Blogg took his boat out again at 4.40 a.m., with the ropes still round her propellers, and reached the wreck at 8 a.m. to find conditions somewhat moderated. He took off 44 survivors who were landed at Yarmouth at 11.30 a.m. Coxswain Johnson had also gone out again but, finding the wreck deserted, returned to station about the same time.

DUMBLE James Edward, Coxswain, Sheringham Lifeboat	**BRONZE**

13 November 1941

30–31 October 1941: About 1 a.m., the Montreal s.s. *Eaglescliffe Hall* was reported to be drifting ashore at Cley, Norfolk, about five miles west of Sheringham in a strong north-easterly gale and very heavy seas. She did not ask for a lifeboat until 9.23 a.m. In the conditions – a northeast gale, very rough seas and hard squalls of rain and sleet – launching was very difficult. After traversing a steep pebble beach, a narrow channel, a sandbank and an outer ledge of rocks, the Liverpool class motor lifeboat *Forester's Centenary* got clear at 11.15 a.m. and went alongside the steamer, which had both anchors down, having drifted through a boom defence. Fifteen of her crew were taken off and landed. On the following day, after a tug had arrived, the crew were returned to the steamer together with a salvage officer and supplies of food.

UPPERTON James Thomas, Second Coxswain, Shoreham Harbour Lifeboat   **SILVER**

PHILCOX Henry, Mechanic, Shoreham Harbour Lifeboat   **BRONZE**

11 December 1941

16 November 1941: In a strong south wind and heavy swell, H.M.M.S. *President Briand* was suffering engine problems at 1 a.m. off Shoreham Harbour, Sussex, and was in danger of being carried ashore. The Watson class motor lifeboat *Rosa Woodd and Phyllis Lunn* launched and stood by until 9.30 a.m. at which time a tug was on her way out. After returning to station, the Coxswain was taken out in the pilot cutter to pilot in the minesweeper. A further call came at 9.45 a.m. because the minesweeper and tug were being driven ashore, and the lifeboat put out again under the command of Second Coxswain Upperton. The tug was found trying to haul the minesweeper clear in worsening weather and shallow water. Then the tow ropes parted, the minesweeper struck and rolled heavily with seas breaking over her. Ignoring the presence of land mines, the lifeboat went alongside six or seven times and removed all 22 men including her own Coxswain.

COMISH John, Coxswain, Ramsey Lifeboat   **BRONZE**

12 February 1942

20 November 1941: With the south-south-easterly wind blowing strongly on a very dark night, the 193 ton Aberdeen steam trawler *Strathairlie* ran ashore at Skellig Bay, north of Ramsey, Isle of Man. In the heavy on-shore sea, it was impossible for the self-righting motor lifeboat *Lady Harrison* to get close enough to take off the trawler's crew. Coxswain Comish anchored, dropped down on his cable and managed to get two lines on board the casualty. Then hauling on these lines just far enough for a man to jump aboard when a sea had passed and hauling out again on the cable before the next sea, all 15 men were in turn successfully rescued.

CROWTHER Walter Digory, Coxswain, Plymouth Lifeboat   BRONZE

12 March 1942

13 January 1942: In a wind varying from south to south-west accompanied by heavy rain squalls over very rough seas, a R.A.A.F. Sunderland flying boat with two men on board was carried on to rocks in Jennycliff Bay, Plymouth, Devon. She had been carried between the cliffs and the pier by a coastal vessel dragging her anchor. The Barnett class lifeboat *Robert and Marcella Beck* left her moorings at 3.38 a.m. Reaching the area, Coxswain Crowther tried unsuccessfully to get a line to the flying boat using a line-throwing gun. He then took his boat in closer to facilitate attempts with a heaving cane. After several attempts, the two men on board the flying boat managed to seize a line and make it fast. The lifeboat then towed the aircraft into the Cattewater and returned to her station at 7.12 a.m.

THOMSON James, Coxswain, Campbeltown Lifeboat	**SILVER**
NEWLANDS Duncan, Second Coxswain, Campbeltown Lifeboat	**BRONZE**
BLACK Duncan, Bowman, Campbeltown Lifeboat	**BRONZE**
LISTER John Hubert, Reserve Mechanic, Campbeltown Lifeboat	**BRONZE**
LANG James, Crew Member, Campbeltown Lifeboat	**BRONZE**
McGEACHY Joseph, Crew Member, Campbeltown Lifeboat	**BRONZE**
McLEAN Duncan, Crew Member, Campbeltown Lifeboat	**BRONZE**
SPEED Neil, D.S.M., Crew Member, Campbeltown Lifeboat	**BRONZE**

21 May 1942

19 January 1942: In the absence of the regular lifeboat, the temporary Watson class motor lifeboat *Duke of Connaught*, stationed at Campbeltown, Argyllshire, launched at 8.45 a.m. in an increasingly strong wind and rising seas. Two vessels, the fishing boat *Anna Maria* and the Antwerp m.v. *Mobeka*, had gone ashore in Carskey Bay, on the southern coast of Kintyre but, in spite of attempts by rocket apparatus, only one of the crew of the former had reached the shore. Of the crew of 53 men in the motor vessel, nine had been saved by rocket apparatus when Coxswain Thomson arrived in the bay after a journey of 25 miles. In worsening conditions, exacerbated by showers of sleet and snow, and with a damaged rudder, he took the lifeboat round the ship's bows into her lee and saved the remaining 44 men, then set course for Campbeltown. After four miles, the engine failed and with the sail hoisted, the Coxswain put about and sailed into Dunaverty Bay to effect repairs. When the engine failed once more, he returned under sail to Dunaverty where the survivors were landed. The lifeboat crew returned to Campbeltown by road.

Coxswain Thomson was also awarded the British Empire Medal.

MURPHY Patrick, Coxswain, Newcastle, Co. Down Lifeboat	**GOLD**
MURPHY William, Second Coxswain, Newcastle, Co. Down Lifeboat	**SILVER**
AGNEW Robert, Mechanic, Newcastle, Co. Down Lifeboat	**SILVER**
LENAGHAN William James, Bowman, Newcastle, Co. Down Lifeboat	**BRONZE**
McCLELLAND Thomas, Assistant Mechanic, Newcastle, Co. Down Lifeboat	**BRONZE**
McCLELLAND Patrick, Crew Member, Newcastle, Co. Down Lifeboat	**BRONZE**
ROONEY Patrick, Crew Member, Newcastle, Co. Down Lifeboat	**BRONZE**

21 May 1942

21 January 1942: In a south-east gale with very heavy seas, rain and sleet, a convoy of ships missed its way in the morning, a number of them going ashore near Ballyquinton, Co. Down, northern Ireland, . As the Cloughey lifeboat was already on service, the self-righting motor lifeboat *L.P. and St. Helen* launched at 5 a.m. with a voyage ahead of 20 miles in limited visibility. Reaching the scene, Coxswain Murphy found seven ships ashore but only one, the Liverpool s.s. *Browning*, was capable of being reached. Seventeen of her crew had been taken ashore by life-saving apparatus; one of the remaining 39 had shot himself in the hand while destroying horses. The Coxswain made several attempts to reach the vessel from windward but without success. Switching to the lee side, he manoevred the lifeboat through a dangerously narrow channel into a small lagoon of calm water and took off all survivors. The lifeboat was now seriously overloaded, but the Coxswain took the only way out and crossed the reef of rocks at full speed, judging the time to perfection. With no chance of returning to Newcastle in the conditions, he landed the survivors at Portavogie, a small fishing village.

Coxswain Murphy was also awarded the British Empire Medal.

McLEAN John Buchan, Coxswain, Peterhead Lifeboat	**GOLD**
WISEMAN David Falconer, Mechanic, Peterhead Lifeboat	**SILVER**
HEPBURN Alexander Wilson, Assistant Second Coxswain,	
Peterhead Lifeboat	**BRONZE**
STRACHAN William, Acting Bowman, Peterhead Lifeboat	**BRONZE**
SUMMERS William, Assistant Mechanic, Peterhead Lifeboat	**BRONZE**
CORDINER George, Crew Member, Peterhead Lifeboat	**BRONZE**
GOWANS Alexander, Crew Member, Peterhead Lifeboat	**BRONZE**
STRACHAN Alexander, Crew Member, Peterhead Lifeboat	**BRONZE**

12 March 1942

23–26 January 1942: In a series of rescues extending from the morning of the 23rd to midday on the 26th, the Watson class motor lifeboat *Julia Park Barry of Glasgow* went out four times to three ships aground in Peterhead Bay, Aberdeenshire. During the whole of this period, south-south-easterly gales were blowing with gusts up to 105 miles per hour, there were blinding snow storms and tempestuous seas, and intense darkness made navigation extremely difficult. In 75 hours, the crew had less than 12 hours rest, they stood by for 54 hours and were at sea for nine and three-quarter hours. In the course of these activities, they rescued 44 men from the Whitby s.s. *Runswick*, 36 from the Whitby s.s. *Saltwick* and 26 from the Glasgow s.s. *Fidra*.

BENNISON William Henry, Lieutenant, C.G.M., R.N.V.R **Coxswain, Hartlepool Lifeboat**	**GOLD**
JEFFERSON Herbert William, Mechanic, Hartlepool Lifeboat	**SILVER**
GILCHRIST Thomas, Bowman, Hartlepool Lifeboat	**BRONZE**
HORSLEY Robert, Assistant Mechanic, Hartlepool Lifeboat	**BRONZE**
WALLACE Edward, Emergency Mechanic, Hartlepool Lifeboat	**BRONZE**
COULSON Richard, Crew Member, Hartlepool Lifeboat	**BRONZE**
HORSLEY William, Crew Member, Hartlepool Lifeboat	**BRONZE**
PEARSON Herbert, Crew Member, Hartlepool Lifeboat	**BRONZE**

12 March 1942

26 January 1942: With an easterly gale blowing and fierce snow squalls, the London s.s. *Hawkwood* went ashore in a rough sea, half a mile north of the Tees North Gare Jetty at Hartlepool, Co. Durham. The Watson class motor lifeboat *The Princess Royal (Civil Service No. 7)* launched at 7.35 a.m. and, on arrival, found the wreck in two parts lying in water too shallow for approach, therefore Coxswain Bennison returned to station. He went out again in the afternoon and, with heavy seas breaking into the lifeboat, took off five men from the fore part of the wreck and landed them. A third trip to rescue men on the aft part was unsuccessful. The remaining survivors were later saved by rocket apparatus.

STEWART Neil (Junior), Coxswain, Wick Lifeboat   **BRONZE**

8 October 1942

21 September 1942: At 2.25 a.m. the Watson class motor lifeboat *City of Edinburgh* launched into pitch darkness and torrential rain to help the tug *St. Olaves* and the motor barge *Gold Crown*, both ashore west of Duncansby Head on the Ness near John o'Groats, Caithness. With a north-easterly gale blowing, a very high sea and a dangerous cross swell, the two vessels could not at first be found, but finally were sighted at dawn; 27 men were taken from the barge and four from the tug. The rescued men were all very cold and exhausted, but the lifeboatmen revived them with rum.

WINTER James, Captain, Acting Coxswain, Peterhead Lifeboat   **BRONZE**

14 January 1943

15 December 1942: With the regular Coxswain ill, Captain Winter, the 69 year old Harbour Master, took his place and launched the Watson class motor life boat *Julia Park Barry of Glasgow* at 3.50 a.m. The Aberdeen trawler *Loch Wasdale* was lying on the Skerry Rocks off Buchan Ness, Aberdeenshire, in heavy seas and a strong south-south-easterly wind. When the lifeboat reached her, the trawler was found with her stern under water and seas breaking over her. In atrocious conditions, Captain Winter took the boat alongside and took off 12 men just before she sank.

SLINEY Patrick, Coxswain, Ballycotton Lifeboat	**SILVER**
WALSH Michael Lane, Second Coxswain, Ballycotton Lifeboat	**BRONZE**
SLINEY Thomas, Mechanic, Ballycotton Lifeboat	**BRONZE**
SLINEY William, Crew Member, Ballycotton Lifeboat	**BRONZE**

14 January 1943

23–24 December 1942: The Dublin s.s. *Irish Ash* was in distress south of Power Head, Co. Cork, Ireland, in a south-south-west gale, rough sea and heavy rain squalls. When the Barnett class motor lifeboat *Mary Stanford* arrived at 1.30 p.m., the casualty was south of the Ballycotton lighthouse, drifting north-north-west with her pumps out of action. Coxswain Sliney stood by, with one absence to take a message ashore, until 9 p.m., when the steamer's engines had been repaired. The engines broke down again four miles from Ballycotton Island and, with the wind increasing, the vessel began to drift rapidly towards the island. After helping her to anchor, the lifeboat refuelled at Ballycotton and returned to stand by again. When the steamer's engines had been repaired once more, the lifeboat escorted the casualty to safety in Queenstown. She returned to station at 6.30 p.m. after 30 hours on service.

CROSS Robert, G.M., Coxswain, Humber Lifeboat	**GOLD(2)**
RICHARDS George, Reserve Mechanic, Humber Lifeboat	**SILVER**
STEPHENSON George , Bowman, Humber Lifeboat	**BRONZE**
CROSS Samuel, Assistant Mechanic, Humber Lifeboat	**BRONZE**
HARMAN Sidney, Crew Member, Humber Lifeboat	**BRONZE**
MAJOR William, Crew Member, Humber Lifeboat	**BRONZE**
SHAKESBY George William Henry, Crew Member, Humber Lifeboat	**BRONZE**

11 February 1943

6–7 January 1943: In a full easterly gale, a very dark overcast night and frequent snow storms, the Watson class motor lifeboat *City of Bradford II* put out at 10.50 p.m. and took off five men from a floating anti-aircraft defence unit which had broken free and had become entangled in the boom defence. The lifeboat returned to station at 11.20 p.m., cast off again at 3.10 a.m. and found H.M. Trawler *Almondine* lying on her side on the Binks with a strong spring flood tide swirling over the sands. In a succession of runs, 19 men were taken off before the trawler floated away and disappeared with her Captain and officers still on board. The survivors were landed at 6.15 a.m. at which time it was reported that the trawler, which had drifted into the entrance to the River Humber, had been taken in tow by a tug.

ARMITAGE Benjamin Stanton, Boatman, West Kirby Sailing Club	**BRONZE**
JONES Herbert, Coxswain, Hoylake Lifeboat	**BRONZE**
WIDDUP William G., Station Officer, H.M. Coastguard, Hoylake	**BRONZE**

8 April 1943

6 February 1943: During a rough sea and strong westerly wind, two men in a 14 foot dinghy, making from Hilbre Island for West Kirby Sailing Club in the River Dee estuary, were in danger of being swamped and flung against the sea wall. Realising that launching a lifeboat would take too

long, Coxswain Jones and Mr. Widdup took life-saving apparatus to the scene by car. With Mr. Armitage, they launched a small boat and rescued the two men who had managed to anchor their dinghy. Coxswain Jones was then 65 years old.

JONES Richard, Coxswain, Holyhead Lifeboat   BRONZE

JONES John, Mechanic, Holyhead Lifeboat   BRONZE

11 March 1943

12–13 February 1943: In a heavy south-westerly gale and very rough sea on the morning of the 12th, the 3,067 ton Ellerman Papayani Co. s.s. *Castillian* ran on shore on the East Platters, part of the Skerries, off the north-western part of Anglesey. She had previously been sheltering in Church Bay to the south, but this had proved to be exposed, and she was seeking a better position. The Barnett class motor lifeboat *A.E.D.* put out at 5.25 a.m. with a reduced crew of six men. Reaching the casualty, Coxswain Jones found the steamer with heavy seas pounding her weather side in an ebbing tide, and with her bows on the rocks. The Captain refused to allow anybody to be taken off but, because of the deteriorating conditions, changed his mind. In a number of approaches, 47 officers and men were able to jump into the lifeboat; they were landed at 10 a.m. on the 13th. The wreck sank at 2 p.m.

SOAR Joseph, Doctor of Music, Honorary Secretary, St. David's R.N.L.I.   BRONZE

DAVIES Gwillym Jenkin, Crew Member, St. David's Lifeboat   BRONZE

8 April 1943

28–29 February 1943: A man was reported trapped on the cliffs near Llanunwas, Solva, Pembrokeshire. The Watson class motor lifeboat *Swyn-y-Mor (Civil Service No. 6)* launched at 10.35 p.m. On arrival at the scene at 11.30 p.m., the lifeboat remained 500 yards from the bottom of 200 feet high cliffs. The Second Coxswain, D.J. Lewis, and one of the crew went ashore in the boarding boat and found the man, 40 feet up the cliff on a ledge, unable to move up or down. Returning to the lifeboat, the Second Coxswain reported that it was impossible to reach the man from below. Gwillym Davies volunteered to climb down from above. Dr. Soar, the Second Coxswain and Davies then returned ashore. Davies found a way to the top of the cliffs where coastguardmen lowered him on the life saving apparatus. Davies reached the man, they were both let down to the foot of the cliffs, and were all taken off to the lifeboat. Apart from the light of the signal lamp, the whole rescue had taken place in pitch darkness and lasted two hours.

MATTHEWS Thomas Hendy, Harbour Pilot, Porthleven   BRONZE

9 September 1943

23 March 1943: In an attempt to rescue an army Sergeant swimming in heavy seas at Porthleven, Cornwall, an army Lieutenant himself got into difficulties. Mr. Matthews, who lived nearby, made provisions for dealing with them if they should be washed ashore then launched an 18 foot motor pilot boat. He had to hoist it over baulks of timber placed across the inner harbour. This was achieved with two helpers, who remained in the boat with him. They took her through the outer harbour and round to the shore where they rescued the totally exhausted Lieutenant. Unfortunately the Sergeant was dead.

MUGGRIDGE John Edward, Coxswain, Hastings Lifeboat   **BRONZE**

HILDER William R., Mechanic, Hastings Lifeboat   **BRONZE**

20 May 1943

31 March 1943: When the self-righting motor lifeboat *Cyril and Lilian Bishop* arrived at 5.50 a.m., H.M. Trawler *Caulonia* was found broadside on to the sea in broken water, off Jury's Gap, seven miles west of Dungeness, Kent, with her forepart under water and her after-gun just visible. Seventeen of the trawler's crew had left her already. Coxswain Muggridge took his boat into the heavy seas breaking over the trawler, amid floating wreckage, and brought off the seven remaining survivors. Coxswain Muggridge was killed a few days later when his fishing boat struck a mine, and Mechanic Hilder was killed two months later in an air-raid.

WATTS WILLIAMS William, Coxswain, St. David's Lifeboat   **BRONZE**

20 May 1943

25–26 April 1943: With the Angle lifeboat under overhaul, the Watson class motor lifeboat *Swyn-y-Mor (Civil Service No. 6)* launched at 10.45 p.m. to a tank landing craft in difficulties off St. Ann's Head, Pembrokeshire. By the time she arrived on the scene, after an 18 mile journey in heavy seas and a gale, and with floating mines in the area, the landing craft (one of two) had sunk with heavy casualties. Arriving at 1 a.m., the lifeboat immediately took part in the search, and rescued one man from the sea. After daylight, having managed to avoid a floating mine a few yards ahead, she returned to station at 8.30 a.m. So that the lifeboat would be available for further service, Coxswain Watts Williams, exercising great skill and judgement, took her up the slipway and rehoused her.

SINCLAIR Murdo, Coxswain, Barra Island Lifeboat   **SILVER**

11 November 1943

5 September 1943: In the absence of the regular boat, the reserve Watson class motor lifeboat *Duke of Connaught* launched at 9 a.m. and proceeded on a 40 mile journey to Idrigil Point, Loch Bracadale on the Isle of Skye where the 9,000 ton London s.s. *Urlana* was stranded under high cliffs. The lifeboat left in a gale with continual rain, heavy seas and nil visibility but, about 2.15 p.m., the weather cleared so that she could see the wreck and the s.s. *Thurland Castle* from the same convoy standing by her. The gale, however, continued unabated, the wreck was swept by heavy seas and, as Coxswain Sinclair was rounding her stern, a collision with a motor boat was narrowly avoided. The motor boat, full of *Urlana*'s survivors, was taking them to the *Thurland Castle* where other survivors had also been taken. The motor boat's engine broke down soon afterwards and only after great difficulty did the lifeboat tow her to the rescue vessel, before setting out for Carbost on the opposite side of Loch Bracadale. She reached there at 6 p.m., despite her engine stopping on the way. The weather forced her to remain there until the 7th.

MOORE James Orr, Mechanic, Barrow Lifeboat   **BRONZE**

MOORE Frank, Assistant Mechanic, Barrow Lifeboat   **BRONZE**

11 November 1943

27 September 1943: A small fishing boat *Seabird* tried to take refuge near Piel Island, south-east of Barrow-in-Furness, Lancashire, but, under the influence of a gale and heavy flood tide, drifted

into mid-channel on her way to shore. Her plight was recognised by Mechanic Moore and his son, who, realising there was insufficient time to launch the lifeboat, put out in a 12 foot punt through the pitch darkness and took the two crewmen to safety before the fishing boat sank.

SPURGEON Albert, Coxswain, Lowestoft Lifeboat BRONZE(2)

11 November 1943

30 September-1 October 1943: In a light wind and heavy ground swell, the Watson class motor lifeboat *Michael Stephens* put out at 10 p.m. in the dark and foggy night to *H.M.M.S. 106*. The mine-sweeper had gone ashore about one and a half miles south of Lowestoft harbour, Suffolk, where she had stuck fast on a sea defence groyne about 100 yards from shore at Kirkley. Taking off all the vessel's confidential books and gear, the lifeboat landed them at the naval base then returned to the casualty. The Coxswain was injured en route when he was thrown against the binnacle which cut open his jaw. On this trip to the badly listing ship, he took off wireless sets and other gear which he also landed at the base. Returning once more, Coxswain Spurgeon took off ten men, hauled out into deep water and anchored until daylight. He then put the crew back on board the casualty and stood by until a motor naval boat came out. The whole service took ten and a half hours.

MATTHEWS John, Coxswain, Moelfre Lifeboat SILVER(2)

EVANS Richard Matthew, Second Coxswain, Moelfre Lifeboat BRONZE

WILLIAMS Robert, Mechanic, Moelfre Lifeboat BRONZE(2)

11 November 1943

21 October 1943: On a very dark night, in a very rough sea and a southerly wind, a R.A.F. Vickers Whitley bomber aircraft crashed into the sea off Anglesey and four men escaped in their rubber dinghy, which was seen beating against rocks to the north of Dulas Island, three miles from Moelfre. The Watson class motor lifeboat *G.W.* got away at 1.45 a.m. at low tide, then, on reaching the scene was faced with shallow water, rocks and intense darkness, Coxswain Matthews went straight in with Second Coxswain Evans prone on the bows as a lookout. Lifting one of the airmen straight out of the sea, the Second Coxswain passed a line to the dinghy, which was towed to a slightly safer place where the other three airmen were taken into the lifeboat.

PEDDLESDEN Leonard Alfred John, Coxswain, Newhaven Lifeboat SILVER

PARKER Frederick Arthur, Second Coxswain, Newhaven Lifeboat BRONZE

LOWER Richard William, Mechanic, Newhaven Lifeboat BRONZE

CLARK Benjamin Jack, Bowman/Signalman, Newhaven Lifeboat Post. BRONZE

EAGER Alfred James, Acting Assistant Mechanic, Newhaven Lifeboat BRONZE

HOLDEN Stephen, Crew Member, Newhaven Lifeboat BRONZE

MOORE Harold Charles, Crew Member, Newhaven Lifeboat BRONZE

WINTER Stanley, Crew Member, Newhaven Lifeboat BRONZE

13 January 1944

23–24 November 1943: With a full gale blowing, the Watson class motor lifeboat *Cecil and Lilian Philpott* launched at 9.45 p.m. in torrential rain and very bad visibility but found nothing at the position given. She was then re-directed to a position nearer Cuckmere, over four miles to the east and, off Hope Gap, found H.M. Trawler *Avanturine* only 300 yards from a rocky lee shore in extremely shallow water very close to a reef. Dropping anchor, Coxswain Peddlesden started veering down to the trawler when it appeared out of the darkness drifting rapidly from the position at which it was thought to be anchored. In the inevitable collision, the lifeboat was very seriously damaged and lost her mast and wireless. Bowman Clark was swept away and lost, the Coxswain and three men were badly injured; only the two Mechanics and one man on the deck were unscathed. The lifeboat escorted the trawler to a place of reasonable safety, then returned to station at 0.30 a.m.

DISTIN Edwin William, Coxswain, Salcombe Lifeboat **BRONZE**

13 July 1944

4–5 December 1943: After breaking away from her tow in an easterly gale on a cold, wet night, Admiralty Salvage Craft *L.C. 18* went ashore at the lower end of the Skerries, three miles east of Start Point, Devon. It was thought that the Watson class motor lifeboat *Samuel and Marie Parkhouse* could not be made available as her Mechanic was ill and the Second Mechanic had died that day. A former Mechanic took charge of the engines whilst the Honorary Secretary, Mr. H.W. Richards, a man of 65, went as a crew member. The lifeboat launched at 10.15 p.m. The casualty was found to be very high out of the water and dragging across the bank, rolling heavily. Coxswain Distin took the lifeboat right alongside four times before the craft's ten man crew could be induced to jump on board. They were landed safely at 1.30 a.m.

WATKINS James, Coxswain, Angle Lifeboat **SILVER**

20 April 1944

18 December 1943: With a south-westerly gale blowing and in very rough seas, the small Rotterdam m.v. *Thor* was seen, in the early evening, to be in difficulties off St. Ann's Head at the entrance to Milford Haven, Pembrokeshire. Approaching the mid-channel buoy, she was overwhelmed by a following sea and thrown on to her beam ends. The Watson class motor lifeboat *Elizabeth Elson* launched at 5.30 p.m. and found a tug standing helplessly by the casualty, some of the crew having already abandoned the motor vessel. The 67 year old Coxswain Watkins searched the area and picked up two survivors. Going around to the leeward, he took the lifeboat through floating gear and wreckage and dragged two others survivors from the wreck on veering lines; two more were able to jump on board from the bottom of the *Thor*. The tug rescued one man, but three others were drowned.

MERCER Joseph Richard, Coxswain, Walmer Lifeboat **BRONZE**

9 March 1944

18 January 1944: The Watson (Beach) class motor lifeboat *Charles Dibdin (Civil Service No. 2)* launched at 1.25 a.m. to two motor boats aground near the East Goodwins, two and a quarter miles from No. 2 buoy. In a fresh south-west wind and rough sea with the tide low, Coxswain Mercer took the lifeboat across the sands, avoiding wrecks on a night made dark by mist and rain. He found H.M. Motor Anti-Submarine Boat *No. 25*, whose engine-room had been on fire, with both propeller shafts driven through her bottom and all her after part under water. Then, in four difficult operations, 13 men and the confidential books were taken off. A search for the other vessel proved unavailing as she had been able to free herself. The lifeboat beached at her station at 5.15 a.m.

McLEOD John, Coxswain, Thurso Lifeboat   **BRONZE**

20 April 1944

8 February 1944: In a northerly gale with high seas and storms of sleet and snow, the Watson class motor lifeboat *H.C.J.* launched at 2.30 p.m. to two objects, thought to be dinghies, two miles to seaward of Melvick Bay, and 13 miles west of Thurso. On approaching the Bay, the seas became confused, and broken water covered the area. At 4.30 p.m., two rafts were sighted, and Coxswain McLeod made for the one nearer to the shore. After removing two survivors from this, he approached the other raft but found all five men aboard were dead. The bodies were taken into the lifeboat, which reached Wick at 7.10 p.m. Both rafts had come from the Norwegian s.s. *Freidig*, which foundered when her cargo of grain had shifted in passage from Aberdeen to Liverpool.

GAMMON William John, Coxswain, Mumbles Lifeboat   **GOLD**
DAVIES William Gilbert, Mechanic, Mumbles Lifeboat   **BRONZE**
ACE Thomas John, Bowman, Mumbles Lifeboat   **BRONZE**

14 December 1944

11–12 October 1944: After the frigate H.M.C.S. *Chebogue* was torpedoed in mid-Atlantic, she was towed into the Bristol Channel and anchored in Swansea Bay but, when a sudden south-westerly gale arose, she started to drag her anchors. The Watson class motor lifeboat *Edward Prince of Wales* launched at 7.15 p.m. in a strong gale, accompanied by squalls of rain and heavy breaking seas; she found the frigate with her stern already aground. In a series of 12 very hazardous approaches, with the lifeboat rising and falling like a lift, all 42 men were taken off the frigate. One of them fell and broke his leg, another man fell between the two vessels and was snatched to safety by Coxswain Gammon, who was badly bruised by another survivor falling on to him. Everybody was landed at Mumbles but, unable to use the slipway, the lifeboat had to make for Swansea, where she arrived at 2 a.m.

CANN Sydney, Coxswain, Appledore Lifeboat   **BRONZE**

14 December 1944

18 October 1944: The concrete caissons used in constructing the Mulberry Harbour on the invasion beaches of Normandy were known as Phoenixes, and *Phoenix* 194 was under tow in the Bristol Channel in a south-westerly gale and the heaviest seas seen for years. The *Phoenix* had broken adrift from her tugs and sent out distress signals. In spite of conditions over Appledore Bar, the Watson class motor lifeboat *Violet Armstrong* launched at 3.55 p.m. and set off on the journey of 18 miles. After two corrected locations had been received, she came up with the *Phoenix* at 8 p.m., five miles south-south-west of Scarweather Lightship. In a series of difficult operations, the crew of seven men was removed and landed at 11 p.m. at Ilfracombe, Devon.

ORCHARD William, Second Mechanic, Padstow Lifeboat   **SILVER**

8 February 1945

23 November 1944: As the Coxswain and Second Coxswain had only recently been appointed, the Second Mechanic was in command of the Barnett class motor lifeboat *Princess Mary* when she launched to the aid of the Oslo s.s. *Sjofna* ashore inside the breakers under high cliffs, one mile

south of Knap Head, north of Bude, Cornwall. After travelling 28 miles, the lifeboat arrived at 6.25 a.m. to find the smaller Clovelly lifeboat in position but unable to make contact. Acting Coxswain Orchard anchored and let down to the casualty, but was unable to get a line on board. He re-anchored in a different position and was now successful in setting up a breeches buoy. He had taken off seven men when the line was carried away. Before he could re-establish contact, the remaining 12 were rescued by life saving apparatus from the cliff top. The lifeboat reached Padstow at 4.15 p.m., and had been out over 12 hours.

SANDERS Frederick Collier, Coxswain, Torbay Lifeboat　　　　**SILVER**
HARRIS Richard Trewaves, Mechanic, Torbay Lifeboat　　　　**BRONZE(2)**
8 March 1945

17 December 1944: With only six men on board, instead of the normal crew of eight, the Barnett class motor lifeboat *George Shee* slipped her moorings at 0.43 a.m. and headed through a south-easterly gale, heavy seas and torrential rain toward Hollicombe Point, between Paignton and Torquay, Devon. There she found the tug *Empire Alfred* less than 50 yards from the shore inside the surf line. At the third attempt, Coxswain Sanders took off the 14 men on board. *Yard Craft 345*, which had been under tow by the tug, was lying closer inshore but, the lifeboat, unable to reach her, took the tug's survivors to Brixham, reaching there at 4.50 a.m. Returning to the scene, Coxswain Sanders managed, in spite of the shallow water, to get alongside, took off five men and landed them also at Brixham at 7.50 a.m.

WATKINS James, Coxswain, Angle Lifeboat　　　　**BRONZE(2)**
13 September 1945

16 July 1945: It had been blowing hard all night, when the Watson class motor lifeboat *Elizabeth Elson* launched at 12.20 p.m. through rough seas and a dangerous ground swell. The ex-German s.s. *Walter L.M. Russ* had gone ashore 50 yards from the western extremity of Grassholm Island, and heavy seas were making a clean sweep over her, little being seen above them. When the lifeboat arrived, a breeches buoy was rigged and three men were brought off, in a rescue operation taking two hours. Coxswain Watkins learned that the remainder of the vessel's crew was on the island and, after a prolonged search and difficult approach, six men were rescued. The survivors were landed at Angle, at 10.30 p.m., but no trace was found of eight other men known to have been on board.

PETERS William, Coxswain, St. Ives Lifeboat　　　　**SILVER**
10 January 1946

24 October 1945: The Bideford auxiliary ketch *Minnie Flossie* went ashore at Hell's Mouth Cove, east of Godrevy Island, after being swept out of St. Ives Bay, Cornwall, by a west-south-westerly gale accompanied by heavy squalls of wind and rain. When the Liverpool class motor lifeboat *Caroline Oates Aver and William Maine* launched at 6.43 a.m., she found the ketch lying on her beam ends and sinking close inshore. In view of the extreme urgency, Coxswain Peters drove straight in, despite heavy seas, and the owner and his wife were snatched off just before another sea swept over the lifeboat and sank the ketch. They were landed at St. Ives at 8.15 a.m.

BLOOM Thomas Henry, Coxswain, Walton and Frinton Lifeboat BRONZE(2)

14 February 1946

21–22 December 1945: In a strong east-south-easterly wind, intense darkness and rain, two R.N. motor fishing vessels *96* and *611* went ashore on North East Gunfleet Sands, about five miles from Walton, Essex. The Ramsgate class motor lifeboat *E.M.E.D.* launched at 6.15 p.m. and 65 year old Coxswain Bloom took his boat alongside one of them but help was refused. As he took his boat back into deeper water, distress signals were soon made by both vessels. There was no direction from which either vessel could be approached in deep water and, as the tide had started to flow, the lifeboat was driven over the sands and 11 men were taken off in spite of the lifeboat's rudder being put out of action during the operation. They were landed at Brightlingsea.

HARLAND John Robert, Crew Member, Whitby No. 1 Lifeboat SILVER
MURFIELD Harry, Coxswain, Whitby No. 1 Lifeboat BRONZE

11 April 1946

23 February 1946: After the Whitby, Yorkshire, fishing fleet had put out, a north-north-westerly gale sprang up forcing seas to break right into the narrow harbour and over the piers. The Watson class motor lifeboat *Mary Ann Hepworth* was already outside the bar to escort the fishing boats in, but as the sixth boat, *Easter Morn*, was approaching, a large sea buried her. Signals from people on the nearest pier indicated that a man from the vessel was in the water. Seeing this, Coxswain Murfield took the lifeboat toward him and a lifebuoy on a line was thrown, but the man made no effort to reach it. It was obvious that he was unconscious therefore, without hesitation, Mr. Harland jumped overboard in his oilskins and lifebelt, seized the man and grabbed the lifebuoy. They were both hauled back on board and, after landing, the man recovered.

NEWLANDS Duncan, Coxswain, Campbeltown Lifeboat BRONZE(2)

16 May 1946

16–17 March 1946: In a south-south-easterly gale, rough seas and poor visibility, the American s.s. *Byron Darnton*, in ballast from Copenhagen to Gourock, went ashore on the south side of Sanda Island, off the Mull of Kintyre, immediately below Sanda Lighthouse. The Watson class reserve lifeboat *Duke of Connaught* put out at 11.40 p.m. but, on reaching the casualty, was unable to get any response from her and anchored in Sanda Roads on the north side of the island at 4.10 a.m. At daybreak she set out once again, but damage to her rudder forced her to return. Local reports were received that there were people on the wreck and they were seeking help by lifeboat. Coxswain Newlands set out again. Closing the steamer from astern, the lifeboat went alongside, took off all 54 passengers and crew, and landed them at Campbeltown at 4.30 p.m.

MURT John Tallack, Coxswain, Padstow Lifeboat SILVER

12 September 1946

12 August 1946: The Singapore s.s. *Kedah*, under tow by a tug from Barrow-in-Furness to Antwerp, Belgium, was reported making little headway in a fresh westerly gale and very heavy seas off St. Ives Head, Cornwall. The St. Ives lifeboat was called out, but was compelled to return when the weather worsened. The Watson class motor lifeboat *Princess Mary* launched at 5 p.m.

and made for St. Agnes Head, 25 miles to the south. She arrived at 8.30 p.m. to find the steamer three-quarters of a mile east-north-east of the Head, with a parted tow. Even with her anchors down, she was dragging toward the shore and yawing considerably in a very confused sea. The lifeboat sustained damage in trying to get alongside but, at the third attempt, Coxswain Murt drove her alongside at full speed, and enabled the ten men to jump to safety.

WATTERS John, Coxswain, Fowey Lifeboat   **BRONZE**

15 May 1947

23 March 1947: With Coxswain Watters in charge, the Watson class reserve lifeboat *The Brothers* launched at 4.40 a.m. in a whole gale, a dark night and heavy seas. The auxiliary m.v. *Empire Contamar* had run on to Callyvardor Rock, Par Bay, Cornwall, but the Coxswain had to search the Bay before he found her, fast on the Rock with only her bow and poop visible. The seven man crew was waist deep in water on the poop. In a difficult operation a line was got on board, the men were taken off and all landed at Fowey, 50 minutes after the lifeboat had reached the wreck.

MADRON Edwin Francis, Coxswain, Penlee Lifeboat   **SILVER**
DREW John Batten, Mechanic, Penlee Lifeboat   **BRONZE**

19 June 1947

23 April 1947: Her fighting career ended, the battleship H.M.S. *Warspite* was under tow from Portsmouth to a Clyde breakers' yard, when she broke away in a strong gale and rough seas off Cudden Point, at the eastern end of Mount's Bay. The Watson class motor lifeboat *W. & S.* launched at 2 p.m. and found the warship aground on Mount Malpas Ledge, off Marazion, near St. Michael's Mount, Cornwall. It proved impossible to get alongside and the lifeboat withdrew to Newlyn Harbour. After an hour and a quarter, she put out again. In worsening conditions, Coxswain Madron found the battleship in Prussia Cove with her bow head-on to wind and seas, her forecastle awash and seas breaking around B turret. He then took his boat into a narrow channel between the wreck and the rocks and spread oil in the area. Avoiding an outswung boat, he drove alongside and the eight men jumped one at a time into the boat. They were landed at Newlyn at 7.45 p.m.

JONES William Stephen, Second Coxswain, New Brighton Lifeboat   **BRONZE**

13 November 1947

22 September 1947: Forts of various types were built in different estuaries around Britain during the Second World War as a protection against air and surface attack. A gale with rain squalls and breaking seas 20 feet high was threatening the Queen's Fort in the Mersey Estuary. and there was concern for the six men stationed in it; the Barnett class lifeboat *William and Kate Johnston* launched at 2.45 p.m. Under command of Second Coxswain Jones, his first time in charge, she was brought under the lee of one of the fort's towers, a position without effective shelter, and held there until each of the marooned men jumped one at a time into the lifeboat. The actual rescue took 40 minutes.

MACLEOD Kenneth, Fisherman   **BRONZE**

11 December 1947

14 October 1947: Three men were out lobster fishing in their motor boat *Village Bell*, off the Isle of Skye when, at the entrance to Loch Pooltiel, in a strong wind and moderately rough sea, a rope fouled their propeller. They anchored, but the anchor chain carried away and the boat was thrown on to the rocks. The three men were able to scramble on to them, but they were at the foot of unclimable cliffs. Their danger was seen, and Mr. Macleod put out immediately followed by a larger rowing boat containing six men. He rowed two miles to the spot, backed in and took off the men one by one. After being transferred to the larger boat, which was too big to get close to the rocks, all were landed safely after a hard pull.

UPTON Frederick, Coxswain, Walmer Lifeboat   **SILVER**
CAVELL, Cecil Percy, Mechanic, Walmer Lifeboat   **BRONZE**

12 February 1948

2–4 January 1948: In a moderate wind, moderate seas, mist and rain, the Italian s.s. *Silvia Onorato*, Adriatic to Rotterdam, ran ashore on the Goodwin Sands, off Deal, Kent, one and a half miles west-south-west of the East Goodwin lightvessel. The Watson (Beach) class motor lifeboat *Charles Dibdin (Civil Service No. 2)* launched at 3.19 p.m. and Coxswain Upton took her straight across the Sands in confused seas, but, when she arrived, the crew refused to leave the ship. Standing by all night, the Coxswain approached the steamer again at 7 a.m. then, after the Captain again refused, he returned to shore to refuel. This situation lasted until the evening of the 4th when, with a gale imminent and no hope of the steamer being pulled off the Sands, 28 Italians, two German stowaways and a dog were taken off and landed at Walmer at 6.15 p.m. The service lasted 51 hours of which 45 of them had been at sea.

PALMER, Frederick James, Coxswain, Weymouth Lifeboat   **BRONZE**

8 July 1948

6–7 June 1948: When 15 miles west of Portland Bill, Dorset, a converted 110 ft. naval motor launch, now the twin screw motor yacht *Mite*, suffered failure of both wireless and engines. With a fresh wind increasing, two of her crew volunteered to make for the shore and seek help. The Coastguard had seen the dinghy driving ashore and alerted the Weymouth lifeboat station. Five minutes after the dinghy landed, the Barnett class lifeboat *William and Clara Ryland* slipped her moorings and reached the yacht, now anchored, at 4.30 p.m. The owner requested a tow and, reluctantly, Coxswain Palmer agreed. In seriously worsening conditions on a course wide of Portland Bill, the lifeboat towed the yacht for 12 miles. After the tow parted for the third time at 8.30 p.m., two miles off the Shambles, the yacht's three man crew was taken off and landed at 0.30 a.m. The yacht was washed ashore later near Lulworth Cove.

UPPERTON, James Thomas, Coxswain, Shoreham Harbour Lifeboat   **SILVER(2)**

14 October 1948

8 August 1948: Early in the morning, in a gale, a rough sea and a heavy swell, the yacht *Gull* was seen off Shoreham, Sussex, being driven along the coast out of control with her sails torn.

The Watson class lifeboat *Rosa Woodd and Phyllis Lunn* launched and, hoisting sail to help her engines, gave chase. She caught up with the yacht at the entrance to Newhaven Harbour, a distance of 14 miles. In her desperate attempt to enter the harbour, the yacht gybed and became a water-logged wreck in broken, shallow water. Coxswain Upperton took his boat alongside and, in two trips, rescued three men, two women and a boy. He landed them at Newhaven, and then returned to Shoreham, arriving there at 3.30 p.m. after seven hours at sea.

SHACKSON, Percy, Bowman, Clovelly Lifeboat	**BRONZE**
BRAUND, William, Assistant Mechanic, Clovelly Lifeboat	**BRONZE**

13 January 1949

30–31 August 1948: Two young Americans were swimming and wading around Baggy Point, North Devon, at the north end of Barnstaple Bay, when they were caught by the rising tide before they could reach their destination in Croyde Bay. With the wind off-shore, the sea was breaking around the rocks making it impossible for them to swim off. The self-righting motor lifeboat *City of Nottingham* launched at 9.45 p.m. with an 11 foot dinghy lashed across her gunwhale, reached the scene at 11.20 p.m., anchored and sent the dinghy, manned by two volunteers, Shackson and Braund, into the area of submerged rocks. The young Americans were dragged clear, picked up by the lifeboat and, at 1.45 a.m. landed at Clovelly.

PALMER, Frederick James, Coxswain, Weymouth Lifeboat	**SILVER**
McDERMOTT, James, Mechanic, Weymouth Lifeboat	**BRONZE**

19 May 1949

2 April 1949: In heavy rain driven by a strong south-westerly wind and dense banks of fog over a rough sea, the old dockyard steam tug *H.L.S. 161*, in passage from Plymouth to London, was reported in difficulties west of Portland Bill and drifting northwards. The Barnett class lifeboat *William and Clara Ryland* slipped her moorings at 6.35 a.m. and, after searching in the fog, found the tug, her steering almost out of action, broadside on to the Chesil Beach 50 yards away. Losing no time, Coxswain Palmer took his lifeboat alongside, managed to get a tow on board, and pulled the tug off just in time to avoid certain death for the four men on board. It was then 8.20 a.m. Two hours later they reached Weymouth.

LEADBETTER James, Coxswain, Fleetwood Lifeboat	**BRONZE**

19 May 1949

3–4 April 1949: The Watson class lifeboat *Ann Letitia Russell* launched in a strong south-west wind, torrential rain and very heavy seas to the Stranraer auxiliary ketch *Alpha* in difficulty near the North Scar Sandbank. When the lifeboat arrived, the ketch was bumping over the sandbank. Coxswain Leadbetter took the boat in and got a line on board but, trying to tow her off, the ketch's windlass was torn out of her deck. He then took off the crew, seven men and a boy aged ten, and arrived back on station at 4.35 p.m. At low tide in the evening, six of the ketch's crew walked across the sands and re-boarded her although the weather was worsening. As no trace of the casualty could be seen at daybreak, the lifeboat launched again at 7.20 a.m. and, after searching, found her in a worse position than before on Clarke's Wharf Sandbank. In a difficult operation of considerable danger, the six men were taken off and landed at noon.

KING, Thomas James, Coxswain, St. Helier Lifeboat	**GOLD**
BOUTELL, Philip, Acting Second Coxswain, St. Helier Lifeboat	**BRONZE**
GUBBEY, Kenneth S., Reserve Mechanic, St. Helier Lifeboat	**BRONZE**
TALBOT, David Robert, Acting Assistant Mechanic, St. Helier Lifeboat	**BRONZE**
KING, Charles George, Crew Member, St. Helier Lifeboat	**BRONZE**
NICOLLE, Reginald John, Crew Member, St. Helier Lifeboat	**BRONZE**
STAPELY, George , Crew Member, St. Helier Lifeboat	**BRONZE**
STEVENS, Lionel Percival, Honorary Secretary,	
St. Helier R.N.L.I.	**BRONZE**

8 December 1949

13–14 September 1949: After the reserve Watson class lifeboat *Hearts of Oak* had spent six hours in an unsuccessful search for a French military aircraft, she was directed to deal with the St. Helier yacht *Maurice Georges*, which was reported to be in difficulties near Demie de Pas, to the east of St. Helier, Jersey. The lifeboat crew had already been out for more than eight hours in an unfamiliar boat, in a fresh westerly wind, rain squalls and a rough sea. They located the yacht deep among rocks without her engine; Coxswain King went straight in with his searchlight on and with men in the bows to warn him about the numerous rocks. A line was passed to the yacht, which was towed out without damage and all returned to St. Helier at 0.30 a.m., nine hours after launching. The Honorary Secretary went out as a member of the crew.

JONES, Richard, Coxswain, Holyhead Lifeboat	**BRONZE(2)**

8 December 1949

25–26 October 1949: In a whole northerly gale with violent squalls and a rough sea, the Watson class lifeboat *M.O.Y.E.* launched in a dark night to the Liverpool s.s. *Mayflower*, which had run ashore on Salt Island Point at the entrance to Holyhead harbour, Anglesey. She reached the wreck in ten minutes and, with the tide ebbing, Coxswain Jones took the lifeboat alongside, and held her there while seven men jumped on board. The Master and Chief Engineer were both taken off later by breeches buoy from the shore.

IRWIN, Cecil George, Coxswain, Ilfracombe Lifeboat	**SILVER**
CANN, Sidney, Coxswain, Appledore Lifeboat	**BRONZE(2)**

12 January 1950

13 November 1949: On passage from Newport to Genoa, Italy, with 5,000 tons of coal, the Bilbao s.s. *Monte Gurugu* sank south of Lundy Island in a full north-westerly gale and tremendous seas. Appledore lifeboat, the Watson class *Violet Armstrong*, launched at 6.45 a.m. in heavy broken seas and Coxswain Cann set course past Baggy Point to Woolacombe Bay (Morte Bay). At 8.45 a.m., after a search, an empty and badly broken ship's lifeboat was found. Continuing the search, five bodies and one living survivor were found before the exhausted lifeboat crew made for Ilfracombe, and arrived there at 11.45 a.m. The Ilfracombe lifeboat, the Liverpool class *Richard Silver Oliver*

launched at 7.18 a.m. and made her way into Woolacombe Bay, past Bull Point and Morte Point, where, just before 9 a.m., a ship's lifeboat was found. Coxswain Irwin took the lifeboat between the ship's boat and the breakers ten yards away and, after 23 men had been taken on board, pulled out, and reached Ilfracombe at 10.30 a.m. The search was continued without success until 8.30 p.m. The final total of men drowned was 13.

LE RICHE Silver Harry , Acting Coxswain, St. Helier Lifeboat **BRONZE**
12 January 1950

19–20 November 1949: On a dark night with a moderate northerly wind, the Poole auxiliary ketch *Hanna*, on passage from Plymouth to Jersey with carbonate of lime, went hard and fast on to L'Etacq reef between Sark and Grosnez Point, north-west Jersey. The Watson class lifeboat *Elizabeth Rippon* launched at 10.50 p.m., cleared the pier heads and negotiated the Corbière inner passage to find the ketch with her head toward shore with heavy seas breaking over her. Second Coxswain Le Riche took the lifeboat in through a narrow channel, the only one leading to the wreck and, laying alongside, took off her three man crew; using the same channel, he pulled out and landed at St. Helier at 2.30 a.m.

KAVANAGH Edward, Coxswain, Wicklow Lifeboat **BRONZE**
9 November 1950

10–13 September 1950: On a fine day, with calm seas and a light breeze, the Glasgow m.v. *Cameo*, coal-laden, went aground on Arklow Sandbank, 14 miles from Wicklow, Co. Wicklow, Ireland. The Watson class lifeboat *Lady Kylsant* launched and reached the scene at 12.30 p.m. Help was refused and she returned at 3.10 p.m. Next day, with a gale now raising broken water on the sandbank, she went out again to stand by while efforts were being made to refloat the casualty. Towlines were passed between a tug and the casualty, but these soon parted; still the *Cameo*'s Master refused to abandon ship. Coxswain Kavanagh returned to Wicklow again at 7.20 p.m. Next evening (the 12th) the Master of the *Cameo* finally asked for the lifeboat, which launched for the third time at 9.20 p.m. Anchoring to windward, the Coxswain veered down on his cable alongside the *Cameo*, threw lines on board her and took off the eleven crewmen. They all returned to Wicklow safely at 4 a.m..

JONES William Stephen, Second Coxswain, New Brighton No. 2 Lifeboat **BRONZE(2)**
12 October 1950

16 September 1950: At 8.45 p.m., the Barnett class lifeboat *Edmund and Mary Robinson* launched with Second Coxswain Jones in command and drove through a southerly full gale with frequent rain squalls. The Arklow three-masted schooner *Happy Harry* was lying alongside the training wall, six and a half miles from New Brighton, Cheshire with her anchors dragging. This wall was a substantial revetment of limestone rubble, 12 feet wide. Heavy seas were breaking over the schooner but, steering the lifeboat through a gap in the wall, Second Coxswain Jones took her alongside. The four members of the schooner's crew jumped into the lifeboat and were landed at New Brighton at 11.15 p.m.

POWER Patrick, Coxswain, Dunmore East Lifeboat BRONZE(2)
POWER Richard, Second Coxswain, Dunmore East Lifeboat BRONZE

8 February 1951

14 December 1950: While returning to port in a south-easterly gale and snow squalls, the local fishing boat *St. Declan* was driven ashore near Falskirt Rocks, off Swines Head, two miles from Dunmore, Co. Waterford, Ireland. In order to try to arrest her drift, her fishing nets had been thrown out. However, when the Watson class lifeboat *Annie Blanche Smith* arrived on the scene, the fishing boat was within minutes of going ashore. In the most difficult circumstances, Second Coxswain Power took the lifeboat near enough for Coxswain Power to throw a line from the boat. The fishing boat was towed out, then brought into harbour at midnight.

JOHNSTON Alfred, Coxswain, Longhope Lifeboat BRONZE

14 June 1951

12–13 April 1951: In a strong south-westerly gale, the Gothenburg motor tanker *Oljaren*, bound from Curacao to Stockholm with diesel oil, went ashore on the west side of Muchal Skerry, Pentland Firth. At 1.40 a.m., the Watson class lifeboat *Thomas McCunn* launched, but on arrival the tanker's crew elected to stay on board. The lifeboat stood off until 1.00 p.m. that afternoon and then was able to take off 24 men; all the others stayed aboard. Coxswain Johnston took the lifeboat back to Longhope, where they landed at 3.30 p.m. Another trip to the wreck was wasted when the Captain again refused to be taken off. A third trip was made at 2.35 p.m. on the 13th and, in accordance with the owner's orders, the Captain and 15 men were taken off and landed at 5.45 p.m.

SLAUGHTER Edward Alfred, Mechanic, Flamborough Lifeboat BRONZE

12 July 1951

15 May 1951: When a boy fell into the sea from the top of 150 foot cliffs between Flamborough Head, Yorkshire, and the lifeboat station, the Liverpool class lifeboat *Howard D* launched in heavy rain and on the ebb tide. The boy, still alive, was seen lying on a rock ledge, but the lifeboat could get no closer than 80 yards. After an unsuccessful attempt by the Second Coxswain, Mr. Slaughter, a powerful swimmer, reached a flat topped rock with a rope, 20 yards from the boy, and then waded shoulder deep to reach him. Finding the boy to be too badly injured to transfer to the lifeboat, arrangements were made to take him up the cliff by stretcher. This done, Mr. Slaughter returned to the lifeboat which returned to station at 6.15 p.m.

DOP William, Second Coxswain, Porthdinllaen Lifeboat SILVER

20 September 1951

8–9 August 1951: A man and his two nephews in the auxiliary yacht *Waterbell* were forced to anchor close in to Porth Oer, Caernarvon, ten miles south of Porthdinllaen, in a mass of breaking water. When the Watson class lifeboat *Charles Henry Ashley* arrived half an hour after midnight, it was pitch dark and the wind was increasing. Second Coxswain Dop, in charge, took her alongside between the yacht and the rocks, which enabled the three men to jump aboard. He brought the lifeboat out stern first and returned to station at 5.30 a.m.

WILSON Alfred Robert, Crew Member, Margate Lifeboat   **BRONZE**

8 November 1951

2 September 1951: In rough seas and a westerly gale, the Chichester yacht *Girlanda* was found shortly after midnight anchored 100 yards north of Margate Harbour wall with seas rebounding from the wall over her. The Watson class lifeboat *North Foreland (Civil Service No. 11)* was brought alongside, but the yacht's two occupants were unable to move from their cockpit. Mr. Wilson managed to board the casualty, laid on the deck with seas washing over him, held on to the mast with one hand and used the other to secure a line. After he had released the yacht's two anchors, she was towed by the lifeboat to safety in the harbour. Shortly after this service, the lifeboat went out again and took two men off the Rochester yacht *Sir Gobbo*.

LARBELESTIER Edward, Coxswain, St. Helier Lifeboat   **SILVER**

8 November 1951

27–28 September 1951: In a fresh south-south-westerly wind, storms of rain and a very heavy swell, the French yacht *Santa Maria* of Cartaret went ashore on rocks a mile east of St. Helier, Jersey, Channel Islands. A two hour search in complete darkness was necessary before the Watson class lifeboat *Elizabeth Rippon* found the yacht in a small sheltered gully between two high ridges of rock, at anchor with two ropes around a rock pinnacle. Going in, Coxswain Larbelestier took the lifeboat alongside. After waiting for more tide, he brought out the yacht and towed her to St. Helier, where he arrived with the three men at 1.40 a.m.

WALKER John, Coxswain, Dover Lifeboat   **BRONZE**

8 November 1951

27–28 September 1951: Late on a very dark night with heavy rain squalls, Coxswain Walker, on his way along the Eastern Harbour Arm at Dover, Kent, saw the small Amsterdam yacht *Akeco* anchored just outside, in a strong southerly onshore wind and with her anchor dragging. The Barnett class lifeboat *Southern Africa* launched without waiting for the last two men of her crew to arrive. In a very confused, violent and dangerous sea, she reached the yacht at midnight to find her little more than 100 yards from the cliffs in Fan Bay, broadside on to wind and sea. Getting a line across, a tow was secured and the yacht was brought safely into harbour at 0.30 a.m.

PENNYCORD Leslie Charles, Coxswain, Selsey Lifeboat   **BRONZE**

10 January 1952

17–18 November 1951: The 163 ton Costa Rican m.v. *Swift*, Brittany to Boston, Lincolnshire with a cargo of onions, developed engine trouble and drifted toward rocks near Selsey, Sussex, but managed to anchor seaward of the Pullar Bank. The lifeboat *Canadian Pacific* launched and reached the casualty at 8.45 p.m. At the same time, H.M.M.S. *Marvel* arrived but lay off to windward. Half an hour later, the tug *Alligator* joined then and passed a line to the motor vessel. Disaster struck as the towing hawser fouled the tug's propeller and parted; the tug drifted helplessly across Middle Bank Grounds and anchored. *Swift*'s end of the tow, lying on the sea bed, acted as an anchor. The minesweeper departed at 2.30 a.m. leaving the lifeboat on watch all night in heavy seas, shoal water and a south-westerly gale. At daybreak, the casualty was seen to be on top of the Pullar Banks, where Coxswain Pennycord went alongside three times and took off six men who were landed at 8.10 a.m.

SHEADER John Nicholas, Coxswain, Scarborough Lifeboat   **BRONZE**
MAINPRIZE Thomas Jenkinson,
   Assistant Mechanic, Scarborough Lifeboat   **BRONZE**
DALTON Frank, Bowman, Scarborough Lifeboat   **Post. BRONZE**
10 January 1952

9–10 December 1951: In a westerly gale with snow squalls, the 499 ton Dutch m.v. *Westkust,* from Bo'ness to Hamburg with a cargo of coal dust, was reported to be sinking 26 miles east by north of Scarborough. Her cargo had shifted and she was making water and listing 35 degrees. Her bilge pumps were choked; one of her two lifeboats had been lost and the other damaged. At 11.30 a.m. the self-righting lifeboat *E.C.J.R.* launched and at 2.30 p.m. a wireless message from the *Westkust* gave a revised position of 21 miles east of Flamborough, 20 miles south of the original position. Finally reaching the casualty at 7 p.m., the lifeboat put two of her crew on board – Mr. Mainprize, the Assistant Mechanic, and Mr. Dalton, the Bowman. Although he had hoped to bring his vessel into harbour, the Captain soon after decided to abandon ship. Coxswain Sheader took the lifeboat alongside and the ten man crew of the *Westkust* jumped into her. The Flamborough lifeboat, which had arrived just before, stood by. On the Scarborough lifeboat's next approach, Mr. Mainprize jumped safely aboard, but at that moment a sea separated the two vessels and Mr. Dalton was left hanging full length from the *Westkust*'s rail. A rogue sea crushed him between the two vessels, fracturing his pelvis. He fell on to the lifeboat which made at once for Bridlington, but before she arrived, at 1.30 a.m. next morning, Dalton was dead.

UPTON Frederick, Coxswain, Walmer Lifeboat   **SILVER(2)**
CAVELL Cecil Percy, Mechanic, Walmer Lifeboat   **BRONZE(2)**
14 February 1952

13–14 January 1952: The Watson (Beach) class lifeboat *Charles Dibdin (Civil Service No. 2)* launched at 11.10 p.m. in intense darkness with patches of mist and a south- westerly gale which brought stinging rain. She spent the next two and a quarter hours searching the Goodwin Sands before she found the 4, 000 ton La Rochelle s.s. *Agen.* The casualty, on passage from Dakar, Senegal to Hamburg, was aground and had broken in two with a 40 foot gap between both parts. With the tide ebbing fast, Coxswain Upton decided to wait until conditions improved. At 6.15 a.m., he steered between the two parts and took off 37 men from the fore-part, all except the Master who refused to leave. After landing these men, he returned and persuaded the Master to leave and completed the service which had lasted for 11 hours.

THOMAS Henry Owen, Torbay Lifeboat   **BRONZE**
13 March 1952

30–31 January 1952: In a whole south-south-westerly gale accompanied by frequent squalls of rain and sleet with poor visibility and a very heavy sea, the Barnett class lifeboat *George Shee* launched to search for a vessel in difficulty four miles north-east of Berry Head, near Brixham , Devon. After an hour and a half the Royal Engineer's tug *Trieste* was found off the mouth of the River Exe, a mile from Straight Point, riding to sea-anchors with her main steam-pipe burst. In several approaches with the tug yawing violently and spray from breaking seas blowing to a height of six feet, Coxswain Thomas took off 11 men, five of them prostrate with sea-sickness, and landed them at Brixham Harbour at 2 a.m. The tug was towed to Dartmouth later.

KIRKALDIE Douglas Stephen, Coxswain, Ramsgate Lifeboat   **BRONZE**

9 October 1952

20–21 August 1952: The New York s.s. *Western Farmer*, Norfolk, Virginia, to Bremen with coal, collided with the Norwegian tanker *Bjorgholm* 18 miles east -south-east of Ramsgate, Kent. Both the Dover lifeboat *Southern Africa* and the Ramsgate lifeboat *Prudential* launched, the former diverted to Walmer to pick up a doctor. When the *Prudential* arrived the steamer was anchored one and a half miles north of Sandettie Bank buoy and had started to break up. Coxswain Kirkaldie took off seven of the crew, an operation made much more difficult by leaking diesel oil. The ship's Master ordered all of his crew into the two ship's lifeboats which got clear just before the wreck broke into two. The Ramsgate lifeboat took on board men from one boat and a man who had jumped into the sea. The Dover lifeboat took the 13 men from the second boat, but five men still remained on the wreck's stern part which was partly awash and drifting. Coxswain Kirkaldie went alongside, took them off and landed them at Ramsgate at 3.16 a.m.

MACDONALD Malcolm, Coxswain, Stornoway Lifeboat   **BRONZE**

13 November 1952

18–19 September 1952: The Barnett class lifeboat *William and Harriot* left her moorings at 11 p.m. on the 18th in a moderate north-north-easterly wind and heavy swell. She faced a 65 mile passage to Sula Sgier, which is 35 miles north-north-east of the Butt of Lewis, Outer Hebrides. The four man crew of the local boat *Mayflower* had been collecting young gannets for salting but their vessel had been sunk by backwash from the cliffs and they had been marooned on the rocks since the previous afternoon. Reaching the scene at 7.30 a.m., Coxswain Macdonald found the men on top of a 120 foot cliff, but they refused to entertain any attempt at rescue from there suggesting that it be tried from a nearby cove. He waited until after mid-day when the weather had moderated, then took the lifeboat in to the cove. Passing a line ashore, the four men were hauled into the boat using veering lines. They were landed at Stornoway at 8.15 p.m.

METCALFE Tony William   **BRONZE**

11 December 1952

21 September 1952: The sailing boat *Tit Bit* capsized in a slight sea and westerly breeze off Shellness, at the east end of the Isle of Sheppey, Kent, and a man and a boy were thrown into the water. The incident was seen by 15 year old Tony Metcalfe who put out in a ten foot outboard motor dinghy and hauled the boy on board, but the boat sank in the efforts to get in the man who weighed 18 stone. The three of them then clung to the *Tit Bit*; a number of rescue attempts were made by different vessels and eventually they were successful.

PRICE Denis Richard, Coxswain, Margate Lifeboat   **SILVER**

11 December 1952

7 November 1952: In a whole north-westerly gale and very heavy sea, the auxiliary barge *Vera* went ashore near the Mid-Barrow Lightship on the north side of the Thames Estuary. All three Essex lifeboats were out on services, and although it was over 20 miles from Margate, the Watson class lifeboat *North Foreland (Civil Service No. 11)* launched at 3.10 a.m. and battled through rain and sleet squalls with the gale against her. She reached the wreck at 6 a.m. and found two men clinging to the mast rigging which was visible above the water. Coxswain Price took the lifeboat over the barge's deck and the survivors slid down the rigging to safety after being there for almost five hours. Frozen and wet through they were landed at Brightlingsea at 9.45 a.m. before the lifeboat returned to Margate.

NELSON Hugh, Coxswain, Donaghadee Lifeboat   **BRONZE**
McCONNELL William, Coxswain, Portpatrick Lifeboat   **BRONZE**

12 March 1953

31 January 1953: The waters between Ireland and Scotland, known as the North Channel, are notorious for the treacherous nature of the weather. Twenty -five miles wide, the Channel is the passageway between the Irish Sea and the eastward tongue of the Atlantic Ocean traversed regularly by the passenger/vehicle ferry running between Stranraer, Wigtownshire, and Larne, Co. Antrim. This was the scene of the worst peacetime disaster in 25 years involving a British merchant vessel. Setting out from Stranraer at 7.45 a.m., the 2,694 ton m.v. *Princess Victoria*, with 176 people on board, benefited from the shelter of Loch Ryan for the first eight miles of her regular, seemingly routine, run. Then, rounding Milleen Point and heading for Northern Ireland, she encountered tremendous north-westerly gale force winds driving over savage seas with squalls of sleet and snow gusting up to 75 miles per hour. Lost to sight, it was not surprising that conflicting reports were made regarding her position and condition. The relentless, punishing seas had burst open her rear car-deck doors and flooded in, so sealing her doom. Portpatrick lifeboat, the Watson class *Jeanie Speirs*, slipped at 11 a.m. and, by a minor miracle, left the small harbour heading northwards on a wild goose chase inspired by a wildly inaccurate report. Meanwhile, the Donaghadee lifeboat *Sir Samuel Kelly* had launched at 1.15 p.m., also on a highly inaccurately determined heading. Corrections were issued and both boats now made for a point about seven miles east of the entrance to Belfast Lough, where the ferry had foundered at 2 p.m. Here Coxswain Nelson took 29 survivors from a ship's lifeboat, one man from another boat and one from a raft, while Coxswain McConnell picked up two from rafts. These were all taken to Donaghadee. Ten survivors were taken from the sea by other

vessels but 133 people were lost. Both Coxswains were awarded the British Empire Medal. Lifeboats from Cloughey and Newcastle, Co Down, were also involved in the search for survivors.

RICHARDS Thomas Benjamin, Coxswain, Tenby Lifeboat   SILVER

THOMAS William Raymond, Bowman, Tenby Lifeboat   BRONZE

ROGERS William Henry George, Mechanic, Tenby Lifeboat   BRONZE

12 November 1953

21–22 September 1953: The Watson class lifeboat *John R. Webb* was launched at 9.42 p.m. in a full west-south-westerly gale with heavy rain squalls. Pumps in the St. Gowan lightvessel, 15 miles west-south-west from Tenby, Pembrokeshire, had failed and she was in danger of sinking. Setting course for the casualty, Coxswain Richards took the lifeboat through Caldy Strait, inside Caldy Island, in extremely rough seas. Reaching the lightvessel at 1.10 a.m., he took off her seven man crew in three approaches through high seas and heavy swell with huge waves breaking over both vessels. They were landed at Tenby at 3.30 a.m.

TAYLOR Eric Charles, Coxswain, Whitby No. 1 Lifeboat   BRONZE

10 June 1954

15 April 1954: With most of the Whitby fishing boats at sea in deteriorating weather conditions and Coxswain Taylor in one of them, the No. 1 Watson class lifeboat *Mary Ann Hepworth* launched at 9.30 p.m. under command of ex-Coxswain Richardson in a north-north-easterly gale and very rough seas. The lifeboat escorted in some of the smaller boats, and Coxswain Taylor himself came in unescorted in his own keel boat. At 10.20 p.m. he took over command of the lifeboat. The fishing boat *Foxglove*, trying to return to port, was hit by a heavy sea which put her engine out of action and swept out one of her crew, but he was picked up by the lifeboat. The fishing boat, meanwhile, had been carried on to rocks outside the eastern breakwater. Coxswain Taylor took the lifeboat through a gap in the rocks but, on his first attempt was unable to take off any crew. At the next attempt, all three men were rescued. After landing the survivors, the lifeboat resumed escorting fishing vessels.

LAMEY George, Coxswain, Clovelly Lifeboat   BRONZE

16 September 1954

27–28 July 1954: The 90 ton motor ketch *Progress,* of Bideford, was in distress under the lee of Lundy Island, with the trawler *Hosanna* standing by. The owner of the ketch, his wife and 12 year old son had planned a voyage to New Zealand via the Bahamas. The Liverpool class lifeboat *William Cantrell Ashley* launched at 5.10 p.m. into a very rough sea, in a westerly gale. The engines of the *Progress* had broken down and she was made fast astern of the trawler. Once the ketch was safely anchored, the trawler proceeded to Milford Haven, and the lifeboat returned to Clovelly, and arrived there at 4,35 a.m. on the 28th. At 1 p.m. the lifeboat was called out as the ketch was again in trouble, drifting up channel. Pushing through rough seas, Coxswain Lamey took the lifeboat through the Hartland Race, and reached the *Progress* at 3.15 p.m. He took the lifeboat repeatedly alongside the starboard side of the yacht and it took ten attempts before finally the three crew, a cat, some new-born kittens and a canary were taken on board the lifeboat. Clovelly was reached at 7.50 p.m.

BRADFORD Harold John, Coxswain, Exmouth Lifeboat　　　　　**BRONZE**

11 November 1954

19–20 September 1954: In a dark night, heavy rain squalls and a considerable swell, the Starcross cabin cruiser *Nicky* ended inside a rock ledge near Maer Rocks at the approach to the estuary of the River Exe. The Liverpool class lifeboat *Maria Noble* launched just before midnight and approached the casualty from the eastward keeping the wind and sea on her port bow. Using the last of the flood, Coxswain Bradford drifted alongside the vessel three times and took off five men before the cruiser sank.

HARVEY William James, Coxswain, Newhaven Lifeboat　　　　　**SILVER**

13 January 1955

27 November 1954: At 4.50 a.m., the Watson class lifeboat *Cecil and Lilian Philpott* launched in response to a call from the Danish auxiliary schooner *Vega*, which was listing in a severe gale 25 miles south-west of Beachy Head. After an extremely rough passage, the lifeboat reached the schooner to find that she had a 30 degree list and was rolling wildly with her deck cargo of timber loose and with the booms swinging violently. Finding it impossible to go alongside, Coxswain Harvey ordered a breeches buoy to be rigged. A crewman from the *Vega* jumped into the sea with a line round his waist. He was hauled aboard the lifeboat and the breeches buoy was bent on the line. The seven other crew were brought into the lifeboat in 20 minutes. They were landed at Newhaven at 12.40 p.m.

PARKINS Curtis E., Captain, United States Air Force,
　66th Air Rescue Squadron　　　　　**SILVER**

13 January 1955

27 November 1954: Gales of exceptional force had been blowing for several days off the East Kent coast and, early in the morning, it was noticed that the South Goodwin light vessel had disappeared. Lifeboats at Ramsgate, Dover and Walmer were warned and, during the night, the first two launched and carried out searches of the Goodwins without success. At daylight, the vessel was located on her beam ends, lying on her side where she had drifted. The Walmer lifeboat launched. The combined efforts of all three boats could not detect any survivors, therefore a call was made to 66th Air Rescue Squadron, U.S.A.F., which provided a helicopter from its base at Manston, Kent, near Ramsgate. A second sortie at 9 a.m. by Captain Parkins noticed a solitary figure – a Ministry of Agriculture and Fisheries bird watcher – clinging to the light vessel's superstructure. Ignoring the normal rules, the helicopter was brought down to 30 feet and, in spite of the wreckage and spray, the lone survivor was plucked from his refuge and landed safely at Manston.

This was the first R.N.L.I. medal to be awarded to any pilot of any aircraft and also the first service given by a helicopter when lifeboats, although present, were unable to render the necessary help.

WATTS WILLIAMS William, Coxswain, St. David's Lifeboat	**SILVER**
WALSH Richard, Coxswain, Rosslare Harbour Lifeboat	**SILVER**
JORDAN George G., Mechanic, St. David's Lifeboat	**BRONZE**
DAVIES Gwillym Jenkin, Assistant Mechanic, St. David's Lifeboat	**BRONZE(2)**
DUGGAN William, Second Coxswain, Rosslare Harbour Lifeboat	**BRONZE**
HICKEY Richard Michael, Mechanic, Rosslare Harbour Lifeboat	**BRONZE**

13 January 1955

27–28 November 1954: The 20,125 ton Liberian tanker *World Concord*, in ballast from Liverpool to Syria, broke in two during exceptionally violent storms in the Irish Sea, off the Pembrokeshire coast. The two pieces drifted apart with the Master and six men on the fore-part and 35 men on the aft-part. At 8.28 a.m., the St. David's Watson class lifeboat *Swyn-y-Mor (Civil Service No. 6)* launched. She reached the aft-section, 15 miles north-north-west of the South Bishop Lighthouse at 11.45 a.m. and, in a fresh southerly gale, continuous rain and violent seas, Coxswain Watts Williams took off the 35 survivors, one at a time. The Rosslare lifeboat *Douglas Hyde* launched at 3.50 p.m., finally reaching the fore-section at 7.10 p.m. Coxswain Walsh decided to stand by until daylight – 12 hours in dreadful conditions. At 8.30 a.m. in a gale which had the wreck running before it, the lifeboat went alongside in the heavy swell and violent seas. The seven survivors were taken off in 15 minutes and landed at Holyhead. It is doubtful if the rescue could have been completed without the help of the aircraft carrier H.M.S. *Illustrious*, which was the first ship to answer the S.O.S. from the tanker at 3,30 p.m. The Rosslare lifeboat had been at sea for 26 hours.

LETHBRIDGE Matthew, Coxswain, St. Mary's Lifeboat   **BRONZE**

10 March 1955

21–22 January 1955: In a dark night with a moderate west-north-west wind blowing and dense fog, the Panamanian s.s. *Mando* went ashore between the Menavaur Rock and Gold Ball Rock, north of the Isles of Scilly. The Watson class lifeboat *Cunard* launched at about 9.00 p.m. in a moderate swell, but had to make a wide detour around Samson and Bryher Islands because of the imminent low tide. She reached the steamer just after 10 p.m. Coxswain Lethbridge's approach was made very difficult by a considerable swell, falls and other ropes, also the presence of two ship's boats on the ends of long painters. He managed to get the lifeboat alongside and took on board the entire crew of 25 men who left by means of a Jacob's ladder. With the ship's boats, loaded with the crew's personal possessions, in tow together with a 30 foot gig which had arrived from Bryher, the lifeboat, now on a rising tide, returned by the channel between Tresco and Bryher. She reached St. Mary's at 0.30 a.m.

ALLCHORN Thomas, Coxswain, Eastbourne Lifeboat   **BRONZE(2)**

14 July 1955

6 May 1955: On 26 April the Piraeus s.s. *Germania* ran ashore east of Beachy Head, Sussex, and during the next ten days salvage work proceeded. At 4.20 p.m. on the 6th, distress signals were displayed and the Beach class lifeboat *Beryl Tollemache* launched in a fresh south-west gale, rough sea and overcast sky. On her way, she encountered the salvage boat *Endeavour* which she towed to safety in the lee of Eastbourne Pier and then did the same for the salvage boat *Moonbeam* despite the tow rope parting four times. In the course of the second rescue, a piece of driftwood drawn into her starboard propeller bent the shaft, but Coxswain Allchorn resumed his service to the *Germania* which he reached at 9.30 p.m. By this time, a fresh gale was blowing over a rough sea and the

night was very dark; the wreck was found with her stern and bows resting on different rocks and her back broken. In spite of many difficulties, 16 men were taken off and landed at Eastbourne.

PARKINSON Joseph Harold, Coxswain, Lytham St. Anne's Lifeboat   **BRONZE**
15 September 1955

3 July 1955: In the afternoon of the 3rd the yacht *Penboch* anchored one mile north of Southport pier, Lancashire, on an ebb tide in a strong westerly squally wind. With the weather deteriorating, the Watson class lifeboat *Sarah Townsend Porritt* launched at 6.26 p.m. and managed to get into Pinfold Channel down river, then anchored off Great Brow Bank to wait for the tide. The yacht was now lying on her port bilge. At 9 p.m., Coxswain Parkinson made three unsuccessful attempts to close the yacht. At 9.45 p.m. the yacht's mast carried away and one anchor parted. In the violent sea, the lifeboat anchored and veered down; five men were able to jump to safety.

CAREY Reginald, Second Coxswain, Lizard Lifeboat   **BRONZE**
9 February 1956

2 January 1956: Shortly after midnight, the 779 ton m.v. *Citrine*, of Glasgow, bound from Llandulas for London with a cargo of limestone, wirelessed that her forehatch had stove in and that she needed help. She was three miles east of the Lizard, and a fresh gale was blowing from the north-west. The Coverack lifeboat *William Taylor of Oldham* launched at 1.20 a.m., and the Lizard's *Duke of York* at 1.25 a.m. The Coverack boat reached the casualty first at 1.50 a.m. The *Citrine* was well down by the head, with her stern to the wind, and the Master was trying to beach his ship on Kennack Sands, about a mile north of Cadgwith. The Lizard lifeboat arrived at 2.05 a.m. At 2.30 a.m., the *Citrine* hit the bottom and began to sink. Seven crew were thrown into the sea when trying to launch one of the ship's boats. The Coverack lifeboat rescued four, the Lizard boat the other three. Three men were left on board. Coxswain Carey took his lifeboat full speed ahead over the port quarter of the *Citrine* which was listing heavily towards him. As he reversed off, the three men each grabbed one of the lifeboat's lifelines and were dragged clear of the vessel just before she sank.

BOYES Michael Alec, Schoolboy, Birchington   **BRONZE**
8 November 1956

18 May 1956: Two boys, aged 14 and 15, were sailing a ten foot dinghy in a fresh north-westerly wind and rough sea, when it capsized in Minnis Bay, near Birchington, Kent. One of the rescuers to put out was Michael Boyes, aged 14, who launched his ten foot single-seater canoe. After paddling for 20 minutes, he reached the dinghy and, with the two victims grasping the canoe's stern, made for shallow water where they were able to wade ashore. He beached his canoe over a mile west of the point from which he had set out an hour before.

WALKER John, Coxswain, Dover Lifeboat **BRONZE**

20 September 1956

29 July 1956: A south-south-westerly gale caused the Barnett class lifeboat *Southern Africa* to be launched at 10.30 a.m. to the yacht *Straight Flush* which was in difficulties two miles from Dover, in a rough sea and strong gale. Securing a tow, Coxswain Walker brought her, with her four man crew, into harbour at 12.15 p.m. The gale strengthened to hurricane force, and he launched again at 1.15 p.m. as a number of yachts in harbour were dragging their anchors. The Coxswain went first to the *Mermaid* near Castle Jetty, but was too late; he carried on to the *Tawi*, anchored just west of the jetty and after several attempts three men were brought off. The *Sonia* then asked for a tow; this was too risky, but it was possible to take off five men. Finally a man and his son were saved from the cabin cruiser *Madame Pompadour* just before she broke up.

GRANT Douglas Alfred, Coxswain, Selsey Lifeboat **SILVER**

20 September 1956

29 July 1956: With widespread south-westerly gales sweeping the coasts, the *Maaslust*, a Dutch boeier of 40 tons, was seen in distress heading towards West Wittering , Sussex; her sails had blown away in rough seas and heavy rain squalls. The Watson class lifeboat *Canadian Pacific* launched at 12.10 p.m., but lobster pot lines freed by the storms fouled her propellers, thus reducing her speed. She pressed on around Selsey Bill towards the boeier which was surrounded by rocks in steep seas and with so much spray that there was almost nil visibility. After an initial attempt to assist, the yacht *Bloodhound* was then seen in greater danger. Coxswain Grant steered to windward and took off seven men and two women. He returned to the *Maaslust* from which, in dreadful conditions, he took off three men, one woman , one child and a baby. During this rescue the lifeboat was damaged and her rudder jammed. Making for Portsmouth, he came across another yacht, the *Coima*, which had been driven from an anchorage in St. Helen's Roads, and took off three men. All the survivors were landed at 4.45 p.m at Portsmouth.

TART George, Coxswain, Dungeness Lifeboat **BRONZE**

20 September 1956

29–30 July 1956: Winds of hurricane force were blowing off Dungeness, Kent, when the Watson (Beach) class lifeboat *Charles Cooper Henderson* launched at 12.55 p.m. to go to the assistance of the m.v. *Teeswood,* but the boat capsized shortly before the lifeboat arrived at 1.30 p.m. The s.s. *B.P. Distributor* picked up six men from the wreckage and directed the lifeboat to the main body of survivors. An Italian liner of 20,000 tons was also near, drifting down on the lifeboat in an attempt to rescue one man in the water. Avoiding the liner, Coxswain Tart picked up the man. In all the lifeboat rescued 10 men, but one was dead. The Coxswain headed for Littlestone and landed the survivors. The lifeboat headed out again in response to a distress call from the yacht *Crevette* which, however, was taken in tow by a steamer. Back at the station at 8.50 p.m., the lifeboat was called out yet again at midnight to the yacht *Right Royal*. After a lengthy search, the yacht was reported safe alongside the Dyck lightvessel. The lifeboat finally returned to base at 11.30 a.m. She had spent 18 of the last 22 hours at sea.

ROWDEN Harold, Owner, Fishing Boat *Audrey Russell*, Whitstable   **BRONZE**

20 September 1956

29–30 July 1956: A dinghy was in difficulties and sheltering to the leeward of Street Stones, a narrow shingle bank off Whitstable, Kent, but this protection would disappear as the tide rose. The 20 foot whelk boat *Audrey Russell* was launched at 1.30 p.m. with Mr. Rowden and two other men on board. In south-westerly hurricane force winds, the boat was forced to pass round the seaward end of the Street Stones. Going alongside the starboard side of the dinghy, they took off a man and a woman and, cutting her anchor rope, brought the dinghy back into harbour at 2.15 p.m., escorted in the later stages by the Margate lifeboat.

WEST Henry Emery, Coxswain, Sheringham Lifeboat   **SILVER**
CRASKE Edward C., Mechanic, Sheringham Lifeboat   **BRONZE**

13 December 1956

31 October 1956: The 1,598 ton s.s. *Wimbledon*, laden with coal, was in trouble 13 miles north of Cromer, Norfolk and was making for shore at Blakeney. Her Master had already been washed overboard. The Liverpool class lifeboat *Forester's Centenary* launched at 9.03 a.m., and set course for the Blakeney bell buoy. After taking off eight men while seas swept over the steamer, Coxswain West transferred them to another ship and stood by. He was asked at 1.55 p.m. to remove the remainder of the ship's crew. Several attempts were necessary because of the dangerous conditions but, by 2.30 p.m., all ten men had been saved. Four of them were transferred to another vessel; the remaining six survivors were landed at Wells-next-the-Sea at 3.30 p.m., by which time the *Wimbledon* had sunk. The lifeboat did not return to Sheringham until 4 November because of continuing foul weather. During the service, the Mechanic was up to his armpits in water more than once and had to hold the radio microphone above his head to keep it dry.

LEWIS David John, Coxswain, St. David's Lifeboat   **BRONZE**

13 December 1956

8 November 1956: At 5 p.m., in a moderate south-south-westerly gale, overcast sky and a very rough sea, the Watson class lifeboat *Swyn-y-Mor (Civil Service No. 6)* launched to help a French trawler *Notre Dame de Fatima*, which had broken from a tow six miles east of St. Ann's Head, Pembrokeshire. After several attempts, Coxswain Lewis went alongside and took off her eight man crew and, at 8 p.m., set course for Milford Haven, considering it too dangerous to re-enter Solva harbour. Approaching St. Ann's Head, the lifeboat twice filled with heavy seas and rolled heavily over to port. One of her crew, Ieuan Bateman, was lost overside and his body was recovered next day.

SALES John Wood, Coxswain, Lerwick Lifeboat   **BRONZE**

14 March 1957

28 December 1956: After drifting for nearly 24 hours, the Swedish m.v. *Samba* was located 68 miles south-east of Bressay, Lerwick, Shetland Islands on the 27th with two trawlers standing by and a tug making for her. At 11.50 a.m. on the 28th, as the tug was unable to take the motor vessel in tow, the Barnett class lifeboat *Lady Jane and Martha Ryland* left the harbour in a south-easterly

gale, a rough sea and poor visibility. After changing her course due to false reports on the casualty's position, the lifeboat headed for a position two miles south-east of Bard Head on Bressay. Shortly after 3 p.m. the tug took off six men by floating down a rubber dinghy, but then the line parted and the dinghy was lost. Arriving on the scene at 4 p.m., Coxswain Sales took off the five remaining men in a rescue which involved six approaches to the *Samba*, now under the cliffs at Ord headland. There had been no time to lose – shortly after, the *Samba* drove on to the rocks and disappeared.

STONALL George, Coxswain, New Brighton Lifeboat **BRONZE**

12 December 1957

5 November 1957: After being in trouble earlier in the morning, the 211 ton Castletown, Isle of Man coaster *J.B. Kee*, was found to be in difficulties again with a 45 degree list to port; her cargo of gravel had shifted. Huge seas were sweeping over her and she was lying beam on to the wind and sea one and a half miles south of Liverpool Bar at the mouth of the River Mersey. The Barnett class lifeboat *Norman B. Corlett* left her mooring at 9.20 a.m. and Coxswain Stonall took a direct route over the sands. Reaching the coaster, he made the only approach – to the starboard bow; the lifeboat crew lined the deck and seized the six crewmen as they slid down into the boat. The lifeboat reversed clear of the *J.B. Kee*; and the survivors were landed at New Brighton at 11.45 a.m.

BATES Mark, Coxswain, Kilmore Lifeboat **SILVER**

13 February 1958

19–20 December 1957: In a fresh south-south-westerly gale and moderately rough sea, the Liverpool class lifeboat *Ann Isabelle Pyemont* launched at 11.40 p.m. and set course for the Lorient trawler *Auguste Maurice* near Ballyteige Bay, five miles west of Kilmore, Co. Wexford, Ireland. Low in the water with her head to the east-south-east, the trawler was listing heavily to port and rolling dangerously, but Coxswain Bates went alongside and two of the trawler's crew were able to scramble to safety on board the lifeboat; six more were able to do so on the second run. Another man scrambled across, but the Master was reluctant to follow and had to be grabbed by the neck at the third attempt to bring him into the lifeboat. The rescued men were landed at Kilmore at 1.40 a.m. The trawler later drove ashore and broke up.

PETERS Michael, Mechanic, St. Ives Lifeboat **SILVER**
ROACH Daniel, Coxswain, St. Ives Lifeboat **BRONZE**
PAYNTER Daniel, Signalman, St. Ives Lifeboat **BRONZE**

18 September 1958

9 August 1958: A party of two men, two girls and a boy climbed down into Smuggler's Cave, near Hellsmouth, east of Godrevy Point, Devon, but when they tried to get out, one man fell and injured his head. The other man succeeded in getting out through the cave's mouth. The Liverpool class lifeboat *Edgar, George, Orlando and Eva Child* launched at 7 p.m. in a light wind, overcast, mist and drizzle, with a dinghy in tow. Manned by four men, including Signalman Paynter, the dinghy proceeded to the cave where four explorers were found in the dark. On the way in to the cave the dinghy was holed and sank, therefore the Signalman swam out to the lifeboat to alert the Coxswain to the situation, but after the difficult swim, he was too weak to seize the line thrown to him. Michael Peters jumped overboard and brought him back to the lifeboat. Peters then swam into the

cave with a line while Coxswain Roach manoeuvred the lifeboat into the most suitable position. Using the line, Peters brought in a heavier line and with it a breeches buoy and lifejackets. Everybody was hauled out of the cave, taken on board and landed safely at 9.45 p.m.

MOORE Roland, Coxswain, Barrow Lifeboat	**BRONZE**
	13 November 1958

24–25 September 1958: The Watson class lifeboat *Herbert Leigh* launched at 7.18 p.m. and headed through a west-south-westerly gale, frequent heavy rain squalls and reduced visibility to the Morecambe Bay lightvessel, on which there was a man needing hospital treatment. She travelled 16 miles past Barrow Bar light buoy and Lightning Knoll buoy through short steep seas. The lightvessel, when reached, was pitching violently. The Coxswain took the lifeboat along the port side of the vessel, the sick man was grabbed and hauled on board without injury to him or damage to the lifeboat. The lifeboat then headed to Moelfre where there would be a good lee to land the patient, who happened to be a native of Anglesey. The lifeboat reached Moelfre at 5.10 a.m. after covering 41 miles from the lightvessel.

SALES John Wood, Coxswain, Lerwick Lifeboat	**SILVER**
MOUAT Andrew Duncan, of Baltasound	**BRONZE**
	11 December 1958

16–17 October 1958: The Soviet trawler *Urbe* sank near the Holm of Skaw, an uninhabited rocky islet off the north-eastern corner of Unst. She was one of a fleet of some 30 vessels which had been fishing off the Shetlands. The Barnett class lifeboat *Claude Cecil Staniforth* launched at 9.30 p.m. and proceeded 53 miles north in the teeth of a northerly gale. En route, the lifeboat called at Baltasound to pick up Mr. Mouat who had a good knowledge of the waters around Unst and had volunteered to act as pilot. On arrival at the scene, the lifeboat's crew were able to see three survivors sheltering behind a high boulder – searchlights had been set up on Unst to help in the rescue operations. A rocket line was fired ashore from the lifeboat and, by this means, the three men who included the skipper of the trawler were brought on board. At 5.20 a.m., the lifeboat then headed for Norwick Bay where it took on a small local boat with which it returned to the Holm. There Mr. Mouat with three lifeboat crew searched for any further survivors, without success. The lifeboat then continued a wider search during which two bodies were recovered. Returning to Baltasound, the survivors were cared for, then the lifeboat set out for Lerwick at 2.40 p.m. Shortly afterwards the Coxswain was directed to return to Baltasound to hand over the survivors and bodies to the Russian authorities. This he did, and so finally he reached Lerwick at 9.20 p.m.; by that time he had been without sleep for 41 hours.

KIRKPATRICK Daniel, Coxswain, Longhope Lifeboat	**SILVER**
	4 April 1959

4 February 1959: The 93 ton Aberdeen trawler *Strathcoe* was reported hard ashore on the west coast of Hoy, in a gully between 500 feet high cliffs. The site was eight miles from Longhope and 11 miles from Stromness. When the Barnett class lifeboat *Archibald and Alexander M. Paterson* arrived about 4 a.m., the casualty was listing at 45 degrees, her trawl gear was a tangled mass over

her side and seas were breaking over her funnel. With the Stromness lifeboat standing by as a radio-telephone link, Coxswain Kirkpatrick veered down, got a line across to the trawler and started to take off survivors. The first man reached the lifeboat after being washed out of the breeches buoy. After waiting for the tide to ebb, the remaining 13 men were taken into the lifeboat by breeches buoy and were landed at 10.22 p.m.

DERHAM Kenneth, Avon Café Proprietor, Christchurch   **SILVER**

11 June 1959

30 March 1959: Returning from a pleasure trip, a 30 foot motor fishing vessel capsized at the entrance of Christchurch harbour, Hampshire, in a very heavy breaking sea and showery weather. After being told that the three occupants were some 250 yards off shore, Mr. Derham, who had undergone a serious operation only six months before, with help launched his rowing boat. Standing up in the boat and push-rowing, he negotiated the surf and backwash and dragged a 15 year old girl on board. Then, with a 19 year old man clinging to the transom, he took the boat back stern first between the groynes and landed the two survivors safely. The girl's father drowned.

DAWSON Thomas Douglas, Coxswain, North Sunderland Lifeboat   **BRONZE**

17 September 1959

12 July 1959: In a strong west-south-westerly wind and a heavy ground sea, a canoe capsized close under the western shore of Inner Farne Island, off the coast of Northumberland. Its sole occupant managed to scramble 12 feet up the rock face to a ledge. The Liverpool class lifeboat *Grace Darling* launched at 3.30 p.m. and went to the scene. Coxswain Dawson realised that the man could not grasp a rope if it had been fired to him since he was clinging to the ledge. None of the lifeboat's crew could swim, but all had volunteered to try to reach the shore. After the lifeboat had been veered down until her stern was 60 feet from the shore, Coxswain Dawson himself went overside with a line. Reaching the man, the Coxswain found that he could not swim either. A lifebelt was dragged ashore, put round the man then used to pull him into the boat.

GILLIES James, Coxswain, Islay Lifeboat   **BRONZE**

10 December 1959

27 October 1959: The Tarbert motor fishing vessel *May* ran ashore on a reef immediately east of the Black Rock Buoy in the Sound of Islay, off the west coast of Scotland. At 9.30 a.m., the Watson class lifeboat *Charlotte Elizabeth* launched through a whole gale, gusting to hurricane force. After steaming for an hour and a half, she found the casualty and, after making an unsuccessful attempt to fire a line aboard, a line was floated down from the *May*. A breeches buoy was rigged and four men were taken off. Coxswain Gillies returned them to Port Askaig at 4.30 p.m.

DUTHIE Alexander John, Acting Coxswain, Fraserburgh Lifeboat   **BRONZE**

KIRKNESS Frederick Alexander, Mechanic, Fraserburgh Lifeboat   **BRONZE**

14 January 1960

27 October 1959: On the 27th the Watson class lifeboat *Duchess of Kent* launched under the command of Mr Duthie, a local fisherman; her Coxswain and Second Coxswain were away fishing. Tremendous seas were running and, just outside the harbour, the boat was spun around twice, but undeterred the Acting Coxswain set course toward the motor yawl *Ocean Swell* and the motor fishing vessel *Star of Faith* and started to escort them toward the harbour. Four miles north-east of Rattray Head, the *Ocean Swell* shipped a heavy sea and rolled over onto her beam ends then righted herself. Acting Coxswain Duthie went alongside, took off two men, and then continued to escort the *Star of Faith* to Peterhead, which was reached at 8.30 p.m., after nine hours on service.

EVANS Richard Matthew, Coxswain, Moelfre Lifeboat   **GOLD**

OWENS Evan, Mechanic, Moelfre Lifeboat   **SILVER**

FRANCIS Donald Murlay, Second Coxswain, Moelfre Lifeboat   **BRONZE**

OWEN Hugh, Crew Member, Moelfre Lifeboat   **BRONZE(2)**

JONES Hugh, Crew Member, Moelfre Lifeboat   **BRONZE**

10 December 1959

27 October 1959: Late in the morning of the 27th in Dulas Bay, north Anglesey, the 506 ton Cardiff s.s. *Hindlea*, from Manchester to Newport in ballast, was seen dragging her anchor in a strong gale which had veered suddenly. In view of the extreme urgency of the situation, the reserve Watson class lifeboat *Edmund and Mary Robinson* launched at noon with only five men in her crew. By 1.55 p.m., the steamer was within 200 yards of the rocks, when the Captain ordered abandon ship. The crew gathered on the port side of the poop deck from where the eight men jumped, one at a time. Coxswain Evans had to make ten runs before they were all on board the lifeboat. With the engines still running, the ship's propeller continued to revolve far out of the water; this presented a grave hazard as did the hurricane force gusts of over 100 miles per hour amid tremendous seas. This was Hugh Jones' first service.

WATSON Albert, Coxswain, Cromarty Lifeboat   **SILVER**

WATSON John, Mechanic, Cromarty Lifeboat   **BRONZE**

11 February 1960

7–8 December 1959: In a south-south-easterly near gale, rough seas and with an overcast sky, the 360 ton Leith coaster s.s. *Servus*, Methil to Kirkwall with coal, was drifting with her propeller shaft broken, one mile off shore near Dunbeath, Caithness. The Watson class lifeboat *Lilla, Marras, Douglas and Will* launched at 4.45 p.m. and, after a 40 mile journey, reached the coaster at 1.40 a.m. to find her yawing violently and dragging towards the shore. Coxswain Watson twice ran alongside, took off eight men, and landed them at Cromarty at 7.47 a.m.

THOMAS Henry Owen, Coxswain, Torbay Lifeboat   **SILVER**
HARRIS Richard Trewaves, Mechanic, Torbay Lifeboat   **BRONZE(3)**

11 February 1960

7 December 1959: In response to a call for help from a drifting lighter, the Barnett class lifeboat *Princess Alexandra of Kent* launched at 9.35 p.m. in overcast conditions with frequent fierce rain squalls and a south-east whole gale. The Dutch tug *Cycloop*, sheltering in Tor Bay with three lighters, had cut one adrift after her propeller became fouled by its rope. When Coxswain Thomas arrived, he found the lighter aground, half a mile south of Torquay; on board were two men with a cargo of steel pipes. In spite of heavy seas sweeping the length of the lighter, one of the men and a small dog jumped into the lifeboat, but the other, older man hesitated and lost his chance. No amount of manoeuvring could bring the lifeboat into a suitable position for his rescue. He took hold of a rope but dropped into the sea and was hauled unconscious on board by boathook. Members of the lifeboat crew tried to revive him with artificial respiration, but without success.

POWER Patrick, Coxswain, Dunmore East Lifeboat   **BRONZE(3)**

12 January 1961

4 October 1960: Two barges, sheltering in Dunmore Bay, Co. Waterford, Ireland, were reported to have set sail in worsening weather, one towed by the other. The Watson class lifeboat *Annie Blanche Smith* slipped her mooring in anticipation and, soon after she passed the pierhead lighthouse, saw one of the barges very near the rocks, lying across the wind with her engine broken down. The other barge had been cut adrift. The first barge was being driven ashore inside the Laweesh Rock by the wind and ebb tide. After two unsuccessful attempts, Coxswain Power drove the lifeboat on to the broken down barge and the solitary man on board was hauled over the bow. Although the second barge had no engine, with her 40 tons of ballast she had drifted more slowly, and Coxswain Power was able to put two men on board to take her into Dunmore.

CUNNINGHAM Samuel, Coxswain, Portrush Lifeboat   **SILVER**
McMULLAN Robert, Second Coxswain, Portrush Lifeboat   **BRONZE**

12 January 1961

22 October 1960: In a fresh south-east wind and moderate to rough sea with deteriorating overcast conditions, the 10,392 ton Piraeus s.s. *Argo Delas* went ashore on the islet of Tor Beg, near Inishtrahull lighthouse, about fives miles north east of Malin Head, Co. Donegal. The Watson class lifeboat *Lady Scott (Civil Service No. 4)* launched at 3.05 a.m. and proceeded 24 miles to the scene. The Coxswain took the lifeboat alongside the wreck several times and took off 14 men, despite seas breaking over the ship and escaping oil making her deck slippery. In addition to the damage already occasioned to the lifeboat, a rope fouled her port propeller. Coxswain Cunningham then transferred the survivors to H.M.S. *Leopard,* which had been standing by, and made for the lee of Tor More Rock, where the obstruction was cleared. The lifeboat stood by while the other 15 men were transferred from the steamer by helicopter before returning to Portrush at 5.20 p.m.

CARTER Thomas John, Master Mariner   **SILVER**
HENDERSON Charles F., Carpenter   **SILVER**

9 February 1961

25–26 October 1960: At 10.20 p.m. two coastal tankers, s.s. *Arkendale* and s.s. *Wastdale*, collided near the dock entrance at Sharpness, on the River Severn. The two vessels, one containing 200 hundred tons of diesel oil and the other nearly 350 tons of petrol, drifted upstream locked together, and then collided with the Severn railway bridge causing two spans to collapse. Fire broke out and, with the vessels grounded upstream at Purton, Captain Carter, Master of another tanker, and Mr. Henderson, newly arrived in the area from Glasgow, put out in a dinghy at 11.45 p.m. and carried out a search. In the intense heat and over an extremely large fall of tide, they picked up an oil covered man who was swimming in the river and landed him at 2.30 in the morning.

STONEHOUSE John, Coxswain, Teesmouth Lifeboat   **BRONZE**

21 September 1961

1 June 1961: The Watson class lifeboat *Sarah Jane and James Season* launched at 10.20 a.m. into a gale and a very rough sea to help the 20 ton yawl *Sybil Kathleen*, Hamble to Norway, in difficulties in Skiningrove Bay, near Redcar, Yorkshire. Dismasted 120 miles north-east of the Tyne, she had reached the coast short of fuel and with insufficient power to make headway against the wind. Having laid oil to windward, Coxswain Stonehouse passed a line at the fourth attempt and towed the yawl to the lee of Hartlepool, Co. Durham.

HERNON Coleman, Coxswain, Galway Bay Lifeboat   **BRONZE**
MULLEN Bartley, Assistant Mechanic, Galway Bay Lifeboat   **BRONZE**
JOYCE Thomas, Crew Member, Galway Bay Lifeboat   **BRONZE**
QUINN Patrick, Crew Member, Galway Bay Lifeboat   **BRONZE**

8 March 1962

16 January 1962: The Rotterdam coaster s.s. *June* ran aground in a gale on the reefs off Mutton Island, near the entrance to Galway docks. At 12.30 p.m., the Watson class lifeboat *Mabel Marion Thompson* put out from Kilronan, 24 miles from the casualty. The coaster was found with a 20 degree list to port, her bows on a rock but, with the weather improving, her Master decided not to abandon her. The lifeboat put into Galway docks but set out again at 7.15 p.m. when the weather deteriorated. She towed with her a small boat and carried an extra man with local knowledge and the owner of the *June*. The gale was now gusting with rough seas, hail and rain squalls, and the *June*'s crew had taken refuge on Mutton Island. Coxswain Hernon took the lifeboat as close to the lighthouse landing as possible and Bartley Mullen and Thomas Joyce then brought off six survivors in the small boat. Patrick Quinn replaced Bartley Mullen and several attempts were made to return to the landing. Eventually, after twice being swamped, two other men and a dog were taken off. All survivors were landed at Galway at 11 p.m.

MACDONALD Malcolm, Coxswain, Stornoway Lifeboat   SILVER
MACLEOD John, Mechanic, Stornoway Lifeboat   BRONZE
MACDONALD John, Assistant Mechanic, Stornoway Lifeboat   BRONZE

10 May 1962

30–31 January 1962: In a storm force wind blowing over a rough sea, the motor fishing vessel *Maime,* with two men and a woman on board, broke down as she was leaving Stornoway, Lewis, and drifted on to the rocks off Battery Point, Stornoway Bay in overcast conditions with rain and sleet showers. The Barnett class lifeboat *The James and Margaret Boyd* reached the casualty at 8.35 p.m., but, as the Bowman was injured by a flare, returned to harbour and came back to the wreck at 9 p.m. After a number of unsuccessful attempts, a line was got on board the vessel. The Coxswain instructed the vessel's crew by loud hailer to clamber over the rocks with a line secured to each of them. One man did make the attempt, but without a line he was washed away and drowned. The Coxswain then borrowed a rubber raft from H.M.S. *Malcolm* which was at anchor in the Bay. The raft was floated down but the two survivors still made no effort. Coxswain Macdonald then veered down and, using the raft, he and John Macdonald boarded the casualty and dragged the survivors into the lifeboat. They were landed at 3.40 a.m.

SEMPLE Walter, Coxswain, Cloughey Lifeboat   BRONZE

10 May 1962

7 March 1962: In a south-easterly gale blowing over a very rough sea and broken water, the 260 ton Dutch coaster *Frida Blokzijl* was drifting ashore in the afternoon near the fairway buoy in Strangford Lough, Co. Down, . The Liverpool class lifeboat *Constance Calverley* put out and, one mile south of the Butter Pladdy buoy, reached the casualty, which was using her engines to keep off the lee shore because her steering gear was out of action. Coxswain Semple had to make seven attempts before four men jumped from the coaster, but the Master decided to remain on board. Those in the lifeboat were landed at Portavogie at 4.35 p.m. After that the weather deteriorated, and the casualty dragged towards the shore. The lifeboat returned to the coaster and, at his own request, the Master was taken off on a second attempt. He was landed at 7.30 p.m.

JENNINGS Arthur Daniel, Captain. Harbour Master, Alderney   BRONZE

14 June 1962

28 March 1962: In bad weather with a fresh south-south-easterly breeze and poor visibility, the m.v. *Ridunian,* on passage from Alderney to Guernsey, with 150 tons of grit and gravel, struck Barsier rock while passing Corbet rock; it was too rough to lower the ship's boats. Two attempts by inflatable raft were unsuccessful, but the ship was also transporting a ten man raft which the seven man crew took to just before the motor vessel slipped off the rock and sank. Orders were given for the St. Peter Port, Guernsey, lifeboat to launch. Captain Jennings was also advised, who then collected a scratch crew and launched the Trinity House pilot cutter *Burhou* (a converted motor fishing vessel), which made for the Swinge channel and, in poor visibility, sighted the Clouque rocks at 8.40 p.m. and started to search the area. The search was transferred to the area of the Berhou reefs where the raft was sighted; all seven men were taken off and landed at Alderney harbour at 9.45 p.m.

PARKINSON Harold, Coxswain, Lytham St. Anne's Lifeboat **BRONZE**

20 September 1962

21 July 1962: With a near gale blowing over a rough sea, the seven ton motor ketch *Lone Seeker* went aground between Peet's Light and Salter's Bank on the north side of the River Ribble channel. After waiting for the tide to flood, the Watson class lifeboat *Sarah Townsend Porritt* went down channel at 11.05 a.m. and over the training wall. A line was fired to the ketch, but this parted and the line gun was lost overboard on the second attempt. In worsening conditions, Coxswain Parkinson decided to take the lifeboat alongside, but this proved to be impracticable, although he managed to get a heaving line on board the ketch, which was then towed into deeper water. The ketch was found to have surprisingly little damage, and she continued up river under her own power.

CAMPINI Harold Louis, Coxswain, Rhyl Lifeboat **SILVER**

8 November 1962

17 September 1962: Hovercraft *VA – 3001* was employed during the summer in ferrying between Rhyl and Hoylake, Cheshire, across the mouth of the River Dee. At the end of season, she was moored at Rhyl waiting to be towed to Liverpool. She broke adrift in the early hours of the 17th and her crew tried to take her out to sea under power in a west-north-west gale with rough seas and poor visibility. The Liverpool class lifeboat *Anthony Robert Marshall* launched at 1.17 a.m. and made for the hovercraft, which was drifting rapidly towards the promenade. There was no place on the casualty to which Coxswain Campini could make a line fast. He took the lifeboat alongside the hovercraft which enabled the three men to jump off seven minutes before the it hit the promenade. The lifeboat had to wait an hour for a lull before she could enter the harbour.

CANN Sidney, Coxswain, Appledore Lifeboat **SILVER**

14 February 1963

17–18 November 1962: In a gale and very rough seas, the tanker R.F.A. *Green Ranger* broke loose from the tug *Caswell*, which was towing her off Hartland Point at the southern end of Bideford Bay, Devon. The Clovelly lifeboat launched, but had to return as she could not make the Point in the conditions prevailing. The larger Watson class lifeboat *Violet Armstrong* launched from Appledore at 6 p.m. and set course for Hartland Point, and searched close inshore as far as Knap Head. An hour later, a searchlight from H.M.S. *Agincourt* showed the wreck to be located on rocks under the cliff near Long Peak beach, with seas breaking over her forecastle and her starboard side awash. Coxswain Cann ran down alongside her, but the loud hailer brought no response. At 3.15 a.m., he received information that the tanker's crew had been rescued already by life-saving apparatus. The lifeboat returned to Appledore and arrived there at 8.45 a.m.

FAWCUS Thomas, Coxswain, Blyth Lifeboat **SILVER**
KERR John, Bowman, Blyth Lifeboat **BRONZE**

14 February 1963

18 November 1962: The 200 ton m.v. *Paullgate,* lying inside the Fairway Buoy off Blyth, Northumberland, broached to with a 35 degree port list in a near northerly gale, rough sea and heavy swell. The Watson class lifeboat *Winston Churchill (Civil Service No. 8)* launched and

reached the casualty; Coxswain Fawcus took off two men from her bilge keel. The Captain remained on board intending to enter the Tyne and asked the lifeboat to stand by, but the motor vessel ran out of fuel at the river entrance, and drifted through the piers at flood tide. Bowman Kerr scrambled on board and secured a line from the lifeboat which kept the casualty clear of the shore until a tug arrived.

PETIT Hubert Ernest, Coxswain, St. Peter Port Lifeboat	**GOLD**
PETIT John Hubert, Crew Member, St. Peter Port Lifeboat	**BRONZE**
PATTIMORE Eric Clifford, Mechanic, St. Peter Port Lifeboat	**BRONZE**

11 April 1963

5–6 February 1963: The Barnett class lifeboat *Euphrosyne Kendal* left her moorings at 3.45 p.m. in a near gale from the south, rough seas and overcast weather. The 1,995 ton Norwegian m.v. *Johan Collett*, 14 miles west-north-west of Les Hanois lighthouse at the south-west corner of Guernsey, in passage from Tunis to Ghent, Belgium, was in difficulty; her cargo of zinc concentrates had shifted. Fourteen of her crew had been transferred, and a South African frigate was standing by. When the lifeboat reached her at 6.30 p.m. they found the motor vessel lying stopped, beam on to the wind and waiting for a tug. In four runs, Coxswain Petit took off the Chief Engineer and two apprentices before the tug arrived. After the tow had been connected and the wind force had risen to Beaufort strength ten, the Coxswain made six more runs and saved the remaining six men. All survivors were landed at St. Peter Port at 6.45 a.m.

TAYLOR Francis Robert, D.S.M., Second Coxswain, Wells Lifeboat   **BRONZE**

10 October 1963

18–19 May 1963: At low tide, the Frinton cabin cruiser *Seamu* went aground in a strong west-north-west breeze and rough sea at the entrance to Blakeney harbour, Norfolk. Second Coxswain Taylor (acting as Coxswain) launched the Liverpool class lifeboat *Cecil Paine* and reached the casualty at 10.50 p.m., but his first approach was frustrated by a sandbank and, when he started the second run, the wind had strengthened to a near gale. Four further attempts were necessary before he could get alongside and drag two men aboard. The lifeboat was back on station at 3.15 a.m.

HOULIHAN Joseph, Motor Mechanic, Valentia Lifeboat   **BRONZE**

12 December 1963

2 September 1963: Seeing a small dinghy capsize off the shore at Valentia, Co. Kerry, Ireland, Motor Mechanic Houlihan launched the station boarding boat in a north near gale and pulled for the dinghy, already 200 yards north-north-east of Reenagiveen Point. He found two men in the water, dragged one, near collapse, into the boarding boat, and told the other, a clergyman who was much heavier, to hang on to the transom. He returned to the beach in a journey of great difficulty and landed the two men. He later returned to the scene and recovered the capsized dinghy.

HICKEY Richard, Coxswain, Youghal Lifeboat **BRONZE**

12 December 1963

27 October 1963: The French trawler *Fée des Ondes* went ashore in Ardmore Bay, Co Cork, in a strong south-east breeze with mist and limited visibility, and the Liverpool class lifeboat *Herbert John* launched at 6.30 a.m. By the time Coxswain Hickey had travelled the seven miles to the casualty, seven of the trawler's crew had already landed in an inflatable dinghy but, in addition to the Master and one man, two helpers from the shore were also aboard. With the vessel lying about 300 yards from the shore, rolling heavily, the lifeboat anchored to seaward and veered alongside several times, but the Master refused to leave. At 11 a.m., the trawler drove toward the shore into more rocks and, holed, began to list. The Master then decided to leave. When the lifeboat veered down in the difficult conditions all four men jumped aboard and were landed at Youghal at 12.30 p.m.

SCOTT Lionel Derek, Coxswain, Mumbles Lifeboat **SILVER**

13 February 1964

18 November 1963: On the evening of the 17th, the Amsterdam m.v. *Kilo*, with a deck cargo of drums of sodium, was making for Swansea. The deck cargo was on fire and there had been heavy explosions, but the ship was in no immediate danger. Both Padstow and Tenby lifeboats were called out, but their instructions were cancelled. At 3.20 a.m., the Watson class Mumbles lifeboat *William Gammon – Manchester and District XXX* launched in a severe thunderstorm with winds up to 65 miles per hour. After an extremely severe passage, the vessel was sighted in the light of a parachute flare dropped by a Shackleton aircraft. Despite the mass of flames over the sea ahead and downwind, Coxswain Scott decided to go alongside, but two attempts failed. On the third try, with the flames dying down, the vessel's Captain decided to make for the Mumbles, and beached at 4.50 a.m. in Mumbles Bay with the lifeboat alongside. Three-quarters of an hour later, the flames increased and spread to the inflammable cargo in the holds – the lifeboat took off all the crew. As the tide made, the vessel was seen to refloat in the continuing torrential rain and thunderstorm, and the fire began to die down. Putting the Captain and Chief Engineer back on board, the lifeboat escorted the vessel under tow to Swansea Dock.

PLUMMER John Robert, Coxswain, Caister Lifeboat   **BRONZE**

13 February 1964

13 December 1963: The Lowestoft trawler *Loch Lorgan* went aground in heavy, breaking seas and a wind gusting to gale force, on the Middle Caister shoal off the Norfolk coast. The Liverpool class lifeboat *Jose Neville* launched just after midnight in a rough sea and poor visibility and, on reaching the shoal, ran straight in, bows first, alongside the trawler which enabled seven men to jump on board. During this time, seas were breaking over both vessels continually, sometimes filling the lifeboat's cockpit. Exercising considerable skill, Coxswain Plummer withdrew and reached Gorleston at 2.15 a.m. Later the trawler appeared to have refloated, and her crew was taken back out to her but they could not get aboard.

KIRKPATRICK Daniel, Coxswain, Longhope Lifeboat   **SILVER(2)**

9 April 1964

3–4 January 1964: The Watson class lifeboat *T.G.B.* launched at 10.26 p.m. in a fresh to moderate southerly breeze, and made good progress to the Aberdeen trawler *Ben Barvas* which was ashore on the Pentland Skerries, north-east of John o' Groats, in a very steep sea. In this area of turbulent seas, it was obvious that it would be impossible to go alongside the trawler, therefore Coxswain Kirkpatrick hauled off to the south-west, anchored and veered down to a suitable position, and fired a rocket line by which means a breeches buoy was rigged. The exhausting work of hauling in the nine crewmen was made more difficult by oil from the trawler's fractured fuel tanks covering everything. After leaving the scene, the lifeboat picked up five more survivors from another trawler to which they had earlier been transferred and all 14 were landed at St. Margaret's Hope at 4.30 a.m.

POWER Patrick, Coxswain, Dunmore East Lifeboat   **BRONZE(4)**
WHITTLE Stephen, Second Coxswain, Dunmore East Lifeboat   **BRONZE**
POWER John, Assistant Mechanic, Dunmore East Lifeboat   **BRONZE**

17 September 1964

11 March 1964: The Dutch m.v. *Jan Brons*, of Delfzijl, went on to rocks off Ardnamult Head near Dunmore East harbour, Co. Waterford, Ireland, and, by the time the Watson class lifeboat *Annie Blanche Smith*, with her boarding boat in tow, reached there a near gale was blowing from the south-east over a rough sea. Coxswain Power had to abandon the first attempt to go alongside by boarding boat, and, when a breeches buoy was being set up, the lifeboat's anchor started to drag. After moving to another anchorage, the breeches buoy was rigged successfully. With the help of the boarding boat manned by the Second Coxswain and Assistant Mechanic, six survivors were brought into the lifeboat; the trawler's Master, Mate and Chief Engineer remained on board to be rescued eventually from the land.

OXLEY Walter Jonas, Coxswain, Walton and Frinton Lifeboat   **BRONZE(2)**

11 June 1964

15 March 1964: In a gale and extremely rough seas, visibility was less than half a mile in heavy rain when the Watson class lifeboat *Edian Courtauld* launched at 3.50 a.m. to the 498 ton Dutch m.v. *Merak* aground near the Sunk lightvessel. After an extended search in poor conditions, the

lifeboat came up with the casualty near the south-east Shipwash buoy, but Coxswain Oxley was asked to stand by. At 10 a.m., he was asked to take off the crew. In three runs, a woman and eight men were removed. A short while later, the motor vessel washed clear, and the Captain and a crewman were put back on board to drop anchor; then the Engineer was put back on board. After standing by for two tugs to arrive, the lifeboat landed the woman and five men at Walton Yacht Club.

NICHOLAS Henry, Coxswain, Sennen Cove Lifeboat BRONZE(2)

11 June 1964

24 March 1964: The 90 ton Belgian trawler *Victoire Roger* ran ashore at Land's End, Cornwall, in wet, foggy weather with the wind blowing from the south-west over a moderate swell. When Coxswain Nicholas sighted the trawler from the Watson class lifeboat *Susan Ashley*, she was on fire in Camper Cove with her crew standing on the poop, so he decided to go alongside at once. He took off four men, but a heavy sea then intervened, driving the lifeboat into the cove. In a second approach, he succeeded in recovering the Master, who had a broken arm. All five men were landed in Newlyn at 6.15 a.m.

Coxswain Nicholas won this medal at the age of 62, nearly 45 years after the first award for a service on 30 November 1919.

O'CONNOR Patrick BRONZE

McCARTHY William, Sergeant, Garda Siochana BRONZE

17 September 1964

29 June 1964: With a strong west-north-westerly breeze blowing and a moderate sea and swell, the 32 foot fishing boat *Beal Eairbeirt*, containing two men, stranded near Bird Rock off Clahaneleesh, Co. Kerry, Ireland. On learning this, Mr. O'Connor and Sergeant McCarthy put out from Meenogahan in a curragh, which had not been in the water for a year. They went through broken water immediately, then, after a difficult two mile journey, pulled the men into the curragh and landed them on Clahaneleesh beach at 11 a.m. One of the men was unconscious when picked up and, despite attempts at resuscitation, was dead when they landed.

McLOUGHLIN Joseph, Coxswain, Howth Lifeboat BRONZE

8 October 1964

14 July 1964: The Arklow trawler *Ros Cairbre* left Howth in a full southerly gale, but her engine broke down and she was being swept on to a lee shore, north of Howth lighthouse, Co. Dublin, Ireland. In the absence of the regular boat, the reserve Watson class lifeboat *H.F. Bailey* put out at 9 p.m. and, after two and a half miles against a very rough sea and flood tide, the casualty was found under cliffs on the north side of Freshwater Bay. Coxswain McLoughlin went alongside the trawler almost immediately and made fast; he drew the casualty clear and, with her crew of six men aboard, towed her to Howth.

BOWDEN John Richard, Second Coxswain, Appledore Lifeboat   **BRONZE**

10 December 1964

11 September 1964: Just before 3 p.m., in the absence of the Coxswain, Second Coxswain Bowden launched the reserve Watson class lifeboat *Cecil and Lilian Philpott* to the yacht *Volunteer*, stranded on the bar near the entrance to the River Taw. He landed two of his crew on the sandbank, and they gave advice to the yacht's crew who decided to remain on board the yacht until she refloated. The lifeboat stood by as the conditions deteriorated. The yacht was damaged and swept broadside up on to the bank. Finally, in a complex operation, Bowden took off two men and two women and landed them safely.

COYDE Harold, Coxswain, Torbay Lifeboat   **SILVER**

HARRIS Richard Trewaves, Mechanic, Torbay Lifeboat   **BRONZE(4)**

11 February 1965

22 December 1964: In a gale and heavy swell, the Danish coaster m.v. *Northwind* went aground in broken, heavy water on a small beach between two outcrops of rock under Hollicombe Gas Works, near Torquay, Devon. When the Barnett class lifeboat *Princess Alexandra of Kent* arrived at 3.45 p.m., the crew were being taken ashore by breeches buoy. As Coxswain Coyde was trying to veer down to the coaster, he was informed that her Master and Chief Officer were going to remain on board. Later, while still standing-by the casualty, he was told that they had been taken ashore; the lifeboat then returned to her station after over four hours on service in exceptionally difficult conditions.

This service was described tersely as 'stood by vessel'.

LAKER Donald Shipway, Crew Member, Weymouth Lifeboat   **BRONZE**

8 July 1965

29 May 1965: In the early afternoon, the yacht *Dehra* went aground to the north of the pier at Weymouth, Dorset, in a moderate wind and a short, choppy sea with spray breaking over her. Successive efforts were made to help her by the Barnett class lifeboat *Frank Spiller Locke*, a small boat, and by rockets. The Coxswain decided that to wait any longer would mean the yacht being driven up the beach on her beam ends. Mr. Laker went overside and swam to her with a line, after stripping to his underclothes. With the tow secured and the yacht's owner and one of his crew injured, the lifeboat held the yacht's head to wind until she refloated with the tide and was taken into harbour.

INNES Ian, Master, Fishing Vessel *Branch*   **BRONZE**

10 March 1966

28 October 1965: At 9.16 a.m., the fishing vessel *Branch* began to search for a lobster boat in trouble off Golspie, Sutherland, but, when the vessel was reported safe, Mr. Innes headed for Helmsdale. Nine minutes later the lobster boat *James's* was reported in difficulty off Ousdale, four miles north of Helmsdale, with the Skipper and his two sons on board. By 10 a.m., the weather had deteriorated sharply. On arriving at Helmsdale, two small vessels accompanying the *Branch* entered the harbour. The *James's* refused a tow and tried to follow the small boats in a steep, confused and breaking sea; she was overturned 50 yards short of the entrance. The *Branch* hauled the Skipper and one son on board, but the other son was swept well into the

channel. Giving chase, Mr. Innes could see a hand above the water and he grasped it from a most precarious position, then both he and the near victim were dragged to safety by the men on deck.

ELLIOTT Gordon Harvey, Coxswain, Padstow Lifeboat   **SILVER**

13 January 1966

23 November 1965: The Barnett class lifeboat *Joseph Hiram Chadwick* slipped her moorings at 3.50 p.m. in a gale gusting to violent storm and pushed through a very rough sea and poor visibility to the fishing vessel *Deo Gratias* off Padstow Bay, Cornwall. When Coxswain Elliott found her, she was riding head to wind with her mizzen carried away, then she broached and sheered about violently while drifting rapidly downwind. The two men on board wanted to abandon ship, but two attempts to get a line on board failed. Waiting for a lull, the lifeboat's bow was pushed against the casualty's starboard quarter and both men were hauled in. Although the lifeboat had sustained some damage and the weather was deteriorating, the men were landed at Padstow at 7.20 p.m.

EVANS David Winston, Coxswain, New Quay Lifeboat   **BRONZE**
FOWLER Evan George Sydney, Mechanic, New Quay Lifeboat   **BRONZE**
REES David, Police Sergeant, Glamorganshire Constabulary   **BRONZE**

10 November 1966

7 August 1966: At 0.40 a.m., the Liverpool class lifeboat *St. Albans* launched in a breeze and choppy sea, tasked to search the coast between the River Drewy and Gilfach-yr-Halen, Cardiganshire. Just before midnight, three boys had been reported missing either on the cliffs or on the beach in the Llwyn Celyn area, which was being searched by coastguards. Despite the treacherous nature of the bottom with its outlying rocks, Coxswain Evans took the lifeboat as close to the cliffs as possible. At about 1.45 a.m., his searchlight picked out a 16 year old boy, stranded on a ledge about 20 feet up the cliff. With conditions preventing the lifeboat from getting near, Mechanic Fowler and Sergeant Rees stripped off and swam in, taking a light nylon rope with them. While the lifeboat was anchored, the rope was used to rig a breeches buoy and the youth was taken into the boat. The swimmers then recovered a body together with a mortally injured youth and the Coxswain brought the lifeboat on to a small beach so that they could be taken on board. Sadly the second boy died before the lifeboat reached New Quay at 2.30 a.m. Sergeant Rees, son of a former Honorary Secretary, was on leave and volunteered for service in the lifeboat.

WILSON Michael Ormond, Second Officer, Crew Member, Tenby Lifeboat   **SILVER**
RICHARDS Joshua William, Bowman, Tenby Lifeboat   **BRONZE**

10 November 1966

27 August 1966: When five boys and a girl were cut off by the tide at Waterwynch, a mile from Tenby, the Watson class lifeboat *Henry Comber Brown* launched in a moderate south-easterly wind and towed a small rowing punt to the vicinity. Bowman Richards hauled the punt close to the shore and kept it there by great skill and strength, while Mr. Wilson swam from it on five occasions and brought off five of the children through a heavy swell. One boy had swum to the punt unaided. Mr. Wilson, a Merchant Navy officer, was on leave and went out as a member of the crew.

BLOOM Frank, Coxswain, Walton and Frinton Lifeboat BRONZE

12 January 1967

17–19 November 1966: When the Watson class lifeboat *Edian Courtauld* slipped her moorings at 12.30 p.m. on the 17th, a strong north-north-westerly wind was blowing, squalls were frequent and the sea was rough with a heavy ground swell. Arriving at the Long Sand bank near the Sunk light vessel, the casualty, with four vessels in attendance, was found to be the 2,831 ton Panamanian s.s. *Ypapanti,* Newcastle to Lisbon with a cargo of coke. Already the weather had worsened, but Coxswain Bloom took the lifeboat alongside. The Master refused to let anybody leave and the lifeboat stood by but returned to Walton at 6 p.m. after a huge sea filled her wheelhouse. Returning to Long Sand, but receiving no indication that the steamer's crew wished to leave, he took the lifeboat back to station at 4.40 a.m. on the 18th. After conditions worsened, he went out again and, at 11.45 a.m. 11 men were taken off, one at a time, and landed at Walton at 2.20 p.m. Next day, it was decided that rescue would have to be by helicopter, so the five men remaining were lifted by an aircraft from Manston, Kent, and transferred to the lifeboat, which landed them at 6.33 p.m.

BYRNE Philip, Coxswain, Arranmore Lifeboat SILVER

13 July 1967

26–27 November 1966: With a north-westerly gale blowing, a very rough sea and poor visibility, conditions were so bad that a helicopter could not be used. The Watson class lifeboat *W.M. Tilson* slipped her moorings at 7.45 p.m. and proceeded to Tory Island off the coast of Donegal, Ireland, where a ten-year-old boy, seriously ill with acute appendicitis, needed hospital treatment. The 21 mile voyage took two and a half hours, but it proved impossible to go alongside the jetty because of rocks. Coxswain Byrne stood off while the boy and his father were brought out in a large curragh. The boy and his father were then landed at Burtonport, Donegal at 3.30 a.m. after a voyage through rough seas and gale force winds. Conditions were so bad that when the lifeboat returned to her station, her crew could not land until 5.30 a.m.

Veering down on a wreck

HARVEY Harold Harknett, Lieutenant Commander, V.R.D., R.N.R. Inspector of Lifeboats North West	**GOLD**
ALCOCK Thomas, Coxswain, Holyhead Lifeboat	**SILVER**
JONES Eric Samuel, Mechanic, Holyhead Lifeboat	**SILVER**
JONES William John, Second Coxswain, Holyhead Lifeboat	**BRONZE**
WARD Francis, Acting Bowman, Holyhead Lifeboat	**BRONZE**
SHARPE Jack, Acting Assistant Mechanic, Holyhead Lifeboat	**BRONZE**
DRINKWATER David Graham, Crew Member, Holyhead Lifeboat	**BRONZE**
HUGHES John Michael, Crew Member, Holyhead Lifeboat	**BRONZE**
STEWART Brian Gordon, Crew Member, Holyhead Lifeboat	**BRONZE**
EVANS Richard Matthew, Coxswain, Moelfre Lifeboat	**GOLD(2)**
OWENS Evan, Mechanic, Moelfre Lifeboat	**SILVER(2)**
FRANCIS Donald Murphy, Second Coxswain, Moelfre Lifeboat	**BRONZE(2)**
OWEN Hugh, Bowman, Moelfre Lifeboat	**BRONZE(3)**
DAVIES William Maynard, Assistant Mechanic, Moelfre Lifeboat	**BRONZE**
EVANS David T., Crew Member, Moelfre Lifeboat	**BRONZE**
JONES Hugh, Crew Member, Moelfre Lifeboat	**BRONZE(2)**
JEAVONS Jocelyn David, Captain. Crew Member, Moelfre Lifeboat	**BRONZE**

12 January 1967

2–3 December 1966: When the 1,287 ton Greek s.s. *Nafsiporos* broke down 20 miles north of Lynas Point, Anglesey, a north-westerly gale was blowing over a heavy sea with poor visibility. At 10.30 a.m., the Barnett class lifeboat *St. Cybi (Civil Service No. 9)* put out from Holyhead with Lieutenant Commander Harvey, who was visiting the station at the time. The Moelfre Watson class lifeboat *Watkin Williams* had already been to sea on another service since 7.40 a.m. and was secured half-way up the slip when she was called at 2.22 p.m . to help the Holyhead lifeboat, which had already reached the casualty. Meanwhile, the steamer was drifting approximately south-west, after the towline from a Russian ship had parted. At 3.25 p.m., she scraped close past the Ethel Rock Buoy and finished up close to West Mouse Rock, rolling violently. The Holyhead lifeboat was badly damaged in trying to go alongside and Coxswain Alcock went to supervise operations from the deck; with the crew's consent, Lieutenant Commander Harvey took his place at the wheel. As the Holyhead lifeboat ran in for the first attempt, Coxswain Evans arrived and made the second attempt, but could not persuade anybody to leave. Lieutenant Commander Harvey made another run and a man was snatched from the steamer's jumping ladder. With the boat manoeuvring alongside, four others were taken off just before a ship's boat crashed on top of the lifeboat. While the wreckage was being cleared, Coxswain Evans went alongside and took off ten men; the steamer's Captain and three men remained on board by choice. All 15 survivors were landed by both boats at Holyhead at 6.30 p.m., then Coxswain Alcock took his boat back to stand by until the steamer was taken in tow by a tug just before 7 a.m.

NICOLSON John Robert, Coxswain, Aith Lifeboat **SILVER**

11 May 1967

19 February 1967: In strong winds gusting to gale, heavy rain and sleet showers, there was a strong choppy sea in Aith Voe, and the Aberdeen trawler *Juniper* went aground on Papa Stour in Fogla Skerry, Shetland. The Barnett class lifeboat *John and Frances MacFarlane* put out at 5.48 a .m. and, when she reached the north side of Papa Stour, saw seven trawlers standing by the casualty in Lyra

Sound between Lyra Skerry and Papa Stour. Because of rocks and skerries, Coxswain Nicolson took the lifeboat around the west side of Fogla Skerry then went through a narrow channel and alongside the trawler to take off the trawler's 12 man crew. The lifeboat was damaged when twice struck by the trawler. At times the lifeboat rose and fell some 12 to 15 feet. The survivors were landed at 9.35 a.m.

LETHBRIDGE Matthew (Junior), Coxswain, St. Mary's Lifeboat	**SILVER**
GUY Ernest Roy, Second Coxswain, St. Mary's Lifeboat	**BRONZE**
BURROW William Richard, Mechanic, St. Mary's Lifeboat	**BRONZE**

21 September 1967

22–23 May 1967: The motor yacht *Braemar*, chartered to an ITN crew covering the completion of Francis Chichester's round the world trip, sprang a leak in very heavy seas and a near gale force wind 28 miles from Bishop Rock. The Watson class lifeboat *Guy and Clare Hunter* launched at 6.48 a.m. and set course past St. Agnes Point, then, at 9 a.m., the yacht reported that her engines had failed and she was drifting. When Coxswain Lethbridge came up with the yacht at 10.30 a.m., 13 miles from Wolf Rock, a motor vessel was already trying to take her in tow. After several attempts, the lifeboat managed to get a line on board. With the yacht taking more water, 15 men and a woman were dragged into the lifeboat with great difficulty, but the Master and two men remained on board the yacht, which was taken under tow and eventually entered Mount's Bay where the pilot cutter took her into Newlyn.

KING John Edward, Coxswain, Bridlington Lifeboat   **BRONZE**

9 May 1968

4–5 February 1968: In snow and sleet with 16 degrees of frost, the Hamburg coaster s.s. *Maria F* dragged her anchors about one mile east by south of Bridlington Harbour, Yorkshire. The Oakley class lifeboat *William Henry and Mary King* launched at 4.34 p.m. with Second Coxswain John Simpson in charge. With heavy seas sweeping the coaster, it was impossible to put a man on board. The lifeboat returned to harbour at high water and embarked the Coxswain, who had just returned from a day's leave. With the coaster grounded and pounding badly, the lifeboat put out, anchored and veered down but, once again, was defeated by the conditions. It was therefore decided to try to approach the casualty from a new position. While manoeuvring, both propellers fouled on the anchor cable. After one had been cleared, the lifeboat returned to the beach where the other was freed. Putting out again, she found conditions too bad to remain alongside for rescue except that the coaster's cook – a woman – jumped, was injured and had to be taken ashore. In improving conditions, a tug was sent for and the lifeboat stood by until it arrived. The lifeboat had been at sea in appalling conditions and sub-zero temperatures for more than 20 hours.

JAPPY George Alexander, Coxswain, Buckie Lifeboat   **BRONZE**

9 May 1968

21 February 1968: The reserve Watson class lifeboat *George and Sarah Strachan* put out at 1.05 p.m. to the motor fishing vessel *Mistletoe* aground off the mouth of the River Spey, rolling and pounding 350 yards from the beach. Three other fishing vessels were standing by but two attempts

to set up a tow with one of them failed when each time the line parted. The *Mistletoe*'s crew refused to use the breeches buoy rigged from the shore. Coxswain Jappy took the lifeboat alongside and the six men jumped from the coaster. They were landed at Buckie at 4.50 p.m.

KIRKPATRICK Daniel, Coxswain, Longhope Lifeboat   **SILVER(3)**

19 September 1968

1 April 1968: The Grimsby trawler *Ross Puma* went on shore on the island of Hoy in the Orkneys, in a north-westerly wind approaching gale force with heavy sleet and snow. The Watson class lifeboat *T.G.B.* put out at 2.56 a.m. to find the casualty on the Little Rackwick Shoals about 50 yards off shore under high cliffs. Coxswain Kirkpatrick anchored to windward and veered down to within 20 yards, but attempts to take off the crew by rocket line failed. Although in danger from rocks, the lifeboat brought off 15 fishermen by hauling them across the gap between the two boats on a liferaft. First seven men, then eight men were rescued and landed at Longhope at 6.30 a.m.

SCOTT Lionel Derek, Coxswain, Mumbles Lifeboat   **BRONZE**

14 November 1968

3 October 1968: The Watson class reserve lifeboat *Cunard* launched at 0.25 a.m. in squally weather to help the sand dredger *Steepholm*, which had gone aground with a crew of seven men on Tusker Rock, near Porthcawl, Glamorgan. During her approach, the dredger's crew took to the liferafts and, nearing the casualty, Coxswain Scott altered course towards the Ogmore River where he considered that the rafts would have drifted. Coming up with the roped together rafts, and helped by the Porthcawl inshore rescue boat, six men were taken on before the lifeboat returned to the dredger and took off the Master at the second attempt. All survivors were landed at Swansea, and the lifeboat returned to Mumbles at 5.45 a.m.

OFFER Eric Thomas, Coxswain/Mechanic, Dun Laoghaire Lifeboat   **BRONZE**

18 September 1969

15 June 1969: In windy, squally weather, very heavy rain and intense darkness, an 18 stone, 62 year old man was thrown into water when his dinghy overturned while rowing to his yacht in Dun Laoghaire harbour. Another man who had also been capsized in a dinghy tied him to a motor cruiser for safety and swam ashore for help. Coxswain Offer drove to the coal pier, climbed down to the dredger moored alongside, and crossed over a motor boat to get to a 15 foot dinghy. The other man (weight 15 stone) who had sought help fell into the water and had to be dragged into the dinghy. Mr Offer sheared off to the motor cruiser and the older man was hauled in, but the dinghy sank under the combined weights of the three men. The Coxswain swam with the older man to the motor boat and secured him to it then, with great difficulty pulled both men on board. After a rest, all were able to climb ashore.

STEWART Robert Wade, Crew Member, Amble Inshore Lifeboat   BRONZE
SCOTT Andrew Barton, Crew Member, Amble Inshore Lifeboat   BRONZE
HENDERSON William, Coxswain, Amble Lifeboat   BRONZE
STEWART James, Crew Member, Amble Lifeboat   BRONZE

15 January 1970

29 September 1969: R.A.F. Pinnace *No. 1386* capsized about half a mile from north pier head while trying to enter Amble Harbour, Northumberland, in a heavy swell. The D class inshore lifeboat made for the pinnace at 6.34 p.m. and the Watson class lifeboat *Millie Walton* put out at 6.39 p.m. with some non-lifeboatmen among her crew. When two men were spotted clinging to a lifebuoy, the inflatable lifeboat went in through heavily breaking water, hauled them on board and took them to the harbour. The lifeboat reached the scene and found one man with seas breaking over him clinging to the pinnace. As Coxswain Henderson went alongside, James Stewart jumped on to the hull of the casualty and helped the man into the rescue boat. Knocking was heard from inside the pinnace and as she could not be righted, it was towed into harbour where, after a number of unsuccessful attempts, the one man in the wreck was cut free. Three bodies were recovered later from among the rocks.

The awards to Robert Stewart and Andrew Scott were the first medals for a service carried out in an inshore lifeboat.

BRYAN John, Coxswain, Great Yarmouth and Gorleston Lifeboat   BRONZE

15 January 1970

9–10 November 1969: In a gale, rough sea and heavy swell, the Watson class lifeboat *Khami* left her moorings at 7.35 p.m. to help the Danish m.v. *Karen Bravo* which was hove to with her cargo shifted and with engine trouble. She was found in the vicinity of Cross Sand lightvessel at 9.35 p.m., and Coxswain Bryan noticed that she was pitching heavily with a list of 20 degrees and with heavy seas breaking over her bows. The wind was now gusting to force ten over a very rough, confused sea and heavy swell, a situation worsened by intense cold and rain squalls. In seven approaches, five men were taken off, and the lifeboat stood by as the motor vessel's Master corrected her list and brought her into Gorleston harbour at 3 a.m.

SHEADER William, Coxswain, Scarborough Lifeboat   SILVER

15 January 1970

23 November 1969: Shortly after noon, the yacht *Sheena*, a converted ship's lifeboat, overturned in South Bay pitching the occupants into the sea. The Oakley class lifeboat *J.G. Graves of Sheffield* launched through rough seas, a north-easterly wind and in overcast conditions. The first survivor was recovered from a rock-strewn area after the lifeboat had filled several times. He was in such a bad condition that he had to be landed at once. Coxswain Sheader then brought another man ashore who, unfortunately, died soon afterwards. After efforts to find a third man proved unsuccessful, the two fishing vessels were escorted into the harbour, one of them under tow.

WALSH Dermot, Coxswain, Valentia Lifeboat **SILVER**

16 June 1970

20–21 February 1970: The 650 ton Limerick m.v. *Oranmore*, in distress with her engines broken down, lay nine miles north-north-west of Brandon Head, Co. Kerry, Ireland, in a rough sea and a heavy Atlantic swell. The Barnett class lifeboat *Rowland Watts* with Coxswain Walsh in charge slipped her moorings at 6.05 p.m., began a 42 mile journey and arrived at 11.15 p.m., in darkness. Two hours later, with the lifeboat still standing off the stricken vessel,the Master signalled he wished some of his crew taken off. The lifeboat made its first run in, snatching one man, then two more in a similar run. After the decision had been made to abandon ship completely, a nylon rope was passed and the lifeboat taken alongside enabling seven men to jump, in turn, to safety. The Mate fell into the sea and, although he was recovered, died. With her port propeller fouled by a rope, the lifeboat made for Kilrush Harbour landing the ten men and the body at 6.15 a.m.

LETHBRIDGE Matthew (Junior), Coxswain, St. Mary's Lifeboat **SILVER(2)**
GUY Ernest Roy, Second Coxswain, St. Mary's Lifeboat **BRONZE(2)**
BURROW William Richard, Mechanic, St. Mary's Lifeboat **BRONZE(2)**

16 June 1970

21 February 1970: North of the Isles of Scilly, the 450 ton Lidkoping (Sweden) m.v. *Nordanhav* was in trouble, listing heavily in squally weather, a very rough sea and heavy swell with poor visibility. The Watson class lifeboat *Guy and Clare Hunter* launched and found that H.M.S. *Ulster* was standing by the completely helpless casualty and illuminating her by searchlight. Down by the head, the motor vessel was listing badly in an unstable condition. Coxswain Lethbridge closed without delay and kept his boat alongside skilfully, enabling all of the ten man crew to transfer. They all landed at St. Mary's at 1.02 p.m. after a 35 mile passage and a 12 hour service.

HARLAND William, Coxswain, Whitby Lifeboat **BRONZE**

9 September 1970

15 July 1970: The Watson class lifeboat *Mary Ann Hepworth* launched at 5.10 a.m. to the fishing vessel *Gannet* and reached the casualty half an hour later to find the engine swamped and the rudder jammed. Although conditions at sea were very bad, the two man crew refused to leave, and Coxswain Harland decided to tow the fishing vessel to Scarborough, Yorkshire; however the two men had to be taken off as the vessel began to fill with water. At 8.30 a.m. the Scarborough lifeboat met the Whitby boat, still towing the casualty, but shortly afterwards the tow line parted and the fishing vessel was left adrift to be recovered later in the day.

MADDRELL Alfred Dennis, B.E.M., Coxswain, Port Erin Lifeboat **BRONZE**

9 December 1970

9 September 1970: At 6 a.m., the coaster s.s. *Moonlight* was reported to be in trouble five miles north of Chicken Rock, the southernmost point of the Isle of Man. The Watson class lifeboat *Matthew Simpson* launched in a south-south-westerly gale, very rough sea with poor visibility and through worsening squalls. A liferaft sighted by an aircraft was found to be empty when the

lifeboat arrived. About 11 a.m., another raft was sighted and this was secured alongside. The two occupants were found to be the sole survivors and in a very poor condition. After a very difficult operation, they were brought into the lifeboat, which headed for Port Erin where they landed at 1 p.m.

HARDY Ronald James, Coxswain, Swanage Lifeboat   **BRONZE**

9 December 1970

12 September 1970: After returning from a previous service, most of the crew of the Rother class lifeboat *J. Reginald Corah* were still in the boathouse when they were asked to launch again. She slipped her moorings at 5 p.m. A youth was trapped by the rising tide in a cave to the west of Blacker's Hole where the lifeboat arrived half an hour later to find a big swell breaking heavily at the foot of the cliff, its backwash creating a nasty, confused sea. The youth was standing on a ledge at the back of the cave, the floor was awash and covered with boulders. After the lifeboat had veered down as near as possible, he was brought out using the inflatable dinghy.

WHITTLE Stephen, Coxswain, Dunmore East Lifeboat   **SILVER**

10 March 1971

25 November 1970: The fishing boat *Glenmalure* was about to drive into Hook Head, the southernmost point of Co. Wexford, Ireland; the foul weather and cross seas were so violent that they alone damaged her bilge keel. When Coxswain Whittle arrived on the scene in the Watson class lifeboat *Douglas Hyde*, he found that the fishing boat was just 50 yards from the rocks with her crew on their liferaft. In spite of possible danger from trailing ropes and nets, he took his boat alongside the liferaft twice and removed three men; another man had been swept away and an extended search for him was to no avail. The skipper of the *Glenmalure* was also the Coxswain of Kilmore Quay lifeboat.

BRUNTON David, Crew Member, Dunbar Lifeboat   **BRONZE**

10 March 1971

23 December 1970: It was very cold with rain and a southerly gale when a youth reported that his brother had been washed off the rocks at the entrance to Dunbar Harbour, East Lothian. The Watson class lifeboat *Margaret* slipped her moorings at 2.20 p.m., negotiated the narrow entrance in a very heavy swell with a rough confused sea, and then headed for the scene where a man was sighted face down in the water supported by the air trapped in his clothes. Because it was difficult for the boat to get close to the casualty, David Brunton dived in and swam to the man and supported him. After getting into difficulties himself, a second crew member jumped into the sea and facilitated the rescue of both men.

HODDER John Leslie, Crew Member, Lyme Regis Inshore Lifeboat   **BRONZE**

10 November 1971

14 March 1971: While working on The Cobb at Lyme Regis, John Hodder heard cries for help; the inflatable lifeboat being out of action, he ran around the harbour to alert the Skipper and owner of the motor fishing vessel *Barbarella*. The vessel put out at 7.40 p.m. in a north-westerly

wind and short choppy sea. The Skipper's son and another boy had been out in their fishing dinghy hauling pots but had got into difficulties. About 500 yards offshore, the Skipper's son was seen in the water; John Hodder dived overside followed immediately by the boy's father, who had to be rescued a short time later. Mr. Hodder was then found supporting the boy and, cold and exhausted, they were landed without delay. Extensive searches by the vessel together with another fishing boat, the Exmouth lifeboat and a naval helicopter failed to find the other boy.

SCOTT Lionel Derek, B.E.M., Mumbles Lifeboat SILVER(2)
9 June 1971

12 April 1971: Leaving his wife to call out the inflatable lifeboat, Coxswain Scott put out in a dinghy fitted with an outboard motor to assist a boy reported clinging to an upturned canoe drifting out to sea towards Mumbles Head, Glamorgan. In poor weather and turbulent, confused seas, he drove the unstable dinghy towards the boy who, by now, was very exhausted. Coxswain Scott unshipped the outboard, took him on board, then re-shipped the engine and headed shorewards. The inflatable lifeboat came up with them and took the casualty on board, retrieved the canoe and together with the dinghy returned to shore.

STOCKFORD John Henry, Crew Member, Barmouth Inshore Lifeboat SILVER
PUGH Colin, Crew Member, Barmouth Inshore Lifeboat SILVER
HAWORTH Robert Airdrie, Doctor. Honorary Medical Adviser, Barmouth SILVER
9 September 1971

21 June 1971: After falling over the cliffs at Friog, Merioneth, south of the Afan Mawddach Estuary, a woman was lying 80 feet below, badly injured, in a small cove cut off by the rising tide. As it was impossible to get the woman up the cliff, the D class inflatable lifeboat was launched at 4.03 p.m., backed up by the Barmouth lifeboat. With the surf and waves breaking over her, the lifeboat beached and landed Dr. Haworth. The casualty was attended to and strapped into a mountain rescue stretcher and then carried to an adjoining cove where it was easier for the inshore lifeboat to beach and take off the woman. She was landed at the Friog end of Fairbourne beach and was handed over to a waiting ambulance at 5 p.m. but she died about five hours later.

TRIGGS Harold, Coxswain, Hoylake Lifeboat BRONZE
8 December 1971

27 August 1971: In a strong west-north-westerly wind and a very heavy, steep breaking sea, the Liverpool class lifeboat *Thomas Corbett* launched at 10.27 a.m. She followed a route around Hilbre Island, through Welshman's Gut, and headed for a small boat off West Hoyle Bank. On reaching the position nothing could be seen of the *Diane* but the top of her wheelhouse down to the grab rails to which two men were clinging desperately. Coxswain Triggs took the lifeboat through the shallow water across the bank and came up with the wreck, where the first survivor was brought safely on board. The other man, however, would not let go of the rail but on a second run he was snatched from his position by two members of the lifeboat crew. Although holed and flooded, the lifeboat returned to Hilbre and landed the two men.

BURNS John Gilbert Victor, Helmsman, Trearddur Bay Inshore Lifeboat   **BRONZE**
WILLIAMS Edmund Michael Owen, Crew Member,
  Trearddur Bay Inshore Lifeboat   **BRONZE**

10 November 1971

2 September 1971: In bad sea conditions with a south-west wind, a dinghy capsized about 50–100 yards south-west of Cod Rocks, Trearddur Bay, Holy Island, Anglesey. The D class inflatable lifeboat left Porth Diana by the northern channel and by the time the casualty was reached it had been righted only to capsize again. With both survivors clinging to it, the dinghy was drifting towards Cod Rocks. An attempt to pull her clear of the surf was unsuccessful, so the lifeboat turned and picked up one man without difficulty then, in spite of heavy backwash, brought out the second.

FORREST Donald Malcolm, Mechanic, Holyhead Lifeboat   **BRONZE**
JONES Gareth Ogwen, Crew Member, Holyhead Lifeboat   **BRONZE**
HUGHES John Michael, Crew Member, Holyhead Lifeboat   **BRONZE(2)**

8 December 1971

3–4 September 1971: At 10.25 p.m., the Barnett class lifeboat *St. Cybi (Civil Service No. 9)* launched in response to red flares fired by the yacht *Sinbad*, six miles north of the Skerries, off the north-west of Anglesey. During his approach, Coxswain Jones was told that a man on the casualty had suffered a heart attack and refused to be moved as he had been provided with oxygen equipment by the *Friesian Express* which had reached the casualty first. A member of the yacht's crew shouted that three unconscious men were trapped below. The lifeboat went alongside and five crew members were transferred to the casualty. In difficult and dangerous circumstances, in confined spaces, an unconscious man was rescued from the main cabin, one from a small forward cabin and another from the heads. The unconscious heart patient was strapped into a Neil Robertson stretcher, then moved from the main cabin with great difficulty. All four men were landed at Holyhead at 4 a.m. Carbon monoxide poisoning resulting from a cracked exhaust pipe together with a calor gas leak were the reasons why the crew lost consciousness.

POCKLEY George Robert, Coxswain, Flamborough Lifeboat   **BRONZE**

8 December 1971

22 September 1971: A small boat, apparently unmanned, was seen floating close to the cliffs near Bempton, Yorkshire. In hazy weather, an east-south-easterly wind and a moderate swell, the Liverpool class lifeboat *Friendly Forester* launched at 8.05 p.m. Coxswain Pockley reached the scene and found two men and a dog stranded on shore, after being thrown out in the breakers when trying to land under the cliffs. Despite the configuration of the cliffs making a rescue by that route very difficult, Coxswain Pockley took in the lifeboat. By means of a breeches buoy and a crewman who swam ashore, both men and the dog were brought to safety and landed at Flamborough.

FOX John Alfred, Coxswain, Shoreham Harbour Lifeboat BRONZE

12 January 1972

19 October 1971: In worsening weather, the drilling rig *William Allpress* was anchored three-quarters of a mile off Rustington, Sussex, awaiting a tug to tow it to Portsmouth. It was necessary to take off the crew, who had had no food or sleep for three days and were suffering from sea sickness. The Watson class lifeboat *Dorothy and Philip Constant* launched at 2.10 p.m. in a very heavy sea and a swell and a south-westerly gale with generally very poor visibility. Because of the irregular shape of the casualty and with heavy seas breaking over her, Coxswain Fox circled the rig to assess the situation. Finally with all fenders made up into one large fender, he put his bow alongside until four men had been pulled on board. Repeating this manoeuvre, the Master was also saved. The lifeboat headed back to Shoreham and reached there after three hours at sea.

DENNISON Robert Hunter, Staff Coxswain, Kirkwall Lifeboat BRONZE

8 March 1972

8 November 1971: In deteriorating weather conditions, the 70-foot Clyde class lifeboat *Grace Paterson Ritchie* went to the aid of the Danish fishing vessel *Clupea* which had broken adrift and was aground to the east of Kirkwall pier. Other Danish fishing vessels also broke away and in the end the lifeboat also saved the *Rosslau*, the *Anne Stranne*, the *Kami* and a total of 20 fishermen. First the *Rosslau* and *Anne Stranne* were towed clear of Kirkwall pier, then Coxswain Dennison anchored and veered down, made contact with the *Clupea* and towed her down to the *Rosslau* which took over the tow. The operation was then repeated to tow out the *Kami*. All four vessels then took shelter at Shapinsay.

KING John Edward, Coxswain, Bridlington Lifeboat BRONZE(2)

8 March 1972

24 January 1972: The Oakley class lifeboat *William Henry and Mary King* launched at 4.30 a.m. into a southerly near gale and rough sea to the motor fishing vessel *My Suzanne*, which, with her engines failed, was drifting helplessly on to the shore under Sewerby cliffs, near Flamborough, Yorkshire. Anchoring near the casualty, Coxswain King veered down towards the casualty, fired a rocket over her and passed a line followed by a cable. Setting up the tow, the fishing vessel was found to have broached broadside to the beach, rolling and grinding her bilges on the rocky bottom, but, as the lifeboat took the strain, the casualty's engine was started and she was pulled clear. At this stage, the cable fouled the lifeboat's port propeller but, using the starboard one, the lifeboat escorted the vessel into harbour.

PAVEY Alfred Thomas, Coxswain, Weymouth Lifeboat BRONZE

14 June 1972

4–5 February 1972: The gas tanker *Methane Princess* reported the Yacht *Nomis* in distress off Portland Bill, with the skipper in need of medical attention. The Barnett class lifeboat *Frank Spiller Locke* left her moorings at 10 p.m. with the Honorary Medical Adviser on board. A south-south-east gale was blowing over a very rough sea, and the *Methane Princess* reported that she had had to abandon her tow. Reaching the casualty shortly after midnight, Coxswain Pavey took the lifeboat alongside allowing the bowman and Dr. Parkinson to jump on board. As it was impossible to transfer the Skipper to the lifeboat, the Coxswain decided to tow the yacht to Weymouth. He took a route to avoid the Portland Race, and for a while the *Methane Princess* provided a lee by steaming alongside. Near the Shambles Lightship, the lifeboat turned for Weymouth, and the tanker continued on passage up Channel. With conditions a little easier, the lifeboat and the *Nomis* reached harbour at 3.30 a.m.

HELMER Martin, Crew Member, Southwold Inshore Lifeboat   **BRONZE**

PILE Patrick, Crew Member, Southwold Inshore Lifeboat   **BRONZE**

8 March 1972

6 February 1972: Early in the morning, Mr. Pile saw a small fibre-glass dinghy heading out of Southwold harbour, Suffolk, with four people on board and, anticipating trouble in the strong east-south-easterly wind and heavy seas, he rushed to the lifeboat house where he found Mr. Helmer. They launched the D class inflatable lifeboat at 10.13 a.m. and headed into the sea. The dinghy was found upturned between the harbour and Walberswick, with four bodies floating nearby, two boys of 13 and 16, a youth 18 years and a man weighing 18 stone. All four were dragged into the lifeboat, which made for Walberswick beach where two fishermen helped to land the bodies. The boys and the youth were revived, but the man, their father, was dead on arrival at hospital.

WOOD Reuben, Coxswain, Aldeburgh Lifeboat   **BRONZE**

14 June 1972

10 April 1972: With all local fishing boats returned except one, the Watson (Beach) class lifeboat *The Alfred and Patience Gottwald* launched at 10.10 a.m. into a very rough sea with a gale and frequent heavy squalls. She came up with the motor fishing vessel *Ocean Pride* approaching treacherous shoals one mile south of Aldeburgh. Heading towards the beach, the fishing vessel crossed the outer shoal, but was overwhelmed by a huge wave on the inner shoal and sank. Coxswain Wood took his lifeboat straight to the spot and picked up two of the crew immediately. The third crew member was recovered only after skilful manoeuvring of the lifeboat.

BROWN Walter Lewis, Coxswain, Falmouth Lifeboat   **BRONZE**

8 November 1972

8 August 1972: In a very rough sea and a gale, the Swedish schooner *Mina* was drifting on to a lee shore under Dodman Point, near Mevagissey. The relief Watson class lifeboat *The Princess Royal (Civil Service No. 7)* launched at 4.10 a.m., and reached the casualty at 6 a.m. A first attempt at a tow failed, and the assistance of a tug was requested. When the *Mina*'s anchor cable parted at 7.30 a.m., the lifeboat immediately went alongside, took off eight of the crew, including four girls, and left two crew on board. A tow line was established and the lifeboat was able to hold the position of the *Mina* off Dodman Point until the tug arrived at 9.45 a.m. The tow was transferred and Falmouth harbour finally reached at 3.30 p.m.

GIBBIN Douglas, Crew Member, Hartlepool Inshore Lifeboat **BRONZE**

14 February 1973

1 October 1972: When a sailing dinghy capsized in a fresh wind and choppy sea by the break-water at North Gare, Hartlepool, Co. Durham, the Atlantic 21 rigid inflatable lifeboat put out but was unable to approach the casualty because of the confused sea. Mr. Gibbin jumped into the sea and supported one survivor until he could be rescued. Some delay was experienced when the lifeboat had engine trouble, which left Gibbin in the water for a considerable time. The second occupant of the dinghy was rescued from the breakwater by members of the local fire brigade.

LEITH George, Coxswain, Lerwick Lifeboat **SILVER**

14 February 1973

13 December 1972: In storm conditions with the wind blowing over a very rough sea, two trawlers came adrift in Lerwick Harbour, Shetland Isles, and went aground on Bressey Island. One of them refloated, but the other, *Granton Osprey*, remained hard aground. The Barnett class life boat *John Gellatly Hyndman*, temporarily on station, put out at 6.40 p.m. and less than 20 minutes later was hove to off the casualty. Coxswain Leith twice brought the lifeboat in, bow on, and took off the nine men although, at times, completely enveloped in solid water.

MACKAY Malcolm, Acting Coxswain, Islay Lifeboat **BRONZE**

14 March 1973

25 December 1972: The 200 ton Greenock coaster *Raylight* reported she had broken down five miles north of Skervuile, sound of Jura. The reserve Watson class lifeboat *Mabel Marion Thompson* launched at 4.15 a.m. into a south east gale and very rough sea. At 7.30 a.m. the coaster was found at anchor some 500 yards from the shore, and, as a tug was reported on the way, the lifeboat decided to stand by. At 11.30 a.m. the tug abandoned the attempt to reach the *Raylight* as the weather was too bad. A German vessel the *Alexandra S* had also arrived on the scene, and the lifeboat helped fix up a tow between the two ships which broke soon after. The lifeboat continued to stand by until at 3.35 p.m. the *Raylight* was only 115 yards from shore. The crew of three them took to a rubber dinghy and, with fine seamanship, Coxswain Mackay manoeuvred the lifeboat so that the men could be plucked from the dinghy. At 4 p.m. the lifeboat set out on the 22 mile journey to Port Askaig, and arrived there at 7 p.m.

LESLIE Jack, Coxswain, Longhope Lifeboat **BRONZE**

11 April 1973

9–10 February 1973: Shortly before midnight, the trawler *Ross Tern* went ashore on Tarf Tail, Swona Island in the Pentland Firth. Six of her crew took to the liferaft, and five others remained on board, clinging to her superstructure. The Solent class lifeboat *The David and Elizabeth King and E.B.* slipped her moorings in a gentle breeze and smooth sea, although there were frequent snow showers. In confused seas, a moderate swell having arisen, the survivors were taken from the raft. Coxswain Leslie then brought the lifeboat's bow against the trawler's transom stern in a very restricted channel and enabled the five men to be taken off safely. All the 11 men were landed at St. Margaret's Hope on South Ronaldshay at 2.30 a.m. in heavy snow showers.

MACKAY Malcolm, Coxswain, Islay Lifeboat **BRONZE(2)**

10 October 1973

27–30 March 1973: The 1,100 ton coastal tanker *Olga*, in passage from Liverpool to Bergen, Norway, went aground on Bhride Island (Eilean Bhride) off the south-east coast of Isla, Inner Hebrides, on the evening of the 27th, and the reserve Watson class lifeboat *Mabel Marion Thompson* put out in a fresh breeze, moderate sea and overcast conditions with a 14 mile passage ahead of her. At 0.27 a.m. on the 28th, Coxswain Mackay conned the lifeboat alongside the tanker and whilst three of the crew jumped into his boat, the remainder stayed on board. He stood by but, after a few hours, the three insisted that they be landed as soon as possible, and he took them to Ardbeg pier at 7.15 a.m. He returned to the casualty while a tug made attempts to tow her off. When these proved unsuccessful, the Master still refused to leave his ship. The lifeboat, after standing by, returned first to Port Ellen early on the 29th, and proceded later to Port Askaig, where her crew stood down after having been on duty 38 hours. The weather in the casualty area worsened, the lifeboat launched again then, at 1.30 a.m. on the 30th, started to take off the survivors in an operation made more difficult by the ship's Master who by now needed a stretcher. Nevertheless, all seven men were landed safely at Port Askaig at 6.05 a.m.

KING John Edward, Coxswain, Bridlington Lifeboat **SILVER**

13 November 1973

2 April 1973: In north-north-easterly storm force winds accompanied by a rough sea, the Grimsby vessel *White Knight* was dragging her anchor near the South Smithic Buoy off Hornsea, Yorkshire. The Oakley class lifeboat *William Henry and Mary King*, which had launched previously to deal with another vessel, was diverted to the *White Knight,* which was heading into a hurricane after leaving the shelter of the Smithic Shoal in reduced visibility. The fishing vessel was sighted lying broadside on to the seas and rolling heavily, but, by 1.06 p.m., Coxswain King had gone alongside and five men had been taken off. Because of the horrific conditions the Coxswain had to nurse his boat back to Bridlington in the bitter cold and reached the harbour at 3.48 p.m.

GROVE John Walter, Helmsman, Horton and Port Eynon Inshore Lifeboat **BRONZE**

10 October 1973

2 July 1973: Four persons stranded on Worms Head (Penrhyn-gwyr), at the southern end of Rhossili Bay, Glamorgan, were trying to swim to the mainland against a strong flood tide. The D class inflatable lifeboat was launched at 6.20 p.m. Realising the urgency of their task, Helmsman Grove took his boat close inshore into broken water where the swimmers were becoming separated, and three of the four were picked up. One of them, an apparently lifeless 20 year old girl, needed medical attention urgently therefore the Helmsman took his craft through the heavy surf and past jagged rocks into a gully, where the swimmers were landed. The fourth person was rescued by rocket line.

PEARSON Benjamin, Helmsman, North Berwick Inshore Lifeboat **BRONZE**
RUSSELL Alexander, Crew Member, North Berwick Inshore Lifeboat **BRONZE**

12 December 1973

26 July 1973: Bathers in East Bay, to the east of North Berwick Harbour and some 500 yards from the lifeboat station, were reported to be in difficulties. The D class inflatable lifeboat *Blue Peter III* (one of the lifeboats provided by the sale of paperback books collected by viewers of the programme) launched at 3 p.m. and shortly after a man was spotted close to the rocks, struggling in the heavy swell. With difficulty he was hauled aboard. During the rescue two very heavy seas hit the ILB in succession, and the survivor was injured in the shoulder. Another man was noticed floundering in the water, but by the time *Blue Peter III* reached the position he had disappeared. No trace of him was found. The survivor was then landed, and the ILB, with an extra crew member (James Pearson) on board, returned to search unsuccessfully until 4.30 p.m.

 T*he three crew members received Blue Peter's gold badge, its highest award for outstanding achievement, during the broadcast on 20 December 1973.*

WILLACY Keith, Helmsman, Morecambe Inshore Lifeboat **BRONZE**

10 October 1973

4 August 1973: Off the oil jetty in Heysham harbour, Lancashire, two men were adrift in a small dinghy with a south-westerly gale blowing, short steep seas and limited visibility. They were sighted on a sandbank and, after the D class inflatable lifeboat found that she could get no nearer than 30 feet, Helmsman Willacy went over the side on a lifeline. After this proved unsuccessful, he shifted his anchorage and veered down through the surf to take the men on board.

FOX John Alfred, Coxswain, Shoreham Harbour Lifeboat **BRONZE(2)**

10 October 1973

5 August 1973: The Watson class lifeboat *Dorothy and Philip Constant* launched at 3.15 a.m. in a south-south-westerly gale and rough seas, and set course, with only 600 yards visibility, for the yacht *Albin Ballad*, which was broached to under bare poles with sails flapping in the water. Finding the casualty due south of Littlehampton, Sussex, with large waves breaking over her, and her three man crew seasick and exhausted, Coxswain Fox put the lifeboat's starboard bow against the yacht amidships which enabled two lifeboatmen to scramble on board. In spite of the tow parting once and being re-established, the yacht was finally towed into Shoreham harbour at 7.25 a.m.

FARO Dennis, Helmsman, Eastney Inshore Lifeboat **BRONZE**

13 November 1973

5 August 1973: At 5.40 p.m., the air-sea rescue helicopter having failed to lift two men from the yacht *Jo of Ryde* near Langstone bar, off Eastney, Portsmouth, the McLachlan lifeboat A 508 launched in south-south-westerly gale force winds. At the second attempt, Helmsman Faro placed his bow alongside, took off the two injured men, returned through very rough and confused seas and landed them at 6.20 p.m.

HOLMES William John Rees, Coxswain, Angle Lifeboat   **BRONZE**

10 October 1973

5–6 August 1973: In a south-south-westerly storm, rough seas and a heavy swell, the oil-tanker *Dona Marika* ran aground at Wooltack Point, Lindsway Bay, west of Milford Haven, Pembrokeshire. The Watson class lifeboat *Richard Vernon and Mary Garforth of Leeds* launched at 9.35 p.m. The tanker's cargo of high octane fuel precluded the use of rockets therefore, with the very grave risk of explosion, Coxswain Holmes went alongside seven times, but the marooned crew refused to leave. The lifeboat stood by until, with the conditions improved, rescue was achieved from the shore. The lifeboat was at sea for nine and a half hours.

JONES Donald, Helmsman, Rhyl Inshore Lifeboat   **BRONZE**

13 November 1973

7 August 1973: Two boys, cut off by the tide, were clinging to the perch which marked the sewer outfall between Rhyl and Prestatyn, Flintshire, half an hour before high tide. The D class inflatable lifeboat, which launched in a near westerly gale with heavy surf on the beach, filled with water immediately and ran down to the perch – a post with a cage on top – where the boys were clinging to the cage. Avoiding a submerged concrete wall and a groyne, Helmsman Jones approached the scene and both boys were taken off safely. With their added weights, the craft filled with water again, and had to be beached at Splash Point, half a mile to the west.

RICHARDSON Keith, Assistant Mechanic, Walton and Frinton Lifeboat   **BRONZE**
BARRETT Jack, Crew Member, Walton and Frinton Lifeboat   **BRONZE**

12 December 1973

15 August 1973: Returning from a call to the Kentish Knock lightvessel, the Watson class lifeboat *Edian Courtauld* was diverted at 9.47 p.m. Reaching Pye Sand, north of Stone Point in Walton Backwaters, Essex, she found a speedboat ashore with the lifejacketted occupants up to their waists in water. In the choppy seas and dark night, the lifeboat grounded about a cable from the casualty, where Keith Richardson and Jack Barrett went overside in their underclothing and lifejackets taking a line with them. Wading and swimming, they reached the speedboat to find two men, one with an artificial leg, two boys and a girl; all of them needed much reassurance. Returning to the lifeboat, Mr. Barrett helped in refloating her thus enabling the Coxswain to take her to within five yards of the casualty. The five persons were then taken on board and landed at Walton.

BERRY Michael Edward, Coxswain, St. Helier Lifeboat   **SILVER**

13 November 1973

18 September 1973: In a west-south-westerly gale, a very rough sea and heavy swell, the Watson class lifeboat *Elizabeth Rippon* slipped her moorings at 8.30 p.m., in heavy rain squalls and poor visibility, to assist the French yacht *Bacchus* at anchor and extensively damaged east of La Sambue rock, amidst many rocky outcrops. After grounding four times, the lifeboat was taken in by Coxswain Berry, and four men and two girls were removed from the yacht and three men were taken from a Fire Service Zodiac which was taken in tow (the Zodiac had launched from La Motte to assist the yacht, but sea conditions were too severe). All nine were landed at St. Helier at 10.10 p.m.

ROWLEY Thomas, Second Coxswain, Scarborough Lifeboat   **BRONZE**

13 November 1973

29–30 September 1973: In storm force north-north-westerly winds and very rough seas, the *Eun Mara an Tar*, an ex-harbour motor launch, was in difficulties off Castle Point, Scarborough, Yorkshire. The Oakley class lifeboat *J.G. Graves of Sheffield* launched at 11.35 p.m and found the casualty four miles off Clayton Bay, south-east of Scarborough, running before the weather, at the mercy of wind and sea, under power but with her steering gear broken down. Deciding that it would be too dangerous to attempt to take off her crew, Acting Coxswain Rowley took her in tow, but conditions were so severe that the tow line parted three times before harbour was reached at 2.46 a.m.

PIKE Barry John, Mechanic, Torbay Lifeboat   **SILVER**

8 May 1974

5 October 1973: The Hatch class inshore lifeboat slipped her moorings at 3.50 p.m. in a near south-south-easterly gale to help a woman in the sea off Meadfoot Beach, near Torquay, Devon. Very rough seas and shoal water prevented the lifeboat from closing on the casualty's estimated position, but Mechanic Pike, sighting the woman's body, jumped overboard fully clad to her rescue. Rough seas threw him on to the beach, but, although exhausted, he re-entered the sea several times until, near complete collapse, he succeeded in bringing her body ashore. She was found to be dead from a severe head injury.

FARRINGTON Arthur, Coxswain, Seaham Lifeboat   **BRONZE**

13 March 1974

11 November 1973: Eighteen anglers, fishing from the drum head of North Pier, Seaham, Co. Durham, were cut off at 4.30 p.m. and in danger of being swept off by heavy seas. The Oakley class lifeboat *The Will and Fanny Kirby* launched and although frequently thrown clear by the surge of confused seas and swell, Coxswain Farrington took the lifeboat into the corner where the drumhead joined the main pier, and the anglers, two or three at a time, jumped into her. One of them had to be rescued from the sea, but everybody was landed at 5.30 p.m. The Coxswain sustained a broken wrist and head injury when a particularly violent sea fell on the boat.

BARCLAY Paul S., Doctor, M.C., T.D., Honorary Secretary,
Cromer R.N.L.I.   **BRONZE**

13 March 1974

15 November 1973: The 300 ton deep sea trawler *Boston Jaguar* suffered a gas cylinder explosion, which left her 37 miles from Cromer, Norfolk, at night without steering gear, in a strong gale-force wind and very rough sea. Her Mate had died and a crew member had suspected internal injuries. Helicopter help could not be contemplated until daylight, and transfer to a nearby trawler was not to be countenanced. As four doctors in the area were either unavailable or had no sea experience, Dr. Barclay, although liable to seasickness, elected to go himself and boarded the trawler in very dangerous conditions to deal with the casualty. Both doctor and patient were flown off at 6.50 a.m.

GIBBS Kenneth Edward, Coxswain, Torbay Lifeboat **BRONZE**
10 July 1974

16–17 December 1973: In a strengthening wind, the Barnett class lifeboat *Princess Alexandra of Kent* slipped her moorings at 7.50 p.m. and set course for a position about 40 miles south-east of Torbay, Devon, where the Guernsey fishing vessel *Petit Michel* was lying, disabled with starboard beam to the wind. A solitary survivor remained on board. Bringing the lifeboat round to the windward side, Coxswain Gibbs sprayed storm oil on the waves, passed a lifejacket to the trawler and lay alongside for sufficient time to enable the man to jump on board. Abandoning the casualty, the lifeboat returned to Torbay at 7 a.m.

DARE John, Coxswain, Plymouth Lifeboat **BRONZE**
10 July 1974

16 January 1974: When the Danish coaster *Merc Enterprise* got into serious difficulties 23 miles south of Plymouth, Devon, the Barnett class lifeboat *Thomas Forehead and Mary Rowse* left Millbay Docks at 2.17 p.m. As the boat cleared the breakwater, she met a full hurricane and, crossing the Tinker Shoal, was swept continually by heavy breaking seas; her crew in the wheelhouse were up to their waists in water. Helicopters and a Russian trawler had by now recovered survivors, but, hearing the news that seven men were still missing, Coxswain Dare carried on and only called off the search at 5.20 p.m. on receipt of a direct order from the Deputy Launching Authority.

BROWN Albert, Coxswain, Workington Lifeboat **BRONZE**
10 April 1974

27–28 January 1974: The Watson class lifeboat *City of Edinburgh*, on temporary duty, cleared the harbour at 9.25 p.m. after the fishing vessel *Kia Ora* had reported that she had broken down off Hestan Island, at the mouth of Auchencairn Bay, Kirkcudbright, and was dragging her anchor in severe weather conditions. Finding the casualty half a mile north-east of the island, Coxswain Brown went alongside in extremely rough seas and sleet showers. At the second attempt, he took off six men and a ten year old boy and landed them at Workington at 2.05 a.m. At one moment during the rescue, the Coxswain had been thrown from the wheel by the violence of the storm.

HOUCHEN Michael Stafford, Staff Coxswain, Clovelly Lifeboat **BRONZE**
8 May 1974

6 February 1974: At 2.20 a.m., the Clyde class lifeboat *Charles H. Barrett (Civil Service No. 35)* slipped her moorings to go to the aid of the trawler *St. Pierre*, reported to be flooding with her pump unable to cope, 26 miles from Hartland Point, west of Clovelly. When sighted, the trawler did not appear to be in immediate danger of sinking and Coxswain Houchen felt that it would be best to tow her, with her crew on board, to an anchorage off Lundy Island in the Bristol Channel. A tow was passed at the third attempt, but two hours later the steep seas off Lundy Race stove in the trawler's transom and both vessels were in danger of broaching. A safe anchorage was reached about 10 a.m., the trawler was pumped out and she was then towed to Ilfracombe which they reached about 5 p.m.

TART Tom Richard, Coxswain, Dungeness Lifeboat SILVER
THOMAS Peter Edward, Assistant Mechanic, Dungeness Lifeboat BRONZE
8 May 1974

11 February 1974: Caught up in a violent south-south-westerly gale raging in the Channel, the 399 ton m.v. *Merc Texco*'s cargo shifted and a seaman's leg was badly crushed. Three attempts by a helicopter failed to lift him off. The Watson class lifeboat *Mabel E. Holland* launched over the beach at 5 p.m. in the worst conditions experienced up to that date. When he reached the motor vessel, Coxswain Tart had to manoeuvre alongside twice before the injured man could be taken off with the help of Peter Thomas, the first aider who had managed to scramble on board with a stretcher. After a rough passage, the lifeboat beached safely at Dungeness at 7.30 p.m.

FRYER Trevor, Helmsman, Tynemouth Inshore Lifeboat BRONZE
ARKLEY Frederick, Crew Member, Tynemouth Inshore Lifeboat BRONZE
8 May 1974

10 March 1974: After going to the boathouse in anticipation, two lifeboatmen launched the D class inflatable lifeboat at 3.43 p.m. after the tug *Northsider*, which had gone to help an oil exploration vessel, was driven on to rocks swept by breaking seas. With Trevor Fryer at the helm, a young boy was taken off the tug and landed. The inflatable lifeboat returned, escorted by the Tynemouth lifeboat, to find the tug now driven under the cliffs and in danger of breaking up. In three runs, the three crew members were taken off by the inshore boat and put aboard a police launch.

KNOTT Thomas Victor, Coxswain/Mechanic, Lowestoft Lifeboat BRONZE
GIBBONS Peter, Second Coxswain, Lowestoft Lifeboat BRONZE
10 July 1974

13 April 1974: The yacht *Sarina* dragged her anchor and went aground five cables east of Benacre Ness, south of Kessingland, Suffolk, in a north-easterly near gale with large breaking waves. In trying to reach her, the Watson class reserve lifeboat *Canadian Pacific* grounded twice, but Coxswain Knott took her close enough for Second Coxswain Gibbons to jump on board where he found two men and two women on the yacht totally exhausted by their passage from Dover. Peter Gibbons secured a towline by which the lifeboat brought out the casualty stern first into deeper water and then resecured the tow line at her bow. The yacht was taken to Hamilton Dock, Lowestoft.

BIRD Albert, Coxswain, Aberdeen Lifeboat SILVER
JACK Ian, Mechanic, Aberdeen Lifeboat SILVER
10 July 1974

13 April 1974: The Barnett class reserve lifeboat *Hilton Briggs* slipped her moorings, at 9.30 p.m. in light airs and a slight swell, to carry out a particularly dangerous service four and a half miles out to sea. The Leith trawler *Netta Croan* (268 tons), on passage from Granton to the fishing grounds, was circling out of control, burning fiercely over the entire stern so that her crew could neither stop her engines nor steer her. Approaching her, Coxswain Bird handed over the wheel to Mechanic Jack to enable him to command both deck and helm operations, then, with both vessels travelling at about nine knots, the lifeboat went alongside the forward end of the main deck and

took off 12 men within a minute. Throughout the whole operation, the lifeboat was threatened with fire, explosion and the possibility of being rammed. Later a search was made for a missing crew member who had fallen into the sea. He was not found.

BROWN Edward Beverley, Helmsman, New Brighton Inshore Lifeboat   **SILVER**

MIDDLETON Robin, Crew Member, New Brighton Inshore Lifeboat   **SILVER**

11 September 1974

9 June 1974: Shortly after midnight the Atlantic 21 lifeboat *B 509* launched in a strong westerly breeze, with two extra men on board, to assist the motor fishing vessel *E.B.H.*, anchored in confused seas on a sandbank near Perch Rock Light, New Brighton. As the lifeboat attempted to veer down to the casualty, the fishing vessel's cable parted and she drifted towards a submerged groyne. Helmsman Brown drove over the groyne on to the deck of the listing vessel and rescued two of her crew. Robin Middleton jumped on board and rescued a third man, who had an injured leg, from the rigging.

THOMAS Mervyn Lloyd, Helmsman, New Quay Inshore Lifeboat   **BRONZE**

22 January 1975

30 July 1974: Following a report that a small motor boat had been seen drifting about half a mile north of Trwyn-Croi, Cardigan, the D class inflatable lifeboat was launched at 5.43 p.m. Reaching the area, some four miles south of the station, the motor-boat, with one man on board, was sighted anchored about 150 yards from the base of the cliffs. Two men had swum ashore. One of them could be seen on a rock, exhausted, with surf breaking over him. The second man had reached the top of the cliff safely. Helmsman Thomas took the lifeboat in through rough confused sea, anchored and backed under power towards the cliff. Using oars, the lifeboat got close to the man who was taken on board with difficulty. Back at the motor boat, the owner refused to leave. The survivor, who was in poor shape, was landed at Cwmtydu, a mile to the north, and the lifeboat returned to the motor boat. It then stood by until the arrival of the New Quay offshore lifeboat at 7.05 p.m. which towed the motor boat to Llangranog, two miles south.

WILLIAMS David William, Crew Member, Aberdovey Inshore Lifeboat **BRONZE**

11 December 1974

10 August 1974: As the motor cabin cruiser *Lady Jane* was crossing Dovey Bar, off Aberdovey, Merioneth, a man was seen to fall overboard in a strong west-north-westerly wind and rough sea. Atlantic 21 rigid inflatable lifeboat *Guide Friendship I* launched and found the man suffering from exposure and shock, clinging to a life jacket. The lifeboat was informed that three children were still aboard the cruiser. Shortly after, wreckage was sighted on South Bank, one child was on the sandbank and two in the water. The lifeboat could not reach them in the shallow water, but David Williams waded and swam to the children and, with the help of another crew member, brought them ashore through heavy surf.

THAYERS Sydney Ronald Stanley, Helmsman,
   Eastney Inshore Lifeboat **BRONZE**
HAWKINS William Charles, Operational Swimmer,
   Eastney Inshore Lifeboat **BRONZE**
FARO Dennis, Crew Member, Eastney Inshore Lifeboat **BRONZE(2)**

13 November 1974

7 September 1974: The inflatable lifeboat *D 184* launched at 3.43 a.m. in south-south-westerly storm force winds with an overcast sky making the visibility poor. She pushed through very rough seas at full speed towards Langstone Channel, where the motor cruiser *Valon* was found with a man and his 11 year old son lashed in. By the light from a Coastguard mobile patrol on shore, the two were taken on board in a very difficult operation due to the cruiser snubbing her anchor and shipping seas over her bow. Because of the conditions, the return journey was completed at a very much slower pace.

JONES Griffith John, Coxswain, Porthdinllaen Lifeboat **BRONZE**

22 January 1975

20 September 1974: In a gale, the Porthdinllaen lifeboat, Watson class *Charles Henry Ashley*, launched after dark to search for two people lost from the tender of a yacht moored in the bay. Coxswain Jones, who was on leave, watched the launch with his 14 year old son, Eric, from a cliff and, in the light of a turning vehicle, spotted a man clinging to an isolated rock, north of the boathouse. They ran down, launched and manned the boarding boat. Negotiating extremely narrow channels in confused seas, they reached the exhausted man, pulled him a board and brought him to safety. An inscribed wrist watch was awarded to Coxswain Jones' son.

MARTIN John Herbert William, Coxswain/Mechanic, Hastings Lifeboat **SILVER**
WHITE George Douglas, Second Coxswain, Hastings Lifeboat **BRONZE**

22 January 1975

27 September 1974: The motor fishing vessel *Simon Peter* was in distress in the morning during a strong gale, two and a half miles south-west of Rye harbour, Sussex. It was raining heavily and large seas were breaking on the beach, but the reserve Oakley class lifeboat *Jane Hay* launched successfully from her carriage and engaged with the Dungeness lifeboat in a prolonged search guided by Lydd airport radar. She reached the fishing vessel at 12.42 p.m. to find her wheelhouse stove in. Amidst a worsening gale and mountainous seas and exercising supreme judgement and

seamanship, Coxswain Martin made two approaches. On the second approach, Second Coxswain White leaned across to the casualty and, at risk of being crushed, made fast the head-rope. The three crew were then dragged on board, the headrope was chopped away, and the lifeboat cleared the wreck.

BRYAN John, Coxswain/Mechanic,
   Great Yarmouth and Gorleston Lifeboat   **BRONZE(2)**

12 March 1975

13 December 1974: In gales which had sprung up overnight, a French tug was towing a barge carrying a 500 foot jack platform, when the tow was cut 45 miles east-south-east of Gorleston, Norfolk, by the 493 ton coaster m.v. *Biscaya*, bound from Rotterdam to the Humber with a cargo of sulphur. The Waveney class lifeboat *Khami* slipped her moorings at 1.54 a.m. and made good speed to the coaster, which was reached, listing and drifting to the south-south-east, at 6.30 a.m. The coaster was drifting with her steering gear out of action and, when her list increased to 45 degrees at 10.45 a.m., three of her crew took to the liferaft from which they were rescued by the lifeboat. Three men remained on board the casualty, so Coxswain Bryan took the lifeboat into her lee and removed them, just before she sank. The service was completed at 6.25 p.m.

DAVY Peter, Doctor, Honorary Medical Adviser, Hastings Lifeboat   **SILVER**

12 March 1975

23 December 1974: An explosion occurred in the morning on the Argentinian warship *Candido de Lasala*, off the coast of Sussex, and medical help was required. The Oakley class lifeboat *Jane Hay*, on temporary duty, launched with Dr. Davy on board. After the lifeboat had made one and a half miles through a fresh south-east by east breeze and a moderate sea, the doctor was taken on board a helicopter. He was smashed against the lifeboat's stern and washed into the sea but, after being recovered, he carried on to the warship and tended the casualties before being transferred with one of the wounded to hospital. He sustained seven broken ribs.

RICHARDS William Trevelyan, Coxswain, Penlee Lifeboat   **BRONZE**

10 September 1975

25 January 1975: West-south-west winds gusting to hurricane force were blowing when the crew of the motor vessel *Lovat* was reported to be abandoning ship 24 miles south-west of Lizard Point, Cornwall. The Watson class lifeboat *Solomon Browne* launched at 6.55 a.m. and, after leaving the shelter of the land, was subjected to violent conditions in poor visibility, but Coxswain Richards drove on at full speed. One of the helicopters co-operating in the search rescued two survivors but, tragically, 11 lives were lost. The arduous and unhappy task of recovering five of the bodies fell to the lifeboat, and they were landed at Newlyn after a service lasting seven and three-quarter hours.

SHEARER William, Helmsman, Berwick-on-Tweed Inshore Lifeboat   **BRONZE**

10 September 1975

31 May 1975: A trimaran capsized in a rough sea outside the Berwick-on-Sea harbour entrance

and the D Class inflatable lifeboat launched at 4.35 p.m. Reaching the scene, they first hauled an unconscious woman from the sea, who was not wearing a lifebelt. Two men clinging to the upturned hull reported that a second woman was trapped underneath. Speeding back to the harbour, the lifeboat landed the first woman and returned with an axe with which the trimaran's hull, by now driven ashore, was breached. The second woman was freed and was picked up by helicopter.

RUDDY Martin Charles. Boy Scout, 1st Ilfracombe Troop   **BRONZE**

8 October 1975

7 June 1975: In the afternoon, Martin Ruddy, a 14 year old Scout, was rowing his new 9 ft inflatable dinghy close to the shore on Tunnels Beach at Ilfracombe, when he saw a speedboat, half a mile to seaward, with her occupants signalling for help. Although he had been warned of the dangerous cross currents and rocks in the vicinity, he responded immediately and, after 20 minutes, reached the casualty, which was already sinking. He succeeded in getting the four people and a dog on board his dinghy, then made the arduous and dangerous trip back to the shore.

PETIT John Hubert, Coxswain, St. Peter Port Lifeboat   **BRONZE(2)**
ROBILLIARD John Harry, Emergency Mechanic, St. Peter Port Lifeboat   **BRONZE**

8 October 1975

15 July 1975: At 1.45 a.m. on completion of a service to a fishing vessel, the Arun class lifeboat *Sir William Arnold* left her moorings to assist the tanker m.v. *Point Law* aground on Le Puits Jervais on the extreme south-west tip of Alderney. As there was no immediate danger to the tanker's crew, Coxswain Petit waited until first light when, in gale force conditions, he held the lifeboat just clear of the rocks, while crew member Robilliard brought off six of the crew (one on a stretcher) in the lifeboat's inflatable dinghy; he rowed backwards and forwards on five exhausting occasions. The remaining six men were taken from the tanker by helicopter.

COATES Michael Raymond, Helmsman, Whitby Inshore Lifeboat   **BRONZE**

12 November 1975

25 July 1975: The D class inflatable lifeboat launched at 6.20 p.m. to help a man clinging to the crumbling cliff face near Saltwick Nab, close to Whitby, Yorkshire. He was in danger of losing his hold and of being swept away by the heavy, breaking sea. The lifeboat anchored off and, with crew member David Wharton remaining on board, Helmsman Coates swam to the foot of the cliff attached to a line and persuaded the man to slide down into the sea. They were then both hauled on board.

BOWRY Charles Henry, Coxswain/Mechanic, Sheerness Lifeboat   **BRONZE**

21 January 1976

16 August 1975: The Waveney class lifeboat *Helen Turnbull* slipped her moorings at 1.28 a.m., cleared Garrison Point, Sheerness, Kent and headed at full speed down Medway Channel towards West Barrow Buoy where the motor sailing yacht *Eladnit* had lost her rudder and gone aground in

a south-westerly near gale and heavy broken water. As there was danger that the lifeboat herself might ground, Coxswain Bowry anchored and two crew members were veered down in the inflatable dinghy. On learning that among the five people on board there were two children and two adults overcome by seasickness, the Coxswain towed off the casualty and transferred the crew to the lifeboat. The yacht was then towed to Sheerness.

HODGSON Brian William, Crew Member, Whitby Inshore Lifeboat   **BRONZE**

10 December 1975

18 August 1975: A report was received that a small boat had been swamped in rough seas 400 yards off shore, seaward of the Metropole Hotel, Whitby, Yorkshire, and her two man crew washed overboard. One man was seen in the water outside the line of breaking surf and a second man, a non-swimmer, on the edge of the surf. Crew member Hodgson entered the water to help the first man whilst the D class inflatable lifeboat went directly to the other. After rescuing this man, the first man and his rescuer were recovered just as they were about to be swept into the surf.

MORRIS Julian, Helmsman, Weston-super-Mare Inshore Lifeboat   **BRONZE**

10 December 1975

13 September 1975: On a very dark night, the McLachlan class lifeboat *A 504* launched at 10.31 p.m. in an easterly gale and rough sea with squally showers. A motor boat was reported wrecked at the base of a sheer cliff in a small cove, midway along the north side of the Brean Down peninsula, south-west of Weston-super-Mare, Somerset. The five men on board were now standing on a rocky ledge and were in danger of drowning in the rising tide. After making one run in through rough and confused seas, frequently grounding on submerged rocks , Helmsman Morris approached again and heaved a line ashore so that four men were hauled out to the lifeboat. The fifth man waded out, and all were landed at Ferry Stage, Uphill, at 11.20 p.m.

KENNETT David George, Coxswain/Mechanic,
    Yarmouth (Isle of Wight) Lifeboat   **SILVER**

21 January 1976

14 September 1975: The Oakley class lifeboat *The Earl and Countess Howe* launched in a gale and very heavy rain at 1.22 a.m. to the sloop *Chakya of Ardgour,* which was drifting in heavy confused seas seven miles south of the Needles Channel, Isle of Wight. When the lifeboat reached the area, the gale had increased to storm force and backed to the north. The yacht was moving violently but, with superb timing and expert seamanship, Coxswain Kennett went alongside twice and snatched off the five man crew. The weather did not ease on the way back and, with rescued and rescuers exhausted, cold and soaked, the lifeboat finally reached Yarmouth at 6.45 a.m.

BLOOM Frank, Coxswain, Walton and Frinton Lifeboat   **SILVER**

18 February 1976

14–15 September 1975: The yacht, the *Tsunami,* was in trouble on the south side of Long Sand, off Clacton-on-Sea, Essex, in a near gale and in overcast conditions with heavy rain. The Watson class lifeboat *Edian Courtauld* slipped her moorings at 4.42 p.m. Lying at anchor under bare spars, the yacht was reached at 6.52 p.m. Coxswain Bloom took his lifeboat alongside to take off three men, but the owner and another man refused to leave. A towline was passed on a second approach and the yacht was towed clear, taken up the Walton River and secured to a mooring at 4 a.m. The tow had lasted over nine hours at a speed of just over two knots.

LIDDON Arthur, Coxswain/Mechanic, Dover Lifeboat	**SILVER**
HAWKINS Anthony George,	
Second Coxswain/Assistant Mechanic, Dover Lifeboat	**BRONZE**

18 February 1976

1–2 December 1975: The 1,199 ton Cypriot coaster m.v. *Primrose*, loaded with phosphate, suffered a loss of steering gear in storm force winds gusting up to 100 miles per hour three miles east of the breakwater at Dover, Kent. Two cross-channel ferries gave help. The Waveney class lifeboat *Faithful Forester* slipped her mooring at 10.37 p.m. and set out for the casualty. She was laid over on her beam ends as she left the harbour. The crew of the coaster had managed to jury rig steering gear, but the violent weather was driving the vessel towards the Goodwin Sands. At 11.30 p.m., the lifeboat reached her and advised that a course should be steered for Dover. With no pilot or tug able to get out in the violent weather, Coxswain Liddon stayed on scene and, with the ferries, piloted the coaster into the harbour at 4.12 a.m.

KING Peter James, Crew Member, Calshot Lifeboat	**BRONZE**
SMITH Christopher James, Crew Member, Calshot Lifeboat	**BRONZE**
STREET John Anthony, Crew Member, Calshot Lifeboat	**BRONZE**

21 July 1976

29–30 January 1976: Just after 10 p.m., in responding to a call for help, an inshore rescue boat, a Boston whaler belonging to Hamble Rescue, was driven ashore on the saltings. She was en route from Hamble, Hampshire, to Ashlett Creek, when both engines failed as she tried to find the channel. The Keith Nelson type lifeboat *Ernest William and Elizabeth Ellen Hinde* slipped her moorings at 10.20 p.m., towed her inflatable boarding boat through a gale with sub-zero air temperatures and anchored at the entrance to Ashlett Creek. Using the boarding boat, crew members Peter King, Christopher Smith and John Street found the first casualty about 11 p.m. and took a man ashore. About 11.30 p.m. they sighted the Hamble Rescue boat and, taking turns, dragged their boat through the marsh. The two Hamble crew were taken on to the boarding boat which was then driven and hauled over the marsh back to the lifeboat, which was moored back at Calshot at 1.15 a.m.

BLAIR Alan, Crew Member, Aberystwyth Inshore Lifeboat	**BRONZE**

19 May 1976

22 February 1976:Two men were trapped inside the hull when the motor cruiser *Annabel II* capsized in heavy surf near the harbour entrance at Aberystwyth, Cardiganshire. At the time, the inflatable lifeboat was temporarily off service and cover was being provided by the motor fishing vessel *Western Seas*. She put out, manned by seven men, all but one of them lifeboat men, and found the casualty in a very heavy ground swell, surf and shallow water, off the north harbour arm. Crew member Blair, on a line but hampered by his clothing and lifejacket, reached the

upturned cruiser and, although there was no sign of life, dived three or four times in low visibility to reach the victims, but to no avail. He then fixed a tow line, and the *Western Seas* began to tow the motor cruiser but the tow broke and Alan Blair was then hauled on board. The cruiser later drove on shore where two bodies were recovered.

BEGG Charles, Acting Coxswain, Aberdeen Lifeboat **BRONZE**
21 July 1976

12 March 1976 The Barnett class lifeboat *Ramsay-Dyce,* with Second Coxswain Begg in command, slipped her moorings at 6.54 p.m. and headed for Aberdeen Bay, where the Leith motor fishing vessel *Karemma* was out of control, her steering gear broken down, in a near gale and rough, heavy seas. A tug had already abandoned her efforts because of damage, but Begg took the lifeboat alongside the fishing vessel, now driving towards the beach, and, in three runs, took off the five man crew. The lifeboat returned to station after one and a quarter hours.

WHITTLE Stephen, Coxswain/Mechanic, Dunmore East Lifeboat **BRONZE(2)**
17 November 1976

9 July 1976: An open boat was seen to go on to rocks near Falskirt Rock, off the southern coast of Co. Wexford, Ireland. The Waveney class lifeboat *St. Patrick* launched, and cleared the harbour at 3.05 a.m. in a heavy swell with the wind increasing to force five, accompanied by driving rain. The search and approach to the casualty were made more difficult by the large number of salmon nets and lobster pots in the area, but Coxswain Whittle brought the lifeboat into the very narrow and shallow channel, where a buoy was thrown to one man, who was hauled on board. There was no sign of the other crew member.

KNOTT Thomas Victor, Coxswain/Mechanic, Lowestoft Lifeboat **BRONZE(2)**
17 November 1976

16 August 1976: Michael Knott, the pilot cutter Coxswain, was in Lowestoft Bridge Control station when he heard a radio message that the harbour tug *Barkis* had overturned. He ran across the harbour bridge to his 16 knot cutter, and collected his father, Coxswain Knott, on the way. They arrived at the scene of the capsize at 8.40 a.m. and hauled a first survivor out of the water. A second survivor was seen, face down in the water. Coxswain Knott jumped into the sea, but, despite valiant efforts, could not get the man into the cutter. Michael Knott then got his father back on board. A third survivor was rescued from the sea and a fourth from the upturned hull of the tug.

DEW John, Crew Member, Torbay Lifeboat **BRONZE**
17 November 1976

23 August 1976: A speedboat was wrecked and went ashore under overhanging cliffs in Forest Cove, towards the northern end of Start Bay, Devon, ten miles south of Torbay. The temporary duty Barnett class lifeboat *Princess Alexandra of Kent* launched at 2.41 p.m. in a fresh easterly breeze producing rough seas and arrived in the cove at 4 p.m. to find six adults, eight children and

an Alsatian dog stranded on the beach. Crew member Dew swam ashore with a line. Pairing one adult with a child in the breeches buoy as far as possible, he swam beside them on seven journeys to the lifeboat. They were then landed at Dartmouth. A professional diver, John Dew acted as crew member whenever he was home on leave from Nigeria.

HENDY Frank, Boatman, Howth Yacht Club　　　　**BRONZE**

17 November 1976

28 August 1976: While a race from Abersoch, Cardigan, was being timed into Howth harbour, the yacht *Sula Bassana* grounded heavily about 11.30 p.m. when trying to pass inside the buoys marking rocks off the end of the East Pier. Frank Hendy, the Howth Yacht Club boatman and former lifeboat mechanic, put out in a launch with another man. Although a strong easterly breeze was causing a very heavy and confused sea on the rocks, he took the launch alongside the yacht and, after her sails had been hoisted, managed to tow her clear and into the harbour.

ROBERTS Glyn, Crew Member, Porthdinllaen Lifeboat　　　　**BRONZE**

19 January 1977

31 August-1 September 1976: Hearing that a boy was trapped on a cliff at Porth-y-Nant, the Watson class lifeboat *Charles Henry Ashley* launched at 11.15 p.m. with a boarding boat (fitted with an outboard motor) in tow. On arrival, the boarding boat, manned by the Second Coxswain and crew member Roberts, was despatched inshore. Finding a channel between the rocks they landed and Roberts climbed the near vertical 170 foot cliff to the boy about 80 feet up and persuaded him to descend. When about 30 feet from the bottom, Roberts fell to the beach, but climbed back and brought the boy the rest of the way down.

JONES William John, Coxswain, Holyhead Lifeboat　　　　**SILVER**

19 January 1977

11 September 1976: A yacht with her sails blown out and without power was in distress 23 miles south-west of Skerries Lighthouse, north-west Anglesey, with a north-easterly gale blowing over very rough seas in heavy rain. A merchant vessel stood by, after trying to put a line on board. The Barnett class lifeboat *St. Cybi (Civil Service No. 9)* launched at 1.29 p.m., but, on approaching, a line streamed by the yacht fouled her port propeller. Nevertheless, Coxswain Jones made an approach on one engine and rescued the four man crew. An unsuccessful search was made inshore on the return journey when a red flare was sighted.

JORDAN Joseph Robert, Nature Reserve Warden　　　　**BRONZE**

19 January 1977

25 September 1976: Two duck shooters out walking on Stiffkey Marsh, Norfolk, tried to return to the mainland after fog had reduced visibility; they became lost as the tide rose to danger level. With water up to their chests, they signalled with a torch and fired a shotgun, which alerted Joseph Jordan. Knowing the area well, he felt his way along the now submerged footpath, boarded a dinghy and, after a difficult row, brought the two men back and led them to safety.

ALLEN Robert William, Coxswain, Whitby Lifeboat   **SILVER**
ROBINSON Richard Martin Kildale, Helmsman, Whitby Inshore Lifeboat   **BRONZE**

17 March 1977

30 September 1976: The fishing vessel *Admiral Van Tromp* went aground in thick fog and a heavy swell under cliffs in the vicinity of Whitby High Light, Yorkshire. The reserve Watson class lifeboat *William and Mary Durham* launched at 3.26 a.m. On arrival at the casualty, Coxswain Allen decided to wait for more favourable sea conditions but, at 4.14 a.m., the Master of the fishing vessel reported that he could wait no longer as his ship, heeled to port, was being swept by the heavy seas. Three attempts by the lifeboat to get alongside were unsuccessful. Two men were recovered ashore and three were missing. One was seen on a rock, and the D class inflatable, under Helmsman Robinson, drove in at full speed on to a ledge. The man was grabbed as a large sea broke over the rock and washed the boat back into the sea.

HARDY Ronald James, Coxswain, Swanage Lifeboat   **BRONZE(2)**
MARSH Victor Albert Charles, Second Coxswain/Mechanic, Swanage Lifeboat   **BRONZE**

17 March 1977

14 October 1976: At 1 p.m., the Rother class lifeboat *J. Reginald Corah* launched in a south-south-westerly storm force wind and very rough sea to take over the tow of the French yacht *Campscharles* from the Russian trawler *Topaz*. Reaching the rendezvous about three miles north-east of Peveril Point, Swanage, Dorset, Coxswain Hardy brought the lifeboat alongside the trawler and took off two yachtsmen. In casting off the towlines, one of them fouled the lifeboat's rudder and starboard propeller. Both engines had to be stopped while an attempt to clear them was made by Second Coxswain Marsh. The rudder was cleared, and the Coxswain decided to proceed on the port engine only. One of the lifeboatmen, with a towline, was put back on the yacht which was then towed in to Poole at 4.20 p.m.

PITMAN Victor James, Acting Coxswain, Weymouth Lifeboat   **SILVER**

19 January 1977

14 October 1976: The 52 ton yacht *Latifa* was in distress off Portland Bill, Dorset, in a storm force south-westerly wind and worsening sea conditions. She had damaged sails, a shattered main boom, split mast and jammed halyards. A Navy frigate, acting as escort, could not take anybody off. At 5.28 p.m., the Arun class lifeboat *Tony Vandervell* launched and, with the wind worsening to a hurricane and after being thrown almost on to her beam ends several times en route, she reached the yacht. A line was passed at the third attempt and Second Coxswain Pitman began the tow to Weymouth which was reached at 8.55 p.m.

The leadership and determination of Victor Pitman, on his second trip in command, under daunting circumstances, were inspiring and courageous. His crew who had an average age of 50 saved eight lives under the worst conditions any of the participants could remember.

BOWER Keith William, Acting Coxswain, Torbay Lifeboat	**GOLD**
BOWER Stephen James, Mechanic, Torbay Lifeboat	**BRONZE**
HUNKIN William John, Assistant Mechanic, Torbay Lifeboat	**BRONZE**
BROWN Richard R., Crew Member, Torbay Lifeboat	**BRONZE**
DAVIES Nicholas, Crew Member, Torbay Lifeboat	**BRONZE**
DEW John, Crew Member, Torbay Lifeboat	**BRONZE(2)**
MILLS Michael, Crew Member, Torbay Lifeboat	**BRONZE**

17 March 1977

6 December 1976: Six miles south-east of Start Point, Devon, the m.v. *Lyrma* was in trouble with her radar out of action, her steering gear broken down and listing in a southerly gale and huge seas. The Arun class lifeboat *Edward Bridges (Civil Service No. 37)* slipped her moorings at 1.15 a.m. under command of the Second Coxswain. Attempts to take off the crew by helicopter were abandoned; Second Coxswain Bower closed the casualty's starboard quarter and four men were taken off in the first five approaches, but the lifeboat was damaged in the next effort. Despite this, two more survivors and the Master were taken off in three more passages and the last two survivors were picked up from a liferaft. The lifeboat reached Torbay at 5. a.m.

LETHBRIDGE Matthew (Junior), B.E.M., Coxswain, St. Mary's Lifeboat	**SILVER(3)**

18 May 1977

13 February 1977: At 2 a.m. in a moderate to fresh south-westerly breeze and a very heavy swell in the area of Bishop Rock Lighthouse, to the west of the Isles of Scilly, the French trawler *Enfant de Bretagne* was reported aground on a rock near Pednathise Head. The Watson class lifeboat *Guy and Clare Hunter* launched at 2.15 a.m. and headed south between the islands of Annet and St. Agnes, then steered south-westwards. At about 2.50 a.m., she encountered the smell of diesel oil and noticed pieces of polystyrene in the sea. After sighting the remains of a vessel at the base of some rocks, east of Pednathise Head, Coxswain Lethbridge carried out an extended and thorough search of the area, which was bestrewn by many uncharted rocks, with narrow gaps between them. The search in heavy swells among breakers was abandoned at 10.50 a.m. after one body was recovered.

WARNOCK Anthony William, Coxswain, Padstow Lifeboat	**SILVER**
ENGLAND Trevor Raymond,	
Second Coxswain/Assistant Mechanic, Padstow Lifeboat	**SILVER**

16 November 1977

17 July 1977: The yacht *Calcutta Princess* was reported to be in difficulties in a south-westerly gale and confused seas off Dinas Head, Devon. The Oakley class lifeboat *James and Catherine Macfarlane* launched at 5.34 p.m. On arrival, Coxswain Warnock had to manoeuvre the lifeboat between the yacht and the rocks, some submerged, before towing her to safety with a man, a woman and a dog on board. During the operations, the tow parted once, injuring a crew member, and was re-established when the yacht was only 25 yards from Bull Rock. The rescued were then taken on board the lifeboat.

BLISS Peter David, Helmsman, St. Agnes Inshore Lifeboat **SILVER**
26 April 1978

17 July 1977: A surf boarder off Porthtowan, Cornwall was swept by a fresh to strong westerly wind, with mist, rain and a heavy surf in to the sheer sided Flat Rocks Cove. After bouncing off rocks, he landed at the head of a shingle beach. In trying to climb to safety, he fell and broke his wrist. The D class inflatable lifeboat *Blue Peter IV* was launched at 4.30 p.m. and drove to the scene at maximum speed. Swamped continuously by breaking waves, Helmsman Bliss drove the lifeboat through dangerous surf over barely covered rocks, beached, picked up the injured man and took him to Porthtowan beach, before returning to St. Agnes at 6.45 p.m.

BROWN Bruce George, Coxswain/Mechanic, Walmer Lifeboat **BRONZE**
16 November 1977

4 August 1977: The Watson (Beach) class lifeboat *Beryl Tollemache*, on temporary duty, launched at 9.38 a.m. in foggy weather to the cabin cruiser *Shark*, aground inside the drying line on the Goodwin Sands, south-west of the South East Goodwin Buoy. The rising tide was moving the cruiser farther up the sand, so Coxswain Brown drove the lifeboat on to it and took off two adults and two children. Placing two of his crew on board, he towed off the casualty. Nearing Ramsgate with the cruiser settling, he decided to take off his two men but the Second Coxswain became trapped by his leg in the cabin. The other crewman already on board could not help him as 'he was too large'. Coxswain Brown jumped on board and, with great difficulty, managed to free him. After all three men had regained the lifeboat, they headed for Ramsgate, landing the survivors and the injured man.

MARJORAM John, Helmsman, Aldeburgh Inshore Lifeboat **BRONZE**
16 November 1977

17 August 1977: In a gale over a rough sea, the yacht *Spreety*, manned by her owner and his 11 year old son, was in difficulties off Aldeburgh, Suffolk. An attempt was made to launch the Beach Watson class lifeboat, but this proved impossible so the inflatable lifeboat *D-111*, whose crew was still under training, launched at 8.45 a.m. Making the first few yards under oars, the engine was started and Helmsman Marjoram drove her, filled by heavy seas, to the casualty, where the boy was taken off and lifted by helicopter. The inflatable lifeboat stood by until the yacht was taken in tow by the Aldeburgh offshore lifeboat and then accompanied her to the River Ore.

JONES William John, Coxswain, Holyhead Lifeboat **BRONZE(2)**
25 January 1978

4 September 1977: The relief Barnett class lifeboat *Thomas Forehead and Mary Rowse* launched at 9.37 p.m. in a gale and very rough sea to help the yacht *Gika* in distress, south-west of South Stack. The lifeboat searched until shortly after 3 p.m. before finally sighting the casualty. At a second attempt a tow was successfully passed and made fast by the *Gika*'s skipper who then transferred to the lifeboat. At 6.35 p.m. the lifeboat and her tow entered Holyhead harbour. The other crew member had been rescued by helicopter.

PETIT John Hubert, Coxswain, St. Peter Port Lifeboat   **BRONZE(3)**

26 April 1978

11–12 November 1977: In a gale, gusting to violent storm winds, and heavy rain squalls, the 25 ft sloop-rigged *Canopus* was close to shore, south-east of Pleinmont Ledge in the vicinity of Les Hanois Lighthouse, off south-east Guernsey. The Arun class lifeboat *Sir William Arnold* slipped her moorings at 10.30 p.m., but, when she reached the yacht, heavy seas made it extremely difficult to bring the lifeboat alongside. Nevertheless, Coxswain Petit made four approaches and took off four occupants. After failing to secure the yacht for tow, the survivors were landed at St. Peter Port at 0.37 a.m.

PENGILLY Horace Eric, Coxswain/Mechanic, Sennen Cove Lifeboat   **SILVER**

22 February 1978

16–17 November 1977: The 499 ton coaster *Union Crystal* was in trouble in a strong gale, rain squalls and very high seas, 12 miles north of Cape Cornwall, north of Land's End. Two lifeboats were launched, the St. Ives boat and the Rother class lifeboat *Diana White*, which put out at 7.43 p.m. reared, plunged and twisted in the difficult conditions. Coxswain Pengilly had to fight hard to retain control. Twenty minutes earlier a final message was received that the casualty, listing with her cargo of rock salt shifted, was sinking. The lifeboat remained at sea for nearly six hours, searching for survivors, but only one was rescued by a helicopter. Sadly Coxswain Pengilly died in January 1978, a few weeks after the service.

WEST Arthur Charles, Coxswain, Falmouth Lifeboat   **BRONZE**

26 April 1978

28 November 1977: At 9.45 p.m., the Thames class relief lifeboat *Rotary Service* slipped from her moorings in a near gale to help a jack-up barge *Mer d-Iroise*, in tow of a tug, 11 miles east of the Lizard, Cornwall. The barge, 110 feet long and 70 feet wide, had one leg at each corner, extending 40 feet below water and 70 above. The six men on board were all wearing lifebelts ready to abandon ship. With the deck under water, the barge was moving violently, but Coxswain West held the lifeboat alongside until all six men were dragged on board.

COCKING Thomas (Senior), Coxswain, St. Ives Lifeboat   **SILVER**

22 February 1978

24 December 1977: In a storm and phenomenally high sea, the Danish coaster *Lady Kamilla* foundered off the coast of Cornwall and her crew abandoned ship. When news of the disaster reached land, a search by the Padstow, St. Ives and Clovelly lifeboats, helicopters and various surface craft was instituted. The St. Ives Oakley class lifeboat *Frank Penfold Marshall* launched at 0.44 a.m., headed north, then, at 2.25 a.m., was redirected towards the Portreath/Porthtowan area. Heading there at full speed, a massive breaking sea rolled the lifeboat almost 90 degrees to port , but Coxswain Cocking retained control, although the cockpit was almost filled with water. When she righted, he resumed the search which lasted for six and a quarter hours.

    The Padstow lifeboat was out for 14 and three-quarter hours: the Clovelly lifeboat also for 14 and three-quarter hours.

WALSH Thomas Francis, Coxswain, Kilmore Lifeboat   **SILVER**
DEVEREUX John James, Acting Mechanic, Kilmore Lifeboat   **BRONZE**

25 January 1978

24 December 1977: The Oakley class lifeboat *Lady Murphy* launched at 1.50 a.m. in a west-south-westerly gale and rough sea, after red flares had been seen off Bannon Bay, towards Saltee Island, off Co. Wexford, Ireland. After a prolonged, fruitless search, Coxswain Walsh turned for home in worsening sea conditions. About a mile south-south-west of Forlorn Point, a very high breaking sea capsized the boat. When she righted, the Acting Second Coxswain was missing, the engines were restarted, and he was picked up after a search. Continuing her journey she was capsized again with only three men remaining on board; when she righted, all except one man were brought back on board. A second launch with a new crew failed to find him. His body was later found on the shore at Meanstown.

PETIT John Hubert, Coxswain, St. Peter Port Lifeboat   **SILVER**

26 April 1978

1–2 February 1978: The oil rig *Orion* was being driven aground at night in west-south-westerly gales and rain showers, after parting from her tow with the German tug *Seefalke*. Her four legs and platform were mounted on a tanker hull, the legs extending to about 250 feet above the waterline. The relief Barnett class lifeboat *The John Gellatly Hyndman* slipped her moorings at 9 p.m., and Coxswain Petit managed to take off one man from the oil rig before it went ashore on the north-west corner of Guernsey. He rescued another man from the sea, where he had been catapulted by a tautening scrambling net. With the rig aground, the remaining men were rescued by a helicopter whilst the lifeboat stood by.

MARSHALL Patrick John, Acting Coxswain, Plymouth Lifeboat   **BRONZE**
ALCOCK Cyril, Mechanic, Plymouth Lifeboat   **BRONZE**

26 July 1978

15 February 1978: In a violent west-south-westerly storm, accompanied by very heavy snow and a very rough sea, the fishing vessel *Elly Gerda* went aground on rocks, ten miles south of Rame Head, at the south end of Whitsand Bay, Cornwall. The Waveney class lifeboat *Thomas Forehead and Mary Rowse II* launched at 10.50 a.m. and reached the casualty. Second Coxswain Marshall twice took the lifeboat alongside the vessel, which was hard up against a vertical rock face, while Mechanic Alcock hauled off two men. They reported that the Skipper had gone overboard, but he was subsequently found to be on the casualty. Shortly after, the *Elly Gerda* was washed off the rocks and escorted by the lifeboat into Looe harbour.

DYER George Edward, Coxswain, Torbay Lifeboat   **BRONZE**

26 April 1978

19 February 1978: The Arun class lifeboat *Edward Bridges (Civil Service No. 37)* slipped her moorings in Brixham harbour at 12.33 p.m. in a full east-south-easterly gale, rain and poor visibility. Shortly before, the pilot cutter *Leslie H* had left harbour but had got into difficulties, and, with her steering jammed, was drifting southwards one and a quarter miles east of Berry Head, Devon.

At 12.50 p.m., Coxswain Dyer brought the lifeboat alongside her to take off two men; the Master remained on board to secure a towline and was then taken off. In the course of the tow, made erratic by a jammed rudder, a massive wave struck the lifeboat and washed one of her crew overboard, but he was recovered. Afterwards the tow broke, the cutter was abandoned and then sank. The survivors were landed at 1.30 p.m.

MORRIS William Thomas, Coxswain, St. David's Lifeboat　　　　　　**BRONZE**

26 July 1978

11 March 1978: In a moderate north-north-easterly wind and confused seas, *M.F.V. 7*, a Royal Navy tender, her engine broken down, was being carried in the direction of the Carreg-Trai Rocks, near St. David's Head, Pembrokeshire. The Watson class lifeboat *Joseph Soar (Civil Service No. 34)* launched at 12.30 p.m. Setting out at full speed, Coxswain Morris took the lifeboat north of Ramsey Island, where the casualty was sighted drifting towards Daufraich. Intercepting her short of Moelyn Rock and avoiding many other treacherous rocks, the casualty was towed clear and the tow passed to the fleet tender *Grassmere*. The lifeboat was back at St. David's at 5.10 p.m.

JONES Evan David, Coxswain, Barmouth Lifeboat　　　　　　**BRONZE**

24 January 1979

22 November 1978: In passage from Barmouth, Merioneth, to Beaumaris, Anglesey, the motor fishing vessel *Boy Nick* went aground on the sands of North Bank, just outside the harbour in a westerly gale and very rough sea. The relief Liverpool class lifeboat *B.H.M.H.* launched at 9.50 p.m. and drove through breaking seas, close to the harbour bar, grounding frequently. Coxswain Jones took the lifeboat past a bank of rocks, went alongside and took two men from their liferaft.

HOLMES William John Rees, Coxswain/Mechanic, Angle Lifeboat　　　　　　**BRONZE(2)**

28 February 1979

1 December 1978: About midnight, the fishing boat *Cairnsmore*, in passage to Scotland, was seen to be in trouble five miles south-west of the Hats and Barrels, 11 miles west of Skomer Island, and, at 0.30 a.m., the Watson class lifeboat *Richard Vernon and Mary Garforth of Leeds* launched. She set course through a south-easterly near gale, rain and sleet, and arrived at the casualty in worsening conditions. Coxswain Holmes stood by while a tug took her under tow; her crew sheltered as best they could. One man, who fell in the water, was picked up by the lifeboat which was now requested to take the other two men off the casualty. This done, they were landed at Milford Haven at 1.06 p.m.

CURNOW Arthur Lawrence Vivian, Coxswain, Torbay Lifeboat　　　　　　**BRONZE**

28 February 1979

2 December 1978: The fishing trawler *Fairway* broke down and was drifting towards the shore near Branscombe, Devon. Realising that the conditions would prevent the Exmouth lifeboat putting out, the Arun class lifeboat *Edward Bridges (Civil Service No. 37)* slipped her moorings at 2 a.m. in heavy rain. Soon after setting out, the lifeboat ran into such severe weather that she had to reduce speed, but, reaching the casualty at 3.45 a.m., Coxswain Curnow took off six men in two approaches and landed them at Brixham at 6.30 a.m.

McCORMACK Richard Seamus, Acting Second Coxswain,
   Rosslare Harbour Lifeboat   **BRONZE**

28 February 1979

7 December 1978: At 11.55 a.m., the relief Watson class lifeboat *Sir Samuel Kelly* launched, with Richard McCormack in command, to the fishing boat *Notre Dame du Sacre Coeur,* sinking off Tuskar Rock, east of Carnsore Point, Co. Wexford, Ireland, in a violent south-easterly storm force wind and a very rough sea. Reaching the casualty in waves 30 feet high, the lifeboat went alongside and took off two men, one at a time. After checking that nobody remained, the fishing boat was abandoned. Rosslare Harbour was regained at 2.45 p.m.

BOWRY Charles Henry, Coxswain/Mechanic, Sheerness Lifeboat   **BRONZE(2)**

29 March 1979

30 December 1978: In a strong north-easterly gale, a heavily overcast night, snow flurries, moderate to poor visibility and rough breaking seas, the cabin cruiser *Ma Jolie II*, overdue in passage from St. Katharine's Dock, London, to the Medway, was in trouble near Cinque Port Marshes in Gillingham Reach, off Gillingham, Kent, where there was an existing wreck. The yacht had struck the wreck, lost her propeller and was now dragging her anchor. Coxswain Bowry, in spite of many yacht moorings and very little sea room, took the Waveney class lifeboat *Helen Turnbull* into the shallow water three times and rescued the two man crew who were landed at Gillingham Pier at 10.20 p.m..

BEVAN Brian William, Superintendent Coxswain, Humber Lifeboat   **SILVER**

29 March 1979

30–31 December 1978: The Dutch coaster *Diana V* was in distress 74 miles from Spurn Head, Yorkshire, near Well Bank, her cargo of maize having shifted. The Arun class lifeboat *City of Bradford IV* slipped her moorings at 2.10 p.m., and encountered a strong easterly gale, very heavy seas and heavy snow showers as soon as she left the river. After travelling 25 miles, Coxswain Bevan was forced to return to Grimsby to effect repairs to a fractured oil pipe and set out again shortly after 9.30 p.m. The coaster was now 28 miles from Spurn. Reaching the casualty at 11 p.m., the lifeboat made three approaches and was thrown against the heaving, listing ship by the breaking seas before a 12 year old girl, a woman and four men were taken off. The Skipper of the *Diana V* remained on board to save his ship. Escorted by the lifeboat and H.M.S. *Lindisfarne* which had been standing by since 4 p.m., the coaster finally reached the River Humber at 2 p.m. on the 31st. The lifeboat landed the rescued crew at Spurn Point.

PETIT John Hubert, Coxswain, St. Peter Port Lifeboat   **BRONZE(4)**

29 March 1979

4–5 January 1979: In an easterly hurricane, poor visibility and snow showers, the heavily listing 2,200 ton Greek m.v. *Cantonad* sank in the English Channel, 35 miles west-south-west of Portland Bill. The Arun class lifeboat *Sir William Arnold* slipped her moorings at 9.09 p.m. and set out at full speed and carried out a 12 hour search, during which one huge sea rolled her over 45 degrees, threw Coxswain Petit out of his seat and rendered him unconscious for a few moments. A crew member broke two ribs. During the search, two bodies were recovered.

GRANT Michael John, Coxswain, Selsey Lifeboat   **SILVER**

30 May 1979

10 January 1979: At 4.10 a.m., the Oakley class lifeboat *Charles Henry* launched into a violent southerly storm, very rough seas and heavy rain on a bitterly cold morning. The 2,650 ton Panamanian cargo vessel *Cape Coast* was taking water in her engine room, had developed a list and was dragging her anchor near Nab Tower, off Bembridge, Isle of Wight. Thrusting her way through the tremendous seas, the lifeboat reached the casualty at 5.20 a.m. to find her decks being swept continuously by huge waves. Coxswain Grant manoeuvred in three times and took off her entire crew of 20 men. Throughout the operation, the coaster rolled and pitched violently; several times the lifeboat was picked up and driven hard against the vessel by large seas. The survivors were landed at H.M.S. *Vernon,* Portsmouth at 10 a.m.

BEVAN Brian William, Superintendent Coxswain, Humber Lifeboat   **GOLD**
BAILEY Dennis, Second Coxswain, Humber Lifeboat   **BRONZE**
SAYERS Barry (Bill), Mechanic, Humber Lifeboat   **BRONZE**
SAYERS Ronald, Assistant Mechanic, Humber Lifeboat   **BRONZE**
BAILEY Dennis (Junior), Crew Member, Humber Lifeboat   **BRONZE**
JORDAN Peter, Crew Member, Humber Lifeboat   **BRONZE**
ROLLINSON Sydney, Crew Member, Humber Lifeboat   **BRONZE**
STOREY Michael Barry, Crew Member, Humber Lifeboat   **BRONZE**

29 March 1979

14 February 1979: The Arun class lifeboat *City of Bradford IV* slipped her moorings at 0.15 a.m. and headed towards the Panamanian m.v. *Revi,* sinking slowly 30 miles north-east of Spurn lightvessel in a north-easterly storm, very heavy seas and snow storms. When she arrived at the casualty, Coxswain Bevan took her alongside 35 times before all four men were taken off. The last survivor – the Captain – was still on board when the lifeboat narrowly escaped disaster as a massive wave caused the motor vessel to smack down beside her. Coxswain Bevan rammed the throttles full astern, and the Arun's power pulled her clear by only a matter of inches. The Captain was then recovered from the stern rails, and the survivors were landed at Grimsby at 5 a.m.

WALKINGTON Fred, Coxswain, Bridlington Lifeboat BRONZE
29 March 1979

15 February 1979: With a blizzard and a violent north-easterly storm blowing, the German freighter *Sunnanhav* was in a desperate situation eight miles north-east of Flamborough Head, Yorkshire, when the Oakley class lifeboat *William Henry and Mary King* launched in seven degrees of frost at 9.45 a.m. Not long after the lifeboat had left Bridlington Bay, Coxswain Walkington was informed that the freighter had regained limited power. Then a big sea filled his cockpit and the radar went dead. A further message reported restoration of full power, he therefore abandoned the service. On the way back to Bridlington, the lifeboat was struck by a huge wave which knocked her over to starboard, which operated the engine cut-out. The engines were restarted, and she made harbour at 7 p.m. in such cold conditions that the diesel was freezing in the funnel during refuelling.

COX David James, Coxswain, Wells Lifeboat SILVER
BEVAN Brian William, Superintendent Coxswain, Humber Lifeboat BRONZE
29 March 1979

15–16 February 1979: The Roumanian freighter *Savinesti*, with 28 people on board, was dragging her anchor and was in danger of running aground with engine failure, 37 miles south-east of Spurn Point. The Oakley class lifeboat *Ernest Tom Neathercoat* was launched at Wells, Norfolk, at 10.24 a.m., in temperatures well below freezing point and with huge seas washing right over her. She reached the casualty and stood by until the Arun class lifeboat *City of Bradford IV*, which had slipped her moorings at 11.24 a.m., reached her to take over the service. When Coxswain Cox took his boat back into Wells, she had been at sea for over 11 hours; the return journey was completed with snow blowing into the aft cockpit. Coxswain Bevan eventually escorted the casualty into the River Humber after 15 hours at sea.

  At the Presentation of Awards at the Royal Festival Hall on 22 May 1979, Brian Bevan received his bronze, silver and gold medals, the first time that, at the same meeting, any lifeboatman had received all three medals.

HALL Simon Peter, Robin Hood's Bay BRONZE
23 January 1980

10 June 1979: Two youths launched a homemade raft from Robin Hood's Bay, south-east of Whitby, Yorkshire, in the afternoon, but heavy seas washed it towards Gunney Hole, and it began to break up. One of them tried to swim to safety but got into trouble. Simon Hall, aged 16, rowed out in a small 8 ft dinghy and single handedly, through breaking seas, brought the youth to safety at a moored fishing boat from which they were taken by Whitby inshore lifeboat. The other youth had swum safely ashore.

HODDER John Leslie, Helmsman, Lyme Regis Inshore Lifeboat BRONZE(2)
JONES Colin Ian, Crew Member, Lyme Regis Inshore Lifeboat BRONZE
28 November 1979

13 August 1979: The yacht *White Kitten*, with two men, two women and a five-year-old boy on board, was lying in broken water off Beer Head; all the crew were exhausted and had been with-

out sleep for 51 hours. Because of the heavy weather causing short, steep seas, the Atlantic 21 rigid inflatable lifeboat *U.S. Navy League*, which launched at 7.47 p.m., carried an extra crew member for the seven mile westward journey. They reached the scene, and the women and the boy were transferred to the lifeboat, whilst one of the lifeboat crew (a sailing instructor) took over the yacht handling. The wind force had increased to gale, gusting storm. Helmsman Hodder landed the women and boy at Lyme Regis at 8.45 p.m., returned and then escorted the yacht, now being sailed by Colin Jones, safely into harbour.

JONES Thomas Henry (Harry), Coxswain, Hoylake Lifeboat **BRONZE**
23 January 1980

20 September 1979: The catamaran *Truganini* was in trouble in a severe gale gusting to storm force and a very rough sea, on West Hoyle Bank, off Point of Ayr, Flintshire. At 9.26 a.m., the relief Oakley class lifeboat *Will and Fanny Kirby* launched and found the casualty anchored in shallow water on a lee shore, rolling and pitching violently in confused and breaking waves. Being too risky to take off the three occupants who were exhausted, Coxswain Jones put two of his crew on board, and the catamaran was towed to Mostyn Harbour, Flint. The lifeboat returned to station at 1 p.m.

ENGLAND Trevor Raymond, Coxswain, Padstow Lifeboat **SILVER(2)**
24 April 1980

15 December 1979: The Greek freighter *Skopelos Sky*, listing in an on shore westerly hurricane and very high seas in Portquin Bay, five miles north-east of Trevose Head, was in considerable trouble. The Oakley class lifeboat *James and Catherine Macfarlane* launched at 9.52 a.m. Arriving on the scene, Coxswain England went alongside five times but the freighter's crew could not be taken off. He stood by with the lifeboat acting as the only communications link between the casualty, a helicopter and the coastguard. The helicopter lifted off the survivors as darkness fell, just before the freighter was driven hard on to rocks. The lifeboat returned to Padstow at 7 p.m.

HAWKINS Richard John, Coxswain/Mechanic
Great Yarmouth and Gorleston Lifeboat **BRONZE**
23 July 1980

22 December 1979: The fishing vessel *St. Margarite* went aground on Scroby Sands off Yarmouth, Norfolk, in a north-easterly strong breeze with rough steep seas and a very heavy easterly swell. As the fishing vessel was in danger of breaking up, the Waveney class lifeboat *Khami* launched and headed across the sandbanks. Coxswain Hawkins made two approaches. One man was taken on board on the second attempt and another man fell into the sea, but was rescued. The fishing vessel shortly after floated off the sandbank. A lifeboatman was put on board, a tow established and she was then taken to Gorleston, where later she sank at her moorings.

VOICE Kenneth Frederick David, Coxswain, Shoreham Harbour Lifeboat　　**SILVER**

24 April 1980

21 January 1980: With 22 men, two women and two children on board, the 3,500 ton Greek cargo vessel *Athina B* was in difficulties on a lee shore, one and a half miles from Shoreham, Sussex. In a severe south-easterly gale with violent seas breaking over her she lay almost beam on to tide and sea. The Watson class lifeboat *Dorothy and Philip Constant* slipped her moorings at 8.40 a.m. and, in three approaches, took off the women and children, then landed them. The lifeboat returned, took off 11 men and landed them at Shoreham. The cargo vessel floated clear and, eventually, went ashore on Brighton beach, where the lifeboat made an approach at 9.35 p.m. and a further ten men threw themselves on to the deck of the lifeboat. The last man fell into the water, but was picked up, and everybody was landed at 11.50 p.m.

BOWRY Charles Henry, Coxswain/Mechanic, Sheerness Lifeboat　　**SILVER**

23 July 1980

19–20 March 1980: In the evening, during a strong gale, the radio ship *Mi Amigo* was dragging anchor in the vicinity of North West Long Sand Beacon, off the Thames Estuary, 24 miles north-east of Sheerness, Kent. The Waveney class lifeboat *Helen Turnbull* launched at 6.16 p.m., but met rough, breaking seas and had to reduce speed because of driving spray and heavy seas. On arrival, she found the casualty aground on Long Sand Shoal. After Coxswain Bowry had stood by for three hours, the radio ship refloated, but rolled and pitched violently, shipping heavy seas overall. He had to make 13 approaches before the four survivors could be taken off, and the ship sank soon afterwards. The lifeboat returned to Sheerness at 3 a.m.

REYNOLDS Robert Glynne, Helmsman, Cardigan Inshore Lifeboat　　**BRONZE**

26 November 1980

15 August 1980: An 18 ft motor cruiser was reported in serious trouble in Cardigan Bay. At 1.20 p.m. the D class inflatable lifeboat launched into moderate surf but on the bar the seas were esti-mated to be 16 feet or more, with heavy dumping surf. Reaching the casualty, Helmsman Reynolds drove the lifeboat on to the cruiser amidships and the two crew members grabbed a boy who was firmly grasping a dog. An attempt to rescue the woman on board was frustrated as she was holding firmly on to her husband. Another approach was made and the owner of the cruiser was grabbed. The man, the boy and the dog were landed on the beach, and the lifeboat returned to the casualty. Again Helmsman Reynolds drove the bow of the lifeboat on to the cruiser and the remaining couple were pulled on board.

WHITE Graham, Helmsman, Withernsea Inshore Lifeboat　　**BRONZE**

26 November 1980

30 August 1980: At 5.12 p.m., a three man diving party was reported overdue and, with the Humber lifeboat already on service, the D Class inflatable lifeboat was launched at 5.20 p.m. and headed for a well-known wreck area. A near gale was blowing, and the lifeboat made best possible speed with following, breaking seas; the diving boat was seen three miles east-south-east of Withernsea. Realising that in deteriorating weather a return would be made increasingly difficult,

Helmsman White shouted instructions to the divers to leave their boat and jump into the lifeboat immediately she came alongside. This was achieved within seconds and, with great difficulty, all three men were landed at Withernsea in the heavy breaking seas.

JOHNSON Ian Jones, Coxswain/Mechanic, Troon Lifeboat   **SILVER**

26 November 1980

12 September 1980: In Irvine Bay, off Irvine Harbour, Ayrshire, the Dutch dredger *Holland I* was in danger of parting her moorings in a gale. The Waveney class lifeboat *Connel Elizabeth Cargill* launched at 3.55 p.m. in poor visibility, deteriorating weather and heavy seas, which laid her on her beam ends several times during her passage. Reaching the dredger, Coxswain Johnson made an approach, avoided anchor cables, and took off one man. Another four men were then rescued, one at a time, and all were landed safely.

MACDONALD Malcolm, Coxswain/Mechanic, Stornoway Lifeboat   **SILVER**

19 March 1981

29 September 1980: Just after midnight, the Solent class lifeboat *Hugh William Viscount Gough* launched in a gale, poor visibility and very heavy seas. The motor fishing vessel *Junella* had run aground on rocks off Eilean Trodday, north of the Isle of Skye. She lay with her bow high above water with breaking seas swirling around her stern, while her sister ship stood by illuminating the scene. Coxswain Macdonald manoeuvred the lifeboat to the casualty's starboard quarter and held her bow against the pilot ladder for 40 minutes while 29 men transferred. They were all landed after a three hour return journey.

DUNSTER Frank Sidney, Helmsman, Hayling Island Inshore Lifeboat   **BRONZE**

19 March 1981

14 December 1980: The yacht *Fitz's Flyer*, her rudder broken, was in danger of being driven by a gale on to a lee shore off Eastoke Head, Hayling Island, Hampshire. The Atlantic 21 rigid inflatable lifeboat launched at 1.20 p.m. On Chichester Bar and around Chichester Bar Beacon, visibility was poor with very high waves, driving spray and pouring rain, but, in spite of heavy seas forcing the two boats apart, Helmsman Dunster ran in eight times and took off four men. On two occasions, the lifeboat's twin engines stalled but were restarted immediately.

COSTER Alan Percival, Helmsman, Lymington Inshore Lifeboat   **BRONZE**

19 March 1981

17 December 1980: Helmsman Coster, who was also the Assistant Harbour Master, put out in the 18 ft harbour launch with a colleague to help the fishing vessel *Al Mor*, which was flashing her lights at the entrance to the River Lymington, Hampshire. Reaching the vessel, he found that she was in an inaccessible shoal area and was being driven on to a lee shore. Unable to help the two men, he returned to shore. With a second colleague, he launched the Atlantic 21 rigid inflatable lifeboat and made full speed to the river entrance, where a gale was causing rough seas in the shallow waters. Unable to get the lifeboat to the sinking casualty, Coster slipped overboard and swam

20 yards to reach her. When the fishing vessel sank, her two man crew jumped on to the mud; Helmsman Coster led them through half a mile of marshes, mud and gullies to rendezvous with the lifeboat at Pylewell from where they proceeded to Lymington.

TRIGG Roger Edward, Helmsman, Southwold Inshore Lifeboat   **BRONZE**

19 March 1981

16 January 1981: The local fishing vessel *Concord*, broken down east of Southwold Harbour, Suffolk, was dragging her anchor in heavy seas. At 4.38 p.m ., the Atlantic 21 rigid inflatable lifeboat was launched in a south-south-easterly gale and confused seas caused by a heavy swell. Helmsman Trigg, who was also Harbour Master, put one of his crew on board the casualty, which was taken in tow by a sister fishing vessel m.f.v. *Broadside*. The lifeboatman was transferred from the *Concord* to the second boat. Nearing the harbour entrance, the towline parted, injuring the lifeboatman, and the *Concord* was driven aground. The lifeboat was forced through the heavy seas intending to take off the survivors, but the tow was repassed and the casualty was pulled clear by the Atlantic 21. The tow was then transferred to the *Broadside*, while the lifeboat escorted both vessels to Lowestoft. The tow parted on four occasions and each time the lifeboat helped re-establish it.

MASSARELLI Michael, Acting Coxswain, Porthdinllaen Lifeboat   **BRONZE**

2 December 1981

25 April 1981: With a north-easterly gale blowing and a rough sea, an inflatable dinghy had capsized in Porthdinllaen Bay, Cardiganshire, throwing the two occupants into the water near submerged rocks, 120 yards from the beach. The Watson class lifeboat *Kathleen Mary* launched at 3.42 p.m. and, on reaching the casualty, a line was thrown to one man who was hauled to safety. Second Coxswain Massarelli made two more approaches with seas breaking over the boat and, as the second approach was made, the second man lost his grip on the dinghy and was washed down to the lifeboat and pulled on board.

RAYMENT Clive Richard, Helmsman, Cromer Inshore Lifeboat   **BRONZE**

16 September 1981

1 May 1981: The D Class inflatable lifeboat was launched from the beach at 12.19 p.m. to help the crew of the crab boat *George William* that had been swamped and sunk off East Runton, Norfolk. Her two man crew had been thrown into the water. The weather was fine with good visibility, but a fresh to strong north-north-easterly breeze was creating a rough sea and a heavy on shore swell. Helmsman Rayment took the lifeboat down over the shallows, where waves were breaking, manoeuvred around the capsized craft and debris and then picked up the two men. At 12.37 p.m. the lifeboat was beached on Cromer's Fisherman's Beach.

WIGNALL Arthur Robert, Coxswain, Lytham St. Anne's Lifeboat   BRONZE
PEARSON Brian, Assistant Mechanic, Lytham St. Anne's Lifeboat   BRONZE

16 September 1981

6 June 1981: The yacht *Morag*, in a south-west by west gale and very rough sea, was heading into more dangerous waters and was rolling heavily off South Shore, Blackpool, Lancashire. The Watson class lifeboat *City of Bradford III* slipped her moorings at 3.20 p.m. The yacht was found a quarter of a mile off shore on the Crusader Bank, three-quarters of a mile from St. Anne's Pier, apparently abandoned and towing an inflatable dinghy close behind. A man could be seen in the water, seemingly clinging to her stern. Assistant Mechanic Pearson leapt into the inflatable dinghy, then jumped into the sea to drag the man clear as his lifeline had become entangled in some way. He dragged the man round to the port quarter clear of the lifeboat's bow and climbed on to the yacht to secure a line to the lifeboat as another crewman jumped into the yacht, cut the lifeline and pulled the survivor into the casualty. Coxswain Wignall, in spite of only having one engine available, drove straight on to the yacht and took off the survivor and the second lifeboatman. Pearson had already been ordered back on board the lifeboat.

HUTCHENS Maurice, Coxswain/Mechanic, Sennen Cove Lifeboat   SILVER

2 December 1981

19 September 1981: The Rother class lifeboat *Diana White* launched at 8.45 p.m. in a west-south-west gale, heavy rain squalls and a very rough sea. The 500 ton Icelandic coaster *Tungufoss*, with a cargo of maize, was heeled over four miles south of Longships Lighthouse, west of Land's End, with eight men on board. When the lifeboat reached her, Coxswain Hutchens found that three others had been lifted off by helicopter. After two attempted approaches, the lifeboat was manoeuvred as close as possible. Three men from the coaster had got into liferafts attached to her stern; they floated towards the lifeboat and were snatched aboard. Two more men, who tried to jump into the liferafts but missed, were dragged from the water into the lifeboat, followed by two others who were taken off the coaster as her list increased. The last man – the Master – was lifted off by a helicopter as the sea started to engulf him.

JAMES Roderick Harold, Crew Member, Hayling Island Inshore Lifeboat   SILVER
DUNSTER Frank Sidney, Helmsman, Hayling Island Inshore Lifeboat   BRONZE(2)

27 January 1982

19 September 1981: In a south-easterly near gale, a teenage boy was seen clinging to the post of a groyne, some 20 yards out to sea, opposite the Golden Nugget Cafe, Eastoke, Hayling Island, Hampshire, with very rough, confused seas breaking over him. The Atlantic 21 rigid inflatable lifeboat had already been engaged in services to two windsurfers, a dinghy and a yacht but, when at 5.20 p.m., Helmsman Dunster was told of the boy's predicament, he closed with the scene. Two attempts by shore helpers had already been made, and the lifeboat made four unsuccessful attempts to rescue. Then, when she came to within 30 feet of the boy, Roderick James entered the water and, as the exhausted boy let go and disappeared, he grabbed him and made for the shore. After landing him safely to shore helpers, Mr. James regained the boat at the lifeboat station which continued to deal with vessels in distress until 7.50 p.m. During services that evening, seven people were rescued from two sail-boats, a cabin cruiser, a yacht and a catamaran as well as the boy on the groyne. Help was also given to other craft.

GILCHRIST Alexander Charles, Coxswain/Mechanic,
  Campbeltown Lifeboat   **SILVER**

24 March 1982

2 October 1981: The Arun class lifeboat *Walter and Margaret Couper* slipped her moorings at 7 a.m., when the trawler *Erlo Hills* went ashore off the east coast of Rathlin Island, Co. Antrim, northern Ireland, two miles south of Altacarry Head. By the time that the lifeboat reached the scene, the northerly wind had reached near gale force giving short, steep, breaking waves, but she still managed to pass a towline between the casualty and another trawler. The casualty was towed off, and the other trawler departed. Shortly after, the trawler's steering gear jammed, her main engine broke down, and she began drifting to the shore. Her Master refused to allow the crew to be taken off. Coxswain Gilchrist secured a tow but, buffeted by large waves, the lifeboat could hardly make headway, so the other trawler returned and took up the tow again. After it had parted four times, the attempt was abandoned. Later, in six approaches, the lifeboat took off 14 men and landed them at Campbeltown at 8.30 p.m.

RICHARDS Joshua William, Coxswain, Tenby Lifeboat   **BRONZE(2)**

24 March 1982

7 October 1981: The catamaran *Helen M* was anchored in a dangerous position off Pendine, Carmarthenshire, in a south-westerly gale, very rough seas and a heavy swell. The Watson class lifeboat *Henry Comber Brown* launched at 9.30 p.m. Two of the catamaran's crew had rowed ashore, but, unable to return, this had left the owner on board on his own. The lifeboat anchored and Coxswain Richards veered down to lift the anchor cable and tow the casualty clear. Two lifeboatmen had managed to scramble aboard the catamaran when the anchor cable parted. After a second anchor was let go, a tow was passed and the catamaran was brought to safety.

JOHN Frederick George, Coxswain/Mechanic, St. David's Lifeboat   **BRONZE**

24 March 1982

18–19 October 1981: Towing two other tugs, the *Vernicos Giorgos*, with a rope around her propeller, was dragging her anchors in the northern part of St. Bride's Bay, Pembrokeshire, in a strong south-westerly gale and very rough seas. By the time the relief Watson class lifeboat *Charles Henry Ashley*, which had launched at 9.56 p.m., arrived, the two tugs being towed were already on the rocks; their crews were on board the *Vernicos Giorgos* which was riding at two anchors but was being dragged towards the rocks with waves breaking over her. In five approaches, Coxswain John took off three men, but another five, deciding to remain, were lifted off by helicopter when the tug grounded after midnight.

COX David James, B.E.M., Coxswain, Wells Lifeboat   **BRONZE**

24 March 1982

20 November 1981: With a north-westerly gale blowing over a very rough sea, the fishing vessel *Sarah K*, her engine room flooded, was in difficulties, two and a half miles north of Brancaster, north-west Norfolk. The Oakley class lifeboat *Ernest Tom Neathercoat* launched at 2.39 p.m., proceeded at full speed to the casualty, which was near Woolpack Buoy, west-north-west of Scolt Head and stood by while a helicopter lowered a pump to the trawler. At 5.24 p.m. the fishing vessel's large foremast broke and, the helicopter having withdrawn, Coxswain Cox made four

approaches and took off the four man crew. At 6.15 p.m. with the wind moderating, the Skipper was put back on the *Sarah K* to put down the anchor. This done, he was taken back on to the lifeboat which headed back to Wells.

GALLICHAN David Walter, Coxswain, Beaumaris Lifeboat   **BRONZE**

24 March 1982

13 December 1981: The angling launch *Wygyr* was in difficulties at the northern end of the Menai Straits, off Puffin Island, in a strong south-south-easterly gale rising to storm force and a blizzard. The Watson class lifeboat *Greater London II (Civil Service No. 30)* launched at 12. 45 p.m., after her crew experienced difficulties in reaching the boathouse because of seas washing over the catwalk. The windscreen iced up almost immediately and Coxswain Gallichan posted lookouts. After a search, the launch was found and taken in tow with the towline doubled up. When one line parted, two men were taken on board the lifeboat: shortly afterwards, the other line gave way and the casualty was blown ashore at Trwyn Du, Anglesey, where she broke up. The lifeboat continued up the straits to Menai Bridge. Visibility was so poor that the manager of the Gazelle Hotel was asked to put the hotel's lights on to assist navigation. The two men were landed at Menai Bridge at 4.40 p.m.

SCALES Michael John, Coxswain, St. Peter Port Lifeboat   **GOLD**

BOUGOURD Peter Nicholas, Second Coxswain, St. Peter Port Lifeboat   **BRONZE**

VOWLES Robert Lewis, Mechanic, St. Peter Port Lifeboat   **BRONZE**

MARTEL Alan Frederick, Assistant Mechanic, St. Peter Port Lifeboat   **BRONZE**

BISSON Peter John, Crew Member, St. Peter Port Lifeboat   **BRONZE**

BOUGOURD John Philip, Crew Member, St. Peter Port Lifeboat   **BRONZE**

HAMON Richard James, Crew Member, St. Peter Port Lifeboat   **BRONZE**

WEBSTER John, Crew Member, St. Peter Port Lifeboat   **BRONZE**

24 March 1982

13 December 1981: The Ecuadorian m.v. *Bonita* was listing heavily in the middle of the English Channel, nearly 40 miles north of Guernsey, Channel Isles. Thirty six people were on board, including women and children. A southerly storm, gusting to hurricane force, was blowing with driving snow and sea spray, reducing visibility to 200 yards. Slipping her moorings at 2 p.m., the Arun class lifeboat *Sir William Arnold* maintained full speed, despite broaching eight times, and eventually arrived on the scene at dusk. Despite ropes, drums and large pieces of timber floating in the vicinity, Coxswain Scales made *50 approaches* to the casualty during three and a half hours and took off 29 people. Five crew were saved by helicopter, and one by a tug. One man drowned. Ten runs were made to rescue just one man who could not hold on to the heaving line which was being used. The lifeboat landed the survivors at Brixham, Devon, at 11.13 p.m.

BEVAN Brian William, Superintendent Coxswain, Humber Lifeboat   **BRONZE(2)**

24 March 1982

13–14 December 1981: The Arun class lifeboat *City of Bradford IV* slipped her moorings at 11.18 p.m. with a south-westerly storm blowing over very heavy seas in heavy snow. The coaster *Harry Mitchell*, north of Humber lightvessel, had developed a 30 degree list after her cargo had shifted, and when the lifeboat arrived, the winds were gusting to violent storm. Nevertheless, Coxswain Bevan took the lifeboat alongside eight times to take off three men, but the Master and Mate decided to stay on board. She was escorted very slowly by the lifeboat into the Humber estuary, where a pilot boarded her at 5.42 a.m. The three rescued men were then put back on the coaster.

RICHARDS William Trevelyan, Coxswain, Penlee Lifeboat	**Post. GOLD**
MADRON James Stephen, Second Coxswain/Mechanic, Penlee Lifeboat	**Post. BRONZE**
BROCKMAN Nigel, Assistant Mechanic, Penlee Lifeboat	**Post. BRONZE**
BLEWETT John Robert, Emergency Mechanic, Penlee Lifeboat	**Post. BRONZE**
GREENHAUGH Charles Thomas, Crew Member, Penlee Lifeboat	**Post. BRONZE**
SMITH Kevin, Crew Member, Penlee Lifeboat	**Post. BRONZE**
TORRIE Barrie Robertson, Crew Member, Penlee Lifeboat	**Post. BRONZE**
WALLIS Gary Lee, Crew Member, Penlee Lifeboat	**Post. BRONZE**

27 January 1982

19 December 1981: The 1,400 ton coaster *Union Star* reported engine failure eight miles east of Wolf Rock Lighthouse, which is in deep water south-west of Land's End. The Watson class lifeboat *Solomon Browne* launched in south-east by east hurricane force winds, mountainous seas, a heavy ground swell, driving rain and very poor visibility. Arriving at the scene, Coxswain Richards made a number of approaches during which four people on the casualty's deck jumped into the lifeboat. In turning 50 yards from the steep-to rocky shore, the lifeboat was overwhelmed. All her crew and the survivors from the coaster were lost. In spite of lengthy searches by helicopters, two other lifeboats, fishing vessels and coastguard search teams, no survivors were found.

WARD Eric Thomas, Helmsman, St. Ives Inshore Lifeboat   **BRONZE**

30 June 1982

8 April 1982: Two youths and two young men in a sailing dinghy, leaving St. Ives harbour in a strong northerly breeze and rough broken seas, were seen in difficulties a mile clear of the harbour, heading towards Hayle Bar. The dinghy capsized and the crew were seen clinging to her; the D Class inflatable lifeboat launched at 4.35 p.m. The course was set and full speed maintained although, while approaching, she was taking on more water than her self-bailers could clear. Within minutes of arrival, all four survivors were on board, but the water in the lifeboat was level with the top of her sponsons. As she tried to clear the casualty, her propeller was fouled by a halyard. Crew member Allen jumped overboard to hold the bow head to sea, while efforts were made to free the propeller. This done, the lifeboat set out to return to St. Ives. Crew member Thomas treated the survivors for hypothermia. An increased speed caused Allen to fall out of the lifeboat, but he was quickly recovered. The harbour was reached at 4.55 p.m., and the four survivors and Allen were taken to hospital.

FOSSETT Robert Terence, Helmsman, Southend-on-Sea Inshore Lifeboat   **BRONZE**

24 November 1982

2 May 1982: When the motor fishing vessel *Mary* broke down due west of Maplin Edge Buoy, off Shoeburyness, Essex, another fishing vessel tried to take off her crew, but was unable to go

alongside. The Atlantic 21 rigid inflatable lifeboat launched at 5.12 p.m. in a westerly gale and heavy confused seas. As she approached, she broached several times and was laid over on her starboard sponson, but still her crew managed to snatch the two fishermen at the first attempt. Her return journey proved to be extremely difficult, and the two fishermen were transferred to the Sheerness Waveney class lifeboat, which had been called out. Both boats returned to Southend Pier.

WARD Eric Thomas, Helmsman, St. Ives Inshore Lifeboat BRONZE(2)

24 November 1982

15 July 1982: The D Class inflatable lifeboat launched at 9.27 a.m. in a slight, gentle breeze and went to the area of the Western Carracks, three miles west of St. Ives, Cornwall, where the yacht *Ladybird* was aground off Whicker Point. The yacht was found to be unmanned, but it was thought that her liferaft, close inshore nearby, could be holding somebody. Helmsman Ward anchored and veered the lifeboat down through very broken waters among dangerous rocks, where her propeller was damaged by one of them. A helicopter established that the liferaft was empty; the lifeboat withdrew and returned to St. Ives. No survivors were found.

BROWN Edward Beverley, Helmsman, New Brighton Inshore Lifeboat BRONZE

24 November 1982

29 August 1982: The yacht *Ocea* was reported in difficulty just north of Great Burbo Bank, off Blundellsands, Lancashire. The Atlantic 21 rigid inflatable lifeboat *Blenwatch* launched at 2.10 p.m. in a strong south-south-westerly breeze, gusting to gale force, and in very heavy seas. By the time the yacht was reached, she had crossed the main channel and was heading northwards towards very rough waters on the shallows of Taylor's Bank. Helmsman Brown made two approaches and put a man on board the yacht to secure a towline. The casualty was then taken in tow through very heavy seas to the mouth of the River Ribble, where the tow was transferred to the Watson class lifeboat from Lytham St. Annes. After considerable difficulty, the lifeboat recovered her own crewman and put the two survivors on board the Watson before returning to station which was reached at 8.35 p.m.

CLARK Peter Hewitt Peterson, Coxswain/Mechanic, Lerwick Lifeboat BRONZE

26 January 1983

21 September 1982: At 1.10 a.m., the Arun class lifeboat *Soldian* slipped her moorings and cleared harbour, heading for the Out Skerries, north-west of Whalsey, Shetland Isles, where the yacht *Hermes of Lune* was dragging her anchor in Northeast Mouth during a storm, rough seas and torrential rain. Despite the rough weather and restricted visibility, Coxswain Clark took two men from the yacht and stood by for the remainder of the night; the Skipper remained on the yacht. With returning daylight, the storm eased, and the lifeboat's inflatable dinghy was used to run a line ashore from the yacht. After the wind eased to a south-westerly near gale, one of the yachtsmen was put back on board and the other taken to Lerwick which was reached at 9.35 a.m.

WILLACY Keith, Helmsman, Morecambe Inshore Lifeboat **SILVER**

23 March 1983

17 October 1982: With a strong breeze rising to a south by east near gale, a rough sea and confused water, a windsurfer was reported in difficulties in Half Moon Bay, near Heysham, Lancashire. The D Class inflatable lifeboat was launched at 4.35 p.m and, with waves breaking right over and filling the lifeboat, Helmsman Willacy steered through a narrow channel towards the open bay and started to search. The windsurfer was discovered 40 feet up an old oil pier concrete dolphin, a quarter of a mile out to sea. The structure was approached with care, as the man had fixed his board fast to the access ladder blocking his way down and obstructing any approach by the lifeboat. Finally, the man was told to jump into the water where he was quickly lifted into the lifeboat and landed at Heysham at 5.30 p.m.

HATCHER Charles George, Coxswain, Blyth Lifeboat **BRONZE**

23 March 1983

7 December 1982: As the Waveney class lifeboat *William and Jane* was about to set out for a rough weather exercise, she was told of the fishing vessel *Castle Cove* taking water five miles north-north-east of the River Tyne. Slipping her moorings at 6.30 p.m., the lifeboat drove through the dark overcast evening, sleet showers, rough seas and heavy swell to find that the fishing vessel's engines had stopped shortly after her arrival. After being taken in tow to the River Tyne, the casualty started to sink. The tow was slipped and Coxswain Hatcher went alongside to rescue three men. The *Castle Cove* sank five minutes later, 500 yards north of Tyne North Pier.

BERRY Michael Edward, Coxswain, St. Helier Lifeboat **BRONZE**

23 March 1983

14 December 1982: The Norwegian yacht *Festina-Lente*, her engine and steering gear broken down, was a mile south of St. Helier, Jersey, in a fresh to strong breeze and moderate to rough sea. The Waveney class relief lifeboat *Faithful Forester* set out at 1.56 p.m. and the casualty was soon found. She had been swept into a bottleneck among rocks from where another yacht had tried, unsuccessfully, to rescue her, while six fishing boats stood by helplessly. Realising that there was no hope of towing the yacht clear, Coxswain Berry drove the lifeboat into the heavily broken water. Two survivors leaped on board, and the lifeboat was driven out stern first. The rescue operation had taken only five minutes.

LEE Kenneth Verdun, Petty Officer, Trinity House Pilot Vessel *Valour* **BRONZE**
WARNER Barry James, Seaman, Trinity House Pilot Vessel *Valour* **BRONZE**
WRIGHT Michael Anthony, Second Officer, Trinity House Pilot Vessel *Patrol* **BRONZE**
WAKELIN Thomas Edward, Seaman, Trinity House Pilot Vessel *Patrol* **BRONZE**

23 March 1983

19–20 December 1982: Just before 11 p.m., two ferries *European Gateway* and *Speedlink Vanguard* were in collision near Cork Spit Buoy, off Felixstowe, Suffolk, and the former developed a heavy, increasing list. All available craft were alerted in the heavy gale and short steep seas. The Trinity House pilot vessel *Valour* managed to take off 28 people by driving her stern against one of

European Gateway's lifeboats, which acted as a bridge between the ship and the pilot boat; three men were recovered from the sea. Meanwhile, another Trinity House pilot vessel, *Patrol,* had arrived and a search was made amidst the floating debris; two men were picked up. Fifteen more survivors were taken by *Patrol* from the *European Gateway.*

ROGERS John Desmond, Helmsman, Portaferry Inshore Lifeboat **BRONZE**

23 November 1983

19 December 1982: At 6.40 p.m. in a gale, high seas and darkness, Helmsman Rodgers launched the C class Zodiac inflatable lifeboat and headed for a sheltered gully on the west side of Janes Rock in Strangford Lough, Co. Down, northern Ireland, where the yacht *Frieda* was stranded with her keel wedged between two rocks. After a survivor had been taken on board the rescue vessel, a search for a missing man took place down wind to the eastern shore of the lough in a storm force south-westerly wind and with the lifeboat continuously awash. The search was unsuccessful and the lifeboat returned to base at 10 p.m. The missing man was recovered safely next day on Dunsy Island on which he had managed to land.

FORRESTER Robert Allen, Helmsman, Flint Inshore Lifeboat **BRONZE**

4 May 1983

26 February 1983: On a cold, dark evening with a fresh to strong north-westerly breeze, the cabin cruiser *Heron II* was in difficulty one mile south-east of Mostyn Dock, Flint, in the River Dee Estuary. The D Class inflatable lifeboat was launched into the Dock at 8.05 p.m. Leaving the dock entrance, she had to cross heavy, breaking and confused seas to reach the cruiser which was aground with an anchor out. Helmsman Forrester took the lifeboat alongside, and the two lifeboat crew had to board the cruiser to carry off one of the two survivors who had collapsed.

HILL Arthur Maclean, Crew Member, Largs Inshore Lifeboat **SILVER**

23 November 1983

24 July 1983: The Atlantic 21 rigid inflatable lifeboat *Independent Forester Liberty* launched at 7.44 p.m. to a casualty off Fairhaven, on the east side of Great Cumbrae Island. Within a few minutes various craft could be seen around a capsized motor cruiser with only her bow above water. Two men had already been picked up by a yacht, and a third unconscious man rescued by a motor-boat. A young girl was still trapped in the cabin. Helmsman Strachan asked crew member Hill to get in the water and investigate the hull as it was impossible to right the cruiser. At the third attempt, Arthur Hill got under the cabin top and found the girl in a small air pocket. After a first unsuccessful attempt, Hill pushed the girl down which enabled Helmsman Strachan to grasp her legs from the other side and pull her clear. Hill followed unaided. The girl was taken into the Atlantic 21 and was joined by the two survivors taken into the yacht. All were landed in to medical care shortly after 8 p.m. The survivor in the motor boat was pronounced dead by a doctor on one of the boats.

BERRY Michael Edward, Coxswain, St. Helier Lifeboat **SILVER(2)**

23 November 1983

3 September 1983: In a strong west-south-westerly gale, pitch darkness and very large waves, the Waveney class lifeboat *Thomas James King* launched at 3.39 a.m. Coxswain Berry took her three miles in among rocks in Clement's Bay, south-east of St. Helier, Jersey, near Demie de Pas light tower, where the French yacht *Cythara* was drifting. With her mainsail and jib still hoisted, the yacht was rolling and pitching heavily. After taking off two men and a woman, Coxswain Berry manoeuvred his way out of the maze of rocks, striking them twice in the process.

GRANT Michael John, Coxswain, Selsey Lifeboat **SILVER(2)**

25 January 1984

9–10 September 1983: A yacht, the *Enchantress of Hamble,* was aground in Looe Channel, half a mile south-west of Selsey Bill, Sussex. The Oakley class lifeboat *Charles Henry* launched at 7.20 p.m. into a southerly gale, very rough seas and poor visibility. She located the yacht about 30 minutes later, in shallow water between The Streets. Coxswain Grant went close in despite his boat hitting the bottom regularly. After one wave had filled the cockpit waist high, he went alongside the yacht and took off two women and two men, then passed a line to the two men remaining on board. When a tow had been established, these two were taken on board the lifeboat. The women were landed at Selsey in the inshore lifeboat whilst the Oakley continued to Portsmouth, arriving there at 1.10 a.m.

MUNDAY David Frank, Helmsman, Selsey Inshore Lifeboat **BRONZE**

25 January 1984

5 October 1983: The D Class inflatable lifeboat was launched at 9 p.m. in darkness, into a strong south-westerly breeze to aid the 54 ft motor cruiser *Joan Maureen*, lying on the lee side of Kirk Arrow Bank where, in heavy spray and with waves rebounding from the sea wall, she was lying at the seaward end of a timber groyne. After a first unsuccessful approach, Helmsman Munday drove the lifeboat hard against the cruiser. Crew member Delahunty leapt aboard with the lifeboat's painter. The three young men were pulled or jumped into the lifeboat, followed by Delahunty. The lifeboat then headed for Selsey.

COCKING Thomas (Senior), Coxswain, St. Ives Lifeboat **SILVER(2)**

21 March 1984

3 January 1984: At 5 p.m., the relief Oakley class lifeboat *The Vincent Nesfield* was launched in rain squalls and was driven by a north-north-westerly gale to the West German tug *Fairplay X* which, while trying to pass a towline to the Netherlands coaster *Orca*, had fouled her propeller. Reaching the tug, which was in danger of running aground in Hayle Basin, Coxswain Cocking made several runs and took off seven men, whom he then landed. The Coxswain put out again at 10.36 p.m. and took seven approaches to rescue the seven men from the Dutch coaster. After a very rough return passage, the seven were landed at 11.45 p.m.

SINCLAIR William Swanson, Captain. Coxswain, Kirkwall Lifeboat   **BRONZE**

21 March 1984

22 January 1984: The fishing vessel *Benachie* parted her moorings and went ashore at 9.15 a.m. on the south side of the Island of Rousay, in the Orkneys. After the Clyde class lifeboat *Grace Paterson Ritchie* slipped her moorings, Coxswain Sinclair successfully made the passage from Kirkwall to the casualty despite a full blizzard, a violent south-south-westerly storm and heavy seas. He found the casualty grounded among rocks, rolling heavily and with waves breaking over her. The lifeboat anchored, veered down, and a line was successfully put on board, which enabled the fishing vessel with her three occupants to be pulled clear of the rocks.

SCALES Michael John, Coxswain, St. Peter Port Lifeboat   **BRONZE**

21 March 1984

24 January 1984: The Liberian freighter *Radiant Med* developed a serious list and capsized in the English Channel during a strong west-north-westerly gale gusting to storm force. The Arun class lifeboat *Sir William Arnold* slipped her moorings at 1.28 a.m. and set off at full speed. She reached the freighter's lifeboat containing nine survivors and, after manoeuvring alongside, took them on board. Coxswain Scales had to carry out the operation in the dark with massive seas, and severe hail squalls. He then searched the area until 4.30 a.m., before returning to harbour at 6.13 a.m.

McKAY Donald, Coxswain/Mechanic, Wick Lifeboat   **BRONZE**

21 November 1984

25 June 1984: The relief Solent class lifeboat *The Royal British Legion Jubilee* launched at 11 a.m. and headed out at full speed towards Sinclair Bay, Caithness, where a salmon coble was in trouble off Ackergill, in a strong breeze, gusting to gale force. The presence of staked salmon nets and creels in the area restricted the approach to the casualty, which was 200 yards from shore among rocks and breaking seas. After an unsuccessful attempt to veer down a breeches buoy, Coxswain McKay got a Speedline on board, followed by a towline, and towed the coble with her crew of three to safety in Ackergill Harbour.

MITCHELL Peter Robert Charles, Coxswain/Mechanic,
    Lizard-Cadgwith Lifeboat   **BRONZE**

27 March 1985

3 September 1984: After losing her rudder, the yacht *Bass* was being towed by a similar vessel two and a half miles from Looe Bar, Cornwall, in a near gale and rough sea. The Oakley class lifeboat *James and Catherine MacFarlane* launched at 6.26 p.m. and caught up with the two yachts half a mile off Prah Sands, west of Porthleven. The vessel under tow was pitching and rolling heavily, sheering badly and shipping seas occasionally. Coxswain Mitchell was able to pass a heaving line, then a tow rope, and then take over the tow. Despite the tow parting once, he brought the *Bass* and her three crew into Newlyn at 11.45 p.m.

CLEMENCE David William, Coxswain, Ilfracombe Lifeboat **BRONZE**

21 November 1984

9 September 1984: The yacht *Liberty* was dragging her anchor close in to the Rapparee Rocks, just outside the Ilfracombe outer harbour entrance. One of the two men on board had radioed that his skipper appeared to be dead. The Oakley class lifeboat *Lloyds II* launched at 5 p.m., in a gale and very rough seas. The Rocks were only 20 yards from sheer cliffs and dan buoys prevented Coxswain Clemence from going right alongside. He got within ten feet of the yacht, passed a tow rope and pulled her clear. The Captain's body and one survivor were landed at 6.00 p.m. in Ilfracombe.

MARTIN John (Joe) Henry William, Coxswain/Mechanic,
** Hastings Lifeboat** **BRONZE**

27 March 1985

20 November 1984: The relief Oakley class lifeboat *Calouste Gulbenkian* launched at 8.23 p.m. into a strong westerly gale and heavy breaking seas, in response to a request from the Irish container ship *Bell Rover*. Sailing down the English Channel, she had reported a sick man who needed to be taken ashore. Meeting her seven miles south-east of Hastings, Sussex, Coxswain Martin approached the container ship with the sick man, weighing 22 stones, already on a pilot ladder. He was dragged into the lifeboat which had the Honorary Medical Adviser on board and landed at Hastings at 10.20 p.m.

CLARKE Alan John, Helmsman, Hunstanton Inshore Lifeboat **BRONZE**

26 June 1985

31 March 1985: A windsurfer was seen to be in trouble among sandbanks off Brancaster, Norfolk, where he was lying on his board, unable to reach the shore. The Atlantic 21 rigid inflatable lifeboat *Spirit of America* launched at 4.30 p.m. in a westerly gale. Helmsman Clarke took the lifeboat into the shallow water and reached the exhausted man, although she grounded on two occasions and was filled with water by each rolling sea. As the windsurfer was blown alongside, he and his board were taken into the lifeboat and landed at 5.30 p.m.

BISSON Peter John, Second Coxswain, St. Peter Port Lifeboat **BRONZE(2)**

27 November 1985

11 August 1985: The Arun class lifeboat *Sir William Arnold* slipped her moorings at 9.50 a.m. in a southerly gale, high seas and swell, and headed for the French yacht *Matam II*, which was anchored below the cliffs at La Corbière, on the south-west coast of Guernsey. Second Coxswain Bisson, in command, had to negotiate many rocks before he could get close enough. The lifeboat's inflatable dinghy was then launched with three crew members on board and a towline was passed to the yacht, which was towed clear and taken into St. Peter Port with her three man crew.

MAIDEN Robert Nolan, Coxswain, Hartlepool Lifeboat **BRONZE**

8 May 1986

10 November 1985: In a violent north-easterly storm and heavy breaking high seas, the Dutch coaster *Anne* was dragging her anchor. Shortly after midnight, she ran aground on Long Scar Rocks near Hartlepool, Co. Durham. The Waveney class lifeboat *The Scout* slipped her moorings and, on reaching the scene, Coxswain Maiden took her in four times. While rescuing the four man crew, the lifeboat was twice swept by heavy seas which broke over and around the casualty. The coaster's Captain remained at risk on board, but as the tide fell, the immediate danger passed.

PAVITT John William, Helmsman, Appledore Inshore Lifeboat **BRONZE**

25 June 1986

1 December 1985: On relief duty, the Atlantic 21 rigid inflatable lifeboat *Long Life I* launched at 1 p.m. in a southerly gale and 20 foot waves to help a windsurfer in trouble off Croyde, at the north end of Barnstaple Bay. The man could be seen clinging to his board in confused seas, south of Asp Rock, and in imminent danger of being swept thereon. Helmsman Pavitt ran straight in towards the surfer, took him and his board on to the lifeboat, and landed them at 2.11 p.m. Winching the surfer up by helicopter had been considered too dangerous.

CANNON Ronald Nicholas, Coxswain/Mechanic, Ramsgate Lifeboat **SILVER**

19 March 1986

26 December 1985: In rapidly deteriorating weather, the French trawler *Gloire à Marie II* went aground in a storm, south of Ramsgate, Kent. The Waveney class lifeboat *Ralph and Joy Swann* left her moorings at 8.15 p.m. after she first experienced great difficulty getting her crew on board from the pier. Despite hazardous conditions in the shallows, Coxswain Cannon manoeuvred the lifeboat close to the trawler, and two lifeboat crewmen boarded her. A tow was passed and the casualty brought off. The tow was then dismantled and the trawler, with her seven man crew, escorted into Ramsgate harbour under her own power.

HOGG John Adrian, Captain. Coxswain, Tynemouth, Lifeboat **SILVER**

10 September 1986

15 April 1986: The fishing vessel *La Morlaye*, with a crew of three, had been towed for 27 miles from the fishing grounds where her nets had fouled her propeller. The tow had parted in the east-

south-easterly gale, and *La Morlaye* was now only 400 yards off Whitley Bay, north of Tynemouth. The Arun class lifeboat *George and Oliver Turner* launched at 1.15 a.m. to find the vessel lying in very shallow water. After making near successful attempts to tow off the casualty, Coxswain Hogg took the lifeboat alongside, and the three men jumped to safety on board.

SHAW Stephen Eric, Coxswain, Alderney Lifeboat   **BRONZE**

10 September 1986

4 May 1986: After a rough crossing, the yacht *Sea Victor*, on passage from Exmouth to Guernsey, found her engine had developed major difficulties. Without power and taking in water, she was in trouble about five miles west of Platte Fougère lighthouse in heavy seas and with a southerly gale force wind. As the St. Peter Port lifeboat had been diverted to another yacht in greater need, the Alderney Brede class lifeboat *Forester's Future* slipped her moorings at 1.30 a.m., headed towards the yacht, and reached her at 2.30 a.m. In the darkness, the scene of the rescue was illuminated by a French helicopter while Coxswain Shaw made ten passes which enabled a crewman to jump on board the yacht. A woman and two men were then transferred to the lifeboat. Finally a towline was passed. The crewman and the yacht's Skipper stayed on board whilst she was towed to St. Peter Port, where she was handed over to the harbour launch at 7.15 a.m. The lifeboat reached Alderney at 9.30 a.m.

SHAW Stephen Eric, Coxswain, Alderney Lifeboat   **BRONZE(2)**
HARWOOD Martin John, Second Coxswain, Alderney Lifeboat   **BRONZE**

7 May 1987

25 August 1986: A yacht, the German owned *Seylla II*, was in trouble three miles north-east of Alderney with a broken rudder in a southerly storm – a situation made more difficult because the occupantswere only able to speak German. The Brede class lifeboat *Forester's Future* slipped her moorings at 7.40 p.m., and, helped by an unknown German-speaking radio station, established the yacht's position as south-east of Quenard light, east of Race Rock. Coxswain Shaw took his boat alongside, which enabled Second Coxswain Harwood to jump on board and organise a successful tow. The yacht and her six occupants – two men, two women and two children – were brought safely into harbour at Braye just after 9 p.m.

STRINGER Ian, Helmsman, Eastbourne Inshore Lifeboat   **BRONZE**

25 March 1987

9 December 1986: Filming a stunt for a new James Bond film at Beachy Head, Sussex, an outboard powered Dory capsized while recovering equipment from beneath the cliffs, and pitched the three man crew into the heavy sea and swell. The D Class inflatable lifeboat *Humphrey and Nora Tollemache* launched, with a crew of two, and threaded her way through dangerous rocks and shallows covered intermittently by breaking seas and surf. The three men were picked up and transferred to the safety launch *Trinitas* as the weather worsened. Attempts had been made to save the Dory and the film equipment, but to no avail.

CASTLE Robin, Coxswain/Mechanic, Sheerness Lifeboat   BRONZE

25 November 1987

16 October 1987: In the west-south-westerly hurricane force winds sweeping south-east England and the English Channel, the Waveney class lifeboat *Helen Turnbull* was forced to leave her normal berth and, in total darkness due to a power blackout, to secure alongside the pumping plant quay at Queenborough, Isle of Sheppey. Then, alerted to two men in a small angling boat in danger off the Isle of Grain, she put out with safety lines rigged aft of the wheel-house; every man on board had his lifejacket lights switched on. Both men were picked up and brought on board, but, in manoeuvring to get clear, a violent gust of wind forced the lifeboat's stern aground. For 30 minutes Coxswain Castle and his crew tried unsuccessfully to free her, but, at 8 a.m., the main engines were shut down and everybody else stayed below with all water-tight doors closed, while the Coxswain and Second Coxswain remained in the wheelhouse. At 1.30 p.m., against advice, the younger angler succeeded in walking ashore. The lifeboat refloated in moderating weather at 6.17 p.m. and after pulling her off gently, Coxswain Castle returned the *Helen Turnbull* to her Sheerness berth.

SARGENT Derek John, Coxswain/Mechanic, Weymouth Lifeboat   BRONZE

27 January 1988

16 October 1987: In south-south-westerly hurricane conditions, the catamaran *Sunbeam Chaser* was reported to be stationary, under bare poles, with engine and steering problems, 12 miles south of Portland Bill. The Arun class lifeboat *Tony Vandervell* slipped her moorings at 1.20 a.m. and forged through the adverse conditions in which she sustained damage. She reached the casualty and Coxswain Sargent took her in twice to save the occupants. Refusing to acknowledge her attempts, the owner veered away each time. Eventually three men, a woman and a youth were taken off, but the owner stayed on board. Finally he made Weymouth harbour at 9.30 a.m. in company with the lifeboat, having missed the Shambles by 100 yards. Throughout the whole operation the Skipper ignored the lifeboat.

COUZENS Roy William, Acting Coxswain, Dover Lifeboat   SILVER
ABBOTT Michael Frederick, Acting Assistant Mechanic/Emergency Coxswain
   Dover Lifeboat   BRONZE
BRUCE Robert John, Crew Member, Dover Lifeboat   BRONZE
McHUGH Dominic William, Crew Member, Dover Lifeboat   BRONZE
RYAN Christopher William, Crew Member, Dover Lifeboat   BRONZE
TANNER Eric St. John, Crew Member, Dover Lifeboat   BRONZE
BUCKLAND Geoffrey Ian, Crew Member, Dover Lifeboat   BRONZE

23 March 1988

16 October 1987: The south-south-westerly hurricane drove the 1,600 ton vessel *Sumnia* against the Admiralty Pier at Dover, Kent, close to the western entrance, where she was pinned by the terrible conditions against the west end of the southern breakwater. After initial problems, the Thames class lifeboat *Rotary Service* put to sea about 7 a.m. with one propeller fouled by rope. She arrived to find the bulk carrier moving violently in 20 foot high seas and with waves up to 60 feet high breaking over Admiralty Pier. Acting Coxswain Couzens took the lifeboat close to the breakwater, on the lee side, to find two men had been washed overboard. While rescuing them, he was thrown

heavily against the steering controls and bruised his rib cage. A third survivor was sighted among the wreckage and recovered. The three men were landed, and the lifeboat returned to continue the search for survivors. During this search the Coxswain collapsed and his place was taken by Michael Abbott. The lifeboat immediately returned to the tug haven and, on arrival, the Acting Coxswain was taken to hospital, where he was diagnosed as having suffered a heart attack.

HORROCKS Keith, Helmsman, Blackpool Inshore Lifeboat   **BRONZE**
DENHAM Philip, Helmsman, Blackpool Inshore Lifeboat   **BRONZE**
23 March 1988

6 January 1988: A small vessel fired a red flare off Blackpool, Lancashire, and another vessel, half a mile away, capsized. Both D class inflatable lifeboats, based on Blackpool, launched in north-westerly winds and violent broken seas. *D 310* under Helmsman Horrocks searched the area of the capsized vessel and found one man floating face downwards, but he was pronounced dead on arrival at hospital. Helmsman Denham took out *D 300* and was able to rescue the survivor from the other craft, which was about to capsize in the surf. Both lifeboats then combined to search for nearly two hours for other survivors but without success.

CLARKE Alan John, Helmsman, Hunstanton Inshore Lifeboat   **BRONZE(2)**
23 November 1988

7 February 1988: With a four man crew, the Atlantic 21 rigid inflatable lifeboat *Spirit of America* launched at 5.45 p.m., in darkness and a southerly near gale, to evacuate an injured crewman from the King's Lynn motor fishing vessel *Portunus*, which was disabled and under tow eight miles north of station, in the mouth of the Wash. On arrival the wind had strengthened to a strong gale, also steep seas and a tide running with squalls of sleet and snow. With very little room for manoeuvre and in virtually zero visibility, the man was grabbed and hauled aboard the inflatable lifeboat at the second attempt, then conveyed to shore and landed at 7.33 p.m. to be taken to hospital.

THOMSON Peter Neville, Coxswain/Mechanic, Whitby Lifeboat   **BRONZE**
BOTHAM Nicholas Simon, Helmsman, Whitby Inshore Lifeboat   **BRONZE**
29 June 1988

9 April 1988: The yacht *Cymba* was driven towards the shore after capsizing off Whitby harbour. The D Class inflatable lifeboat *Gwynaeth* launched at 8.40 a. m. followed by the Waveney class lifeboat *White Rose of Yorkshire*. After negotiating heavy breaking seas at the harbour entrance, Helmsman Botham turned west towards the casualty which was in very rough broken water. The inflatable lifeboat picked a man from the water, but on examination found him to be dead. Meanwhile, Coxswain Thomson had taken his lifeboat inshore because the yacht was being driven inland with a survivor in the water on the stern side, apparently attached to her in some way. Heading in toward her, the lifeboat was struck by two large seas; this incident persuaded the Coxswain to take her in stern first through atrocious sea conditions. He managed to secure the man at the third approach, and the survivor was dragged alongside the lifeboat, lifted in, and later landed at Whitby. The lifeboat then went back to sea to escort fishing vessels into harbour – a regular duty.

SINCLAIR William Swanson, Captain. Coxswain, Kirkwall Lifeboat   **BRONZE(2)**

24 January 1989

13 September 1988: At 7.18 a.m. the Arun class lifeboat *Mickie Salveson* cast off to help the 500-ton bulk cement carrier *BC Mercurius* drifting towards the shore with engine failure, two and a half miles off Noup Head, Westray, Orkneys. Four of the casualty's crew had already been lifted off by helicopter, but her Master and Chief Engineer were still on board. When the lifeboat arrived at 9 a.m. the wind had risen to Force 8. As the ship's Master indicated that he wished to be towed clear rather than taken off, the lifeboat passed a line to the casualty, fighting the increasingly severe seas and wind. The fight to save her took more than two hours during which the line parted twice due to the violent movements of both vessels. At one stage the casualty was only 300 yards from shore, but Coxswain Sinclair managed to coax her to a safe anchorage then stood by for two and a half hours until a tug arrived to take over. The lifeboat returned to station after a service lasting 13 hours.

RAINES Graham Alan, Crew Member, Hayling Island Inshore Lifeboat   **BRONZE**

24 January 1989

9 October 1988: Early in the afternoon the Atlantic 21 rigid inflatable lifeboats launched independently from both Portsmouth and Hayling Island, in response to a report that the 32 foot yacht *Dingaling* was in difficulties. On passage from Cowes to Chichester the yacht had broached to and, when the Hayling Island boat found her at 1.24 p.m., she was wallowing near Chichester Bar, under a storm jib with her propeller fouled. A man was seen floating on his back and, after a helicopter had failed to recover him, Crew Member Raines leapt into the water and swam to him to give support. As he approached, the yachtsman wrapped his legs around the rescuer and they were forced under the surface by the inflatable driven sideways by the breaking seas. As they surfaced the other crewman, who tried to help, was thrown into the water beside them, then grabbed hold of Raines with one hand and a lifeline with the other. Whilst the Helmsman was manoeuvring the lifeboat on one engine, the Portsmouth craft arrived on the scene, and one of her crew pulled Raines and the victim into the Hayling Island boat. The Portsmouth boat stood by and confirmed the yacht was empty although water-logged. A woman who had been picked up by a rescue helicopter was found to be dead on arrival at hospital, but the man recovered.

CATCHPOLE John William, Coxswain, Lowestoft Lifeboat   **BRONZE**

24 January 1989

19 October 1988: The coaster *Medina D* had stranded four and a half miles north of Lowestoft station and was taking water. The Tyne class lifeboat *Spirit of Lowestoft* slipped her moorings half an hour after midnight and set out in an east-south-east Force 8 gale. Visibility was worsening to poor with frequent rain squalls and as the lifeboat cleared the harbour she met heavy confused seas. When the casualty was sighted on the south side of Crofton Channel she was being pounded by seas breaking across her decks, therefore Coxswain Catchpole and his crew manned the upper conning position. Weather, wind and visibility had all worsened and the coaster was lying with a pronounced list to starboard in driving rain and blown spray. The lifeboat started the first approach only to be forced off course by a huge sea. Circling, she made a second approach and took off three men before another very large sea forced her to retire. The last crew member and the Master were taken off during the third approach which

took place while breaking seas were creating a very dangerous situation. Shortly after the lifeboat cleared the scene at 1.12 a.m., the coaster capsized and sank. The survivors were landed at 1.40 a.m.

RALSTON Thomas, Coxswain/Mechanic Mallaig Lifeboat   **BRONZE**

21 March 1989

27 October 1988: The Mallaig Arun class lifeboat *The Davina and Charles Matthews Hunter* successfully towed the motor fishing vessel *Galilean* to a safe mooring at Loch Nevis in Force 11 northerly winds and stormy conditions. The crew of two was rescued and the vessel saved. Coxswain Ralston displayed great determination and courage and a high degree of skill in taking the lifeboat into a hazardous area and then in manoeuvring both lifeboat and casualty to safety.

CLARK Peter Hewitt Peterson, Coxswain/Mechanic, Lerwick Lifeboat   **BRONZE(2)**

21 March 1989

13 January 1989: The fishing vessel *Boy Andrew* went aground near Bressay Lighthouse, head into a gully at Trebister Ness, in an area known as The Nizz. Shortly after 5 a.m. the Lerwick Lifeboat, the 52 ft Arun class *Soldian,* proceeded to the casualty. Some of the crew of the *Boy Andrew* were then ferried to the lifeboat in the *Soldian*'s Y class inflatable. An initial attempt by the lifeboat to tow off the fishing vessel failed as it was stuck fast on a falling tide.

Later in the morning, after landing some of the survivors at Lerwick, the *Soldian* returned to the scene in rapidly deteriorating weather conditions. A 200 ft fishing vessel, the *Altair*, also arrived to render assistance and help to tow off the *Boy Andrew*. As the Skipper was alone on the casualty, two men from the *Altair* were transferred by a helicopter from Sumburgh, and the winchman also stayed aboard to help. After one abortive attempt, the tow line was secured, and at 1.08 p.m. the *Altair* pulled the *Boy Andrew* clear, stern first. She immediately began to sink, therefore Coxswain Clark moved in at full speed, crossed ahead of the sinking bow on to *Boy Andrew*'s weather side and placed the lifeboat's port shoulder to the casualty's port quarter. The three fishermen were pulled aboard the lifeboat, but the helicopter winchman slipped and fell between the two boats. With full engine power, the Coxswain manoeuvred clear before the winchman was crushed, and the wash from the lifeboat carried him clear of the sinking vessel. The helicopter then moved in and retrieved the winchman from the sea. The time was 1.12 p.m. when the lifeboat reported to the Coastguard that the *Boy Andrew* had sunk and that everyone had been saved.

MACDONALD Malcolm, Coxswain/Mechanic, Stornoway Lifeboat   **BRONZE**

21 March 1989

13 February 1989: Late in the afternoon, Stornoway lifeboat, the 52 ft Arun class *Sir Max Aitken II,* proceeded to the crabber *Westward* which had anchored off Holm Island but was dragging seawards and in need of assistance. The wind was blowing from the north-west at hurricane force. At 5.20 p.m. the casualty was sighted, lying across wind and sea on a westerly heading with her anchor out. She was rolling heavily and shipping seas across her open foredeck. Her two man crew was in the tiny wheelhouse forward. Coxswain Macdonald approached the casualty across the wind and finally succeeded in holding the lifeboat alongside the stricken boat long enough for the two crew members to be snatched to safety.

This was accomplished in spite of a 15 foot swell, driving spray and rain together with a wind so strong that the lifeboat crew had to turn their heads down wind just to breath air into their lungs.

CHANT David J.O., Coxswain/Mechanic, St David's Lifeboat　　　　　**BRONZE**

3 May 1989

26 February 1989: St David's 47 ft Tyne class lifeboat *Garside* was launched at 9.40 a.m. following distress calls from m.f.v. *Stephanie Jane*, which had lost power and was dragging her anchor five cables south of the South Bishop lighthouse. In winds of severe gale Force 9, gusting to hurricane Force 12 with very rough seas, and close to rocks, Coxswain/Mechanic David Chant skilfully positioned the lifeboat allowing a towline to be passed to the fishing vessel. Due to the extreme weather conditions and the difficulty of the tow, the two vessels were not safely berthed and the survivors landed at Milford Haven until 2.45 p.m.

STEENVOORDEN David L., Helmsman, Cleethorpes Inshore Lifeboat　　　**BRONZE**

16 January 1990

30 July 1989: The Cleethorpes D class inflatable lifeboat was launched into a north-north-west wind of Force 7 to 8 at 10.21 a.m. to locate and escort five canoeists on a charity paddle from Grimsby to Cleethorpes. In confused seas up to 10 ft high the lifeboat was continually full of water as she searched for, and located, the casualties in driving rain, with spray reducing visibility to almost nil at times. Continually full of water, the lifeboat, with the five survivors and three crew aboard, made slow progress in the severe weather resulting in the transfer of the canoeists to the Pilot Launch *Neptune* for landing at Grimsby. The heavily laden lifeboat needed three attempts to transfer the casualties, the 6 ft to 7 ft seas knocking the bow away on the first two attempts.

Before returning to station the crew were alerted to a yacht in trouble at Spurn Point. The worst of the squall had passed, but the wind was still north north west Force 5 when the lifeboat reached the 20 ft yacht *Serenus* and found her aground, beam on to the seas. Rigging from a broken mast section cluttered the deck and surrounding water, yet the lifeboat passed a tow in the shallow water and refloated the yacht, eventually taking her and the two occupants to Grimsby.

RACE Peter Roland, Coxswain, Teesmouth Lifeboat　　　　　　**BRONZE**

16 January 1990

26 August 1989: The fishing vessel *Gang Warily* had been driven aground in the dark at the foot of a sheer 360 ft cliff, with 12 ft seas breaking heavily and driven by an onshore Force 7 wind. Redcar's Atlantic 21 lifeboat *Lord Brotherton* was first on the scene but was unable to approach closely because of underwater rocks. Crew Member Peter Hodge swam ashore with a line, and he was being pulled back to the lifeboat with the survivors when the line snagged on a rock. Crew Member Hodge was pulled under water until he was able to free the line and subsequently was washed back ashore with the two survivors.

The Teesmouth Tyne class relief lifeboat *Owen and Ann Aisher,* with Coxswain Race at the helm, then entered the surf bow first, using her engines to hold station as she eased towards the cliffs, the seas breaking heavily over the stern of the 47 ft lifeboat. About 150 ft from the shore the Tyne's small inflatable X Boat was launched with Crew Member Christopher Jones aboard. The oars were soon knocked from his hands, and the small boat was carried ashore by the wind and seas as the crew aboard the lifeboat kept the line taught enough to ensure clearance of the rocks.

Once ashore Crew Member Jones took the three men aboard the inflatable while the Coxswain edged the lifeboat closer still, the Tyne's steel bow twice striking on submerged rocks. When all was ready, the lifeboat eased astern through the breaking waves, pulling the inflatable to seaward. Although the heavily laden dinghy was going through the seas rather than over them the manoeuvre was successful and the inflatable was brought alongside the lifeboat and the four men pulled aboard – a task accomplished at 10.13 p.m.

By 10.40 p.m. the survivors had been landed at Teesmouth by the Tyne.

THOMAS William Alan, Coxswain, Tenby Lifeboat   **SILVER**

16 January 1990

22 September 1989: Following a report that Motor Fishing Vessel *Seeker* was in difficulties with m.f.v. *New Venture* attempting a tow, Tenby's 47 ft Tyne class lifeboat *RFA Sir Galahad* was launched at 4.20 p.m., with Coxswain Alan Thomas at the helm. The lifeboat arrived at the scene in Rhossili Bay at 5.15 p.m. to find that m.f.v. *Seeker* had been washed up the beach. Her crew had been assisted ashore by the Coastguard and airlifted by helicopter. However, a third fishing vessel, the *Silver Stream,* was now struggling to keep off the beach. The wind was west north west, Force 8–9, with poor visibility through rain squalls, whilst 30 ft very rough seas were breaking.

Coxswain Thomas realised that it would be impossible to tow either of the two vessels clear and so with great care and courage, he manoeuvred the lifeboat inside the surf line to maintain close contact. While they battled to clear further offshore, a very large sea rolled *Silver Stream* over, revealing her keel. Amazingly, she recovered but was part full of water and her lone Skipper was trapped in his wheelhouse by loose gear on deck. Coxswain Thomas saw that the man was in grave danger and, with outstanding skill and determination, he drove the lifeboat up to the fishing vessel, into exactly the right position for the Skipper to be pulled through the wheelhouse window by lifeboatmen on deck.

The lifeboat continued to keep close contact with m.f.v. *New Venture* as she slowly managed to steer clear and make for Tenby. Once moored in Tenby Roads, her two exhausted crew were transferred to the lifeboat and brought ashore.

KENNETT David George, Coxswain, Yarmouth (Isle of Wight) Lifeboat   **BRONZE**

16 January 1990

28–29 October 1989: During the morning of 28 October, the 495 ton high sided cargo vessel *Al Kwather I* was reported in trouble three and a half miles east of Peveril Point. There was a south-westerly, severe gale Force 9 blowing. Her cargo of cars was loose on deck. The Swanage relief Rother class lifeboat *Horace Clarkson* first located the casualty at 11.30 a.m. and stood by in winds approaching hurricane force. At 3.10 p.m. the Yarmouth relief Arun lifeboat *Margaret Russell Fraser* took up position astern of *Al Kwather I*, and this allowed the Swanage lifeboat to return to her station. The Arun stood by for an hour. Then, as the casualty was in no imminent danger, she proceeded to Swanage for the crew to recuperate and some damage repairs to be effected.

Shortly after midnight, however, the Master of the *Al Kwather I* reported engine problems and requested that he and his crew be taken off. The Yarmouth and Swanage lifeboats therefore both put to sea at 12.40 a.m. As the Yarmouth lifeboat, the faster boat, approached the ship all her lights went out, and the lifeboat crew used their searchlight to pinpoint her position. They could see her listing to port and lying broadside on to the seas, rolling violently. The lifeboat edged close to the stern of the vessel where the casualty's crew, all wearing lifejackets, had gathered on the poop deck and rigged a cargo net over a stern door. Coxswain Kennett managed to position the lifeboat against the door. Several times the lifeboat and merchant ship collided as the Coxswain fought to reposition the lifeboat as she rolled and ranged up and down the casualty's stern. A crew member from the *Al Kwather* could be seen clambering down the cargo net. He then virtually rolled on to the lifeboat. The second survivor to disembark caught his foot in the net and at one stage fell below the level of the lifeboat's deck. Coxswain Kennett, alert to this, pulled the lifeboat astern. As he did so, crew members succeeded in hauling the man on board.

As news had arrived that the rescue helicopter was on its way, the remaining six crew members from the casualty decided to wait for its arrival. The Yarmouth lifeboat took up a position to windward, and the Swanage lifeboat, which had arrived on the scene ten minutes after the Yarmouth boat, moved to leeward of the casualty to cover for any accidents. By 2.12 a.m. the helicopter airlift of the six remaining crew members was completed and both lifeboats returned to their respective stations.

COLEMAN Shane Gordon, Coxswain, Lowestoft Pilot Boat
  (also Second Coxswain/Mechanic Lowestoft Lifeboat)   **BRONZE**
27 June 1990

26 January 1990: Soon after midnight, Shane Coleman, Coxswain and sole crew member of the Lowestoft pilot boat, had just transferred a pilot on board the 240 ft coaster *Oakham*, when he saw the coaster collide with a 60 ft tug. It was a dark night and a Force 9 to storm Force 10 wind from the south west was driving spray through the air. The tug *Impulsion*, which had been struck by the coaster's bow on her port quarter, began to list heavily to port. Shane Coleman immediately steered the pilot boat around the coaster's stern and towards the rapidly sinking tug. By the time he reached her, the stern was already under water at a 50 degree angle and the sea was full of cordage and flotsam from the tug.

Her three crew members were standing on top of the wheelhouse which was only four feet above the surface of the water. As Coleman made a fast approach towards the starboard side of the casualty, his port engine stalled after picking up something around the propeller. He increased speed on the starboard engine and drove up to the starboard side of the tug's wheelhouse, allowing the three survivors to step aboard. He put the starboard engine astern, but at a distance of 12 feet this engine stalled as the propeller also picked up a rope. Coxswain Coleman was uncertain if he would be pulled under as the tug sank, and asked the Coastguard for lifeboat assistance. At 12.50 a.m. the tug sank and although the stern of the pilot boat was pulled down it remained above the water. Eleven minutes later Lowestoft lifeboat was alongside and able to take the three survivors aboard.

HEADING Peter Robert, Helmsman, Aberystwyth Inshore Lifeboat   **BRONZE**

GORMAN Robert James, Skipper, Fishing Vessel *Seren-y-More*   **BRONZE**

15 January 1991

18 September 1990: The Aberystwyth C class lifeboat, with Peter Heading at the helm, was launched following a report that the 18 ft yacht *Otter*, with one man aboard, was in difficulties some three quarters of a mile from shore. There was a fresh wind with 5–6 ft seas and hazardous 'wind over tide' conditions at the bar. Clearing the bar safely, the lifeboat came up to the casualty to find that the yacht's engine had failed and the occupant was tired, cold and distressed. Helmsman Heading decided to take the yacht in tow, and Crew Member Mike Harris managed to climb aboard the yacht with a line.

As the weather worsened, concern was expressed that the lifeboat would experience difficulties in towing the yacht over the bar. Local fisherman Robert Gorman, who was also a member of the lifeboat crew, agreed to launch his own 32 ft fishing boat *Seren-y-Mor* to assist. Four other men with lifeboat experience agreed to act as crew. In deteriorating conditions, Helmsman Heading decided to pass the tow over to the *Seren-y-Mor*. After careful and expert manoeuvring, under very difficult circumstances, the tow was successfully passed. Aboard the yacht, Crew Member Harris fashioned a drogue from a gas bottle to counter broaching. Despite some tense moments, all three craft were skilfully and safely steered across the bar and into the harbour.

DOUGAL James A, Acting Coxswain/Assistant Mechanic, Eyemouth Lifeboat   **SILVER**

26 March 1991

6 October 1990: Soon after 4 p.m. a dramatic change in weather conditions led to hurricane force winds springing up from the north along the east coast of Scotland. The coastline between Dunbar and Eyemouth is popular with divers, and it soon became clear to Coastguards that a number of sub aqua enthusiasts had been caught out at sea in the hurricane.

Three lifeboats were alerted, including Eyemouth's relief 44 ft Waveney *44.001* which launched at 4.49 p.m. with Assistant Mechanic James Dougal at the helm. Taking the lifeboat out of the narrow harbour entrance into the face of the 100 knot hurricane was only the first great hazard the Acting Coxswain was to encounter. Twenty foot seas were running into the entrance and crashing over the sea walls. Visibility was virtually non-existent in the rain, spume and spray.

Clear of the dangerous rocks near the harbour entrance, James Dougal headed for St Abbs where a group of divers had been caught in the storm. The lifeboat met seas of 35 ft head on, the Acting Coxswain reducing power as he negotiated each one. The 44 ft boat rolled violently as she drove on, her side decks awash.

By 5.15 p.m. the lifeboat was off St Abbs Harbour, with visibility about 50 yards, wind 90 knots and the seas still breaking at a height of 35 ft over the rocky outcrops. From his position on the harbour wall, the Auxiliary Coastguard in Charge at St Abbs had miraculously spotted two of the divers in the water. He then lost sight of them in the spray and all he could see of the lifeboat was her searchlight beam. With that as his only reference he guided the lifeboat to the scene.

Less than 200 feet from the lifeboat's starboard side lay the Cathedral Rock, the same distance to port jutted the Ebb Carr Rocks. Neither were visible and the heavy spray made them undetectable by radar. Still the Acting Coxswain persevered. His crew, lifelines secured, were out on deck scouring the sea for the divers, whom they spotted still conscious and close to a creel buoy.

On the third attempt James Dougal succeeded in bringing the lifeboat close enough for a crew member to throw a heaving line to the divers. Both were able to grab it and they were hauled against the lifeboat's starboard shoulder and then on to the boat.

There were still two divers missing south of St Abbs. Eyemouth lifeboat began a search for them but her Acting Coxswain became concerned about his two survivors who were becoming severely sea sick. However, an attempt to land them at St Abbs had to be abandoned when it became clear that entering the harbour would endanger the lifeboat. Instead the lifeboat continued to search for the other divers until 7 p.m. An attempt was made to winch the two survivors into an RAF helicopter, but the weather forced this attempt to be abandoned too.

By 7.45 p.m. darkness made further searching impossible and Forth Coastguard suspended the operation. The lifeboat headed south for Eyemouth only to find that there was no safe way into the harbour which forced the Coxswain to continue on to Burnmouth. On reaching this destination a power cut had extinguished the harbour leading lights but, thanks to the resourcefulness of local fishermen, car headlights were positioned to guide the lifeboat safely into harbour. Her survivors were landed into the care of the Scottish Ambulance Service.

WILLIAMSON George Lamont, Skipper/Owner, Salmon Workboat *Challenge*, Burra, Shetland

BRONZE

26 March 1991

8 October 1990: At about 9.15 p.m., Mr George Williamson was informed that the boat *Vidra* had been wrecked on Burwick Holm and lobster fisherman Ralph Pottinger was stranded on the island. As a Coastguard helicopter had been unable to winch the man clear, Mr. Williamson spoke by radio to fishing boats in the area and immediately set off for Scalloway Harbour.

At 9.33 p.m., Mr. Williamson and a volunteer crew of three set out to sea in his 36 ft salmon work boat *Challenge*, towing an 18 ft flat-bottomed boat *Conquest*. The sky was overcast with heavy rain. Storm Force 10 south-westerly winds whipped up driving spray from the sea.

As Burwick Holm came in sight, four large fishing vessels could be seen lying off the island helping to light the scene, but unable to come close enough to recover the survivor. The wind was gusting Force 11, creating confused steep seas between the islands. With some difficulty, Mr. Williamson safely negotiated a route between salmon cages and creel markers into the lee of Burwick Holm. Transferring to *Conquest*, with Mr. Theodore Fullerton as crew, Mr. Williamson drove the boat to the north east corner of the island, running it on to the shingle. With an Auxiliary Coastguard searchlight illuminating the area from the Ness of Burwick, Mr. Pottinger crossed the island and boarded *Conquest*. Mr Williamson brought the boat off the shingle and all three men were back aboard *Conquest* by 9.57 p.m.

Progress on the return journey among the cages and creels was slow and hazardous. With skill and determination Mr. Williamson navigated the boats, crew and survivor into Scalloway Harbour, where they were met by an ambulance crew at 10.20 p.m.

TOMLINSON Jonathan Richard (Rick), Photographer

BRONZE

3 September 1991

16 April 1991: Rick Tomlinson, a former crew member of the Port St Mary lifeboat, Isle of Man, and Nick Keig, a well known and experienced yachtsman and President of Peel lifeboat station, were afloat on Lough Swilly in *Vulture*, a 17 ft rigid inflatable, for a publicity photography assignment with the Lough Swilly 16 ft inshore lifeboat, when a Mayday call was received. The 30 ft fishing vessel *Ross Revenge* had suffered machinery failure at the entrance to the Lough and was in

danger of being swept against a cliff face. Both inflatables made for the casualty but it was soon apparent that winds up to gale force and seas of some 20 feet were beyond the lifeboat's operational capabilities. The lifeboat remained in more sheltered waters while *Vulture*, aided by radioed navigational advice from the local RNLI, reached the casualty, which was drifting some 20 feet from the rock face below Pollst Head and in danger of being swept against the cliff. With Rick Tomlinson in command and Nick Keig at the helm, they manoeuvred the *Vulture* to the starboard bow of the casualty, which was lying port shoulder to sea, and a line was passed and secured. A tow was commenced immediately with the line set at 40 feet, and the fishing vessel was drawn clear of the cliff face.

Taking instruction and advice from the lifeboat station, the *Vulture* manoeuvred at slow speed through the narrows between Swilly Beg and Stookan Ore rock. It was difficult to maintain a steady course with the sea on the port quarter, so the towline was lengthened to 80 feet. Once clear of the narrows, the casualty was towed to Port Salon, arriving at 2.15 p.m.

The *Ross Revenge* was baled out and her crew were able to restart the engine. *Vulture* escorted the fishing vessel towards Rathmullen and was met by the Lough Swilly lifeboat off Macamish Point. On arrival at Rathmullen, the lifeboat transferred the survivors to the lifeboat station.

HARTLAND John Robert, Helmsman, Withernsea Inshore Lifeboat　　　　BRONZE

27 November 1991

15 May 1991: At 4.40 p.m., Humber Coastguard alerted Withernsea station that the 24 ft yacht *Frangipani* was in difficulties two and a half miles offshore and the D Class lifeboat was launched at 4.50 p.m., with John Hartland at the helm. The wind was northerly Force 5–6 with heavy breaking 6–8 ft waves.

The lifeboat was driven as fast as conditions would allow and reached the casualty at 5.20 p.m. where two occupants had stowed the sails and set the engine running slow ahead. The Skipper was slumped, complaining of engine fumes, and Hartland decided to take him aboard the lifeboat.

The wind was gusting Force 7, with moderate visibility and rough 15 ft seas. Loose gear and ropes in the water meant that Hartland's only possible approach would have to be on the port side. As all the crew held the lifeboat alongside the casualty, a very large sea reared up, taking both craft up a wall of water. As it subsided, the sick man rolled out of the yacht and was grabbed by the lifeboatmen.

The remaining yachtsman aboard *Frangipani* had only nine hours sailing experience, thus a decision was taken that lifeboatman Paul Theobald should be transferred to the craft. This was achieved at the first attempt and Theobald took control to await the arrival of Humber's Arun class lifeboat.

The Witherness lifeboat then made for shore, where the sick man was carried to a waiting ambulance. He later made a full recovery in hospital. The yacht was taken in tow by the Humber lifeboat, Withernsea crewman Theobald staying aboard for the duration of the two and a half hour trip back to Grimsby.

COTTER Kieran, Coxswain, Baltimore Lifeboat **BRONZE**
5 May 1992

30–31 October 1991: At 5 p.m., the 120 ft fishing vessel *Japonica* had engine failure some 13 miles west of the Fastnet Rock. The relief 47 ft Tyne class lifeboat *Good Shepherd*, under Coxswain Cotter, launched and finally reached the casualty after two and a half hours in a southerly storm Force 10. As the *Japonica* was being driven closer to the rock-bound shore, it was decided to attempt a tow; this was finally achieved after an hour and ten minutes in appalling conditions. The lifeboat then began to tow the casualty towards the safety of Bantry Bay. After having to reconnect the tow once, they reached the Bay shortly after 6 a.m. The *Good Shepherd* started on the return journey to Baltimore but had to put in to Castletownbere to land a crew member for medical attention and to repair a blocked fuel filter. There the lifeboat received a further radio call reporting another vessel in difficulties to the south of the Fastnet Rock. After repairs the Tyne sailed at 1.25 p.m. heading back into the full force of the weather as she rounded Mizen Head and pressed on towards the Fastnet.

The new casualty was the 60 ft sailing vessel *Atlantic Adventurer* which was having trouble with her auxiliary and sailing under a storm jib in an onshore wind from the south which had moderated slightly to gale Force 8 but gusting Force 9. Conditions were worsened by the rough sea with over a 20 ft swell. *Good Shepherd* reached the yacht at 4 p.m. and found her making six knots under a small storm jib. As her crew were exhausted, a tow was passed, a process which took some 15 minutes. The casualty was then taken to the safety of Baltimore Harbour, which she reached at 6.50 p.m. The two services lasted 26 hours.

WELLS David Howard, Helmsman, Clacton-on-Sea Inshore Lifeboat **BRONZE**
18 March 1992

1 November 1991: Early in the afternoon, the 29 ft yacht *Two Niner* with six persons on board went aground on the south side of Buxey Sand. Clacton's Atlantic 21 *Institute of London Underwriters* with David Wells at the helm was launched at 2.38 p.m., experiencing rough head seas, continual rain, and reduced visibility. The yacht was located at 3.10 p.m., listing heavily to port. The wind was south-south-west Force 7–8 and very rough 6 ft breaking seas were causing violent motion to the yacht. With great skill and care, Helsman Wells manoeuvred the starboard shoulder of the lifeboat against the port quarter of the casualty, to enable crew member Terry Bolingbroke to board the yacht. A towline was secured and slowly the yacht was moved off the sand. Once clear of Buxey Sand, the tow was slipped.

During the return voyage to Clacton, when passing Knoll Buoy, a particularly large sea broke from the darkness, burying the bow and suddenly impeding the progress of the lifeboat. Helmsman Wells fought to regain control and once clear found that lifeboatman Thomas Ridley was missing. Helmsman Wells turned the lifeboat immediately to retrace his course. As they strained to find any sign in the gloom, Bolingbroke caught sight of a flash of light ahead – the retro-reflective tape on Ridley-s lifejacket had reflected the lifeboat's navigation lights. Fifty yards ahead, Ridley was located and quickly recovered, though not without hazard since it required both lifeboatmen to help him aboard, which left the lifeboat beam on to the sea.

The Clacton lifeboat was back on station by 7.26 p.m., five hours after the service had begun.

SMITH Frank Yeoman, Coxswain/Mechanic, Salcombe Lifeboat   BRONZE

18 March 1992

8 January 1992: Salcombe-s Tyne class lifeboat *Baltic Exchange* was launched at 1.48 a.m. to stand by the 1,200 ton coaster *Janet C* carrying 1,300 tons of cargo and disabled just over two miles south east of Start Point with total power failure. The lifeboat, with Coxswain/Mechanic Smith at the helm, arrived at the casualty at 2.30 a.m.; the sea was rough with wind south south west Force 7, gusting 8–9. After several attempts a tow was connected, the coaster being then only half a nautical mile off Start Point. Thirty minutes after the tow was established, *Janet C* had been pulled away to nearly one nautical mile from Start Point. While awaiting the arrival of a tug the tow was continued; it broke once but the crew reconnected it within 15 minutes. The tug arrived at 5.20 a.m. and the Salcombe lifeboat stood by until the tow was well secured, leaving the area at 6.03 a.m. to arrive back on station at 7.30 a.m.

On board during the service were Staff Coxswain John Marjoram, who was there to deputise for Frank Smith who was due to attend the London Boat Show, and a film cameraman and sound recordist from Central TV making the programme 'Lifeboat'.

HODGE Peter William, Senior Helmsman, Redcar Inshore Lifeboat   BRONZE

18 March 1992

19 January 1992: A man and a woman, in their fifties, together with a dog were trapped beneath high cliffs at the base of Hunt Cliff, with the incoming tide breaking all round them. The Redcar Atlantic 21 lifeboat *Leicester Challenge* under the command of Senior Helmsman Peter Hodge was launched shortly after 1 p.m. to proceed the four and a half miles to the scene, and arrived there at 1.25 p.m. An 11–13 ft swell was breaking directly onshore and to a position some 130 yards off.

After dropping the anchor some 200 feet from shore, Hodge manoeuvred the lifeboat towards the shore, from where crew member Barry Wheater swam ashore to make fast a line. In shallow water the engines were stopped and tilted clear to avoid damage from the rocks.

Crew member Derek Robinson then went ashore with the stern line to assist Wheater and to help prevent the lifeboat being drawn seaward. Meanwhile the seas were lifting the lifeboat and pounding her against the rocks. At 1.40 p.m., with crew member Mark Reeves on the anchor warp and Wheater and Robinson ashore, Hodge assisted the two casualties, a Mr and Mrs Darling, and their dog into the lifeboat. They were fitted with lifejackets, wrapped in foil blankets and given the crew's gloves.

The crewmen ashore returned, the stern line was cut and the crew took up station in the bow to haul the lifeboat into deeper water. Still grounding heavily, she was hauled clear where the engines were lowered and started at the first attempt. The anchor rope was then cut and the lifeboat was driven out through the surf.

BISSON Peter John, Coxswain, St Peter Port Lifeboat   SILVER

25 November 1992

29–30 August 1992: Whilst already at sea, the St Peter Port Arun class lifeboat *Sir William Arnold* received a very broken Mayday from the 50 ft yacht *Sena Sioria* some 20 miles north west of the Hanois lighthouse on the south-west tip of Guernsey. The wind was Force 7–8, gusting force 9. Reaching the casualty shortly after 2 a.m. on the 30th, Coxswain Bisson decided to evacuate the people on board. On a first run, three people were snatched from the *Sena Sioria* before the lifeboat had to back off. The second run was aborted when one engine developed problems. On the third run, three more survivors were grabbed by the lifeboat crew on the foredeck. The Coxswain then saw the yacht's mizzen mast begin to fall towards the lifeboat and started to back away. The mast landed on the foredeck and, as the lifeboat backed off, the crew were dragged forward against stanchions and sails; consequently the Coxswain took the lifeboat ahead, back alongside the yacht, while the debris were cleared and two injured crew treated.

A helicopter arrived shortly thereafter and took off the two injured men. The lift took a full hour as the lifeboat was moving violently in the rough seas. When the helicopter returned at 4.30 a.m., the three crew remaining on the yacht jumped into the sea one at a time and were winched to safety, with the lifeboat standing by. Both injured lifeboat crew made a full recovery.

JAMES Roderick Harold, Helmsman, Hayling Island Inshore Lifeboat   **SILVER(2)**
DUNSTER Frank Sidney, Crew Member, Hayling Island Inshore Lifeboat   **SILVER**
19 January 1993

25th October 1992: At 11.50 a.m., the Coastguard received a Mayday from the 75 ft ketch *Donald Searle* which had anchored at the eastern end of Chichester Bar after her sails had been blown out in a 50 knot westerly gale and her engines had failed. There were 17 people on board, and the yacht was dragging her anchor as she was hurled about in 15 to 20 ft breaking seas. As the Hayling Island Atlantic 21 was already out on a service, Frank Dunster launched his own 28 ft rigid inflatable *Hayling Island* and headed for the casualty, which by now was in very shallow water and close to the Target Wreck. He took his boat alongside the ketch's starboard quarter and, at the second attempt, took off the first of the crew, and then a female crew member who had to be recovered from the sea between the two boats. Dunster, knowing the Bembridge lifeboat and a helicopter were on the way, headed back to Hayling Island lifeboat station and landed the two survivors at 12.35 p.m.

Meanwhile, Roderick James, in the Atlantic 21 *Aldershot,* was heading towards the casualty through very steep seas, such that at one stage the lifeboat stood on end. He reached the casualty at the same time as the helicopter and, in a series of five approaches, took five people off the *Donald Searle*. A lifeboat crew member was put on to the ketch to enable the helicopter winchman to be hauled towards the yacht. Two more people were taken on to the Atlantic 21 which then headed back to the station and landed all seven survivors.

The Bembridge lifeboat arrived at 12.42 p.m. to help. During a very difficult approach, the two vessels made heavy contact as the ketch was thrown 20 ft to leeward by a sea, damaging both boats. One survivor was pulled on to the lifeboat, but the Coxswain then decided it would be safer for the helicopter to complete the rescue. All seven remaining crew of the *Donald Searle,* the Hayling Island lifeboat crew member and the helicopter winchman were safely aboard the helicopter by 12.52 p.m.

Roderick James was the first inshore lifeboat crew member to win a second silver medal (his first was awarded in 1981).

CLARK Peter Hewitt Peterson, Coxswain/Mechanic, Lerwick Lifeboat   **BRONZE(3)**
24th March 1993

17–18 January 1993: About 11 p.m. on 17 January, Lerwick-s Arun class lifeboat *Soldian* proceeded at full speed to reach m.f.v. *Ardency* which had broken down 16 miles east-south-east of Bard Head and was taking water with her pumps not working. The wind was from the west at about 50 knots creating a very rough sea, whilst very heavy rain reduced visibility. A helicopter from Sumburgh reached the *Ardency* shortly after midnight but could not lower salvage pumps to the vessel because of the severe motion. By the time the lifeboat reached the casualty, the wind was gusting Force 14, and Coxswain Clark manoeuvred the lifeboat off her bow. At the second attempt a heaving line was passed and a tow started that eventually allowed the helicopter to lower the pumps on board. For five hours the lifeboat towed the *Ardency* slowly towards some lee from the land. At 5.35 a.m. the tow-line broke and it took three quarters of an hour before it could be re-established. Shortly thereafter, the *Ardency*'s engineer managed to get her engines working again, but the Coxswain left the tow in place until Lerwick Harbour was reached about 08.15 a.m.

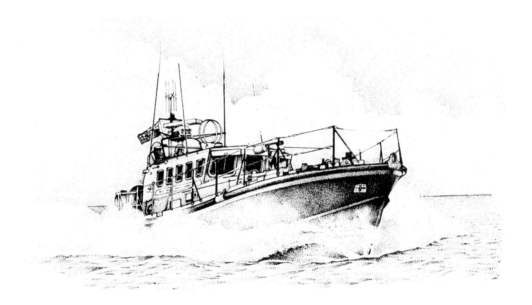

PEARSON John, Helmsman, Whitby Inshore Lifeboat **BRONZE**
13 April 1993

20 February 1993: At 11.30 a.m., Humber Coastguard requested Whitby lifeboat station to provide help to two 6 metre rigid inflatable boats (RIBs) to the east of the harbour. One had capsized with two men on board, one of whom was picked up by the other boat. Whitby's Tyne Class Lifeboat *City of Sheffield* proceeded on service, followed by the D class inflatable, although the latter was not fully checked out for the season and had no radio on board. Reaching the shallow area known as Whitby Rocks, the second man from the RIB was seen in the water. With only 3 ft of water under the Tyne, the D class inflatable sped inshore. Helmsman Pearson had to take the lifeboat past the survivor to carry out a 'snatch turn' on the back of a sea to return for a head-to-sea approach. On the second attempt, the man was recovered and hauled aboard. Taking the D class straight out into the seas, the boat left the water completely on several occasions. Eventually she reached the *City of Sheffield* and the survivor transferred to be landed in Whitby Harbour at 12.11 pm.

McDOWELL Ian, Helmsman, St Bees Inshore Lifeboat   **BRONZE**

24 November 1993

31 July 1993: The fishing vessel *Coeur de Lion* was aground in Fleswick Bay off St Bees Head, stuck on an outcrop of rocks 35–40 yards offshore, listing to starboard with heavy seas breaking on to her decks. The 'C' class inflatable lifeboat launched at 7.25am, with Alistair Graham at the helm, and with Helmsman Ian McDowell, Marcus Clarkson and Paul McDowell in the crew. An initial attempt to get alongside the casualty was thwarted when a large wave hit her, pushing the lifeboat away and damaging her engines on the rocks. Helmsman Graham decided to beach the lifeboat for repairs which was accomplished with difficulty, with Graham sustaining injury when the boat fell on top of him. Ian Mcdowell then tied a length of line around his waist and walked into the surf to get out near the *Coeur de Lion* to shout to the survivors to hold on. With new propellers fitted, the lifeboat, only Ian McDowell and Marcus Clarkson on board, powered away from the beach towards the casualty, striking numerous rocks on the way. In two difficult approaches the two men jumped from the fishing boat in to the lifeboat, which then headed directly back to St Bees, arriving there at 8.30 a.m. A helicopter recovered Graham and Paul McDowell from Fleswick Bay. The fishing vessel broke up shortly after the two crew had been rescued.

BENNETT Barry, Coxswain, St Mary's Lifeboat   **BRONZE**

24 November 1993

12 September 1993: At 5.21 p.m. the Arun class lifeboat *Robert Edgar* headed for Porth Cressa Bay on the island of St Mary's, where two yachts were anchored in an east-south-east severe gale, with a ground swell and breaking sea. The bay faces south-east and is very rocky. First the lifeboat provided a lee to enable the yacht *Aurea* to get clear of the bay and head for St Mary's. Then Coxswain Bennett took the lifeboat back in to the bay to the 25ft Folkboat *Bacarole*, still at anchor with the sole crew member sheltering in the stern. After several attempts a heaving line was passed over, but almost immediately this parted when the lifeboat had to be manoeuvred over a set of large breaking waves. A second line was got aboard and a tow was being established when the yacht was knocked flat and broke her mast. The Coxswain immediately decided to evacuate the survivor. At a second attempt, the lifeboat was brought close to the yacht, and the man jumped to be grabbed by the crew. A minute later *Bacarole* sank. The survivor was landed shortly after 6 p.m. at St Mary's.

DAVIES Richard William, Coxswain, Cromer Lifeboat   **BRONZE**

18 January 1994

13 October 1993: The Cromer 47 ft Tyne Class lifeboat *Ruby & Arthur Reed II* was launched at 3.20 p.m. to the aid of the 30 ft Kingfisher class yacht *Happy Bear* which had sent out a distress call. Heavy seas were lashing the boathouse doors as the lifeboat launched down the slipway and, on reaching the water, she was completely buried in the sea. At 3.45 p.m., and about three or four miles out, radio contact was established with the yacht and, at 3.57 p.m., she was sighted about a mile from the shore at Trimmingham, with storm jib set and engine going ahead. She was in great difficulty as the gear was not engaging properly, and she was being violently tossed around in shallow breaking sea. The Skipper was hanging on as best he could; his four man crew were below deck. A gale force wind was still blowing, visibility remained poor, and the breaking sea was up to 35 ft. As

Coxswain Davies considered it too dangerous to approach the casualty because it was likely to cause her serious damage, he asked the Skipper to maintain course with the lifeboat.

At 4.57 p.m., with daylight fading and the casualty's gearbox becoming even less effective, the Coxswain decided it was time for the tow line to be passed. The lifeboat manoeuvred off the casualty's weather beam and came up into the sea as the tow line was passed across. The Skipper and one of his crew went forward and secured the tow while another took the helm. The tow got under way at 5.07 p.m. and the lifeboat set course for the Cockle Gateway off Winterton. During the tow one large sea broke right over the casualty, leaving the Skipper's head just visible above the water. Another time the yacht broached right around so that the lifeboat and yacht were stern to stern.

At 6.00 p.m. weather conditions eased but, as the yacht's Skipper was nervous about bringing the craft into Great Yarmouth himself, during the approach Second Coxswain William Davies jumped across from the lifeboat to the yacht and took the helm. The lifeboat and yacht tied up alongside the Town Quay at 7.38 p.m. Weather conditions made it impossible for the lifeboat to return to Cromer for another five days.

CLARK William John, Joint Second Coxswain, Lerwick Lifeboat   **BRONZE**

18 January 1994

17–18 November 1993: The Lerwick 52 ft Arun class lifeboat *Soldian* was launched at 11.10 p.m. with Joint Second Coxswain Clark at the helm in the absence of the Coxswain on leave. The 3985 ton Kaliningrad registered *Borodinskoye Polye*, a factory trawler, had gone ashore on the Unicorn Reef in the northern approaches to Lerwick with 73 people on board. A south-westerly gale was blowing, visibility was poor, with a nine foot swell. The tide was creating waves up to 16 foot high close to the casualty. The vessel was aground lying beam to the sea, with her bows rolling from side to side and pitching on the rocks. Just after midnight, the lifeboat began to approach the casualty on the lee side where a jumping ladder had been rigged just aft of midships. By 1.20 a.m., after 35 approaches to the ship, 37 survivors had been taken on board. The lifeboat crew had had to contend with the lifeboat rising and falling up to 20 feet in the swell, fuel oil being forced out of vent pipes from the factory ship's ruptured tanks spraying the deck, and being bombarded with the survivors' personal belongings in suitcases as they were thrown on to the lifeboat.

The remaining 36 persons on board were winched to safety by a rescue helicopter. During the rescue, Lerwick Harbour Trust Pilot vessels were also at the scene.

Eight days previously in the early hours of 9 November the lifeboat had been called out after a Latvian registered trawler ran ashore on rocks near Kirkabister Light. Joint Second Coxswain William Clark and his crew snatched three survivors from a liferaft just minutes before it would have been driven ashore on to rocks. All the rescue services were involved in the joint operation, and in all 59 people were saved. On this occasion William Clark was awarded the Thanks of the Institution on Vellum.

BOWDEN Michael, Coxswain, Appledore Lifeboat   **BRONZE**

29 March 1995

31 March 1994: The Appledore Tyne class lifeboat *George Gibson* slipped her moorings just after 11 a.m. in response to a Mayday call from the fishing vessel *Torridge Warrior* near Bideford Bar Buoy. The vessel had one engine out of action, and its dinghy had been washed overboard.

Coxswain Bowden used his helm and throttles to make the quickest passage he could through extremely heavy seas. The casualty was sighted on the edge of the surf, and the lifeboat approached the *Torridge Warrior* on her starboard quarter. A tow line was passed successfully at the first attempt, and the vessel was then pulled clear of the Bar. A course was set for Ilfracombe since conditions prevented a return to Appledore. Although an RAF helicopter was called to the scene, the two crew refused to abandon the vessel.

The Ilfracombe Mersey class lifeboat *Spirit of Derbyshire* launched shortly after noon to assist in the tow, and reached the two boats half an hour later. At 1.30 p.m. the sampson post on the *Torridge Warrior* pulled out and the tow rope whipped through the wheelhouse destroying the instrument panel and controls. The casualty was then without any power. The Ilfracombe lifeboat, with Coxswain Andrew Putt at the helm, re-established a tow and, with the Appledore lifeboat now as escort, the *Torridge Warrior* was finally brought into Ilfracombe harbour at 7 p.m.

BROCKMAN Neil, Coxswain/Mechanic, Penlee Lifeboat	**BRONZE**
GEORGE Terence, Coxswain/Mechanic, Sennen Cove Lifeboat	**BRONZE**

29 March 1995

6–7 October 1994: The wooden hulled crabber *Julian Paul* was disabled with a fouled propeller four miles south west of the Longships Lighthouse. Weather conditions were deteriorating when the Sennen Cove Mersey class lifeboat *The Four Boys* launched at 3.30 p.m. with Coxswain George in command. The casualty was found to be lying across the weather and rolling heavily. A tow, successfully connected at the first attempt, commenced at 4.05 p.m., and the casualty was brought round head to sea. Little headway could be made against the tide, and the Penlee lifeboat was then called out to assist. The Arun class lifeboat *Mabel Alice* found the others despite poor visibility by means of VHF-DF and Sennen Cove lifeboat-s searchlight being shone into the sky.

A decision was made to attempt a tow of the heavily-laden crabber by both lifeboats to improve the rate of progress. The second tow was established by the Penlee lifeboat, and by 6 p.m. a speed of three knots was achieved. At 6.17 p.m. the Sennen Cove lifeboat's tow line snapped. As the Penlee lifeboat was towing well, the second line was not re-established and the *Four Boys* stood by as escort. In worsening conditions, the *Julian Paul* was towed to Newlyn Harbour where they arrived at 12.55 a.m. on the 7th.

CLARK Peter Hewitt Peterson, Coxswain/Mechanic, Lerwick Lifeboat	**SILVER**

17 January 1995

31 October 1994: The 10,074 ton Russian factory ship *Pionersk*, with 155 people on board, ran aground during the night at Trebister Ness, about three miles south of Lerwick. The Arun class lifeboat *Soldian* set out at 1.16 a.m. and by 1.30 a.m. was alongside *Pionersk*. The casualty's midships section lay on rocks with her bow facing seaward and her port side to the shore. She was yawing violently in a heavy swell. Coxswain Clark decided to start taking the crew off from an accommodation ladder over the stern; only four survivors had been rescued when the ladder was damaged and rendered useless. The lifeboat was then manoeuvred around the stern of the casualty, between her and the rocky shore.

The wind was gusting storm Force 10 causing extremely difficult handling conditions. Coxswain Clark had to make *between 70 and 80 approaches* to recover 63 men, one at a time, from a pilot ladder over the ship's port side. The rescue operation was carried out in extremely hazardous conditions – bunker oil was leaking into the sea; large grips and bags thrown from the high deck level on to the lifeboat; refrigerant gas escaping from broken pipes; and the lifeboat working in total darkness. With 67 survivors on board, the lifeboat returned to Lerwick at 3.10 a.m. and, after landing them, immediately returned to stand by until the remaining crew had all been rescued by helicopter. The Station Honorary Secretary reported: 'I have never seen a Coxswain and crew so physically and mentally shattered after a service. They really did give their all'.

ROBERTS Stuart Ian, Helmsman, Porthcawl Inshore Lifeboat   **SILVER**
29 March 1995

30 December 1994: A surfer was reported to be in difficulties off the breakwater at Coney Beach, Porthcawl. He was caught in the riptide and waving for help. Although the conditions were well outside the operating limits for a D class lifeboat, it was decided to launch with Stuart Roberts, an extremely able and experienced seaman, at the helm. He was assisted by crew members Carl Evans and Wayne Evans. The launch, at 1.55 p.m., was very difficult as the wind pinned the lifeboat to the breakwater, with waves about four metres high. Despite the difficult and dangerous conditions, and the lifeboat constantly filling with water, the surfer was reached within two or three minutes. A first attempt by Wayne Evans to grab the casualty into the lifeboat was abandoned as a huge wall of broken water hurtled towards them. Helmsman Robert powered the boat forward, and the wave went right through the lifeboat, swamping it with white water. At a third attempt, the surfer was pulled into the boat, but the elastic cord was still attached to the surfboard, and the force of dragging the man on board shot the surfboard into the lifeboat and nearly knocked out the Helmsman. He was saved by his 'bump cap' which was dented. Turning the lifeboat square to each wave and keeping her just ahead of the following seas, Roberts ran her straight up on to the sandy beach.

PEARCE Richard, Helmsman, Brighton Inshore Lifeboat   **SILVER**
EBDELL Martin John, Crew Member, Brighton Inshore Lifeboat   **BRONZE**
PURCHES Edward J.A., Crew Member, Brighton Inshore Lifeboat   **BRONZE**
16 January 1996

7–8 September 1995: Just before midnight on 7 September, a message was received at Brighton Marina inshore lifeboat station that two girls had been swept off the beach and into the sea. They were then caught by the undertow and trapped under the Palace Pier, some 20 yards offshore. Because of an earlier service, the Atlantic 21 inshore lifeboat *Graham Hillier and Tony Cater* was fully manned and launched immediately. In order to reach the girls, Helmsman Pearce had to drive the lifeboat under the pier and manoeuvre within a very tight space in order to keep clear of the dangerous surf. Whilst maneouvring, an underwater spike punctured the inflatable sponson. Despite this, the crew managed to reach the girls. One girl was grabbed by Purches and brought aboard. Ebdell's legs were trapped and a finger broken when the lifeboat became pinned under a metal support. As the lifeboat dropped into a trough, Ebdell's legs became free, and he managed to grab the arms of the second girl and pull her into the lifeboat.

Once clear of the pier, Helmsman Pearce manoeuvred into a relatively clear area of water. At 0.47 a.m. Newhaven-s Arun class lifeboat *Keith Anderson* arrived, the casualties and the lifeboatmen were taken on board, and the lifeboat taken in tow.

WILLIAMSON Crispin, Helmsman,
  Little and Broad Haven Inshore Lifeboat | **BRONZE**

22 November 1995

23 September 1995: A family of two adults and four children were stranded at the base of a cliff on a rising tide after their dinghy had been swamped at Nolton Haven beach. The wind was westerly Force 5, gusting 6 with six feet waves when, at 3.41 p.m. Little and Broad Haven's D class inflatable lifeboat *Sybil* was launched. Reaching the scene, Helmsman Williamson decided first to rescue the mother and the four children (aged between 6 and 12) who were stuck on a rock ledge. He anchored the lifeboat and veered down to a rocky outcrop to allow crew member Brian Dilly to leap ashore. He then carried the children, one at a time, to the end of the outcrop and threw them to crew member Dai Love, who caught them in the well of the boat. Finally the mother was rescued. The five were landed at a nearby beach before the lifeboat returned to rescue the father who, in going for help, had climbed a cliff and was stuck some 50 feet up. The St David's Auxiliary Cliff Rescue Team had been called out and for the next hour the lifeboat stood off to direct the rescue teams. An Auxiliary Coastguard and the casualty were lowered to the beach and taken off by the lifeboat. By 5.21 p.m., the last casualty had been landed at Druidston.

The lifeboat returned to the abandoned dinghy to rescue personal gear, including house keys. The dinghy was holed and could not be saved.

MASON David Victor, Coxswain,
  Great Yarmouth and Gorleston Lifeboat | **BRONZE**

27 November 1996

29 August 1996: The 33 ft yacht *Olline* was reported in trouble 28 miles north-north-east of Great Yarmouth, taking water in Force 11 winds and mountainous seas. One of the six people on board was thought to have a broken neck. The Trent class lifeboat *Samarbeta* put to sea at 5 a.m. heading towards the casualty which was finally sighted at 6.45 a.m. A helicopter had arrived earlier but had been unable to put a doctor on board the yacht. The doctor provided medical advice to Steve Bartram, a first aider and Emergency Mechanic, who volunteered to go aboard *Olline*. Only at the fifth attempt did Bartram manage to leap into the yacht's port rigging. The injured man – later found to have a broken collar bone – was wedged securely in place for the trip home. Coxswain Mason then tried to pass a tow-line. This was successful only at the fourth attempt when the lifeboat was brought close alongside the yacht. Starting at 8.45 a.m., a long, slow tow ensued, with the lifeboat and yacht reaching Great Yarmouth at 4 p.m.

This was David Mason's first service as Coxswain. Steve Bartram was awarded the Thanks of the Institution on Vellum.

CATCHPOLE John William, Coxswain, Lowestoft Lifeboat | **BRONZE(2)**
FIRMAN Ian, Coxswain/Mechanic, Aldeburgh Lifeboat | **BRONZE**

27 November 1996

29 August 1996: Lowestoft's Tyne class lifeboat *Spirit of Lowestoft* and Aldeburgh's Mersey Class lifeboat *Freddie Cooper* were both involved in a long, arduous service in storm force winds and extremely heavy seas when they answered a Mayday call from the yacht *Red House Lugger*. She was on passage from Holland with her Skipper, a schoolmaster, and four 16 and 17 year old pupils on board. The yacht was about 30 miles south east of Lowestoft. The two lifeboats reached the casualty about 10.15 a.m. to find the cargo ferry *Norking* standing by to provide some shelter. With

great difficulty, Coxswain Firman put his boat alongside the *Red House Lugger* and three of the crew were snatched to safety. Second Coxswain Shane Coleman was then put aboard the yacht from the Lowestoft boat and helped the remaining people on to the *Spirit of Lowestoft*. It was then decided to tow the yacht to Harwich, which they finally reached at 7 p.m.

Aldeburgh lifeboat was at sea from 8 a.m. to 8 p.m. whilst the Lowestoft boat returned to her station shortly after 11.30 p.m.

At one point during the rescue, the Aldeburgh lifeboat was laid over by a wave until the wheelhouse windows on the port side were under water. No crew were injured, but one of them had been completely immersed and his automatic lifejacket had inflated. Second Coxswain Shane Coleman was awarded the Thanks of the Institution on Vellum.

HAW Christopher, Coxswain, Swanage Lifeboat   **BRONZE**

27 November 1996

28–29 October 1996: The relief Mersey class lifeboat *Lifetime Care* launched at 7.45 p.m. to go to the assistance of the 90 ft yacht *Be Happy* which was 22 miles from Anvil Point. She had lost her sails and one engine, and was taking water through a broken window. The wind was Force 9–11, with heavy squalls, poor visibility, and very rough seas caused by the tail-end of a hurricane. On the way to the casualty, the lifeboat's radar went down and one engine developed problems. Aided by the searchlight of a helicopter, the lifeboat finally reached the yacht at 9.20 p.m. In the prevailing conditions a tow was impossible, and the yacht was drifting eastwards. The lifeboat went alongside the yacht to evacuate four crew whilst the Skipper stayed at the helm. As the two craft came together, they both rolled with such violence and speed that the lifeboat rails were crushed inboard injuring four of the lifeboatmen. One, Chris Coe, received a broken arm. Nevertheless, the four yachtsmen jumped aboard the lifeboat, followed shortly after by their Skipper. The Decca Navigator on the lifeboat had now failed, and the helicopter therefore escorted the *Lifetime Care* back to Swanage arriving at ten minutes after midnight. *Be Happy* subsequently went ashore on the Isle of Wight.

R.N.L.I. Headquarters, Poole

Honorary Medals

Gold Medals	Voted	Reason
1. Sir William Hillary, Bart	10 March 1825	Founder of the Institution
2. Captain G.W. Manby RN	10 March 1825	For his invention of mortar apparatus for saving lives from shipwreck
3. HM King George IV	14 May 1825	The first Patron of the Institution
4. Dr Manners Sutton Archbishop of Canterbury	14 May 1825	Presided at inaugural meeting on 4 March 1824
5. HRH The Duke of York	14 May 1825	As a Vice Patron, he presided at the first anniversary dinner on 25 May 1825
6. Thomas Wilson, MP	18 April 1826	The first Chairman of the Institution. He served from 1824 to 1852
7. HRH The Duke of Sussex	May 1826	As a Vice Patron, he presided at the second anniversary dinner on 18 May 1826. He subsequently returned the Medal which was awarded to Lieutenant J. Lindsay RN on 7 February 1827
8. Captain G.W. Manby RN (Gold Boat)	15 December 1830	For his 'method for forcing boats from a flat beach through heavy surf'
9. HM King William IV	30 March 1831	The second Patron of the Institution
10/11. George Palmer MP (Gold Medal and Gold Boat)	3 March 1853	For the 'invaluable services rendered by the lifeboats built on his plan during the past 25 years'; also for his great attention to the lifeboat affairs of the Institution.
12. James Peake	3 February 1859	For his design of the lifeboat adopted and used by the Institution
13. Sir Edward G.L. Perrott, Bart	7 March 1872	For long and valuable service – for 20 years Chairman of its preparatory committees

Gold Medals	Voted	Reason
14. Thomas Chapman, FRS	5 April 1883	On his retirement as Chairman of the Institution (1873 – 1883)
15. Vice-Admiral John Ross Ward RN	7 June 1883	On his retirement as Chief Inspector after 31 and a half years in that post
16. Koninklijke Noord en Zuid Hollandsche Redding Maatschappij	18 November 1924	Centenary of the foundation of the North and South Holland Lifeboat Society on 11 November 1824
17. Koninklijke Zuid-Hollandsche Maatschappij tot Redding, van Schipbreukelingen	18 November 1924	Centenary of the foundation of the South Holland Lifeboat Society on 20 November 1824
18. Deutsche Gesellschaft zur Rettung Schiffbrüchiger	10 December 1964	Centenary of the foundation of the German Lifeboat Society on 29 May 1865
19. Société Centrale de Sauvetage des Naufragés	10 December 1964	Centenary of the founding of the Central French Lifeboat Organisation in 1865
20. HRH Princess Marina, Duchess of Kent	12 January 1967	25 years as President (1943–1968)
21. HM Coastguard	9 February 1972	150th anniversary of its foundation on 15 January 1822
22. Koninklijke Noord en Zuid Hollandsche Redding Maatschappij	11 September 1974	150th anniversary of its foundation
23. Koninklijke Zuid-Hollandsche Maatschappij tot Redding, van Schipbreukelingen	11 September 1974	150th anniversary of its foundation
24. Administration de la Marine, Belgium	7 September 1988	150th anniversary of the foundation of a Belgian lifeboat service on 30 October 1838
25. Nippon Suinan Kyusai Kai	28 June 1989	Centenary of the foundation of the Japanese Lifeboat Society in November 1889
26. United States Coast Guard	28 March 1990	Bi-centenary of the establishment of the Revenue Marine, later the Revenue Cutter Service in 1790

Gold Medals		Voted	Reason
27.	Norsk Selskab til Shibbrudnes Redning	26 March 1991	Centenary of the foundation of the Norwegian Lifeboat Society on 9 July 1891
28.	Instituto de Socorros a Naufragos	14 January 1992	Centenary of the foundation of the Portuguese Lifeboat Society on 21 April 1892
29.	HRH The Duke of Kent KG	23 March 1994	25 years as President (1969–1994), a position he still holds

Silver Medals		Voted	Reason
1.	William van Houten	14 May 1836	President of the Rotterdam Shipwreck Society. He sent models of a lifeboat and carriage he had invented
2.	William van Houten	28 July 1841	For the Royal Academy at Leiden to add to its collection of medals of the world
3.	Commander Clement La Primaudaye RN	13 September 1888	On his resignation as District Inspector for the Western District after 9 years in that post
4.	Svenska Sallskapet for Raddning af Skeppbrutne	11 April 1957	50th anniversary of the founding of the Swedish Lifeboat Society on 1 June 1907
5.	Norsk Selskab til Skibbrudnes Redning	12 May 1966	75th anniversary of the founding of the Norwegian Lifeboat Society on 9 July 1891
6.	Professor Edgar A. Pask OBE, MD, MA, MB, BChir, DA, FRARCS (Posthumous)	14 July 1966	For his ceaseless work and outstanding devotion to the cause of saving life at sea as Honorary Medical Adviser to the Institution
7.	Svenska Sallskapet for Raddning af Skeppbrutne	24 November 1982	75th anniversary of the founding of the Swedish Lifeboat Society on 1 June 1907
8.	Slysavarnafelag Islands	23 March 1988	60th anniversary of the founding of the Icelandic Lifeboat Society on 29 January 1928

The London Tavern, Bishopsgate where the inaugural meeting of the
Institution was held on 4 March 1824.

The Plates

Sir William Hillary, Bart (1771–1847), Founder of the Institution

In February, 1823 he published a pamphlet 'An Appeal to the British Nation on the Humanity and Policy of forming a National Institution for the Preservation of Lives and Property from Shipwreck'. As a result, a public meeting was held in London on 4 March 1824 at which the formation of the 'National Institution for the Preservation of Life from Shipwreck' was approved.

Sir William was awarded an honorary gold medal as Founder in 1825 (p. 405). He also won three gold medals for services in the Douglas, Isle of Man lifeboat (pp. 18, 28 and 29). This picture, taken from a portrait which hangs in the Headquarters of the RNLI at Poole, shows Sir William wearing the Institution gold medal below the insignia of a Knight of Malta.

The first woman to be awarded a
medal was Grace Darling who
received a silver medal in 1838
(p. 60).

Nineteen other silver medals have been awarded – the last in 1888 – to women. These included four to the sisters Prideaux-Brune and one to Miss Nora O'Shaughnessy of Padstow in 1879 (see p. 166). This illustration of their exploit appeared in 'The Story of the Sea', edited by Sir Arthur Quiller-Couch in 1895.

Read letter from Capt Sparshott — and letter enclosed from Capt Neale Inspect: Com' at Whitby of the 16 Dec'. stating the loss of the Sloop "Northfield" on the 12th Decem' when Lieut. Jones — with his Crew immediately proceeded to the Spot, and with his usual intrepidity Lieut. Jones watched the receding of the Sea and rushing through the Water gained the Vessel, procured a Rope and took it on shore; in doing so he ran great risk of his Life, for the Sea carried him off his legs two or three times before he succeeded in handing the Rope to the Men on shore, by which means the lives of the 4 people composing the Crew of the Vessel were saved, and she immediately after went to pieces —

Resolved

That the Gold boat be presented to Lieut. Jones to be attached to the Gold Medallion presented to him last Year —

Photograph of a page from the Minutes Book of the Committee of Management meeting held on 5 January 1831 awarding a second gold medal (the gold boat) to Lieutenant Richard Jones RN of HM Coastguard at Whitby (p. 31).

Redcar lifeboat 'Zetland', [buil]t in 1800, in which Coxswain [Rob]ert Shieldon won the silver [med]al in 1857 (p. 114).

The steam lifeboat 'Duke of Northumberland', in service from 1890 to 1922. The Chief Engineer, Arthur Simmons, was awarded the silver medal in 1895 (p. 203).

[Pad]stow steam tug 'Helen [ ]n station from 1901–29. [Cap]tain, Joseph Atkinson, was [awarded] the bronze medal in 1928

Joseph Rodgers, seaman, of the
'Royal Charter', awarded the gold
medal in 1859 (p. 121). This
portrait appeared in the Illustrated
London News of 26 November
1859.

...wain Robert Hook of Lowestoft, awarded the silver medal in 1859 ...23).

Henry Freeman, the sole survivor of the Whitby lifeboat 'Lucy' which capsized on service on 9 February 1861. He was awarded the silver medal (p. 128).

...in Edgar West Woods, Gorleston, awarded the silver medal in ... 191).

Coxswain James Cable of Adeburgh. He was awarded the silver medal in 1891 (p. 192), a second silver in 1893 (p. 199) and a third silver in 1900 (p. 212).

The Scottish author R.M. Ballantyne was at Liverpool with his brother
awaiting the arrival of family members on the 'Royal Charter' which was
wrecked at Moelfre in November 1859 (p. 121). The scenes he later
witnessed at Moelfre made a great impression on him, and he decided to
support the lifeboat cause. His book 'The Lifeboat: A Tale of our Coast
Heroes' was published in 1864. He gave lectures to raise funds, and in
1866 a lifeboat named 'Edinburgh and R.M. Ballantyne' was sent to the
new station at Port Logan, Wigtownshire.

This illustration is a reproduction from the publicity pamphlet issued to
advertise the book.

The Penzance lifeboat 'Richard Lewis' going out to the 'North Britain',
wrecked in Mount's Bay on 6 December 1868. Five silver medals were
awarded to men who took part in the rescue (p. 147).

Coxswain Stephen Clayson of Margate, awarded the silver medal in 1905 (p. 216).

Coxswain John Owston of Scarborough who received the silver medal for five services in October 1880 (p. 168).
He retired on pension in December 1911. He was born in 1844 and was appoi: Coxswain in 1871. Altogether he assisted in saving 230 lives.

This illustration from the Rev. T. Stanley Treanor's book 'Heroes of the Goodwin Sands' shows Coxswain James Laming of Kingsdown, Coxswain Richard Roberts of North Deal and Coswain John Mackins of Walmer.

Laming was awarded the silver medal on his retirement in 1907 (p. 223). Roberts won three silver medals (pp. 173, 201 and 222). Mackins received the Thanks of the Institution on Vellum for a service in 1901.

The five survivors of the Ramsgate crew which went out to the 'Indian
Chief' in January 1881. From left to right: Thomas Friend (age 81 years):
Thomas Cooper (79 years): Henry Belsey (82 years): Charles Verion
(80 years): and David Berry (81 years). Each man received the silver
medal (p. 169).

The photograph was taken on 14 April 1926 at the naming of the new
Ramsgate motor lifeboat 'Prudential'.

FOUNDED 1824.

ALL COMMUNICATIONS
SHOULD BE ADDRESSED TO
THE SECRETARY,
ROYAL NATIONAL
LIFE-BOAT INSTITUTION.

ROYAL NATIONAL LIFE-BOAT INSTITUTION.

(Supported solely by Voluntary Contributions.)

Patron—HER MOST GRACIOUS MAJESTY THE QUEEN.
President—HIS GRACE THE DUKE OF NORTHUMBERLAND, K.G.
Chairman—SIR EDWARD BIRKBECK, BART., M.P., V.P.
Deputy Chairman—COL. FITZROY CLAYTON, V.P.
Secretary—CHARLES DIBDIN, ESQ., F.R.G.S.

14, JOHN STREET, ADELPHI, LONDON, W.C.

8th Jany 1891

My dear Sir,

I have very great pleasure in informing you that the Committee have to-day decided to grant your retiring Coxswain J. H. Smallridge, in recognition of his long and good service, the sum of £25, their second service clasp to be affixed to his medal and a Certificate of Service framed. — I am sure that both he and your Committee will be gratified at their award.

I enclose a Cheque for the money and the Certificate will be forwarded as soon as it is ready, will you kindly obtain the medal and send it home in order that we may have

have the clasp affixed Smallridge's Signature of Voucher and return sort of acknowledgment the Committee

Claude W. S. Gould
Bra...

Coxswain James H. Smallridge of Braunton was awarded the silver medal in 1871 (p. 153) and a second service clasp on his retirement in 1891 (p. 188).

The letter announcing the award of the second medal was sent to the Honorary Secretary at Braunton: it is signed by Charles Dibdin, Secretary of the RNLI from 1883 to 1910.

H. Gartside-Tipping

tenant Henry Gartside-
ing RN. He was Inspector of
rish District of the RNLI for
ears and received the silver
l on his resignation (p. 195)
92.

vented the Tipping's plates,
d after him, which enabled a
y lifeboat to be transported
deep mud and soft sand.

LIFEBOAT TRANSPORTING CARRIAGE.
(WITH TIPPING'S WHEELPLATES.)

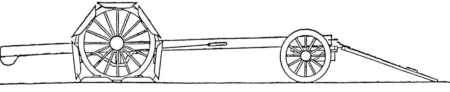

ELEVATION.

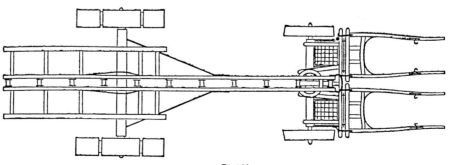

PLAN.

Coxswain William Henry Baker
of Padstow, awarded the silver
medal in 1911 (p. 228).

Coxswain William Stanton of the North Deal Reserve lifeboat award
silver medal in 1916 (p. 240) and a bronze medal in 1919 (p. 246).

Coxswain William Johnston of
Stromness, awarded the bronze
medal in 1922 (p. 250). He
received a second bronze in 1929
(p. 260).

silver medallists in 1913 featured in this montage in the February
4 Lifeboat Journal (p. 230–2).

Six silver medallists of 1915 and early 1916 are shewn in this group from
the May 1916 Lifeboat Journal (p. 235–7).

ur silver medallist for services at Sennen Cove (p. 247) and
gland (p. 248) are shewn in this group from the May 1920
at Journal.

This service at Fishguard was rewarded with one gold, three silver and
nine bronze medals (p. 249). The February 1921 Lifeboat Journal
reported the events in detail.

Twelve medal winners of 1914. Three gold medals and nine silver medals were awarded (p. 233–4).
Back row: J. Wickham, W. Duggan, W. Power, A. Cunningham, J.S. Brownlee, R. Eglon, G. Peart
Front row: E. Wickham, T. Holmes, R. Smith, T. Langlands, J.T. Swan

At the Annual General Meeting in London on 28 April 1921, the Princ of Wales, President of the Institution, inspected the Fishguard lifeboat and met the crew. He was accompanied by the Earl Waldegrave, Chairman of the RNLI. The boat and crew had been brought to Londo by train (p. 249).

...dal winners from Holy Island at the Annual General Meeting in ...don on 29 March 1922.

The group includes (from left to rights) Thomas Stevenson, Miss D. Cromarty, Coxswain George Cromarty, Mrs Cromarty and Second Coxswain William Wilson.
Mrs and Miss Cromarty represented the women of Holy Island who had helped launch the lifboat on service (p. 250) and received a special letter of thanks on their behalf.

Two gold medallists: Coxswain John Swan of Lowestoft (p. 251) and Coxswain Robert Smith of Tynemouth (p. 233).

As part of the Centenary celebrations in 1924, seven of the eight
surviving gold medallists were received at Buckingham Palace on 30 June
by King George V. Each man received the Empire Gallantry Medal
(replaced in 1942 by the George Cross).

This picture shows the men leaving the Palace: from left to right:
Coxswain John Swan, Lowestoft (p. 251); Coxswain Henry Blogg,
Cromer (p. 241); Coxswain William Fleming, Gorleston (p. 251);
Coxswain Robert Smith, Tynemouth (p. 233); Coxswain John Howells,
Fishguard (p. 249); and Major Herbert Burton, Tynemouth (p. 233).

Captain Thomas McCombie, Kingstown (p. 205) is not included in the
photo.

Because of ill health the Rev. John O'Shea, Waterford (p. 227) was unable
to attend.

Bronze medal winners in 1924: from left to right. Second Coxswain Thomas Patton and Coxswain Andrew Tose of Runswick (p. 253), and Coxswain Richard Payne of Newhaven (p. 253).

winners at the 1928 Annual General Meeting:
w: Second Coxswain Roberts and Captain Jones, Moelfre (p. 256); Coxswain Upcraft, Southwold
); Coxswain Fleming, Great Yarmouth & Gorleston (p. 257); Second Coxswain Balls and Coxswain
Cromer (p. 257).
 Row: Coxswain Lethbridge, Second Coxswain J.T. Lethbridge and Charles Jenkins, St Mary's, Isles of
p. 256); Coxswain Spurgeon, Lowestoft (p. 257); Bowman Williams, Moelfre (p. 256).

Medal winners at the 1929 Annual General Meeting. From left to right:
Coxswain Robinson, Second Coxswain Nicholson and Mechanic Scott,
New Brighton (p. 259); Second Coxswain Sim, Fraserburgh (p. 229);
Coxswain Baker, Padstow (p. 258); Captain Atkinson, Padstow (p. 259);
Hugh Mackay (p. 258).

The medallists photographed on
the roof of Grosvenor Gardens
prior to the 1931 Annual General
Meeting at which they received
their awards from the Prince of
Wales.
They are, from left to right,
Front Row: Coxswain Barnes,
Selsey (p. 262); Mrs Polly
Donkins of Cullercoats (who
received a gold brooch for
'distinguished service'); Coxswain
Fenton, St Andrews (p. 262); and
Mr John Cahill, Tralee (p. 262);
Back Row: Coxswain Hood,
Hartlepool (p. 261): Bowman
Davies, Cromer (p. 262); and
Coxswain McPhail, Thurso
(p. 263).

edal winners examine their
ards after the Annual General
eting of 1932. On the left is
xswain Swanson, Longhope
263); on the right Coxswain
mpbell, Portpatrick (p. 263).

The rescue of the crew of the Daunt Rock lightship by the Ballycotton
lifeboat was the outstanding service of 1936 (p. 269). The photograph, taken
at the awards ceremony, shows, from left to right, Coxswain Patrick Sliney, his
wife, his son William and Sir Godfrey Baring, Bart, Chairman of the RNLI.

The Duke of Kent, President of the RNLI from 1936 to 1942, speaking to Coxswain Cocking, Second Coxswain Peters and Bowman Matthew Barber of St Ives at the 1938 Annual General Meeting (p. 272).

This picture shews Princess Marina, Duchess of Kent, presenting his gold medal to Coxswain McLean of Peterhead (p. 294). Princess Marina was President of the RNLI from 1943 to 1968.

swain C.A. Johnson, Great Yarmouth & Gorleston, awarded bronze
...als in 1922 (p. 251), 1938 (p. 274), 1939 (p. 280) and 1941 (p. 291),
...the silver medal in 1941 (p. 289).

Coxswain W.D. Crowther, Plymouth, awarded the bronze medal in 1942
(p. 293).

...nant W.H. Bennison, Coxswain of Hartlepool lifeboat, awarded the
...edal in 1942 (p. 295).

Dr Joseph Soar, Honorary Secretary at St David's, awarded the bronze
medal in 1943 (p. 297).

At the Annual General Meeting in 1946, seven men who had won gallantry medals since the end of the war received their awards: *Back row, from left to right*: Coxswain Watkins, Angle (p. 302); Coxswain Peters, St Ives (p. 302); Coxswain Murt, Padstow (p. 303); Crew Member Harland, Whitby (p. 303). *Centre row*: Coxswain Newlands, Campbeltown (p. 303); Coxswain Murfield, Whitby (p. 303). *In front*: Coxswain Bloom, Walton & Frinton (p. 303).

At the Annual General Meeting in 1953, 15 year old Tony Metcalfe receives his bronze medal from HRH Princess Marina, Duchess of Kent (p. 313).

...swain E.W. Distin, Salcombe, awarded the silver medal in 1939
...80) and the bronze medal in 1944 (p. 300).

Coxswain Thomas King, St Helier, awarded the gold medal in 1949
(p. 307).

...ain H.J. Bradford, Exmouth, awarded the bronze medal in 1954
...).

Coxswain George Tart, Dungeness, awarded the bronze medal in 1956.
Coxswain Tart is one of a family long connected with the lifeboat service
(p. 318).

For rescuing survivors from the South Goodwin lightship in November
1954, Captain Curtis E. Parkins, US Air Force, received the Institution's
silver medal (p. 315).
The crew of the helicopter, left to right: Captain Curtis E. Parkins, Major
Paul L. Park, Airman First Class Elmer H. Vollman and Captain W.R.
Kusy.

...hard Evans of Moelfre, awarded the bronze medal in 1943 when he ... Second Coxswain (p. 299). Then as Coxswain he has twice been ...rded the gold medal (pp. 323 and 335).

Coxswain L.D. Scott, The Mumbles, who was awarded the silver medal for a service in November 1963 (p. 329), the bronze medal in 1968 (p. 337) and a second silver in 1971 (p. 341).

...vain David Kennett, Yarmouth, Isle of Wight, awarded the silver ... for a service in September 1975 (p. 356).

© Margaret Murray

Coxswain Trevor England, Padstow, awarded silver medals for services in 1977 (p. 361) and 1979 (p. 369).

Medal winners from Stornoway following a service in January 1962 (p. 326): from left to right, Coxswain Malcolm Macdonald, Mechanic John Macleod and Assistant Mechanic John Macdonald.

Presented with medals at the Annual General Meeting in 1968 are, from left to right, Coxswain Lethbridge, Second Coxswain Guy and Mechanic Burrow of St Mary's (p. 336); Coxswain Byrne, Arranmore (p. 334); and Coxswain Nicolson, Aith (p. 335).

r services in 1970, three of the dallists are shown at the 1971 nual General Meeting. They , from left to right: Mechanic rrow, St Mary's for his second nze medal (p. 339); Coswain sh; Valentia (p. 339); and xswain Whittle, Dunmore East 340).

The three members of the Holyhead lifeboat who received medals for a service in September 1971: from left to right, Mechanic Forrest; Crew Member John Hughes; and Crew Member Gareth Ogwen Jones (p. 342).

Above: Posing on the Embankment outside the Roy[al] Festival Hall, medal winners [prior] to their presentation at the 197[?] Annual General Meeting. Fro[m] left to right: Coxswain Leith, Lerwick (p. 345); Coxswain Pavey, Weymouth (p. 343); Coxswain Wood, Aldeburgh ([p.] 344); Coxswain Brown, Falm[outh] (p. 344); Crew Member Gibb[s], Hartlepool (p. 345); Coxswai[n] Mackay, Islay (p. 345); Cox[swain] Leslie, Longhope (p. 345).

Left: Presented with their me[dals] at the Royal Festival Hall in [197?] are from left to right, Coxsw[ain] Liddon and Second Coxswa[in] Hawkins of Dover (p. 357); [Coxswain] Martin Ruddy (p. 355); and Coxswain Petit and Mecha[nic] Robilliard, St Peter Port (p.

77, Coxswain Matthew Lethbridge, St Mary's, was awarded his
ıd silver medal (p. 361).

Helmsman David Bliss of the St Agnes Inshore Lifeboat was awarded the
silver medal for a service on 17 July 1977 (p. 362).

Superintendent Coxswain Brian Bevan, Humber, and his crew from the
service on 14 February 1979. Brian Bevan was awarded the gold medal,
and each of the crew received the bronze medal (p. 367).
In the photograph behind Coxswain Bevan are, from left to right: Second
Coxswain Dennis Bailey, Snr., Mechanic Bill Sayers, Assistant Mechanic
Ronald Sayers, Crew Members Michael Storey, Peter Jordan, Sydney
Rollinson and Dennis Bailey, Jnr.

For a service in Lyme Regis inshore lifeboat on 13 August 1979,
Helmsman J.L. Hodder and Crew Member C.I. Jones each received the
bronze medal (p. 368).

Coxswain J.H. Petit of St Peter Port has been awarded one silver medal
(p. 364) and four bronze medals (pp. 328, 355, 363, 366).

Coxswain Peter Hewitt Clark, Lerwick, awarded bronze medals in 1
(p. 377), 1989 (p. 388) and 1993 (p. 397), and the silver medal in 19
(p. 401).

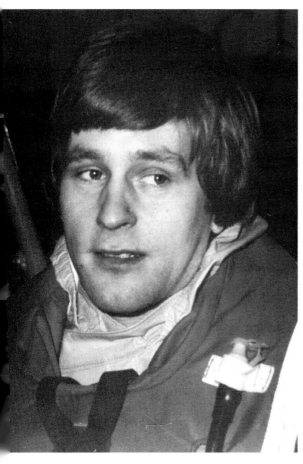

Member Arthur Hill of the Largs inshore lifeboat who was awarded lver medal for a service on 24 July 1983 (p. 379).

Coxswain D.W. Clemence, Ilfracombe, awarded the bronze medal in 1984 (p. 382).

in/Mechanic Robin Castle, Sheerness, one of the medal winners he great storm of October 1987 (p. 385).

Photo F. Broomhead

Coxswain W.A. Thomas, Tenby, awarded the silver medal for a service in September 1989 (p. 390).

[PORTABLE EDITION FOR THE POCKET.]

TREATMENT OF THE APPARENTLY DROWNED.

ROYAL NATIONAL LIFE-BOAT INSTITUTION.

Incorporated by Royal Charter—Supported solely by Voluntary Contributions.

PATRON—HIS MOST GRACIOUS MAJESTY THE KING.

VICE-PATRONS— { HER MAJESTY QUEEN ALEXANDRA. { HIS ROYAL HIGHNESS THE PRINCE OF WALES, K.G.

DIRECTIONS FOR RESTORING THE APPARENTLY DROWNED.

THE leading principles of the following Directions for the Restoration of the Apparently Dead from Drowning are founded on those of the late DR. MARSHALL HALL, combined with those of DR. H. R. SILVESTER, and are the result of extensive inquiries which were made by the Royal National Life-boat Institution in 1863–4 amongst Medical Men, Medical Bodies, and Coroners throughout the United Kingdom. These Directions have been extensively circulated by the INSTITUTION throughout the United Kingdom and in the Colonies. They are also in use in His Majesty's Fleet; in the Coast-guard Service; at all the Stations of the British Army at home and abroad; in the Light-houses and Vessels of the Corporation of the Trinity House; the Metropolitan and Provincial Police Forces; the London County Council Schools; and the St. John Ambulance Association.

I.

Send immediately for medical assistance, blankets, and dry clothing, but proceed to treat the Patient *instantly* on the spot, in the open air, with the face downward, whether on shore or afloat; exposing the face, neck, and chest to the wind, except in severe weather, and removing all tight clothing from the neck and chest, especially the braces.

The points to be aimed at are—first, and *immediately*, the RESTORATION OF BREATHING; and secondly, after breathing is restored, the PROMOTION OF WARMTH AND CIRCULATION.

The efforts to *restore Breathing* must be commenced immediately and energetically, and persevered in for one or two hours, or until a medical man has pronounced that life is extinct. Efforts to promote *Warmth* and *Circulation*, beyond removing the wet clothes and drying the skin, must not be made until the first appearance of natural breathing; for if circulation of the blood be induced before breathing has recommenced, the restoration to life will be endangered.

II.—TO RESTORE BREATHING.

TO CLEAR THE THROAT.—Place the patient on the floor or ground with the face downwards and one of the arms under the forehead, in which position all fluids will more readily escape by the mouth, and the tongue itself will fall forward, leaving the entrance into the windpipe free. Assist this operation by wiping and cleansing the mouth.

If satisfactory breathing commences, use the treatment described below to promote

1.—INSPIRATION.

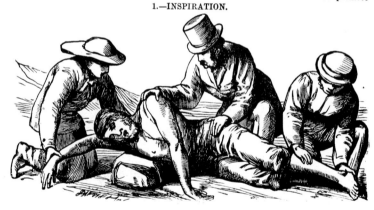

The 'Treatment of the Apparently Drowned', as described in this pocket edition, first appeared in the Lifeboat Journal in July 1864.

The following is a copy of a Handbill circulated on the Coasts of the United Kingdom by the Institution, for the purpose of informing Boatmen and others that it encourages laudable exertions to save Life from Shipwrecks:—

TO BOATMEN AND OTHERS.

To encourage prompt and energetic exertions in time of Danger on the part of Boatmen and Others, by quickly putting off to save Life in CASES of WRECKS on the Coasts of the British Isles, either by

SHORE-BOATS OR ·OTHER MEANS,

The Royal National Life-boat Institution

GRANTS

Rewards of Money or Medals.   In all cases the Rewards are given without further delay than is necessary to obtain proof of the merits of each case, and to ensure their being paid to the right parties.

Application to be made to the Secretary.   By Order of the Committee.

Reproduced from The Life Boat Journal, May 1888

CAPTAIN MANBY'S MORTAR LIFE-LINE.

Many early rescues were made using Manby rockets. Captain G.W. Manby (1765–1854) was awarded an honorary gold medal in 1825 for the invention of his rocket apparatus, and an honorary gold boat in 1830 (p. 405).

Medals of the RNLI

King George IV
1824–1862

Reverse
1824–1903
1912 to date

Victoria
1862–1903

King George V
1912–1937

Hillary
1937 to date

Edward VII
1903–1912

Reverse
1903–1912

Appendix I

MAIN TYPES AND VARIATIONS IN RNLI MEDAL DESIGN

John Hayward

Type 1 1824–1862

Obverse: Head of King George IV facing left; 'W. WYON MINT' and '1824' below truncation; 'ROYAL NATIONAL INSTITUTION FOR THE PRESERVATION OF LIFE FROM SHIP-WRECK GEORGE THE FOURTH PATRON' in two lines around head.

Reverse: Three men in a lifeboat – one rescuing a survivor from a broken spar; 'W. WYON MINT' on left of spar; 'LET NOT THE DEEP SWALLOW ME UP' (Psalm lxix.15) above.

Metal: Gold; Silver.

Design: By William Wyon RA (after Henry Howard RA), later Medallist and Chief Engraver to the Royal Mint. Interestingly Wyon portrayed himself as the rescuer in the reverse design. The deterioration of the obverse die led to a new one being cut (circa 1851) – some minor changes included the relocation of '1824' from beneath the truncation to a central position towards the rim, between a more compressed outer line of inscription; 'MINT' was removed from below the truncation and 'W. WYON' was realigned.

Suspension:

a. Many of the earliest medals (circa 1825–1831) with the exception of some gold awards were pierced below the rim and above the King's head to accept a small ring interlinked with a larger 'ribbon' ring. A small number of the first silver medals were issued without piercing.

b. A band of the appropriate metal with an integral central 'eye' was applied to the rim of the medal (circa 1833), a small ring interlinked with a larger 'ribbon' ring was attached to the eye.

c. The well known 'Dolphin' suspension made its debut on medals issued (circa 1852) – this comprised a central ball shaped swivel above a hand fretted claw of flattened form – two uniface dolphins, cast and chased, face each other, their tails uppermost, were attached to the swivel at their heads – a ribbon suspension bar was soldered to the flat reverse of the dolphin's tails; due to the hand finished element a large number of minor suspension variations exist; some non-standard suspensions have been noted, including a swivel ring and bar on the gold medal voted to Sir William Hillary (1828) and a swivel ring on the silver award to Mr Robert Parrott (1856).

Size: Varies from 34.80mm to 36.00mm diameter (including those medals with applied bands); thickness varies 2.40mm to 3.90mm (including obverse and reverse rims).

Type 2 1862–1903

Obverse: Head of Queen Victoria with a chaplet of oak leaves facing left; 'L.C. WYON' below truncation; 'ROYAL NATIONAL LIFE-BOAT INSTITUTION. FOUNDED IN 1824. INCOR-PORATED 1860. VICTORIA PATRONESS' in two lines around head.

Reverse: Unchanged

Metal: Gold; Silver.

Design: The new obverse die by Leonard Charles Wyon, Modeller and Engraver to the Royal Mint, was employed upon medals issued in 1862, two years after Queen Victoria granted a charter of incorporation to the Institution – the obverse also carried the new title of the Institution which had been altered in 1854; a number of minor changes made to the obverse include – a slight 'ageing' or fullness of the Queen's profile made in two stages, the designer's name, which appeared well spaced and in a straight line on the earlier issues, became more compressed and followed the curved truncation line on the later issues; William Wyon's reverse used throughout quite often displayed on the medal an unwillingness to replace a worn die (mostly in the 1860s and 1870s); obverse and reverse rims were given a knurled effect (circa 1892).

Suspension:

a. Dolphins, ribbon suspension rod and ball swivel were machined in one piece (circa 1868) and at the same time, the hand fretted claw was replaced by the more conventional variety, not unlike the official double claw fitted to campaign medals.

b. The claw was later strengthened by the addition of a rivet completely through the claw and medal.

Size: Varies from 35.50mm to 36.00mm diameter; thickness varies from 2.20mm to 4.20mm (including obverse and reverse rims).

Type 3 1903–1912

Obverse: Bust of King Edward VII in ermine cape facing left; 'G.W. de SAULLES' below bust; 'KING EDWARD VII PATRON' around head; 'ROYAL NATIONAL LIFE-BOAT INSTITU-TION. FOUNDED 1824. INCORPORATED 1860' within a border.

Reverse: A Coxswain/Superintendent standing before a seated female figure of 'Hope' - an anchor and lifebelt in the background – a crewed lifeboat on wheeled trolley at sea edge – oars at the ready.

Metal: Gold, Silver.

Design: These new dies by George William de Saulles, Chief Engraver to the Royal Mint, were first employed in 1903 and the first medal of this type was voted to Thomas William Rowntree on 13 August of that year – the two following entries in the RNLI medal book list John Stewart and Hector Robinson with silver awards but they are both recorded as receiving the old Queen Victoria type – their service took place only three days earlier than Rowntree's! One die variation was noted during the issue of this type – the knurling to the obverse and reverse rims of the gold issue.

Suspension:

a. Dolphins were struck from obverse and reverse dies for the first time and a separate ribbon rod let into the tails of the dolphins.

b. A new single claw was introduced, this was secured to the medal by a rivet – this method was successfully employed on contemporary official campaign medals, for example, South Africa, 1899–1902.

Size: 38.00mm diameter; thickness varies from 2.40mm to 3.50mm.

Type 4 1912–1937

Obverse: Head of King George V facing left; 'B.M.' (Bertram MacKennal A.R.A.) on truncation; 'ROYAL NATIONAL LIFEBOAT INSTITUTION' above head; 'GEORGE V' to left; 'PATRON' to right; 'FOUNDED 1824 INCORPORATED 1860' below.

Reverse: As for Types 1 and 2

Metal: Gold, Silver, Bronze from 1917.

Design: The obverse die for this new type was designed by Bertram MacKennal A.R.A. The reverse reverts to the original Wyon design. The prow of the boat appears clearer and is further from the rim; this is probably due to the increased diameter of the medal. For the same reason the lettering is further from the rescuers.

Suspension:

The ribbon rod is once again manufactured separately and is brazed to the centre point of the dolphins's tails.

a. Each dolphin's head is attached to a central swivel ball suspension.

b. Size: 37.00mm diameter; thickness of the silver examples is 4.30mm.

Type 5 1937 to date

Obverse: Head of Sir William Hillary Bart., the founder, facing left (on his accession to the throne, King George VI directed that only medals awarded by him personally should carry his effigy); the name of the Institution appears in smaller lettering than Type 4; 'FOUNDED' '1824' appear separately at either side of the head; 'SIR WILLIAM HILLARY, BT.' below; 'A.G. WYON SC' in small capitals below truncation.

Reverse: Same as Type 4.

Metal: Gold, Silver, Bronze.

Design: The obverse die was designed by Alan G. Wyon, F.R.B.S.

Suspension: The double dolphin suspension surmounts the older style double claw, although somewhat small than later Victorian types.

Size: 37.00 mm diameter; thickness 4.00mm

Methods of Recognising Extra Services

a. A miniature rowing boat, gold for gold awards, silver for silver awards; these were suspended from two short chains; some were attached to the medal ribands and others were suspended from the medal itself. The award of boats appears to have been phased out about 1835.

b. The practice of awarding another medal for subsequent services was discontinued around the middle of the nineteenth century, when second, third and subsequent service clasps were issues and fixed to the suspension of the medal.

Ribbon

Blue

Naming

A recipient's name was engraved on the rim; generally speaking all medals are engraved on the rim in varying styles together with the date the award was voted. There are exceptions with some of the earliest issues which just bear the names of recipients. These particulars sometimes appear on the reverse of boats and always on the reverse claps

Honorary Gold Medal and Gold Boat awarded to Captain G.W. Manby RN (p. 405)

Appendix II

CURRENT LIFEBOAT STATIONS
(AS AT 31 DECEMBER 1996)

Aberdeen, Grampian
Aberdovey, Gwynedd
Abersoch, Gwynedd
Aberystwyth, Dyfed
Achill, Mayo
Aith, Shetland
Aldeburgh, Suffolk
Alderney, CI
Amble, Northumberland
Angle, Dyfed
Anstruther, Fife
Appledore, North Devon
Aran Islands, Galway
Arbroath, Tayside
Arklow, Wicklow
Arran (Lamlash), Strathclyde
Arranmore, Donegal
Atlantic College, South Glamorgan
Ballycotton, Cork
Ballyglass, Mayo
Baltimore, Cork
Bangor, Down
Barmouth, Gwynedd
Barra Island, Western Isles
Barrow, Cumbria
Barry Dock, South Glamorgan
Beaumaris, Gwynedd
Bembridge, Isle of Wight
Berwick-upon-Tweed, Northumberland
Blackpool, Lancashire
Blyth, Northumberland
Borth, Dyfed
Bridlington, Humberside
Brighton, East Sussex
Broughty Ferry, Tayside
Buckie, Grampian
Bude, Cornwall

Bundoran, Mayo
Burnham-on-Crouch, Essex
Burry Port, Dyfed
Calshot, Hampshire
Campbeltown, Strathclyde
Cardigan, Dyfed
Clacton-on-Sea, Essex
Cleethorpes, Humberside
Clifden, Galway
Clogher Head, Louth
Conwy, Gwynedd
Courtmacsherry Harbour, Cork
Courtown, Wexford
Craster, Northumberland
Criccieth, Gwynedd
Cromer, Norfolk
Cullercoats, Tyne and Wear
Donaghadee, Down
Douglas, Isle of Man
Dover, Kent
Dun Laoghaire, Dublin
Dunbar, Lothian
Dungeness, Kent
Dunmore East, Waterford
Eastbourne, East Sussex
Exmouth, South Devon
Eyemouth, Borders
Falmouth, Cornwall
Fenit, Kerry
Fethard, Wexford
Filey, North Yorkshire
Fishguard, Dyfed
Flamborough, Humberside
Fleetwood, Lancashire
Flint, Clwyd
Fowey, Cornwall
Fraserburgh, Grampian

Galway, Galway

Girvan, Strathclyde

Great Yarmouth & Gorleston, Norfolk

Happisburgh, Norfolk

Hartlepool, Cleveland

Harwich, Essex

Hastings, East Sussex

Hayling Island, Hampshire

Helensburgh, Strathclyde

Helvick Head, Waterford (from 4 Feb 1997)

Holyhead, Gwynedd

Horton and Port Eynon, West Glamorgan

Howth, Dublin

Hoylake, Merseyside

Humber, Humberside

Hunstanton, Norfolk

Ilfracombe, North Devon

Invergordon, Highland

Islay, Strathclyde

Kilkeel, Down

Kilmore Quay, Wexford

Kilrush, Clare

Kinghorn, Fife

Kippford, Dumfries & Galloway

Kirkcudbright, Dumfries & Galloway

Kirkwall, Orkney

Kyle of Lochalsh Highland

Largs, Strathclyde

Larne, Antrim

Lerwick, Shetland

Little & Broad Haven, Dyfed

Littlehampton, West Sussex

Littlestone-on-Sea, Kent

Lizard (The), Cornwall

Llandudno, Gwynedd

Lochinver, Highland

Longhope, Orkney

Looe, Cornwall

Lough Swilly (Buncrana), Donegal

Lowestoft, Suffolk

Lyme Regis, Dorset

Lymington, Hampshire

Lytham St Annes, Lancashire

Mablethorpe, Lincolnshire

Macduff, Grampian

Mallaig, Highland

Marazion, Cornwall

Margate, Kent

Minehead, Somerset

Moelfre, Gwynedd

Montrose, Tayside

Morecambe, Lancashire

Mudeford, Dorset

Mumbles (The), West Glamorgan

New Brighton, Merseyside

New Quay, Dyfed

Newbiggin, Northumberland

Newcastle, Down

Newhaven, East Sussex

Newquay, Cornwall

North Berwick, Lothian

North Kessock, Highland

North Sunderland, Northumberland

Oban, Strathclyde

Padstow, Cornwall

Peel, Isle of Man

Penarth, South Glamorgan

Penlee, Cornwall

Peterhead, Grampian

Plymouth, South Devon

Poole, Dorset

Port Erin, Isle of Man

Port Isaac, Cornwall

Port St Mary, Isle of Man

Port Talbot, West Glamorgan

Portaferry, Down

Porthcawl, Mid Glamorgan

Porthdinllaen, Gwynedd

Portpatrick, Dumfries & Galloway

Portree, Isle of Skye

Portrush, Antrim

Portsmouth, Hampshire

Pwllheli, Gwynedd

Queensferry, Lothian

Ramsey, Isle of Man

Ramsgate, Kent

Red Bay, Antrim

Redcar, Cleveland

Rhyl, Clwyd

Rock, Cornwall

Rosslare Harbour, Wexford

Rye Harbour, East Sussex

Salcombe, South Devon
Scarborough, North Yorkshire
Selsey, West Sussex
Sennen Cove, Cornwall
Sheerness, Kent
Sheringham, Norfolk
Shoreham Harbour, West Sussex
Silloth, Cumbria
Skegness, Lincolnshire
Skerries, Dublin
Southend-on-Sea, Essex
Southwold, Suffolk
St Abbs, Borders
St Agnes, Cornwall
St Bees, Cumbria
St Catherine, Jersey, CI
St Davids, Dyfed
St Helier, Jersey, CI
St Ives, Cornwall
St Mary's, Isles of Scilly
St Peter Port, Guernsey, CI
Staithes and Runswick, North Yorkshire
Stornoway, Western Isles
Stranraer, Dumfries & Galloway
Stromness, Orkney
Sunderland, Tyne and Wear
Swanage, Dorset

Teesmouth, Cleveland
Teignmouth, South Devon
Tenby, Dyfed
Thurso, Highland
Tignabruaich, Strathclyde
Tobermory, Strathclyde
Torbay, South Devon
Tramore, Waterford
Trearddur Bay, Gwynedd
Troon, Strathclyde
Tynemouth, Tyne and Wear
Valentia, Kerry
Walmer, Kent
Walton and Frinton, Essex
Wells, Norfolk
West Kirby, Merseyside
West Mersea, Essex
Weston-Super-Mare, Avon
Weymouth, Dorset
Whitby, North Yorkshire
Whitstable, Kent
Wick, Highland
Wicklow, Wicklow
Withernsea, Humberside
Workington, Cumbria
Yarmouth, Isle of Wight
Youghal, Cork

Appendix III

CLOSED LIFEBOAT STATIONS

This list includes all places where there have been RNLI lifeboat stations which no longer exist. At some places, lifeboats were operated by other associations prior to being taken over by the Institution. In such cases, the original date of establishment has also been listed.

The following stations which will be found in the current station list (Appendix II) are not included:

a. stations which have closed and subsequently been re-opened (eg Alderney)

b. offshore stations which have closed but where inshore lifeboats are now operated (eg Blackpool)

c. current operational stations which at one time had two or more boats with separate boat houses where one or other of these has been withdrawn (eg Montrose).

Station	County	Estab pre- RNLI	Taken over or estab by RNLI	Closed	Comments
Abergele	Denbighshire		1868	1869	Station moved to Llandulas q.v.
Ackergill	Caithness		1878	1932	
Alnmouth	Northumberland	1852	1853	1935	
Ardmore	Co Waterford		1858	1895	
Ardrossan	Ayrshire	1807	1869	1930	
Atherfield	Isle of Wight		1890	1915	
Ayr	Ayrshire	1802	1859	1932	
Bacton	Norfolk	1823	1857	1882	
Balbriggan	Co Dublin		1875	1898	
Balcary (Auchencairn Bay)	Kircudbrightshire		1884	1931	
Ballantrae	Ayrshire		1871	1919	
Ballywalter	Co Down		1866	1906	
Bamburgh Castle	Northumberland	1786	1882	1897	A lifeboat was placed here in 1786 by the Crewe Trust, in service for several years (the original station fell into disuse before 1824).
Banff & Macduff	Banffshire		1860	1907	Transferred to Whitehills 1924 q.v.
Banff			1907	1924	
Barmston	Yorkshire		1884	1898	

Station	County	Estab pre-RNLI	Taken over or estab by RNLI	Closed	Comments
Blackrock (Dundalk)	Co Louth		1859	1935	See also Giles Quay
Blakeney	Norfolk	c1825	1861	1935	
Boulmer	Northumberland	1825	1852	1968	
Bournemouth ILB	Hampshire		1965	1972	
Brancaster	Norfolk		1874	1935	
Braunton	North Devon	1848	1855	1919	known as: Appledore No.3 1852–1862 Braunton 1862–1894 Appledore No.3 1894–1897 Appledore No.2 1897–1919 (Appledore No.1 (estab 1825) still operational)
Brighstone Grange	Isle of Wight		1860	1915	
Boadstairs	Kent	1850	1868	1912	
Brooke	Isle of Wight		1860	1937	
Buckhaven	Fifeshire		1900	1932	Original proposal was to call station Buckhaven & Methil.
Buddon Ness, Dundee	Angus	1830	1861	1894	
Bull Bay	Anglesey		1868	1926	
Burnham-on-Sea	Somerset	1836	1866	1930	
Cadgwith	Cornwall		1867	1963	
Cahore	Co Wexford		1857	1916	
Caister	Norfolk	1846	1857	1969	
Cambois	Northumberland		1899	1927	Name of Blyth No.2 station between these dates.
Carmarthen Bay	See Ferryside				
Carnsore	Co Wexford		1859	1897	
Carrickfergus	Co Antrim		1896	1913	
Castletown	Isle of Man	1826	1856	1922	Lifeboat presented to Isle of Man District Association by RNLI in March 1826. The original station ceased to function some years before RNLI station of 1856.
Cemaes	Anglesey		1872	1932	
Cemlyn	Anglesey	1828	1855	1919	
Chapel	Lincolnshire		1870	1898	

Station	County	Estab pre-RNLI	Taken over or estab by RNLI	Closed	Comments
Capman's Pool	Dorset		1866	1880	Sometimes referred to as Isle of Purbeck.
Chichester Harbour (West Wittering)	Sussex		1867	1884	Lifeboat moved to Littlehampton.
Church Cove, Lizard	Cornwall		1885	1899	
Cloughey	Co Down		1885	1965	
Cloughey/ Portavogie	Co Down		1965	1981	
Clovelly	North Devon		1870	1988	
Corton	Suffolk		1869	1879	
Coverack	Cornwall		1901	1980	
Crail	Fifeshire		1884	1923	
Cresswell	Northumberland		1875	1944	
Crimdon Dene ILB	Co Durham		1966	1993	
Cromarty	Cromartyshire		1911	1968	
Cruden Bay	See Port Errol				
Culdaff	Co Donegal		1892	1913	
Dartmouth	South Devon		1878	1896	
Deal	See North Deal				
Derrynane	Co Kerry		1844	1855	
Donna Nook	Lincolnshire	1829	1864	1931	
Dornoch Firth & Embo	Sutherlandshire		1886	1904	
Drogheda	Co Louth		1856	1926	
Dublin	See Poolbeg				
Duncannon	Co Wexford		1869	1886	Station moved to Fethard
Dundalk	See Blackrock & Giles Quay				
Dungarvan	See Helvick Head				
Dunwich	Suffolk		1873	1903	
Dymchurch (No.27 tower)	Kent		1826	1838	Known as Dungeness 1826–1836.
Easington	Yorkshire		1913	1933	
Fenit (Tralee Bay)	Co Kerry		1879	1969	
Ferryside	Carmarthen		1835	1960	Known as: Laugharne 1835–1843 Carmarthen Bay 1860–1892 Ferryside 1892–1960

Station	County	Estab pre-RNLI	Taken over or estab by RNLI	Closed	Comments
Folkestone	Kent		1893	1930	See also Hythe.
Formby	Lancashire	1776	1894	1919	
Giles Quay (Dundalk)	Co Louth		1880	1912	
Gourdon	Kincardineshire		1878	1969	
Greencastle	Co Donegal		1864	1928	
Greenore	Co Louth		1894	1920	
Greystones	Co Wicklow		1872	1895	
Grimsby	Lincolnshire		1882	1927	
Groomsport	Co Down		1858	1920	
Hauxley	Northumberland	1852	1853	1939	
Hayle	Cornwall		1866	1920	
Helvick Head	Co Waterford		1858	1969	Known as Dungarvan 1859–1900. Dungarvan Bay (Helvick Head) 1900–1908 and Helvick Head (Dungarvan Bay) 1908–1969.
Hilbre Island	Cheshire	1848	1894	1939	
Holy Island	Northumberland	1802	1865	1968	
Hope Cove	South Devon		1878	1930	
Hornsea	Yorkshire'	1851	1854	1924	
Humber Mouth ILB	Lincolnshire		1965	1980	
Huna	Caithness		1877	1930	
Hythe	Kent		1876	1940	Known as Hythe, Sandgate & Folkestone 1876–1893.
Irvine	Ayrshire	1834	1860	1914	
Isle of Arran	See Kildonan				
Isle of Purbeck	See Chapman's Pool				
Isle of Whithorn	See Whithorn				
Johnshaven	Kincardineshire		1890	1928	
Kessingland	Suffolk	1855	1867	1936	
Kildonan	Isle of Arran		1870	1901	
Killough	Co Down		1901	1914	Lifeboat kept at Rossglass, but manned from Killough, and called Killough.
Killybegs	Co Donegal		1941	1945	War time emergency station
Kimmeridge	Dorset		1868	1896	
Kingsdowne	Kent		1866	1927	
Kingsgate	Kent		1862	1897	
Laugharne	See Ferryside				
Littlehaven	Pembrokeshire		1882	1921	ILB estab Litle and Broad Haven 1967
Littlestone	See New Romney				

Station	County	Estab pre-RNLI	Taken over or estab by RNLI	Closed	Comments
Llanaelhaiarn	Caernarvonshire		1883	1901	
Llandulas	Denbighshire		1869	1932	
Llanddwyn	Anglesey	1840	1855	1907	
Llanelli	Carmarthenshire	1852	1854	1863	Station moved to Pembrey 1863 q.v.
			1869	1870	Lifeboat placed on Pilot Ship near Llanelli, which was wrecked in October 1870.
Londonderry	See Greencastle				
Lossiemouth	Elginshire		1859	1923	
Lynmouth	North Devon		1869	1944	
Machrihanish	Argyllshire		1911	1930	
Maryport	Cumberland		1865	1949	
Methil	See Buckhaven				
Mevagissey	Cornwall		1869	1930	
Middlesborough	Yorkshire	1836	1855	1895	
Moray Firth	See Nairn				
Morthoe (or Morte Bay)	North Devon		1871	1900	
Mostyn	Flintshire	1835		1851	
Mullion	Cornwall		1867	1908	
Mundesley	Norfolk	1811	1857	1895	
Nairn (Moray Firth)	Nairnshire		1878	1911	Known as Moray Firth 1878–1892.
Newburgh	Aberdeenshire		1877	1965	In early days known as River Ythan.
Newlyn	Cornwall		1908	1913	
Newport	Pembrokeshire		1884	1894	
New Romney	Kent		1861	1929	Known as Littlestone 1861–1871.
Northam Burrows	North Devon	1852	1855	1897	Known as: Appledore No.1. 1856–1861 Appledore. 1861–1870 Appledore No.1 1870–1889 Appledore 1889–1894 Appledore No 1 1894–1897 See also Braunton
North Deal	Kent		1865	1932	
Pakefield	Suffolk	1840	1855	1922	
Palling	Norfolk	1852	1857	1930	
Pembrey	Carmarthenshire		1863	1887	Moved from Llanelli q.v. Moved to Burry Port 1887 (closed 1914: reopened with ILB 1973)

Station	County	Estab pre- RNLI	Taken over or estab by RNLI	Closed	Comments
Penmon	Anglesey	1831	1855	1915	
Penzance	Cornwall		1826	1917	Closed 1828–1853.
Pill ILB	Somerset		1971	1974	
Point of Ayr	Flintshire	1826	1894	1923	
Polkerris	Cornwall		1859	1922	Station moved to Fowey 1922
Poolbeg	Dublin	1820	1862	1959	
Portavogie	See Cloughey				
Port Erroll (Cruden Bay)	Aberdeenshire		1877	1921	
Port Eynon	West Glamorgan		1884	1916	ILB estab 1968 Horton & Port Eynon.
Porthleven	Cornwall		1863	1929	
Porthoustock	Cornwall		1869	1942	
Porth Rhuffydd	Anglesey		1891	1904	
Portland	Dorset		1826	1850	
Portloe	Cornwall		1870	1887	
Port Logan	Wigtownshire		1866	1932	Also known as Port Nessock.
Purbeck, Isle of	See Chapman's Pool				
Queenstown	Co Cork		1866	1920	
Rhoscolyn	Anglesey	1830	1855	1929	
Rhosneigr	Anglesey		1872	1924	
Robin Hood's Bay	Yorkshire	1830	1881	1931	
Rogerstown	Dublin		1874	1882	
Rossglass	Co Down		1825	1835	See also Killough and St John's Point.
Rosslinks (Holy Island No.2)	Northumberland		1868	1908	Then transferred to the Island.
Runswick	Yorkshire		1866	1978	From 1978 ILB station Staithes and Runswick.
Ryde	Isle of Wight	1869	1894	1923	
St Agnes	Isles of Scilly		1890	1920	
St Andrews	Fifeshire	1800	1860	1938	
St Annes	Lancashire		1881	1925	
St John's Point	Co Down		1835	1843	Rossglass lifeboat housed at St John's Point 1835–1843.
Saltburn	Yorkshire	1849	1858	1922	
Sandgate	See Hythe				
Seaham	Co Durham	1856	1870	1979	
Seascale	Cumberland		1875	1895	
Seaton Carew	Co Durham	1823	1857	1922	
Seaton Snook	Co Durham		1907	1909	Under control of Seaton Carew.

Station	County	Estab pre-RNLI	Taken over or estab by RNLI	Closed	Comments
Sidmouth	South Devon		1869	1912	
Skateraw	East Lothian		1907	1943	
Solva	Pembrokeshire		1869	1887	
Southend (Cantyre)	Argyllshire		1869	1930	
Southport	Lancashire	1812	1860	1925	
Southsea	Hampshire		1886	1918	
Stonehaven	Kincardineshire	1854	1867	1934	
ILB			1967	1984	
Stronsay	Orkney Islands		1909	1972	Closed 1915–1952
Studland	Dorset		1826	1852	
Sutton	Lincolnshire	1844	1864	1913	
Theddlethorpe	Lincolnshire	1828	1864	1882	
Thorpeness	Suffolk		1853	1900	
Torquay	South Devon		1876	1923	
Totland Bay	Isle of Wight	1870	1885	1924	
Tralee Bay	See Fenit				
Tyrella	Co Down	1838	1860	1899	
Upgang	Yorkshire		1865	1919	
Varne					
Light Vessel ILB	Kent		1971	1972	Temporary station.
Watchet	Somerset		1875	1944	
West Hartlepool Beach	Co Durham	1847	1869	1906	
West Hartlepool Dock	Co. Durham	1854	1869	1894	
Westport	Co Mayo		1857	1860	
West Wittering	See Chichester Harbour				
Wexford	Co Wexford		1859	1927	
Whitburn	Co Durham	1830	1854	1918	
Whitehaven	Cumberland	1804	1865	1925	
Whitehills	Banffshire		1924	1969	See also Banff.
Whitelink Bay	Aberdeenshire		1878	1905	
Whithorn, Isle of	Wigtownshire		1869	1919	
Winterton	Norfolk	1823	1857	1924	
Woodbridge Haven	Suffolk	1825	1851	1854	
Worthing	Sussex	1852	1865	1930	
ILB			1964	1967	
Yealm River	South Devon		1878	1927	
Ythan River	See Newburgh				

Appendix IV

**CLOSED LIFEBOAT STATIONS
OPERATED BY ORGANISATIONS
OTHER THAN THE RNLI**

Station	Opened	Closed	Operated by
Bawdsey Haven, Suffolk	1801	1825	Suffolk Association boat moved to Woodbridge Haven
Boarhills, Fife	1865	1895	Boarhills Lifeboat Society
Caernarvon	1834	1853	Caernarvon Harbour Commissioners
Frinton, Suffolk	1901	1917	Frinton Lifeboat Committee
Gibraltar Point (Boston Deeps), Lincolnshire	1825	1830	Spilsby District Association and from 1827 by Lincolnshire Coast Shipwreck Association
Helmsdale, Sutherland	1909	1939	Helmsdale Lifeboat Committee
Huttoft, Lincolnshire	1835	1844	Lincolnshire Coast Shipwreck Association
Landguard Fort, Suffolk	1821	1826	Suffolk Association
	1845	c1864	
Liverpool, Lancashire	1839	1894	Mersey Docks and Harbour Board Station closed on take over of the Board's boats by the RNLI in 1894
The Magazines, Cheshire	1827	1863	Mersey Docks and Harbour Board Station closed when RNLI opened station at New Brighton
Orford, Suffolk	1826	1835	Suffolk Association
Saltfleet, Lincolnshire	1827	1829	Lincolnshire Coast Shipwreck Association. Boat moved to Donna Nook.
Scratby (California), Norfolk	1854	c1883	Boat manned by local Scratby fishermen
Sizewell (Gap), Suffolk	1826	1851	Suffolk Association boat manned from Aldeburgh

Index of Medal Awards

Index of Lifeboats Involved in Medal Services

This index includes all services where lifeboats, whether of the RNLI or of other organisations, have been involved.

Index to Shore Boat Services

Services where lifeboats are not involved in the actual rescue are termed 'Shore boat services'. Services have been listed by geographical location. Where services occurred at sea – e.g. in the English Channel or Atlantic Ocean – they have been so indexed. In some cases, lifeboats have been present, and these have also been indexed under the separate 'Index of Lifeboats Involved in Medal Services'.

Medal Awards – 1997

Since the finalisation of the production of this book, medals have been awarded in 1997. Brief details are given below. These are not included in the indexes on previous pages.

SUTHERLAND Albert, Coxswain, Fraserburgh Lifeboat **BRONZE**
25 March 1997

16–17 February: A nine hour service in the Tyne class lifeboat *City of Edinburgh* in extremely adverse weather conditions to the fishing vessel *Hope Crest* which was taking water some 50 miles N.E. of Fraserburgh. Despite massive seas throwing the two vessels around, the two vessels were brought together so that a portable pump could be passed over. The *Hope Crest* and six crew reached Fraserburgh safely at 2.30 am.

STRINGER Ian, Helmsman, Eastbourne Inshore Lifeboat **SILVER**
16 September 1997

7–8 April 1977: Eastbourne's D class lifeboat was launched, despite the darkness and poor weather conditions, to go to the aid of a man trapped on a beam under the pier. Helmsman Stringer took the lifeboat in under the structure three times before the man could be saved.

REES Jeremy, Coxswaim, Angle Lifeboat **BRONZE**
16 September 1997

5 May 1997: Angle's Tyne class lifeboat *The Lady Rank* was launched to assist the motor vessel *Dale Princess* which had anchored in North Haven, Skomer Island, to effect engine repairs. Her anchors were dragging in Force 8 wind, and the vessel was in danger of being driven ashore. Coxswaim Rees took the lifeboat near enough to connect a tow, despite the treacherous backwash from the cliff. The boat and her crew were towed to Milford Haven.

CLARK Peter Hewitt Peterson, Coxswain/Mechanic, Lerwick Lifeboat **GOLD**
SIMPSON Richie, Second Coxswain, Lerwick Lifeboat **BRONZE**
LAURENSON Brian, Emergency Mechanic, Lerwick Lifeboat **BRONZE**
THOMSON Peter, Emergency Mechanic, Lerwick Lifeboat **BRONZE**
LEASK Ian, Crew Member, Lerwick Lifeboat **BRONZE**
GRANT Michael, Crew Member, Lerwick Lifeboat **BRONZE**
21 January 1998

19 November 1997: The refrigerated cargo vessel *Green Lily* had developed engine trouble, and tugs were attempting to take her in tow. The Coastguard helicopter had also been scrambled.

The Lerwick Severn class lifeboat *Michael and Jane Vernon* arrived on the scene at 1.50 pm with the casualty only 1!s miles from shore. Then, as the RNLI Divisional Inspector reported:

> Coxswain Clark demonstrated enormous courage, leadership, determination and seamanship. He made the decision to try and rescue the crew after it appeared that all other hope had gone. The towline had parted, the helicopter could not work the casualty. He manoeuvred the lifeboat in limited searoom, which was further reduced with each passing minute, in 15 metre breaking seas and violent Force 11 winds. His incredible skill in handling the lifeboat and taking her alongside the violently rolling casualty ensured his crew were safe and that survivors could be taken off. When he finally drove the lifeboat clear with five survivors on board, there was less than 200 yards to the shore. The crew of the lifeboat are an example of teamwork, courage and tenacity.

Finally, a tug managed to fix a tow and pull the casualty's bow head on to the wind. This enabled the helicopter to rescue the remaining ten crew. Sadly, in doing so, the Coastguard winchman, William (Bill) Deacon, was lost overboard when a huge wave had broken over the ship.

The five survivors rescued by the lifeboat were landed at Lerwick at 3.20 pm.

One Honorary Gold Medal was voted on 21 January 1997 to the Finnish Lifeboat Service – **Suomen Meripelastusseura** – to mark the Centenary of its foundation on 27 March 1897.

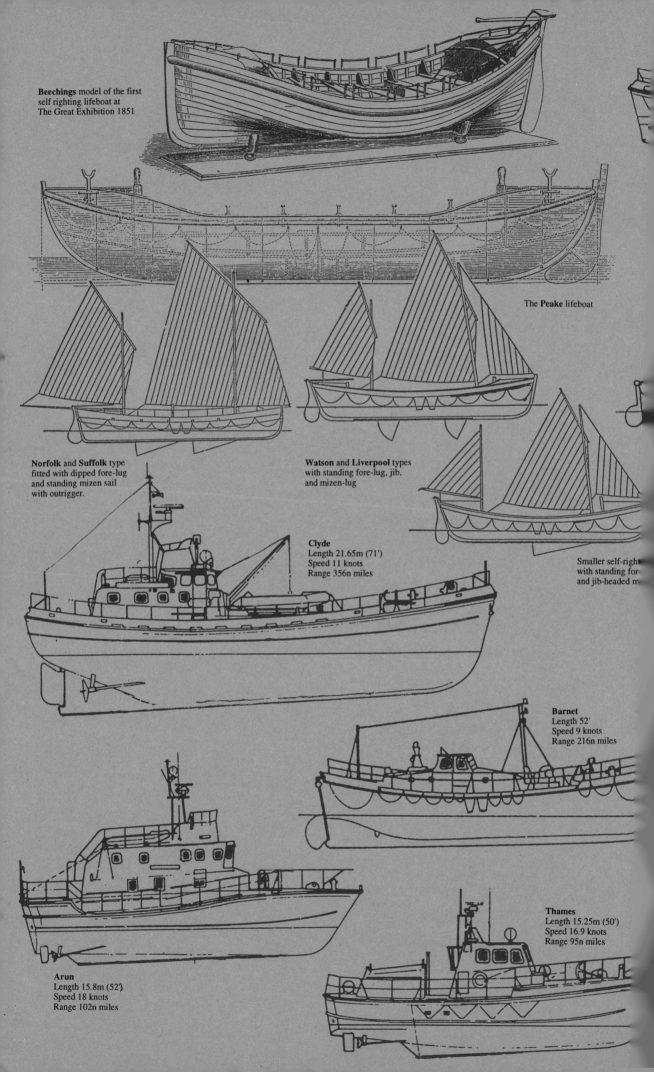

Beechings model of the first self righting lifeboat at The Great Exhibition 1851

The **Peake** lifeboat

Norfolk and **Suffolk** type fitted with dipped fore-lug and standing mizen sail with outrigger.

Watson and **Liverpool** types with standing fore-lug, jib, and mizen-lug

Smaller self-righ[t] with standing for[e] and jib-headed m[izen]

Clyde
Length 21.65m (71')
Speed 11 knots
Range 356n miles

Barnet
Length 52'
Speed 9 knots
Range 216n miles

Arun
Length 15.8m (52')
Speed 18 knots
Range 102n miles

Thames
Length 15.25m (50')
Speed 16.9 knots
Range 95n miles